HISTORY

OF THE

TOWN OF WESTFORD,

IN THE

COUNTY OF MIDDLESEX, MASSACHUSETTS,

1659—1883.

BY

REV. EDWIN R. HODGMAN, A. M.,

Member of the New England Historic Genealogical Society.

PUBLISHED BY
THE WESTFORD TOWN HISTORY ASSOCIATION.

LOWELL, MASS.:
MORNING MAIL COMPANY, PRINTERS.
1883.

Notice

In many older books, foxing (or discoloration) occurs and, in some instances, print lightens with wear and age. Reprinted books, such as this, often duplicate these flaws, notwithstanding efforts to reduce or eliminate them. The pages of this reprint have been digitally enhanced and, where possible, the flaws eliminated in order to provide clarity of content and a pleasant reading experience.

History of the Town of Westford, in the County of Middlesex, Massachusetts 1659-1883

By:
Rev. Edwin R. Hodgman

Originally published:
Lowell, Massachusetts
1883

Reprinted by:

Janaway Publishing, Inc.
732 Kelsey Ct.
Santa Maria, California 93454
(805) 925-1038
www.JanawayGenealogy.com

2016

ISBN: 978-1-59641-373-3

Made in the United States of America

PREFACE.

"To write a great history," says one, "requires a great imagination; but no man of imagination can deal with a famous epoch without seeking to know it and to depict it in due proportion and detail."

The compiler of this book makes no pretensions to a great imagination nor to any special qualifications to write history. He has diligently sought for facts, and has aimed to present them in a clear and lucid manner. The history of the early New England towns is the history of men who constituted a part of the winnowed wheat which Old England sent to these shores in the seventeenth century, and which grew to wonderful ripeness in the wilderness.

The settlement of some parts of this town was almost cotemporary with the settlement of Chelmsford; and it is fair to presume that at least two hundred and twenty years have passed since the axe of the pioneer began to level the forests on the eastern border. In a country like this, the record of so long a period is full of stirring events and noble achievements; and it has been the purpose of the compiler to set these forth in such a way as to instruct and stimulate the reader. A careful study has been made of the records of Chelmsford, which was the mother-town; and the facts in regard to the settlement of the west precinct have been sought out and presented. The records of deeds in the office of registration at East Cambridge have been examined and much valuable information has been obtained. The archives of the State House in Boston have also been examined with much painstaking. Search has been made in the records of neighboring towns, and several town histories and family genealogies have been consulted. Two journeys were made to Vermont in order to learn the facts in regard to the settlement of Cavendish, Ludlow, Mount Holly, and other towns; and several towns in New Hampshire were visited for a similar purpose.

The records of the town are in a fair state of preservation, and so, too, are the records of the first church during the ministry of Mr. Hall; but no record has been found of the ministry of Mr. Scribner. See p. 274. Note. It is to be regretted that, during the late civil war, certain papers and documents belonging to the town and once stored in the attic of the first parish meeting-house, were removed and sold.

The number of pages in this volume was limited by the contract of the Town History Association with the compiler; but it was found necessary to exceed that number; and even then, with the addition of one hundred pages, much important genealogical matter has been excluded. For this reason, families who came here after the year 1800 are not found in the tables, and of those who were here before that date the record had to be abridged for want of space.

The completion of the work has been delayed by the ill health of the compiler, and by other causes. It now goes from his hands after much toil, with a real diffidence on his part, but with the consciousness that he has done what he could. It would have been better in matter and form, if strength and opportunity had permitted him to make it so.

The compiler gratefully acknowledges his indebtedness and obligations to many persons who have aided him in preparing the volume; especially to Julian Abbot, Esq., of Lowell, George E. H. Abbot and sister, of Groton, Samuel A. Green, M. D., of Boston, Sherman D. Fletcher, Edward Symmes, Nathan S. Hamblin, John M. Fletcher, George B. Hildreth, David P. Lawrence, and others, of Westford. He is under special obligations to Rev. Thomas Wilson of Eaton, Madison County, New York. While he resided here Mr. Wilson made a careful study of the records of the first church, and compiled an interesting summary of its history, which he very kindly loaned to the compiler. In some cases the language of Mr. Wilson has been used where it justly and tersely described the facts.

To the members of the Westford Town History Association the compiler hereby tenders his sincere thanks for their confidence and sympathy, their courtesy and forbearance, as expressed in various ways, and for their generous aid in the execution of his task. Nor can he forbear, in these acknowledgments, to mention — but without her knowledge or consent — the name of an only daughter, Harriet M. Hodgman, to whom many thanks are due for long-continued assistance in copying, arranging, and proof-reading.

EDWIN R. HODGMAN.

Westford, March 7, 1883.

WESTFORD TOWN HISTORY ASSOCIATION.

THE following record explains the origin of this Association:

At a meeting of persons interested in the matter of compiling and publishing a history of this town, held in the Town Hall, March 15, 1879, the following business was transacted, namely:

1. Chose George T. Day, Chairman; Edwin R. Hodgman, Secretary; and Sherman D. Fletcher, Treasurer.

2. Voted to accept the preamble and articles presented by William E. Frost, containing an agreement to form an Association to prepare and publish a History of Westford.

The agreement is as follows:

It is proposed by the undersigned to publish a History of the town of Westford, Mass., in a well-bound octavo volume of not less than 400 pages, printed on paper of good quality and in clear type; the work to comprise such portions of the authentic colonial, revolutionary, civil, educational, and religious history of the town as can be compiled from the town records, and gathered from other reliable sources; and to be issued on or before the first of July, 1880, in an edition of 600 copies, and sold to the inhabitants of Westford at $2.00 a copy, and to non-resident purchasers at such price, not less than $2.00 a copy, as a majority of the undersigned may hereafter agree upon.

In order to secure the publication of the Town History above described, and according to the above-mentioned specifications and limitations,

We, the undersigned, do severally agree, and legally bind ourselves to pay into the treasury of this Association such sum, not exceeding fifty dollars, as may be assessed upon us severally, to defray the expense of compiling, printing, binding, and selling the above-mentioned History of Westford; *provided* that the following precedent conditions are accepted by the Association, and faithfully complied with, namely:

First—That the sum of $200, appropriated by the town for the publication of a Town History, be paid into the treasury of this Association.

Second—That the sum required, in addition to the amount appropriated by the town, to defray the expense of compiling and publishing a History of Westford, be assessed equally on the members of this Association.

Third—That all money received by members of this Association or by their agents, from the sale of the Town History, be paid into the treasury; and that the balance remaining in the treasury after the payment of all bills for compiling and publishing the Town History, be divided equally among the members of the Association.

Fourth—That responsible committees be appointed to discharge the following duties, viz.: 1st, to audit all bills payable by the Association; 2nd, to canvass the town for subscribers for the work, before its publication; 3rd, to contract with the compiler and the publishers of the work; 4th, to take charge of the edition when published.

Fifth—That the compiler of the Town History be elected by the Association.

Sixth—That the History be submitted to the Association for inspection before its publication.

Seventh—That the preceding obligation and agreement, with conditions annexed, have no binding force and be null and void, unless signed by eighteen or more responsible citizens and tax-payers of Westford.

Alvan Fisher.	Wm. E. Frost.
George T. Day.	Abiel J. Abbot.
J. Henry Read.	Edward Prescott.
John W. Abbot.	Sherman D. Fletcher.
Allan Cameron.	Sherman H. Fletcher.
William Reed.	William L. Kittredge.
Arthur Wright.	Gilman J. Wright.
Albert P. Richardson.	W. H. H. Burbeck.
George W. Heywood.	Nahum H. Wright.

3. Voted that the Secretary shall inform certain persons of the wish of this Association that they should join it.

4. Voted that a committee of five persons be appointed to audit all bills payable by the Association, to contract with

the compiler and the publishers of the work, and to take charge of the edition when published.

5. Chose Alvan Fisher, George T. Day, William E. Frost, J. Henry Read and William Reed for that Committee.

6. Voted to adjourn to Saturday evening, March 22, at 7.30 o'clock.

EDWIN R. HODGMAN, Secretary.

WESTFORD, March 22, 1879.

The Town History Association met according to adjournment, and transacted the following business:

1. Voted that the size of the type and quality of the paper be determined by the committee of five who were chosen at the first meeting.

2. Voted that Edwin R. Hodgman be requested to offer proposals for compiling the Town History.

3. Voted that the Chairman and Secretary be made permanent officers of this Association and be empowered to call meetings whenever the interests of the Association shall require them, during the existence of the Association.

4. Voted that the name of this society be the Westford Town History Association.

5. Voted to adjourn to Friday evening, April 4th, at 7.30 o'clock.

WESTFORD, April 4, 1879.

At an adjourned meeting of the Association, held at the residence of the Chairman, the following business was transacted:

1. The Secretary having read proposals for compiling the History of the Town of Westford, it was voted to accept his proposals, to wit: four hundred dollars in cash and twenty-five bound copies of the work when published—and he will assume only the responsibility of compiling, composing, and reading proofs.

2. Voted to take the binding of the Report of the State Board of Education as a *sample*—the price being eighteen cents per copy.

3. Voted to adopt the following resolution: That the Secretary be requested to prepare a Prospectus of the contemplated History, and cause one thousand copies to be printed, with the view of circulating the same in order to obtain subscribers to the work.

4. Voted to appoint Gilman J. Wright canvassing agent for the Association, and with him all parties shall be requested to correspond and to order the book.

HISTORY OF WESTFORD.

PART I.—CHAPTER I.

FROM THE SETTLEMENT TO THE INCORPORATION—ONCE PART OF CHELMSFORD—INDIANS—EARLY SETTLERS—EXTENSION—EARLY HOMESTEADS—ROADS—THE STRUGGLE FOR A PRECINCT—FAMILIES BELONGING TO THE PARISH OF LITTLETON—EXTRACTS FROM RECORDS—PRECINCT ESTABLISHED, 1724—FIRST MEETING-HOUSE—BRIEF HISTORY OF THE PRECINCT.

HISTORY gives voice to achievement and concerns itself with the deeds of men in their social, religious and political relations. It takes note of the field of action as well as of the actors upon it, and shows how the force of human reason and the energy of the human will combine to produce results that are worthy to be treasured up and transmitted to posterity.

The territory now to be described was once a part of the new world opened only a few centuries ago to the march of a christian civilization. It was a wilderness, the haunt of wild beasts and savage men; and the primeval solitudes were unbroken. The scene can be pictured only by the imagination.

> Then these broad vales and quiet hills
>   Responded to the piercing cry
> Of wolf or wild cat; at these rills
>   Drank trembling fawns, so coy and shy.
> Forests with thick, umbrageous gloom
>   Spread far and wide; wild fruits matured
> Unplucked by man; the choice perfume
>   Of flowers no human foot allured;

> The hawk and raven built their nest
>   Unscared ; the timid fish, uncaught,
> Swam the deep pools, and nature dressed
>   In pristine garb, with grace untaught,
> Looked queenly in the eye of heaven.
>   Lowly and sweet the anthem then
> At blush of morn or calm of even.
>   Along each winding stream and glen
> Stretch groves of pale, deciduous trees ;
>   The slopes are crowned with evergreen.
> No woodman's axe hath humbled these ;
>   No vandal's touch hath marred the scene.
> The circling hills in order stand,
>   The crown is on Monadnoc's brow,
> And, rippling over rock and sand,
>   The gentle river floweth now
> Untrammelled to the boundless sea.

Such was its primitive state, the hunting-ground of the Pawtuckets or Wamesits, who owned the Great Neck, as it was called, between the Merrimack and the Concord rivers, on which the city of Lowell stands; and of the Nashobas, a small tribe that lived near Nashoba Hill.

The town of Westford was originally a part of Chelmsford, and its early history is involved in the history of that town. From the land allotments recorded in Chelmsford and from old deeds, it appears that the meadow and plain in the southwest part of Westford were called Great Tadmuck;* the swamp on the east side was called Tadmuck; and these were sometimes designated as Farther Tadmuck and Hither Tadmuck; and the region about the east burying-ground was known as Little Tadmuck. The hill on which the central village stands bore the name of Tadmuck. No proof has been found that this name was given to any territory north of Stony Brook, and no Indian name of this stream has been discovered. The early deeds also mention Nubanussuck Pond and Kissacook Hill, north and west of the brook, and these are each Indian appellations.

---

* This name is variously spelled in the old documents Tadnoc, Tadnick, Tadnuck and Tadmuck. The last is more general and is adopted as the true one.

Some of the favorite haunts of the Indians are still known, where they built their wigwams and planted their corn. These were generally near a stream or spring, but sometimes on a warm hillside. One of their resorts was on the east side of Boutwell's Meadow, about one mile from the Centre, and near the house of Oren Coolidge. Stone tools and flints have recently been found there, and are now in the possession of Mr. Coolidge.

Another resort was an island in Providence Meadow, on which their implements have been found. Still another on the slope near the lone tree west of George Drew's house, and there probably they raised patches of Indian corn, after the manner of Indian husbandry. Yet another was on the hill east of Eli Tower's, where a flat rock is shown upon which the squaws kindled their fires and baked Indian cake in the best style of Indian cookery.

But Forge Pond was the rallying point of the tribes. It is to be regretted that the Indian name of this pond has not been preserved. On its banks they were accustomed to gather for feasting and dancing, and for purposes of Indian hospitality and friendship. On the eastern margin two places are shown where the encampments or lodges were fixed, which are indicated by slight excavations and the finding of arrow-heads. Old Andrew, the Indian, who sold his *warre* (weir) at the outlet to the town of Groton before 1680, was doubtless a fisherman (an expert in the business), but driven away by the encroaching white man. No trace of their abiding at or near Nubanussuck is known to the compiler; but it is fair to presume that they often went there as well as to other ponds in the north part of the town. By those clear and quiet waters no doubt the Indian maidens had their toilet, and by the setting sun their graceful forms were mirrored in the limpid stream. These freeborn children of solitude have passed away, but still the waters shimmer in the sunlight and remind us of the sad fate of a vanished race.

During the Indian wars that occurred between the years 1675 and 1760 the town of Chelmsford was not seriously harmed, although kept in constant fear of an attack. The Indian sachem, Wannalancet, "was always peaceable and true to the English"; and the first minister, Rev. John Fiske, and Maj. Henchman, an influential magistrate, are said to have cultivated his friendship "with successful assiduity." At one time, after a long absence, Wannalancet called on Mr. Fiske and inquired of him whether the people in Chelmsford had suffered greatly during the war. Mr. Fiske replied that they had been highly favored, for which he desired to thank God. "Me next," said the sagacious sagamore, intimating that through his influence this town had been exempted from the calamities that had befallen many others.*

There is a tradition, however, that a party of Indians once came to the house of one of the early settlers in the night, and made noises like swine and other annoying demonstrations. The man went out but did not return. His wife barred the doors and remained with her children until morning, and on going out she found the head of her husband, stuck upon a pole.

There is also a tradition that before the settlement a battle was fought between the Nashoba Indians and the Wamesits. The battle-ground, it is said, was a triangular piece of ground on the north side of Frances Hill, near the residence of the late Trueworthy Keyes.

In due time a change came over the wild domain of nature. The white man enters, and we have to do with a new order of things. The plantation of Chelmsford was granted in 1653, May 18, and incorporated two years afterward, 1655, May 29. The first petitioners for the grant, twenty in number, were of Concord and Woburn. These were joined by others, chiefly the company of Rev. John Fiske, from Wenham, making thirty-nine in all. Of the Concord families, the Adamses, the Fletchers, Hartwells and Proctors became largely influential in the settlement; while

---

*Allen's History of Chelmsford, page 157.

the Butterfields, Chamberlins, Fosters, Hildreths, Nuttings, Parkers and Wrights from Woburn, contributed very much to its establishment and growth. The Barretts and Spaldings from Braintree, John Bates from Hingham, Solomon Keyes from Newbury, and Cornelius Waldo from Ipswich, were also excellent men. Thomas Henchman, of the Wenham company, "was for many years a leading character, and became a large land-holder."—(*Allen.*)

The early grant to Chelmsford, according to a plan to be seen at the State House in Boston, was in the form of a parallelogram, with its longer lines running east and west. The northwest corner was near the house of the late Col. Benjamin Osgood, in Westford, and the shorter line on the west end is almost identical with a part of the present boundary line between the two towns. This tract proving too small for them and withal the soil being barren and stony, the proprietors asked for more land, and the General Court granted their request.

Mr. Eliot, in behalf of the praying Indians, also petitioned for an enlargement of their grant. "In answer to to these petitions," says Allen, "the Court, on conference with the committee who established the bounds of Chelmsford, and on examination of a plot of the said plantations and of the tract of land by both parties petitioned for, *granted* that the Indian plantation be extended one mile from the northeast angle of Chelmsford, abutting on Merrimac and Pawtuckett eastward, taking in John Sagamore's planting ground, and the end of the said mile to determine the Indian plantation. For the rest of the land petitioned for by both towns, it was ordered that Chelmsford north and south lines abutting on Tadmuck be extended (the south to Groton line*), the north from the northeast corner or angle three miles upon Merrimac River and thence a south-

---

* This prolonged the line running west from Concord River to a point near Nashoba Hill. Nashoba was made an Indian town in 1654 by request of Rev. John Eliot. Gookin, writing in 1674, says it was the sixth praying Indian village and lieth in the centre between Chelmsford, Lancaster, Groton and Concord. In 1682 Groton had taken into its bounds nearly half of the Indian plantation and claimed three hundred and

west line to Groton. And this whole tract was to remain in community unto the town of Chelmsford and Pawtuckett.'

"To this additional grant," continues Mr. Allen, "which contained all Westford and the northerly part of Chelmsford, the Indians had a common right with the inhabitants of Chelmsford. But whether they availed themselves of it at all, or made a compromise with the people of Chelmsford for any particular parcel of land, is not certainly known. It is probable, however, that the Indians gave up their right in this grant in consideration of some parcel of land, or some immunity or privilege. For in 1660 the Indians of Pawtuckett and the inhabitants of Chelmsford entered into an agreement which was sanctioned by Court, to exchange lands and to settle the boundaries between them." (History of Chelmsford, pp. 14, 15.)

By this agreement in 1660 this township of Westford ceased forever to be the hunting-ground of the red man, and became the abiding place of a civilized race, who brought with them a hardy energy that could subdue forests, and a wise forecast that built up a community in which liberty was a cherished principle, and in which, above all, *religion* was a governing policy and an inspiring motive.

> Not from the court or council hall,
>   Not from the home of wealth and pride,
> From titled ranks, or great or small,
>   With greed of gain unsatisfied,
> Came they who first a pathway cleared
>   Through the wide forest, thick and drear,
> Built their rude cabins and upreared
>   A house for Him whom all revere.
> Strong, hardy men, with instincts true,
>   Laid the foundations of the town;
> They kept a noble end in view,
>   And worked for God, not for renown.

---

fifty acres of Nashoba—that is to say, of the portion held by the English. The line between Nashoba and Chelmsford was indefinite for some time. When Littleton was incorporated, in 1714, it included Nashoba, excepting a portion on the northwest side which now belongs to Groton, and also Concord Village, or New Grant. It may be that a triangular slip, on the northeastern side of the original Nashoba, is now included in Westford.

There is nothing to show that the territory now known as Westford was ever accurately surveyed by compass and chain, and the farms or lots marked off. But each man chose his land, and the town sanctioned his act and confirmed his title by recording it. This record, however, was often made years after he had seized the land. In this way the early inhabitants held their homesteads by actual seizure or appropriation from the domain of nature. As there was no regularity in these proceedings, the boundaries are often exceedingly indefinite and hard to trace, unless there is some natural object, such as a pond, or brook, or hill, to aid one. This could hardly be otherwise, when the whole region was a forest and no artificial landmarks had been set up.

At first the settlers were obliged to look for springs of water for their own use, and to search out and appropriate the meadows and swamps in order to procure hay for their cattle. Tadmuck, Great Tadmuck and Little Tadmuck were their hay-fields, as were also the swamps near Nubanussuck, Long-Sought-For and Keyes Ponds. Hence it was that Thomas Adams was allowed six acres at a place "called Providence," on the east side of Tadmuck Hill, "with a little swamp running down from the southeast corner." Also, "six acres at '*None Such*.'" Daniel Blodgett had four acres at Little Tadmuck, and Isaac Learned seven acres at Great Tadmuck. John Wright likewise had three acres at "Farther Tadmuck," and three acres at "Heather Tadmuck." This was in 1659, only six years from the beginning of the plantation; and these are probably the earliest allotments of land within the present limits of Westford. It is possible that one or two allotments were made a little earlier than this, to men whose heirs afterward became permanent residents; but if so, the records are silent concerning them. Esdras Read, who came from Wenham, probably in the spring or summer of 1654, was elected to office to manage the public affairs of the place at a general meeting holden on the 22nd of November,

1654. This was the first meeting. He did not remain long, for in 1660, the records say, "John Webb is admitted to purchase all the rights and privileges formerly granted by this town of Chelmsford to Esdras Read." He seems to have reserved a piece of meadow in Little Tadmuck, of which mention is made in 1674. In 1661 he removed to Boston, where he died in 1680; and his grave-stone is now standing in Copp's Hill burying-ground. (History of the Read family, p. 151.) His grandson, Thomas, with his wife, came here in 1685, and to them the town made an assignment of "four acres of land formerly granted to William Good." (*Gould?*) To this he also added by private purchase a tract of land lying on Tadmuck and Stony Brooks, upon which he built a house. It stood on the slope of the hill west of School House No. Two. His son, Thomas, Jr., owned the farm now known as "the Read Farm" in 1740, when he sold it to his son Joseph. (Transcript of deed.) This farm was alienated in 1876, having been in possession of the Reads for about one hundred and forty years.

Solomon Keyes, from Newbury, in 1664 had a grant of land on the north side of Frances Hill, and there he fixed his home, having married in Newbury in 1653 *Frances Grant*. From her no doubt the hill took its name. There is reason to suppose that he was here at a time still earlier than the date of his allotment. He appears to be the first permanent settler in the town of Westford and his family is the oldest in town. Not far from this time Joseph Butterfield seems to have settled on Frances Hill, and later the Wright family, on or near the farm now occupied by Edwin E. Heywood.

The Chamberlin homestead was in Chelmsford, not far from Westford line, and is now occupied by Charles Sheahan. The pioneer was Thomas Chamberlin, who was born in England, probably; came first to Charlestown, was next of Woburn, and was of the first company that peopled Chelmsford. His grandson, *Samuel*, born in 1685, lived in the south part of this town. He (Samuel) was a man of some distinction. His name often occurs in connection with the town or province affairs, and he was one of the original members of the first church here, formed in 1727. He died in 1769 in his eighty-fourth year.

The Fletcher homestead was in Chelmsford, but the family early spread into Westford, especially into the valley of the Stony Brook and the southwest part, and became very numerous and influential.

The Hildreth homestead was about midway between the Centre and the South Village of Chelmsford. This family also spread into Westford. A tract of land containing some five hundred acres on the east side of the town, came into their possession. It is not easy to give the exact boundaries. It included the houses, with land attached, of Augustus Bunce, George Porter Wright, the Drew brothers (Thomas and George), Isaac G. Minot and Julian Hildreth. Providence Meadow was its northwestern limit, and the house of Edward Symmes stands not far from its eastern border. The Hildreths also took up two or three farms south and east of Tadmuck Hill, or that spur of it known as Prospect Hill. Four or five houses there were at one time known as *Hildreth Row*.

The Parkers owned homesteads near what is now South Chelmsford, and the Proctors in the neighborhood of Heart Pond. Samuel Proctor, son of Robert, settled near Sparks Hill before 1700. At an early date these families were quite numerous in the south part.

Thomas Blodgett, Jr., occupied a tract of forty acres on the west side of Tadmuck Hill, including the farm of the late Amos Heywood. Joseph Underwood, from Reading, held a tract on the east side of the hill, including the farms of Albert P. Richardson, the Ira Leland heirs, and A. and E. G. Spalding. The homestead of Arthur Crouch was near Underwood's. Robert Conant lived near the house of Charles L. Fletcher. Samuel Underwood owned three hundred acres east of Providence Hill, including the farm of the late Abbot Read.

Thomas Kidder settled near Nonesuch Hill. He was son of John and Lydia, and was born in 1690. He married Joanna, daughter of Joseph Keyes, in 1716. Peter Dill, and after him Benjamin Robbins, had a farm near Nashoba Hill, and near him was Jonathan Hartwell, on the farm now occupied by Asaph B. Cutter. The Fosters— Moses and Elias—lived on the farms now owned by Henry P. Ruggles and the Millard heirs.

In 1679, Samuel Fletcher took up a piece of land on the west side of Great Tadmuck (twenty-six acres) the bounds of which were renewed in 1709. This was a part of Calvin Howard's farm. He subsequently made additions to his original grant until he owned about four hundred acres, extending to Sparks Hill and "Mackrill Cove," including the farm of Henry A. Hildreth, on which his grandson William settled about 1730, and the farm of Atwood Brothers.

Joshua Fletcher, Jr., owned a large tract in the vicinity of Boutwell's Meadow, extending southwest to Hop-Yard Swamp, southeast to the farm of the late Horace Pratt, including the farms of Stephen E. Hutchins, George Hartford and Rufus Patten. William Read, said to be a sea captain, had twelve acres on the east side of Boutwell's Meadow and Benjamin Butterfield a few acres adjoining, both parcels now included in the farm of the Coolidge brothers.

In the vicinity of Stony Brook was the farm of John Comings, who in 1707, or before, bought land and buildings near the present home of George B. Dupee. Adjoining him on the south was the allotment of John Spalding whose son Timothy seems to have settled upon it. Still further up the brook was the Bixby farm, including the farm of John Warren Day and the homestead of the late John Waldo Cumings.

The land in the vicinity of Brookside was originally in the possession of William Fletcher and Nathaniel Langley. The land west of the railroad at Westford Station was first held by Josiah Burge, whose house stood near the residence of the late Asia Nutting. He gave his name to Burge's Pond near by.

Ensign Joseph Keyes, before 1722, was in possession of land at Humhaw Brook, a small affluent of Keyes Pond; and west of this was land owned by Thomas Read. Andrew Spalding settled on the north side of Keyes Pond, and beyond, north, was the farm of John Bates. At the head of Long-Sought-For Pond was the small farm of Simon Rumrill, who probably came from Enfield, Connecticut. He purchased of Joseph Spalding in 1727.

"In 1683, further provision was made for the ministry by a grant of ten acres of meadow for the use of the ministry forever. This land was in the northwest corner of the town near to Groton, in a place called Snake Meadow. It was leased to John Spalding and Arthur Crouch for a succession of years, for four shillings a year, payable in corn at two shillings per bushel. It was given up to Westford as their part of the ministerial lands, when that town was incorporated in 1729." (History of Chelmsford, p. 27.)

In the vicinity of the ministry meadow was the allotment to Jonathan Butterfield, in 1728, of "four acres at a hill called Millstone Hill." Also, of Jacob Wright, who lived on the Lyon place.

In 1669 the town of Chelmsford granted to Thomas Henchman, William Fletcher and Josiah Richardson, a parcel of land to encourage the erection of another saw-mill. This was a tract of land now principally in Westford, but partly in West Chelmsford. It included the mill-site, now unused, on the tributary of Stony Brook, at Westford Corner. The brook is the outlet of Nubanussuck Pond and is called Saw-mill Meadow Brook, in the old deeds. This was the first mill of any kind within the limits of Westford, and the second saw-mill in Chelmsford, the first standing on River Meadow Brook in the southeast part. Neither of them were on Stony Brook. On this stream, from Forge Pond to its mouth, there are at least seven mill-sites, with a height of fall varying from eight to twenty-two feet, but not one of them had been used at this date, 1669. The water-power at Forge Village, then in Groton, was first used about 1680, and this was the first point at which a mill was built on the brook.

In 1724, William Chandler, clothier, of Andover, but last from Billerica, bought of Nathaniel Longley twenty acres, on both sides of Stony Brook. This included the mill-site at Brookside, and soon after he built a fulling-mill and grist-mill. On that spot the business of dressing cloth was carried on for about one hundred and forty years.

The first garrison house in this town was probably built near the residence of Solomon Keyes, on Frances Hill. The foundation is still remaining; another stood at Brookside, near the stone-yard of Noah Prescott. The house of Samuel Fletcher, near the present residence of Calvin Howard, was one of them; it was torn down in 1814. There was one at Forge Village—the old Prescott house, burned in 1876. Undoubtedly there were others that were long ago demolished. It is supposed that the only one now standing is the house occupied by Eli Tower. These were strongly built with brick or stout oak planks between the studs, and the upper story sometimes projected over the lower one. In this way the people sought to protect themselves against the Indians. When night came on and the deep gloom of the forest settled down upon them, the women and children hastened to these houses, and in them they often heard the yell of the savage startling the night air. Be it remembered that King Philip's war occurred only twenty-two years after the planting of Chelmsford, and it may be that men from this settlement were engaged in that contest.

In 1663 the town of Chelmsford laid out a highway from Chelmsford to Groton, and this is the account of it on Chelmsford town-book: "Beginning at Beaver Brook Bridge and running over the north side of Robins' Hill, through Richard Hildreth's yard to the west end of Heart Pond, over the swamp to Chamberlin's Meadow, and so on towards Groton on the east side of Tadmuck Great Meadows."

This route was indirect and circuitous. The road passed by the Elias Sweetser place, now occupied by Benjamin M. Fletcher, to a point near the house of George Hutchins, where it turned through the meadow around the Gilbert Parker house and across Nonesuch Brook, near the old Parkerville school-house, then led westward past Balch's, Martin's, E. J. Whitney's, Captain Smith's, and the West Burying Ground to Forge Village. The next road opened in the territory of Westford was probably the one leading from Deacon Isaiah Spalding's, in Chelmsford, over Frances Hill to the Stony Brook Valley. It was laid past Warren Hunt's and School House No. Two, over Tadmuck Brook, up the valley to the bridge at Westford Station. Afterward it was extended past Warren Day's to Boutwell's Hill and over Boutwell's Brook, and came out near Forge Village, where it intersected the Groton road, mentioned above. These roads soon became thoroughfares for towns on the west. Over the southern one passed a large share of the travel from Groton and Lancaster to Boston, crossing Billerica Great Bridge, as it was called. This bridge, sometimes called Hill's Bridge, was built in 1658, removed higher up the river in 1662, and again removed in 1699. It was erected and supported at the joint expense of Chelmsford, Groton, Dunstable, Dracut, Westford and Billerica. Groton obtained an act of exemption in 1699. (History of Chelmsford, p. 76.) Townsend was also compelled to help support it. (p. 18.) Dracut, Dunstable and Westford were holden till 1737, and Chelmsford till 1792.* (p. 77.)

The other road became the highway to Salem, which, before its decline, afforded a better market than Boston. Pork and rye were the chief articles of traffic, and these had to be transported by ox-teams, or on horseback; for in those days there were no wheeled vehicles save the lumbering ox-cart or wagon. Dr. Holmes' "one-hoss shay" was not yet introduced, and express wagons are a modern invention.

---

* Lancaster people came through Littleton. The house now occupied by Asaph B. Cutter was once a tavern for the accommodation of travellers.

The land north and west of the Railroad Station is now covered with a forest of pines which are cut and sold for fuel. The early settlers put the forests of their day to a different use. They tapped the pines and made tar and turpentine, and these products were probably carried to Salem. The town controlled the business so far as this: It gave permission to persons to use so many trees, and the license was recorded in the town-book. Among those who carried on the business were John Wright, who was licensed to use five hundred trees; Moses Parker, five hundred; and Thomas Robbins, three hundred and fifty. The ridge of land on which the North Burying Ground stands, was called *Tar-kiln Hill*, and it marks one place where these articles were manufactured. The region was afterward cleared and sown with rye; but the forest has again taken possession. Moreover, these two roads indicate the drift of population. The early expansion of Chelmsford plantation was northward and westward. Hence it was that the west precinct was so early and rapidly settled. The comparatively level and open lands of the Stony Brook Valley were taken up next after a few homesteads on Frances Hill. They also seized the lands in Nonesuch, now Parkerville, and pushed on quite early to the plain lands on the margin of Great Tadmuck Meadow.

In 1713 the struggle began for the erection of the west part into a precinct. Again and again were petitions sent in without avail. Apparently in response to the first one, the following vote was passed: "March 2, 1713. Voted, that the town doth not esteme those petitioners that did petition to be a separate precinct *capable* at present."

While the question was pending the town of Littleton was incorporated, November 2, 1714; and the residents of that town doubtless selected their earliest location for a meeting-house and training-field, or common, near the boundary line of Chelmsford with the expectation that a portion of the westerly part of that town lying so remote from the centre would at a future time be annexed to Littleton. Seven families were thus annexed for parish convenience and so remained until the west parish of Chelmsford was formed, when they were disannexed from Littleton by the General Court and included in said west parish, and Littleton took early measures for removing their centre about one mile southwesterly of their early location. The names of persons thus associated with Littleton were Joshua Fletcher, Josiah Whitney, Benjamin Robbins, Moses Foster, Joseph Hildreth, John Read and Samuel Chamberlin. (History of Chelmsford, p. 35.)

"1716, May 5. At a meeting of the inhabitance legaly warned in order to the choyse of gospel minister, the Rev. Benjamin Shattuck chosen. These men was chosen, namely, Joshua Fletcher, Walter Powers, and Samuel Dudley, to treat with Mr. Shattuck." (Records of Littleton.)

"1717, March 16. There was a vot past that the Inhabitance of Littleton joyne with the naiboring famelies of Concord and Chelmsford in a petition to the General Court to be layd oaf to us. There was also a vot past that two men of those of Concord and Chelmsford should be chose for assessers to assisit those of Littleton in making rates."

"1717, May 8. It was agreed upon that those of Concord and Chelmsford that paid to the minister's settlement, should have the same privilege in the meeting-house according to there pay as others have." (Littleton Records.)

About the same date, namely, January 4, 1716, the Chelmsford records have the following vote: "Voted that paying arrears those that have been petitioned to be dismissed from paying toward the support of the minister here any further—it is voted that they be dismissed provided they bring a certificate from Littleton Clerk that they pay towards the support of the minister there, so long as they pay to the minister at Littleton." (Book B, reversed p. 29.)

"Littleton, March 4, 1716-'17. This may certifie whom it may concern that Joshua Fletcher, Joseph Hildreth, Moses Foster, Benjamin Robbins, Josiah Barrett, and Josiah

Whitney are obliged to pay to the minister at Littleton. Samuel Dudley, Town Clerk."

"March 3, 1718–'19. John Read and Samuel Chamberlin are freed from paying to the minister, they bringing a certificate from Littleton." (Records of Chelmsford.)

Benjamin Robbins, Josiah Whitney, Joshua Fletcher, David Bixby, Moses Foster, Joseph Butterfield, Josiah Barrett, Joseph Hildreth, and John Proctor petitioned to be set off to Littleton, and their petition was denied March 17, 1719–'20. On the same day John Proctor, David Bixby and James Burn also presented a petition which was denied.

These requests seem to relate to the privilege of attending public worship. But the following vote appertains to the troublesome question of a new parish.

"Voted that William Fletcher, Benjamin Adams, and Captain Jonas Clark give reasons why the petition of Joseph Underwood, John Comings, and Jonas Prescott should not be granted." This was in 1724. Shortly after a denial was in like manner given to Joseph Underwood and twelve others who wanted a school-master who could preach to them.

These extracts reveal the progress of the controversy which was earnest and protracted.

"We have already mentioned," says Allen, "the unsuccessful attempt of the west part of the town to become a distinct parish or precinct. This year, 1724, they again stated their inconveniences and complaints to the General Court, who granted them leave to be erected into a separate religious society by the name of the West Precinct of Chelmsford. This act passed in May. In December following a committee was chosen by the town to make an equitable division between the old town and the new precinct. The Court ordered that the town should pay one hundred pounds to the west parish for their proportionable expense in building a meeting-house." (History of Chelmsford, pp. 36 and 37.) This was the house which the old town voted to build in 1710, which was erected in 1711 and finished and accepted by the town in 1712.

"Chelmsford, Nov. 10, 1725. Att a meeting of the Committee of the east precinct of the old town, it was ordered that Lieut. Wm. Fletcher of the sd precinct should receive the assessment that was made to pay Mr. Stoddard his Sallery and to pay the west precinct for there part of the meeting-house in the east precinct *as pr the General Court's order.*"

So it was not until the west parish had appealed to legislative authority that payment was made. The amount paid was one hundred pounds.

Among other records of bills paid was this: "To Ens. Chamberlin for three days going down to the General Court for to wait on the Committee in there making report concerning the two precincts."

As soon as the General Court gave them leave to be a parish, the people took measures to build a house of worship, and the following seems to be the first recorded vote concerning it:

"May 5, 1724. Pay Ens. Chamberlin for nine days attendance on the surveyor in surveying the town and setting the meeting house spott." (Records Book B, p. 176.) This house was begun in 1724, but was not completed for several years. It stood near the site now occupied by the Church of the First Parish of Westford.

It is evident that notwithstanding the decree of the General Court, the people of the old town did not assent to the organization of the new parish any farther than they were obliged to by law. For it was not until the year 1727, three years after the act of Court, and fourteen years after the first agitation of the matter, that they withdrew all opposition and recognized the west precinct. After so long a test of their patience and strength of purpose, they were then considered "*capable*" of self-government. The records give no hint of any feeling of triumph on the part of those who dwelt upon the hills and in the valleys of Tadmuck; but we may suppose that even then, those grave men believed with Galileo, that the *world moves*.

It appears from the records of the precinct, that Joseph Butterfield was collector in the year 1725-'26, when the amount of taxes put into his hands for collection was thirty pounds eleven shillings and four pence — less than one-third of the whole town assessment. But subsequently there was an additional sum of fifty pounds "towards finishing the meeting-house."

In the year 1726-'27, when Ebenezer Wright was treasurer and Timothy Spalding collector, the tax levied was the sum of two hundred and fourteen pounds and three shillings. In the year 1727-'28, William Fletcher was treasurer and Samuel Chamberlin collector, to whom was committed "the assessment granted to defray the charge of the ordination and the last finishing of the meeting-house; that is, the sum of fourty pounds twelve shillings and eight pence." In 1728-'29, William Fletcher was treasurer and Paul Fletcher collector, and another assessment was made of "fourty-two pounds seven shillings and one penny, to defray the last finishing of the meeting-house." The records of subsequent years show that this "last finishing" was the rock of Sisyphus to them, which, after being rolled up the hill, always rolled down again, till in 1771 the house was sold, another having been erected to take its place.

The most significant event in the brief history of the precinct was the formation of a church, November 15, 1727. In the chapter on ecclesiastical affairs this will be properly noticed. The town was incorporated September 23, 1729, and assumed an independent existence, taking its place among the grandly historic towns of Middlesex County.

Seventy-six years had then elapsed since the first blow was struck in the forests of Chelmsford. To one who has witnessed the sudden and wonderful growth of towns in the Western States of the Union, this must seem but a snail-like progress. Compared with the present that was indeed the day of small things. But those years were the years of *beginning* in a country where wealth had not accumulated for generations; and those beginnings were *seminal*, containing in them the germs of that completer civilization, that more enlightened faith, and that broader charity which mark the steps of true progress and determine the value of all worthy achievement. Those early efforts to make the solitary places glad were not misdirected. The new paths were rough, but the men who trod them were men who feared God and loved his cause.

> The old world cast them out with hate;
> The new world took them in with love;
> And here they built a Christian state,
> With faith and hope in God above.
>
> Debtors to man's lore or skill,
> They bore the stress of constant toil;
> With patience and unconquered will,
> They strove to make a stubborn soil
>
> Pay tribute to unwearying care.
> Unlearned they were, uncouth and rough;
> But men of faith and men of prayer;
> Men fashioned of the sternest stuff.
>
> Were they not heroes, though their names
> Are blazoned not on martial rolls?
> *True men* whose sterling virtue shames
> The meanness of some modern souls?

CHAPTER II.

FROM THE INCORPORATION TO THE BEGINNING OF THE REVOLUTIONARY WAR—THE CHARTER—FIRST TOWN MEETING—ADDITION OF TERRITORY FROM GROTON—FIRST TAX LIST—EARLY HOMESTEADS—OLD ROADS—SOLDIERS IN LOVEWELL'S EXPEDITION—NOTICE OF THE EXPEDITION TO CUBA, 1740—SOLDIERS AT THE SIEGE OF LOUISBURG, 1745—FRENCH NEUTRALS—FRENCH AND INDIAN WARS—EXTRACTS FROM TOWN RECORDS—REMONSTRANCE AGAINST THE STAMP ACT—SYMPATHY WITH THE BOSTON BRETHREN—THE SECOND MEETING HOUSE, 1770-'71.

THE long struggle for the right to be a precinct was now ended, but the people were not long contented with this. They desired the full privileges of a Town by enactment of the General Court. Accordingly a committee was appointed to draw up a petition, present it and enforce it by the usual arguments and appeals. This committee consisted of Joseph Underwood, Joshua Fletcher and Benjamin Robbins. The date of their appointment does not appear on the records, but "December 25, 1728, it was ordered that William Fletcher, Treasurer of sd Precinct shall pay to Joseph Underwood for going to the General Court to procure us a township the sum of 2 pounds. Also, to Joshua Fletcher for money paid for entering two petitions and other expenses in ordere to our being set off a seperate township the sum of one pound, two shillings." Also, voted, August 28, 1738, almost nine years afterward, "to allow Benjamin Robins one pound ten shillings for his going to boston to git us a Township."

The General Court acceded to their request and granted the following

Charter.

ANNO TERTIO REGNI REGIS GEORGII SECUNDI.

An Act for Erecting the West Precinct of the Town of Chelmsford into a Township by the name of Wesford.*

Whereas, the Inhabitants of the West Precinct in the Town of Chelmsford in the County of Middlesex, have addressed this Court, setting forth the many difficulties they now labor under as a Precinct, which might be effectually remedied if they were constituted a Township:

Be it therefore enacted by the Lieut. Governor, Council, and Representatives in General Court assembled and by authority of the same,

That the lands contained in the said Precinct, as they are hereafter set forth and described, be and hereby are set off and constituted a distinct and separate Township by the name of Wesford. The bounds of the said Township to be as follows: Beginning at the South East Corner at a Heap of Stones, being the bounds between Chelmsford and the said Town of Wesford, thence running north to a chestnut tree marked and stones about it, so running on a straight line north to a tree marked at Coll. Tyng's Farm, thence Westwardly upon Coll. Tyng's Farm or Dunstable line to a heap of stones, thence Southerly by Groton line till it come to Littleton land, then upon Littleton land Southerly or Southeasterly, till it come to Concord Line, thence easterly on Concord Line to Bounds first mentioned. And that the Inhabitants of the said lands as before bounded and described, be and hereby are vested with the Powers, Privileges, and Immunities that the Inhabitants of any of the towns are or ought by Law to be vested with.

Sept. 20, 1729. This Bill having been read three several times in the House of Representatives,
    Passed to be enacted.
        J. QUINCY, Speaker.

Sept. 23, 1729. This Bill having been read three several times in Council,
    Passed to be enacted.
        J. WILLARD, Secretary.

---

* This was the mode of spelling the word used by the Town Clerks generally, until 1744, after which time the practice changed to Westford, which without doubt is the true orthography. "Engrost Bill for a new Town by the name of Westford." Massachusetts General Court Records, Vol. 14. September 23, 1729.

By the Honble the Lieut. Governor. I consent to the enacting of this Bill.

Wm DUMMER.*

The neighboring town of Bedford received its charter on the same day, and if it be allowed the priority, then Westford was the twenty-eighth town in the county in the order of incorporation or settlement.

There is no record on the town books of any town meeting held during the autumn of 1729. Probably there was no real necessity for one, inasmuch as the Committee of the Precinct, at a meeting held September 2d, of that year, had made all needful provision for the next fiscal year.

THE FIRST TOWN MEETING.

" Wesford, March the 2d, 1729-'30.

At a General Town meeting of the freeholders and other inhabitants of the sd town Regularily Assembled to Chuse Town officers for the year ensuing.

Dea. John Commings Chose moderator for the work of the day.

Voted to Chuse five Selectmen for the year ensuing.

Dea. Joshua Fletcher Chose the first Selectman. Dea. John Commings Chose the second Selectman. Samuel Chamberlin Chose the third Selectman. Ins. Joseph Keyes Chose the fourth Selectman. Thomas Reed Chose the fifth Selectman. Dea. Joshua Fletcher Chose Town Clerk. Samuel Faset, Town Treasurer.

Constables — Aaron Parker and Aquila Underwood. Surveyors of Highways, Elias Foster, Ephraim Hildreth,

---

* William Dummer had been acting Governor for a year then, in place of William Burnet who was appointed Governor by the King, and came to Boston in July, 1728. He died September, 1729, and Lieut. Governor Dummer was again in charge. George II. succeeded his father, George I., in 1727, and reigned thirty-three years. He died October 25, 1760, " universally lamented."

Henry Wright, and Andrew Spaulding. Tithingmen—Benjamin Robins, and James Hildreth Jun.

Fence Vewers—Joseph Hildreth Jr. and William Reed.

Hogg reaves—William Butterfield and Ebenezer Hildreth.

The above named persons were Sworn to the faithful Discharge of their Respective oficeses as the law directs.

JOSHUA FLETCHER,
Town Clerk of Wesford.

Voted the day above sd that swine shall goe at large. ——that Samuel Fletcher Senier's head shall be left out of the rates for the year ensuing. Voted the day above sd to Joine with Capt. Jonas Prescott, Ebenezer Prescott, Ebenezer Townsend, and Abner Kent, all of Grotton, in Petioning to the General Court in ordere to their being anext to Wesford Township. Voted—the Selectmen shall apoint a man to Joine with the above sd Persons in Petioning to the General Court in ordere to their being anext to Wesford Township.

JOSHUA FLETCHER,
Town Clerk of Wesford."

Under date of January 7, 1730–'31, the Selectmen ordered Samuel Faset, Treasurer of said town to pay

"To Joshua Fletcher for going to the General Court with Capt. Jonas Prescott in ordar for the families living in that part of Grotton to be anext to the Town of Westford for money and time expended the sum of 2£—11s. 7d."

The petition of Captain Prescott and others met with a favorable response, as will be seen from the following enactment of the General Court:

"A petition of Jonas Prescott, Ebenezer Prescott, Abner Kent, and Ebenezer Townsend, Inhabitants of the town of Groton, Praying that they and their Estates contained in the following Boundaries, viz: Beginning at North East corner of Stony Brook Pond, from thence extending to the Northwest Corner of Westford, commonly called Tyng's

Corner, and so bounded Southerly by said Pond, may be set off to the Town of Westford for their greater convenience in attending public worship.

In the House of Representatives: Read and Ordered that the Petitioners within named, with their Estates according to the Bounds before recited, be and hereby are to all intents and purposes set off from the Town of Groton and annexed to the Town of Westford.

In Council, read and Concurred, September 10, 1730.

J. BELCHER."

(Massachusetts General Court Records, Vol. 14, p. 386.)

The territory thus joined to this town was triangular in shape, the base of the triangle being the shore of Forge Pond, and the sharp point Tyng's Corner on Millstone Hill. In the description it is not definitely said that a portion of Forge Pond was included, but this was really the case, since the bound or monument fixing the southeast corner is on the Littleton side. Nearly one hundred years afterward, namely in May, 1827, the Selectmen of the two towns ran the boundary lines between them and erected permanent monuments where none had been previously erected, and the lines and monuments are thus described: "Beginning at a stone post on Millstone hill marked G. W. T. at the ancient pillar of stones, thence running South 10° West 186 rods to a stone post near the house of Oliver Wright; thence South $12\frac{1}{4}$° West 386 rods to another stone post on Clay-pit hill; thence South 12° West 252 rods to another stone post near the house of Capt. Nathan Brown; thence South $10\frac{1}{4}$° West 49 rods and 20 links to the shore of Forge Pond, so called, and thence the same course into said Pond [and over?] to a heap of stones the corner of Littleton." (Miscellaneous Records of Westford, p. 216.)

The line of this triangle on the side next to Westford, began on the southeastern shore of Forge Pond and crossing the pond it passed a little west of the house now occupied by George Wright, over or near the spring in the bank, now covered up, over the brook and Kissacook Hill, west of the Poor House, and onward across the old stage-road from Lowell to Groton, to Millstone Hill.

Probably there was no computation of the area of this triangle at any time. Only four men are named as the owners of it, but they, it is supposed, held titles to only a portion, and the remainder was wild or "common" land.

This was the only acquisition of territory the town has ever made, and there has been no loss, except possibly such as might occur in the adjustment of disputed lines between it and the adjacent towns. In this it has been more fortunate than some others whose domain has become narrow by division and apportionment. A dispute did arise about the boundary line between Littleton and Westford as the following extract from the records will show: "1756. In the month of April the bounds Between our town and Groton and Littleton, Acton and Chelmsford were renewed as the Law directs and their was no desputes on any of the bounds except the old Despute Between Littleton and our town." The Westford records do not show what were the grounds of dispute, nor how the matter was settled. It may fairly be inferred from them, however, that this town was not the aggrieved party.

In 1755, Samuel Adams and John Glenny, living in the north part of the town, sent a petition to the General Court to be set off with all their lands and annexed to Dunstable. The town opposed them, and through its committee presented a remonstrance; and the prayer of the petitioners was refused. In 1756, Thomas Read, Esq., was paid "for money expended, time and horse journeys to Boston in behalf of this town to save any part of it from being set off to Carlisle." This attempt at division was also unsuccessful.

THE FIRST TAX-LIST.

The names are copied as they stand on the book, but the sum that each person was assessed is not given. For a long time the tax-payers were divided into two lists, called the North and South; and each list was put into the hands of a constable for the collection of the taxes.

THE SOUTH LIST.

Samuel Procter,
Joseph Buterfeild,
Nathaniel Boynton,
Thomas Barrit,
James Burn,
Joseph Buterfeild, Jun.,
John Buterfeild,
James Brown,
Wid. Tabitha Blodgett,
Samuel Chamberlin,
Amos Davice,
Joshua Fletcher,
William Fletcher, Jr.,
Samuel Fletcher, Jr.,
Timothy Fletcher,
Wid. Elizabeth Fletcher,
Elias Foster,
Moses Foster,
Ephraim Hildreth,
Jonathan Hartwell,
Joseph Hildreth,
Joseph Hildreth, Jun.,
Ebenezer Hildreth,
Ephraim Hildreth, Jun.,
James Hildreth,
James Hildreth, Jun.,
Thomas Heald,
Aaron Parker,
Joseph Procter,
Jonathan Procter,
Thomas Procter,
Ezekiel Procter,
Nathan Procter,
Walter Powers,
Benjamin Robins,
John Reed,
Thomas Robins,
John Reed, Jun.,
William Barit,
Ebenezer Spaulding,
Joseph Temple,
Wid. Joannah Kydar,
Ephraim Buterfeild,
Hugh Smith.

The number of names in this list is forty-four, and the sum assessed is £59 11s. 11d.

THE NORTH LIST.

Samuel Adams,
Josiah Burge,
David Bixby,
Wid. Elizabeth Buterfeild,
Benjamin Buterfeild,
William Buterfeild,
Edward Bates,
John Blodget,
Dea. John Commings,
William Chandler,
Ephraim Chandler,
Ephraim Craft,
Thomas Reed,
William Reed,
Jonathan Reed,
Simon Rumrill,
Ser. Timothy Spaulding,
Timothy Spaulding, Jun.,
Andrew Spaulding,
Ebenezer Townsend,
Joseph Undarwood,
Aquila Undarwood,
Ebenezer Wright,
Jacob Wright,

William Fletcher,	Henry Wright,
Paul Fletcher,	Ebenezer Wright, Jun.,
Joseph Fletcher,	Ins. Joseph Keyes,
Jonathan Fletcher,	Joseph Keyes, Jun.,
Jonas Fletcher,	Abner Kent,
Samuel Faset,	Jabez Keep,
Adam Gould,	Joseph Pollard,
Josiah Heald,	James Pollard,
Capt. Jonas Prescott,	William Shed,
Ebenezer Prescott,	Jonathan Cleaveland.
Jonas Prescott,	

In this list there are forty-five names, and the sum assessed is £65 6s. 1d. The whole amount in the two lists is £125. The number of names in the two lists is eighty-nine. Of these, four were widows and five of the men paid only a poll tax, and hence there were only seventy-eight men who were owners of real estate. To these early sovereigns of industry the town was chiefly indebted for its subsequent development and growth; and, as in the mind of the real lover of history a degree of interest bordering on the fascination of romance attaches to these founders of the town, an attempt has been made to fix their homesteads and to indicate as far as practicable the residence of each. In the absence of any regular plot of the town, and in view of the long time that has passed since they lifted up their axes upon the thick trees, this has been no easy task. After a thorough searching of the books of Chelmsford and of the numerous volumes in the Registry of Deeds, in East Cambridge, the following are the materials that have been gathered:

THE SOUTH LIST.

Samuel Procter lived near the present residence of Amos Leighton, and his farm included a portion of Sparks Hill. His house stood in the field near Mr. Leighton's, and on the same side of the road. The original owner seems to have been Peter Talbut. In 1714 Henry Sparks, of Concord, sold to Samuel Proctor, "all the lands that my honored father Henry Sparks possessed in Chelmsford, lying near Farther Tadmuck." The older Sparks married Martha Barrett, of Chelmsford, and died 1694.

Joseph Butterfield lived on Frances Hill, near Chamberlin's corner.

Nathaniel Boynton; on the farm of Coolidge Brothers.

Thomas Barrett lived in the extreme south part of the town, a mile or more from Parkerville. No open road at present leads to the spot.

James Burn, or Bourne, as the name is spelled on the Chelmsford books, lived probably on the farm of Samuel N. Burbeck. He is said to have been a potter by trade, and that his yard was in the field in the rear of the houses of Nathan S. Hamblin and John W. Abbot.

Joseph Butterfield, Jun., owned land near Deacon Calvin Howard's, recently in possession of John Pierce, of Hyde Park. The house stood not far from Deacon Howard's. He died before August 16, 1741.

John Butterfield; not known with certainty, but probably near Boutwell's meadow.

James Brown; not ascertained.

Tabitha Blodget, widow of Thomas; on the Amos Heywood place.

Samuel Chamberlin lived in Nonesuch, now Parkerville, near the house of George H. Elliot, somewhere in the triangle now formed by the roads.

Amos Davice; nothing known of him. There is no record of his marriage, and probably he had no homestead.

Joshua Fletcher; on the farm now occupied by Robert J. Taylor.

William Fletcher, Jun., lived on the farm now occupied by Henry A. Hildreth.

Samuel Fletcher, Jun.; on the Calvin Howard place.

Timothy Fletcher; on the farm of Rufus Patten.

Elizabeth Fletcher, widow of Samuel Fletcher, Sen. She probably lived with her son Samuel, Jr., on the Howard place.

Elias Foster; on the Lieut. John Hildreth place, lately occupied by Morris Millard.

Moses Foster owned the land near the house of Henry P. Ruggles and school-house Number Four. He petitioned for a way to his house, and he may have lived away from the public road.

Ephraim Hildreth; on the Julian Hildreth place.

Jonathan Hartwell; on the farm now owned and occupied by Asaph B. Cutter.

Joseph Hildreth; on the farm of Isaac G. Minot.

Joseph Hildreth, Jun.; on the farm of the late Abijah Hildreth.

Ebenezer Hildreth; in that part of the town called "Texas," on or near the Hapgood place.

Ephraim Hildreth, Jun.; on the farm now owned by the heirs of Abel Fletcher.

James Hildreth; on the farm now occupied by Charles A. Wright.

James Hildreth, Jun.; not certainly known, but probably on the farm lately owned by J. Boynton Read.

Thomas Heald; near Forge Village, on the shore of the pond, on the farm of David P. Lawrence. He soon removed to a farm near Jeptha Wright's.

Aaron Parker; on the spot on which the house of George Hutchins stands.

Joseph Procter; in Parkerville, near the junction of the two roads at the school-house.

Jonathan Procter; in the southeast part, near Pond Brook.

Thomas Procter; on or near the present residence of Frederick Martin.

Ezekiel Procter; not fully determined, but probably near Thomas Procter.

Nathan Procter; on the farm now owned by Capt. Jacob Smith.

Walter Powers; it seems probable that he owned the farm now occupied by John Wayne, near Nashoba Hill and on the line of the Nashua and Acton Railroad. He was assessed a few times in the town and county lists, but paid no poll tax. The farm was in possession of Joseph Hooker as early as 1740.

Benjamin Robbins, near Nashoba Hill and southeast of Asaph B. Cutter's, on an old road laid out in 1720, now seldom used.

John Reed; probably the son of Thomas Read, sen. His farm was near E. J. Whitney's.

Thomas Robbins; in southeast part, near the house of John Hutchins, Jr.

John Reed, Jun. His farm was near Amos Leighton's. It was occupied a few years ago by Alpheus and Annan Reed.

William Barrett, on the premises now occupied by George Yapp — the old tavern stand of Timothy Hartwell.

Ebenezer Spaulding; near T. J. Wheeler's.

Joseph Temple; in the region called "Texas," or in that vicinity.

Joanna Kidder, widow of Thomas Kidder; at Nonesuch Hill, southwest of the Gilbert Parker house.

Ephraim Butterfield; not known.

Hugh Smith. He paid only a poll tax, and probably had no homestead.

THE NORTH LIST.

Samuel Adams; in the extreme north part, near Allen R. Perham's.

Josiah Burge; in the Stony Brook Valley, south of the railroad station.

David Bixby; on the homestead of the late John Waldo Cummings.

Elizabeth Butterfield, widow of Benjamin Butterfield (son of Joseph), who died before 1715. She lived on Frances Hill.

Benjamin Butterfield, son of Benjamin and grandson of

Joseph, lived on the east side of Boutwell's Meadow, near Oren Coolidge's.

William Butterfield, brother of the preceding, lived on Frances Hill.

Edward Bates; north of the present residence of Dennis Burke, and west of Long-Sought-For Pond.

John Blodget; on the Amos Heywood place, on the west side of Tadmuck Hill.

Deacon John Commings; in the valley of the Stony Brook, near the Westford railroad station. His farm included the land now owned by George B. Dupee and Sarah Cummings.

William Chandler; at Brookside. He was the owner of a fulling-mill there, built about 1725.

Ephraim Chandler, cousin of William; on the northwest side of Flushing Pond.

Ephraim Craft; near Alvan Fisher's.

William Fletcher, the father of Capt. Amos; in the valley of the Stony Brook, near William Taylor's.

Paul Fletcher; near Boutwell's Meadow.

Joseph Fletcher; near Tadmuck Brook, on the farm owned by the heirs of Joshua Decatur.

Jonathan Fletcher; in the valley of the Stony Brook, northwest of the railroad, near Thomas Horan's.

Jonas Fletcher; in the valley, near Jeptha Wright's.

Samuel Fassett; near Providence Hill and the sources of Tadmuck Brook. His house stood near the land of Isaac W. Green.

Adam Gould; not known. He paid only a poll tax and probably had no estate.

Josiah Heald; at the centre, near the residence of Artemas W. Cummings.

Captain Jonas Prescott lived in Forge Village. His house stood on the promontory formed by the brook and the margin of the pond.

Ebenezer Prescott, son of Captain Jonas, lived in Forge Village.

Jonas Prescott, son of Captain Jonas, in Forge Village.

Thomas Read; on Frances Hill, owner of the farm so long known as the "Read Farm."

William Read lived on the farm now owned by Oren and Edward C. Coolidge.

Jonathan Read, brother of William. He owned land on Tadmuck Hill, near the Kendall A. Wright place, but his residence is not known.

Simon Rumrill owned a farm of ten acres at the head of Long-Sought-For Pond, near the brick tavern.

Timothy Spaulding; on the farm of Luke L. Fletcher.

Timothy Spaulding, Jr., probably had no homestead, but lived with his father, Timothy Sen. He died in 1734.

Andrew Spaulding lived north of Keyes Pond on the farm recently occupied by John Morrison.

Ebenezer Townsend; in Forge Village.

Joseph Underwood; on the eastern slope of Tadmuck Hill. His house stood nearly opposite of the residence of the late Ira Leland.

Aquila Underwood; on Tadmuck Hill, near the house of N. Harwood Wright.

Ebenezer Wright; on the farm now occupied by Edwin E. Heywood.

Jacob Wright; on the Lyon place.

Henry Wright; near the house of Isaac W. Green.

Ebenezer Wright, Jr.; on the homestead of his father, Ebenezer Wright, Sen.

Joseph Keyes; on Frances Hill, near the residence of the late Trueworthy Keyes.

Joseph Keyes, Jr.; on Humhaw Brook, the present homestead of George Keyes.

Abner Kent; in Forge Village.

Jabez Keep; in Forge Village.

Joseph Pollard; had no homestead and paid only a poll tax. He soon removed to Nottingham West, now Hudson, N. H.

James Pollard; without homestead. He subsequently settled in the Centre, where he kept a tavern, on the premises now held by Mrs. John W. P. Abbot.

William Shedd; also without homestead, and no information respecting him can be gleaned from the town records.

Jonathan Cleaveland; not ascertained. Perhaps he was a son of Samuel Cleaveland, who lived near the old mill-site in Providence Meadow.

OLD ROADS.

The two roads early laid out by the Town of Chelmsford through the present territory of Westford are described on pages 12 and 13. One of them is constantly referred to in the old deeds as the Groton Road and the other as the Stony Brook Road. Two others are also frequently mentioned, namely: the Long-Sought-For Road, which, crossing the brook near Westford Corner, led over the plain to Long-Sought-For Pond; and the Tadmuck Road, which led by Minot's Corner and intersected the Groton road near Amos Leighton's.

Inasmuch as the description of highways often enables the inquirer to fix the homesteads of the early settlers, the transcripts of many of them are here given. They are sometimes very indefinite, but in many instances they help us to a knowledge of natural objects and indicate the progress of settlement. Some of them were only private ways that have long since been forsaken; others became thoroughfares, which are now much travelled.

At the second annual town meeting, held March 1, 1730–'31 a committee was chosen "to view the highways and take account what each person will have for satisfaction for damage done in their property, and make report to the town. Paul Fletcher, Samuel Chamberlin and Thomas Read, Committee for sd business."

At a meeting of the selectmen, held in April, 1732, "to divide the highways and private or particular ways to each surveyor their part of ways to keep in repair and men to do the services," the following assignment was made:

1. "Thomas Procter should repair the Country road from Elias Foster's field fence to Concord line, and the way

from Samuel Fitches house by Reed's and Burn's to the meeting house; and all the ways east and southeast from sd way from Chelmsford, Concord and Littleton lines you are to repair, and all the men who dwell in said limits are appointed to assist in sd work as the surveyor shall appoint."

The western boundary of this highway district began at Fitch's, now John Murphy's place, and ran from thence to George B. Hildreth's; then, turning back, it ran by Amos Leighton's to Minot's Corner; turning again, it passed George P. Wright's and wound around Blake's Hill, by J. Boynton Reed's to the meeting-house.

2. "That William Barrett should repair the way from Benjamin Robinses to the meeting house, and the way from Joshua Fletcher's by Boynton's to the bridge by the Wid. Blodgett's; and all the wayes over Tadmuck [swamp] to Littleton line, and all the wayes within the sd limits; and all the men who dwell in the sd limits, and Mr. Joseph Underwood's family, are appointed to assist in sd work," etc.

The eastern boundary of this district began at the old Robbins' house, near Nashoba, and ran by Atwood Brothers and "Mackril Cove," to Mrs. Daniel Flagg's and onward to the meeting-house. It also included the road from Robert J. Taylor's, past Miner's Corner and Rufus Patten's, to the house of Ai Bicknell.

3. "That William Read should repair the Country road from Groton line to the town way that goes from Capt. Prescott's to the meeting house, and from thence to the meeting house, and so to Ebenezer Wright's, and so by sd Wright's to Chelmsford line, and so by Chelmsford line to Stoney brook, and all the Bridges over Stonney brook (being in wayes laid out), and all the wayes northerly from the first mentioned way to Stoney brook; and all the men who dwell in the sd limits (excepting Mr. Joseph Underwood's family) are appointed to assist in sd work," etc.

The southern limit of this district was the road from Groton line at Swan Brook, near the Abraham Prescott place, through Forge Village, over the plain through Boutwell's Meadow and a piece of woodland now owned by the heirs of John W. P. Abbot, past the Heywood place, by the Common and the East Cemetery, to Chamberlin's Corner, turning there to the Chelmsford line beyond Edwin E. Heywood's, then turning back to Chamberlin's Corner and over Frances Hill to Brookside. A part of this line is no longer used, namely: from the plain over Boutwell's Meadow to the Bixby Hill.

4. "That William Chandler should repair all the wayes on the north side of Stonney brook (except Groton road), and all the men (excepting the families set of from Groton) who dwell in sd limits are appointed to assist in sd work," etc.

It will be seen that this fourth district included nearly one-half of the town. That half, however, was not so densely peopled as the other. This seems to be the first time the town was divided into highway districts.

In the year 1744, fifteen years after the incorporation, a description of several roads in this town which had been laid out by the old town, and which had been copied from Chelmsford books, was put upon record by a vote of the town. (See Records, Vol. I, pp. 213–17). These transcripts are here given in an abbreviated form:

1. "Chelmsford March 14, 1721–'22. A Highway laid out from the town to Groten Road by Capt. Jonas Prescott's field which way begins by the corner of Lt. William Fletcher's pasture wall, . . . and so by many bounds till it comes to Westford line, near to Joseph Keyes' fence; from thence . . . to Jacob Butterfield's land, and then between the land of Jacob Butterfield and Thomas Read . . . to Thomas Read's house; from thence by the land of Thomas Read, Jonas Fletcher, Joseph Fletcher, Timothy Spalding, and John Comings, and from thence by marked trees . . . until it comes to Groten road by Capt. Prescott's field. The sd way was laid out through a piece of Joshua Fletcher's land, which lieth on the most westerly side of Boughtall's brook."

This is the road up the Stony Brook Valley, a part of which must have been in use long before the date of this transcript.

2. "Chelmsford Feb. 11, 1722-'3. Two highways laid out, . . . firstly a highway beginning at a white oak standing at the southeasterly corner of Thomas Read's orchard fence, leading northerly to a white oak at the east end of sd Read's stone wall . . . to Samuel Fletcher's land and then turns by the dividing line between sd Fletcher's land and the land of Thomas Read, and so runs through sd Fletcher's land aboute seventy-three rods and a half, down to Stoney brook, . . . and runs over the brook, . . . through Fletcher's land . . . until it comes to a pine tree which is Samuel Fletcher's corner, and from thence straight to Jonathan Fletcher's land . . . and so a bridele way through Samuel Fletcher's meadow and thence the most convenient way to the meadow of Thomas Read, Joseph Fletcher, and Jonas Fletcher; and so through the meadow of Jonas Fletcher by the dividing line between his and Samuel Fletcher's meadow."

This road began near School-house Number Two and ran past William Taylor's, over the bridge by the railroad, turning to the left and passing near Thomas Horan's, and extending to some point near the north burying-ground, or perhaps to some point near the railroad station.

3. "2$^{dly.}$ A Highway beginning at Joseph Keyes' field and as the path goes to Stoney brook and over sd brook and then leading toward Nathaniel Langlee's house within about four rods of the southerly side of his house, and from sd house to the road to Long-Sought-for." [Amended in 1740, Vol. I., p. 172.]

This road was laid out by the house of the late Trueworthy Keyes and across the brook at Brookside Station, by the house now owned by the heirs of Hiram H. Decatur to the road across the sandy plain.

4. "A Highway Laid out in Chelmsford June 15, 1719, over the meadow of Ens. Joseph Keyes."

This was the meadow at Keyes Pond through which Humhaw Brook flows. The road has been discontinued.

5. "Chelmsford, May 13, 1719. A highway of three rods wide laid out, beginning at a white oak tree marked at

the line between Littleton and Chelmsford, running as the path now is by marked trees . . . until it comes to the highway which is laid to the meadow of Auther Crouch, Deceased."

This is the road beginning at the corner near Joseph Whitney's and running to Calvin Howard's. Arthur Crouch owned a meadow northwest of Dea. Howard's.

6. "Chelmsford Nov. 1, 1726. Joshua Fletcher, Samuel Chamberlin [and] Benjamin Adams, being a Committee appointed by the Selectmen to lay out Highways in the west part of the Town, proceded and laid out a highway beginning at the west precinct meeting house where they took off a piece of Robert Cunnant's land at the southeasterly corner of his land . . . and thence westerly to a great white oak tree in land that was laid out to Mr. Edward Emerson; and on the southern side of the sd meeting house the sd way began at a stake and heap of stones and to be three rods wide, running through the land laid out to Mr. Emerson westerly, . . . thence through the land of Paul Fletcher and common land to the dwelling house of Thomas Blodget Jr. . . . thence by said Blodget's house as near as the path now goes to Paul Fletcher's, by Boutall's meadow; and Jonas Prescott Jr and Thomas Heald was by Paul Fletcher's consent and the committee's consent, allowed a bridle way to pass and repass through the land and meadow of Paul Fletcher to go over a narrow place of Boutall's meadow to and from meeting, . . . provided the sd Prescott and Heald make a causeway over said meadow at their own cost; and also the liberty to pass and repass as above mentioned, through the land of Joshua Fletcher on the westerly side of sd meadow unto the sd causeway."

This road is now a part of Main Street, at the Centre. It passed by the Amos Heywood house, which stands on or near the site of Thomas Blodget, Jr's., house, and turned to the left about half-way down the Bixby Hill and so led through the woods to Boutwell's Meadow. (See p. 3 of this Ms.)

7. "Chelmsford, October 31, 1726. Town highways laid out by the Selectmen's order. . . . A town highway beginning at Groten road to the east of Samuel Chamberlin Jun. his dwelling house against sd Chamberlin's field . . . thence running northeasterly acrost sd Chamberlin's land unto the path that goes from Aaron Parker's house by the southwesterly corner of sd Chamberlin's stone wall, and to be a bridle way so far; . . . then the sd way runs by the sd Chamberlin's land or stone wall which is on the west, thence by a line of marked trees through Aaron Parker's land until it comes within about three rods of Joseph Hildreth and Ephraim Hildreth's fence, from thence bounded easterly by sd fence and westerly by marked trees unto the road that leads from town to Tadmuck, and acrost sd way through some land left for a highway and the land of Joseph Spalding and the land of Mr. Edward Emerson unto the west precinct meeting house."

This road began near W. F. Balch's and ran northeast to the corner where it made a sharp turn and led by John Wilson's to Minot's Corner, thence to a point nearly opposite George Drew's house, where it turned around Blake's Hill and by the Boynton Reed farm to the centre.

8. "On the day above sd [Oct. 31, 1726] laid out a town way, beginning against the way that leads to Littleton by Joseph Butterfield's, and running by the house of Nathaniel Boynton. Bounded northwesterly by the land of Joshua Fletcher to a rock and heap of stones near said Boynton's shop, thence between said Boynton's shop and dwelling house, and thence by marked trees . . . unto the land of Benoni Perham deceased, and through one corner of sd Perham's land over a rocky gutter and so as the path now goes to the highway laid out from the Precinct meeting house to Boutals meadow by Thomas Blodget Jr's. The land was left for a highway in the Division of Commons."

This began at Ai Bicknell's and led by O. and E. C. Coolidge's to the meadow on the west.

9. "On the day above sd [Oct. 31, 1726] a town way laid out issuing out of the road at the easterly end of

Robert Cunnant's dwelling house, running northerly through a corner of Robert Cunnant's land, a slip of common land and Josiah Burge's land and the land of Timothy Spalding, and between the land of Deacon Comings and said Burge's unto Stoney Brook road at Josiah Burge's northwesterly corner of his field."

This is now the street leading from Charles L. Fletcher's to the railroad station.

10. "Chelmsford, May, 1722. Laid out a highway beginning at the house of Ens. Joseph Keyes to and over the meadow of William Langlee and to and over the meadow of John Steavens . . . then turning by Keyes Pond, thence by the land of Josiah Burge and between [through?] the land of John Comings upon a brow, thence by marked trees on the westerly side to a causeway."

This began at the house now occupied by George Keyes, and ran past the John Morrison house, Jacob Blodget's Corner, the North Burying-ground, through the woods, by Thomas Horan's to the bridge near the railroad, not long since known as the Willard Fletcher Bridge. A part of it had been previously laid out.

11. "On the day above sd, laid out a highway beginning at Groten road near the saw mill and over Stoney Brook below the saw mill through the land of John Comings and several others which were owners of sd saw mill, about 60 poles, thence by the land of John Comings, William Langlee, Ens. Keyes and Josiah Burge by marked trees, and thence by marked trees on the southerly side to the highway from the old sawmill to the above sd causeway."

The saw-mill here mentioned was at the railroad station, and the road passed back of George B. Dupee's house, over the brook, and probably led in the direction of Thomas Horan's and intersected the now travelled road near Mr. Horan's. It has been discontinued.

12. "Chelmsford Dec. 26, 1722. A highway laid out beginning at the Pond Plain to the west of Aaron Parker's old house and runs to John Foster's field, and from thence

as the path now runs to Aaron Parker's land that he purchased of Isaac Barron."

This was doubtless a private way, not now in use.

13. "On the day above sd, a highway laid out issuing out of the road that goes to Peter Procter's and is to run on the northerly side of Aaron Parker's meadow-fence and before sd Parker's house, and thence to Groten road by the land of Samuel Chamberlin."

This began at the old road which once passed through the east part of None Such Meadow and run by George Hutchins' to W. F. Balch's.

14. "On the day above sd there was a highway laid out through Samuel Procter's land which was Sparkes, about twenty rods in length . . . as the path now goes towards James Burn's field and from thence to sd Burn's wall, and so by marked trees by Burn's wall to John Read's land on Spark's hill."

This was a short road near Amos Leighton's, and is now a link connecting other roads.

15. "Chelmsford May 6, 1723. A highway was laid out from Jonathan Hartweil's westerly to Littleton highway."

Hartwell lived on the farm now owned by Asaph B. Cutter.

16. "Another highway laid out the day above sd from Groten road to the highway that goes from Stoney brook to Groten mill . . . Begins at a black oak on the north side of Groten road by a spruce swamp called the hop yard, which oak is the bounds of Joshua Fletcher's land, and so southeasterly by sd Fletcher's land to James Hildreth's land and so east by sd Hildreth's land to the highway that goes from Stoney brook to Groten."

This began at Miner's Corner and led toward the Nashua and Acton railroad, and turned into the main road on the plain, west of the railroad bridge.

17. "February 21, 1707. A highway laid out from Stony Brook to John Richardson's mill, beginning at the highway that leads from John Snow's to the meeting house."

The mill of John Richardson was probably at the mouth of Stony Brook, and John Snow lived perhaps in the vicinity of Brookside.

18. "February 21, 1707. A highway laid out from Stony brook houses through the land of Joseph Butterfield and so over Frances hill by Joseph Keyes . . . and Flaggy meadow plain . . . and by the east end of Henry Farwell's house into the country road."

This is an earlier transcript of the road leading over Frances Hill by Warren Hunt's. (See No. 1.)

19. "Also we laid out a highway from Arthur Croutches house and by the houses of Little Tadmuck and by the house of Joseph Parkhist and as the way is drawn, until it comes to Stoney brook way."

The starting-point was the dwelling of Arthur Crouch, which, according to the land allotments, must have stood near the Centre School-house. The road led past the Common and Town House, and down the hill by the house of widow Ira Leland, and probably turned to the left near C. F. Keyes', and leading northward, terminated at the brook near Eli Tower's. That portion of it which lies between C. F. Keyes' and Mr. Tower's has been given up.

20. "A highway laid out to Great Tadmuck for the inhabitants of Stoney and elsewhere in the town; beginning at the old way and so through the land of Joshua Fletcher Jr.—beginning at a rock on the right hand and on the left a stake, and by the bounds of Samuel Foster on the left hand . . . and so by marked trees till it comes to a little sponge [bog-hole?] and thence through to the meadows westward." (May 28, 1707.)

This began at the corner, near Robert J. Taylor's and ran past the West Burying Ground to the corner in the woods, on the old road leading by Rufus Patten's.

21. "A highway laid out which began about forty rods beyond Ens. John Snow's house westerly and was laid through sd Snow's land by a line of marked trees . . . and from sd Snow's land the highway was laid to the highway which leads to Groten." . . .

22. "On the same day there was a highway laid from Ebenezer Wright's house west to his field bars."

Mr. Wright lived near Edwin E. Heywood's. Probably his house stood away from the public road, and this was a short road giving him egress to the travelled highway.

23. "November 7, 1718. Laid out a highway which began on Tadmuck road near Aaron Parker's house . . . from thence over the brook by marked trees blazed or marked three ways. The way runs by Peter Procter's and Thomas Kidder's to Ephraim Hildreths land."

This probably started near School-house Number Five, and ran southward over Nonesuch Brook to the Kidder place, now deserted.

24. "On the same day [Nov. 7, 1718], laid out a highway which began on the east side of the Gutt on Groten road . . . from thence along by Joseph Hildreth's to Arthur Croutche's."

The "Gutt" was a piece of low land east of Amos Leighton's. From this, the road was laid by Samuel N. Burbeck's to Minot's Corner, and from thence to the Centre, to a point near the School-house. From the Gutt, so called, to Minot's Corner it now forms a part of the main travelled road from Littleton to Lowell; and from the Centre to the Corner, a part of the road to Boston.

These were the highways established by the old town. After the incorporation others were speedily added to the list as the following records will show.

(*a*). "Westford September 22, 1730. "A way laid out to Dunstable line . . . beginning at a stake and heap of stones on the west side of Andrew Spalding's shop and near the east end of sd Spalding's barn, and so by marked trees to Dunstable line."

Andrew Spalding lived on the John Morrison place, and this road led by School-house Number Eight, and by Dennis Burke's and John F. Banister's to the town line.

(*b*). "Also, a way laid out the day above sd . . . from Edward Batteses over the meadow till it comes to the meadow near Long-Sought-for pond . . . and so to a black oak tree near the pond, and from Ephraim Spalding's house by marks on the south or southwesterly side till it comes to the way that goes to Rumrill's."

Edward Bates lived north of Dennis Burke's, and this road led out to the pond, thence by John Dane's to the brick tavern.

(c). "Also, a way laid out from Jacob Wright's field by Jonas Fletcher's, and so over Stoney brook to Bouttle's [Boutwell's] hill to the mill road."

Jacob Wright lived on the Bradley V. Lyon place, and this road led by Jeptha Wright's through the village of Graniteville to the hill west of J. Warren Day's. These appear to be the first roads laid out by the Selectmen of Westford.

"Westford May 14, 1731. Town ways laid out by the Selectmen of sd town and allowed by the town March 6, 1731–'2."

1. "A way through the land of Joshua Fletcher, beginning at the Country road east of sd Fletcher's field . . . thence easterly to a new field and so on the south side of sd field, as the path now goeth, to the way by Boynton's."

2. "A way beginning at the above sd way at a rock and heap of stones, from thence to a walnut tree near the draw bars that lets into sd Fletcher's pasture, from thence to a stake and heap of stones by Joshua Fletcher's land . . . and the sd Fletcher gave the land (which the above sd ways takes) to the town forever for sd use."

These roads have probably been changed or partly given up, but they are supposed to be in the vicinity of Jonathan T. Colburn's and George H. Hartford's. It may be that the road from the house of the late Daniel Flagg to Mr. Hartford's represents them in part.

3. "A town way laid out the day above sd, beginning at the Country road by a rock and heap of stones which is Joshua Fletcher's bounds, and so bounded on the southeasterly and easterly side by sd Fletcher's land to the town way by Boynton's which goes to the meeting house

in sd town; and bounded on the southeasterly and easterly side of sd way on the land of Left. William Fletcher, Gershom Procter, Deces. [deceased] William Barrett, Joseph Hildreth, and Nathaniel Boynton to the above sd way."

This has not been determined with certainty.

4. "A town way laid out beginning at the Country road that leads to Groton at a field called the ginril [general] field and bounded on the northerly side by sd field fence, eastwardly until it comes to a town way that runs cross sd field . . . thence to a pine tree standing on the brow of a hill, thence to a stake at Boutl's [Boutwell's] meadow, so called, thence to the southerly side of Timothy Fletcher's house to a town way that leads to the meeting house. Laid out pursuant to a vote passed March 5, 1732."

This runs from Miner's Corner near Hop Yard Swamp, to Rufus Patten's.

5. "Westford May 15, 1732. A town way laid out from the way that goeth upon the eastwardly side of Mr. Joseph Underwood's homestead to Joseph Hildreth's — beginning at a white oak which is Mr. Underwood's corner bounds, and so bounded on the northerly side of sd way by Mr. Underwood's land to the broock that runs out of Providence medoo, and upon the easterly side of sd way by Mr. Hall's medow and on the westerdly side by Capt. Prescott's medow, and on the southerly side by Ebenezer Spalding's land to the way first mentioned."

This led from a point nearly opposite Mrs. Ira Leland's to Providence meadow and onward to a point near George Drew's. It has been entirely discontinued.

6. "A town way laid out . . . from the way that leads from Stoney broock to Groton: beginning on boutl's [Boutwell's] hill . . . thence running between David Bigsby's house and barn, thence to a white oak being the most northerly corner of Wido Bloged's land."

This led from the hill west of J. Warren Day's, by the house of the late J. Waldo Cumings to the top of the hill.

7. "Westford November 5, 1736. A highway laid out for Jonathan Procter and others to come to the meeting house: beginning a red oak by Jonathan Procter's land . . . and so as the path goes through some of Benjamin Hildreth's land, and then through the east side of Cuckson's land to the highway that leads to the meeting house by Cowdrey's, and then turning through Capt. Jonas Prescott's land to the highway that leads to the meeting house by Ephraim Hildreth's."

Jonathan Procter lived near Pond Brook, and this road led through the land of Benjamin M. Fletcher to the house of Mrs. Eunice Hildreth, and thence to Josiah Vose's.

8. "Westford June 9, 1736. Laid out a private and particular for Mr. Hall, Capt. Prescott and Benjamin Robbins to go to Providence: beginning on the north side of the way that leads to Joseph Hildreth's, then running easterdly to a black oak tree . . . then to a stump on the ridge hill by the dug-way, then to a black birch by the fordway; then on the southeasterly side of Mr. Hall's meadow and Mr. Benjamin Robbin's meadow and on the westerly side of the way by Capt. Prescott's meadow, then to a white oak tree, from thence to the way that leads to Joseph Hildreth's."

The meadows here mentioned lie east of Providence Meadow and between the land of George Drew and Julian Hildreth.

9. "Westford February 25, 1737-'8. A private and particular way for Timothy Adams and for others to go to Little Tadmuck."

This was on the east border of the town. It never became a public road.

10. "In February, 1740, the Selectmen renewed the bounds in part of the road leading up the Stony brook valley: beginning near the old sawmill . . . then to a stake by Oliver Spalding's wall near his dwelling house, thence to a black oak near the bounds of Oliver Spalding and Josiah Burge," thence by various bounds to land, "now improved by Thomas Comings, thence to a stake one rod

south from Mr. Thomas Coming's house; thence to a pine stump at the foot of Boutwell's hill, thence running acrost Boutwell's brook to a tree which is a bound for Jonas Prescott's land."

This renewal concerns the old road from Westford station to Forge Village — a part of it which none of the transcripts very clearly define. It is plain that changes have taken place since the date of this renewal.

11. "Westford December 25, 1741. Upon the desire of Mr. Joseph Temple, laid out a private road for the said Temple to go to meeting: beginning near said Temple's house and running westwardly and northwardly to a road that was formerly laid out for Jonathan Procter."

12 and 13. "Westford February 20, 1750. A highway laid out—beginning about 20 rods southerly from Samuel Adams' house, thence through Daniel Blodget's land 60 rods and through said Adams' land 100 rods, thence through Samuel Perham's land about 80 rods to the land of Ephraim Chandler at the northeast end of said Chandler's land. Then laid out a way . . . beginning near sd Chandler's field fence . . . then southerly through Jonathan Keyes' land . . . to the land of Samuel Perham and so through sd Perham's land about 40 rods to James Spalding's land . . . and so to the way that leads to Thomas Smith's."

The first of these led from Allen R. Perham's to the north end of Chandler's farm, being the northern part of the road now leading from Mr. Perham's to Flushing Pond; and the second led from Chandler's homestead along the margin of the pond to a point on the old stage road near T. J. Sherburn's.

14. "Westford, Nov. 8, 1751. "A highway laid out through the home place of Ephraim Chandler, leading toward Samuel Adams'; beginning at the south side of his field by Jonathan Keyes land . . . from thence [by various bounds] to a red oak marked for highway bounds by land of Nathaniel Barrett's, still leading toward Samuel Adams."

This led northward from Flushing Pond and intersected No. 12, above, and made a continuous road from the pond to Allen R. Perham's.

15. "Westford, Aug. 27, 1752. Laid out a town way through a part of Henry Richardson's land . . . turning out of an old highway and running easterly about twenty poles . . . to a stake standing in or near Chelmsford line."

This was a short road running east from Westford Corner.

16. "Westford, February 14, 1736. A highway laid out from Stoney brook bridge by David Fletcher's, to the road by Mr. Hall's old field to Henry Richardson's. Sd way began about one rod north of said bridge at an old way, and thence northerly as the path now goes till it comes near Ruben Fletcher's barn, then turning eastward till it comes to a new cleared field, thence turning northerly till it comes into the road above mentioned."

This began at the railroad bridge north of William Taylor's, and ran to the road that leads to Moses Edwards' and the "corner."

17. "Westford, February 13, 1756. Laid out a town road that goes by Jacob Fletcher's to that road that leads to David Fletcher's: beginning at a heap of stones southerly of sd Jacob Fletcher's dwelling house, it being Mr. Bowen's northeasterly corner bounds, then westerly . . . till it comes into the road by the sd David Fletcher's dwelling house. The road is not proposed for a cart-way but only for convenancy for man and horse."

William Bowen lived on the Warren Hunt place, and Jacob Fletcher north of him; and the road ran down the hill to Alvin G. Polley's. Long discontinued.

18. "Westford, February 28, 1757. A town way laid out in exchange for the old way through the land of Nathaniel Boynton against the lane leading down to the house of Benjamin Butterfield, deceased."

This was a change in the road near the house of the Coolidge Brothers.

19. "March 5, 1759. Voted to accept the transcript of a bridle way laid out from Jonas Prescott Jr.'s and so by Capt. Prescott's and Timothy Prescott's [land] and John Cowdrey's to Groton bounds."

This began near George W. Blodget's, in Forge Village, and running west of Kissacook hill, came out by the house once owned by Asa Wright, on the line of the Nashua and Acton Railroad, and onward to Groton line.

20. "February 20, 1759. A town way laid out, beginning at a town way laid out by Jacob Wright Jr.'s dwelling house and running northerly until it comes to a black oak by the land of Ephraim Wright."

This began at school-house No. 9, and led to the house of Edwin Gould.

21. "February 3, 1757. A town way laid out . . . beginning at a town way by Jacob Wright's field, . . . northerly between the lane of Jacob Wright and his son John, till it comes to Hide's hole, so called, to a rock on land left for a highway . . . thence to a stake and stones on Thomas Heald's land, and by land of Benjamin Dutton . . . to Ebenezer Prescott's land and so by marked trees to Groton old line."

This led from the Lyon place by Erastus Wright's and Hezekiah Cummings' to the corner of James Woods' and on to Groton line. A part of it over Hide's Hole has been given up.

22. "May 15, 1761. Voted to accept of transcript of town way from Chelmsford line by William Blodget's and Samuel Fassett's and to Henry Richardson's field, and so by Josiah Spalding's into the country road."

This began at the town line east of Oak hill, and came out by Andrew Fletcher's to the Woodward place at the foot of Nubanussuck Pond.

23. "November 26, 1763. A town way laid out, beginning at an old way near Caleb Wright's dwelling house, running easterly near the back side of sd Wright's house to a stake and stones at Chelmsford line."

This was a short road southeast of Edwin E. Heywood's.

24. "March 4, 1763. A town way laid out (in exchange of a way) beginning at a town way a little below Lt. Leonard Spalding's dwelling house . . . thence southerly to a stake and stones at a stone wall near John Hildreth's barn at the old way."

This is probably the road leading from T. J. Wheeler's to George P. Wright's.

25. "December 20, 1762. A town way laid out, — beginning at the old burying ground near Ebenezer Fletcher's dwelling house, thence from sd burying yard southerly to a black oak tree by Mr. Thomas Comings' stone wall . . . thence southerly to a stake and stones by Mr. Daniel Raymond's land, thence southerly through sd Raymond's orchard, — thence southeasterly to a plum tree between sd Raymond's house and barn. To be a bridle way with gates."

This leads from the east cemetery by C. F. Keyes' to the Abbot Read farm.

26. "March 4, 1763. A town way, beginning at a town way that leads from Lieut. Samuel Chamberlin's by Aaron Parker's and so by Jacob Robbins' to Chelmsford . . . running southeasterly and southerly to a black oak tree, it being a corner bound of Philip Robbins' land."

This marks the road from Benjamin M. Fletcher's to John Hutchins'.

27. "February 14, 1764. A town way beginning on Tadmuck road, so called, near Mr. Benjamin Farmer's dwelling house" . . . running northerly by various bounds . . . "to a plumb tree between Daniel Raymond's house and barn."

This is the identical plum tree mentioned in No. 25, above, and the transcript points out the continuation of the road from the Abbot Read place to the road near Josiah Vose's.

28. "March 2, 1765. A town way turned and laid out a little southerly of Dea. Andrew Spalding's house,

and running westwardly crossing a brook where the bridge now is, and as the path goes . . . to a dwelling house of Jonathan Keyes."

This was a change from the meadow to the hard ground of the road from the John Morrison place to George Keyes'.

29. "March 2, 1763. A town way beginning at Thomas Read Jun's land and so running southeasterly . . . to a stake and stones near the corner of Jonathan Keyes' barn, thence easterly to sd Keyes' house."

This is the road leading from George Keyes' in the direction of Alien Fisk's.

30. "February 20, 1767. A town way . . . beginning at a black oak tree, (by the old town way that leads from Major Thomas Read's to Chelmsford by Jonathan Keyes') then running southerly bounded on Ens. Amos Fletcher's land to a black oak tree, thence southerly to a white oak tree on Eleazer Read's land, thence southerly to a stake in the stone wall near sd Fletcher's corner bound, thence by sd wall to the old town way."

In the Stony Brook valley, near William Taylor's. (?)

31. "January 12, 1767. A town way beginning on the south side of Nashoba Brook at a stake by Jonathan Robbins' land, running northerly by Barrett's stone wall . . . and northerly to a white oak tree by the path at the northeast corner of Joseph Hooker's field . . . and so on to a white oak at the corner of Mr. John Read's stone wall, and thence by sd wall to Groton road. To be a bridle way."

Starting at Nashoba Brook, near the hill, this road or path led eastward of John Wayne's and into or near to the present road above Wayne's, and toward the road that goes to E. J. Whitney's.

32. "October 9, 1772. A town way . . . beginning at a stake by Jonathan Keyes' land bounding southerly to a stake on Ephraim Wright's land, thence across the meadow on the causeway to a stake near the brick yard,

thence by the east end of said Wright's dwelling house to the old town way."

The way from George Keyes' to Edwin Gould's.

33. "Nov. 26, 1770. A town way . . . beginning at Groton road about one-quarter of a mile from Abner Kent's dwelling house, thence southerly and westerly to a little white oak by the dug-way near the bridge, thence over the bridge by Ebenezer Hadley's and John Hadley to Littleton line."

This began at Miner's Corner and ran over the brook to the farm of Joseph F. Prescott, and to the town line.

34. "Feb. 8, 1771. A town way . . . beginning at a stake at the old town way near John Raiter's dwelling house, running southeasterly to a pine tree by Jonathan Keyes' field . . . then easterly to a black oak tree by the road that leads from William Spalding's to Samuel Fassett's."

This leads from a point near T. J. Sherburn's by Adam Taylor's, and enters the road west of School-house No. 7.

35. "Feb. 14, 1772. A town way from that road that leads from Daniel Whitney's — to Groton road, so called, near to Moses Keyes' dwelling house:— beginning at a pine tree by the afore [first] mentioned road, running southerly to a pine tree by Simeon Wright's land . . . about twenty poles westerly of sd Simeon Wright's barn; then running southerly and bounding on the land of Samuel Wright and Moses Keyes on the easterly side of sd road till it comes to Groton road near the sd Moses Keyes' dwelling house."

The Groton road here mentioned seems to be the road from Carlisle station to Parkerville. The road appears to start from a point near the Burnham Smith place, and it led by William M. Vose's to Dupee's Corner.

36. "Dec. 7, 1778. A town way beginning at a town way a little below Silas Read's dwelling house and running southerly . . . to a white oak tree near the land of Willard Read, thence to a heap of stones over the brook

. . . by the dwelling house of Mr. Francis Leighton to Littleton to line."

This led from the old Groton road, by John Wayne's to John Murphy's house which was the house of Francis Leighton. It was laid out as a bridle way many years before, but was then made a permanent highway.

These appear to be the principal highways established by the town for the space of fifty years after its incorporation.

SOLDIERS IN LOVEWELL'S EXPEDITION.

In the second expedition of Capt. John Lovewell, of Dunstable, against the Indians, in 1724 — sometimes called the Winnepesockett expedition — there was an Ebenezer Wright; and he, no doubt, was from Chelmsford, West Precinct, and lived on Frances Hill, within the present limits of Westford. Samuel Fletcher was also in that expedition, and he, too, was of Westford, and was, perhaps, the Samuel who settled on the place now owned by Calvin Howard. He was afterwards known as Capt. Samuel.

In the third and last expedition of Capt. Lovewell, which terminated in that sanguinary battle, "nigh unto Pigwacket," in which Lovewell was slain, there was one *Solomon Kies*. In the list of Capt. Lovewell's men he is said to be of *Billerica;* but Rev. Henry A. Hazen, in his Genealogy of Families in Billerica, says: "The name (Keyes) has been occasionally on the tax-lists, but no family is recorded." Judge Asa Keyes, in his Genealogy of the Keyes Family, published in 1880, says of this Solomon and of his part in Lovewell's Fight: "Solomon Keyes, in some accounts of this fight, has been accorded to Billerica, as was also the birth of his father, the son of Solomon and Frances. But no record of the birth of either father or son has been found in that place, and both are recorded in Chelmsford, where the second Solomon lived and where Capt. Solomon probably passed his early life." (Keyes' Gen., p. 131.) The truth seems to be that he was a Westford man whose early home was on Frances Hill, at or near the residence of the late Trueworthy Keyes. The story of his adventures is thus given in Abbot's History of Maine, as quoted by Judge Keyes: "Solomon Keyes received three bullet-wounds, and was apparently dying. To save his dead body from being mangled by the savages, he rolled himself down the beach to a canoe which chanced to be there. Almost senseless, he succeeded in creeping into it. A gentle breeze blew the canoe across the pond, diagonally, and landed it but a short distance from the stockade fort, into which he contrived to creep." "Later in life," says the Judge, "he removed to Western (now Warren), Mass., then a part of Brookfield. . . . Capt. Solomon lived thirty years after the fight at Pequawket, and was killed at Lake George, Sept. 8, 1755, in the French and Indian War." (Keyes' Gen., p. 131.)

Lovewell's Fight took place May 8, 1725. Col. Tyng, of Dunstable, wrote to Lieut. Gov. Dummer, May 14, saying: "I received your orders about eleven of the clock & I forthwith sent to Capt. Willard for twelve of his best men, & to Robert Richardson for fifteen of his Snow Shoe men," etc. These snow-shoe men were a company in Chelmsford, under the command of Capt. Robert Richardson and Lieut. Joseph Parker. It numbered forty men, of whom fourteen lived in the West Precinct, and these are their names:

Samuel Fletcher, who was in the Winnepesockett expedition.

Joseph Keyes, son of Joseph and Joanna, and cousin of Capt. Solomon. He was then 26 years old.

Josiah Spalding, born 1706; then 19 years old. He settled at the foot of Nubanussuck Pond.

Nathan Procter, born 1698; then 27 years old.

John Procter, Jr., born 1694; 31 years old.

Benjamin Robbins, son of Benjamin and Hannah, born 1708; 17 years old.

James Burn, born 1696; 29 years old.

Joseph Underwood, probably son of Joseph; age not known.

Joseph Fletcher, afterwards Captain, born 1689; 36 years old.

Josiah Burge, born 1696; 29 years old.

Simon Rumrill; age not known.

Thomas Read, Jr., born 1687; 38 years old.

THE EXPEDITION AGAINST CUBA.

Great Britain declared war against Spain, Oct. 23, 1739, and the next year an expedition against Cuba was undertaken. "An American regiment consisting of about 3600 men was raised on this occasion. In this expedition, the northern colonies furnished a considerable number of troops and sustained a great loss of men, principally in an uncommon mortality which prevailed in the army." (Holmes' Annals.)

Five companies of one hundred men each were raised in Massachusetts, who embarked for Cuba, Sept, 23, 1740. Of these five hundred men only about fifty returned. They were paid off and dismissed, Oct. 24, 1742. One of these companies was under the command of Capt. John Prescott, of Concord. Shattuck says of him: "When the unfortunate expedition to Cuba was proposed, he entered readily into the views of the government, and enlisted a company of one hundred men from this neighborhood." (History of Concord, p. 245.)

In his company, there is reason to believe, were the following men from Westford:

Ephraim Fletcher, aged 30, enlisted July 14, 1740. He was the son of Dea. Joshua, and was born March 12, 1710. He returned in safety, and was afterwards engaged in other wars.

William Skinner. He signed a receipt for bounty (five pounds), Sept. 10, 1740.

Oliver Spalding, aged 29, enlisted July 15, 1740. (Mass. Archives, Vol. 91, pp. 333-'4.)

SOLDIERS AT THE REDUCTION OF LOUISBURG, 1745.

"After the peace of Utrecht (1713), the French, as a security to their navigation and fishery, built the town of Louisburg on the island of Breton, and fortified it with a rampart of stone from 30 to 36 feet high, and a ditch 80 feet wide. There were 6 bastions and 3 batteries, containing embrasures for 148 cannon and 6 mortars. On an island at the entrance of the harbor was planted a battery of 30 cannon, carrying 28 pounds shot, and at the bottom of the harbor, directly opposite to the entrance, was the grand or royal battery of 28 cannon, 42-pounders, and 2 18-pounders. The entrance of the town on the land side was at the west gate, over a draw-bridge, near which was a circular battery mounting 16 guns of 24-pounds shot. These works had been twenty-five years in building; and, though not finished, had cost the crown of France not less than thirty millions of livres. The place was deemed so strong and impregnable as to be called the Dunkirk of America. In peace it was a safe retreat for the ships of France bound homeward from the East and West Indies. In war it gave French privateers the greatest advantage for ruining the fishery of the northern English colonies and interrupting their entire trade. It endangered, besides, the loss of Nova Scotia. . . . The reduction of this place was, for these reasons, an object of the highest importance to New England.

"Early in January, 1745, Gov. Shirley communicated to the General Court the plan which he had formed of attacking Louisburg. The proposal was at first rejected; but it was finally carried by a majority of one voice. . . . Forces were raised, and William Pepperrell, Esquire, of Kittery, was appointed commander of the expedition. This officer sailed from Nantasket on the 24th of March, and arrived at Canso on the 4th of April. Here the troops, joined by those of New Hampshire and Connecticut, amounting collectively to upwards of 4,000 men, were detained three weeks waiting for the ice which environed the island of Cape Breton to be dissolved. On the 30th of April the General landed his troops. The next object was to invest the city. With extreme difficulty, cannon were drawn, for 14 nights successively, through a morass to the camp. The men, with straps over their shoulders and sinking to their knees in mud, performed the service which horses or oxen on such ground could not have done. On the 16th of June (1745) articles of capitulation were signed. This expedition was one of the most remarkable events in the History of North America. . . . The plan for the reduction of a regularly constructed fortress, was drawn by a lawyer, to be executed by a merchant, at the head of a body of husbandmen and mechanics." (Holmes' Annals of America.)

In that memorable campaign, Massachusetts furnished 3250 men; New Hampshire, 304, and Connecticut, 516. *Westford was nobly represented there.* Dr. Jonathan Prescott, of Littleton, was a captain of engineers in the siege, and a few men from Westford were in his company, while others were connected with other officers. It has been found difficult to bring together the facts concerning them. But in Volume 74 of the Massachusetts Archives, there is a petition of soldiers who went to the reduction of Louisburg, for aid from the State. It is dated 1751. Among the names are these which, there is scarcely any reason to doubt, were the names of Westford men: Enoch Cleaveland, Zacre [Zachariah] Robbins; Jonathan Procter for Jacob Procter and Ephraim Procter, deceased. Enoch Cleaveland for Jonathan Cleaveland, deceased. Benjamin Robbins for Jonathan Robbins, deceased. To these should be added James Hildreth, Jr., who, as the town records plainly say, " departed this life at Cape Bretton Oct. 11, 1745." He was the son of Richard and Dorcas Hildreth, and was born in 1701.

Two large volumes of manuscript, entitled the Pepperrell Papers, are now in possession of the Massachusetts Historical Society, and from these the names of soldiers in that siege have been collected and may be seen at the State House. Unfortunately the lists are not complete and the residences are not given. From that transcript a few names have been copied, of men who are supposed to hail from Westford.

In Capt. Gershom Davis' company, William Skinner, Ephraim Fletcher, Jonathan Cleaveland.

In Capt. Williams' company, Francis Kidder, "joyner."

In Capt. Hunt's company, Jonathan Robbins, corporal.

In Capt. Smith's company, Jonathan Fletcher.

In Capt. Prescott's company, Joseph Prescott.

In Col. Choate's regiment, Lieut. Obadiah Perry, who received his commission at Louisburg, June, 1745.

Ebenezer Wright was appointed Ensign, April 15, and Benjamin Butterfield, Ensign, October 29, 1745.

FRENCH NEUTRALS.

The peninsular of Nova Scotia which had been ceded to the English in 1713, was inhabited by French people who adhered to the Catholic religion. Its boundaries were unsettled. The English claimed to the St. Lawrence, but the French insisted on restricting them to the peninsular of Acadie or Nova Scotia. While commissioners were discussing these claims, the French occupied the contested country and erected forts to defend it. Against these forts an expedition was sent out in 1753. The command of it was given to Lieut. Col. Monckton. The New England forces were commanded by Gen. Winslow, of Marshfield. The troops embarked at Boston on the 20th of May, and in the following month they seized the strongholds and took possession of the country. A difficult question then arose: What ought to be done with the inhabitants? They claimed to be neutrals, but some of them had fought against the English. An offer was made to such of them as had not been openly in arms, to be allowed to continue in possession of their country, if they would take the oath of allegiance without qualification. But they unanimously refused it. It was then determined to disperse them among the British colonies. To prevent the re-settlement of those who escaped, the country was laid waste. (Holmes' Annals.)

In Volume 23, p. 3, of Massachusetts Archives, there is a list of the vessels that brought more than a thousand of these French Neutrals to the port of Boston:

	CLASS.	NAME.	COMMANDER.	No. Men.
1	Sloop.	Three Friends.	Captain Carlisle.	160
2	. . .	Dolphin.	Captain Farnum.	227
3	. . .	Endeavor.	Captain Nichols.	125
4	. . .	Sarah and Mary.	Captain Purington.	151
5	Sloop.	. . . .	Captain Percy.	205
6	Schooner.	. . . .	Captain Davis.	209
Total	. .	. . . . .	. . .	1077

These arrived November 5, 1755. A second company came after December 27, 1755, and before January 23, 1756. Some of these embarked for France, and others were distributed among the towns of Massachusetts. At least six of these persons were sent to Westford. It would seem from the account that they were sent by the Sheriff of the County in September, 1756. Later in that year several items concerning them are recorded on the town book: "Pay to Mr. Nathaniel Boynton 2£ 10s. for what he let the french people have since they came to town etc."

In the same volume, p. 347, there is an account rendered by the Selectmen, in which the following names appear:

"Maudlin Robeshaw, a female, aged 83; Maudlin Robeshaw, a female, aged 41; Frederick Robishaw; Lise Robishaw, aged 15; Lisebe Robishaw, aged 11; Mary Robishaw, aged 8 years." Signed by John Abbot, Jonas

Prescott, Jabez Keep, William Fletcher, Joseph Dutton, Selectmen of Westford. The bill of expense amounted to £8. 8s. Account rendered to February 7, 1757. Of these persons it is said: "The old woman very helpless and often sick; the young man sick of the fever and *ago* the great part of the spring and summer past."

"MIDDLESEX ss. To his excellency Thomas Pownal Esq. Capt. General and Governor in Cheafe in and over his majesties province of the Massachusetts Bay in New England &c and the Honorable his Council: The Desiar of the Town of Westford and pray that your Excellency and Honours would be pleased to allow to ye Town of Westford the sum hereafter mentioned, viz, the sum of Ten pounds five pence and two farthings lawful money for supporting ye French Family that Lately came from Nova Scotia, that are now in Westford,—which sum the sd Town of Westford has expended for ye french family aforesd. sence ye Tenth day of November 1757. In providing a House for them to live in and Nessessaryes for their support—there Being one old woman as she says she is 87 years of age—ye others have been very sickly and Not able to do But Very Little of their one support and could not any waise Comfortably subsist with Less Than the Town has laid out for them. Westford January ye 22nd 1759. Samuel Fletcher, Samuel Read, Amos Fletcher, Nathaniel Boynton, Selectmen of Westford."

In Volume 24, p. 466, of Massachusetts Archives, these names are mentioned: Mary Maudlin Robinshaw, 44; Eliz. Ruhard, 17, and Mary Ruhard, 11. This list varies from that given elsewhere, and it is probable that changes were made which are not made known explicitly. Apparently the last account was rendered to the Governor and Council, January 11, 1761.

"These may certifie to your Honours that there hath been paid out of our Town Treasury in Westford the sum of nine pounds lawful money for one year past for the Necessary support of the french family which was sent to Westford, being six in Number, and one of said persons being a very aged person of about Eighty Nine years of age and another of said persons very weakly and Not able to maintain herself, which sum etc. Jonas Prescott, John Abbot, Nathaniel Boynton, Selectmen."

REMOVAL OF THE FRENCH FAMILY.

"MIDDLESEX. Charlestown, April 6, 1761. To the Selectmen of the Town of Westford in sd County, Greeting.

By virtue of the Power and Authority given by the Great and General Court to Samuel Danforth, Will'm Brattle, Samuel Livermore, Charles Prescott and James Russell, Esq'rs You are hereby forthwith to cause to be removed from your town to the Town of Littleton, Mary Maudlin Robesheau, Frederich Richar, and Betty Winnett, and that there remain in your town Mary Maudlin Robesheau, aged about 44 years, Eliz'th Richar, and Mary Richar; and make return of your doings to sd Samuel Danforth of their being removed as aforesaid and the charge of removing them. S. Danforth pr. order of the Committee."

"Westford April 14, 1761.

Be it remembered that by order of the abovesd Committee, the abovesd Mary Maudlin Robesheau and Betty Winnett were conveyed to Littleton and delivered up to Mr. Thomas Warren one of the Selectmen of sd Littleton; and that Frederich Richar living at Charlestown was Notified to repair to Littleton also; and a return sent down of the Removeal of sd french persons and cost of removing them." (Town Records, Volume 1, p. 403.)

Thus, at the end of five years, one-half the number was assigned to Littleton, and four years afterward one of the three who remained died in Cambridge. The fate of the other two is not known.

"Westford May 20, 1765.

Voted to leave the French affair relating to the town of Cambridge against Westford to the Selectmen to make further enquiry," etc.

"Voted that the town treasurer shall borrow twelve pounds lawful money and give his note in behalf of the town for six months on Lawful interest till paid to ennable him to pay the town of Cambridge their cost in supporting Magdalene Rubishaw Jun. in her last sickness, death and burial." (Town Records, Volume II., p. 34.)

While these outcasts were in town, they lived near the present residence of the Coolidge Brothers, and Nathaniel Boynton, who then occupied the Coolidge farm, furnished them with a house and garden. Numerous entries are made upon the town book in regard to the cost of supporting them; but no intimation is given that any of them died here. Their expatriation was a cruel act and their fate was a sorrowful one. To that band of exiles, so rudely forced from their homes in the "Acadian Land," can be traced the beautiful *Evangeline*, whose story has been so charmingly set forth by Longfellow:

> "Far asunder, on separate coasts, the Acadians landed;
> Scattered were they, like flakes of snow, when the wind from the northeast
> Strikes aslant through the fogs that darken the Banks of Newfoundland.
> Friends they sought and homes; and many, despairing, heart-broken,
> Asked of the earth but a grave, and no longer a home nor a fireside."

SOLDIERS IN THE FRENCH AND INDIAN WARS.

1748. In the History of Northfield, Massachusetts, p. 267, there is a description of Serg. Thomas Taylor's encounter with the Indians near Fort Dummer. Henry Chandler, of Westford, it is stated, was killed in that skirmish, which occurred July 14, 1748. He was the son of William and Susanna Chandler, and was born in this town (at Brookside) March 29, 1727. He was 21 years of age. Fort Dummer stood a short distance below the present town of Brattleborough, Vt. It was built in 1723.

1754. In Capt. Phinehas Osgood's company, Col. Winslow's regiment, in defence of the eastern frontier,

Hezekiah Corey, of Westford, served from April 23 to November 8, 1754. He was born in Chelmsford in 1736, and was the son of John and Ruth Corey. He removed to New Ipswich about 1762, and was one of the early settlers of that town.

1755. In Capt. Jonathan Butterfield's company, in the expedition to Crown Point, Robert Butterfield was a sergeant. He was the son of Jonathan and Elizabeth, and was born in 1716. He died near Lake George, October 23, 1756, at the age of 40.

1755, September 18. In Capt. Samuel Dakin's company (Col. Brown), on the same expedition, was Ebenezer Hildreth, of Westford.

1755, September 21. In Capt. Daniel Fletcher's company, under the command of Col. John Cummings, were Daniel Brooks, Paul Fletcher, Ezekiel Procter, Jr., Benjamin Kidder, Hezekiah Corey, Francis Leighton, Joseph Hooker and James Blodgett. Also, at Lake George, Isaac Patch, Zachariah Willis and Oliver Procter.

1756. Ephraim Fletcher was taken captive at Oswego, at the time (August 14) when Forts Oswego and George surrendered to the French under Montcalm. Fourteen hundred men belonging to the regiments of Gov. Shirley and Gen. Pepperrell were then taken prisoners. In the Fletcher Genealogy (p. 18) it is stated that Ephraim Fletcher enlisted in the French war and never returned home; and of his brother, Zechariah, it is said he enlisted with his brother Ephraim in the French and Indian war, and like him, never returned. At Lake George, Benjamin King.

1757. In Capt. Thomas Hartwell's company were Samuel Blodgett and Richard Russell.

In Capt. Samuel Davis' company, John Bigelow, Ebenezer Hildreth, Samuel Wright, Timothy Fletcher and Simon Hunt.

In the alarm list, whereof Samuel Davis was captain, Mark White, Jr., Samuel White and Daniel Brooks.

In Capt. Samuel Bancroft's company, Samuel Fassett.

1757. " A Muster Roll of the Company in his Majesty's Service to Springfield, under the command of

>Jonas Prescott, of Westford, Captain.
>Gershom Fletcher, Clerk, of Westford.
>Samuel Parker, Sergeant, of Westford.
>Thomas Wright, Sergeant, of Westford.
>John Wright, Private, of Westford.
>Oliver Wright, Private, of Westford.
>Moses Burge, Private, of Westford.
>Samuel Adams, Jr., Private, of Westford.
>Joel Wright, son of Ebenezer, Private, of Westford.
>Peter Butterfield, son of William, Private, of Westford.
>John Robbins, Private, of Westford.
>Nathaniel Hill, Private, of Westford.
>Joseph Cummings, Private, of Westford.
>Joshua Fletcher, Private, of Westford.
>Hezekiah Corey, Private, of Westford.
>John Hadley, Private, of Westford.
>Nathaniel Barrett, Private, of Westford.

The above muster Roll is for pay for an alarm for the relief of Fort William Henry, for August 15, 1757. Capt. Jonas Prescott made solemn oath that the several officers and soldiers did duty according to the time therein set." The distance travelled, as appears on the roll, was 180 miles, and the time of service one week and six days. (Massachusetts Archives, Volume 96, p. 3.) Fort William Henry was taken by Gen. Montcalm, August 9, 1757. Before hearing of its surrender this company started for its relief, and went as far as Springfield. After learning the fact, it seems to have returned home.

1758. In this year three expeditions were planned; one, under Gen. Amherst, against Louisburg, which had been given up to France, in 1748, by the treaty of Aix la Chapelle; one, under Gen. Abercrombie, against Ticonderoga and Crown Point; and one, under Gen. Forbes, against Fort DuQuesne. Gen. Amherst was successful in taking Louisburg, July 26; and Fort DuQuesne was taken November 25, and named Pittsburg. But Gen. Abercrombie was repulsed at Ticonderoga, July 8. He sent Col.

Bradstreet to reduce Fort Frontenac, on Lake Ontario, which he accomplished, August 27.

These achievements were very significant and they effectually dispelled the gloom which rested upon the colonies at the close of the previous year. In the expedition against Ticonderoga men from Westford bore an active part. These are their names: Jonathan Sprague, Benjamin Pollard, Aaron Blood, Richard Wyer, Caleb Huston, James Blodgett, Amaziah Hildreth and Thomas Mead; and they were probably connected with the company of Capt. Thomas Lawrence, of Groton, who was killed in that campaign.

At the battle of Half-Way Brook, July 20, Simon Wheeler was killed and Joel Crosby was taken captive. Oliver Wright was reported missing. He was a sergeant in Capt. Lawrence's company. In that company, also, were Leonard Spalding (Second Lieutenant, afterwards promoted First Lieutenant). Joseph Hartwell, Josiah Butterfield, Benjamin Farmer, Benjamin Nutting, Benjamin Richardson, Zachariah Willis and Simon Wheeler.

1759. In Capt. Daniel Fletcher's company, for the reduction of Canada, were Thomas Hildreth, Cæsar (negro servant of Gershom Fletcher), Josiah Prince and Benjamin Pollard.

In Col. William Lawrence's regiment, Capt. Leonard Whiting's company, under General Amherst: Isaac Cummings, aged 17, son of Thomas; Reuben Wright, aged 19. son of Thomas; William Parker, aged 17, servant of John Wright; Joseph Pollard, aged 21; Benjamin Pollard, aged 17, son of Joseph; Aaron Blood, aged 19, ward of Ephraim Chandler; Jonathan Sprague; Richard Wyer, aged 21; Isaac Patch, ward of Joshua Fletcher; Caleb Huston, aged 18, ward of Nathan Procter; Thomas Hildreth, aged 18, son of Benjamin; James Blodgett, aged 25; Zachariah Willis, aged 18, servant of Philip Robbins; Amaziah Hildreth, aged 21; Thomas Mead, aged 56; Oliver Procter, aged 38; Benjamin King, aged 37.

"Worcester, April 30, 1759.
"Billeting of Capt. Leonard Whiting's Co. in the first Battalion, Brig. Gen. Ruggles Reg. from the day of enlistment. Men's names:

Leonard Whiting, Captain.

Richard Wyer,	Aaron Blood,
James Blodgett,	Isaac Cummings,
Caleb Huston,	Amaziah Hildreth,
Benjamin King,	Thomas Mead,
Joseph Pollard,	Benjamin Pollard,
Isaac Patch,	Obadiah Perry,
Jonathan Sprague,	Reuben Wright,
Jonas Wright,	Zachariah Willis."

In his Genealogy of the Early Families of Billerica, Rev. H. A. Hazen states that Capt. Leonard Whiting was in command of a company at the surrender of Quebec.

1759. Another billeting roll of this company, having the name of Oliver Procter added, bears date, May 11, 1759; and from this the names of Wyer, Blood and Mead are wanting.

Reuben Wright was in the hospital at Albany from November 23 to December 9, and discharged. Thomas Mead was there for the same length of time, and also discharged. Ephraim Fletcher, from May 31 to June 14, and discharged. Isaac Patch, from October 17 to October 20; and Caleb Huston, for the same period. Oliver Procter from September 1 to September 25; also, from September 30 to October 14.

1760. Muster Roll of Capt. Leonard Whiting's company. The return made out and signed, Boston, February 27, 1760. The following names appear: Richard Wyer, Aaron Blood, James Blodget, Isaac Cummings, Caleb Huston, Amaziah Hildreth and Thomas Hildreth.

Probably Captain Whiting's company were paid off at this time. If so, the names of several men from Westford who enlisted in it, are not found in the list above. Perhaps some of them were transferred to other companies, and some had died.

1760. In Capt. Oliver Barron's company were Benjamin Read, son of Joseph, who died at Crown Point, October 1760; also, Silas Wright, son of Ebenezer, who served at Crown Point.

1760. Caleb Gleason, of Westford, servant of Thomas Adams, was in Capt. Aaron Willard's company from February 20 to December—forty weeks.

1761. Muster Roll of Capt. Jonathan Butterfield's company: February 28, Leonard Spalding, First Lieutenant; Hezekiah Corey, Sergeant; William Reed, Abraham Butterfield and Peter Butterfield.

Richard Whitney, servant to Cummings, was also in Capt. Aaron Willard's company, April 2nd.

1762. January. List of officers commissioned — First Company, in Westford: James Pollard, Captain; Timothy Fletcher, Lieutenant; Amos Fletcher, Ensign. Second Company: Samuel Fletcher, Captain; Joseph Read, Lieutenant; Zachariah Robbins, Ensign.

1762. Abijah Procter served twenty-four weeks and six days in Capt. Farrington's company.

1762. In Capt. Leonard Whiting's company were John Dunn, Joseph Darling, George Crowder, Josiah Blood, Ephraim Craft, [reported] dead, Samuel Fassett, [reported] dead, Samuel Foster, and Joel Fletcher, son of Timothy.

1763. In the same company as reported this year, were Joshua Parker, William Pierce, Benjamin Adams, James Blodgett, Abraham Bennett, Nathan Boynton, Amos Boynton, Samuel Clark, Salmon Dutton, Joseph Darling, David Fish, David Keyes, John Meeds, Joseph Parker, Leonard Parker, Joseph Robbins, Thaddeus Read, Jonathan Robbins, David Rumrill, Ebenezer Willis.

By the conquest of Montreal, in 1760, the entire reduction of Canada was accomplished and the British forces were triumphant. As peace was not yet established, the military organizations were kept up in order to be ready for any call. In 1762 fears were entertained lest Canada and the American fishery might be restored to the French, and an addition was made to the quota of Massachusetts, making the number of men 3,270. On the 10th of February, 1763, a definitive treaty of peace was signed at Paris, and soon after ratified. By the second article, France renounces and guarantees to Great Britain all Nova Scotia, or Acadie, and likewise Canada, the island of Cape Breton, and all other islands in the gulf and river of St. Lawrence. (Holmes' Annals.)

1771. At this date there were two military companies in Westford, belonging to the Sixth Regiment. Their officers were as follows: First Company — Amos Fletcher, Captain; Jonas Prescott, Jr., Lieutenant; Nathaniel Boynton, Ensign. Second Company — Jonathan [Joseph ?] Boynton, Captain; Moses Parker, Lieutenant; Jonathan Carver, Ensign.

EXTRACTS FROM THE TOWN RECORDS.

Plan for a New County. In the year 1734, the project was agitated of making a new county which should comprise the towns in this vicinity. This town passed the following vote in regard to it.

"September ye 2nd day, 1734.

"Voted to choose three men for a comity to Joyne with the comity of the negibrin [neighboring] towns in pertisoning the grate and ginril cort of this province to be erected into a county in such manner as they agree on, provided that this town be not charged with any cost of sd comity or of manigen of sd petison. Mr. Joseph Underwood, Capt. Thomas Read, and left. Samuel Chamberlin chose a comity to act in behalf of this town in this affair.

JONAS PRESCOTT, Town Clerk."

Previous to the establishment of the State line between Massachusetts and New Hampshire, in 1740, several towns now in New Hampshire, were regarded as belonging to Middlesex County. Nottingham West, now Hudson, passed the following vote:

"September 7, 1734.

"The Town by vote signified its desire that if a new County is obtained, the Shire town may be at Chelmsford or Dunstable."

The reason why the plan was not carried out may be found in the fact that soon after, by the running of the line between the two States, several towns were assigned to New Hampshire, and the necessity for a new county no longer existed.

In 1763 a similar project was agitated, and it was kept before the people for several years. In 1767 this town passed the following vote in regard to it:

"May 21, 1767.

"Voted that Capt. Jonas Prescott, Capt. Jabez Keep, and Capt. William Fletcher, agents for the Town of Westford in behalf of a new County, shall still Proceed for some Releaf either for a new County or that Concord may be the Shire Town."

New County Road. "August 9, 1736 It was put to vote whether they will joyne with severil of the nabring towns for the contery Rode they have petisoned for . . . and it past in the negatife. Chose Capt. Jonas Prescott, Dea. John Comings, Thomas Read a Commity to meet and treet with ye Hon^d Cort's commity who ware apinted by said Cort to inquire into the Nesesty of the way petisoned for from Westford meeting House thrugh part of Chelmsford, Billerica, Bedford, Lexenton, and the said Commity are directed to do what they can to prevent and hinder the way petisoned for from coming to Westford."

"September 28, 1736.

"Voted to alow the Cometty 2 — 15 — 4 for time and money expended in going to bedford."

"February the 7th, 1736–7. Pay Capt. Jonas Prescott, Dea. John Comings, and Thomas Read for time and money expended in going to bedford to meet the Court's Comety."

INCORPORATION TO BEGINNING OF REVOLUTIONARY WAR. 69

Fishways. "March the 1st day 1735-6. Voted to chos two men for a comity to vew the dams across stonne brook with the cost of making conveaninces for the fish to run and report to the selectmen of what the cost may be. Benjamin Robens and Jonas Prescott Jun. Comity for said work."

This seems to be the first vote of the town in regard to the passage of shad and alewives from the Merrimack River to Forge Pond. In those days when fish were abundant, it was an important matter to have them pass the dams and reach the pond.

"September 28, 1736.
"Voted to be at further cost for the fish coming up in the spring. Chose Mr. Benjamin Robens and Mr. Jonas Prescott a Comety to prosacout the matter aboght the fish and to agre with John Richardson to make a convanent sluse for the fish to com up in the spring."

John Richardson owned the mill at the mouth of Stony Brook, in North Chelmsford.

The practice of choosing a Fish Committee or Fish Wards, every year, continued until the year 1826 — almost a century. Nahum H. Groce, Zaccheus Read, and Benjamin Osgood were chosen for that year, and they appear to be the last committee appointed.

Deer-Killing. In 1739, December 7, Jabez Keep and William Fletcher, Jr., were chosen "to inform of all breeches of act of law that is relating to kiling of deer." After this, two men were annually elected deer-reeves until the year 1773. Thomas Adams and Pelatiah Fletcher were chosen in that year.

Land Bank. The origin of the Land Bank is thus explained in Hildreth's History of the United States:

"Two companies were started [in 1740]; one, known as the 'Silver Scheme,' proposed to issue £150,000 in notes redeemable in silver at the end of fifteen years; the 'Manufactory Scheme' or 'Land Bank' undertook to circulate double that amount to be redeemed at the end of twenty years in colonial produce. The Silver Scheme was patronized by the merchants and traders; the Land Bank by the farmers and mechanics. The notes of the Land Bank were largely pushed into circulation. That company had eight hundred stockholders and held complete control over the House of Representatives. The Manufactory scheme remained unsettled for several years and proved ruinous to many persons." (History of the United States, Vol. II., p. 380, seq.)

"Westford May 25, 1741.

"At a meeting of the freeholders and other inhabitants Reguerly assembeled at the meeting hous in said Westford . . . Whereas the town of Westford have taken under consideration the grate diffikelty they labor under for want of a meedom of trade by reason of the provence bills being so skase amounge us,

"Therefore Voted and mutoally agreed that the Land Bank or Manificttery Bills, so cald, shall pass and pay all town debts that shall arise in said town for all servis don in public afaires the year current in said town on all accounts what so ever except spicashall contracts.

"Voted for the ese and benfit of the town that who so ever shall be choes to serve and Represent them at the grat and generll court shall have no pay out of the provences Treasury, but bring a list from the Clark of the house of Representives atested what his serves for time travel and atendance come to and he shall Receve the land Bank or Manifictirye bills, so called, as they now pass or shall pass for and shall give the town a discharge therefor."

Bounty on Squirrels and Blackbirds. "An account of the number of squirrels and Blackbirds killed in this town in the year 1741: The number of gray and ground squirrels is 4762; The number of old blackbirds is 403; The number of young blackbirds is 339; and their has been paid out of our town stock for the above named squirrels and blackbirds the sum of £85—15—10, and the Selectmen have given Dea. Henry Wright, Town Treasurer, a certificate to Mr. William Foye Esq. provence Treasurer, for to Receive the above sd sum of £ 85 — 15 — 10."

"February 1742. At a meeting of the Selectmen . . . it appeared that their has been paid out of our town stock this present year the sum of £ 115 — 3 — 8 for 6554 gray and [ground] squirrels and for 345 old blackbirds and 393 young blackbirds; and the Selectmen Did Draw a Certificate to Mr. William Foye Esq. Provence Treasurer to Receive the sd sum of £ 115 — 3 — 10 into our Treasury again."

The Province tax of Westford for the year 1742 was £ 53. 13 s. 4 d., less than half the bounty-money drawn from the county.

No Supper. "September 13, 1742. Voted that, the Town Officers shall have no supper at their annual meeting upon the town's cost."

It would hardly seem a proper time to be niggardly when so many squirrels and blackbirds had been killed. But eight years later the restriction was made more oppressive.

"September 17, 1750. Voted that the town officers should have no subsistence at the annal meeting in March *for seven years* to come from this Date on the town's cost."

What that long-suffering body of men, the town officers, had done to deserve such treatment does not appear; but perhaps the following order of the Selectmen helps to explain it.

"February 27, 1750. Pay to James Pollard the sum of 10 s. 5 d. for 13 Dinners Last March meeting of town officers."

It was only an item of reform in the early civil service.

Training Field. "May 21, 1744. Voted and chose Capt. Thomas Read, Lt. Jonas Prescott, Jr. and John Abbot as a Committee for to treat with Mr. Joseph Underwood about bying a piece of Land for the Convenancy of a training field Round the meeting house half an acre more or less as they see fit."

"March 24, 1748. Pay to Mr. Joseph Underwood the sum of 5 £ for the land which the Com^tee bought of Mr. Underwood for a training field."

The land so acquired is now the Common in the central village.

"March 2, 1767. Voted to purchase the piece of land Latly added to the training field in Westford on the east of the meeting house."

Bounty on Wolves. "May 22, 1749. Voted to give one pound more than the Law gives to any Person of Westford that shall kill a grown wolf in sd Westford or take the track of any wolf and follow sd wolf till he or they kill it, and If Groton Littleton Dunstable Hollise Townshend Lunenburg and Harvard will Joyn with us to give something to the incouraging any Persons for kiling the wolves as the Selectmen of the above sd towns have agreed viz Groton 2 £ Littleton £ 1 — 2 — 6 Dunstable 12 s. — 6 d. Hollise 10 s. townshend 10 s. Lunenburg £ 1 — 5 — 0, Harvard £ 1. . . . then the town of Westford agreed to give one pound to any person of the above sd towns that shall kill a grown wolf or take the track of any wolf in any of sd towns and kill it where they will, upon a certificate under the hand of the Selectmen of the above sd towns or either of sd towns that there has been a grown wolf killed and the ears cut as the Law Directs."

Tony's Island. "In the year 1751 Enoch Cleaveland with his whole family, also Sarah Tony with her child, were all warned to depart."

In Rev. Willard Hall's Record of Baptisms occurs the following:

"1751 Nov. 24. Sarah Tony [negro] adult. Frances Tony Daugh^r of Sarah."

This Sarah was perhaps a servant in the family of Enoch Cleaveland, who lived near the old mill-site in

Providence Meadow. An island in the meadow is still known as Tony's Island.

Warning out Strangers. By a law of the Province, enacted in 1692-'93, it became necessary to warn all strangers to leave the town; and if such warning was not given within three months, then all such persons were to be reputed inhabitants of the town, and if any of them became sick or poor then the town was obliged to aid them. Great care was taken to comply with the law, as the lists of persons warned clearly show. If any person duly warned by the constable did not depart in fourteen days, he was conveyed out of town by the constable or by his order.

"Sept. 1756. Be it remembered that Edmond Marble of Stow was warned out of our town and old Mr. Kemp of Billerica. Also Lydia Stratton and Lydia Stratton Jun. and one child more."

"1757 Lydia Russell, Sarah Willis, Mary Patch and Anna her Daughter were warned out of town."

"1759 John Wright and Sarah his wife, Sarah and Mary their children, Isaac Kent and Mary his wife; Mary, Elizabeth, Abigail, and Isaac their children. Also Eason Dix and Daniel Dudley and Hannah his wife & Daniel their child. Also hannah Blanchard and Sarah, Daniel and Moses her children, and Josiah Kemp Jr."

"Sept. 1760 William Park, Margaret Brown and William, James, and John her children; Eleazer Taylor, Sarah Love; also Mary Lawrence, Jacob Ames and his brother."

"1761. Isaac Holt and Mary his wife, Obadiah and Mary their children; Jonathan Fish and David Fish."

"1762. John Bigelo & Grace Bigelo his wife, and Lucy, Bulah, Sarah, Silas, Simeon, Molly, Grace, and Eunice Bigelo their children, and Judah Wheeler, all which came from Acton. Isaac Patch and Elizabeth his wife, & their son, John Avery Patch, which came from Groton."

"1762. Hugh Smylie and Mary his wife, Thomas, David, William, Alexander, Sarah, and Mary their children, all Lately came from Willton in Newhampshire. Dorcas Wheeler, wife of Samuel Wheeler, of Acton; and Mary French who lately came from Shrewsbury; and Theophilus Mansfield."

"1763. Nowel Dodge and Prissilla his wife, Joseph, Elijah, Sarah, hannah, Deborah & Delileth their children, lately came from Groton; Lucy Turner from Pepperill, Eleazer Fish from No. 1, so called in Newhampshire, Lucy Avery from Townsend, Mary Searls and Experience Harwood from Dunstable, Zerviah Lawrence Anna Lawrence from Pepperill, Isaac Parker from Groton; Ephraim Wheeler and Rebecca his wife, Lucy, Oliver, Rebecca, Lois, Jesse and Mary their children, all from Acton; Thomas Perry from Lexington, Lydia Perry from Acton, Samuel Farnsworth from No. 4 in Newhampshire."

In many cases the persons so warned remained and became useful citizens. The vigilance and care of the early inhabitants for the welfare of society in the punishment of idlers and vagabonds were always apparent; while the deserving *poor* were provided for according to the dictates of a genuine philanthropy. The fathers believed in all proper restraints and correctives of immoral conduct, and did not hesitate to punish offenders with a just severity.

"1762. Pay Ephraim Hildreth Jun. for making a New pair of Stocks."*

Meeting-House Bell. "March ye 1, 1762. Voted to raise a sum of money sufficient to Purchase a meeting House bell with what is Raised by subscription."

"September 20, 1762. Voted and chose Capt. Jonas Prescott, Capt. Samuel Fletcher and Deacon John Abbott a Comm.tt to Purchase a meeting house bell for sd Westford.

---

* Stocks: A machine consisting of two pieces of timber in which the legs of criminals are confined by way of punishment.—*Webster.*

Voted that the sd Committe shall Purchase a bell for sd Town of about five hundred and fifty pound weight."

" November 25, 1763. Voted to Receive the meeting house bell lately purchased by a Committee chosen by the Town for that purpose. Voted and chose Capt. Jonas Prescott, Capt. Samuel Fletcher, Dea. John Abbott, Capt. Jabez Keep, and Nath! Boynton as a Committee to hang the sd meeting house bell. Voted the bell shall be hung south-westerly from the meeting house bordering on or twelve feet in Mr. Eben! Stone's Land. Voted that the bell shall hang fifteen feet high and the Belfrey be as wide as the Committee shall think proper. Voted that the Selectmen shall appoint a man to ring the sd bell."

" Copy of a subscription for a meeting house bell. £27—9—0. Nath! Boynton Town Clerk.

" Westford February 19, 1762.

" We the subscribers do promise to pay into the Town Treasury of sd Westford in twelve months from the date hereof the sums of money set against Each of our Names in part to purchase a good meeting house Bell for the use of sd Town, Provided that the Inhabitants of sd Westford do at their anaual meeting in March Next vote to Raise the Remainder of the money for such a bell as the Town shall think Proper and Convenant for sd Town ; and on conditions as aforesaid we bind ourselves and our heirs to pay the money set against Each of our Names as aforesd as witness our hands :

	£	s.	d.
Samuel Chamberlin	0	12	0
Jonas Prescott	2	8	0
James Pollard	2	8	0
John Abbott	1	4	0
Nath! Boynton	1	4	0
Benjamin Carver	1	4	0
Joshua Fletcher	1	4	0
Zechariah Hildreth	1	4	0
Joseph Boynton	1	4	0
Timothy Underwood	1	4	0
David Dutton	0	12	0
Phinehas Hildreth	0	18	0
Ephraim Hildreth Jun.	1	4	0

	£	s.	d.
Eben^r Stone	0	18	0
Amos Hildreth	1	4	0
Thomas Comings	1	7	0
Jabez Keep	0	18	0
Benjamin Fletcher	1	4	0
James Dutton	0	12	0
Moses Burge	1	4	0
Timothy Prescott	0	12	0
Jonathan Spaulding	0	12	0
William Spaulding	0	12	0
Asa Bixby	0	12	0
Pelatiah Wright	0	12	0
Thomas Smith Jun.	0	12	0

"Westford April ye 2 : 1763.

"The above is a True copy of the subscription for a meeting house bell for sd Westford which I have Rec^d into my office in order to Receive the money.

"JOSEPH BOYNTON, Town Treasurer.

"Westford Decr 1763, the above Named subscribers have all paid the money into the Treasury which they subscribed."

"Westford June 14 1763.

"To Lieut. Joseph Boynton, Town Treasurer. You the sd Treasurer are ordered to pay Capt. Jonas Prescott, Capt. Samuel Fletcher & Dea^n John Abbott as a Committee chosen by sd Westford to provide a meeting house Bell for sd Town or to the major Part of sd Committee the sum of £27—9—0 which is the sum total of what is subscribed in sd Westford towards Purchasing sd bell. Also, you the sd Treasurer are ordered to pay out of the Treasury to the sd Committee or to the major part of them the sum of £27—11—0 in order to enable them (with the sum subscribed above mentioned) to purchase a good bell for sd Westford.

By order of the Selectmen.

NATH^l BOYNTON, Town Clerk."

"December 5, 1763. Pay to Capt. Jonas Prescott £3—4s for cash that he paid towards Purchasing the meeting house bell over and above what was ordered and for his Journey to boston to Receive sd bell."

"December 19, 1763. Pay to Ephraim Hildreth Jun! the sum of 12s for bringing the meeting house bell from Boston."

The land on which the belfry stood was conveyed to the town by the following deed:

"Whereas The Town of Westford hath lately Builded a New Building in the Middle of sd Town known by the Name of a Bellfree (so called) and as it now standeth on the Land of Ebenezer Stone and is now used for the Hanging and Ringing the Meeting House Bell that belongeth to the sd Town of Westford.

"Now Know Ye that I Ebenezer Stone of Westford in the County of Middlesex, Trader, in consideration of the Love and Good Will I bare on my mind to sd Town of Westford, Have given granted Bargained and sold and do by these presents give grant bargain and sell and Freely and Fully and absolutely convey and confirm unto the sd Town of Westford, the land on which the sd Bellfree above mentioned Now Standeth so long as the Town of Westford shall see cause to use and improve the same piece of land for a Bellfree to Ring Westford meeting house bell on; and if the Town of Westford aforesd shall cease to use and improve the sd peice of land for the purpose afore mentioned, then this conveyance to be nul and void. Otherwise so long as sd peice of land is improved by sd Town of Westford for the purpose above mentioned this conveyance shall Remain in full Force and vartue as witness my hand and seal this Twenty Third Day of May A. D. 1764 in the Fourth year of his Majesties Reign.

EBEN! STONE [L. S.]

Signed sealed and delivered in presents of us

JONAS PRESCOTT
SAMUEL FLETCHER
BENJAMIN CARVER
THOMAS KIDDER
OLIVER BATES."

This deed is to be found in Volume II., page nineteen, of the Town Records. Inasmuch as the clerk did not sign it as if recorded by him, it is probably the original draft and the signatures are genuine autographs.

The dimensions of the belfry are not given except that the bell was to "hang fifteen feet high," and it was to "be as wide as the Comm^tee think proper." It is evident, however, that it was not a mere skeleton of frame-work, but a building framed, boarded, clapboarded, plastered, painted and glazed.

The coming of the first bell ever brought to town was an event of some significance to the people. Its glad peals were to call them to the house of God, and its solemn tolling was to announce the passing of many a soul from earth to heaven.

The records show the sums paid for work and materials: Asahel Wyman found the irons; Phinehas Hildreth, laid the underpinning; Capt. Jabez Keep furnished "15 hundred of bords"; Benjamin Carver, a white pine tree; Abner Kent, "an iron plate for the axeltree"; Ebenezer Stone, "nails and other things"; Joseph Boynton, "clabords"; James Dutton, "477 feet of bords"; Thomas Comings, Jr., "slit work and plank"; Timothy Underwood, timber, and widow Thankful Chase, "one crooked beam." Joseph Dutton, Jr., was paid "for 4 days' works"; Capt. Samuel Fletcher, "for work Nails and other service"; Dea. John Abbot, Zechariah Hildreth, Amos Hildreth, and Oliver Adams, of Chelmsford, "for work"; Capt. Jonas Prescott, "for work planck & slitwork"; Henry Wright, Jr., "for twenty eight days' work;" and Nathaniel Boynton, "the sum of £14—10, for work & stuf & Painting and glazing and plastering,"—the largest item of the account.

The bell was bought in the autumn of 1763, but probably it was not put in position until some time in the spring of 1764. The belfry was "southwesterly of the meeting house." The meeting-house of that day stood much nearer the Common than the present one does, and the site of the belfry was near the corner of the lot on which the Academy stands.

The First Bell-Ringer. "Westford February 22, 1765, Pay to Ebenezer Stone the sum of £1 for ringing the meeting house bell the year past."
Mr. Stone was doubtless appointed as soon as the bell was ready for use, and he was therefore the first to make it ring out over the hills and valleys of Tadmuck.

Gloves. "April 4, 1763. Lieut. Joseph Boynton, Pay to Mr. Ebenezer Stone £1—1—4 for nine pair of Gloves that he provided for ye funeral of Mrs. Boynton."

Copying Records. "September 30, 1765. Voted to transcribe the Record of Births and Deaths all out of the old Book into the new Book bought for that use in order as they ought to be. Voted and chose John Abbot and Mr. Nathaniel Boynton a committee for that service to transcribe the Births and Deaths above mentioned."

Deeds of Charity. "January 6, 1766. Pay John Abbot the sum of 8s. for a great coat Jacoat and Briches which he found for William Bowen by the Selectmen's order—sd Bowen being under such low circumstances that he was like to suffer with cold, he being so naked that he was like to freeze with cold and the Selectmen thought it a Deed of Charity to Relieve him at his Desire."

"February 10, 1766. Pay Dea. Henry Wright the sum of £1 for milk Butter and Cheese and six yards of all wool Cloath for womans gounds and making them up for John Blodget's wife and girl."

Singing. "May 21, 1767, voted and granted the third, fourth & fifth seats in the Frunt gallery to those Persons that have been taking pains to learn to sing Ruleable in the Congregation and to aney others that shall be disposed to learn to sing by Rule."

This vote indicates that some attention began to be paid to the science of music. Generally the psalm or hymn had been "deaconed off," that is, read one line at a time by the deacon, and so caught up and sung by the congregation.

Civil Action. "September 1, 1767. Voted Not to pay Doctor Jeremiah Robbinson's Acc! as set forth in the write. Voted to Defend the Action commenced against sd Westford by Jeremiah Robinson. Voted that Mr. Thomas Kidder and Nath! Boynton shall be a Committee to Defend the action commenc! against sd Westford by Doctor Jeremiah Robinson."

This was a suit to recover fees for doctoring some of the town's poor. Dr. Robinson came from Marblehead and removed from Westford to Littleton.

Mending the Bell. "November 20, 1767. Pay to Nath! Boynton the sum of 13s—4d for a Journey to Hanover for instructions for mending the Town bell."

There was a foundry established in Hanover quite early and to that probably he went for his instructions.

The Early Burying-Grounds. "There are burial-grounds where, as Tennyson beautifully says: 'The stone-cut epitaph remains after the vanished voice and speaks to men.' And what tales do they not tell us? Every name we read in rugged and half-worn capitals recalls some page of romantic history, some career over which the archæologist may linger with affectionate remembrance; wafts legendary stories from the dim twilight of the past, and recalls traditions which years may have buried amid the lumber of our recollections."

It is a fact worthy to be mentioned, that the first burying-place in Westford was not near the meeting-house. It was the custom to lay out a lot around or very near the sanctuary. This was so in Concord, Chelmsford and Groton, and in nearly all the old towns. The practice is a very old one, perhaps started by the Celts in the 6th Century or possibly by the Romans. St. Columba, who founded the monastery at Iona, on the west coast of Scotland, marked off a space in the chapel or oratory for the repose of the dead. Later, such a place was called "God's Acre," the term being first used, it is supposed, by the Germans. In Westford, the oldest burial-ground is a mile east of the meeting-house, and is not, therefore, a *church*-yard. Indeed, the early settlers never used the word *church* to designate the house of worship or the place of burial. Inasmuch as the eastern portion of the town was first settled, the spot was selected long before the precinct or town was formed. The oldest head-stone bears this inscription: "Abram Wright, died 1702." But burials may have taken place before this; and as the records of Chelmsford give no information about it, it is perhaps impossible to fix the time when the first grave was made there.

"May 20, 1751. Voted that Capt. Fletcher, Lt. Prescott and Mr. Ebenezer Wright be a Com^{tt} to search out the bounds of the Burying Place and make report to the next meeting."

"August 19, 1751. Voted that the Com^{tt} shall continue to do somewhat further about the burying places."

"March 6, 1752. Voted to continue the Former Comittee that was chosen to search up the bounds of the buring place and Renew the same if they may be found."

"May 18, 1752. Voted to refer the article about the buring place to the next meeting, and the Com^{tt} chosen for that service are Desired to get the assistance of some of the Elderly people of sd town to assist them in finding out the bounds of the burying Place If they may be found."

"September 25, 1752. Voted to Ad Thomas Read Esq. Mr. Josiah Burge, Ens. Samuel Fletcher, and Mr. James Pollard to the former Com^{tt} chosen to search up the bounds of the buring place, and sd Com^{tt} to go and make the bounds of the buring place where they think they ought in Justice to bee."

It is implied in these votes that very little was known about it. The Committee made the following report:

"We the subscribers being a Com.ᵗᵗ to Renew the Bounds of the Buring Place Between Mr. Daniel Brooks and Mr. Josiah Brookses Land—is as followeth to wit: Begining at ye corner of the ston wall which was Sa.ᵘ Underwood's corner then Running Partly Easterly By ye Land of Mr. Daniel & Josiah Brookses Land aboute Eight Rods to a stake and stons then Running Northardly aboute three rods to a stake and stons By ye ston wall, then Running westerly aboute fifteen Roads to a stake and stons by the Highway as the fence Now stands, then Turning at ye End of ye ston wall which ye Town Built for the Burying Place Southardly aboute four Roads, Then Turning and Running Partly Easterly a Boute seven Roads to ye corner of ye ston wall where we Began.

"Dated at Westford ye 19: day of February 1753. Jo.ˢ Fletcher, Jonas Prescott, Ebenezer Wright, Tho.ˢ Read, Sa.ᵘ Fletcher, James Pollard."

"Westford February 19ᵗʰ 1753. We the subscribers have Renewed the Bound of the Burying Place with the Com.ᵗᵗ within Named against our Land & do Consent to said Bounds. Daniel Brooks, Josiah Brooks, Thomas Cumings. Record [ed] by me Jos Read Town Clerk."

"May 23, 1753. Voted to Except of the old Burying Place as the Com.ᵗᵗ Bounded it out and the Transcript To Be Recorded."

"May 15, 1754. Voted and chose Ens. Sa.ᵘ Fletcher & James Pollard a Com.ᵗᵗ to make ye Town's part of ye fence Betwene Mr. Brookes Land and the Buryind Place & to make a Hors block and Set it up there and also to make a conveneant Gate & put it up for conveniance of going into the same."

Additions were soon after made to it as will be seen by the following extract:

"May 18, 1768. Voted to Exsept of ye Com.^{tte} Report Relating to ye old Burying Yard & also Returned Thanks to Mr. Thomas Cumings & Josiah Brooks for ye land they Generously gave to ye Town for an adition to ye old Burying Yard. Ye Com.^{tte} Report is as follows, viz:

"Westford March ye 3, 1768. We the subscribers chosen by ye Town a Com.^{tte} to settle ye line Betwene the old Burying place & Mr. Thomas Cumings Land and also to Treat with him aboute purchasing a piece of his Land adjoyning to said Burying place for a adition to ye same— accordingly we have settled ye Line Betwene said Cumings Land and the sd Burying place & have measured of aboute 18 rods of his Land Joyning to ye southerly side of said Burying place by his Consent & bounded oute ye same by Taking a Plan of said peace of Land & on said Burying Place & have also measured of a peace of Mr. Josiah Brookes Land by his Consent for an adition to said Burying Place of aboute 30 rods of ground which we found would accomodate better than to Take a peice of either of their Lands Seperate & said Thomas Cumings and Josiah Brooks have Generasly offered to Give each of their peices of Lands bounded oute by them and ye Com.^{tt} for an adition to ye Burying place to the Town forever for that use, provided the Town will exsept of the same & fence ye Burying Place & grant Liberty to said Parties to feed the same by putting into said place calves or sheep But no large Cattle or hogs that may Damnifie ye same. Ye Bounds of sd Burying Place may more fully appear by the plan of the same Taken by Mr. Ebenezer Prescott by our desire Said parties above mentioned are to have ye above mentioned improvement of but only in & by Their own Persons & also Mr. Brooks to have ye apples Growing on the same.

JONAS PRESCOTT,
JOHN ABBOTT, } Com.^{tte}
SAM^{l.} FLETCHER,

"Westford May ye 18th 1768. We the subscribers freely consent to ye within Com— Report & freely Give ye

Land within mentioned to the use of the Town forever with ye within Reserve

THOMAS CUMINGS,
JOSIAH BROOKS.

"Voted that Mr. Josiah Brooks shall have ye Liberty of gethering ye apples that grow on ye adition made to ye old Burying yard untill the Town shall Want to Improve the Land."

North Burying-Ground. "March 5, 1753. Voted to Except of the Land on Tarkil (Tarkiln) hill for a Burying Place as itt was laid out By the Com^{tt}."

The description is thus given:

"March ye 1st 1753. Laid out for a Buring Place a Peace of Land att a Place Called Tarkil hill Being one acer more or less Bounding near where Two Rodes meet a small pine tree marked and a heap of stons Then Runing Northerly By said Rode Thirteen Rods to a small pine Tree marked & a heap of stons about it one the west side of said Rode Then Running westerly fourteen Rods to a pine tree marked and a heap of stons then Southerly Thirteen Rods to a Black Oake tree marked & a heap of stone then one the North Side of a Roade that Leads from Thomas Wright's which was the Road Before mentioned to the first Bound.

JOSEPH FLETCHER, } Com^{tt}"
EBENEZER WRIGHT.

"Westford March ye 1st 1753. We whose Names are underwritten Being owners of the Land above mentioned do freely Give it To the Town for a Burying Place for Ever if they Except it for that use.

EBENEZER WRIGHT,
THOMAS WRIGHT."

"September ye 21 : 1767. Voted to fence the North Burying Yeard with Stone Wall Eight Rods squear: Provided the owners or Claimers of sd land Do give a good title to the sd Town of sd land."

Decr ye 12th 1768. Pay to Thos Wright & Oliver Bates ye sum of £6—1—8 for making 36 rods and a half of Stone wall Round the north Burying Yard."

The West Burying-Ground. " May 15, 1761. Voted and Excepted of half an acre of Land for a burying Place Purchased by Mr. Nathan Procter of Mr. Samuel Parker as may more fully appear by Deed of Sail for sd Land from sd Parker to sd Procter & to the Town of Westford for their use Provided the Town be at no charge in Purchasing sd Land."

This vote shows that the land was a gift from Nathan Procter. Probably it was a part of the estate of Deacon Joshua Fletcher, who owned a large tract of land in the vicinity and whose daughter Sarah married Samuel Parker.

The Cowdry Estate. " May 15, 1761. Voted that the Selectmen of this town shall use Their best skill and Judgment to Preserve and Recover the Estate of the late John Cowdry Deces.^d or aney part of sd Estate that hath been or is in an unjust manner spent & spending by Anna Cowdry widow of the sd Deces.^d."

Warned Out. " September—1764. Sommers Shattuck of Littleton, Abigail Blodgett of Nottingham West in New Hampshire, John Stanley of Charlestown, William Perkins of Topsfield, James Perry of Billerica, Hepsebeth Perry, wife of James Perry, of Lexington, Doctor Jeremiah Robinson and Eunice his wife, Eunice, Winthrop, and Lydia their children from Haverhill or Marlbrough, Nowel Dodge Junr, Martha Dodge and Elizabeth Dodge of Littleton."

" March ye 11, 1766. Benjamin Chamberlin and Susanna his wife, Benjamin and Susanna their children who came last from Dunstable; wid. Sarah Avery from Townsend; Thomas Hardy and Deborah his wife, Hannah Perry and Richard Perry their grandchildren; Thomas Hardy Junr and Lydia his wife; Joseph Bailey and Deborah his wife, Nathaniel, Elizabeth, Joseph Bailey their children all from Bradford; and Samuel Gilson last from Groton."

"September 11, 1766. John Butterfield and Martha his wife, Benjamin, John, Abel, Henry, Kezia and Martha their children who came last from Shirley; Thomas Nutting from Groton; Joel Wright Perham, hannah Perham & Deliverance Perham from Littleton."

"March ye 2, 1767. Thomas Esterbrooks and Experience his wife, Joseph and Joel Esterbrooks their sons last from Dunstable; Samuel Farwell and Mary his wife last from Groton; Nathan Tylor last from Chelmsford; Zechariah Fletcher and Eunice his wife, Eunice and Susannah their children who lately came from Ipswich in New Hampshire; and Elizabeth Lawrence who lately came from the District of Pepperell."

"March 5, 1770. David Keyes and Esther his wife, Charles, David, and Esther their children all brought from Acton; Peter Larkin lately from Boston and his wife Hannah; Benjamin Estherbrook from Dunstable; Jacob Nutting from Groton; Nathaniel Far & Abigail his wife and Abigail and Martha their children."

"September, 1770. Jonathan Fish and Dorothy his wife, Jonathan, Ebenezer and Lucy their children last from Mason in Newhampshire; Joseph Barrett and Marcy his wife and Molly their daughter lately from Chelmsford; Sarah Kemp from Pepperell; Elizabeth Jones from Manchester; Solomon Wheat from Needham; Lydia Phelps from Groton; Jane Corey from Littleton; Joseph Perry from Chelmsford; Samuel Brooks & his wife from Woburn; Azubah Nutting from Waltham; Peter Rollins from Littleton; David Fish & Sarah his wife from Acton; Smith Foster from Billerica; Hannah Woods from Hampshire; Ebenezer Temple from Acton, and Mary Russell from Littleton."

"March 4, 1771. John Fletcher from Chelmsford; Molly Perry from Dunstable; Joanna Farmer and Isacah Keyes from Chelmsford; Thomas Beal and Molly his wife from Ipswich; and Nancy Taggart. Also Patience Wyman from Littleton."

"September, 1772. Francis Goodhue & Lucy his wife and Benesla & Francis their children late from Ipswich; Arthur Dennis and Mary his wife, Mary and Arther their children last from Ipswich; Thankful Chase last from Putney in New York government; Anna Sartell from Groton; Thankful Bennett and Rhoda Bennett from Hollis; William Beal and Anna his wife and Obadiah Beal from Ipswich; Oliver Barrett and Anna his wife and Anna, Ebenezer, Oliver, Joseph and Benjamin their children and Sipeo their negro from Billerica; Benjamin Wheat and Sarah his wife and Sarah, John, and betty their children from New Ipswich; Henry Morgan and Hannah his wife from Townsend; William Fletcher and Sarah his wife last from Mason; and Jack Lane and his wife, Cyrus, Mella, jesse and Ellis their children from Littleton; and wid. Elizabeth Hunt and Abijah Hunt last from Concord."

"1774. Sarah Parker and Mary how from Littleton; Sarah Curtis from Lyn; William Nicoles and Ruth his wife from Concord; Ebenezer Foster and Hannah his wife, Ruth William and Oliver their children from Chelmsford."

Powder and Bullets. "December ye 12: 1768. Pay to Mr. Eben: Stone ye sum of £6 for to buy one Barrill of Powder & ye Rest is to be laid oute in Bullits & Flints which he has undertaken to buy for the Town of Westford."

Remonstrance Against the Stamp Act. Scarcely had the strife between England and France for supremacy in North America come to an end, before the English Government began to impose burdens upon her colonies here which the free spirit of the people would not bear. The Stamp Act was one of a series of legislative usurpations that led to their separation from the mother country. This town, in common with many others, put upon record its emphatic protest against that Act.

"We the Freeholders and other inhabitants of the Town of Westford in town meeting assembled the Thirty-first Day of October A. D. 1765, Voted and chose Lt. Timothy Fletcher, Moderator; then voted: Professing the Greatest Loyalty to our most Gracious Soverain and our Sincere Regard and Profound Reverence for the British Parliment as the most powerful and Respectable Body of men on earth, yet at the same time Being Deeply sencable of the Difficultys and Distresses to Which that agust Assembly's Late exertion of their power in and by the Stamp Act must Necessarily Expose us; think it proper in the present critical Conjuncture of affairs to give the following instructions, viz:

"To Capt. Jonas Prescott our Representative—we trust in your Honesty and fidelity and trust [to the trust?] Reposed in you Beleiveing you have ever served this town in the best way and manner you were capable; and now at a time when American Subjects are every where loudly complaining of arbitrary and unconstitutional Tax laid on us, as we humbly apprehend, and that the town of Westford cannot any longer Remain silent without just Imputation of inexcusable neglect, we therefore would consider what stepts are best for us to take at this alarming time. We think it proper to let you know our sentiments and to give you our instructions thereupon. We are alarmed and astonished at the Act called Stamp Act by which very greaves [grievous] and we apprehend unconstitutional tax is laid on us. We humbly apprehend by the Royal Charter granted to our forefathers that they had power of making Laws for our internal goverment and of leveling taxes invested in the general assembly; and by the same Charter the inhabitants of this Province are intituled to all the Rights and Priviledges of Natural free born subjects of Great Britain. The most essencial Rights of Britan subjects are those of being Represented in the same body which exercised the power of Leveling Taxes on them and having their properties Tryed by Juries. These are the common Privilidges of Mankind, and we apprehend we ware not Represented in Parlament of Great Britain when that sd act was made, and it is certain that this Act admites of our Properties being tryed by Courts of admiltry [admiralty] without a Jury; so at once we are deprived of our most valuable Rights and Privilidges which is contained in our Charter as we humbly conceive, and to have our properties Judged and determined by Strangers to us; that the investing the Authority in the Courts of Admiltry to Deside in Suites Relating to Stamp Duties and other matters to their Jurisdiction, is highly Dangerous to us his Majesty's subjects and our Lyberties. We humbly think that we are intituled to all the Lyberties, Rights, and Privilidges of his Majesties subjects in Great Britain or Elsewhere, and that our Constitution of Goverment in the Province is founded on the natural Rights of Mankind and the noble Princaples of English Lyberty, and therefore is or ought to be perfectly free. We therefore think it our indispensable Duty to ourselves and our Dear Children as it is our undoubted Privilidge, in the most open and unreserved manner but in Decent and Respectfull termes to Declare our Great Dissatisfaction with this Stamp Act, and we think it incumbent on you by no means to Joyne in any measure for countenancing and assisting in the execution of sd Act; but to use your Best Endeavours to have the Rights and Privilidges of the people asserted and vindicated and Left on Record that our children after us may not charge us with the guilt of Tamely giving our Rights and Privilidges away. We further instruct you that you take care that the money in the Province Treasury which is Drawn from the People of this Province may not be applied to any other purpose but what was Evedantly intended in the Act for Supplying the treasury. As to other things of less importance we leave you to act as you think proper; as you in your wisdom shall think best for your constitutants.

TIMOTHY FLETCHER, Moderator."

"Recorded by John Abbott, Town Clerk."

The Stamp Act was passed by the British Parliament, March 8, 1765, and this protest against it was made in the following October. Thus promptly did the patriots of Westford denounce and resist it.

Not long after this the town passed the following vote to encourage industry.

"January 18, 1768. Whereas the Town of Boston hath made the very agreeable and most Important motion (and agreed) to prevent Excessive Use of foreign Superfluities and to Promote and Incourage Industry and the Produce and Mannufactures of this Province—for which motion we the Inhabitants of the Town of Westford now assembled Do Return our most Hearty thanks to the Town of Boston; therefore voted to concur with the Town of Boston in that most important Plan (laid by sd Boston) to Incourage Industry &c, and to Prevent the use of foreign Superfluities &c."

"March 5, 1770. Chose Capt. Jonas Prescott, Capt. Samuel Fletcher, Dea. John Abbott, Mr. Ebenezer Stone & Mr. Thomas Comings as a Committee to take under their consideration the affair Relating to Incouraging Industry and Disaproveing of Importing Goods from Great Britain, and make report."

"Upon report of the Committee appointed to take into their consideration the article of the warrant Relating to encouraging Industry and Discouraging the Importation of British Goods &c.,—Voted unan [imously] that In Imitation of the Laudable example of several Towns of this Province in promoting Frugality & Encouraging Industry, we Do Highly approve of [and] concur with the Patriotic, Commendable, and disinterested agreement of the merchants of the Towns of Boston, Charlestown &c in not importing any goods or Commodities from Great Britain (a few Necessary articles Excepted) as the most direct and legal means of Securing to us our Constitutional Rights & Privilidges and Redressing those Grievances which arise from an Act of Parliment in Imposing Duties on several articles in order to Raise a Revenue in America. Voted unan!y not to Purchase or Procure either direcly or indirectly any Goods or Commodities of any of those persons who have audaciously Counteracted the Laudable Design of the body of merchants in this province or of any that shall Hereafter endeavour to Counteract the aforesd Laudable Design by Importing any goods or Commodities contrary to the aforesd Patriotic, Commendable, disinterested agreement, and do esteem not only those audacious Importers but all and every such person or persons as shall Procure or Purchase any goods whatever of the aforesd Importers as enemies to their country and better calculated for Vassalage than Trade or the Free Enjoyment of their Rights and Privilidges.

"Voted unan!y that whereas the chief support of the C—n—rs [Councillors] arises from the Duty laid on Bohea Tea, not to Purchase or to use the afore sd Tea (cases of necessity excepted) till such time or times as the Reasons for Non-Importation may be Removed."

"January 12, 1773. Voted as follows: Whereas we have received from the Town of Boston a pamphlet containing the proceedings of said Town in consequence of a rumor which now, alas! we find to be too true, viz. that the judges of the Superiour Court are made not only indepen[den]t of the people but absolutely dependent on the crown for their support—this we apprehend to be a very Dangerous inovation and if continued may be attended with the most Dierful consequences: Voted that this Town heartily join in sentiments with their Boston Brethren and are of opinion that our rights appear to be stated by them with great perspicuity and candor, and are sorry they are obliged to say that the infringements and violations of sd rights are too notorious to be denied. That a Committee be chosen to correspond with Boston or any other Town as occasion may require, that so their may be a free.communication of sentiments throughout the province. That this Committee consist of the five following gentlemen, viz. Mr. Samuel Gardner, Capt. Jonathan Minot, Deacon John Abbott, Dr. Asaph Fletcher and Mr. Nathaniel Boynton. That this Committee be desired to Return a respectfull answer to the Boston committee, expressive of the great obligations we are under to the Town of Boston in general and to them in particular for their noble and generous exertions in the cause of their country, and of our readiness to coincide with them in any measures that may be concluded upon as Best for the Redress of those grievances so justly complained of. That as the general court is now sitting, our Representative is hereby instructed to use his utmost endeavours for the removal of those grievances which if persisted in, threaten this country with entire ruin. That the thanks of this Town be given to that disinterested patriot, the Hon. John Hancock Esq. for his care and zeal discovered upon this occasion and for the many sacrifices he has made to the cause of Liberty : and who, altho' a gentleman of independent fortune (perhaps not inferiour to any of the Marblehead gentry) can with the greatest pleasure and satisfaction see others Live and enjoy the sweets of life as well as himself. That an attested coppy of these our proceedings be transmitted to the Boston Committee and that the above gentlemen be Desired to enclose them in their letter to sd Committee, and forward them as soon as may be.

JOHN ABBOTT, Moderator.

"The above said votes were all unanimously passed in a very full meeting.

Recorded by ZAC. WRIGHT."

This, so far as the records show, was the first Committee of Correspondence appointed by the town. Some of the best citizens were members of it, from time to time, and it was the medium of communication with other patriotic men throughout the province for several years.

The following paper, prepared by Dr. Asaph Fletcher, one of the Committee, was adopted by the town :

"March 30, 1774. Wee inhabitants of the town of Westford being Requested by the Com^tt of correspondence for the town of Boston to give our sence of the present Gloomey situation of our Publick affairs, Do find it incumbent on us to comply with so Reasonable and interesting a request, although we can truly say it is with no small regret that we are so frequently Reduced to the unhappy alternative either to yield compliance with the Iron chains of Slavery or by manly opposition to oppose the same: but in faithfulness to our country, ourselves, and Posterity we hold ourselves obligated according to the utmost of our abilities to make Repeated oppisitions against Repeated attempts to extinguish the just Rights and Liberties of this people, or every attempt to annialate our freedom the Price of which was no less than the price of Blood, even the precious Blood of our worthy ancestors.

" Whatever may have been the motive, it is very apparent that the conduct of the British Administration for some years past and in many Respects hath not comported with their good Regards and Desire for the continuance of our American Lyberties, and the assiduity of their plotting the extorting of our money and consequently the compleating of our bondage seems to be obviously confirmed by a Late act of the British Parliment impowering the East India Company to export their teas to America, subject to a duty for the express purpose of Receiving a Revenue &c. But beholding the general union of the colonies with their uninterrupted exertions in the cause of Lyberty, so inspires our Breasts that we are constrained in a perticular manner to essert our readiness on all Necessary occasions to unite with the colinies in general and with this Province in perticular in every constitutional method for the Redress of our greavances and the continuance of our Lyberties : tho' by all which we do not mean to approve of any Riotous or Disorderly conduct or in the least to indicate any Disregard to our Soverain Majesty or the Dignity of his crown. Neither do we Plead for anarchy, but we seek the enjoyment of those charter Privilidges which Americans have long enjoyed heretofore, in which time a happy Harmony subsisted between Great Britain and her colinies. It is the opinion of this town that if the plan of administration so far succeed as that the general Use of Dutied tea should take place among the colonies, it would be attended with very Distructive consequences; nor do wee think that their are any good advantages that acrue from the use of Endia tea, considered without a duty which might not be obtained from vegetable plants of our own production and cultivation. Therefore Resolved that we will not for the futere Purchase or use ourselves or approve to be used in our families any tea or teas whatsoever, subject to a duty untill such Duty shall be Repealed.

1. "Voted that our Selectmen be and hereby are Desired to withhold their approbation for License for Retailing or tavern keeping to all such Person or persons as shall Refuse to comply with the aforesd Resolve.

2. "Voted that the thanks of this town be given to the patriotick inhabitants of the town of Boston for their continued exertions in the cause of Lyberty.

3. "Voted that the committee of correspondence for the town of Boston be and hereby are informed that Mr. Samuel Gardner who was formerly chairman of the committee of correspondence for this town, by Reason of his removal from this town, was by a vote passed at our annual meeting in March last Dismissed from that service, and Mr. Zaccheus Wright, by a vote passed at the same meeting, was substituted in his Room.

"But before we conclude we cannot forbear to mention that the Late conduct of Peter Oliver Esq. cheife Justice of the Superiour court of this Province, by his Refuseing the free grants of this Province for his service, in taking his Sallary out of the Revenue chest &c seems very alarming. Therefore that the aforesd Peter Oliver Esq. by his Late conduct in Refuseing the grants of this Province for his service as cheife Justice, and in taking a Sallary out of those Revenues which ware unconstitutionally extorted from this People without their consent and by his Declarition of Doing so in the future hath merited the full Resentment of the People of this Province and their non-confidence in him and has given the greatest cause for their uneasiness untill he shall be removed from the office of Cheife Justice.

"Recorded by order of the town of Westford

JOHN ABBOT, Town Clerk."

"July 4, 1774. Voted unanimously to take under our consideration the Papers sent from Boston to our town in consequence of sd Boston Harbour being Blocked up. Voted unanimously that the covenant lastly sent to Westford (with some small alteration thereon) should be signed by our town.

"Voted that the Covenant signed by the inhabitants of Westford Relating to Boston affairs be kept or Left in the town Clerk's hands During the town's Pleasure, and also to Return the names of those who do not sine this paper.

"The following votes were passed by the town altho no article was in the warrant to suport the same, but the town desired that a minitue of the same should be kept of them. Voted unanimously that the proportion of money due from our town to suport the committee of congress be taken out of our town treasury and paid.

"Voted unanimously to hold thursday the fourteenth day of July current as a day of fasting in this town, and furthermore If Mr. Hall Decline the same, then to imploy some sutiable person to cary on the Solemnities of sd Day.

"Voted also that the Selectmen provide a new stock of powder and ball and flints for this town's use."

The following order of the Selectmen, dated January 23, 1775, makes it probable that Rev. William Emerson, of Concord, was called to attend the Fast:

"Pay to Mr. Jonathan Keep the sum of £1—15—6—3 for what he paid Mr. Emerson for preaching our fast last summer."

Another order, dated September 8, 1774, shows that the vote to pay "the committee of congress" was carried out.

"Pay to the Hon. Thomas Cushing of Boston the sum of £1—13—1 for our town's proportion to the five hundred pounds granted by the general Court for the use of the Gentlemen appointed for the Congress Committee."

"September 8, 1774. Chose Capt. Joseph Read and Mr. Zaccheus Wright as a Provincial Committee to meet with sd committe or agents at the time and place of their meetings."

"November 25, 1774. Voted not to pay our town's proportion of the Province tax assessed on the inhabitants of Westford to Mr. Harrison Gray treasurer, nor for the assessors to make any Return to Mr. Gray our former treasurer.

"Voted that our town pay their proportion of the Province tax to Mr. Henry Gardener Province treasurer appointed by the Provincial Congress, and that the constables of sd Westford pay their proportion of sd tax to Mr. Gardner upon their Receiving a confirmation from the Provincial Congress."

The Second Meeting-House. Numerous alterations and repairs had been made upon the old house during the forty-four years that had passed since its erection, but they were not of sufficient importance to be noticed here. The new house which the town undertook to build proved the occasion of much contention, and was destined to have a much shorter history.

"September 19, 1768. Voted Not to repair ye old meeting house for a Number of Years.

"Voted to Build a New meeting House.

"Voted to chuse five men as a Com^{tt} to Treat with some proper workman to see How Bigg to Build the sd meeting House & What form to build it.

"Voted and chose Capt. Samuel Fletcher, Dea. John Abbott, Ens. Amos Fletcher, Mr. Nathl Boynton & Mr. Jona. Minot a Com^{tt} on the above affair Relating to Building a New meeting House and to make Report to ye Town this day six weeks at one of ye clock in ye afternoon to which Time the meeting was adjourned."

"October 31, 1768. Voted to Build a Meeting House sixty feet Long and forty five feet wide and 26 or 27 feet posts.

"Voted to raise one Hundred & Twenty pounds L. M. to provide Bords and other Nessessarys for ye Building of the sd meeting house and to be paid into ye Treasury by ye first day of June next.

"Voted to chuse five men to manage ye affair Relating to sd House and chose Capt. Samuel Fletcher, Dea. John Abbott, Mr. Tho? Cumings, Nath! Boynton & Jon? Minot a Com?? to prepare such things as should be Needful for ye Building of the sd meeting House according to their best skill and judgment."

This was the first step in a long series of municipal acts in which the people had little unanimity, as the records plainly show. A year passed away before any thing was really done except to prepare materials.

"September 25, 1769. Voted to set the New meeting house the back side of the old meeting house about sixteen feet from Capt. Pollard's land.

"Voted to let out the New meeting house fraim to Build by the great [gross or job] to some man or men that will do it the cheepest."

"November 21, 1769. Voted to set up a fraim for a New meeting house and underpin the same by the first of September next.

"Voted that the sd New meeting house frame shall be sixty three feet long and forty four feet wide.

"Voted to build three porches to sd meeting house.

"Voted that the Committee chosen in Sept? 1768 to provide Stuff for a New meeting house shall be a Committee to let out the sd meeting house fraim to build by the great."

"January ye 2 : 1770. Voted to sell the Pews or Pew-ground in the New meeting house that shall be built, to the freeholders of Westford to the Highest bidders."

"March 5, 1770. Voted that the Committee appointed to underpin the New meeting house shall take as many of the stones now under the old meeting house as they think proper."

"April 3, 1770. Voted to Raise the New meeting house fraim about the middle of June next if ready to Raise. Chose Capt. Benjamin Fletcher, Daniel Raymond, Ephraim Comings, Timothy Prescott, Oliver Bates, Pelatiah Fletcher and Ephraim Hildreth ye 3ᵈ as a Committee to take into consideration and make inquiry what meathod is best to Raise the New meeting house fraim."

"May 10, 1770. Voted to raise . . . without geens. Chose Capt. Samˡ Fletcher, Jacob Robinson, Moses Burge, Benjamin Fletcher & Amos Fletcher as a Committee to provide subsistence for the men that are chosen to raise the new meeting house fraim; and David Fletcher, Pelatiah Fletcher & Henry Wright Jun. a committee to prepair all Necessary articles to raise . . . withal Except Spick poles. Voted to have one hundred spick poles prepared."

"June 4, 1770. Voted to Raise the New meeting house the third Wednesday of this Instant June. Chose Capt. Jonas Prescott, Dea. John Abbott, Lt. Samˡ Read, Corˡ Thomas Kidder, Thomas Comings and Ephraim Comings as a Committee to attend the workmen at the raising of the New meeting house and to keep off the People out of the way of Hindering the men that shall raise sd meeting house."

In accordance with the vote of June 4th, the meeting-house was raised on the 20th of June, 1770; and at a meeting held July 12th the town voted "to accept the new meeting house fraim . . . with the *Jice* and Sleepers that are Necesary to put into sd fraim. Voted the thanks of the Town to the several Committees for their service, that was chosen by the Town to build the house and underpin the same. Voted to bord and shingle the New meeting house and lay the lower floor this year. Voted to compleat the finishing by the first of October 1771. Chose Capt. Jonas

Prescott, Capt. Joseph Read, Nath! Boynton, Thomas Comings and Thomas Kidder Committee to finish the house and to let out the said finishing to some faithful workman by the great."

"September 24, 1770. Voted to chuse a vandue Master to sell at Public Vandue or to the highest bidders the several proportions of pew-ground."

Against this action the following protest was entered on the records:

"September 24, 1770. We the subscribers being Inhabitants of the Town of Westford and Voters . . . Do Desent Against the vote for selling the pews or the pew-ground in the New meeting house or fraim, we having an interest in said pew-ground.

"JONAS PRESCOTT, and 16 others."

This protest seems to have been heeded.

"October 19, 1770. Voted and granted to Capt. James Pollard and others 25 wall pews for two hundred and sixty-six pounds thirteen shillings and four pence."

At a meeting held February 11, 1771, an attempt was made to sell these pews a second time, and this called out a protest signed by James Pollard and twenty-four others.

"March 4, 1771. Voted and granted to Amos Hildreth and fifteen others sixteen pews behind the body seats below for one hundred and fifty pounds."

It is just to conclude, that for a time, at least, the "body seats" or pews in the middle of the house, were held by the town, while others were sold to individuals.

Damage by Lightning. "August 13, 1771. Voted and chose the three first Selectmen to be a Committee to Repair the breach in the new meeting house Lately made by

Litning. Voted to sell some part of the old meeting house when it can be spaired conveniantly. Voted that the Com.^{te} and Mr. Samuel Hall shall build the pews back of the body of seats and the seats and alleys in proportion of Room as they are in Medford meeting house."

"October 3, 1771. Voted and granted the frunt gallery pews as follows: the east side of the Doore—the 1st to Isaac Comings, the 2nd to Daniel Goodhue, ye 3rd to Samuel Butterfield, 4th to Josiah Fletcher, the west side of the Doore—first Benjamin Read, the 2nd to Gershom Fletcher Jun., 3rd to William Butterfield Jr., 4th to David Goodhue."

"December ye 23^{d} 1771. Voted to accept of the New meeting house as it is finished, excluding the painting and glaizing, provided Mr. Hall make no demand on the Town any further than the agreement with the Committe."

"Voted that the Reverend Willard Hall shall have the use of the first pew next the pulpit stairs so long as he supplies the pulpit.

"Voted that Maddam Hall shall have a seat in the pew adjoining the pulpit stairs provided she outlives the Reverend Willard Hall, so long as she remains his widdow.

"Voted that Mr. Aaron Parker Jr. shall have the old meeting house for twenty pounds lawful money. Chose Capt. Joseph Read, Lt. Amos Fletcher and Timothy Prescott to be a Committe to seat the new meeting house.

"Voted to seat according to pay, age, and honour.

"Voted that real, personal estate, money, and faccuity be Reconed as pay."

It appears that Samuel Hall was the master-builder or contractor who undertook the work; but his residence and personal history cannot be ascertained from the records. The house was only partly finished when it was accepted by the town. It was occupied as early as December, 1771. The first child who was baptized in it was Elijah Wright, son of Henry Wright, Jr., born November 26th and baptized December 22, 1771, by Rev. Willard Hall. There is no hint in the records, either civil or ecclesiastical, of any service of dedication.

"March 2, 1772. Voted to confirm the former titles of all the pews in the new meeting house to the purchasers of sd pews for them their heirs and assigns, for the sums of money allready paid into the treasury by said purchasers.

"October 1, 1773. Pay to Jonas Prescott Esq., Nathaniel Boynton, Thomas Comings and Cor! Thomas Kidder the sum of £10 for their service and expense in letting the finishing of the new meeting house."

The old house, which was sold to Aaron Parker, Jr., was removed to South Chelmsford, and used by the Baptist Church and Society as a house of worship for many years; and when a new house took its place, it was removed to the farm of James Robbins, where it is now used for a barn.

CHAPTER III.

THE WAR OF THE REVOLUTION—ACTION OF THE TOWN IN REFERENCE TO IT—SOLDIERS IN THE ARMY—FORMATION OF THE STATE CONSTITUTION, AND VOTES OF THE TOWN IN REGARD TO IT.

THE period of the Revolution was one of great significance in the history of this town, in common with all other towns of the county and province. Westford troops took part in the first acts of armed resistance to British aggression at Concord and Bunker Hill; and in the long contest which followed, the citizens were enthusiastic in the cause of civil liberty, and worked zealously and perseveringly to secure their grand object. With the exception of three men, there was entire unanimity of feeling and action. Two of these soon repented and espoused the cause of their country. The third was Rev. Willard Hall, the first pastor, who remained steadfast in his loyalty to the king until he died, in 1779. But they deplored the necessity of a resort to arms, as the records plainly show. They counted the cost before they began. They knew that stern endeavor and unflinching resolution were necessary to success; but when once convinced that war was inevitable, they entered the contest with a just conception of the sacrifices which it involved. For they were strong-hearted, believing men, who trusted in God and gave up their property and their lives in battling for their rights.

> Hard was the labor, fierce the strife,
>   That with heroic valor brought
> Our great Republic into life,
>   Our nation's glorious birthright bought

With price untold—*freedom to think*,
To dare and do. No cowards they
From toil or danger e'er to shrink;
They kept their faith and won the day.

Steadily the tide of opposition rose against the measures of the British Parliament, which seemed determined to carry its points at all hazards. Steadily, also, the preparations for defence went on among the colonists.

January 16, 1775, the town voted to raise twenty pounds to purchase arms. Lieut. Zaccheus Wright, Col. John Robinson and Capt. Oliver Bates were chosen a committee to procure them, and February 3d they delivered eight guns to the Selectmen for the use of the town. Not long before this, the town stock of powder had been replenished and everything was made ready for an emergency which was near at hand.

February 27, the town voted " to chuse a committee of inspection of seven men. Chose Capt. Oliver Bates, Dea. Oliver Prescott, Mr. Ephraim Chamberlin, Ens. John Abbot Jun.ʳ Mr. Pelatiah Fletcher, Lieut. David Goodhue and Mr. Joshua Read for said Com.ᵗᵉᵉ of Inspection whose business and duty it shall be to see that the American Congress Association and the Provincial Congress resolves and Recommendations relative thereto, be well and faithfully observed and complied with, and that this town will not fail of lending all necessary assistance to sd Com.ᵗᵉᵉ in the doing of their duty."

The following agreement was recorded on the same day:

"We the subscribers having seen the [articles of] Association drawn up by the grand American Continental Congress, respecting the non-importation, non-consumption, and non-exportation of Goods &c. Signed by the Delegates of this and the Delegates of other Colonies of this Continent, and having attentively considered of the same, do heartily approve thereof and of every part of them, and in order to make the same Association &c., our personal act, do by these presents, under the sacred ties of Virtue, Honour, and the Love of our Country, firmly agree and associate fully and compleatly to observe and keep all & every article and clause in sd Association contained, with respect to Importation, Exportation, and Non-consumption, according to the true intent, meaning & Letter of our said Delegates, and will duly inform and give notice of every Evasion and Contravention of sd agreement as far as we are able, and that we will, as far as we can, encourage and promote a general union herein. As witness our hands this 27th day of February 1775.

"Voted that the above draught of an Association is approved of and that the same be entered in the Town book of Records for Westford, and that the same be signed by the several inhabitants of said Town, and that the Com^{tee} of Correspondence see the same is done or inform the Town at the next Town meeting of every person who shall delay or Refuse to sign the same, that so the Town may take further order thereon as they may think proper.

"JOSEPH READ, Moderator.

"Recorded by Nathl Boynton, Town Clerk."

March 6. "Voted and consented to Conform and abide by the advice of ye Com^{tees} of Correspondence of the Towns of Boston, Charlestown and several other towns, that was Read in our meeting."

THE CONCORD FIGHT, APRIL 19, 1775.

Authorities vary somewhat in stating the facts relating to this fight, some claiming that in Lexington the first resistance was made on the morning of that memorable day, while others affirm that at Concord Bridge the earliest armed resistance was offered to the soldiers of George the Third.

We are now to consider the service rendered by the men of Westford in that struggle. This has never been fully and accurately stated in any account of it. Prominent among the actors then and there, was John Robinson, of Westford, a Lieutenant-Colonel in a regiment of minutemen, of which William Prescott, of Pepperell, was Colonel. Rev. Dr. Ripley, in his account says: "A company from Westford had just entered the bounds of Concord when the fight took place. But individuals from that town were present and engaged in the battle, among whom was the brave Col. Robinson." He also says further on in his narrative: "The situation of Maj. Buttrick, as it was more dangerous and important, has gained him distinguished celebrity and honor. But this ought never to operate as an eclipse upon any other officer on that occasion. There is satisfactory evidence that on the march to meet the enemy, Maj. Buttrick requested Col. Robinson to act as his superior, he being an older man and of higher rank in another regiment; but he modestly declined, and consented to march at the right hand and be considered a volunteer. The late Col. John Buttrick, then a fifer, repeatedly affirmed that he was present and heard the conversation between his father and Col. Robinson. . . . The Americans commenced their march in double file. . . . In a minute or two, the Americans being in quick motion and within ten or fifteen rods of the bridge, a single gun was fired by a British soldier, which marked its way, passing under Col. Robinson's arm, and slightly wounding the side of Luther Blanchard, a fifer, in the Acton Company."

This account was published in 1827, and being prepared by one on the ground and only about fifty years after the fight, when some who saw it were still living, is, without doubt, the best narrative we shall ever have of that conflict. Others who have attempted to describe it, have done little more than repeat the words of Rev. Dr. Ripley. Some slight variations occur, however. Thus, George Bancroft affirms that Col. Barrett gave the order to advance, whereupon "Capt. Davis, drawing his sword, cried, march! His company, being on the right, led the way, he himself at their head, and by his side Maj. John Buttrick, of Concord, with John Robinson, of Westford, Lieutenant-Colonel in Prescott's Regiment."

Frederic Hudson, in his account [Harper's Magazine, May, 1875,] says:

"Among those early on the field from the neighboring towns, was Lieutenant-Colonel John Robinson, of Westford. . . . He was accompanied by the Rev. Joseph Thaxter, Captain Joshua Parker, and private Oliver Hildreth. Mr. Thaxter had been preaching at Westford as a candidate. On the first tidings of danger he hastened to Concord, armed with a brace of pistols, and was in front to receive the first fire of the enemy; and he and William Emerson, the pastor of Concord, were the first chaplains of the Revolution. . . . Maj. Buttrick took command of the Americans in the forward movement. He was accompanied by Lieutenant-Colonel Robinson. In their left hand they held their fusees trailed and marched with Captain Davis and his men."

From all these statements it is clear that Davis, Buttrick and Robinson were marching side-by-side in this first show of armed resistance to British oppression—a noble triad of choice spirits who dared to do and die. Heroically did they lead on the eager troops who sought, not revenge, but liberty; who, as George W. Curtis pithily said, in his oration at Concord, April 19, 1875, "loaded their muskets, not with a ball only, but with a *principle*, and brought down, not a man, but a *system*."

The three companies whose muster-rolls are here given, copied from the originals in the State House, were no doubt in the fight on that day. Rev. G. Reynolds, in a recent address, admits that *two* companies of minute-men from Westford were present, and the heading of the rolls shows that they marched from home that morning.

Captain Underwood's Company. "A List of the Travel and Service of Capt. Timothy Underwood, of Westford, in the County of Middlesex, with the men under him belonging to Colonel William Prescott's Regiment, of Minute-men, who, in consequence of an Alarm made on the 19th of April 1775, marched from home for the defence of this Colony against the Ministerial troops:

OFFICERS.

Timothy Underwood, Captain.
Thomas Cummings, First Lieut.
Philip Robbins, Second Lieut.
Joshua Parker, Sergeant.
James Fletcher, Sergeant.
Timothy Spalding, Sergeant.
John Wright, Sergeant.
James Proctor, Corporal.
Willard Fletcher, Corporal.
Amaziah Hildreth, Corporal.
Thomas Guy, Fifer.
Isaac Parker, Drummer.

PRIVATES.

Oliver Barrett,
Jonas Blodgett,
Josiah Brooks,
Silas Chandler,
William Chandler,
Ebenezer Corey,
Samuel Crafts,
Ephraim Cummings,
Daniel Dudley,
Joseph Dutton,
William Dutton,
Joshua Fassett,
Davis Fisk,
David Fletcher,
Ebenezer Fletcher,
Jeremiah Fletcher,
John Fletcher,
Josiah Fletcher,
Levi Fletcher,
Ebenezer Foster,
John Hildreth,
Silas Howard,
Jonas Kemp,
Abner Kent,
Samuel Keyes,
Stephen Meeds,
John Nutting,
John Parker,
Moses Parker,
James Perry,
Silas Proctor,
Benjamin Read,
Leonard Read,
Oliver Read,
Samuel Read,
Thaddeus Read,
Abijah Richardson,
Wily Richardson,
Jacob Robbins,
Jeremiah Robbins,
Philip Spaldon,
Levi Temple,
Amos Tidd,
Joseph Underwood,
Daniel Whitney,
Ebenezer Wright.—58.

MIDDLESEX ss. December 16, 1775. The within named Timothy Underwood made solemn oath to the truth of the within Muster Roll. Before me, Moses Gill, Justice of the Peace through the Province."

Captain Bates's Company. "A List of the Travel and Service of Capt. Oliver Bates, of Westford, in the County of

Middlesex, and the men under him, belonging to the Regiment of Militia whereof James Prescott, Esq., is Colonel, who, in consequence of the Alarm made on the 19th of April 1775, marched from home for the Defence of this Colony against the Ministerial Troops.

OFFICERS.

Oliver Bates, Captain.
David Goodhue, First Lieut.
John Abbot, Second Lieut.
Thomas Rogers, Sergeant.
Solomon Spalding, Sergeant.

Joseph Prescott, Corporal.
Daniel Goodhue, Corporal.
John Prescott, Corporal.
Timothy Cummings, Drummer.

PRIVATES.

Joseph Wright, Jr.,
John Barrett,
David Bixby,
Ephraim Bixby,
Jacob Bixby,
Levi Bixby,
Abel Boynton,
Nath! Cummings,
David Dutton,
Ephraim Dutton,
Benjamin Estabrook,
Amos Fletcher, Jr.,
Joseph Fletcher,
Josiah Fletcher,

Jonathan Hadley,
John Hadley, Jr.,
Ephraim Heald,
David Holding,
William Nichols,
Nathaniel Prentice,
Jonas Prescott, 3d.,
Timothy Prescott,
Abel Read,
Stephen Read,
Silas Spalding,
Ephraim Wright,
Pelatiah Wright.—36.

COLONY OF MASSACHUSETTS BAY.

December 27, 1775. Oliver Bates, the Captain, being dead, David Goodhue, his Lieutenant, made solemn oath that this Roll by him subscribed, is just and true in all its parts. Before me, Moses Gill, Justice of the Peace through the Province."

Captain Minot's Company. "A list of the Travel and Service of Capt. Jonathan Minot, of Westford, in the County of Middlesex, and the men under him belonging to the Regiment of Militia whereof James Prescott, Esq., is Colonel, who, in consequence of the Alarm made on the 19th of

April 1775, marched from home for the defence of this Colony against the ministerial troops.

OFFICERS.

Hosea Hildreth, Corporal.
Jonathan Minot, Captain.
Zaccheus Wright, First Lieut.
Leonard Procter, Second Lieut.
Aaron Parker, Jr., Sergeant.
Gershom Fletcher, Sergeant.

William Hildreth, Sergeant.
Samuel White, Sergeant.
Nehemiah Green, Corporal.
Amos Wright, Corporal.
Jonathan Minot, Jr., Drummer.

PRIVATES.

Francis Smith,
Cæsar Bason,
Aaron Blood,
Peter Brown,
Job Dodge,
Elijah Hildreth,
Nathaniel Holmes,
Francis Kidder,
Thomas Kidder,
Rogers King,
Francis Leighton,
Abijah Mason,
Thomas Meads,

Benjamin Osgood,
David Parker,
Ebenezer Parker,
Amos Parlin,
Charles Procter,
John Pushee,
Joshua Read,
John Robbins,
John Robbins, Jr.,
Peter Robbins,
Zechariah Robbins,
James Wright. — 36.

PERSONAL TESTIMONY.

Mrs. Jonathan Prescott, a grand-daughter of Colonel Robinson, who died in this town, April 14, 1876, at the great age of ninety-one years, distinctly remembered the colonel, being twenty years old at the time of his death, in 1805. She testified to the compiler of this work that when the alarm came on the night of the 18th of April, he stood not on the order of his going, but mounted his horse and hurried to Concord, leaving orders to his hired man to follow with provisions. She said, likewise, that he was invited to take the command, and the tradition in her family has always been that he did assume it and ordered the troops to fire. Her recollection accorded with the inscription on his gravestone which affirms that he commanded the soldiers at the Bridge.

One of our citizens, Mr. J. Boynton Reed, now living (1881), says that his father, Abijah Reed, went with Colonel Robinson's man to Concord; but the troops had moved on and they followed them to Lexington. Mr. Reed also says that Capt. Oliver Bates received a wound on that day from the effect of which he died July 4, 1775.

"May 25, 1775. Voted that the militia officers lately chosen by the company in this town viz: Captain Jonathan Minot and Capt. Oliver Bates shall have the command of all the men in this town from sixteen years old to sixty, except those that are excused as by the old Province law, and to call them to train &c., as they think proper; and also to take care that the alarm-men are equipt as the old province law directs. Voted that the Selectmen shall take care of the Baggnets. Chose Capt. Joseph Read to serve the town as a Delegate to go to the Provintial Congress for six months. Voted that the Rev. Mr. Willard Hall shall deliver up his arms to the Committee of correspondence of this town."

A similar vote was passed in regard to Daniel Raymond; and he and his son, Daniel Raymond, Jr., were forbidden to go out of town without a pass from the Committee of Correspondence.

"June 5, 1775. Pay to Capt. Joseph Read the sum of three pounds and fifteen shillings for seventeen days service and expenses at the Provintial Congress at Watertown."

This was for attendance upon the session held at Watertown, from April 24th to May 29th.

THE BATTLE OF BUNKER HILL.

In this battle, as well as in the struggle at Concord Bridge, Colonel Robinson participated. He was then in Prescott's Regiment, which occupied the redoubt. A tall man, of commanding presence, he stood in the front, " in shape and gesture proudly eminent," exposed to instant death, yet doing his duty; now leaping upon the parapet, a target for the advancing foe, and now reconnoitering, with the ill-fated McClary, the position of the enemy to find the best way of repelling his persistent attacks; showing himself everywhere the efficient officer and the strong-hearted man.

In the list of companies in this battle there is given one of which Joshua Parker was captain, Amaziah Fassett, first lieutenant, and Thomas Rogers, second lieutenant. Parker and Rogers were from Westford, and Fassett was born here, but was then a resident of Groton. Parker was a sergeant in Captain Underwood's Company, and Rogers held the same rank in Captain Bates's Company, at Concord Bridge. Fassett was taken prisoner at Bunker Hill, and died in Boston, July, 1775.

The following is the muster-roll of Captain Parker's Company, including only the names of Westford men. They were in Col. William Prescott's Regiment.

Captain, Joshua Parker. Date of Enlistment, 1775.	April 12
Second Lieutenant, Thomas Rogers	April 19
Sergeant, Solomon Spalding	April 19
Sergeant, Nehemiah Green	April 19
Sergeant, Silas Procter	April 19
Sergeant, Jonathan Minott	April 19
Corporal, Peter Brown	April 19
Corporal, Obadiah Perry	April 20
Corporal, Levi Temple	April 19
Corporal, Jonas Holden	April 19
Drummer, Isaac Parker	April 19
Fifer, Ephraim Spalding	April 19
Calvin Blanchard	April 19
David Bixby	May 1
Abel Boynton	May 5
William Chandler	April 30
Samuel Craft	April 19
Ephraim Dutton	April 19
Benjamin Esterbrooks	April 19
Levi Fletcher	April 19
Josiah Fletcher	April 19
Joshua Fassett	April 19
Isaac Green	April 19
Ephraim Heald	April 19
Oliver Heald	May 17

Jonathan Hildreth	April 19
David Keyes	May 6
Samuel Keyes	April 19
Thomas Kidder	April 28
Peter Larkin	April 26
John Parker	April 19
John Pushee	April 19
Nath! Prentice	May 2
William Read	May 18
Oliver Read	April 19
Stephen Read	April 19
Francis Smith	April 19
Silas Spalding	April 19
Simeon Senter	April 26
Joseph Underwood	April 19
Robbin Skinner	April 26
James Perry	April 19
Jonas Blodgett	April 19
Nath! Holmes	April 19

Perry Blodgett and Holmes "enlisted into the artillery Company, May 24, 1775." Joseph Minott and Jonathan Hadley, both of Westford, were killed in battle June 17, 1775. Abijah Mason, also of Westford, died in camp July 30, 1775. This return of Captain Parker's Company, in the Tenth Regiment of Foot, commanded by Col. William Prescott, was made Sept. 27, 1775, and without doubt, Minott, Hadley, and Mason were members of it.

The company of Capt. Abijah Wyman, of Ashby, was in Col. William Prescott's regiment in that battle. The return, made Oct. 3, 1775, includes the following men from Westford:

Thomas Comings, Second Lieutenant; Daniel Dudley, Corporal; Philip Robbins, Corporal.

Thomas Robbins,
Oliver Barrett,
Ebenezer Corey,
David Fish,
Abner Kent,
Jeremiah Robbins,

Cæsar Bason,
David Cowdry,
Simeon Kemp,
Thaddeus Read,
Daniel Whitney.

In all 14 men. The return states that "Cesor Bason died June 17."

Mr. Francis Tinker in his sketch of Ashby, in Drake's History of Middlesex County, Vol. 1, p. 223, says that Lieutenant Comings and ten men in Captain Wyman's company, were from Westford, but he does not give names.

In regard to Cæsar Bason, this anecdote is told on good authority. In the battle he found his powder was nearly gone, and putting in his last charge, he exclaimed, "Now, Cæsar, give 'em one more." He fired and was himself shot, and fell back into the trench. Tradition intimates that Leonard Proctor went to Cambridge on the day before the battle and was on or near the ground. Mr. Tinker states that Jacob Bascom, of Westford, was killed. No such name occurs in our records, and there was probably a mistake in putting Bascom for Bason. Bason was a colored man and perhaps the servant of James Burn. There is some uncertainty as to his real name. In 1773 "Ceasor *Burn* was paid 4 shillings for four crows killed in this town."

Colonel Prescott, in a letter to John Adams, says: "I commanded my Lt. Col. Robinson and Maj. Woods, each with a detachment, to flank the enemy, who, I have reason to think, behaved with prudence and courage." It is stated that when the British were advancing some of the Provincials fired without orders, so eager were they for the fray. This made Colonel Prescott angry. "His Lt. Col. Robinson ran round the top of the parapet and threw up the muskets." [Colonel Swett's narrative, p. 34.]

"July 10, 1775. Chose Doctor Asaph Fletcher to represent this town in the great and general Court to be held at Watertown."

"September 18, 1775. Pay to Capt. Joseph Read the sum of 6£ for twenty four days service at the General Court in the year 1775."

"May 20, 1775. Voted that our Committee of correspond call in the assistance of the Committee of Correspond of the neighboring towns to Judge on the conduct of aney persons that have been unfriendly to their Country, and that the Committee publish their proceedings in the public Prints."

"June 14, 1776. Voted to choose three men to be a Committee to Draw up some advice for our Representative. Chose Doctor Asaph Fletcher, Capt. Amos Fletcher, and Ens. Nathaniel Boynton to be said Committee. Voted to accept the Committee's Report, as follows, viz:

"Whereas wee the subscribers were this day chosen and appointed by the Town of Westford as a Committee to take under consideration a resolve of the Collony of Massachusetts Bay on the 7th day of June instant, to advise the person who should be chosen to Represent them in the general Assembly, wheather, should the Honorable Congress for the safety of the Colonies, declare them independent of Great Britain, they the said inhabitants will solemly engage with their lives and fortunes to support them in the measure,—we have taken the same under consideration and report as follows: that it is our Humble opinion that nothing short of a state of independancy will so weel answer for our safety & in case the said Congress should declare a state of independence wee will acquiese theirto and riske our lives and fortunes in support thereof. Voted that a Coppy of said Report be sent to our Representative as soon as may be. Voted to make the Town store of powder to be three hundred weight; to purchase Ball and flints answerable to the powder. Also, to purchase fifteen guns to be added to our store with Cartridge Boxes."

Salt. It was deemed important to have a town stock of this article on hand, and individuals were designated to obtain it. September 18, 1775, Zaccheus Wright, Zechariah Hildreth and Nathaniel Boynton were paid £8 2s. "for salt for the town." January 29, 1776, Nathaniel Boynton was paid £16, 10s. for salt " he purchased in Salem."

December 2, 1776. "Voted that twenty bushels of salt be still kept in store; that all the salt in store above twenty bushels be delivered to the inhabitants of this Town according to pay; and that Dea. John Abbot, Zach. Wright, and Samuel White be a Committee to proportion the salt to the inhabitants according to Last year's rates. Also, that the twenty bushel of salt be Deald out to the poor of the town by Discretion of the Selectmen."

July 21, 1777. Mr. Francis Leighton was paid £9. 17s. for "Transporting Seventy one bushel of salt from Newburyport to Westford."

Watch. "Sept. 16, 1776. Voted to have a watch kep in case of Alarm in Westford; that the Militia officers shall Leave a sufficient number of men for a watch for the safety of the people in case of alarm; and that said watch shall be under the Directions of the Committee of correspond of this town."

Census. Dec. 27, 1776, Zaccheus Wright, Zechariah Hildreth, Jonathan Keep, and Francis Leighton were paid "for numbering the people in this town." This was the first and only Colonial census and it was taken forty-seven years after the town was incorporated. The population at that time was 1,193.

Agreeably to the following Order of Council, the Declaration of Independence, made July 4, 1776, was recorded on the town book, by Zaccheus Wright, town clerk.

"IN COUNCIL, July 17, 1776.

"Ordered that the Declaration of Independence be printed and Copy sent to the ministers of each parish of every Denomination in this State, and that they severally be required to read the same to their Respective Congregations as soon as Divine service is ended in the afternoon of the first Lord's Day after they shall have received it, and after such publication theirof to Deliver the said Declaration to the Clerks of their several Towns or Districts who are hereby required to record the same in their Respective Town or District Books their to remain as a perpetual Memorial theirof.

"In the name and by order of the Council.

"R. DERBY, Jun. President.

"JOHN AVERY, Dept. Sec'y."

Campaigns. "March 25, 1777. Voted to make the Inhabitants of this town equil according to their estates for each Campaign since Concord Battle as to the cost of hiring men &c. Chose Capt. Joshua Parker, Doctor Asaph Fletcher, Dea. John·Abbott and Capt. Amos Fletcher to settle the prise of each Campaign. Chose Maj. Jonathan Minot, Capt. Pelatiah Fletcher and Capt. Zach! Wright as a Committee to Imploy men for the present Campaign, and pay them a bounty for that service. Voted to accept the Committee's Report Respecting the settleing the prise of each Campaign, viz :

The Cambridge Campaign	8 months	£ 2— 8 s.—0 d.
" " "	6 weeks	10 s.—0 d.
The Siege of Boston	2 months	12 s.—0 d.
The Continental Service	1 year	18— 0 s.—0 d.
The Nantasket Campaign	6 months	1—16 s.—0 d.
The Ticonderodge Campaign	4½ months	15— 0 s.—0 d.
The Dorchester Hill Campaign	3 months	18 s.—0 d.
The New York Campaign	2 months	13—10 s.—0 d.
The New York and Jersey Campaign,	3 months	13— 6 s.—8 d.
The Guarding at Boston	10 weeks	8 s.—0 d.

"Voted to give Twenty-four pounds to each man that shall engage for three years or During this unhappy war in the Continental Service. Voted the Thanks of this Town to the person that has given the sum of 6£ 14s. as a donation to this Town to Hire men for the Continental Service. That the Committee that was chosen to hire men, shall receive and pay out the said Twenty-four pounds to each man who shall ingage, and are to take account of what each man has Don in the former and present Campaign."

April 2, 1777. "In compliance to an act" of the General Court, the town adopted and recorded the list of prices fixed by the Court for labor and for articles of common necessity. The list is very long and only a few items are quoted: Good wheat, 6 shillings per bushel; "Good rie" 4s. 6d. per bushel; Good corn 3s. 6d; Pork 4 1-4 pence per pound; Grass-fed beef 2 1-4 pence; Stall-fed beef 3 3-4 pence. Good English hay in the Spring 3s. per hundred; in the field in Hay time 2s.; Shoeing a horse 5s.; a pair of oxen "corkt" 8s. Husbandry labor from the 20th of June to the 20th of August 3s. per day, and from the 15th of November to the 15th of March 1s. 6d. per day. Carpenters and house wrights 3s. 2d. from the 10th of March to the 10th of November, and from the 10th of November to the 10th of March 2s. 8d. per day.

Regulation Act. "May 19, 1777. Voted that the Town injoin the Committee and Selectmen to inforce and se the late Regulating Act put in practice in every particular excepting a few articles that the Court has of late made an alteration in."

Mr. Hall. "July 7, 1777. Chose Timothy Prescott to procure and lay before the Court all the evidence of all the enemical conduct or Disposition toward this or aney of the United States of any of the inhabitants of this town. Voted to accept of the list exibited by the Selectmen at this meeting—the list contains but one person, viz: Rev. Willard Hall whose Conduct is voted to be enemical and dangerous to the State, by a great majority."

Restitution. "Sept. 18, 1777. Voted that the men that Drawed amminition out of the Town Stock on the alarm to go to Road Island shall Return the same into the said Town Store or pay for the same by the middle of October next."

Soldiers' Families. "Nov. 24, 1777. Chose a Committee to support the Familys of such men as are Ingaged in the Continental Service. Chose Capt. Zach: Wright, Thomas Kidder, Ephraim Chamberlin, Thomas Cumings & Rogers King for said service."

Bills of Credit. "We the Freeholders and other Inhabitants of the Town of Westford being assembled at the meeting house in said Westford on the 5th day of December 1777, in consequence of a warrant from the Selectmen for the purpose, to manifest our sentiments on a late Act of the General Court of this State for Drawing the Bills of Credit &c., and for exchanging the same for Treasury Notes to be on annual interest: Deliberation being had thereon, Wee give it as our sentiments (due deference being acknowledged to our Honorable Court) that said act is not calculated for the greatest advantage and Interest of this State. Some of our reasons for these sentiments are these viz: 1. That such vast sums put on interest for three or four years, will greatly increase our accumulated charges. 2. The consequences of which, the great value and scarcity of money at the end of sd term, will render it very difficult (if not impossible) for the Inhabitants of this State to redeem and pay said Notes, even more so than to be immediately assessed for some part of the sum of 400,000 pounds in order for sinking, while there is such a flush of money circulating among us; and so to assess from time to time till the whole sum of £400,000 should be sunk. Therefore voted that our Representative be and he is hereby instructed to exert his influence in the General Court that the Treasurer be immediately directed to desist from giving out any more Notes on interest for Bills of Credit of this State; and to seek for an immediate Repeal of said Act, and that methods may be adopted by the Court for assessing and sinking the Bills of Credit as speedily as may be conveniently, and in such proportion from time to time as the Honble Court shall think proper. In the meantime to prevent counterfeit Bills, that there be a Bank of money emitted for the purpose of exchanging the aforesaid sum of £400,000 . . . till the whole of said sum be sunk in manner as aforesaid. Voted that our Representative be served with a copy of the Report, and that he lay the same before the Court as soon as may be."

Articles of Confederation. "Jan'y 16, 1778. Voted that the articles of Confederation is [are] agreeable to this town, and that our Representative be and is hereby instructed to give his vote, when Properly Required, in favor of the Ratification of the Articles lately agreed upon by Congress, except some unknown important reasons shall indicate to the contrary."

These were articles of "Confederation and perpetual union" between the original thirteen States, and by them the style of the confederacy was to be "The United States of America." They were agreed to in Congress, November 15, 1777.

The foregoing votes of the town show how freely the men of that time used the privilege of giving instructions to their legislators. They had opinions of their own on all public concerns and were not afraid to express them.

Allowance to Soldiers. "Oct. 15, 1778. Voted to allow each man forty dollars for the 4 months campaign to Bennington; four pounds for 2 months campaign to Rhode island; seven pounds to Philip Spalding for garding stores at Cambridge; two pounds per month to each man for the campaign to Rhod island in Col. Roberson's Regiment; ten pounds for the campaign to Stillwater when Burgoin was taken; six pounds for the three months campaign at Cambridge; eight pounds for six months at Cambridge; thirty four pounds for the Rhod island Campaign in Waid's and

Jacobs Regiment; twelve pounds for six weeks at Rhod island; twelve pounds for three and one half months at Boston or Rhod island; two pounds to the men that went first to Bennington; to the men that marched to North for eight months 82£ each; two pounds for turning out and fixing to go to Boston the last alarm; and one pound to each man for turning out upon the alarm to go to Rhod island."

Bounty. "Nov. 10, 1778. Paid to Peter Prescott as bounty when he went to Rhod island £14 5s. 4d; to Jonas Wright £103 5s for his going for 9 months into the Continental service."

"Dec! 14, 1778. Allow Silas Bigelo seventeen pounds thirteen shillings for carrying packs for soldiers to tanton [Taunton]; six pounds to the men that went to Bennington and returned in six weeks."

Even Pay. "Aug. 2, 1779. Voted to make Isaac Powers and Isaac Patch *even* with Thomas Scott and Abel Procter as to their pay for nine months service in the Continental army."

1780. The Committee of Correspondence for this year were Henry Wright, Jonathan Johnson, Thomas. Wright, John Procter, Jr., and Lieut. Timothy Fletcher; committee to hire men for the war, Lieut. Thomas Comings, Lieut. Timothy Spalding, Lieut. Leonard Procter, Lieut. Aaron Parker, Col. Robinson, Isaac Comings and Samuel Fletcher, Jr.

Pay of Soldiers. "Pay to the Selectmen—mileage money to the 17 men lately Inlisted for the State service, 1020 pounds."

This last item indicates the beginning of that depreciation of the currency which operated so disastrously upon the people, especially upon the soldiers who at the end of their long and arduous service were paid in bills that were almost worthless.

Committee to Provide Beef for the Soldiers, According to the Resolve of the Great and General Court. "Nov. 20, 1780. Voted to pay the money in room of Westford's proportion of beef at four Dollars per pound." Accordingly an assessment was made, called the "beef rate"; and, December 11, 1780, the town voted "to have a Corn Rate for the payment of soldiers that was hired into the service for six months and three months."

February 27, 1781. The Selectmen ordered the Town Treasurer to pay, to seventy persons, certain sums, varying greatly, "for what they paid *more* than their proportion of the beef provided for the army, agreeable to a vote passed Nov. 20, 1780."

"Feb. 12, 1781. Voted that the Inhabitents of this Town shall be divided into Classes in order to procure their proportion of soldiers to serve in the Continental Army for three years or during the war, agreeable to the Directions given in a late Resolve of the great and general Court."

In accordance with this vote the town was divided into five classes; and of these Col. Zaccheus Wright was appointed "head" of Class No. 1; Capt. David Goodhue, of Class No. 2; Capt. Leonard Procter, of Class No. 3; Lieut. Thomas Read, of Class No. 4, and Lieut. Aaron Parker of No. 5. To understand the oppressive taxation of that period it is only needful to cite the fact that in this small town of scarcely twelve hundred people, there were then the average rate, the State Silver Money Rate, the Corn Rate, the Beef Rate, the Continental Rate; and in addition to these, the usual Town Rate, Single Rate, Minister Rate and Highway Rate—these altogether drawing very heavily upon the resources of a people whose pursuits were chiefly agricultural, and whose energies had been severely tried by previous conflicts and toils.

1781. The Committee of Correspondence for this year were Francis Leighton, Zaccheus Wright, Joshua Read, Pelatiah Fletcher and Dr. Asaph Fletcher. Committee to hire soldiers, Daniel Raymond, Thomas Kidder, James Fletcher, Samuel Wright and Thomas Read.

1782. So far as the records show, there was no Committee of Correspondence chosen this year, and no committee to hire soldiers, the war being practically ended by the surrender of Cornwallis at Yorktown, October 19, 1781.

1783. Great Britain acknowledged the independence of the United States by the Treaty of Paris, September 3. For eight years the people, with varying fortunes, struggled for the priceless boon of liberty, and now it is in their hands, having been secured by immense sacrifices and hardships and by the loss of many valuable lives. The country was impoverished and its finances were ruined. It is evident that the people of this town felt the burden and the distress as keenly as any. A committee chosen May 6, 1783, to give the usual instructions to their Representative, made the following report, the language of which clearly defines, in two or three particulars, their views of the duties and perils of the hour.

" The Committee appointed to give some instructions to Mr. Francis Leighton, our Representative in the general Court for the year ensuing, report as follows :

" That our said Representative be instructed to exert his utmost influence in the general Assembly to oppose and exclude the declared enemies and traitors of this Country who have, at or since the commencement of the late war, from an inemical Dispo[si]tion to the Rights and Liberties of their native Country, took shelter and protection under the British government,—from returning among us, as such an Indulgence might occasion Internal Broils and many ill consequences. As the Country grones under an enormous debt, contracted in consequence of an Expensive war for eight years,—that our said Representative be instructed to exert his influence in the general Assembly to promote Frugality in the expenditures of the Publick monies and to oppose unnecessary placemen of every kind; that his attendance and dissition on other matters in general is submitted to his best Judgment & descretion, and that he be instructed to give his attendance at Court as much and no more, as shall best comport with the Interest of his constituents and the Public Good.

"SAMUEL WHITE, Chairman."

"Nov. 20, 1783. Voted that the salt that belongs to the Town shall be kept in store for the use of the poor. Also, that the spades and axes that belong to the Town store shall be still kept safe in store, and all the guns and articles of War belonging to the Town to be collected and safely stored."

This was "picking up the tools" after the work was done, as surely they could do with joy of heart, for these were mementos of a success well-earned and significant. These articles, if they had been preserved to this time, would afford rare gratification to the eye and heart of the antiquary; but like many deeds of self-denial and heroism in those days, they have been lost and forgotten. They were now at peace — a peace which was all the dearer because of struggles and conflicts. It was

"Peace, the source and soul of social life;
Beneath whose calm inspiring influence
Science his views enlarges, art refines,
And swelling commerce opens all her ports."

SOLDIERS FROM WESTFORD IN THE WAR OF THE REVOLUTION.

The names of those who were at Concord Bridge, or who pursued the British troops in their hasty retreat, April 19, have already been given, so far as they have been ascertained; and also the names of those who were at Bunker

Hill, under Col. William Prescott. Promptly did these men obey the call to defend their country, and bravely did they meet the shock of arms, many of them being with Colonel Prescott in the hottest of the battle. It will be seen by what follows that the patriotism of the town did not falter during the long and bloody contest that ensued; but her citizens and her soldiers were true to the American flag, even to the end. The names here given have been gathered chiefly from the muster-rolls in the State House in Boston. A few have been added upon testimony that seems reliable.

1775. In Capt. Henry Farwell's company, of Col. William Prescott's regiment, Oliver Hildreth was a private; and in Capt. Samuel Gilbert's company, Zachariah Robbins; also, in Capt. Asa Lawrence's company, Levi Parker.

1776. On the roll of Capt. Jonathan Minot's company, in Colonel Baldwin's regiment, enlisted January 1, 1776, are Jonathan Minot (captain), John Robbins, Elijah Hildreth (drummer), John Fletcher (fifer), Joseph Underwood, Elias Foster, Sampson Fletcher, Josiah Dodge, William Spalding, Hezekiah Hildreth, Henry Wright, John Barrett, Nehemiah Fletcher, Benjamin Osgood, Sampson Read, Joseph Wright, Abijah Richardson, Thomas Nutting, Thomas Smith, John Nutting, Abijah Read, Amaziah Hildreth, Elnathan Read, Aaron Blood — each paid for fifty-two miles. They were "to receive one penny per mile for their rations from their Respective places of Abode and their return to the same." As they were paid for the number of miles between Westford and Boston and back, it is probable they were of the force stationed near Boston.

Field Officers, Middlesex Regiments, 1776. First Regiment, Samuel Thatcher, colonel; Second Regiment, Eleazer Brooks, colonel; Third Regiment, James Barrett, colonel; Fourth Regiment, Henry Gardner, colonel; Fifth Regiment, Samuel Ballard, colonel; Sixth Regiment, Oliver Prescott, colonel. Jonathan Reed, of Littleton, was chosen colonel in place of Colonel Prescott, who was chosen brigadier general. Seventh Regiment, Simeon Spalding, colonel.

In the Sixth Regiment, Colonel Reed, Pelatiah Fletcher of this town was captain of Company 4, and Zaccheus Wright of Company 8. William Hildreth was chosen major in Colonel Spalding's regiment, but declined. Thomas Cummings and Timothy Spalding were lieutenants in Captain Fletcher's company, and Leonard Procter and Aaron Parker in Captain Wright's company.

The Westford men in Captain Fletcher's company, were William Glenne, Peter Wright, Jonathan Johnson, Jr., Ebenezer (Eleazer?) Read, Jr., Ephraim Cummings, Isaac Glenne, William Hardwick, Jacob Wendell, Oliver Heald, James Perry, Robert Skinner, Joshua Fassett, Ephraim Dutton, Raymond Fletcher, Joshua Fletcher, Jr., Jethro Wilkins, Thomas Nutting, Thomas Fitch, John Patch, Levi Parker.

In Captain Wright's company, Francis Smith, Amos Hardy, William Dutton, Samuel Craft, Jeremiah Robbins, Samuel Darbee, Daniel Dudley, Jr., Jacob Robbins, Jr., Jonas Kemp, Stephen Temple, Ebenezer Foster, Samuel Keyes, Smith Foster, Amos Russell, Elnathan Read, Jesse Dudley, Solomon Fletcher, Oliver Barrett, James Magerr, John Nutting.

It seems probable that Captain Wright's company was transferred to Colonel Brooks' regiment, and its roll somewhat changed.

Return of Capt. Zaccheus Wright's company, in Colonel Brooks' regiment, camp on White Plains, October 31, 1776: Zaccheus Wright (captain), Willard Fletcher, Stephen Wright (drummer), Thomas Cummings (fifer), Samuel Read, Abel Read, Amaziah Hildreth, Samuel Adams, Abel Russell, John Hadley, David Bixby, Nehemiah Fletcher, Silas Chandler, Daniel Whitney, Ebenezer Chandler, Benjamin Robbins, Josiah Fletcher. These were in the battle of White Plains, October, 28, 1776.

Captain Wright was in Col. Eleazer Brooks' regiment, from September 27 to November 16—sixty-two days. His travel was two hundred and twelve miles, and he was allowed eleven days to return home. His honorable discharge was dated "North Castle, Nov. 19, 1776." His company was disbanded about this time, and all transferred to Captain Ballard's company, except Solomon Fletcher, Barrett, and Magerr.

Captain Fletcher's company was also disbanded and Peter Wright, Eleazer Read, Johnson, Cummings, Isaac Glenne, Hardwick, Wendell, Oliver Heald, Fassett, Wilkins, Ephraim Dutton, Thomas Nutting, Fitch, Patch and Levi Parker were transferred to Captain Ballard's company; Raymond Fletcher and Joshua Fletcher to Captain Thomas' company, Robert Skinner to Captain King's, James Perry to Captain Whitcomb's, and WilliamGlenne to Captain Brown's.

In Captain Ford's company at Ticonderoga, 1776, from July 25 to December 31, Joel Esterbrooks, Solomon Woods, Moses Chandler, Levi Parker, Willlam Mears, also Pelatiah Wright.

In Capt. Abishai Brown's company, Col. Josiah Whitney's regiment, in service from August 1 to November 1, in camp at Hull, were Silas Procter (second lieut.), Aaron Blood, (serg.), William Dutton, Benjamin Esterbrooks, Elnathan Read, Thomas Nutting, Abijah Reed, Daniel Dudley, Solomon Fletcher, Simeon Read, Joshua Fletcher, Jacob Robbins, Hezekiah Hildreth, James Wright, Joseph Read, Nathaniel Chamberlin, and John Barrett.

In Capt. John Minot's company, Colonel Dike's regiment, in the service of the State from December, 1776, to February, 1777, were Aaron Parker (ensign), Amos Russell, Abel Russell, Smith Foster, David Parker, Thomas Fletcher, David Dudley, Jesse Minot, Thomas Robbins, Raymond Fletcher, Joshua Fletcher, Aaron Parker, Jr., Isaac Chandler, Simeon Kemp, Isaac Parker, Jeremiah Hildreth, Elnathan Read, Jesse Dudley, Solomon Fletcher, Jacob Robbins, Benjamin Esterbrooks, Silas Parlin and Samuel Chamberlin. This company also rendered two months' service at Warwick Neck, Rhode Island. The pay-roll is dated November 12, 1777, and contains the names of Silas Procter (lieutenant),

Benjamin Esterbrooks, Joel Esterbrooks, Simeon Read, William Read, Thomas Cummings and Abraham Wright.

1777. Enlisted in Capt. Reuben Butterfield's company, December 16, 1776, and served to March 16, 1777, Leonard Procter, Daniel Procter, John Dutton, Ebenezer Parker, Jesse Spalding, James Pike, Ebenezer Wright, Isaac Parker, Silas Procter, Nathaniel Chamberlin, Ephraim Dutton, Thomas Nutting, Jonathan Hildreth, John Fletcher, Hezekiah Hildreth, Amos Hardy, William Dutton, Francis Smith, Thomas Nutting, Jr., David Cowdry, Abraham Wright, William Fletcher, John Cowdry, Benjamin Farmer, Levi Fletcher, Daniel Keyes and Willard Hall.

Col. Samuel Thatcher, in his orders to Captain Butterfield, calls this the eighth company drafted to reinforce the Continental Army in consequence of an order of General Prescott, and says: "You are to march sd Co. by the shortest route toward Connecticut through Providence, and to begin your march on Monday Dec. 16. N. B.—You will call on the Com^{tees} of Chelmsford, Dunstable, Dracut, and Westford, as your men are composed from those towns."

Colonel Robinson's regiment seems to have been organized this year. The officers were John Robinson, of Westford, colonel; John Buttrick, of Concord, lieutenant-colonel; Samuel McCobb, major; Joseph Thaxter, Jr., of Westford, chaplain; Asaph Fletcher, of Westford, surgeon; William Little, surgeon's mate; Jabez Brown, adjutant; Nathan Stone, quartermaster; John Ford, of Chelmsford, captain; Simon Edgell, of Framingham, captain; Asahel Wheeler, of Sudbury, captain; Job Shattuck, of Groton, captain; John Lemont, captain; —— Cole, captain; Joshua Parker, captain. This regiment served in Rhode Island from July 5, 1777, to January 1, 1778—six months.

In Captain Parker's company were these: John Parker, Ebenezer Chandler, Thomas Robbins, David Cowdry, John Spalding, Oliver Read, Isaac Chandler, Nathaniel Chamberlin, Philip Procter, Timothy Underwood, Isaac Parker, Benjamin Farmer, Samuel Chamberlin, Josiah Fletcher,

Simeon Kemp, Daniel Whitney, Amaziah Hildreth, Jonathan Nutting, David Prescott, Thomas Scott, Asa Bixby, Oliver Wright, John Underwood, Stephen Wright, Abel Read, Samuel Read, Jonas Wright, Timothy Adams, Thomas Cummings.

Jonas Holden was an ensign in Captain Cole's company.

In Capt. Aaron Jewett's company of militia, from the towns of Littleton, Westford, Groton, Shirley and Townsend, who marched to Bennington upon the alarm, July 1, 1777, in Col. Job Cushing's regiment, were these from Westford: Simeon Read, Jeremiah Fletcher, Joel Abbot, Jonathan Barrett, Jonas Blodgett, David Bixby, Silas Chandler, Daniel Dudley, Hezekiah Hildreth, Oliver Hildreth, Joel Prescott, Josiah Fletcher and James Wright.

A company under Captain Jewett was in Col. Samuel Bullard's regiment of Massachusetts Bay Militia, "who served at North River when General Burgoyne was taken, from the 14th of August, 1777, to the first of December following." On the pay-roll are Oliver Hildreth, Jeremiah Fletcher, John Pushee, Jonas Blodgett, David Bixby, Levi Fletcher, Abijah Hildreth, Jeremiah Hildreth, Abel Procter, and Jonathan Barrett. On another page of the roll it is stated that these marched to Saratoga; and doubtless they were present at the surrender of Burgoyne.

During this year Charles Procter served in Colonel Dike's regiment; and James Perry was a sergeant in a company of Rangers (artillery men), under Major Whitcomb, who served from February 12, 1777, to December 31, 1779—thirty-four months and eighteen days—at 60s. per month, allowed by General Gates.

The Regiment of Col. Eleazer Brooks, of Concord. 1777—1779. In the company of Capt. William H. Ballard: Peter Wright, sergeant, served from March 18, 1777, to December 31, 1779—33 months, 13 days—" for which the nominal sum of 91£ 12s. 9d. has been paid him by the continent."

Francis Smith, served from March 27, 1777, to December 31, 1779.

Jacob Robbins, drummer, from April 1, 1777, to December 31, 1779, at 44 shillings per month.

William Dutton, from April 9, 1777, to December 31, 1779, 32 months, 22 days, at 40s. per month.

Joshua Fassett, from March 9, 1777, to December 31, 1779, 33 months, 22 days.

Smith Foster, from May 17, 1777, to December 31, 1779, 31 months, 14 days.

Isaac Glenney, from March 29, 1777, to December 31, 1779, 33 months, 4 days. He was transferred to Captain Coburn's company.

Amos Hardy, from April 2, 1777, to December 31, 1779, 32 months, 29 days.

Oliver Heald, from April 20, 1777, to December 31, 1779, 32 months, 11 days.

Jonas Kemp, from May 3, 1777, to December 31, 1779, 31 months, 28 days.

John Patch, from May 28, 1777, to December 31, 1779, 31 months, 3 days.

Eleazer Read, from May 28, 1777, to December 31, 1779, 31 months, 3 days.

Amos Russell, from May 25, 1777, to December 31, 1779.

Jonathan Stratton, from April 16, 1777, to December 31, 1779, 32 months, 15 days. Transferred to Captain Alden's company.

Stephen Temple, from April 21, 1777, to December 31, 1779, 32 months, 10 days. Transferred to Captain Coburn's company.

Elnathan Read, from May 28, 1777, to December 31, 1779, 31 months, 3 days.

Jacob Wendell, from May 28, 1777, to December 31, 1779, 31 months, 3 days.

Ephraim Cummings, died.

Samuel Crafts, from April 8, 1777, to December 31, 1779, 32 months, 23 days.

Ephraim Dutton, from April 3, 1777, to December 31, 1779, 32 months, 28 days.

Jeremiah Robbins, from January 1, 1777, to December 31, 1779, 36 months.

Daniel Dudley, from April 10, 1777, to November 11, 1778, 19 months, 1 day. Killed.

Jesse Dudley, from May 28, 1777, to May 17, 1778, 11 months, 19 days. Died.

Ebenezer Foster, from May 1, 1777, to October 1, 1777, 5 months. Died.

William Hardwick, from March 15, 1777, to February 2, 1778, 11 months. Taken prisoner and deserted.

Jonathan Johnson, from March 28, 1777, to December 31, 1779, 33 months, 28 days. Taken prisoner.

Samuel Keyes, from May 28, 1777, to October 7, 1777, 4 months, 19 days. Killed.

Thomas Nutting, from June 20, 1777, to December 7, 1777, 5 months, 19 days. Died.

Jethro Prince, from March 29, 1777, to September 25, 1777, 5 months, 27 days. Died.

Some of these re-enlisted in the same regiment, as follows:

In Captain White's company, William Dutton, corporal, served 12 months, from January 1, 1780.

Francis Smith, corporal, from January 1, 1780, to March 12, 1780.

Jacob Robbins, drummer, from January 1, 1780, to April 1, 1780.

Peter Wright, from January 1, 1780, to March 12, 1780.

Joshua Fassett, from January 1, 1780, to December 31, 1780, 1 year.

Samuel Crafts, from January 1, 1780, to December 31, 1780, 1 year.

Ebenezer Corey, from January 1, 1780, to July 1, 1780, 6 months.

Ephraim Dutton, from January 1, 1780, to April 3, 1780, 3 months, 3 days.

Oliver Heald, from January 1, 1780, to April 20, 1780, 3 months, 20 days.

Jonathan Hildreth, from January 1, 1780, to June 13, 1780, 5 months, 13 days.

Joseph Underwood, from January 1, 1780, to June 13, 1780, 5 months, 13 days.

Jacob Wendell, from January 1, 1780, to July 13, 1780, 6 months, 13 days.

Jonathan Johnson, from January 1, 1780, to December 31, 1780, 1 year. "Prisoner in Canada since May 30."

In Captain Parker's company: Jonathan Stratton, January 1, 1780, to April 16, 3 months, 16 days.

In Captain Coburn's company: James Butterfield, January 1, 1780, to January 27, 27 days. Isaac Glenney (corporal), January 1, 1780, to December 31, 1 year. Jonas Kemp, January 1, 1780, to May 3, 4 months, 3 days. Stephen Temple, January 1, 1780, to April 20, 3 months, 20 days.

Smith Foster "made up for 1780 in Colonel Crane's regiment."

Amos Hardy "made up for his wages in Colonel M. Jackson's regiment."

Jeremiah Robbins was in Captain Ballard's company.

"The amount of pay was multiplied by 32 1-2 to make up for depreciation."

In Colonel Marshall's regiment: Oliver Barrett served from January 2, 1777, to October 7, 9 months and 5 days, and was discharged. Raymond Fletcher, from January 1, 1777, to February 1, 1778, 13 months. Died February 1, 1778.

In Colonel Reed's regiment and Captain Asa Lawrence's company, which went to the assistance of General Gates, were these: Ephraim Chamberlin, Jacob Bixby, Jonas Hadley, Paul Fletcher, Nehemiah Fletcher, Andrew Fletcher, Josiah Fletcher, Benjamin Robbins, Philip Robbins, Benjamin Read, Joshua Read, Leonard Read, Ezekiel

Wright, Thomas Nutting, William Chandler, Samuel Butterfield, Aaron Blood, John Russell, Abraham Wright, Thomas Cummings (first lieutenant), Ephraim Heald.

1778. Pay-roll of Captain Isaac Woods' company, on guard at Cambridge, from April 1 to July 3:

Solomon Spalding, Gershom Fletcher, Zechariah Fletcher, Abel Boynton, Benjamin Esterbrooks, Benjamin Barrett, Benjamin Read, Asa Bixby, Jesse Minott, Oliver Wright, Amos Parlin, Joshua Read, Abel Wright.

Men drafted for nine months' service from the time of their arrival at Fishkill (in Colonel Reed's regiment):

Peter Hildreth, in Company 8, aged 25 years, stature 6 feet. Arrived June 19.

Jonas Blodgett, in the same company, age 20 years, stature 5 feet 8 inches. Arrived June 19.

Ephraim Chamberlin, in the same company, age 22 years, stature 5 feet 7 inches. Arrived July 2.

Jonas Wright, in Company 4, aged 19, stature 5 feet 4 inches. Arrived July 4.

On pay-roll of Captain Simon Hunt's company, in Colonel Brooks' regiment, John Tidd and Gershom Fletcher, who served from February 3, to April 3, 1778.

In Captain Asa Lawrence's company, Colonel Thomas Poor's regiment: John Pushee, Abner Kent, Ebenezer Stone, each served one month and a few days. Also, Isaac Powers, April 20, 1778. Distance from home 220 miles. In the service to August 1, 1778; and after this their stay in the ranks was prolonged, month by month, to October 1. By the record of this company it seems that they went to West Point.

In Captain John Nutting's company, Colonel McIntosh's regiment, Lovell's Brigade: Amos Parlin and Jesse Dutton, served from July 30 to September 12. Also, Thomas Bixby for the same time. Levi Bixby and Isaac Chandler were in Captain Joseph Boynton's company, of Colonel Wade's regiment, and served from July 1, to January, 1779. Asa Bixby in Captain Joshua Parker's company, Colonel Robinson's regiment, for the same period, perhaps. Also, Oliver Hildreth, William Spalding, Benjamin Esterbrooks, and Oliver Procter, in Captain John Nutting's company. (Captain Nutting was from Pepperell.)

1779. On the pay-roll of Captain John Porter's company, second regiment of Massachusetts Militia, Colonel Denny, for three months' service (October, November, and December), are Abel Parker, Thomas Robbins, Benjamin Barrett, Jonas Blodgett, Isaac Chandler, Benjamin Read, Samuel White. In Captain Nathaniel Lakin's company, of Colonel John Jacobs' regiment, November 19, 1779, were Ezekiel Procter, Leonard Procter, Elihu Read, Ephraim Wright, and Samuel Read.

In the new levies from Massachusetts, for service done in the State of Rhode Island: Timothy Adams, Josiah Procter, and Philip Procter. These enlisted July 12, and served 4 months, 19 days.

In Captain Moses Barnes' company, Lieutenant Colonel Pierce, were: Aaron Parker, Joshua Read, Amos Parlin, and Eliakim Read, who served from May 1 to July 1.

CONTINENTAL TOWN AND COUNTY ROLLS.

NAME.	AGE.	STATURE.	COMPLEXION.
Isaac Patch	16	5 ft. 5 in.	Sandy.
Isaac Powers	17	5 ft.	Light.
Aaron Blood	39	5 ft. 8½ in.	Light.
Thomas Scott	17	5 ft. 6 in.	Light.

In Captain Sargent's company of guards, for service in and around Boston, Aaron Parker.

[Two persons bearing the name of Aaron Parker were in the army. One rose to the rank of captain; the other, a young man of 19, served as a private, and is sometimes called junior.]

1780. Pay-roll for the six months' levies that were in the Continental service for 1780, for the town of Westford:

NAMES.	When Marched.	IN SERVICE.		PAY.			Distance From Home.
		Mos.	Days.	£	s.	d.	
David Bixby	July 2, 1780.	5	19	11	8	8	240 miles.
Isaac Patch	July 2, 1780.	5	18	11	4	0	240 miles.
Asa Patch	July 2, 1780.	5	18	11	4	0	240 miles.
Joshua Read	July 2, 1780.	6	10	12	13	4	240 miles.
Winthrop Robinson	July 2, 1780.	5	18	11	4	0	240 miles.
Abel Procter	July 2, 1780.	5	20	11	6	8	240 miles.
Philip Procter	July 2, 1780.	5	14	10	16	8	240 miles.
Josiah Procter	July 2, 1780.	5	20	11	6	8	240 miles.
James Procter	July 2, 1780.	6	10	12	13	4	240 miles.
Ebenezer Barrett	July 2, 1780.	6	10	12	18	4	240 miles.
Job Spalding	July 2, 1780.	6	10	12	18	4	240 miles.
John Russell	July 2, 1780.	5	20	11	6	8	240 miles.
Charles Keyes	July 2, 1780.	5	17	11	2	8	240 miles.
Simeon Russell	July 2, 1780.	5	20	11	6	8	240 miles.
Amos Parlin	July 2, 1780.	5	12	10	16	0	240 miles.
Total				173	12	0	

These were in the seventh division of six months' men, raised to reinforce the Continental Army, which marched from Springfield July 7, 1780, under the care of Captain Dix. A descriptive list is to be found in the muster-rolls (vol. 35, page 188), giving the age, stature, and complexion. The age of each one is quoted, in order to show the material of which the army was composed. David Bixby, 30; Isaac Patch, 17; Asa Patch, 17; Joshua Read, 17; Winthrop Robinson, 17; Abel Procter, 17; Josiah Procter, 17; James Procter, 16; Ebenezer Barrett, 18; Job Spalding, 18; John Russell, 20; Charles Keyes, 16; Philip Procter, 18; Simeon Russell, 19; Amos Parlin, 21 — all under 20 except three.

During this year Hildreth Dutton, Peter Wright, Thomas Cowdry, and Joshua Parker, Jr., served for three months in Rhode Island, in Captain John Porter's company.

1781. Enlisted for three months to reinforce the army of the United States: Silas Procter (lieutenant), Abijah Reed, Leonard Procter, Isaac Corey, Isaac Corey, Jr., Hezekiah Hildreth, Benjamin Robbins, William Bixby, Asa Holden.

In Captain Asa Drury's company: John Chamberlin and Joshua Parker, Jr., served from July 1 to December 1 — five months.

1781. The following is a descriptive list of men who enlisted for the town of Westford:

ENLISTED.	NAMES.	AGE.	STATURE.		Complexion.	TRADE.	TIME.
			Ft.	In.			
May 7,	York Hambleton	31	5	7	Black.	Laborer.	3 years.
April 14,	William Burrows	50	5	3	Light.	Painter.	3 years.
April 26,	John Nutting	42	5	10	Light.	Laborer.	3 years.
April 5,	John Patch	20	5	10	Light.	Farmer.	3 years.
March 16,	David Johnson	17	5	5	Light.	Farmer.	3 years.
April 9,	Simeon Russell	17	5	7	Light.	Farmer.	3 years.
April 5,	Asa Patch	17	5	5	Light.	Farmer.	3 years.
March 16,	Charles Keyes	18	5	4	Light.	Farmer.	3 years.
March 16,	Peter McEwen	22	5	5	Light.	Farmer.	3 years.
March 16,	Oliver Heald	23	6	1	Dark.	Farmer.	3 years.
May 1,	Josiah Brooks	24	5	4½	Light.	Farmer.	3 years.
April 25,	Amos Parlin	21	5	9	Light.	Farmer.	3 years.
July 31,	William Spalding	18	5	9½	Light.	Farmer.	6 months.
March 20,	Thaddeus Read	42	5	9	Dark.	Farmer.	3 years.
July 26,	Jonas Blodgett	24	5	9½	Light.	Farmer.	3 years.

In the same year William Dutton, Joshua Fassett, Samuel Craft, and Isaac Glenney enlisted in the Seventh Massachusetts Regiment, for three years. Joshua Parker (Jr.?) and John Chamberlin were in Capt. Asa Drury's company from July 1 to December 1; and William Bixby, Silas Procter, Hezekiah Hildreth, Benjamin Robbins, Abijah Reed, Peter Wright, Isaac Corey, and Asa Holden, served in Captain Bowker's company, from August 4 to December 4.

1782. It does not appear from the records that any soldiers were hired this year for the Continental Army; but on a roll of officers and seamen belonging to the State sloop "Winthrop," commanded by George Little, 1782, appear the following names: Philip Procter, Leonard Procter, James Procter, Josiah Procter, Zachariah Robbins, Zack Hildreth, and Job Spalding.

May 30, Simeon Kent and Lieutenant Aaron Parker were each paid a bounty for three years' service, of class No. 5; perhaps for time already spent.

Jonathan Jones was present at the surrender of Cornwallis at Yorktown; but it is not known in what regiment he served. He was at Bunker Hill and served through the war. Was at Valley Forge during the terrible winter of 1777-'78.

Paul Fletcher died at Valley Forge.

David Prescott was wounded at Bunker Hill.

Thomas Rogers was killed by the bursting of a cannon on Lake Champlain, October 11, 1776, aged 26 years, 9 months.

Applicants for Pensions. Of those who were in Captain Joshua Parker's company, and who enlisted in April or May, 1775, for eight months' service: Isaac Parker, Obadiah Perry, Silas Procter, John Parker, John Pushee, Nathaniel Prentice, Levi Parker, William Read, Stephen Read, Oliver Read, Solomon Spalding, Ephraim Spalding, Silas Spalding, Robin Skinner, Simeon Senter, Francis Smith, and Joseph Underwood.

In Captain Wyman's company: Thaddeus Read, Jeremiah Robbins, Philip Robbins, and Thomas Robbins.

In Captain Joel Fletcher's company: Philip Smith and Samuel Reed; also, Ezekiel Procter, who had removed to Hollis, and Abel Procter, who had gone to Littleton.

In 1818, Jonas Kemp of this town, was receiving $8.00 per month as a pension, and in 1832, Samuel Read had an allowance of $57.98 per year during his natural life.

In 1832, the following names were on the roll of pensions: Aaron Parker, Aaron Parker, 2nd, David Parker,

Ephraim Reed, Levi Fletcher, Isaac Green, Reuben Leighton, Simeon Procter, Jonas Kemp, Benjamin Robbins, John Pushee, Thaddeus Spalding, Isaac Patten.

Abijah Reed, of Colonel Brooks' regiment, received a bounty of 200 acres of land in Somerset County, Maine, Lot No. 2, 3rd Range.

ALPHABETICAL LIST OF SOLDIERS IN THE WAR OF THE REVOLUTION.

Abbot, Joel
Abbot, John
Adams, Samuel
Adams, Timothy
Barrett, Benjamin
Barrett, Ebenezer
Barrett, John
Barrett, Oliver
Barrett, Thomas
Bates, Oliver
Bason, Cæsar
Bixby, Asa
Bixby, David
Bixby, Isaac
Bixby, Jacob
Bixby, Levi
Bixby, Thomas
Bixby, William
Blanchard, Calvin
Blodgett, Jonas
Blood, Aaron
Boynton, Abel
Brooks, Josiah
Brown, Peter
Burrows, William
Butterfield, James
Butterfield, Samuel
Chafin, David
Chamberlin, Ephraim
Chamberlin, John
Chamberlin, Nathaniel,
Chamberlin, Samuel
Chandler, Ebenezer
Chandler, Isaac
Chandler, Jesse
Chandler, Silas

Chandler, William
Corey, Ebenezer
Corey, Isaac
Corey, Isaac, Jr.
Cowdry, David
Cowdry, John
Cowdry, Thomas
Craft, Samuel
Cummings, Ephraim
Cummings, Nathaniel
Cummings, Timothy
Cummings, Thomas
Darbee, Samuel
Dodge, Job
Dodge, Josiah
Dudley, Daniel
Dudley, Jesse
Dutton, David
Dutton, Ephraim
Dutton, Hildreth
Dutton, William
Esterbrooks, Benjamin
Esterbrooks, Joel
Farmer, Benjamin
Fassett, Joshua
Fish, David
Fisk, Davis
Fitch, Thomas
Fletcher, Andrew
Fletcher, Gershom
Fletcher, Jeremiah
Fletcher, John
Fletcher, Joshua
Fletcher, Joshua, Jr.
Fletcher, Josiah
Fletcher, Levi

Fletcher, Nehemiah
Fletcher, Paul
Fletcher, Pelatiah
Fletcher, Raymond
Fletcher, Sampson
Fletcher, Solomon
Fletcher, Thomas
Fletcher, William
Foster, Ebenezer
Foster, Elias
Foster, Samuel
Foster, Smith
Glenney, Isaac
Goodhue, Daniel
Goodhue, David
Green, Isaac
Green, Nehemiah
Guy, Thomas
Hadley, Jonas
Hadley, Jonathan
Hadley, John
Hambleton, York
Hardwick, William
Hardy, Amos
Heald, Ephraim
Heald, Oliver
Hildreth, Amaziah
Hildreth, Elijah
Hildreth, Hezekiah
Hildreth, Hosea
Hildreth, Jeremiah
Hildreth, Jonathan
Hildreth, Oliver
Hildreth, Peter
Hildreth, William
Hildreth, Zechariah
Holden, Asa
Holden, David
Holden, John
Holden, Jonas
Holmes, Nathaniel
Howard, Silas
Johnson, David
Johnson, Jonathan, Jr.
Jones, Jonathan
Kemp, Ephraim
Kemp, Jonas
Kemp, Simeon
Kent, Abner
Kent, Simeon

Keyes, Charles
Keyes, Daniel
Keyes, Samuel
Kidder, Francis
Kidder, Thomas
King, Rogers
Larkin, Peter
Leighton, Francis
Magerr, James
McEwin, Peter
Mason, Abijah
Meads, Stephen
Minot, Jesse
Minot, Jonathan
Minot, Jonathan, Jr.
Minot, Joseph
Morgan, Henry
Nichols, William
Nutting, John
Nutting, Thomas
Osgood, Benjamin
Parker, Aaron
Parker, Aaron, Jr.
Parker, Abel
Parker, David
Parker, Ebenezer
Parker, Isaac
Parker, John
Parker, Joshua
Parker, Joshua, Jr.
Parker, Levi
Parlin, Amos
Patch, Asa
Patch, Isaac
Patch, John
Patten, Isaac
Perry, James
Perry, Obadiah
Pike, James
Powers, Isaac
Prentice, Nathaniel
Prescott, David
Prescott, Joseph
Prescott, Timothy
Prince, Jethro
Procter, Abel
Procter, Charles
Procter, Ezekiel
Procter, James
Procter, Josiah

THE WAR OF THE REVOLUTION.

Procter, Leonard
Procter, Oliver
Procter, Philip
Procter, Silas
Pushee, John
Read, Abijah
Read, Benjamin
Read, Eleazer
Read, Eleazer, Jr.
Read, Eliakim
Read, Elihu
Read, Elnathan
Read, Joseph
Read, Joshua
Read, Leonard
Read, Oliver
Read, Simeon
Read, Stephen
Read, Thaddeus
Read, William
Richardson, Abijah
Richardson, Wylie
Robbins, Benjamin
Robbins, Jacob
Robbins, Jacob, Jr.
Robbins, Jeremiah
Robbins, John
Robbins, Peter
Robbins, Philip
Robbins, Thomas
Robbins, Zachariah
Robinson, John
Robinson, Winthrop
Rogers, Thomas
Rowe, Tony
Rumrill, Peter
Russell, Abel
Russell, Amos
Russell, John
Russell, Simeon
Scott, Thomas
Senter, Simeon
Skinner, Robert
Smith, Francis
Smith, Thomas
Spalding, Ephraim
Spalding, Job
Spalding, John
Spalding, Philip
Spalding, Silas
Spalding, Solomon
Spalding, Timothy
Spalding, William
Stratton, Jonathan
Stone, Ebenezer
Temple, Levi
Temple, Stephen
Tidd, Amos
Tidd, John
Underwood, John
Underwood, Joseph
Underwood, Timothy
Wendell, Jacob
White, Samuel
Whitney, Daniel
Wilkins, Jethro
Wright, Abraham
Wright, Amos
Wright, Ezekiel
Wright, James
Wright, Joseph
Wright, Jonas
Wright, Oliver
Wright, Pelatiah
Wright, Peter
Wright, Stephen
Wright, Zaccheus
Youngman, Peter

FORMATION OF THE STATE GOVERNMENT.

"May 4, 1778. Voted to choose a Committee to take under their consideration the new form of Government, and make report to the Next meeting. Chose Dr. Asaph Fletcher, Capt. Joseph Read, Dea. John Abbot, Nathaniel Boynton, Francis Leighton, Timothy Prescott,

Capt. Zaccheus Wright, Capt. Amos Fletcher, and Lt. Samuel Read, as a committee for said service."

"May 20, 1778. Voted to send but one man as a Representative from this town, and chose Capt. Joseph Read to represent this town. . . . After hearing the Committee's Report Respecting the new form of government and debating the same, it was moved to be put to vote, and voted for the new form as it now stands four persons; voted against the new form as it now stands fifty four."

"1779. Agreeably to Resolves of the General Court of Feb. 11, 1779, the Inhabitants of the Town qualified to vote for a Representative, assembled on May 21, 1779, to consider and Determine upon the questions contained in sd Resolves; then being present and voted seventy voters, and on the first question, viz, whether they chuse at this time to have a new constitution and form of Government made, voted unanimously in the affirmative on the following condition, viz, that the freeholders and other Inhabitants of this State at large exercise (being called upon therefore) the Right of chusing a State Convention for that purpose. Otherwise, voted unanimously that no Constitution or form of government be made for the present."

"May 11, 1780. Chose a Committee of thirteen men to take under consideration the new form of Government." This committee consisted of Maj. Jonathan Minot, Capt. Zaccheus Wright, Doct. Asaph Fletcher, Rogers King, Capt. Joseph Read, Samuel White, Lt. Jonas Prescott, Timothy Prescott, Capt. Amos Fletcher, Francis Leighton, Lt. David Goodhue, Lt. Leonard Procter, and Dea. Jonathan Fletcher.

"May 25, 1780. Voted unanimously to accept the first article of the declaration of Rights. Voted to accept the second article except the last clause. After long debating on the 3rd article of the Declaration of Rights, it was moved and seconded to see if the Town would accept of the said 3rd article, and 21 voted in the affirmative; the negative being called by the moderator 68 voted in the negative. The reasons for Rejecting the said 3rd article and adopting the

Substitute in its room were voted by 71 men, and 22 voted in the negative."

"May 30, 1780. Voted that the former clause of the 16th article of the Declaration of Rights be amended as follows, viz: the Lyberty of the press and of speech are essential to the Security of Freedom in a State. — That it be added to the last of the 2nd article of the 1st Section and Second Chapter, the following words, viz: *and protestant profession.* That the Seventh article 1st Section 2nd chapter be so amended as to give Power to the Governor in the recess of the General Court to march or transport the Inhabitants of this State for the Relief of a Neighboring State invaded or threatened with immediate danger. That the ministers of the gospel while they officiate as such, and are free from taxation of the estate under their immediate improvement, ought not to be eligible to a Seat in the Senate or House of Representatives. That the 7th article in the 6th chapter be amended as follows, viz: instead of the words — upon the most urgent and pressing occations & for a limited time, not exceeding twelve months', the following be inserted — except in time of War or Rebellion & for a limited time, not exceeding six months. That the Constitution, without fail, be subject to a revisal every ensuing fifteen years. That our Deligate in Convention be left to act according to his Discretion in Regard to Convention (at their next Session) agreeing upon a time when their form of government shall take place without returning the same again to the people.

"Voted to object against the 3rd article of the Declaration of Rights, and that for following Reasons, viz: that it is asserted and taken for granted in the premises of said article — 'that the Happiness of a people and the good order and preservation of civil government, essentially Depends upon Piety, Religion and morality; & these cannot be generally diffused through a Community but by the Institution of the Public Worship of God and by publick Instruction in piety, Religion, &c.' — When both antient History and modern athentic Information concur to evince that Florishing civil states have Existed and still exist without the Legislature's *Instituting* the Public Worship or Publick instruction in piety and the Christian Religion; but rather, whenever such Institutions fully executed by the civil authority, have taken place among a people, instead of promoting essentially their Happiness and the good order and preservation of civil government, it has, we believe, invariably produced impiety, irreligion, Hypocrisy, and many sore and oppressive evils.

"We think the third article, if adopted, will be likely to form such a combination between the Court and Clergy that the libertys of the people will be endangered.

"But not to enter into a detail of the many reasons that might be offered to justifie and Require our Rejection of the said 3rd article, we think it sufficient only to add that we cannot conceive ourselves in any case or Degree to be Intitled to such a Right as is attributed to the people of this Commonwealth in said article of Investing the Legislature with power to authorize or require the several Towns, Parishes, precincts, and other bodies, politic or Religious Societies to make suitable provision at their own expense for the institution of the public worship of God, and for the support of the public teachers of piety and Religion; because we fully believe that the great Head of the Church has in his gospel, made suitable provision for the said Institution of his public worship and for the support of christian teachers of piety and Religion, & that he has never invested any Commonwealth or Civil Legislature as such, by force and penalty to carry these aforesaid Institutions into execution, — all attempts of which, we think, tend to encroch on the unalienable Rights of conscience, and to the marring of the true principles of civil government which last ever ought, in our opinion, to be kept Distinct of Religious gospel institutions. Further it appears to us that the general principles of civil government as contained in the Constitution, without the said 3rd article, properly attended to and acted upon, would much better secure and promote the Happiness of the people and the good order and preservation of civil government, (which we would ever zealosly promote) than retaining and adopting the said third article.

"Therefore from principles of Regard for the good and Happiness of the Commonwealth and the better to secure the unalienable Rights of conscience, and from a sense of Duty to ourselves and posterity, we feel ourselves bound to reject the said third article of the Declaration of Rights, and to enter our sincere protestation against the same—and that our Religious Freedom and the unalienable Rights of conscience may be better secured and established than they are in the Declaration of Rights.

"We recommend the 3rd article thereof to be superceded by the following as a substitute, viz, All men have a natural and unalienable right to worship Almighty God according to their own conscience and understanding, and no man ought or of right can be compelled to attend any Religious worship, or erect or support any place of Worship, or maintain any minister contrary to or against his own free will and consent, nor can any man who acknowledges the being of a God, be justly deprived or abridged of any civil right as a citizen on account of his Religious Sentiments or peculiar mode of religious worship; and that no authority can or ought be vested or assumed by any person whatsoever, that shall in any case interfere with or in any manner controul the Rights of Conscience in the free exercise of Religious Worship.

"Recorded by NATHL. BOYNTON,
Town Clerk."

This "sincere protestation" did not avail; for the third article of the Declaration of Rights, in form as it was agreed upon in Convention held in Cambridge, Sept. 1, 1779, and by adjournment to the 2nd day of March, 1780, was adopted by the people in the following May, and the new form of Government went into effect Oct. 25, 1780. This article remained on the statute-book for more than half a century, and was amended Nov. 11, 1833.—It will be seen that the sentiment of the people here was greatly in advance of the opinions of the people at large, for the article cited and opposed by them was adopted by a two-thirds vote of the commonwealth. And when, in 1833, fifty-three years afterward, it was changed, the amendment embodied the same principle that was contended for in the little town meeting in Westford.

"February 23, 1781. Pay to Doct. Asaph Fletcher for 52 days' service at the Convention held in Boston and Cambridge in settling the Constitution the sum of 936£."

"September 8, 1780. Voted for the Hon John Hancock Esq, to be Governor by sixty votes:

"Voted for Hon. John Perkins Esq to be Lieut Governor by forty three votes.

"For Hon. James Bowdoin Esq. to be Lieut. Governor by one vote.

"Voted as follows for Councillors and Senators:

"For Josiah Stone Esq. of Framingham thirty two votes.

"For Abraham Fuller Esq. of Newtown thirty two votes.

"For Nathl. Gorham Esq. of Charleston Thirty one votes.

"For James Prescott of Groton, twenty eight votes.

"For Eleazer Brooks of Lincoln twenty eight votes.

"For Loammi Baldwin of Woburn four votes."

This was the first election under the State Constitution.

CHAPTER IV.

FROM THE REVOLUTION TO THE CLOSE OF THE CENTURY—STATE OF THINGS AFTER THE WAR—EXTRACTS FROM TOWN RECORDS—THE MIGRATION TO OTHER TOWNS FOR THE PERIOD OF A CENTURY.

ALLUSION has already been made to the severity of the struggle for independence. The present generation know but little about it, and are content to enjoy the blessings secured by it. The resources of the thirteen original States were laid under heavy contribution in order to gain the desired end; and where all did so well, it is perhaps invidious to make comparisons. But the student of history encounters plain facts which should not be overlooked. The Commonwealth of Massachusetts furnished for the war 69,907 soldiers, while New York furnished but 17,781, making a difference of 50,126 in favor of Massachusetts. In adjusting the war-balances after the peace, Massachusetts, as was then ascertained, had overpaid her share in the sum of $1,248,801, in silver money; but New York was deficient in the large amount of $2,074,846.

New Hampshire, though almost a wilderness, furnished 12,496 troops for the continental ranks, or nearly three-fourths of the number enlisted in the Empire State. The whole number of regulars enlisted for the continental service from the beginning to the close of the struggle was 231,959; and all the States south of Pennsylvania provided but 59,943, or 8,414 *less* than the single State of Massachusetts. New England furnished 118,350, or more than one half the number placed at the service of Congress. In a tabular statement compiled from statistics contained in the report of

General Knox, Secretary of War, to Congress in 1790, it appears that the quota fixed and required by Congress of Massachusetts was 52,698 men, but the State furnished 67,907 "continentals," while her militia showed an aggregate of 15,145, and her contingent force was estimated at 9,500, making a total of 92,552 men engaged in the war for a longer or shorter period. This may be contrasted with New York, which furnished but 30,397 men of all descriptions. [See Sabine's Loyalists of the Revolution.]

By referring to the details of the previous chapter, the reader will find that this town was not deficient in the measure of its service for the common defence. It is well to bear in mind the inevitable result of that long-continued draft upon the material resources of the country; the financial distress that followed, the poverty of those who had been soldiers, and the general tendency to demoralization and discord. And it should not be forgotten that many precious lives had been sacrificed, and many men had been disabled by hardships, wounds, and sicknesses, and could not render services to their families for whom they would gladly toil. It is painful to note how many of the soldiers who went from this town became paupers, and had to be supported by the town, some of them through long years of impotence and pain. In some cases, doubtless, their poverty was owing to a natural shiftlessness, or to bad habits contracted in the army. But in many it was due to the fact that they had spent their strength in wearisome campaigns and were unable to work for their own support. Pensions were not granted until many years had passed by, and many a soldier was sleeping in his narrow bed. The phrase, "Not gitable"* often appears upon the records, and signifies the abatement of taxes. Although sometimes put against the name of persons who had removed from town, it was frequently attached to the name of some poor soldier who had risked his life for the common weal.

---

*Instead of this phrase, the words "Not recoverable" were first used by Richard Kneeland, in 1797, and after a time these also disappeared.

"At the close of the war the citizens were left free indeed, and in full possession of the valuable objects which they had fought to obtain. But the price of those objects was high. Their private state-debt amounted to 1,300,000 pounds, besides 250,000 pounds due to the officers and soldiers of their line of the army. Their proportion of the federal debt was not less than one million and a half of the same money. And in addition to this, every town was embarrassed by advances which they had made to comply with repeated requisitions for men and supplies to support the army, which had been done on their own particular credit. The weight of this burden must strike us with great force, if we consider that by the customary mode of taxation, one-third part of the whole was paid by the rateable polls alone. True it is that a recollection of the blessings which this debt had purchased, must have operated to alleviate every inconvenience arising from such a cause, but embarrassments followed which no considerations of that nature could be expected to obviate." [Minott's History of Insurrections, etc., pp. 5, 6.]

EXTRACTS FROM THE TOWN RECORDS.

1784. *County House.* "Voted unanimously that the town will not give their consent that a County house should be built at Cambridge for the use of the County."

1785. *Land.* "Pay to Lieut. Gershom Fletcher 7s. 6d. for rates he paid at Plimoth for this town." This was for land in Plymouth, N. H., given to the town, probably by Lieutenant Fletcher himself. There is occasional reference to it in the records, especially in 1790, 1794, 1808.

Petition Respecting Public Grievances. "July 31, 1786. Voted that the Committee chosen to corrispond with Committees of other Towns of this Commonwealth, relative to our Public Grievances make report of their Doings at the ajournment of this meeting."

"September 4, 1786. Met according to ajournment and voted to concur with the Committee in stating the Public Grievances as exhibited by them. Voted to accept of the Address exhibited by the Committee and that it be publicly read in the meeting-house by the minister after Public servis. Voted that the Petition of Mr Nathan Proctor and others Respecting the Public Grievances with the List of Grievances and the Address exhibited by the Committee be put on File in the Clerk's office." It is to be regretted, in the interest of a complete history, that these documents cannot be found; for they would reveal to us the real sentiments and opinions of the people at that time. The troubles at Concord in connection with the Shay's Rebellion, so called, were then impending, and on the 9th of September, five days afterward, the town of Concord issued an address or circular letter to other towns in the county, "inviting their co-operation in acting as mediators between the government and the opposition."

In response to that circular this town passed the following votes :

"September 11, 1786. Voted to choose a Committee to meet a Committee of the town of Concord at the house of Capt. Oliver Brown, Innholder, in Concord, to confer together and act according to their Discresion. Chose Capt. Jonathan Keep, Timothy Prescott, Col?. Robinson, Ens. John Abbot, and Deacon Samuel Fletcher for said Committee." The conference was held on Tuesday morning, September 12, and twenty-four towns were then and there represented. On that day a company of insurgents, led by Capt. Job Shattuck of Groton, assembled at the Court House in Concord and forbade the holding of the courts. The convention called to act as mediators, endeavored to prevent a riot; but did not at once succeed in dispersing the crowd. The insurgents, however, left the town late on Tuesday evening. The members of the conference adopted the following expression of their sentiments : "This body cannot forbear to express their disagreeable and painful sensations that their endeavors to dissuade from rash and unlawful measures have proved so ineffectual. They declare their utter abhorrence of the measures adopted by the body in arms, and are fully sensible of the high criminality of such opposition to established authority." [See History of Concord, p. 136.]

This is all that the record shows of any participation of the citizens of Westford, by committee or by individuals, in the proceedings at Concord, September 12, 1786. Dea. Samuel Fletcher and Thomas Richardson were paid £1. 7s each, for attending that Convention. In regard to the action of a county convention held at Concord, October 3, by adjournment from August 23, this town passed the following vote:

"Octr. ye 9th 1786. Voted that we approve of the result of the Convention at their ajournment at Concord on the third day of Octr. Instant." That convention met "to seek relief in a peaceable, orderly, and constitutional way; viewing with the greatest abhorrence and detestation the late riotous proceedings of a rash and inconsiderate body of people, in opposing the sitting of the courts of justice," etc. By approving the action of that convention this town forever warded off the imputation of sympathy or interest in the Shay's Rebellion.

Fire-arms. "Octr. 9, 1786. Voted that the Selectmen Lock up the fire-arms and the war utensils belonging to this town and Make report where They be at the next March meeting."

Instructions to Representative. "May 28, 1787. To Dea. Samuel Fletcher: Whereas you are chosen to Represent the Town of Westford in the General Court the year ensuing, the Town Reposing full Confidence in your ability, firmness, and Steady Endeavors to promote the welfair of the Commonwealth in general as well as this town in Particular, and we expect that when you are acting as Representative you at all times Pay a strict adhearance to the Constitution and Laws of the Commonwealth, and in matters that may Come before you in which you have not Particular Instructions, the Town Expect you to use your Best Judgment.

"That you use your Influence that the General Court Be Removed out of Boston to Some Convenient Place in the Country.

"That agriculture, manufactries and Exportation of our mnufactries Be Incouraged as much as Possible and the Importation of foreign Superfluities Be discouraged by an Earnest Recomendation to omitt the use of such of them as are Not Nessary.

"That the tender act Be continued untill there Be a Sufficient Currancy for the Commerce of the People.

"That Peace and Harmony may be Restored to the People of this Commonwealth, you are directed to use your Influence that the disqualifying act Be Repealed, and that all the Peaceable Citizens Be Restored to their former Privilidges. That you use your Influence that all Pentions and Greatuities Be Curtailed, as far as Justice will allow. That the Taxes in futer on Poles & Estates Be Lowered, and Raised on Imports and Excise.

"The above was accepted by the Town and a Coppy given to the Representative."

Delegate to Convention. "Decem^r. ye 3^d, 1787. Chose Jonathan Keep a dellagate to Represent this Town in the State Convention to be holden at Boston on ye 2nd wednesday of January next." This was probably the convention which assembled to consider the question of adopting the federal constitution.

Death of an Indian. "February 13, 1788. Pay to Leonard Parker £1. 10s, for nursing and Taking care of the Indian, James Symonds, when he was sick at sd Parker's house, and the Trouble of sd Indian's funeral when dead."

Shire Town. "May 2, 1791. Voted that our Representive Youse his Influence in the General Cort that an act be passed making Concord the Sheir Town of the County of Middlesex."

" May 7, 1792. Voted that it 'tis the mind of this town unanimously that Concord be the Shir of this County."

Painting the Meeting House, &c. "April 1, 1793. Voted to Culler the meeting-house this season and to make it neer the Culler of Chelmsford meeting-house. Voted the ruf of the meeting house be tard or Cullered as the Committee think best. Voted to cast the meeting house bell over. Chose a Committee to draw a plan and asertain the Caust of making seetes in the gallery for the Singers to set in."

Belfry. " November 22, 1793. Voted to build a belfree at the west end of the meeting house & in the same form as Chelmsford."

Burning of the Second Meeting-House. The records do not give the precise date of this occurrence. But the following sentence will determine it very nearly:

"January 8, 1794. Sold the remander of the Nales at Vendue which were not Pick, up where the meeting house was Burnt to Mr Nathaniel Boynton for 7–6." [Seven and sixpence.]

The vote of November 22d, quoted above, shows that it could not have been earlier than that date. It was probably some time in December, 1793.

New Meeting-House. "January 13, 1794. Voted unanimous [ly] that they would build a meeting house. Voted to chuse a Committeeto report to the next town meeting where the most Convenient plase is to build the meeting house on and the Caust of the land if they conclude to purchase ground to set it on. Voted and chose five a Committee for the above purpose: Zaccheus Wright Esq. Dea. William Hildreth Mathew Scribner, Timothy Prescott, and Col. David Goodhue."

"January 20, 1794. Voted the town Except the report of the Committee to look out a piece of land to Set the meeting house on, and give £20 for the land described and bounded in their report. Voted that the South Side Sill shall be set in a perrilel line from the Southeast Corner of Joel Abbot's house to the southwest Corner of Richard Kneeland's house. Voted to Chuse a Committee of three to take a Conveyance of the land bought of Joel Abbot to the Satisfaction of the town. Voted the meeting house be built 65 feet long, 48 feete wide and 28 feete posts, with a tower at the west end of said house. Voted to have 58 pews on the lower floor and 24 pews in the gallery. . . . Voted the woales [walls] of said house be swelled & the windows be Cased and made flaring; that thare shall be but one pare of stares to go into the Pulpitt; that the Pulpit Canapy & Dea^n. Seete be nearly in the form that Chelmsford meeting house is, and that the pews shall be finished with ballasters as our old meeting house was."

"January 27, 1794. Voted to chuse a Committee of three to contract in behalf of the town with John Abbot and Moses Thomas to build and finish the meeting house agreeable to the several votes of the town; That the inhabitants pay unto Mr John Abbot & Mr Moses Thomas thirteen hundred pounds for building and finishing the meeting house agreeably to the votes of the town."

"August 12, 1794. Voted to pay Mr. Richard Kneeland twelve pounds for land the Committee bought of him for the use of the town." This was in addition to the land bought of Joel Abbot.

"November 1, 1794. Chose John Abbot and Moses Thomas a Committee to dress the Pulpit and Dress itt in Crimson Coler. Voted that the pews be sold on thirsday the 13th day of November 1794."

"Decem^r. 22, 1794 Pay Col. Zach^s. Wright £57 for a note he gave at Boston for a Bell."

Unitarian Church.

"January 5, 1795. Chose a Committee to set the Psalm —Mr Levi Hedge, Col. Benjamin Osgood, and Mr Jeremiah Hildreth."

This was the third house of worship built in Westford and it is still standing, being the property of the First Parish. It is probable that it was first occupied in January, 1795. There is no hint in the records of any service of dedication.

Bounty for Soldiers. "July 25, 1794. Voted that the town of Westford will give a Bounty of one dollar a peece to all the men to be raised for Public Servis out of this town, officers included, and if they actuley march the town votes that each Soldier shall have seven dollars per month as long as they shall serve as soldiers, including State and Continental day, and provided that no more men be Detacht. from the Cavelry in this town than an Equal proportion according to the number of Cavelry that is in town and that they shall have the same pay as the other soldiers have."

This call for soldiers was probably occasioned by the troubles in Pennsylvania and the war with the Indians in the West. The men who enlisted were Sergt. Naeman Nichols, James Procter, Abel Hildreth, Elijah Hildreth, Jr., Benjamin Foster, Jr., Amaziah Hildreth, Nathaniel Cowdry, Jr., John Hildreth, Samson Fletcher, Capt. Thomas K. Green, Abijah Tarbell, Daniel Tarbell, Joseph Tarbell, Elijah Prescott, John H. Cummings, Hezekiah Richardson, Henry Wilson, Luther Boynton, James Pike, Jr., Isaac Wright, Eleazer Heald, Peter Farwell, Joshua A. Abbot, Thomas Dutton, David Fish, Lieut. Josiah Howard, Ens. Elias Parker, Abel Boynton, Ebenezer Nutting, and John Raymond. Also, Thomas Richardson, Jr., "one of the lite horsemen Drafted to march if requested."

Plan of the Town. "October 3, 1794. Voted to chuse a Committee to Survey and take a plan of the town of Westford."

The survey was made by Ebenezer Prescott, as is shown by the following order:

"Feb. 1796. Pay to Ebenezer Prescott $25.33 for 9 days spent in surveying the town and making out a plan."

"Voted that the Hoss Stables behint the meeting house be built nine feet hight."

The proprietors of these stables were: Joel Abbot, Dea. John Prescott, Dea. William Hildreth, Ebenezer Prescott, Lieut. Thomas Read, Joseph Keyes, Elijah Chamberlin, Isaac Cummings, Willard Fletcher, Capt. Jonathan Keyes, Amos Wright, Capt. Peletiah Fletcher, Zaccheus Read, Timothy Cummings, Willis Hall, and Col. Benjamin Osgood.

Selectmen. "March 2, 1795. Voted to chuse But three Selectmen for the year ensuing." Before this the board consisted of five men, and the change was made at this date.

County Road. "Voted that it Be the mind of this town that the County Road from Worsester come into this town Near Stonny Brook pond, so caled."

Singers. "Voted that it tis the Desire of this town that the Singers take their seets provided for them by the town and Asist in singing as formaly as they wish to make no premance." [Preeminence.]

Burning of House. "May 6, 1795. Voted that the Town Treasurer give up the two notes that Joshua Read Jun. gave to this town as a Compensation for the loss he has met with in loosing his house by fire."

Revising the Constitution. "For revision 113 votes; against revision 92 votes."

Stove. "December 6, 1796. Pay Jonathan Carver for tending the mason when putting a stove in the school house." At the centre, probably, where Mr. Carver then lived.

Loss of Military Stores. "April 3, 1797. Voted to give the Representative instructions to petition the General Court for an abatement of the last year's State tax on account of the loss of the meeting house and military stores by fire."

Military Review. "September 4, 1797. Voted to give each man in Capt. Keyes' and Capt. Crosby's Company fifty cents as a gratuity from the town to reimburse them for the expense they may be at in going to the Review at Concord the 26th of this month."

"Oct. 12, 1797. Pay to Capt. Jonathan Keyes the sum of 35 dollars for Victuals and Drink for 70 men on the day of Review at Concord at 50 cents each."

Land of Samuel Craft. Same date. George Abbot was paid for a journey to Weare, N. H., "to get Samuel Craft's land on Record which said Craft has made over to this town for his support."

List of Paupers. March 8, 1799. — Benjamin Foster, Samuel Craft, Jeremiah Temple, Elizabeth Keyes, Elizabeth Wilson, Patience Fish, Margaret Craft, Thaddeus Read, Sarah Hildreth, Widow Mary Barrett, Widow Thankful Read, and Nehemiah Fletcher, Jun.

Losses by Fire. "May 6, 1799. Voted that the Town will help Mr Dutton and Mr Day on account of their losses by fire. Voted to raise one hundred and fifty dollars for the use of Mr Dutton and family." The burning of Joseph Dutton's house took place April 5, 1799. It stood opposite the house of the late Amos Day, which is now occupied by J. T. Colburn.

Death of George Washington. Commemorative services were held in this town February 22, 1800, this being the birth-day occurring next after the death of the Father of his Country.

The committee of arrangements consisted of Richard Kneeland, Joseph Keyes, and Jeremiah Hildreth, who were the Selectmen for that year.

"Voted that the Committee request Mr John Abbot Jr to deliver a Eulogy or Oration on said 22nd of February, and Rev. Mr. Blake be requested to make an Introductory prayer on said day."

Muster. "October, 1800. Pay Samuel Wood the sum of $121.47 cts for providing for 147 men at Concord at the General Muster at 4s 11½d per man as was struck off to him at Vendue by vote of the town." The muster was held August 27 and 28; Jonathan Keyes and Rogers King were captains of the two companies that year, and the total number of men on duty was one hundred forty-seven.

Recovery of Bill Against the Town. 1800. "Pay John Raymond the sum of $53.00 and the further sum of $9.00 which sums are for the purpose of satisfying an Execution against this town in favor of Elijah Flagg."

This was paid to settle a claim brought by Elijah Flagg, probably a son of Dr. Allen Flagg, for medical aid rendered to several of the town's poor by his father.

THE MIGRATION FROM WESTFORD TO OTHER TOWNS.

The following list of men who have gone out from this town to find homes in other towns, has been prepared with much care after extended investigation and inquiry, in order to show what the men of the past have done to help forward the settlement of our country and the advancement of the nation. Next to the evidence of a real and praiseworthy development in the town itself, is the proof that its representatives have achieved for themselves a good name and honorable distinction in other communities. In this respect the town has no reason to be ashamed. Judged by any standard that is just and right, they are deserving of all praise. They "builded better than they knew." Their outgoing was the tread of stalwart men who believed that life is worth living; of men who had an aim and a purpose, and that was to found other communities wherein should be seen in due time the ripe fruits of a true patriotism and a pure religion. They were pioneers, even as were their fathers before them—the vanguard of an advancing civilization. They took with them no ancestral honors, they bore no titles, they filled no official positions, but they won them by industry, honesty, and rightousness. And it is not a little remarkable that in almost every town in which they dwelt, they became the leading men, and were called to fill every office of dignity or trust. In the broader relations of life they became justices of the peace, judges of the courts, military officers, physicians, deacons and ministers, legislators and governors.

In preparing this account it has been thought advisable to group the facts which have been ascertained, and thus, so far as practicable, to give a just view of the whole subject. No attempt has been made to arrange them chronologically, or to put the names in alphabetical order. This would be no easy task, for it will be necessary to go back to the beginning and to continue our researches for the period of a century, and even longer. The year of removal is given where it is known.

Sometime, it would seem not far from the date of incorporation, Solomon Keyes — " Captain Solomon of the Pequawket affair " — removed to Western now Warren, Massachusetts, taking with him his sons, Solomon and David, probably each of them born on the old homestead. Solomon was wounded in the battle of Lake George, was carried to Fort Edward, where he died October 1, 1755. David removed to Albany, N. Y., where he died in 1761.

To Litchfield, N. H. In 1734, Aquila Underwood was authorized by the General Court to call the first town meeting in Litchfield, and at that meeting, which was held

July 29, 1734, he was chosen moderator, town clerk, and first selectman. He held the office of selectman for several years, and was also agent for the town in the movement for a new county. He owned a farm of 228 acres in 1737. He continued to reside there until his death. James Underwood, probably his son, was town clerk in 1762. Also, John Butterfield, 1736; John Barrett, 1736; Jacob Hildreth, 1736; his son Jacob was selectman, 1763; Thomas Barrett, 1740; Isaac Parker (returned); William Read, son of William and Hannah, colonel, a noted bear hunter, was killed at the raising of a building. He gave his name to Read's Ferry. Also, Benjamin Blodgett, son-in-law of Dea. Joshua Fletcher.

To Hollis, N. H. Ephraim Burge, 1760; Ezekiel Procter, about 1771; Ebenezer Townsend, ——; Minot Farmer, about 1773; William Read, about 1760; Wilder Chamberlin.

To Wilton. Levi Bixby, Sampson Keyes, and afterward to Wilton, Me.

To Mason. Samuel Squier, James Snow, Nathaniel Boynton, William Wright, Charles Prescott.

To New Ipswich. Among the grantees of this township, named in the Masonian Charter, executed at Dunstable, April 17, 1750, were Reuben Kidder, Joseph Kidder, John Chandler, and Andrew Spalding, of Westford.

Reuben Kidder heads the list. He was to make settlement on three shares or rights; John Chandler and Andrew Spalding on one each. He was "for the first twenty years the father of the town." He filled important civil offices, was land surveyor, justice of the peace, captain, and colonel. He gave his attention to the cultivation of fruit, and "previous to the Revolution had one of the largest and most valuable orchards in New England, containing the rarest varieties of apples and pears." He was on intimate terms with Gov. Wentworth, who in 1770 conferred on him the title of Colonel of a regiment of militia. From the Masonian proprietors he received a grant of a township of land, subsequently called Washington, in New Hampshire. He assisted in the organization of the church in 1760, and was one of its original members. He had four sons and eight daughters, all of whom lived to adult age, and some of them to be very old. He died in 1793, aged 70. His wife, Susanna Burge, of Westford, died in 1824, aged 88.

Joseph Kidder established his home near the centre of New Ipswich, where he lived until 1770, when he removed to the adjoining town of Temple. He married Rebecca Chamberlin, of Westford.

John Chandler, 1750. The early proprietors entered into an agreement with him to erect the first mills. For this purpose they made a grant of land, including the falls on the Souhegan River, at what is now known as the High Bridge. He was to have the saw mill ready for service by the last of October, 1750, and the corn mill in October, 1751. For his encouragement he was to have one full right in the township without paying the advance money, the lot on which his mills stood including the sites of all the present factories owned by the Columbian Company, and £50 bills of credit, old tenor. He, with William Chandler, of Westford, was bound in the sum of £400, new tenor, equal to $140, to execute the contract. The mills were built according to agreement. In 1768 he sold his property to Capt. Eleazer Cummings, and removed to Camden, Me.

Andrew Spalding. He signed the church covenant October 21, 1760, but probably was never a permanent resident. His son Andrew became a citizen, and also his stepsons by the name of Crosby. He married in 1745, Mrs. Mehitable (Chandler) Crosby of Andover, and her sons, Jonah, Robert, Joel, and Josiah, came to Westford with her. They removed to New Ipswich soon — about 1750; their names, with the exception of Jonah, were in the tax-list for 1763, but they removed to Maine previous to the Revolution. Robert was a selectman in 1762.

Joseph Bates, 1751. One of the original members of the church; an ardent patriot; chairman of the Committee of Safety in 1775; a lieutenant in the war, and present at the capture of Burgoyne. He removed to Jaffrey in 1785, and afterward to the northern part of New York, where he died.

Joseph Parker, born 1742, went to New Ipswich about 1766. "Captain Parker seems to have been fitted by nature for the part he was to act in this town, particularly during the Revolution. He was a daring, energetic man, and had considerable influence over a certain class. He commanded a company of militia, and was prompt to march wherever his services were needed. He was at Cambridge, Ticonderoga, Rhode Island, and at the taking of Burgoyne. He was very popular with his soldiers. He died 1807, aged 66.

Jonathan Parker, brother of Joseph, was an early settler, a soldier, and a pensioner; lived a bachelor, and died 1820, aged 69.

Nathaniel Prentice, born 1755, removed about 1778. He learned the clothier's trade in Westford, probably of William Chandler, and carried on the business in New Ipswich for more than twenty years. He was an industrious, worthy man. Removed to Peterborough, where he died.

Joseph Pollard, born in Billerica, 1702; came to Westford 1737, but soon went to Nottingham West, now Hudson, N. H., and returned here. He and his two sons, Joseph and Benjamin, removed to New Ipswich after a few years.

Thomas Spalding removed about 1760. James Spalding removed but did not remain; he returned to Westford and died here. James, his son, born 1748, settled on the north side of Watatic Mountain, just over the Ashburnham line, but was always socially connected with New Ipswich. For sixty-five years he was a constant attendant at church. When the alarm of Concord fight was given, he started immediately for the scene of action, while his wife, Hannah (Barron), of Westford, and his oldest son, Jonathan, spent the afternoon of that day upon the summit of Watatic, where they saw the smoke of the burning buildings, and distinctly heard the report of the British cannon. His son, Jonathan, born in Westford, settled in Lempster, N. H., and was much engaged in organizing that town.

Simeon Wright, born 1741. He was badly wounded at the raising of Wilton meeting-house in 1773. Died 1786.

Oliver Wright, son of Thomas, born in 1738. Thomas Wright.

Stephen Hildreth, born in 1742, married Esther Manning, of Townsend, 1764, and settled in New Ipswich about 1772. A soldier of the Revolution.

Simeon Hildreth, born 1736, married Hannah Spalding, 1757. His son, Simeon, was a Revolutionary soldier.

Simeon Fletcher, about 1765, killed at the raising of the frame of Wilton meeting-house, September 7, 1773.

Peter Fletcher, son of Ephraim, born 1736, went to New Ipswich about 1762.

Abraham Bennett, who was taxed here in 1759, was in New Ipswich 1767.

Nathan Boynton, son of Nathaniel, born in 1742, was admitted to the church in New Ipswich in 1766, and was taxed there in 1774.

Hezekiah Corey was taxed there in 1763. Married Sarah Fletcher of Westford. A soldier in the Indian Wars; probably he is the man who went with John Chandler to Camden, Me.

Benjamin King, taxed there in 1763.

Abel Wright, 1763.

Jonas Holden, taxed in 1774; probably the man who afterward settled in Mount Holly, Vt.

Arthur Dennis, came from old Ipswich to Westford, and afterward went to New Ipswich.

David Rumrill, taxed there in 1774.

Nathaniel Farr, who married Abigail Foster of Westford in 1768.

John Bigelow and his son Silas, 1787. Silas kept a tavern "on the South Road," which was known as the "Bigelow Tavern."

Henry Fletcher, 1773.

Benjamin Wheat.

The following persons paid taxes there, and are occasionally mentioned in the records of New Ipswich—probably not actual settlers: Ephraim Chamberlin, Thomas Cummings, Benjamin Carver, Ephraim Cummings, Leonard Procter, Henry Wright, Ephraim Burge, James Wright, Timothy Spalding, Benjamin Procter, 1763; Abel Wright, Solomon Woods, Abel Hildreth, Ephraim Hildreth, James Hildreth, Mark White, also Asa Brown. (?)

To Temple. Asa Perry, Jonathan Spalding, Solomon Richardson, who also resided in Jaffrey and returned to Westford.

Eleazer Taylor, 1772.

To Ackworth. Benjamin Parker, M. D., son of David. He practised many years in Ackworth, where he died.

To Deering. Thomas Dutton.

To Amherst. Robert Read. He went first to Litchfield where his brother William settled, and then to Amherst. He was known as Colonel Read, and was for many years the keeper of the jail in that place.

Henry Chandler, son of Moses.

To Nashua. James Baldwin. His son, Josephus, was Deacon of the First Baptist Church and first Mayor of the city.

To Pelham. Jonas Keyes, 1829, son of Issacher Keyes, born 1787, died in 1863.

To Warner. Solomon Spalding; afterward to Waitsfield, Vt., and Saratoga Springs, about 1813.

To Rochester. Thomas Spalding, 1843; then to Haverhill, Massachusetts, and to Madrid, Me.

To Swanzey. Jonas Blodget, a soldier of the Revolution. He died there, 1826. James Underwood.

To Keene. John Butterfield.

To Hillsborough. Zachariah Robbins, Joash Minot.

To Westmoreland. Aaron Chandler. His wife Ruth was dismissed to the church in Nitchawaugue (Petersham), in 1752, and they afterward removed to Westmoreland. Samuel Minot, Timothy, Jonas, Isaac, and James Butterfield, brothers, and sons of Benjamin Butterfield whose homestead was near the house of the Coolidge brothers. Leonard Keep, Thomas Kidder Green.

To Marlborough. Peter Hadley.

To Jaffrey. Benjamin Prescott, 1774. He received a colonel's commission. Oliver Prescott, Thomas Dutton.

To Fitzwilliam. Phinehas Read, 1787; born 1765, son of Joshua. Enlisted at the age of 14 as a private under Captain Tucker, of Salem. Learned the tanner's trade with his brother Benjamin, in Templeton.

To Stoddard. Joshua Read, who served three years in the war of the Revolution and drew a pension. Eliakim Read, John Taylor, Paul Wright, Elnathan Read. Elnathan Read afterward removed to Walpole, and to Cavendish, 1813.

To Rindge. Asa Johnson, Samuel Walter Fletcher.

To Peterborough. John Jewett.

To Nelson. Oliver and Nehemiah Wright, 1783. Thomas Read, son of Thomas and Susanna.

To Hopkinton. Elijah Fletcher, minister of the Congregational Church there; ordained in 1773, died 1786. His daughter, Grace, married Daniel Webster, 1808.

To Washington. Jacob Wright, Daniel Keyes, Israel Keyes, John Mead, Luther Boynton, Jacob Nutting, (returned); Amos Russell, (?) Abel White. (?)

To Littleton. Ziba Wright.

To Plymouth. Joshua Fletcher, about 1775; Congregational minister. Gershom Fletcher, 1773; came back in 1778. Joseph Read, son of Joshua, born 1776. He was afterward a merchant in Thetford, Vt., 1803 to 1833. Removed to Montpelier, where he died; justice of the peace, representative in the Legislature, county treasurer, and judge of Probate.

THE MIGRATION TO VERMONT.

This State was received into the Union in 1791. It was for many years called the New State, being the first one admitted after the Revolution. Many went thither in quest of new homes. The towns of Cavendish, Ludlow, and Mount Holly were settled and organized chiefly by men from Westford.

To Cavendish. Josiah Fletcher, 1781. He was the first town clerk and a selectman, chosen at the first town meeting, held March 12, 1782. Removed to Ludlow, 1785. At the first town meeting he was chosen town treasurer, 1792; was representative in the Vermont General Assembly at Rutland, 1796, '97, 1800, and 1801. "A Christian of the highest character."

Thomas Dutton was one of the grantees of the township in 1762, but he did not go there to reside.

Salmon Dutton, land surveyor. On the list of freemen in Cavendish, 1782; also on the list for that year, Leonard Proctor, Joshua Parker, William Spalding, Ephraim Dutton, William Spalding, Jr., Abbot Roby, Jesse Spalding, Jesse Fletcher. For 1786, Asaph Fletcher, Timothy Hildreth, Samuel Adams, Benjamin Spalding. For 1788, Aaron Parker, Isaac Parker, Jeremiah Hildreth. 1792, Salmon Dutton, Jr. 1795, Solomon Proctor. 1797, Thomas Proctor. 1799, Nathan Boynton. 1801, John Parker, John White, Samuel White, Jr. Salmon Dutton was moderator of the first town meeting in Cavendish, and was chosen first selectman and treasurer. Also, in 1785, chairman of the committee to hire preaching, and later a justice of the peace. The village of Duttonsville in Cavendish received its name from him. He died in 1824, aged 80.

Capt. Leonard Proctor, selectman in 1784 and '85, and afterward held various public trusts. A man of great force of character and skilled in the affairs of the town. The village of Proctorsville, about one mile from Duttonsville, took its name from him. His sons were all active business men. His grandson, Redfield Proctor, son of Jabez, has been governor of Vermont. Captain Proctor died in 1827, aged 93, and was buried in the "Proctor Cemetery" on the hillside, overlooking the valley of Black River and the railroad.

Capt. Joshua Parker. Although his name appears among the freemen of 1782, it is probable that he did not become an actual settler until some years later. He was the father of Dea. Joshua Parker, born in Westford, 1764, for a long time a resident of Cavendish; an officer in the Congregational Church. Captain Parker died in the State of New York.

Ephraim Dutton was a land surveyor, and afterward settled in Ludlow. His son, Joel, removed to Cato, N. Y.

Abbot Roby is probably the man whose birth is recorded in Dunstable as Philip Abbot Roby, son of Samuel, and born 1754. He owned the Patten farm in Westford, went first to Weathersfield, Vt., and then to Cavendish, where he was lister (assessor) in 1783, and selectman in 1784.

Asaph Fletcher, M. D. His house in Westford was the old Byam house, removed in 1875 in order to give place to the present residence of Hon. J. Henry Read. But the old mansion is still to be seen on Main Street. Removed to Cavendish in February, 1787, and during the following summer built for himself a house in a secluded spot over the hill, nearly or quite half a mile from the river. This house, still standing, was built after the old style, with large stone chimney and ample fire-places. In this quaint old structure his son Richard was born, January 8, 1788—the eminent jurist of Boston, who graduated from Dartmouth College in 1806. He afterward erected a substantial dwelling near Proctorsville. During his long life he held many public offices, and was a distinguished and useful man. He was a member of the convention which applied to Congress for the admission of Vermont to the Union; was often a member of the Legislature, for some years one of the judges of the County Court, member of the Council, elector of president, and president of the County Medical Society, before which he gave lectures. He died January 5, 1839, aged 92 years. His son Ryland was governor of Vermont, 1856 and 1857.

William Spalding, son of Josiah, who lived at the foot of Nubanussuck pond. He married Esther Dutton in 1759.

He took with him to Cavendish his sons, John, who died there at the age of 99, William, Asa, Joseph, Zedekiah, Zaccheus, and Jonas, an adopted son. He died in 1805, aged 68.

Samuel White, son of Mark White, born in Acton, 1744. Was selectman in Westford, 1781-82; he removed 1786, and the following year was elected to the same office in Cavendish. He was a man of excellent character and great influence; deacon of the church. His son, Samuel, born in this town went with him. He gave his name to Whitesville, where he carried on the trade of a saddler. His son John, also born here, settled in Cavendish.

Capt. Aaron Parker, removed in 1788, and was selectman in 1790.

Isaac Parker, in the list of freemen for 1788. Son of Moses and born in 1760. Died in Byron, N. Y.

Nathan Boynton, 1799. One bearing this name was in New Ipswich, 1766. It cannot be determined whether the two are identical, but such is the probable fact.

Jeremiah Hildreth, 1788. Returned to Westford about 1794.

Timothy Adams, 1782; Thomas Chamberlin, Elijah Chamberlin, Ebenezer Stone, 1781; Thomas Cummings, Oliver Harris, James Hall. The latter was a British soldier, born at Ashton-under-line, England, who during the retreat of the Regulars from Concord, April 19, 1775, voluntarily surrendered to the Provincials and came to Westford and worked for Ephraim Hidreth, 3rd, whose daughter he married in 1784.

Thomas G. Hildreth; 1788; Nehemiah Green, (?) Isaac Green, Timothy Stone, John Stone, Isaac Patch, Nathaniel Hildreth, Samuel Adams, 3rd, trader (returned), Isaac Heald, Benjamin Wright, Jacob Abbot, Solomon Fletcher, 1787.

Isaac Parker, physician, son of Aaron, Jr., and Dorothy, and born 1752.

Ludlow. In examining the records of this town it is found that the names of Westford men who were early in

Cavendish are repeated, showing that they were concerned in the settlement of the two towns. The first town meeting in Ludlow was held March 31, 1792—ten years after the organization of Cavendish.

Among the grantees of Ludlow were: Josiah Fletcher, Jesse Fletcher, Simeon Read, David Bixby, Levi Bixby, Thomas Bixby, Thomas Chamberlin, Joseph Chamberlin, Ezekiel Wright, Elijah Chamberlin.

These did not all remove there, but they bought land with the intention of going or sending their sons or others to occupy it. Josiah Fletcher, who was the first town clerk of Cavendish, was proprietors' clerk for 1788 and 1790. At the first town meeting Jesse Fletcher was chosen town clerk and first selectman, and Josiah Fletcher, town treasurer; the former remaining in office for sixteen or seventeen years. He was representative in 1798 and 1799.

Simeon Read and Thomas Bixby were a committee to divide the town into school districts in 1794. The former was son of John Read, and was a soldier of the Revolution.

Thomas Bixby, son of Asa, married in Ludlow about 1787, and his wife and five children died in 1825, probably of some epidemic disease.

Stephen Read. The first town meeting was held at his house, and for four successive years. A soldier of the Revolution. At the battle of Bunker Hill.

John Hadley, grand juryman, 1792; William Caldwell, highway surveyor, 1792; Levi Bixby, hog reeve, 1792; Joseph Bixby, married in Ludlow, 1791; Zebulon Spalding, about 1801, son of Zebulon; Phineas W. Spalding, about 1810, son of Zebulon.

To Mount Holly. This town was incorporated November 19, 1792. At the first town meeting Lieut. Silas Proctor was chosen selectman, and John Hadley grand juror. Lieutenant Proctor was at first a resident of Ludlow, but when an act of incorporation was passed for Mt. Holly, the western portion of Ludlow was assigned to it, and his farm near Healdville was transferred to the new town, in which he was long an active and influential citizen. The people entrusted him with various offices for many years. John Hadley also filled places of trust for a long time.

Jonas Hadley was a lister in 1794 and '95; selectman in 1796 and '97; and one of committee to find the centre of the town and a place for a public building in 1798.

Jonas Holden was a surveyor in 1794.

Gershom Fletcher. He removed to Bridgewater, N. H., where he died in 1814; Stephen Fletcher, probably son of Gershom, is mentioned 1801, when he was highway surveyor.

Amos Hadley, brother of Jonas, was sent back to Westford in 1804, to be supported by the town. He was in some way disabled, perhaps by lameness, and unable to work.

Joseph Bixby, surveyor in 1798.

Simon Lawrence, probably the son of Simon of Westford, married Hannah Wilson in Mt. Holly, 1800; Zachariah Lawrence, 1810; perhaps a brother of Simon.

To Plymouth. Walter Fletcher, Reuben Fletcher, 1805; Henry Fletcher, 1800; Isaac Fletcher, 1815. Removed to Enosburgh, Vt., 1819; and to Berkshire, Vt., 1820; Amos Boynton, Isaiah Boynton, 1792.

To Londonderry. Thomas Read.

To Weathersfield. Benjamin Read, son of Benjamin and Abigail; Samuel Adams.

To Reading. Ebenezer Chandler, Jonathan Jones.

To Putney. Leonard Spalding, about 1864; also his two sons, Leonard, who afterward settled in Dummerston, and Reuben. He first went to Westmoreland. Was distinguished for his patriotic exertions in the struggle for independence.

Samuel Minot, town treasurer, in 1778, captain and deacon.

Timothy Underwood, captain of a company of miutemen in 1775; also his sons, Joseph, who was a soldier on Long Island under General Putnam; Timothy, who afterward settled in Westborough, Massachusetts; Phinehas, who settled in New York City; and Russell, who removed to New York State.

To Brattleborough. Benjamin Butterfield, who had resided a short time in Lunenburg; associate judge at the famous trial in Westminster, Vt. He was appointed second assistant justice in 1772. At the "Westminster Massacre," March 4, 1775, a ball entered the sleeve of Benjamin Butterfield, son of the justice.* Jesse Hadley, Ebenezer Hadley.

To Bennington. Jacob Prescott.

THE MIGRATION TO MAINE.

This State, as well as Vermont, attracted to itself many who wished to seek their fortunes in the wide world. Its extensive sea-coast and good harbors had been early discovered and explored, and numerous settlements had been made; but the development of its vast resources was scarcely begun at the period of the Revolution. On the return of peace and the establishment of the Union, many resorted thither to subdue its wild lands and make homes for themselves along its noble rivers and on its beautiful hills, from many of which the ocean can be seen in all its beauty and grandeur. Among them were many from this town, in whose history and achievements there is no room for disappointment or shame.

To Portland. Stephen Hall, son of the first minister.

Sanford. Joseph Temple.

Farmington. Samuel Chandler, Jacob Chandler, Moses Chandler, Levi Spalding.

To Anson. Joel Fletcher, son of Pelatiah.

Wilton. Jeremiah Fletcher, Thomas Flint, Henry Chandler, Moses Chandler, son of William and Susanna.

To Winthrop. Nehemiah Fletcher (returned), Joseph Chandler, Henry Chandler.

---

* See Hall's History of Eastern Vermont, p. 232.

To Pittston. Isaac Fletcher.
Greene. Silas Richardson, about 1808.
Mount Desert. Silas Parker.
"*The Holmes Purchase.*" Samuel Parker.
Union. Waldron Stone.
Oldtown. Samuel Wright.
Benton. Henry Spalding.
Penobscot. Rev. Philip Spalding.
Dead River. Asa Fletcher.
Bath. Abel Boynton, a lawyer.
Augusta. Nathan Oliver.
Litchfield. Abijah Richardson.

MASSACHUSETTS.

The contribution of Westford to other towns of this Commonwealth, especially to those whose incorporation took place at a more recent date, has been large and significant.

To Templeton. Caleb Fletcher, Joel Fletcher (brothers), Joshua Wright, Ebenezer Wright (brothers), are named in the first tax-list of that town in 1763. Joel Fletcher was captain of a militia company, and was in the battle of Bunker Hill. Also a deacon of the Baptist Church. Joshua Wright was selectman eight or nine years, and treasurer five years. Ebenezer was selectman and town clerk seventeen years. Joel Fletcher was representative several times.

Phinehas Read.

Benjamin Read, son of Joshua, born in 1760. "He served three years in the Revolution. Followed the occupation of a tanner. He was a man of distinction and much wealth." Town treasurer nine years. Selectman.

Zaccheus Barrett.(?) The first town treasurer, 1762.

Philip Atwood, Isaac Needham, Moses Wright (?), Edwin Wright.

To Littleton. Parker Underwood, Peter Wright, Ephraim Wright, Isaac Wright, Francis Kidder, captain; Abel

Fletcher, deacon; Joseph Fletcher, Asa Fletcher, James Dutton, Solomon Keyes, 1807; Isaac Spalding, Dr. Jeremiah Robinson, Joshua Blodgett.

To Groton. John Cummings, son of deacon John; David Fletcher, 1796; Ezekiel Fletcher, 1766; John Butterfield, Oliver Spalding, Oliver Fletcher, about 1764; John Keep, Silas Lawrence, John Blodgett.

To Dunstable. Joseph Fletcher, John Wright, Josiah Spalding, son of Abel; Samuel T. Spalding, George W. Spalding, Willard Hall, Nathan Procter, James Spalding.

To Tyngsborough. Matthew Scribner, Joel Keyes, Jonas Keyes, Elihu Read (returned), Hezekiah Hildreth, Jacob Kidder.

To Pepperell. Abijah Boynton, Abiel Richardson, Abel Parker, afterward to Jaffrey; Samuel Horsley and his sons Aaron, Timothy, Joshua, John, Stephen and Thomas; Josiah and Moses Spalding, each to Pepperell and then to Townsend; Hosea Hildreth.

To Townsend. Josiah Burge, Oliver Procter, Joseph Rumrill, Oliver Hildreth, Eleazar Taylor, first to Temple; Peter Butterfield, Eleazar Butterfield, Samuel Spalding, Josiah Spalding, Samuel Horsley, Moses Spalding, Aaron Keyes, Cyrus Fletcher, Isaac Procter.(?)

To Ashby. Waldron Stone, lived a while in Townsend, where he married Rachel Campbell and moved to Union, Me.; Abraham Wright, Elijah Wright, Stephen Mead, Dr. Allen Flagg, Jonathan Carver (returned), Isaiah Prescott, lived there ten years and returned; Thomas Carver, physician.

To Ashburnham. Jonathan Spalding, James Spalding, Benjamin Spalding, afterward to Jaffrey and Marlborough, N. H.; Lyman Fletcher, Joshua Fletcher, John Bates, about 1755.

To Shirley. Oliver Fletcher (returned), Henry Chandler, son of Isaac.

To Harvard. Jonathan Procter, Jabez Keep, Jr., Capt. Jabez Keep.

To Lunenburg. Benjamin Butterfield, afterward to Brattleborough.
To Fitchburg. Ephraim Spalding, Timothy Wilson.
Stow. Nathaniel Cowdry.
Shrewsbury. Rev. Benjamin Stone.
Chesterfield. William Read, son of John.
Bolton. Rev. Phinehas Wright.
Hardwick. Joseph Hooker, Ebenezer Butterfield.
Randolph. Joshua Prescott, Aaron A. Prescott.
Concord. John Keyes.
Bedford. Caleb Blake (returned), Phinehas Chamberlin.
To Upton. Lemuel Perham.
Acton. Samuel Keyes.
Sterling. James Pollard Patten, Joshua Abbot Jewett, Jr., George Davis.
To Westminster. Joseph Spalding.
Rutland. Oliver Wheeler, Jonathan Fletcher.
Salem. Edmund Boynton.
New Bedford. Oliver Prescott, Judge of Probate.
Lowell. Ebenezer Wright, Horatio Fletcher, William A. Wright.
To Marblehead. Joseph Bixby, son of David.
Northborough. Silas Meriam.
Boston. Thomas Craft, Simon Hunt (died in Quincy), Timothy Hunt, Thomas Davis.
To Belmont. Jonathan Varnum Fletcher.
Charlestown. Jacob Wright, son of Joseph; Leonard Read, son of Joel.
To Cambridge. Levi Parker.
Warren. Capt. Luther Trowbridge, and afterward to Tennessee.
To Deerfield. Luther B. Lincoln, representative, died in 1855.
To Dedham. Benjamin F. Keyes, Joseph Wright.
Lawrence. Rufus Read, son of Asa; Henry A. Prescott.

To Gardner. Horace Parker, M. D.; continued in the practice of medicine seven years and died in 1829, in his thirty-fourth year.

OTHER STATES.

To Norfolk, Conn. Aaron Keyes, son of Joash.
Sodus, N. Y. Amos Read.
Richmond, Va. Jabez Parker, M. D.
Athens, Ohio. Leonard Jewett.
New York. John Jewett, Jr.
Wilmington, N. C. Stephen Keyes, teacher.
California. Joshua Keyes.
Lansingburg, N. Y. Benjamin Fletcher.
New York State. Theodore Wood.
Milwaukee, Wis. Cortes Reed.
Sycamore, Ill. Warren Wright.
Ohio. Jotham B. Wright.
Westville, Otsego Co., N. Y. Theodore Woodward.
Monona, Iowa. Parker Woodward.
Indiana. Lemuel Fletcher.
Granville, N. Y. Silas Spalding, a soldier of the Revolution.
To Western Reserve. Rev. Phinehas Spalding, son of James, a Baptist clergyman.
To Virginia. John Patten, Oliver Patten.
Florida. Harrison Reed, son of Seth. Born in Littleton in 1813. His father removed to Westford when he was less than two years old. Governor of Florida in 1876.

CHAPTER V.

FROM 1800 TO 1860 — THE WAR OF 1812 — ITEMS COLLECTED FROM THE TOWN RECORDS.

IN the last chapter the narrative has been brought down to the close of the last century. The going out of so many men soon after the war, took from the town both capital and executive force; and although there is no account of the fact in the enumeration, for want of space, it is yet true that many noble *women*, born on these hillsides, went forth to be helpers of the sturdy pioneer whose axe leveled the forests in the midst of which, in due time, he provided for his family the comforts, if not the luxuries, of a good home. The mothers and the daughters must not be overlooked, in making up our estimate of the value of the contribution made by the early Massachusetts towns to the welfare of the younger States. The pen of the historian has not yet shown in its fullness the influence of woman in the development of New England civilization. It is, indeed, a force too subtle to be expressed in words or measured by statistics. But, however hard it may be to define it, its potency cannot be denied.

For two centuries or more these towns kept on giving in this way, and as the area of the West broadened and the tide of immigration swept onward to the great valley of the Mississippi, all the towns of New England felt the impulse, and gave their best blood and brain to help found those new republics which have since joined the sisterhood of States. In consequence of this the growth in population and wealth in the old towns was necessarily slow; and, accordingly, it appears that this town, in the year 1800, had but *seventy-four* persons more than it had in the census of 1776, twenty-four years before. Meantime, the expenses of supporting the *poor* were large and constantly increasing. As yet agriculture was the chief source of wealth, and the markets were hard to reach and comparatively meagre in their demands.

THE WAR OF 1812.

On the 19th of June, 1812, the government of the United States issued a proclamation of war against Great Britain. "Upon the declaration of war the few regular troops then in the service of the United States were sent off on an expedition into Upper Canada. To man the fortresses on the maritime frontier, the President called upon the Governors of States for militia to be placed under officers of his own appointment. Governor Strong of Massachusetts, Governor Griswold of Connecticut and Governor Jones of Rhode Island resisted the demand, on the two-fold ground that neither of the constitutional exigencies had arisen, and that the militia could not be compelled to serve under any other than their own officers, with the exception of the President himself, when personally in the field. . . . The misunderstanding between the national executive and the executives of these States . . . embarrassed the measures of the State governments. Massachusetts, Connecticut and Rhode Island were at this time destitute of the protection of national troops and exposed to the ravages of an incensed enemy, with scarcely any other than their own resources, and these were constantly decreasing by an onerous system of taxation for the national treasury." (Holmes' Annals, pp. 449 and 467.)

Although "New England experienced very little actual war within its borders, yet it felt its pressure heavily in the paralysis of its peculiar industries and the continual drain upon its wealth of men and money. . . . From the spring of 1813 until the close of the contest, British squadrons were hovering along our coasts and threatening the destruction of our maritime cities and villages. The year 1814 was a specially trying one for New England. The British government had determined and prepared, at the beginning of that year, to make the campaign a vigorous, sharp and decisive one on land and sea."

"The war was unpopular in Massachusetts, and the people were not enthusiastic in its prosecution. Caleb Strong, then Governor, was intensely opposed to it, and it was not until all the territory east of the Penobscot River in the district of Maine was in possession of the enemy that any energetic measures were taken for its defense. On the 6th of September (1814) Governor Strong had issued his orders for the whole of the State militia of all arms to be in readiness to march to Boston at a moment's notice. By the middle of that month there were some five thousand State troops of all arms in service at Boston and on the forts and batteries in the harbor and vicinity, and were retained in service until the middle of November."

Men from Westford were engaged in this war, but the references to it on the records are few and brief. It is known that the company of militia then organized here went to Boston, but the names of officers and men cannot easily be obtained.*

"July 7, 1812. Voted that the treasurer of this town be and he hereby is authorized and required to pay out of the town moneys to each and every soldier who shall produce sufficient evidence of his having been in the actual service of the United States in consequence of the present detachment from this town, whether he be detached in person or takes the place of another, such sum as in addition to what he may receive from the United States and this State, will make the pay of each private amount to twelve dollars per month, and

---

* The original muster-rolls are in Washington, having been sent thither by request of the Pension Department, and no copies or duplicates are held in the office of the Adjutant-General at Boston. But many names of individual soldiers have been gathered from various sources and put upon record in the office.

of non-commissioned officers and musicians to be as much from the town as a private."

"September 5, 1814. Voted to give a bounty to the soldiers that are drafted or may be drafted of four dollars per month when in actual service for the year 1814."

This is all that can be gleaned from the records concerning that war. The names of a few men who were in the service have been ascertained, but the list is brief.

In Lieut.-Col. Jonathan Page's company of detached militia, stationed at Fort Warren, in Boston Harbor, from September 13th to November 7, 1814, were Thomas Pearson, lieutenant; Asa Bixby, Joseph Brown, John Dudley, Jonas Kemp, Robert McGuire, William Parker, Noah Shattuck, 2nd, Joel Wright and Ebenezer Wright. In Captain Abel Tarbell's company, stationed at the same place for the same time, were Francis Leighton, Ephraim Leighton, Jedediah Robbins and Jonathan Swallow. In Captain Stephen Tolman's company, at the same place, were Bethuel Read and Tilley Allen.

Timothy Fletcher was also at Fort Warren for three months.

Oliver Fletcher was killed in battle near Sackett's Harbor. James Kemp was killed and Jonas Kemp was severely wounded in the same battle, probably.

Thomas Spalding enlisted in the service and rose to the rank of captain.

Walter Abbot was a lieutenant on board the United States frigate Chesapeake, and was wounded in the action of that ship with the frigate Shannon, June 1, 1813. He died from the effects of his wound July 12, 1825.

Several men from the north part of the town were members of the artillery company of Groton and served in the war; but as no muster-roll of that company can be found in the archives of Groton, their names cannot all be ascertained. There is, however, good proof that the following persons were enrolled and served at Boston: Imla Keyes, Thomas

Prescott, Roswell Read (drummer), Caleb Wight, Theodore Woodward and Parker Wright.

It seems probable, too, that William Ditson served at Boston, but perhaps not in the Groton company.

Abel Boynton, son of Abel, born in Westford, settled in Bath, Me. He was captain of a company of cavalry in Bath during the war.

ITEMS COLLECTED FROM THE RECORDS.

January 20, 1817. "Voted that the overseers of the poor lay before the town at the March meeting the expenses of the poor the past year. Voted that the selectmen lay before the town the *whole expenses* of the town the past year." This appears to be the first time that these boards were called upon to make a report of this kind.

October 16, 1820. John Abbot, Esq., was chosen " to meet in convention with other towns to revise or alter the constitution of this commonwealth." This convention met in Boston, November 15, 1820. It submitted to the people fourteen articles of amendment, and this town, at a meeting held on the second Monday of April, A. D. 1821, voted yea on nine of them, and nay on the other five.

"November 2, 1823. Voted that the selectmen lay out in arms and equipments the sum of fifty-six dollars, being the residue of the unexpended conditional exempt money in the town treasury, to be under their care for the use of the company of militia. Voted that the town give leave that a stove be put in the meeting house, the same to be made secure from fire and free of expense to the town." *

Poor-Farm. "April 5, 1824. Voted that the town purchase John Read's farm for the sum of $2500." The committee to purchase it were Eliakim Hutchins, Samuel

---

* Heretofore the men had borne the discomfort of cold feet, but the women had foot-stoves, being the favored sex. It was the meeting-house, undoubtedly, and not the stove, that was to be made secure from fire.

Richardson, Zaccheus Read and John Abbot. They had been appointed at a previous meeting to devise the best means of maintaining the poor, and upon their recommendation the town passed the vote cited above and authorized them to buy the farm and stock it. They were also empowered in the following September to receive proposals for a master and mistress to take charge of the workhouse and to report the best and most proper regulations for the same. On the first day of November they made two reports, one in regard to stocking the farm, and one comprising "Bye-laws, or Orders and Regulations of Westford Workhouse." The first declares that the sum necessary to the purchase of farming-tools, provisions, household furniture and stock to commence carrying on the farm will amount to $500, and recommends that the town borrow this sum for the purpose. The by-laws assigned to the board of overseers the inspection and government of the workhouse, with full power to appoint a master and needful assistants; the said master to be a man of temperance, prudence and good moral character. The overseers were required to meet at the house once in two months, and one of them to make a visit to it once in two weeks. The master was required to keep a book wherein should be recorded the names of all inmates and a book of accounts, and also an inventory of all personal property. He is enjoined to reward the faithful and industrious and to punish the idle and disobedient at his discretion by immediate confinement without any food other than bread and water. The Lord's day to be strictly observed and kept. "The use of all spirituous liquors and any liquor, part of which is spirituous, is strictly prohibited, except when ordered by the physician, overseer or master." The first master was Jonathan Hosmer, and the second Otis Haywood.

Copying. "March 7, 1825. Voted to choose a committee to copy off and regulate the town book of records of births and deaths. Voted Benjamin Osgood regulate and copy off town book of records of births and deaths." In accordance with this vote the late Doctor Osgood copied the record as it now stands in a large volume of several hundred pages, and as it was authorized by the town it must be deemed genuine and valid. This volume brings the record down to about the year 1840.

Idleness and Intemperance. "March 6, 1826. Voted that the overseers of the poor continue to take further measures in relation to suppressing idleness, intemperance and profligacy in this place by causing such persons as possess those habits to be sent to the workhouse in Westford, or to the County House of Correction at Concord, and to take measures to retake any person who may elope from said workhouse."

The report of the committee to reckon with the town treasurer for the year 1825, dated April 26, 1826, is recorded on the town book for the first time; also the report of the overseers of the poor. This last shows the reduction of expenses for supporting the poor that year to be $407.33, which saving is thus tacitly attributed to the policy of buying a farm for the town.

Project for a New County. The town held a meeting April 7, 1828, " pursuant to a resolve of the legislature, approved by the governor, March 8, 1828, to wit: 'Shall a new county be formed of the towns of Royalston, Winchenden, Athol, Templeton, Gardner, Westminster, Ashburnham, Fitchburg, Leominster, Lunenburg, Princeton, Hubbardston, Phillipston, Lancaster, Bolton and Harvard from the county of Worcester; and the towns of Groton, Shirley, Pepperell, Ashby and Townsend from the county of Middlesex' . . . and voted in the negative, ninety votes being cast and not one in the affirmative."

In 1831 the town voted on a proposed amendment to the State constitution as follows: Yeas, 8; Nays, 80. In 1835 the selectmen were made a committee to build one stone bridge in a year across Stony brook, "until they are all constructed with stone."

New Burying-Ground. In 1836 the town voted " to grant to Bela Wright and others the privilege of a burying-ground on the north road, between Caleb Wight's and Reuben Wright's, which is to be free of expense to the town."

Poor-House. "April 3, 1837. Voted to choose a building committee of five persons to superintend the building of a poor-house. Voted that Abram Prescott, Levi Heywood, Asia Nutting, Samuel H. Nichols and Horatio Fletcher be said committee." They recommended the erection of a house 39 feet by 40 feet, two stories high, with buttery and well-room in the shed. It was built in the summer and autumn of 1837. The contractor was Daniel W. Hartwell, who failed to finish it at the time agreed upon, October 20th, and the town voted, November 13th, that the committee be instructed to superintend the finishing of it and settle with Mr. Hartwell as they think proper. He had agreed to build it for $2400, but the committee allowed the additional sum of $37.40, and finished it at a total expense for the house and shed of $3002.45. The overseers were authorized to buy new furniture for it, April 2, 1838, and probably it was occupied about that time, Mr. Parker being the master. The number of persons assisted in and out of the poor-house, between the first day of March, 1839, and the eighth day of February, 1840, was fifty-five.

Common Land. In 1837 a committee was appointed to look up the common land, if any there be. It was in 1832 that Asia Nutting took up and fenced a lot of ten acres in Shipley Swamp, near the head of Nubanussuck Pond. This is the last that is recorded in regard to it.

Disposition of Surplus Revenue. May 15, 1837, the town voted to receive its proportion of the surplus revenue of the United States in deposit, and to comply with the several acts passed by the Legislature respecting it. Abram Prescott was appointed agent to receive and receipt for the money to the State Treasurer, and required to pay over the same to the town treasurer, who, in turn, was required to pay with it all outstanding notes against this town and to loan the remainder on good security.

Printing. "March 4, 1839. Voted that the expenses of the town shall be printed for the future, and for 1838, by the selectmen of that year." *

Annual Reckoning. November 11, 1839, the town voted that the committee chosen to reckon with the town treasurer shall do so "on the second or third week in February and that this vote remain in force until repealed with regard to all further committees chosen for that purpose."

Fencing the Common. September 11, 1839. "Whereas it is desirable that the common in the middle of Westford should be fenced, and individuals are willing and ready to subscribe for the purpose of putting up stone posts with one rail between each post: Now, therefore, we the subscribers agree to pay the sums set against our names to such person as shall be chosen at a meeting of the subscribers to be called by J. W. P. Abbot, as soon as twelve names shall be placed upon this paper.

John Abbot	$25 00	
Ephraim Abbot	6 00	
J. W. P. Abbot	5 00	
S. D. Fletcher	5 50	
Trueworthy Keyes	5 00	
Nathan S. Hamblin	7 00	
B. F. Osgood	2 00	
H. P. Herrick	1 50	
Wm. W. Goodhue	3 00	
Augustus Whiting, N. Y.	10 00	
Otis Longley	1 00	
John Davis	50	
Joseph Whitmore	2 00	
Nathan S. Hamblin	50	
John Cutter	50	
Amt. carried forward,	$74 50	
Amt. brought forward,	$74 50	
Joseph Hildreth	2 25	
Albert Leighton	3 00	
Samuel H. Nichols	2 00	
Walter Wright	1 00	
Henry Herrick	2 00	
Avery Prescott	3 00	
Leonard Luce	2 00	
Ira G. Richardson	1 00	
Imla Lawrence	2 00	
Thomas Davis	2 00	
Benjamin Osgood	2 00	
Francis Leighton	1 50	
Jonas Prescott	1 50	
Josiah Webber	1 00	
Jonathan F. Parker	1 00	
	$102 25	

(Records, vol. vii., p. 377.)

---

* In 1840 the edition included 300 copies. Mr. John M. Fletcher has a collection of these annual reports nearly complete. It is the only collection known to the compiler.

"March 2, 1840. Voted that John Abbot and others may build a fence around the common, provided the town be put to no expense on account of the same."

"The trees on the common in the middle of Westford were set out in 1839, and in the fall of 1841 the fence was built by individual subscription.

"JOHN W. P. ABBOT, Town Clerk."
(Records, vol. vi., p. 370.)

"This certifies that Eliakim Hutchins, Jr., on the twen-seventh day of November, A. D. 1847, set out on the southwest side of the common, opposite the Academy, all the spruce and pine trees in the two rows, and this record is made in commemoration of the same.

"JOHN W. P. ABBOT, Town Clerk."
(Records, vol. vii., p. 120.)

Sale of the Land in Plymouth, N. H. In the report of the treasurer for the year ending February 5, 1842, there is this item: Cash received for the Plymouth land, $49.00. Thus, after a period of fifty-seven years — 1784 to 1841 — this land was sold for this small sum, and the mention of it is no more found in the records. John W. P. Abbot was empowered to give the deed in behalf of the town.

Copying Record of Marriages. "March 2, 1846. Voted and chose John W. P. Abbot to collect and copy the marriage records into a book." *

Appended to this is his own certified copy of returns of marriages of Westford parties, which took place in other towns of the State, made by other town clerks, pursuant to an act of the Legislature of 1857.

Celebration at Acton. "September 23, 1851. Voted and chose John Cutter, Samuel Fletcher, Solomon Richardson,

---

* Mr. Abbot attended faithfully to this service and copied them with his own hand in a suitable book bearing this inscription: "Record of Marriages Collected from the Town Books in Westford from 1728 to 1845. John W. P. Abbot, Town Clerk. April 1st. 1847."

D. C. Butterfield, Jonas Prescott and George E. Burt as a committee to confer with the Acton committee." This was to "take action respecting the coming celebration in that town." The town was invited by its committee to be present and participate in the ceremonies at the completion of a monument to be erected in Acton to the memory of Capt. Isaac Davis, who fell at Concord Bridge. Through the influence of Rev. James T. Woodbury, the Legislature, during the session of 1851, made an appropriation of $2000 for that purpose.

Map of the Town. "March 1, 1852. Voted that the selectmen be authorized to procure 500 copies of a map of this town agreeable to Mr. E. Symmes' proposal."

"Nov. 13, 1854. Voted that Edward Symmes be authorized to print, at his own expense and for his own benefit, 100 extra copies of the map of the town of Westford." This map was published in 1855, from surveys made by Mr. Symmes.

Barn at the Poor-Farm. "May 1, 1857. Voted to choose a committee of three to take measures to build a barn or repair the old one at the Poor-Farm the coming year." The treasurer was authorized to borrow $1500 to defray the expense. Nathan S. Hamblin, Charles L. Fletcher and Timothy P. Wright were the building committee. They asked for instructions in April, 1858, and the barn was built some time in that year, for they presented their report March 7, 1859, which was accepted and placed on file.

CHAPTER VI.

THE WAR OF THE REBELLION.

IT may well be doubted whether a war was ever undertaken that involved such stupendous issues and was attended with such momentous consequences as the War of the Rebellion. It is scarcely within the power of rhetoric or demonstration to set them forth too vividly and strongly.

On the part of the Union army it was a war in defence of our homes and our constitutional rights; a war in vindication of all that was dear to us in our political and educational systems, and, in the last analysis, of all that was valuable to us in our Christian faith. It involved the question whether might makes right; whether liberty is the birthright of every human soul, however lowly; whether the all-embracing air and the vivifying sun in the heavens are God's free gift to all his creatures; whether every man, while submitting to the requirements of just law, has a right to himself, to the ownership of his own faculties of body and mind—the right which is inalienable and untransferable to liberty and the pursuit of happiness. It was to decide this point that every battle was fought. Could there be a more momentous strife? Of all the questions that relate to man's earthly destiny, is there one more important? Bad as war is, in itself considered, always and everywhere; repugnant as it is to every humane feeling, and to every principle of the gospel, it is surely in keeping with the facts to say that no more cogent and justifiable reasons ever existed for taking up arms in defence of freedom and home than the reasons which led the patriot soldiers of the North to go forth to victory or to death.

The early wars in the history of the world were wars of conquest mainly—the effort of the stronger tribes or clans to establish a supremacy over the weaker ones.

The campaigns of Alexander and Napoleon were carried on in the interest of a personal ambition. The end sought was the aggrandizement of the leader or of the nation which he represented. Occasionally, indeed, there was a higher motive; sometimes a veritable stroke in behalf of liberty. But in turning the pages of history, where can be found an impulse so fervidly *patriotic*, so undeniably just and true as that which governed the Union army in the memorable contest?

The bombardment of Fort Sumter sent a thrill to every loyal Northern heart that will not cease to be felt until the generation then on the stage shall have passed away. At that time the air was full of anxious forebodings, and men spoke seriously of the gravity of the situation and wondered what would be the result. The winter of 1860-'61 wore away in dreadful anxiety, and on the breezes of spring came the sulphurous breath of war, mingling unnaturally and reluctantly with the fragrance of the violet and the arbutus.

On the 19th of April, 1861, the Sixth Regiment of Massachusetts troops, whose homes were in Lowell, Lawrence and the vicinity, hastening to the aid of the national government, marched through the streets of Baltimore, Md., leaving their dead cruelly slain by the minions of slavery in that disloyal city. This was the first sacrifice made by the defenders of freedom upon the altar whereon, in the succeeding years, so many choice spirits laid themselves down in death for her sake. The great majority of the people of this town were filled with indignation at this unprovoked assassination. Clear proof of this was shown by the eagerness with which men hastened to enlist under the old flag. On the 22nd of April, three days after that occurrence, the names of twenty-one men, all residents of the town and many of them born here, were on the enlistment-roll of what became, a few days later, Company C, Sixteenth Regiment Massachusetts Volunteers, Captain Leander G. King, and were quartered at Groton Junction, now Ayer, for equipment and drill. These were the earliest to enlist, and others joined them soon after.

Subsequently five men of the twenty-one gave their lives to their country, namely: Nathan D. Bicknell, James T. Flint, John Harris, John F. Richards and Patrick Sheahan.

Raising of the Flag-Staff on the Common. " On the eighteenth of April, eighteen hundred and sixty-one, two subscription papers were opened to raise funds for the above purpose, and the persons hereafter named paid the sums set against their names as follows:

John W. P. Abbot .	$12 00	*Amt. brought forward,*	$89 98
John Burbeck . .	1 00	Eli Tower . . .	8 00
John Cutter . .	1 00	Daniel Flagg . .	8 00
Augustus Bunce .	50	George Heywood .	8 00
Susan Howarth .	1 00	Samuel B. Hicks .	50
Rev. E. R. Hodgman	1 00	M. H. Fletcher . .	5 00
J. Barnard Hildreth.	50	George H. Prescott .	8 00
T. H. Hamblet . .	1 00	Dea. A. Rugg . .	1 00
Joseph Hildreth .	2 00	S. D. Fletcher . .	10 00
A. W. Cummings .	5 00	Caleb Wight . .	2 00
J. B. Fletcher . .	10 00	D. A. Dow . . .	2 00
John William Abbot	5 00	John Lanktree . .	5 00
Charles L. Fletcher .	1 00	Jacob Smith . .	2 00
Abel L. Davis . .	1 00	Luther Prescott .	2 00
Rev. George M. Rice	1 00	Calvin Howard . .	2 00
Daniel Falls . .	1 00	John W. Cummings.	2 00
Nathan S. Hamblin .	8 00	Solomon Richardson	8 00
Wm. H. H. Burbeck .	1 00	Zaccheus Read . .	10 00
Oliver Wright . .	8 00	Jesse Wright . .	8 00
Myron Rand . .	1 00	John Rand . .	8 00
Henry A. Hildreth .	8 00	Samuel N. Burbeck .	50
Moses Caryl . .	1 00	Samuel Wiley . .	2 00
Henry Herrick . .	1 00	Peter Swallow . .	5 00
Edwin Caryl . .	1 00	Rev. Leonard Luce .	2 00
George Hutchins .	1 00	Amos Hildreth, 2nd .	1 00
J. B. Hildreth . .	1 00	Gilman J. Wright .	50
Edward Prescott .	2 00	H. A. Hutchinson .	50
William Chandler .	1 00	George T. Day . .	8 00
Cyrus Hamlin . .	1 00	Arthur Wright . .	1 00
Asa Hildreth . .	5 00	Jonas Prescott . .	2 00
Abijah Fletcher .	15 00	Francis K. Proctor .	5 00
J. B. Reed . . .	1 00	William Agnew .	1 00
Eliel Heywood . .	1 00	C. B. Reed . . .	1 00
S. D. Fletcher . .	5 48	William Taylor . .	1 00
Amt. carried forward,	$89 98	Total	$179 98 "

"April 22, 1861. A meeting of the subscribers was held at the hall of the school-house, No. 1, and the following named persons, to wit: Sherman D. Fletcher, Marcellus H. Fletcher and George T. Day, were chosen a committee to collect the subscriptions, erect a flag-staff, procure a flag and do all other things necessary and proper to complete the work." *

"May 18, 1861.—Saturday forenoon. All things being ready, the flag-staff was raised by Samuel Fletcher, of Graniteville, aided by many citizens of the village and other parts of the town. At two o'clock the stars and stripes were run up amid the cheers and hurrahs of a large collection of men, women and children from all parts of the town who had assembled to witness the patriotic scene. The chairman of the committee then called for a song, and "The Flag of Our Union" was sung with a will. An appropriate and patriotic address was given by the chairman, and then the assembly went into the hall under the First Parish Church. The chairman again called the meeting to order and prayer was offered by Rev. Edwin R. Hodgman. Speeches were made by Revs. Leonard Luce, George M. Rice and Edwin R. Hodgman; also by Col. George F. Sawtelle, of Lowell, and Luther Prescott, Esq., of Forge Village, and after singing another patriotic song the assembly returned to the common, and gathering around the flag-staff, with the flag flying aloft, pledged themselves anew to stand by their country and government through weal or woe in the struggle just commenced, and then separated, after giving twelve hearty and rousing cheers *for the whole Union.*

"J. W. P. ABBOT, Chn. Selectmen." †

---

* The flag was purchased of Col. William Beals for the sum of sixty dollars. The main staff or pole was furnished by Abijah Fletcher for fifteen dollars. It is said that he cut the tree for it on his own lot, near Cold Spring.

† It should be added to Mr. Abbot's account of this transaction that Company C, Sixteenth Regiment, in which the twenty men from Westford had just enlisted under the command of Captain L. G. King, were present on that day and took part in the exercises.

This was the inauguration of the conflict here, and this the covenant of the people to be loyal and true. How well that pledge was kept the subsequent action of the town will demonstrate. It is safe to say that the record is an honorable one, and that no citizen will ever blush with shame when he reads the account of patient endurance and heroic sacrifice even unto death. It was a service illumined by the light of intelligent conviction, warmed by the fire of a true patriotism, and made immortal by the surrender of life at the call of duty.

ACTION OF THE TOWN IN REGARD TO THE WAR.

"1861, April 29. At a legal meeting held this day the following preamble and votes were passed:

"Whereas the President of the United States, by proclamation dated the 15th of April, 1861, did call forth a portion of the militia of the several States of the Union to enable him to suppress combinations existing in certain States therein enumerated, against the government and due execution of the laws;

"And, whereas several citizens of this town have manifested their loyalty and patriotism by volunteering their services to the State to be held in readiness to answer any further call that may be made by the President of the United States; therefore,

"Voted that the Board of Selectmen be authorized to furnish clothing, small arms and other articles of personal convenience and comfort to such men as have already, or may hereafter volunteer; also, to render all needful assistance to the families of such volunteers as in the opinion of said Board may be required to make them comfortable in food, clothing and medical aid during the absence of their heads;

"That the selectmen keep a separate account of all money disbursed from this appropriation and report in detail at the next annual meeting, or at an earlier day if the town so require. To enable the Board of Selectmen to carry out these conditions, voted that the treasurer be and he is hereby authorized and empowered to borrow from time to time in the name of the inhabitants of Westford, on the requisition of the selectmen, a sum or sums not exceeding fifteen hundred dollars:

"That the sum of ten dollars per month be paid to each volunteer, so long as he shall serve without disgrace, and that the first month's pay be furnished as soon as he is mustered into the United States service.

"Chose Sherman D. Fletcher, Marcellus H. Fletcher and George T. Day to carry out the above vote."

"1861, July 13. Voted that the appropriation made by a vote of the town on the 29th day of April last past shall be expended according to the provisions of chapter 222 of General Laws, special session, approved May 23, 1861. That the town hereby ratifies, confirms and approves of the payments made by the selectmen pursuant to the vote passed April 29, 1861."

"1862, July 19. Voted that the selectmen be authorized and directed to pay the sum of $125 to every man, not exceeding twenty-three in number, who shall enlist and be mustered into the military service of the United States in answer to the requisition of the President of the United States upon the Governor of this Commonwealth as soon as certificates of the same shall be filed with the selectmen; and that the treasurer of the town, under the direction of the selectmen, be authorized and empowered to borrow, in the name of the inhabitants of Westford, from time to time, a sum sufficient to meet the amount above voted to each person enlisted."

"1862, August 25. Voted to pay to each volunteer who shall enlist for nine months, to make up the quota, $125; that Isaac E. Day, Eli Tower, George B. Hildreth, William Read, 1st, John B. Fletcher, John Morrison and Charles L. Fletcher be a committee to aid the selectmen in obtaining volunteers and getting them mustered into the service of the United States at an early day, without compensation."

"1862, December 17. Voted, that if it becomes necessary and further orders shall be received requiring the additional men called for, the town will endeavor to furnish the same: that all the men be raised for three years, and that the selectmen cause the treasurer to refund and pay back to the other towns that have enlisted men from Westford, which men are counted to Westford, any sum so paid to said men by any town, provided the sum shall not exceed $125 for each person or whether the time was for three years or for nine months: that it be left discretionary with the selectmen to pay such bounty as they may think expedient: that no bounty shall be paid to any person enlisted until a certificate from the Adjutant-General's office, or such other satisfactory evidence as the selectmen may require, shall be exhibited."

"1863, July 29. Voted to pay each conscript that goes to the war, or furnishes a substitute, the sum of $200."

"1864, April 4. Voted to raise $1500 to pay the expenses of filling the quota of October 17, 1863: that the chairman of the Board of Selectmen be directed to certify to the collector of taxes the amount paid by each person and estate on the apportionment made at a meeting of the citizens or legal voters of Westford, December 1, 1863, for the defraying the expense of recruiting or bounties paid to volunteers under the act to authorize towns and cities to raise money for recruiting under the call of the President of the United States for 500,000 men, which certificates shall be received as so much *cash* by the collector in favor of said persons, and the same be allowed to him in his settlement with the treasurer of the town." *

"1864, May 28. Voted that the selectmen be authorized to proceed and procure such number of men as they may believe necessary to fill the next quota of the President."

"1864, August 22. Voted to raise a sum of money in gold, or its equivalent, amounting in the aggregate to $125

' *The apportionment made by the citizens of the town, Dec. 1, 1863, was $1800.

for each recruit that is now, or may be, enlisted under the last call for volunteers by the President of the United States."

" 1864, November 8. Voted that the selectmen be authorized to pay the *eight* re-enlisted men the sum of $125 each. Also, pay to the soldiers who enlisted and were sworn into the United States service in July, 1861, or to their heirs, $125 each, as soon as proper authority can be obtained to pay the same, provided the conditions of the vote passed in 1861 shall be complied with."

" 1864, December 7. Voted that the selectmen proceed and take measures to obtain such a number of recruits as they may deem necessary, not less than fifteen in number, to fill up the quota which will be assigned to the town on the President's call for soldiers."

" 1866, March 5. Voted to pay to every person who enlisted and was counted as one of the quota of Westford, $125, provided he has not already received a bounty from the town; and to pay to all persons drafted in the town, or who furnished a substitute, $300."

The foregoing extracts from the records show how promptly the inhabitants of the town met the demands upon them for men to go to the field of battle, and for money to carry on the war. There was no lack of enthusiasm or effort. In the darkest hours the feeling prevailed that the government must be sustained, and the life of the nation saved at any sacrifice of men or means; and so the patriotism that rose early in its might to espouse a righteous cause, held out until that cause was triumphant.

The following table is designed to exhibit, in a succinct form, the contributions of men made at various times to the Union army. It includes all who served in any capacity, whether natives or residents of the town, aliens or persons from other towns secured to fill out the quotas. It also includes all who were enlisted in behalf of other towns or States, or in the regular army, as well as those who received a bounty but never joined the ranks. And so far as the facts can be ascertained, it shows the time of enlistment or mustering in, the regiment in which the person served, the time of re-enlistment, and the date of discharge by reason of death or expiration of service.

Alphabetical List of Soldiers in the War of the Rebellion.

Enlist'd or Must'd In.	Names.	Regiment.	Re-enlistment.	Expiration of Service.
1864, Jan. 12	Allen, Seth	4th Cavalry		
1864, Dec. 24	Allerton, William	Regular Army		1865, May 24.
1863, Oct. 19	Andrews, Charles E	1st Cavalry		
	Bailey, Harvey N	1st N. H. Cavalry		
1864, Dec. 30	Barry, John	3rd Cavalry, 3 years		
	Bancroft, Gustavus C	42nd N. Y. reg		Killed at Gettysburg, 1863, July 2.
1861, April	Bicknell, Nathan D	16th reg. C	1863, Dec. 27, 11th reg.	1865, July 14.
1861, July 2	Bicknell, Ai	16th reg. C		Died in service, 1862, June 6, at Gaines' Mill, Va.
1861, Sept. 6	Bicknell, James	22nd reg		
1861, Dec. 25	Bean, True A	4th Illinois Cavalry		Discharged, 1865, Mar. 14, disability.
1862, Aug. 5	Billings, Benjamin F	33rd reg. E		Killed, 1863, Jan. 30, at Deserted House, Va.
1862, Aug. 31	Blodgett, George W	6th reg. B		1863, June 3.
1862, Aug. 31	Blood, George A	6th reg. B		1865, June 11.
1862, Aug. 5	Boies, Andrew J	33rd reg. E		1864, July 27.
1861, June 18	Bond, Nathaniel	16th reg. C		1863, April 19.
1861, April 22	Bond, Charles A	16th reg. C		1864, July 27.
1861, July 21	Bostwick, Julius C	16th reg.		
1864, July 29	Brierly, John	V. R. C		
1865, Jan. 7	Bixton, C. R	35th reg. C		1864, Nov. 7.
1861, Nov. 10	Brown, Albert L	28th reg. B		
	Bunce, William	11th reg. Illinois		
	Burnett, John M	Navy		
1861, Sept. 16	Bussey, Peter	26th reg. B	1864, Jan. 3	
1864, Aug. 23	Callaghan, Michael	V. R. C		1865, Feb. 17.
1861, June 28	Callahan, Timothy	16th reg. G		1865, Nov. 17.
1863, Dec. 14	Cain, John	New Batt. Cavalry		1862, Nov. 12, disability.
1864, Dec. 14	Carey, Patrick	2nd Heavy Artillery		
1864, Dec. 24	Carter, Hiram	Regular Army		1864, July 27.
1862, Aug. 18	Carkin, William Oren	16th reg. C		1863, June 3.
1862, Aug. 31	Carney, Thomas	6th reg. K		

1862, Aug. 31.	Calnan, Timothy.	6th reg. B		1863, June 8.
1861, June 29.	Calvert, George W.	16th reg. G.	In U.S. army, 1863, Oct. 9	
1865, Jan. 24.	Chamberlin, James	U. S. Artillery		
1861, April 22.	Chandler, Marcus M.	16th reg. C.		1864, July 27.
1861, July 12.	Christeen, Charles B.	16th reg. G.		1862, June 16, disability.
1861, Sept. 9.	Clark, Frank N.	26th reg. D.		1862, July 27, died at New Orleans.
1863, Jan. 27.	Clark, Henry.	14th Battery		
1861, April 20.	Coburn, Savillion B.	Navy		1865, May 22, died in Westford.
1862, Aug. 31.	Comberbeach, Robert.	6th reg. I.		1863, June 3.
1863, Aug. 24.	Conant, Marcus.	3rd Heavy Artillery		1865, Sept. 18.
1864, Jan. 18.	Corey, Charles E.	26th reg. B.		
1863, Dec. 28.	Corcoran, Cornelius	56th reg.		
	Craig, John W			
1864, Dec. 21	Crocker, Isaac.	Navy		1864, July 27.
1861, April 22.	Cummings, Charles M	16th reg. C.		1865, Feb. 27.
1862, April 22.	Cummings, John A.	30th reg. C.		1862, Aug. 28, died at New Orleans.
1862, April 22.	Cummings, Reuben W.	30th reg. C.		1865, July 14.
1862, July 25.	Daly, Patrick C.	16th reg. G.	1863, Dec. 27, 11th reg.	1862, June 25, disability.
1861, May 25.	Dane, Hiram.	2nd reg.		Killed, 1862, May 25, at Winchester, Va.
1861, May 25.	Dane, William.	2nd reg. G.		Died, 1863, June 30, at Baton Rouge, La.
1862, Oct. 17.	Davis, Ancil	53rd reg. D.		
1864, July 29.	Davis, John	V. R. C.		1865, Nov. 17, order of War Department.
1864, Aug. 1.	Devitt, George A.	13th reg.		1864, Sept. 4, died at Andersonville, Ga.
1861, June 11.	Dinsmore, William	9th reg. F.		
1865, Jan. 28.	Donovan, Dennis.	3rd U. S. Artillery		
	Dow, Darius A.	4th Illinois Cavalry.		
1861, July 2.	Dow, Thomas E.	16th reg. C.		1863, Jan 2, disability.
1864, Dec. 27.	Drew, Dennison S.	13th V. R. C		1865, May 29, rejected recruit.
1864, May 9.	Dubey, Charles.	V. R. C.		
1865, Jan. 13.	Eager, Alexander.	Navy		
1861, April 22.	Falls, George S.	16th reg. C.	1864, Jan. 16, trans. V.R.C	
1864, July 28.	Ferguson, John.	5th Batt. Lt. Artillery		1865, June 12.
1864, May 7.	Fisher, James Ai.	V. R. C.		
1864, Dec. 24.	Fisk, H. G	Regular Army		
1862, Oct. 17.	Fletcher, Albert W	53rd reg. D.		1863, June 14, killed at Port Hudson.
1864, Jan. 14.	Fletcher, Henry F.	59th reg. C.	1865, June12, 2Lt. 57threg	1865, July 30.
1864, Aug. 22.	Fletcher, Joel Albro.	4th H'v'y Art'y M.		1865, June 17.
1861, April 22.	Flint, James T.	16th reg. C.		1862, Aug. 29, killed, second Bull Run battle.

Alphabetical List of Soldiers in the War of the Rebellion.—Continued.

Enlist'd or Must'd in.	Names.	Regiment.	Re-enlistment.	Expiration of Service.
1864, July 30.	French, Alfred	V. R. C.		1865, Nov. 17, order of War Department.
1862, Aug. 5.	Friar, Henry A.	33rd reg. E.		1864, Feb. 1, at Chattanooga, died in service.
1864, April 12.	Furber, David D.	Signal Corps.		
1863, July 21.	Graff, Frederic.	39th reg. C.	1865, June 2, transferred 32nd reg.	
1862, July 31.	Gilson, Albert A.	33rd reg. D.		1865, June 29.
1864, Feb. 29.	Gilson, Thomas	Signal Corps.		1865, June 11.
1861, Oct. 21.	Green, John R.	30th reg. C.		1865, Nov. 17.
1861, April 22.	Graham, James A.	16th reg. C.	1864, Feb. 29, Reg. Army.	1862, June 18, disability. 1867, March 29, discharged.
1864, Mar. 31.	Gray, Henry	1st Cavalry		1865, July 8.
1862, Aug. 31.	Hale, William F	6th reg. E.		1863, July 3.
1864, Dec. 21.	Hall, George L.	Navy, ship Ohio.		
1863, Feb. 2.	Hall, William, Jr	14th Battery.		
1864, Dec. 27.	Hampton, Daniel	V. R. C.		
1863, Sept. 14.	Hannafin, John	3rd H'vy Artillery G.		1865, Sept. 18.
1863, Jan. 27.	Hayden, Henry	3rd H'vy Artillery E.		1864, July 31, died at Washington D. C.
1863, Jan. 31.	Harney, John.	14th Battery.		
1862, Aug. 31.	Hancock, John.	6th reg. E		1863, June 3.
1863, Dec. 6.	Harris, George A.	2nd Heavy Artillery.		1865, Sept. 3.
1861, April 22.	Harris, John.	16th reg. C.		Killed 1862, Aug. 29, at Bull Run.
1864, Mar. 30.	Hildreth, Frederic A.	Signal Corps.		
1861, Sept. 19.	Hildreth, Joseph B.	4th Illinois Cavalry.	Went from Westford to Fall River and enlisted.	
1864, June 8.	Hogan, Patrick	26th reg. G.		
1864, July 22.	Holland, John.	Navy		
1862, Aug. 31.	Hosley, James A.	33rd reg. E.	1864, May 11, to V. R. C.	1865.
1864, May 31.	Howard, Francis P.	6th reg. B.		1863, Feb. 1, died of wounds at Suffolk, Va.
1863, Jan. 27.	Hunter, William	Navy, 1 year.		1865, June 21, from receiving ship Princeton.
1862, Aug. 1.	Hunt, George W	14th Battery.		
1862, Aug. 18.	Hunt, George W.	Navy		
1862, Aug. 18.	Hutchins, John, Jr	Corp. 35th reg. E.		1865, June 9.

THE WAR OF THE REBELLION. 197

Enlisted	No.	Name	Regiment	Promotion/Transfer	Discharge/Death
1863, Aug.	5.	Hutchins, Thomas, J	33rd reg. E		1863, Oct. 29, killed at Lookout Valley, Tenn.
1863, Aug.	5.	Hutchins, Edward E	33rd reg. F		1864, May 15, killed at Resaca, Ga.
1862, May	28.	Hutchins, Warren E	7th Battery		1864, Nov. 29, died at Duvall's Bluff, Ark.
1861, April	25.	Hutchinson, George	16th reg. C	1863, Sept. 1, to V. R. C.	
1860, Nov.	....	Hutchinson, Frank	1st U. S. Battery		1864, July 27.
1861, April	22.	Ingalls, Albert P	16th reg. B		1863, Feb. 4, disability.
1861, April	22.	Irish, Joseph, 2nd	16th reg. B		
		Jackson, Alfred	4th or 6th N. H. reg.		
1861, Oct.	11.	Jackson, James	26th reg. A, 3 years		1862, Oct. 16, disability.
1862, Aug.	31.	Jewett, Franklin M	6th reg. A	1864, Dec. 30, 1st bat.fr.cav	1865, Jan. 23, died at Readville, Mass.
1864, June	24.	Johnson, William	33rd reg. C	1865, June 1, to 2nd reg.	1865, June 25.
1861, May	23.	Jubb, John	16th reg. G		1862, July 21, died at Harrison's Landing, Va.
1862, Aug.	5.	Jubb, William, Serg	33rd reg. E		1865, June 11.
1861, Dec.	11.	Kane, Paul	56th reg. B		1864, drowned.
1863, Feb.	28.	Kearney, George	14th Battery		
1864, April	1.	Keefe, David F	Signal Corps		1865, Aug. 18, died at Sumter, S. C.
1861, Nov.	8.	Keyes, Edward	30th reg. C		1865, July 19, disability.
1864, Aug.	6.	Lavanthal, Louis	59th reg. F	1865, June 1, to 57th reg.	1865, July 28.
1864, Dec.	27.	Lawler, Thomas	13th Battery		
1863, Aug.	9.	Lawrence, George M	33rd reg. A		1864, May 15, killed at Dallas, Ga.
1864, Dec.	25.	Libby, Alexander H	2nd Heavy Artillery		1865, Sept. 3.
1863, Jan.	27.	Lord, Frost	14th Battery		
1862, Aug.	31.	McDonald, James	6th reg. B		1863, June 3.
1862, Nov.	1.	McLaughlin, James	41st reg. G, became 3rd reg. Cav. 1862.		1865, May 20.
1864, July	28.	McManus, James	2nd H'vy Artillery H		1865, Sept. 3.
1864, Dec.	30.	Mahony, Thomas	6th Battery		1865, Aug. 7.
1864, May	7.	McNally, Matthew	7th V. R. C.		1865, Nov. 15.
1861, April	22.	Metcalf, William	16th reg. C, 1st Lieut.		1862, Dec. 28, resigned.
1865, Jan.	25.	Mills, Gustavus J	3rd U. S. Art'y, 3 yrs		
1861, Sept.	21.	Miner, Charles	30th reg. C		1862, July 22, died at Vicksburg, Miss.
1864, Dec.	30.	Morand, Leon	13th Battery, 3 years		1865, deserted at Greenville, La.
1864, Nov.	9.	Morrill, Charles H	34th reg., 1st Lieut.	1863, Dec. 29, 1st H'vy Ar	1865, June 16.
1862, July	29.	Murphy, James	33rd reg. G		1865, June 9, disability.
1864, Aug.	11.	Murphy, Michael J	16th reg.		1865, July 27.
1864, July	28.	Neal, Thomas	V. R. C.		1864, Oct. 14, deserted.
1861, July	2.	Nolan, Timothy	16th reg. C		1865, Sept. 28, disability.
1865, Jan.	20.	Nolan, Michael	30th reg.		

Alphabetical List of Soldiers in the War of the Rebellion.—Continued.

Enlist'd or Must'd in.	Names.	Regiment.	Re-enlistment.	Expiration of Service.
1864, July 26.	O'Brien, Michael	3rd U. S. Artillery		1865, June 11.
1864, July 14.	O'Malley, Thos. F.	1st Artillery		1862, Oct. 9, died at New Orleans.
1862, Aug. 5.	Owens, James	33rd reg. E		1863, June 8.
1862, April 22.	Peabody, Hiram	30th reg. E		Never joined the regiment.
1862, Aug. 31.	Peck, James B.	6th reg. K		
1864, June 21.	Pender, Michael	33rd reg. E		
	Pico, John	In Cavalry Under Gen. Butler.		
	Pico, Peter	In Cavalry		
1862, Aug. 16.	Prescott, George Henry.	35th reg. D	1863, Sept. 7, to V. R. C.	
1863, Sept. 14.	Quinn, Thomas	4th Heavy Artillery		
1861, April 22.	Rand, Myron	16th reg. C	1864, Jan. 4, to 11th reg. and 1865, Apr. 28, to V. R. C.	1864, April 12, disability.
1862, Aug. 7.	Raymond, Joseph	16th reg. C		
1862, Aug. 31.	Reed, Augustus	6th reg. B		1863, Feb. 27, died of wounds, at Suffolk, Va.
1862, Aug. 18.	Reed, Charles B.	16th reg. G		1862, Dec. 6, died at Alexandria, Va.
1862, Aug. 16.	Reed, Luther F.	35th reg. D		1862, Sept. 17, killed at Antietam.
	Reed, Ephraim	4th N. H. Reg.		1866, July 5.
1861, Nov. 28.	Reed, Merrick	30th reg. C		1863, June 8.
1862, Aug. 31.	Reed, William, 2nd	6th reg. B		
1861, April 25.	Richards, John F.	16th reg. C		1863, Oct. 18, died at Richmond, Va.
1862, Aug. 31.	Richardson, Alfred A.	6th reg. B		1862, Dec. 8, died at Suffolk, Va.
1861, Oct. 14.	Richardson, Gardiner H.	2nd reg. E		1864, Oct. 14.
1862, Aug. 18.	Richardson, Milton T.	16th reg. I		1863, Jan. 29, disability.
1863, Aug. 7.	Rockwood, Henry	15th reg. Asst.-Sur.		1863, Sept. 14, dismissed.
1862, Aug. 5.	Savage, James, 2nd	33rd reg. E	1865, Jan. 12, to V. R. C.	
1861, April 22.	Sheahan, Patrick	16th reg. C		1862, Aug. 29, killed at Bull Run.
1861, April 22.	Sherburne, James	16th reg. C		1863, March 4, disability.
1861, Aug. 10.	Shedd, William H.	22nd reg. F		1863, Jan. 10, disability.
1865, Jan. 20.	Shields, Patrick	30th reg.	Unassigned Recruit	

THE WAR OF THE REBELLION. 199

Enlisted	Name	Regiment	Discharged	Remarks
1864, May 11.	Senior, Thomas R	V. R. C		1865, July 12, prisoner.
1863, Dec. 26.	Smith, Alfred	56th reg. B		1863, June 3.
1862, Sept. 8.	Smith, Allen G	6th reg. E		1863, June 3.
1862, Sept. 8.	Smith, Matthew A	6th reg. E		
1864, Aug. 6.	Smith, William	V. R. C		
1864, Aug. 18.	Spalding, Calvin Warren	16th reg. C	1863, April 29, to V. R. C.	
1861, April 22.	Stiles, Milan A	16th reg. C	1864, Mar. 24, to 26th reg.	1865, Aug. 26.
1864, Mar. 24.	Stiles, William W	26th reg. E, corp.		1865, Aug. 26.
1862, Aug. 9.	Stone, Gilmer	33rd reg. G, sergt.		1865, June 11.
1864, May 7.	Strong, Joseph T	V. R. C		
1862, Aug.	Sullivan, Michael	33rd reg. H		1865, June 11.
1862, Aug. 31.	Sweeny, Charles H	6th reg. K, corp.		1863, June 3.
1862, Aug. 18.	Sweetser, Lorenzo	35th reg. E		1863, May 5.
1861, July 22.	Taylor, John Z	17th reg. F		1861, Nov. 9, died at Baltimore.
1864, Mar. 30.	Taylor, Thomas E	Signal Corps		
1861, June 13.	Taylor, William R	11th reg. B		1864, June 24.
1864, April 22.	Tileston, Justin W	26th reg. B		1864, Sept. 19, killed at Winchester, Va.
1862, Aug. 31.	Thorning, Augustus W	6th reg. B		1863, June 3.
1864, April 12.	Tracy, Joseph	Signal Corps		
1863, Dec. 12.	Trudelle, Joseph	56th reg. B		1865, July 12, absent, sick.
1862, Aug. 31.	Tully, Thomas	6th reg. B		1863, June 3.
1861, Oct. 21.	Waterman, Dexter W	30th reg. C	1864, Jan. 2	1864, April 21, died at Westford.
1863, Jan. 27.	Webster, Charles	14th Battery		
1861, April 25.	Wells, William T	16th reg. C		1862, Dec. 20, disability.
1864, April 9.	Walt, Harrison	Signal Corps		
1863, Dec. 17.	Whipple, Daniel	15th Battery	1865, Jan. 14, to 6th Batt.	1865, Aug. 7.
1863, Dec. 15.	White, John	54th reg. F		1865, Aug. 20.
1862, Aug. 31.	Whitney, John H	6th reg. B		1863, June 3.
1862, Aug. 31.	Whitney, William M	6th reg. B		1863, June 3.
1864, July 22.	Wheeler, Alonzo D	42nd reg. E, 100 days		1864, Nov. 11.
1862, Sept. 26.	Wheeler, Isaac G	45th reg. A		1863, July 7.
1862, Aug.	Wilkins, Luther	53rd reg. D		1863, Sept. 2.
1862, Oct. 17.	Wilkins, Luther Edwin	53rd reg. D		1863, July 20.
1862, July 2.	Willis, Andrew L	10th reg. C	1864, March 1, 2nd Cav	1864, July 27.
1864, Aug. 23.	Wilson, Jesse	V. R. C		
1864, July 17.	Woods, J. Everett	6th reg. 100 days		1864, Oct. 27.
1862, Aug. 31.	Woods, Charles G	6th reg. B		1863, June 8.
1862, Sept. 16.	Wright, Albert A	5th reg. I		1863, July 2.

Alphabetical List of Soldiers in the War of the Rebellion.—Concluded.

Enlist'd or Must'd in.	Names.	Regiment.	Re-enlistment.	Expiration of Service.
1862, Sept. 16.	Wright, Edward E.	5th reg. I.		1863, July 2
1862, Aug. 31.	Wright, Ellery C.	6th reg. B.		1863, June 3.
1861, Aug. 3.	Wright, Hannibal.		V. R. C.	
1862, July 14.	Wright, Jefferson.	35th reg. D.		1865, June 27.
1862, Aug. 19.	Wright, Mason A.	35th reg. E.	1864, July 1, to V. R. C.	
1861, April 22.	Wright, Morton G.	16th reg. C, corp.		1862, Oct. 18, disability.
1861, April 22.	Young, James G.	16th reg. C.	1863, Sept. 1, to V. R. C.	

Here are more than two hundred names. Of the men who were credited to Westford, at least *thirty-five* were born here and more than sixty were residents but not natives, making about one hundred that were connected with the town by greater or less strength. It was natural that a deeper interest should be felt by the citizens in their behalf than could be awakened for those who were strangers; and it so happened that the number of martyrs to the country was *thirty-five*, a number corresponding to the number known to be born here.

The full roll of the men who enlisted April 22, 1861, is here given: William Metcalf, Charles M. Cummings, Milan A. Stiles, Marcus M. Chandler, John Harris, Myron Rand, Morton G. Wright, James Sherburne, Thomas E. Dow, Albert P. Ingalls, Timothy Nolan, Charles A. Bond, James A. Graham, James G. Young, George S. Falls, Andrew L. Willis, Patrick Sheahan, Joseph Irish, John F. Richards, Julius C. Bostwick and James T. Flint. These were soon joined by Nathaniel Bond, George Hutchinson, Nathan D. Bicknell and William T. Wells. They remained at Groton Junction a few weeks and removed to Camp Cameron, in Cambridge, where they were joined by Ai Bicknell. Calvin W. Spalding was a recruit in August, 1862. Timothy Callahan, John Jubb, Michael Murphy and Patrick Daly, were also members of Company G.

The regiment first went to Baltimore, where it remained a few weeks, and was ordered to Suffolk, Va. The men witnessed the triumph of the Monitor in Hampton Roads; went from Suffolk to White House Landing; were in "Woodland Skirmish," June 18, 1862, and in the second encounter at Fair Oaks a few days after, and retreated with others to Harrison's Landing. Returning to Yorktown they were soon transported to Aquia Creek and participated in the second battle of Bull Run, August 29, 1862. Some portion of the regiment, it is believed, were in the battle of Antietam. On the 12th of the following December the men took part in the attack on Fredericksburg, where their chaplain, Arthur B.

Fuller, was killed. They were in the battle of Chancellorsville, and in the stoutly contested action of three days' continuance at Gettysburg. During the winter following they were encamped at Brandy Station, Va.

Advancing with Gen. Grant in the spring of 1864, they were in the battle of the Wilderness, in that at Spottsylvania Court House, and at Petersburg, June 16.

They were released at the expiration of their term of service, July 27, 1864.

Of the thirty-two men credited to this town, only nine served out their full time in this regiment, to wit: Bond (Nathaniel), Carkin, Chandler, Cummings, Ingalls, Murphy, Nolan, Bostwick and Willis; four were killed, to wit: Bicknell, Flint, Harris and Sheahan; the following were disabled: Bond (Charles), Irish, Rand, Sherburne, Wells and Wright; one, Richards, died in prison at Richmond.

In the Second Regiment, which went out in 1861 and was in the vicinity of Harper's Ferry, were two brothers, Hiram and William Dane. The first was released on account of disability, and the second was killed at Winchester, Va., May 25, 1862, just one year from the day of his enlistment, being the first martyr to the cause from Westford.

On the 4th day of August, 1862, the President issued a call for 300,000 men to serve for nine months. "The Sixth Regiment, the same which had fought its way through Baltimore, April 19, 1861, was recruited and organized for nine months' service, at Camp Henry Wilson, in Lowell. It was the determination of the governor to have this regiment the first to leave the State. It received orders to report at Washington and left Massachusetts, under the command of Col. Albert S. Follansbee, about September 1st. It remained in Washington until the 13th, when it was ordered to Suffolk, Va." *

---

* To this regiment as first organized, "distinguished honors have been paid, as the historic regiment of the war. Distinguished ladies volunteered to nurse the sick and wounded. Poets sang its praises in heroic verse. The loyal ladies of Baltimore presented it with a national flag. The United States House of Representatives unanimously voted these soldiers the thanks of the House for their 'prompt response to the

In this regiment, under the new organization, were Franklin M. Jewett, sergeant; Ellery C. Wright, corporal; George W. Blodgett, George A. Blood, Timothy Calnan, Francis P. Howard, James McDonald, Augustus Reed, William Reed, Augustus W. Thorning, Thomas Tully, John H. Whitney, William M. Whitney and Charles G. Woods in Company B; William F. Hale, John Hancock, Allen G. Smith, Matthew A. Smith in Company E; Robert Comberbeach in Company I; Thomas Carney, James B. Peck, Charles H. Sweeny in Company K.

In addition to these were Alfred A. Richardson and Gardner H. Richardson, born in Westford, but enlisted in behalf of Groton.

The regiment was in several sharp skirmishes or battles, but in no general engagement like that at Antietam or Gettysburg. The severest test of their courage and endurance was made near Blackwater, at a place called Deserted House, when they were supporting the Seventh Battery. Their position was upon the edge of a swamp and was very much exposed. The engagement lasted two hours, under close range — eight hundred yards. While the men were lying on their faces, a shell from the enemy burst above them, killing instantly George W. Blodgett, taking off the arm of Augustus Reed, and shattering the leg of Francis Howard, so that each of them died, Howard in two days and Reed in four weeks. Blodgett and Reed were intimate friends, were both quite young, only seventeen, and were both brought home for burial. The funeral of each was held in the Union Congregational Church, and they were buried with military honors.

This regiment was at the front under Col. Follansbee, April 11, 1863, when an attack on Suffolk was threatened, and "from this time onward a continual skirmishing was kept

---

call of duty' and their patriotism and bravery in fighting their way through Baltimore to the defence of the capital."

There was one man from Westford in this regiment when it hurried to Washington on the 19th of April, *Charles G. Woods*, who afterward enlisted for nine months in Company B, and served out his full time.

up for twenty-three days, mostly between sharpshooters, gunboats and artillery, though several times the engagements assumed the proportions of smart battles. During the twenty-three days' siege the regiment was severely taxed and much exposed, . . . but it did not fail. May 13th, the regiment with others started towards the Blackwater for the eighth and last time. During the three fights of this expedition the Sixth suffered much. They returned to the Deserted House, May 19th, and bivouacked on the ground for which they fought, January 30th. It next moved under General Corcoran to Windsor, where it remained until the 23rd of May, and arrived at Suffolk after ten days of most fatiguing and exhausting service, which told more on the health of the regiment than all the rest of its hardships combined. On the 26th of May it bade adieu to the scenes of its toils and perils, arriving in Boston, after a delightful voyage, May 29th, and reaching Lowell the same day, where it was mustered out, June 3, 1863.

Thus ended the memorable campaign of this regiment, honorably to itself, and with remarkable exemption from death by disease and battle, considering the number of its engagements and the unhealthy location of its camp, on the edge of the Dismal Swamp.

All who were killed in battle or died of disease were embalmed and sent home for interment—a remarkable fact in the history of a regiment. Not one of its members rests in Virginia soil." *

The Twenty-sixth Regiment was enlisted for three years at Camp Chase in Lowell. Many of its officers and men belonged to the Sixth Regiment in its three months' service. It left Boston for Ship Island, September 21, 1861, and was the first loyal volunteer regiment that reached the Department

---

* The facts here given, as well as those relating to other regiments, are taken mainly from Schouler's "History of Massachusetts in the Civil War," to which volume the compiler is greatly indebted.

It is proper to add that Isaiah Hutchins, a native of this town, was hospital steward in this regiment.

of the Gulf. Westford was represented in it by Brown Bussey, Stiles (Corporal William), Stiles (Milan), and Tileston.

The Thirtieth Regiment, called at one time the Eastern Bay State Regiment, was under the command of Gen. Butler, and was assigned to the Department of the Gulf. It landed at Baton Rouge, La., June 2, 1862, and was quartered in the State capitol, and raised the stars and stripes over its dome, from which they were never struck. It did service at various points in the State of Lousiana, but was in no general engagement. The climate caused a great amount of sickness among the men. Capt. Welles reported that at times not more than seventy men were free from sickness and entirely well. February 15, 1863, the regiment had about four hundred men left for light duty, out of more than one thousand officers and men.

The men from Westford were Edward Keyes, Charles Miner, Hiram Peabody, Merrick Reed and Dexter W. Waterman. Of these Miner died and was buried opposite Vicksburg, and Peabody at New Orleans. Waterman came home sick, and died. The regiment was retained in the service after hostilities had ceased, and was on duty in South Carolina. While there Edward Keyes died at Sumter, August 18, 1865.

The Thirty-third Regiment was organized at Camp Stanton, Lynnfield, and started for the field August 14, 1862. It joined the army of the Potomac, was at Fairfax Court House and Thoroughfare Gap, and in the battles of Chancellorsville and Gettysburg. It joined the army of the Cumberland, near Chattanooga, September 30, 1863. It performed the task of climbing Raccoon Ridge, October 29th, and charging the enemy on the summit and driving him out of his rifle-pits. This was declared by Gen. Hooker to be the greatest charge of the war. In that perilous undertaking Thomas J. Hutchins was killed, and his body was found within ten feet of the enemy's works. William Jubb leaped over the defences and was collared by a stalwart Rebel, who attempted to stab him with a dirk. Buckley knocked down the "Reb." with his musket and saved the life of his comrade. This regiment entered Atlanta, September 3rd, and started with Sherman for the sea, November 16, 1864. The Union troops occupied Savannah, Ga., December 25th, and Raleigh, N. C., April 14, 1865. Gen. Johnston surrendered April 17th.

In this regiment was George M. Lawrence, Company A, who was killed at Dallas, Ga., May 25, 1864. In Company E were Benjamin F. Billings, Henry A. Friar, James Hosley, Albert A. Gilson, James Owens, James Savage, Michael Sullivan, William Jubb (sergeant), and Thomas J. Hutchins. In Company C, William Johnson. In Company F, Edward E. Hutchins (corporal), killed at Resaca, Ga., May 15, 1864. In Company G, Gilmer Stone. Henry A. Friar died at Chattanooga, Tenn., February 1, 1864. James H. Gilson, for several years a resident of this town, was in this regiment. He served for Groton.

The Thirty-fifth Regiment joined the Army of the Potomac in August, 1862. In it were John Hutchins, Jr., George H. Prescott, Luther F. Reed, Lorenzo Sweetser, Jefferson Wright and Mason A. Wright. Reed was killed at Antietam. The regiment was in the battles of South Mountain, Antietam, Fredericksburg and Petersburg.

The Fifty-third Regiment was organized for nine months' service at Camp Stevens, in Groton. It left Massachusetts November 18, 1862, for New York, with orders to report to Gen. Banks at New Orleans, where it arrived January 30, 1863. It was sent to Baton Rouge, March 6th, and was at Port Hudson supporting a battery, where it remained until the surrender of that garrison, July 9th. In an assault made June 14th, this regiment was in the storming party and suffered severely. The men from Westford were Ancil Davis, Albert W. Fletcher, Luther Wilkins and Edwin Wilkins. Fletcher was killed in the assault on the morning of June 14th, and his body was not recovered.

The foregoing account of the movements and operations of several regiments has been given because they contained a larger number than any others of men who were either natives or residents of the town in whose fate the people at home were deeply interested. It is given with no intent to undervalue the patriotism or self-denial of others who went in smaller numbers into other regiments. The heart of the people beat in sympathy with every loyal heart in the Union army, but it was especially tender and true to every one born or domiciliated on the hilltops or in the valleys of this town which, as it faltered not in the struggle for national independence in 1776, wavered not and never grew weary in the effort to save the nation's life in 1861.

The following names are mentioned with hearty approval of the service rendered: The Wright brothers, Albert and Edward, in the Fifth Regiment, who served for the town of Marlborough; Dow, Bean, Hildreth and Bunce in Illinois regiments; Bailey, Jackson and Reed in New Hampshire regiments; Hildreth, Taylor and Wait in the Signal Corps; Hunt and Eager in the navy; the Taylor brothers in the Eleventh and Seventeenth Regiments.

Three or four entered the Regular Army—Hutchinson before the war, and continued in the ranks till it was over. A much larger number entered the Veteran Reserve Corps and received bounties from the town. Two men entered the Fifty-ninth Regiment and the Fifty-sixth. Eighteen or more went into batteries or artillery companies; five into cavalry companies. One is credited to the Fifty-fourth Regiment of colored troops. Some were on guard in the forts in Boston Harbor and at other points. So, in the various branches of military service, this town was well represented; and when the details of achievement are carefully weighed, it will be found that the record of Westford soldiers is honorable and worthy of recognition, reflecting, as it does, in no dim and unsteady light, but in a clear and unmistakable manner, the spirit of patriotism that never was discouraged nor overborne in that long and eventful struggle. In the common defence they could climb precipices in Tennessee, dig trenches in Louisiana and bear with unconquerable patience the vexatious delays and terrible reverses in Virginia.

The apportionment of Massachusetts for nine months' men was 19,090 men. The quota of Westford was twenty-three men. These were to be drafted. But "from the beginning to the end of the Rebellion, the Governor, the city and town authorities and the people of the Commonwealth were opposed to a draft, and labored to avoid it." In obedience, however, to the requirements of the national government, preparations were made for a draft. Each town was required to make an enrollment of its citizens. A copy of the enrollment for this town, dated August 4, 1862, shows a total of two hundred and fifty men. As this town and, indeed, the whole State, furnished the men within a reasonable time, the draft was avoided. But the enrollment made at that time remained as the basis upon which quotas of cities and towns were apportioned from that time to the end of the war.

In answer to a subsequent call a draft was made on the eighteenth of July, 1863, when the lot fell upon the following persons: Luke L. Fletcher, Frank L. Fletcher, A. Bancroft Fletcher, C. H. Danforth, Arthur Wright, Albert P. Richardson, Charles N. Richardson, William Reed, J. Henry Read, J. Blodgett, Fletcher Peckens, Henry Hayden, William H. H. Burbeck, Thomas Drew, George Drew, John Farmer, John Trull, C. H. Decatur, C. Freeman Keyes, John W. Day, Charles E. Walker, Stephen Hutchins — 25. Some of these were released on the ground of manifest disability. Others procured substitutes, and others still paid a commutation fee which the town refunded to them, as well as sums paid for substitutes, in sums of $300 or less.

The following extracts are from a letter on file from John W. P. Abbot, who, as chairman of the Board of Selectmen and recruiting officer, conducted the military correspondence during the war. It is addressed to Hon. Tappan Wentworth in reply to a circular:

"WESTFORD, July 18, 1865.

"DEAR SIR — I find it impossible to give you an answer as [required] in your circular, and therefore I send you this:

Indebtedness of the town, Feb. 8, 1865		$24,407 34
Indebtedness of the town on account of the war:		
Up to Feb. 10, 1862		1,447 81
Up to Feb. 10, 1863		6,795 30
Up to Feb. 10, 1864, there are no bounties or expenses reported as being paid, having been credited in the following year.		
Up to Feb. 1865		16,937 47
Since Feb. 10, 1865, there have been paid:		
Bounties to re-enlisted men . . .	$625 00	
Three more men at $125 each . . .	375 00	
		1,000 00
Total		$26,180 58

Total number of men put into the service to whom bounties have been paid, 160.
Average to each man, $162.62.

"It is impossible to state the times when men were put into the service. There was at several times great difficulty in ascertaining whether the quota was full or not. On or about the first of February, 1865, the Provost Marshal informed me that by his books the town of Westford had a surplus of sixteen men. On the first of November, 1864, the town was in arrears. It is impossible to give any satisfactory explanation."

This estimate is only a proximate one, and does not include the whole expense, nor the whole number of men. In accordance with the vote of March 5, 1866, large sums were paid to cancel the claims of those who had employed substitutes, or paid commutation money. The alphabetical list shows that more men than Mr. Abbot reported must have received at some time a bounty and a certificate of enlistment. It is doubtless true that some received it who never entered the service.

CASUALTIES OF SOLDIERS.

George S. Falls was wounded at Chancellorsville, his leg being broken between the ankle and the knee.

Mason A. Wright was sun-struck in Mississippi, and was in Camp Nelson, Kentucky, for six months, unfit for duty.

Morton G. Wright was wounded in the arm, probably in a skirmish at Fair Oaks.

Myron Rand was wounded below the knee at Gettysburg.

Albert P. Ingalls was wounded at ——— (Glendale ?) He is said to be the first man from Westford who received a wound.

James A. Hosley was wounded in the arm by an explosive ball.

William Bunce was wounded at Fort Donelson and left for dead on the field, but revived; was taken prisoner and carried to Nashville, where he remained in the Confederate hospital until the Union troops took possession of the city.

ROLL OF HONOR.

*"Is 't death to fall for Freedom's right?
He 's dead alone who lacks her light."*

John Z. Taylor died in hospital at Baltimore, November 8, 1861.

William Dane, killed in battle at Winchester, Va., May 25, 1862.

James Bicknell died of typhoid fever at Gaines' Mill, Va., June 7, 1862.

Charles Miner died in hospital opposite Vicksburg, July 22, 1862.

John Jubb died in hospital at Harrison's Landing, July 30, 1862.

Reuben W. Cummings died in hospital at New Orleans, August 20, 1862.

James T. Flint, killed in second Bull Run battle, August 29, 1862.

John Harris, killed in second Bull Run battle, August 29, 1862.

Patrick Sheahan, killed in second Bull Run battle, August 29, 1862.

Luther F. Reed, killed in the battle of Antietam, September 17, 1862.

Hiram Peabody, died in hospital at New Orleans, October 9, 1862.

Charles B. Reed, died in hospital at Alexandria, Va., December 6, 1862.

Alfred A. Richardson, died in hospital at Suffolk, Va., December 9, 1862.

George W. Blodgett, killed at Deserted House, Va., January 30, 1863.

Francis P. Howard, wounded at Deserted House, January 30; died, February 1, 1863.

Augustus Reed, wounded at Deserted House, January 30; died, February 27, 1863.

Albert W. Fletcher, killed in an assault upon Port Hudson, Miss., June 14, 1863.

Ancil Davis, died in hospital at Baton Rouge, June 30, 1863.

Nathan D. Bicknell, killed at Gettysburg, July 2, 1863.

John F. Richards, fell out sick on the march to Gettysburg; was taken prisoner and carried to Belle Isle prison, where he suffered intensely; was removed to hospital, Richmond, Va., and died, October 13, 1863.

Thomas J. Hutchins, killed at Raccoon Ridge, October 29, 1863.

Henry A. Friar, died in hospital at Chattanooga, February 1, 1864.

Dexter W. Waterman, died while at home on a furlough, April 28, 1864.

Edward E. Hutchins, killed at Resaca, Ga., May 15, 1864.

George M. Lawrence, killed at Dallas, Ga., May 25, 1864.

Alfred Jackson, killed while on picket at Petersburg, Va., September 4, 1864.

William Dinsmore, died in prison at Andersonville, Ga., September 4, 1864.

Warren E. Hutchins, died in hospital at Duvall's Bluff, Ark., November 29, 1864.

Franklin M. Jewett, having served nine months in the Sixth Regiment, re-enlisted in the frontier cavalry and died at Camp Meigs, Readville, January 23, 1865.

Henry N. Bailey, died while at home on a furlough, March 8, 1865.

Savillion B. Coburn, died in Westford of disease contracted in the Uuited States service, May 22, 1865.

John W. Craig, died at Haverhill, Mass., while on his way home from the army, June 13, 1865.

William H. Shedd, died in Westford of disease contracted in the army, June 19, 1865.

Edward Keyes, died in hospital at Sumter, S. C., August 18, 1865.

Gardner H. Richardson, died in Lowell of disease contracted in the service, July 11, 1867.

These were the unreturning braves who laid down their lives for their country. Their names are inscribed on a marble tablet in the Town Hall.

> "To live in hearts we leave behind,
> Is not to die."

THE WORK OF THE LADIES OF WESTFORD FOR THE SOLDIERS.

The following paper, which was prepared in November, 1863, exhibits, in a summary way, the work done by the ladies up to that time :

"As a circular has been forwarded to our pastors, requesting that a contribution be taken up throughout the State on

Thanksgiving day in aid of the Sanitary Commission, the sum obtained to be expended in materials and these made up in the town wherein the money is raised, the ladies of the Soldiers' Aid Society think it a suitable opportunity to state what they have been doing since they commenced operations. They do this, not in any spirit of boasting, but of thankfulness that they have been enabled to contribute to the comfort and alleviate the sufferings of the sick and wounded in the hospitals, and that all may be stimulated to continued exertion. Their efforts commenced with the first and largest instalment of our young men in the spring of 1861, these being furnished, in all, with some seventy flannel shirts, the same number of drawers and socks, and a large number of towels, handkerchiefs, pin-cushions, also thread, needles, buttons, etc. But being little aware of the field of benevolence opening before them, no account was kept until they commenced working for the Sanitary Commission. At the outset, in order to procure materials wherewith to work, it was decided that at the meetings held one afternoon in each week each person should pay five cents. This has been their regular source of supply, increased now and then by gifts of money from those unable to attend the regular meetings and from patriotic and large-hearted gentlemen. Twice, through the disinterested exertions of those in sympathy with our cause, have valuable subscriptions been raised, amounting to $134, with important household stores. The members also have given articles of comfort and use as the needs of the Commission required, so that, although the cost of material has been high, they have been enabled to work diligently at the regular times, and many at home, from the resources thus obtained. Since August, 1862, there have been received $191; paid out $171, of which $50 in money was sent to the Sanitary Commission after the battle of Gettysburg. Since that time there have been made up 336 yards of cloth, and of 40 pounds of yarn purchased the greater part has been knit for the Commission, although our own soldiers have been furnished occasionally with socks and shirts, also with mittens, of which 41 pairs have been given. Before August, 1862, hoping the needs would be temporary, no account was kept of money received, but it was disbursed as there was necessity for material. The following articles have been sent to the Sanitary Commission, the receipt of which has been acknowledged with gratitude: 41 quilts, 75 sheets, 55 pillows filled with feathers, hops and husks; 77 pillow cases, 210 shirts, mostly new; 107 pairs of drawers, 81 pairs of slippers, 2 pairs of pants, 1 vest, 142 pairs of socks, 11 dressing-gowns, 282 hankerchiefs, 94 towels and napkins, 2 pieces of flannel, 12 packages of lint, 81 rolls of bandage, 52 rolls of linen and cotton, 40 cushions for limbs, 7 hop poultices, 4 rolls of mutton tallow, 7 bags of herbs, dried berries, hops, etc.; 440 pounds of dried apples, 7 papers corn starch, 8 gallons of pickles, 9 gallons and 27 cans preserves and jellies, 2 gallons currant wine, 1 dish-brush, 6 tin basins, making in all 1300 different articles. There have also been sent to hospitals in Alexandria, Va., whither two persons had gone from Westford as nurses, 3 barrels filled with comforts of various kinds, and a box to each of two of our wounded soldiers as expressive of our sympathy for them and of our appreciation of their bravery and patriotism. The meetings have been held, until the summer just passed, by invitation at the houses of the members, varying from five to twenty, the average scarcely ten. Since that time a room has been offered them gratuitously by Miss Blood, in the house once occupied by John Abbot, Esq. Thither we would earnestly invite all whose hearts are stirred by patriotism to join us Thursday afternoon of each week, feeling assured it will be a life-long satisfaction to them that they have done what they could for their country and her defenders in their hour of need. Any contributions to the society can be handed to the treasurer, Cornelia A. Fletcher.

Westford, November 19, 1863."

This is a review of work accomplished up to this date, but the society continued its benevolent labors until the necessity for them ceased. The amount of receipts, December 8,

1864, as appears by the treasurer's book was $305.69. December 14, 1864, a levee or fair was held to "assist the Soldiers' Aid Society in their work for the Sanitary Commission," the net proceeds of which was $374.51. The aggregate of these two sums is $680.20.

Several years after the war was ended a more complete list of articles sent out to the soldiers was prepared, which is here given: To the Sanitary Commission, $50 in cash as mentioned above: 237 pairs of socks, more than 300 shirts, 222 pairs of drawers, 454 handkerchiefs, 79 sheets, 60 pillows, 86 pillow cases, 15 blankets, 650 barrels of dried apples, 62 gallons of pickles, and 60 pounds of sugar made into jellies; also 100 barrels of dried apples to the Christian Commission, beside other gifts.

It is but an act of simple justice to say that the ladies did nobly, and from the beginning to the close of the war they worked unitedly, diligently and perseveringly to do what they could.

Destination of the Articles. This can be given in a few instances only. Two or three barrels were sent direct to the hospital at Alexandria, Va., in which Miss Emma D. Southwick and Miss Eliza M. Weeks, both from Westford, were employed as nurses.* One barrel was sent to Ship Island, the rendezvous of the troops under General Butler, and a box was sent to the contrabands. But most of the barrels and packages were sent to the Boston office of the Sanitary Commission.

November 2, 1865, a draft of $300 from the Westford Freedman's Aid Society was sent to William Endicott, Jr., treasurer of the New England Freedman's Aid Society, on account of Sarah E. Keyes, teacher of freedmen, which was duly acknowledged. Inasmuch as she stands as a worthy

---

*These were the only ladies who went from this town, but several men were employed in such service. They continued long and acquitted themselves creditably.

"When pain and anguish wring the brow,
A ministering angel thou."

representative of this town in the line of her chosen profession, it is proper that some notice should be taken of her work. Sarah Elizabeth Keyes was born in Westford, July 4, 1839, and was residing here at the time she accepted the position of teacher of the freedmen. She left home for the scene of her toils the last week in October, 1865, and in a few days reached Kinston, N. C., where she entered immediately upon her work. In a letter written six weeks afterward, she gives some account of her experience. "The colored school was first opened in a building formerly used as an academy. Our number increased so rapidly that we found it necessary to have another room, which was secured, and the school divided. We [i. e., her associate and herself] have now three hundred scholars or more in both schools, and some less than one hundred in our evening school. At first there were about fifteen who could read in the Testament (very poorly, though); and others could not read at all. When I had them spell out the name of our beloved Lincoln, their eyes would sparkle with delight. Some of those who scarcely knew their letters when we commenced six weeks ago, are reading nicely in words of three and four letters. I think they learn quite as fast as the scholars in any school at home with which I am acquainted."

"We are living in a house belonging to John C. Washington, one of the 120 rebels who voted for the secession of North Carolina. He has recently obtained his pardon, and will doubtless soon take possession of his property. Our school-house also belongs to him."

She also engaged in Sabbath school work, of which she says: "Sometimes there has been but one other teacher beside myself to instruct and interest a school of eighty or more. I have tried to teach them something of the life of Christ and of their duty to God and one another."

In both departments of benevolent exertion she and her associates had to encounter much opposition. The rich planter ejected them from his premises, and they were obliged to take up with such conveniences as they could find for their schools. One night evil-minded men entered their school-room, broke up the furniture and threw the stove out of doors. But having a purpose of entire consecration to her Lord and Redeemer, she persevered through the winter and spring, and in May was seized with bilious fever, so common in that climate, and died in Kinston, June 5, 1866, aged 26 years and 11 months. Her grave is there. A memorial service was held in the First Parish Church of Westford, June 20, at which brief addresses were given by Rev. E. R. Hodgman and Rev. E. A. Spence. "She hath done what she could." "The righteous shall be had in everlasting remembrance."

In connection with the services of this noble Christian woman, it is proper to mention the name of her brother, Edward Keyes. It may be said of him, with probability, that he served his country *longer* during the war than any other man who went from Westford. He enlisted November 8, 1861, and served until the war was practically ended. His regiment was kept in the service after nearly all the others had been discharged. He died of jaundice in Sumter, S. C., August 18, 1865, aged 37 years and nine months, and was buried there. It may be truly said of him that he enlisted from a religious sense of duty which he carried into his every-day life. His words were: "My country first, my family next. God's promises and blessings are for us if we do his will. So, let me live and die in His service." To these let it be added: "*He dieth well who liveth well.*"

The spirit and example of this brother and sister may be taken as just types of that genuine philanthropy and piety which shone so brightly in the lives of so many devoted men and women in that eventful period. And now the two Carolinas hold their dust. He sleeps in the State which was the birth-place of rebellion, and she in the State in which secession breathed out its last breath at the surrender of Gen. Joe Johnston to the hero of the "March to the Sea."

Miss Emma D. Southwick, after finishing her work in the hospital, went as a teacher among the freedmen of South

Carolina, where she spent some time on her benevolent mission. "Tom," an intelligent colored lad, was brought by her to Westford and placed in school. Afterward he joined the school at Hampton, Va., now under the supervision of Gen. Armstrong.

The town of Westford " was not behind any town of its size and wealth in the Commonwealth in fulfilling every obligation demanded of it by the State or nation during the entire period of the rebellion. It furnished one hundred and seventy-two men for the war, which was a surplus of fifteen men over and above all demands. Four were commissioned officers. The whole amount of money raised and expended by the town on account of soldiers' families and repaid by the State, was $10,525." [History of Massachusetts in the Civil War, vol. ii., p. 469.]

Inasmuch as a statement has been made (p. 145) in reference to the part of Massachusetts in the War of the Revolution, it seems fitting that a similar statement should be made in regard to the War of the Rebellion. The actual number of men furnished by Massachusetts for the service of the United States, of all arms, and including both the army and navy, was one hundred and fifty-nine thousand one hundred and sixty-five — 159,165. In this estimate are not included the five companies who joined the New York Mozart Regiment in 1861, nor the recruits who entered the Ninety-ninth New York Regiment under Col. Wardrop, which, if added, would make the aggregate within a fraction of 160,000 men. The old Commonwealth came out of the war with a surplus of 13,083 men. Her troops were the first to enter Washington and save that city. They also saved the old frigate Constitution in April, 1861, then lying at Annapolis. They were the first to enter North Carolina and the city of New Orleans. The first also to invade Texas and to ascend the Mississippi from New Orleans to Cairo. Colored troops were the first to enter Richmond, thus fulfilling the law of natural and poetic justice and the letter of the sacred text: "The last shall be first."

The number of officers who were killed or died in the military service from Massachusetts was four hundred and forty-two; and the number of enlisted men was twelve thousand five hundred and thirty-four (12,534), as near as can be ascertained. The enrollment made in 1862, preparatory to the draft, was 164,178; the number who paid a commutation fee was 3,623.

In his valedictory address to the Legislature, January 5, 1866, Governor Andrew "fixes the amount expended by the State for the war and paid out of her own treasury at twenty-seven millions, seven hundred and five thousand, one hundred and nine dollars — $27,705,109. This was exclusive of the expenditures of the cities and towns. She had paid promptly, and *in gold*, all interest on her bonds and kept faith with every public creditor." [See History of Massachusetts in the Civil War, vol. 1.]

CHAPTER VII.

THE SEQUEL TO THE REBELLION — PROSPERITY — TOWN HOUSE — TYNGSBOROUGH BRIDGE — EAST BURYING-GROUND — INVITATION TO CONCORD CELEBRATION — CITIZENS' MEETING — DELEGATION — PROPOSED MONUMENT — CENTENNIAL, 1776-1876 — FUNDING THE TOWN DEBT — TOWN HISTORY — COMPLETION OF ONE HUNDRED AND FIFTY YEARS — REMODELLING THE TOWN-HOUSE — REDEDICATION — MEMORIAL DAY.

THE civil war ended April 9, 1865, by the surrender of the Confederate Army under General Lee to the Union Army under General Grant, at Appomattox Court House, Virginia, and the loyal people of the United States rejoiced with unbounded satisfaction because the strife was over. The peace must have been welcomed, too, by those who fought on the other side; for they, far beyond the experience of any portion of the North, had witnessed the terribly destructive force of war. But the joy that was felt in the hour of triumph was soon changed to grief and mourning. Abraham Lincoln, President of the United States, was cruelly assassinated at Washington, D. C., April 15, only six days after the surrender of Lee. By this tragic event the nation was plunged from the height of exultation to the lowest depths of sorrow. The years that followed, years of readjustment and reconstruction, furnished a test of perhaps unequalled severity to all lovers of freedom and republican institutions. Sharp as was the trial and stern as was the discipline, it was all needed and wisely ordained by the great Ruler of nations, who often leads through roughest ways and darkest skies to serene heights and abiding peace. Although the War of the Rebellion was far more sanguinary than the War of the Revolution, it did not impoverish the people. During its continuance nearly every branch of industry was properous, and after it ceased business of all kinds, except ship-building, was brisk and remunerative. On the other hand, the period after the Revolution, as has been shown, was one of poverty and financial embarrassment. There is a marked contrast in this respect between the two periods.

In this town after the war the evidences of material prosperity were numerous and gratifying. Money was abundant, and the people were ready to use it in making their homes more beautiful and in carrying out some plans for public improvement. A pleasing change was soon observable in the central village; a rapid growth took place in the manufacturing villages of Graniteville and the Forge; and, indeed, throughout the town there were indications of thrift and gain.

By the annulling of the school-district system in 1869, agreeably to the provisions of the laws of the Commonwealth, the town assumed the possession of all the school-houses and of all the school property; and the desire was soon manifest of displacing the old and shabby structures and building in lieu of them houses more convenient and attractive. The need of a new town-house was soon felt, and the struggle to obtain one was long and arduous. Numerous meetings were held and various projects were discussed for one or two years, but in the conflict of opinions it was not easy to secure the erection of a building adapted to all municipal wants and requirements.

THE TOWN-HOUSE.

"July 30, 1870. The town voted to choose, authorize and empower a committee of five persons to build a townhouse, the cost of said building (exclusive of the land on which said house may be located) not to exceed eight thousand dollars. Voted that the town appropriate the sum of eight thousand dollars to defray the expense of building, and also authorize and empower the town treasurer, under the written direction of the selectmen, to borrow in the name of the inhabitants of Westford, a sum not exceeding eight thousand dollars to defray the expense of building a town-house. Chose Charles L. Fletcher, Samuel Wiley, George Drew, Nathan S. Hamblin and Ephraim A. Stevens, building committee."

The committee were instructed, before making any contract, "first to ascertain what the entire expense of building is to be, including wharfing, fencing, and everything appertaining thereto, and if it is to exceed eight thousand dollars, all such proposals are to be rejected. Voted to authorize the selectmen to procure a site for the town-house on the Dr. Osgood lot, so called, the lot connected with that on which the (Osgood) house stands."

Being unable, after long continued negotiations, to purchase the lot of the owners thereof, the selectmen resorted to the process of law in such cases provided and authorized, and took the land, agreeably to the provisions of chapter 411, General Laws, session of 1869. *

The house was built in the autumn of 1870. The town, at a meeting held November 8th, gave discretionary power to put in a furnace and build a brick safe for the preservation of the town books and papers, and the committee procured a furnace and built a safe. At the same meeting in November the town voted "to appropriate two hundred dollars for a memorial slab containing the names of all our townsmen who lost their lives in the late war." The building committee procured the tablet and caused it to be erected at the entrance to the lower hall.

February 4, 1871, the town appropriated six hundred dollars for furnishing the town-house. The house was

---

* In May or June, 1873, Eliza Osgood and others, heirs of the late Dr. Benjamin Osgood, petitioned the court against the town for assessment of damages occasioned by the taking of land for a town-house. A sheriff's jury was summoned, who listened to statements and allegations made by witnesses and counsel for both parties, and afterward brought in a verdict in favor of the petitioners, giving them the sum of $778.43 and interest, which was $21.79, making a total of $800.22.

dedicated March 3, 1871, at which time the address was given by Rev. George H. Young, then minister of the First Parish. Prayer was offered by Rev. E. R. Hodgman. The chairman of the building committee presented the keys, after a brief speech, to the chairman of the Board of Selectmen, who responded, and the building passed into the possession and under the control of the town.

March 5, 1871, the town voted "that the selectmen be authorized to appoint some suitable person or persons to take charge of the town-house and town library, the same to be kept in the town-house; and they shall be authorized to pay what, in their judgment, is a fair compensation for the service; and they shall continue to appoint from year to year until otherwise ordered." Also, "that it be left to the selectmen to let the town-house to parties wishing the use of the same, discriminating between citizens of the town and parties out of town in their charges."

TYNGSBOROUGH BRIDGE.

June 3, 1871, the town chose a committee of two by ballot, namely: John W. P. Abbot and Charles G. Sargent, to appear at the meeting of the County Commissioners at Tyngsborough, June 20th, and oppose the laying of any special tax upon this town for building the bridge across the Merrimack River at Tyngsborough.

EAST BURYING-GROUND.

November 4, 1873, the town voted to purchase land of J. Henry Read for the enlargement of the East Burying-ground, according to a plan drawn by Edward Symmes; to pay at the rate of one hundred dollars per acre, and to fence the lot.

INVITATION.

March 1, 1875, the town voted to accept the invitations extended by the towns of Concord and Lexington to attend the celebration in those towns on the 19th of April next.

CITIZENS' MEETING.

At a meeting of the inhabitants of Westford, held at the Town Hall, April 17, 1875, to take action in regard to an invitation to unite in the centennial celebration of the battles of Lexington and Concord, in which this town participated largely, it was unanimously

"Resolved, first, That we accept most heartily the invitation to join in the celebration on Monday, the 19th inst., and impressed with the importance of the event which occurred one hundred years ago, initiating the War of the Revolution with all its glorious results, and remembering the zeal and alacrity with which our grandfathers rushed to the scene of action, to the number of ninety-four true men, with scarce an hour's notice, and faced unflinchingly the British bayonets, we hereby pledge ourselves, as the descendants of those immortal men, to honor their memory and endorse their heroic efforts by a large attendance at the battle-field, taking such places in the procession as may be assigned to us.

"Resolved, secondly, That Mr. Hodgman be invited to communicate for record such historical facts relating to the participation of this town in the doings of that important day as he has been able to glean from colonial records and other sources.

"Resolved, thirdly, That the action of this citizens' meeting, with the resolutions and the facts which Mr. Hodgman may be able to communicate, be recorded in the Town Book, so that our children's children may remember the deeds of their progenitors when another hundred years shall have passed and the events which we celebrate shall call them together for a similar purpose.

"Resolved, fourthly, That it is the duty of the citizens of Westford to erect a monument to the memory of Lieut.-Col. John Robinson and the other Revolutionary soldiers of Westford.

WILLIAM A. WEBSTER, Chairman.
WILLIAM E. FROST, Secretary."

The resolutions were presented by Mr. J. G. Dodge. It was voted that the chairman, Dr. Webster, appoint a committee to nominate a candidate for marshal of the Westford delegation at the centennial, and he appointed Sherman D. Fletcher, Alvan Fisher and William Reed, 1st. They reported the name of Luther Prescott, Esq., who was unanimously chosen. The same committee nominated for assistant-marshals, George T. Day and J. Murray Chamberlin, and they were chosen.

Lieut. Sherman H. Fletcher and Isaac E. Day were appointed a committee to procure a flag for the Westford delegation.

Remarks were made by George T. Day, Nathan S. Hamblin, Luther Prescott and Edwin R. Hodgman, urging the feasibility of petitioning the General Court for permission to raise money by tax for the purpose of erecting a monument to the memory of Lieut.-Col. Robinson and other Revolutionary soldiers of Westford. A motion was passed that the chairman nominate a committee to petition the Legislature for such permission, and George T. Day, Luther Prescott, William Reed, 1st, Alvan Fisher, George W. Heywood, Sherman D. Fletcher, Joseph Henry Read, George Hutchins, Isaac P. Woods and Nathan S. Hamblin were named and chosen. Voted, also, that the sextons of the churches in town be requested to ring the bells at sunrise and at sunset on the 19th inst.

THE CELEBRATION AT CONCORD.

The following persons, constituting the official delegation from Westford, were present, by invitation, at Concord, April

19, 1875, marched in the procession and participated in the exercises of the day, namely: Edwin R. Hodgman, Town Clerk; Isaac P. Woods, Henry Chamberlin and N. Harwood Wright, Selectmen; Sherman D. Fletcher, Town Treasurer; Rev. Leonard Luce, Rev. William A. Cram and Rev. Henry H. Hamilton.

About two hundred of the citizens of Westford were present, nearly all of whom were in the procession, under the marshalship of Messrs. Day and Chamberlin. The delegation carried a banner, on one side of which appeared the name of Col. Robinson.

MONUMENT PROPOSED.

May 22, 1875, a town meeting was held at which a proposition to raise a sum of money, not exceeding two thousand dollars, to be expended in the erection of a monument on the common to commemorate the services of Col. John Robinson and others who bravely participated in the fight at the old North Bridge in Concord, and at Bunker Hill, was *defeated* by a vote of 78 to 51.

CENTENNIAL EXPOSITION.

When the nation had reached the one hundredth anniversary of its independence in 1876, the event was celebrated throughout the Union. The citizens of Westford attended in large numbers the Exposition in Fairmount Park, Philadelphia. This exhibition was an index to the growth and attainments of the nation during a century, in respect to civilization and the useful arts, the invention of machinery, the development of agriculture, the power of mind over matter, the improvement of schools, and in everything that dignifies and embellishes modern society. But it was more than this; a criterion of the world's progress in all departments of human activity, and everyone who saw it, must have acquired from it a broader conception of the immense resources of the human mind and the wonderful achievements of the human race.

FUNDING THE TOWN DEBT.

May 16, 1877, the town voted that the town treasurer be authorized and empowered, under the direction of the selectmen, to borrow in the name of the inhabitants of the town of Westford, the sum of twenty thousand dollars at an interest not exceeding five per cent. per annum; said sum to be applied to the payment of the town debt already contracted, with the privilege of paying the sum so borrowed within ten years by making an annual curtailment of two thousand dollars or more.

TOWN HISTORY.

March 4, 1878, the town appointed George T. Day, Edwin R. Hodgman, Alvan Fisher, William E. Frost and John M. Fletcher a committee to consider the expediency of publishing a town history. This committee reported, March 3, 1879, in favor of the compilation and publication of such a history, and the town voted to appropriate the sum of two hundred dollars to Alvan Fisher and his associates, provided they shall carry out the recommendation of the History Committee, and shall publish, or cause to be published, a history of this town in a volume of four hundred pages octavo, and shall furnish the same to residents of this town at two dollars per copy.

COMPLETION OF ONE HUNDRED AND FIFTY YEARS.

On Tuesday, September 23, 1879, this town completed the one hundred and fiftieth year of its incorporae existence, and the day was observed by an informal and extempore celebration. By invitation of the Town History Association a meeting of the citizens was held in the town hall and brief addresses were made by several persons. Luther Prescott, Esq., gave some account of the occupation of the water-power in Forge Village, which began in 1680, and also the business of smelting iron ore which started soon after. The leader in this enterprise was Capt. Jonas Prescott, the ancestor of the Prescotts in this vicinity. Allan Cameron, Esq., spoke of his residence of twenty-two years in town, and of the improvements which he had witnessed, especially in Graniteville, which has come into prominence during that time. Rev. George H. Young, former pastor of the First Church, happily alluded to his connection with this people and of his interest in them. Rev. M. H. A. Evans followed him, expressing in a similar manner his interest in the welfare of the town. Rev. J. S. Moulton, Preceptor William E. Frost, and Hon. J. H. Read made brief addresses, and Rev. E. R. Hodgman gave some facts respecting the early history and some statistics of population and manufactures. Mr. C. W. Blood gave two cornet solos and was heartily applauded. Excellent singing was furnished by the two choirs who rendered Keller's "American Hymn," "America" and a select "Hymn of Gratitude" with fine effect. The commemoration was truly successful and was heartily enjoyed by those who were present.

REMODELLING THE TOWN-HOUSE.

March 1, 1880, the expediency of repairing and altering the town-house came before the people at the annual meeting, and the selectmen were made a committee to estimate the expense and report to the town at a future meeting. That committee made a report and the town, at a meeting held March 24, 1880, voted to accept and adopt their report which presented a plan and estimate of cost for repairing and improving the house. Three thousand dollars were raised and appropriated to the purpose, and the selectmen were entrusted with the responsibility of carrying out the vote of the town.

Town Hall.

The plan that was adopted, by putting a new front to the building with a tower, not only added to the beauty of the structure, but enabled great improvements to be made in the accommodations for ingress and egress. A gallery was put into the hall and fifteen more feet added to the rear of the building, which addition gave space for a commodious kitchen and one other room on the first floor. On the floor above ante-rooms were made on each side of the stage, which was set back and made more convenient. The entire cost of the alterations and improvements was $3,662.

REDEDICATION.

It was deemed fitting that the completion of the re-modelled and renovated building should receive some public recognition, and accordingly a celebration was arranged for Thursday, December 9, 1880, which was largely attended by the citizens of Westford and of the adjoining towns. Governor Long was invited to be present, and an address was delivered by Rev. Edwin R. Hodgman, by invitation of the committee of arrangements. The address related to the early history of the town and the principal facts have been embodied in this history. Governor Long, in his address on the occasion, recalled the remark of John Adams, that "the four corner-stones of the Commonwealth are the town, the church, the school and the militia," and said that all were fittingly represented in this celebration. He congratulated the citizens of the town on the evidences of growth and improvement, not only in material things, but in culture and refinement, and he called attention to this wonderful growth all over our country. But while we congratulate ourselves on the progress we are making in tangible things, he said the best progress is after all in those principles which have been referred to in the address as possessing and animating those who founded our New England municipalities. Brief addresses were also made by George A. Marden, of Lowell, and Allan Cameron, of Westford. Music was furnished by the Dunstable Cornet Band. In the evening there was a supper and promenade concert.

MEMORIAL DAY.

Although the town contributed its full share to help sustain the burdens of the war, and although the ladies were liberal in the assistance they gave to the sick and wounded, and all the citizens cherished the memory of the dead, there was no public and formal recognition of Memorial day until the year 1882. A detachment from Post 115, Grand Army of the Republic, came from Groton, May 30th, and joined the veterans of Westford in decorating the graves of comrades in our cemeteries. There were ceremonies in the Town Hall in the evening. The Graniteville Cornet Band performed several pieces of martial music. Miss Laura E. Mace, of this town, read with fine effect "Hooker's Battle Above the Clouds." The address was delivered by Rev. E. R. Hodgman. It contained a brief history of the part of Westford in the civil war. Capt. Palmer delivered a brief but effective address, relative to the objects and organization of the Grand Army of the Republic. It was a fitting observance of the day.

CHAPTER VIII.

TOPOGRAPHY — BOUNDARIES — HILLS — PONDS — BROOKS — VILLAGES — LOCALITIES — GEOLOGY — MINERALS — WATER-LEVEL — MORAINES — SOIL — AGRICULTURAL PRODUCTS — FLOWERS.

The Township of Westford is situated in the County of Middlesex and the Commonwealth of Massachusetts. It is in latitude 42° 35′ 40″ N.; longitude 71° 25′ W.

It is bounded on the north by Tyngsborough, on the east by Chelmsford, on the south by Carlisle and Acton, on the southwest by Littleton, and on the west by Groton. It presents on the map an irregular six-sided figure, having its longest measure on the Chelmsford border, a distance of nearly eight miles. The whole number of acres, as given on a map which was lithographed in 1855, is 19,519. By the census of 1875 it contained 5,142 acres of forests; 4,646 acres of unimproved land, and 638 acres of unimprovable land; and there were 232 farms, including 3,567 acres under crops. The whole number of acres taxed in 1882 was 18,000.

The surface is diversified with hill, valley and plain. Large areas, once cultivated, are now covered with forests, which seem to be extending year by year. The highland near the centre was called Tadmuck Hill in the early deeds, and the name was applied, not merely to a single summit, but to a large area. The highest elevation, now called Prospect Hill, originally *Clay-pit*, rises more than three hundred feet above the valley of the Stony Brook at Westford Station. Blake's Hill, Rattlesnake Hill and Sparks Hill are spurs on the south of this, and Bear Hill, little Bear Hill, and Nonesuch Hill are slight elevations in the southeast.

The boundary line between Littleton and Westford crosses Fletcher Hill and Nashoba.* Snake-Meadow Hill is west of Graniteville; Conscience Hill, west of Keyes Pond, received its name from a man of somewhat peculiar traits, who once owned it and was nicknamed *Conscience*. Spalding Hill, lying between Keyes and Long-sought-for Ponds, probably took its name from Dea. Andrew Spalding. Oak Hill, in the extreme north, has granite quarries which have been worked for many years; Flushing Hill, near the pond of the same name; Milestone Hill, at the northwest corner; Kissacook Hill, near the poor-house; Cowdry Hill, west of Snake Meadow; Providence Hill, northeast of Providence Meadow, and Frances Hill, on the Chelmsford line, complete the list. The last one mentioned is a high table-land, from which beautiful views can be obtained of the mountains on the west.

PONDS AND BROOKS.

Forge Pond, on the southwest, is a fine sheet of water with gravelly banks. Only a part of it can be claimed by Westford, for the town line cuts it in twain. The part included in Westford contains 104 acres. Nubanussuck Pond, half a mile from Brookside, has an area of 123 acres. It is much frequented in summer by excursion parties from Lowell and elsewhere. Long-sought-for Pond † comes next, with an area of 107 acres; then Keyes Pond, 40 acres; Burge's, 25 acres; Flushing, 20 acres, and Grassy, 18 acres. These, with the exception of Forge, are all in the northern half of the town; in the southern half there is no collection of water except the arm of Heart Pond. All these have a beauty of their own. Their pure waters sparkle in the sunlight of the

---

* It is said that the meaning of the word Nashoba is *the hill that shakes*, and that the reason is that at certain times rumbling noises are heard and vibratory motions are seen in the hill, indicating some internal convulsions.

† There is a tradition that the name of Long-sought-for was given because a party, who had heard of its existence, started to find it and spent four days before they came to it. Burge's Pond received its name from Samuel Burge, who owned the land near it.

long summer day and reflect the snow-white clouds that float above them. Malarious influences are seldom generated about them, but they send their sweet waters gaily down to Stony Brook, and this sends them to the broad Merrimack, and this, in turn, passes them on with rapid current to the ocean. The pretty little stream that runs from Forge Pond to the Merrimack is worthy of a more poetic name than Stony Brook, albeit it is a benefactor to the people. It has several tributaries. It receives the waters of Nubanussuck Pond through Gilson's or Saw-mill Meadow Brook, near Westford Corner. It takes the waters of Keyes Pond through Dutton's or Keyes Brook, and Keyes Pond is itself connected with Long-sought-for Pond by Spalding Brook. A small brook, without a name, rises near Kissacook Hill and meets the Stony Brook near the Almshouse. Boutwell Brook, on the south side, was once an outlet of Forge Pond, perhaps the chief one, through Hopyard Swamp, but in the progress of centuries the channel was filled up, and the brook now only drains Boutwell Meadow and falls into the Stony Brook at Graniteville. Tadmuck Brook rises in Providence Meadow and takes a northward course to Stony Brook near the railroad bridge. Swan Brook, near the Groton line, empties into Forge Pond. Humhaw Brook is an affluent of Keyes Pond, from the northwest, and so is Snake Meadow Brook from the southwest. Beaver Brook comes in from Littleton and empties into Forge Pond. Nashoba drains the east part of Great Tadmuck Meadow and passes on to Acton. On its way it receives Vine Brook, which rises south of Prospect Hill and flows in near the railroad, and Nonesuch Brook, which drains Nonesuch Meadow; also Butter Brook, which rises near Great Bear Hill, and empties in near Carlisle Station. Pond Brook flows from the eastern border into Heart Pond. On the larger ones there is no lack of mill-sites.

VILLAGES.

Forge. This is the oldest, without doubt. Its good water-power was its chief attraction to the early settlers. It is a pleasant village, stretching along the margin of the pond, having a large school-house, railroad station, ice-house, post-office and store.

The *Central Village* is "beautiful for situation," being built on a commanding eminence, the northern terrace of Tadmuck Hill, which is 238 feet above the level of the railroad at Westford station. The view of the distant mountains in clear weather is especially attractive and inspiring. The stretch of the western horizon is broken into wavy lines by the summits of Wachusett, Watatic, Monadnoc, the Temple Hills, Kearsarge, Joe English Hill and the Uncanoonucks. The White Mountains of New Hampshire can be seen in favorable times. Its elevated position and picturesque scenery entitle it to rank among the loveliest villages of Northern Middlesex. Here are the church edifices of the First Parish and of the Union Congregational Society, the Academy and the Town House—a large building, two stories high, and furnished with modern conveniences for the town offices, a fire-proof vault and room for the town library; also a large hall for public meetings and armory for the Westford Squad of Company F, Massachusetts Cavalry. The common is a gem of rural beauty, not large in extent, but fringed with a double row of evergreen and deciduous trees. Here in the twilight of pleasant summer evenings the young and the old do sometimes gather to listen to sweet music; or in the spell of the witching moonlight the light-hearted sit and while the gladsome hour away. The main street is shaded with elms and maples, and the ample sidewalks tempt to evening promenades amid the perfumes of June or the golden sheen of October. To those who know, there is a lane that leads to "paradise," where green mosses deck the border of the spring, and birds "sing love on every spray." Prospect Hill is within easy reach of the adventurous foot, and is often visited by those who wish to see "the lovely and the wild mingled in harmony on nature's face." The general intelligence and social refinement of the people, the good influence of the Academy and the healthfulness and general thrift that are apparent, together with the neatness and tidiness of dwellings, gardens and enclosures, all conspire to make this a desirable place of residence for all who seek a home far from the mills and shops and counting-rooms of care-worn men.

Graniteville. This village owes its existence primarily to its water-power and to the building of the railroad in 1847. At that time there were only two or three houses in it. Its development is chiefly due to one man, who came there in 1854. It is now a village of several hundred inhabitants, and contains a machine shop, worsted mill, hosiery, milliner's shop, two or three stores, tin-plate worker's shop, large school-house, two railroad stations, postoffice, Methodist Church and reading-room.

Brookside. This is a small village on the eastern border, near Chelmsford line. It enjoys the distinction of being the spot on which the first fulling-mill was built in the town. A worsted-mill, owned by Moore Brothers, is the centre of the only business carried on there.

Parkerville is the name given to a populous neighborhood in the south part of the town.

Nashoba is the name of a postoffice at the Carlisle station, on the Framingham and Lowell Railroad.

There are in all four postoffices, designated as Westford, Forge Village, Graniteville and Nashoba.

LOCALITIES.

Sackatere. This name, which is found in the old deeds, was given to a tract of woodland on the northeast side of Rattlesnake Hill.

Mackrill Cove. This term was applied as early as 1716 to a lot of ten acres, near the farm of Atwood brothers. The first owner was Thomas Adams, the present is George T. Day.

Texas, or the Lost Nation. This designation was applied long since to a region in the south part of the town, on Nashoba Brook. It includes "cat heads" and the old place once owned by James Hapgood, now abandoned to pasturage and forest.

Westford Corner. A name applied to a cluster of houses near West Chelmsford, at the mouth of Saw-mill Meadow Brook. Hard by is the tomb of Issachar Keyes.

Buffalo. The term applied to a rough place, near Tyngsborough line, north of the house of John Banister.

Elsewhere. Name given to a wood-lot of thirty-six acres, northwest of Erastus Wright's.

Hyde's Hole. Name originally applied to a valley near Merrick Reed's.

New Jerusalem, or Advent Corner. A term once used to designate a cluster of houses about half a mile east of the Centre.

Chamberlin's Corner. The vicinity of Chamberlin's blacksmith shop, on Frances Hill.

GEOLOGY.

The prevailing rocks are granite, gneiss and Merrimack schist. Snake-Meadow Hill and Oak Hill are marked and evident upliftings of granite, which displaced the overlying strata of gneiss. Extensive quarries have been opened in both and the traffic in this material has attained large proportions. "The stone used in Boston under the name of Chelmsford granite does not come from Chelmsford, but from Westford and Tyngsborough. In the latter place it is obtained chiefly from bowlders; but ledges are quarried in Westford. I do not know why it has been called Chelmsford granite, unless from the fact that large quantities are carried to Lowell (formerly a part of Chelmsford) to be wrought. This rock is pure granite with no hornblende; and being homogeneous and compact in its texture, it furnishes an elegant stone. Good examples of it may be seen in the pillars of the United States Bank and the (Quincy)

Market House in Boston. These were from Westford.* The Westford granite is connected with an imperfect kind of mica slate, in which it seems to form beds or large protruding masses." (Report on the Geology of Massachusetts by Edward Hitchcock, 1833, p. 16.) In speaking of the granite beds of this vicinity, Prof. Hitchcock gives the direction as northeast and southwest, and the dip or inclination as 60 degrees to 90 degrees northwest—(p. 294.)

Granite bowlders are scattered in great profusion over the town, and are often quarried for building purposes. Their position in the fields often indicates the force of the drift-current that was hurrying them along. In some cases they were carried quite over to the eastern slope of the hill; sometimes they were left on the top, and sometimes on the western side, as if the current had spent its force at that point. Instances of this are numerous. In digging them out of the ground, small round stones are often found lodged about the bowlders on the west side *only*, indicating the line of the drift, which was from the northwest toward the southeast. The layers of gneiss in many places are tilted almost vertically, so that the thickness of the successive folds can be distinctly seen. Noteworthy instances of this can be found near the house lately occupied by Joseph F. Prescott, on the way from Forge Village to Littleton; also near the house of Henry A. Hildreth. A broad ledge, which crops out near the house of William Kittredge, has upon its surface grooves made by glaciers in some far-off geological age. † Rude outlines of the human face have been traced upon it, and the figure is said to be the work of Indians. "The mineral which is generally called andalusite is most abundant in Westford, in mica slate. Numerous specimens can be obtained from thence. It occurs in stone walls from a

---

* Persons are now living here who remember to have seen those pillars drawn by oxen through the town on the way to Boston. That was fifty years ago, perhaps more, and before the existence of railroads.

† Professor Gunning, who once visited the spot, said it was a remarkably well defined instance of glacial action.

hundred rods to a mile east of the village, and may sometimes be found in distinct prisms, greatly resembling specimens from Germany. It is of a reddish color, and sometimes the masses are two and three inches across. Generally they are accompanied by a fibrous mineral resembling talc; but I am not satisfied as to its nature."* [Prof. Hitchcock's Report, p. 345.]

MORAINES.

These are numerous, especially in the north part of the town. These beds of sand and gravel may be heaps of detritus formed during the glacial period, or of silt or wash, left by the subsidence of water. The largest of these is the plain lying between Nubanussuck Pond and Stony Brook, and extending from Westford Corner to Grassy Pond. Much of it is a barren waste with large spaces of clear white sand upon which no vegetation can grow. Another bed lies between Keyes Brook and Snake-Meadow Hill, and it also shows large tracts of utter barrenness. Patten's Plain, so called, lying between Boutwell's Meadow and Forge Village, is evidently a huge sandbank swept into place by the action of water. Another lies northward of Graniteville, being part of the Dughill lot; and smaller ones are found in other localities. These beds seem to indicate that water once covered the entire Stony Brook valley, and when geological changes occurred, it retreated into the basins of the several ponds that now exist on the north and west of Stony Brook valley. There is clear proof that Forge Pond once discharged its waters, or a portion of them, through Boutwell's Brook, but after a long period it wore its present channel to so great a depth that it became the only outlet, the other channel having gradually filled up.† Beds of deposit are

---

* Perhaps this mineral is in reality the Merrimack schist, which prevails here, and of which he makes no mention in his Report.

† Persons now living speak of a rock in Boutwell's Meadow, which, not long ago,

found in the vicinity of Providence Meadow and Pond Brook —much of the land of the old Cookson lot being of this nature. The "divide" or water-shed between Providence Meadow and Pond Brook, is near School-house No. Six, and Heart Pond seems once to have reached an arm up to that point. Similar beds are found in the region of Vine Brook and Nashoba, showing that once, possibly, the waters of Magog Pond in Acton came up to meet the waves of Forge Pond in Great Tadmuck Meadow. If the supposition be admitted, then Tadmuck Hill, with its outstanding spurs, was an island lifted up by internal forces, and covered in due time with forests. These were possible geological facts, which, of course, cannot be proved.

The soil in the north part and some portions of the eastern and southwestern sections is sandy and poor, but along the margin of Stony Brook, below Heywood & Burbeck's mill, it is of good quality. This charming valley, with its level farms, appeals to the sense of beauty in every beholder. The best land for farming purposes is in the south part, on Farwell's Plain and in the vicinity of Parkerville, near which there is an overlaying of clay which produces excellent grass.

AGRICULTURAL PRODUCTS.

These are such as are common to New England. Proximity to the markets of Boston and Lowell encourages the production of small fruits, in which the Atwood Brothers, Augustus Bunce, John Lanktree, Cyrus Hamlin and Albert P. Richardson bear a part. Many farms are devoted to the cultivation of vegetables. Large orchards abound on Frances Hill and Tadmuck Hill, and the annual product of apples is very large. In some years thousands of barrels are shipped to England.

---

was nearly imbedded in the soil, but is now several feet above it; and this fact serves to show the sinking of the meadow after the filling of the mouth of the brook.

FLOWERS.

This is the home of many wild flowers of great beauty and variety. In the springtime the trailing arbutus appears on the margin of Nubanussuck.

> Blushing 'mid the withered leaves,
> Modest, peerless, little thing;
> Lo! this fragrant May-flower weaves
> Chaplets for the brow of Spring.
>
> Blooming in the sunny days,
> Humbly trailing on the ground,
> Coyly shrinking from our gaze,
> Waiting to be sought, if found.

The hepatica, the houstonia and the violet are followed by the wind-flower, the polygala, the arethusa and the ladies' slipper. The lupine, the painted-cup and the twin-flower come with the early summer. This last, called by botanists the *Linnæa Borealis*, has its home in Twin-flower Dell, near the Nashua and Acton Railroad. Its fragrant and delicate blossoms are specially attractive. The mountain laurel grows sparsely in a few places. The lilies and the asters and the golden rods appear with a multitude of others that have not been named; and when the Indian summer is near at hand, the gentian, taking its hue from the clear autumn sky, brings up the rear of the floral procession for the year.

Machine Shop of C. G. Sargent's Sons.

CHAPTER IX.

INDUSTRIES AND MANUFACTURES.

THE first concernment of the early settlers was to provide for the three urgent necessities of human existence—food, clothing and shelter. They had no luxuries, and they resolutely set their faces against all "foreign superfluities." Their chief business was to till the soil. It was no easy task to cut down the forests, dig out the stumps and stones, and get the ground ready for the seed. In the early years little else was done, and the work required much hardship and self-denial. Yet there was a real joy in it, such as the pioneer feels when he starts out to make a home for himself with all its endearments and pleasures. Their houses were built for protection, not for show; their food was plain, but nutritious; their garments were homespun, but neat; their hearts were true and their minds elastic and cheerful. Gradually, as the settlement went on, they gave attention to the manufacturing of such articles as they needed. The peripatetic cordwainer or cobbler, with his supply of tools, made his annual visit to the scattered houses, at which time the "rising generation" were appropriately shod.

Nearly all fabrics for garments were spun and woven at home on the hand-loom. The early deeds show that men were often weavers by trade. The cloth, after it was taken from the loom, must be dressed by the clothier. The first fulling-mill, as has been stated (p. 12) was at Brookside. The first tannery was built on the east side of the town by Zaccheus Wright. Col. Wright, having no children, gave up his property and business by sale or will to Benjamin Osgood, who carried it on at the same place for many years.

Another tannery was situated near the centre of the town, on Heywood Street. The first proprietor was Col. Abel Boynton. After him was John Osgood, then Ira G. Richardson. It is now many years since both of these were abandoned.

Brick-making. This was early begun in the south part. The clay-hills on the farms of George H. Elliott and John Wilson furnished the materials for the purpose. The business was carried on by Aaron Parker and his successors, and by Capt. Jonathan Minot and his sons. The last men who were concerned in it were Addison Parker and David Whitney. The old house, torn down not long since by George Hutchins, and the house now occupied by Wayland F. Balch, were built of brick burned near by. The last kiln was burned by Samuel Wiley.

Coopering. This has been done here, but never on a large scale. The town annually goes through the form of choosing a "culler of hoops and staves."

Pottery. There was once a yard for this in the rear of the residences of Nathan S. Hamblin and John W. Abbot. The clay was dug for a while on the north side of Prospect Hill, where the pit is still to be seen. As this did not prove to be of good quality, clay was afterward brought from another source. Mr. James Burns was the first and perhaps the only proprietor. He lived, it is said, on the farm lately owned by Samuel N. Burbeck, and died at a very advanced age. Fragments of pottery have been found on the site of the old yard.

Lime-burning. This has been practised on a very limited scale. Limestone is found in Chelmsford and Carlisle, and perhaps occasionally crops out in the south part of this town. The ruins of a lime-kiln are to be seen near the so-called Carter place.

Carpet-weaving. The house at Westford Corner, lately occupied by Frederic Parker, was once used for this purpose.

Abbot & Co.'s Worsted Mill, Forge Village.

This was before the invention of power-looms, when all weaving was done by hand.

Potash. A building with its necessary appendages for the manufacture of potash stood on the old road from Asaph B. Cutter's to George Yapp's house, which was once a tavern-stand, at the junction of the two roads.

By referring to page 12, the reader will find the date of the first occupation of the water-power at Forge Village, namely, 1680. Hon. Caleb Butler, in his history of Groton, says: "After King Philip's war and the resettlement of the town, Jonas Prescott built a mill at Stony Brook, near its issue from Forge Pond, now in Westford. Previous to the erection of Prescott's mill, an Indian by the name of Andrew sold his weir at Stony Brook, as appears by the following record: 'The twenty shillings due to Andrew, the Indian, from the town for his *warre* at Stony Brook, assigned by said Indian to Richard Blood, the said Richard Blood assigns it over to James Parker.'" Prior to 1730, Jonas Prescott had "greatly enlarged and improved the works on Stony Brook by erecting forges for manufacturing iron from the ore as well as other purposes."

It is difficult to fix the precise date of the building of the forges, but it was perhaps as early as 1710. This enterprise of working iron was the fourth or fifth of the kind in New England. The ore used was the variety known as bog-iron, and was procured in Groton. The "Groton iron," produced at the forge, was not of very good quality, being brittle, and it was not extensively used. The business was carried on until the year 1865, when the Forge Company ceased to exist. It was not exclusively the process of smelting, but of manufacturing forks and other implements. During this long period of one hundred and fifty or sixty years the Prescotts, descendants of Jonas of Groton, held a controlling interest in the company and managed its affairs, except during the last few years of its existence. Jonas, who died in 1870, five years after the forging ceased, was the owner of forty shares in 1863, and was the last who worked at the business.

The Forge Village Horse Nail Company was formed January 5, 1865. It succeeded to the franchise of the Forge Company, used the water-power and buildings of that company, and put in machinery for making nails. The capital stock was $30,000, with the right to increase it to $100,000. The officers were John T. Daly, president; John F. Haskins, secretary, and Alexander H. Caryl, treasurer. The capital was increased to $100,000 in 1868. The business was prosperous and remunerative for some time, but it gradually declined until 1877, when it came to an end.

In 1854 Charles G. Sargent came from Lowell to Graniteville and entered into partnership with Francis A. Calvert, under the firm-name of Calvert & Sargent. This was six years after the railroad had been constructed through that village, which then contained only three or four houses. They bought the farm and the saw and grist-mill of Thomas Richardson, and the buildings were converted into shops for the manufacture of woollen machinery. These were burned in December, 1855; and soon after mill number one was erected — a two-story building 185 x 52 feet, with a connecting L 40 x 32 feet. Two years later they built mill number two of the same dimensions. A partnership was formed in 1857 by the firm with John W. P. Abbot, for the manufacture of worsted yarns; but being unable to attend to this department of business, Mr. Sargent sold his interest to Allan Cameron in 1857. In 1862 Mr. Sargent bought his partner's interest in the machine-shop, and continued the business in his own name. He invented a number of important machines pertaining to his branch of manufacture. Among them were a wool-washing machine, a burr-picker, a wool-drying machine, a patent atomizer for oiling wool and a metallic waste-card for reducing yarn, thread-waste and soft flannels to wool. In 1877, he built a new mill on the opposite side of the stream. This was finished and the machinery moved into it in January, 1878.

In the State census for 1875, Sargent's mill is said to have one establishment for the manufacture of woollen

Abbot & Co.'s Worsted Mill, Graniteville

machinery, with a capital of $37,522. The value of goods manufactured in that year was $46,011.

By the death of Mr. Sargent in July, 1878, the business passed into the hands of his two sons, under the firm-name of Charles G. Sargent's Sons. Since they have controlled it, it has materially increased from year to year, until their facilities in the new building are not adequate to their needs. They employ, on the average, seventy machinists, and the business is now three times as large as in 1875.

The Abbot Worsted Mills began business in 1855, with John W. Abbot as managing partner, and John W. P. Abbot and Charles G. Sargent as special partners. At first they manufactured fine worsted yarns for the making of braids and upholstery goods, employing about twenty hands. In 1857 Mr. Sargent retired from the firm, and Mr. Allan Cameron became an active partner. In January, 1858, their works, as well as those of Mr. Sargent, were entirely destroyed by fire; but in January, 1859, they again began business in one half of a large stone mill, built by Mr. Sargent, about one-eighth of a mile below the former site. These premises they have continued to occupy to the present time, with frequent additions to give increased facilities for production. When they started anew they began the manufacture of carded yarns, used in making carpets. In 1878, Abbot & Company leased the part of the mill formerly occupied by Sargent & Sons, and also built a stone addition to the mill occupied by themselves, sixty feet long and two stories high, and proceeded to fill it with machinery. Finding this still insufficient to meet the growing wants of their customers, they purchased, in October, 1879, the buildings and water-power at Forge Village formerly occupied by the Forge Village Horse Nail Company, and filled the buildings with improved machinery. Abbot & Company employ 200 hands. The wages paid annually amount to $60,000. The average sales per month are $50,000. The daily consumption of wool (uncleansed) is 8,000 pounds; the yearly consumption is 2,225,000 pounds. These aggregates include all their mills.

The Chauncy Mills were established in Graniteville in August, 1874, Miner H. A. Evans, proprietor. There is one set of machinery for making Shaker socks. One hundred pounds of wool are used, and fifty or sixty dozen pairs of socks are made each day. Thirty persons are employed in the mill, and work is given to many more out of it.

Stone Quarrying. This, as a distinct business, came into existence more than half a century ago. At first ledges were not worked, but the large isolated rocks found in great numbers in the north part of the town. The granite pillars of the Market House in Boston were hewn of huge bowlders left ages ago on a lot of land lying northwest of the old school-house in district number seven, on the old stage road from North Chelmsford to Groton, and were hauled through the centre of the town by twenty yoke of oxen. They were obtained by Charles Hollis.

Isaac Carkin was the first man to open the ledge on Oak Hill. The quarrying began there fifty-five or fifty-six years ago, that is, in 1826 or '27. After Mr. Carkin, Major Jesse Colburn carried on the business for many years, and more recently George W. Merrill. Much of the stone from this source is drawn to the stone-yard at North Chelmsford, but some is hauled into Lowell.

The first quarrying from the ledges on Snake-Meadow Hill was done by Benjamin Palmer, a native of Camden, Maine. He came to this town in March, 1847. At first he worked on bowlders or cobbles, as the quarrymen call them, and his stone was drawn by teams into Lowell. He soon began to work on the ledges, and has continued the business to the present time. He employs twenty-one men, besides four others who get out paving stones exclusively. Also, three horses and one yoke of oxen.

In the summer of 1847 the railroad bridge across the brook was begun, and there was a demand for split stone on the spot. The contract for building the bridge was taken by George Wright and David P. Lawrence; but they

Residence of Mrs. Charles G. Sargent.

relinquished in December, and the bridge was finished by Henry Woods, of Groton.

In 1848 Samuel Fletcher, a native of Groton, engaged in the business, and hired a ledge on the hill. During the summer of that year he drew a large quantity of stone to the landing near the railroad, and had it all ready for transportation when the railroad was opened. It was carried to Lawrence and used in the construction of the dam across the Merrimack River at that place. Mr. Fletcher now owns a quarry on the hill, and two quarries elsewhere. He employs fifteen or twenty men, and the amount of his annual sales is $10,000.

March 1, 1853, William Reed, 1st, a native of Acton, bought of Thomas Hutchins sixty-one acres of land on Snake-Meadow Hill, and in connection with his brother, David Reed, began the business of quarrying. The lot lies on the crest of the hill and is long and narrow. In a year or two the lot was divided between the brothers, William taking the portion on the top of the hill and David the western part, toward and including some part of Cowdry Hill. They still continue the business. William Reed employs about twenty men for eight or nine months in the year. Also six horses and one yoke of oxen. His annual sales run from $8,000 to $12,000.

The ministry lot of twenty acres on Snake-Meadow Hill lies between the lots of William Reed and Benjamin Palmer. It was given to the First Parish by Jonas Prescott, Esq., the father of Dea. John Prescott, who once owned the saw-mill at Graniteville. In 1853, Ephraim Abbot and John W. P. Abbot were authorized to procure a survey of it, and the latter gentleman was given "full power to sell stone from the church lot for the benefit of the church." The quarry on it has been worked by Benjamin Palmer and Samuel Fletcher.

Asa Bond opened a quarry on Cowdry Hill and was afterward associated with his brother Almon Bond. They carried on the business for a year only, for Almon died,

December 10, 1860, and Asa soon after removed to Concord, N. H.

Reed, Palmer and Fletcher supplied a large quantity of stone to George Runels, contractor, to be used in building he State Prison at Concord. It was sent on the Nashua and Acton Railroad.

Noah Prescott has a stone-yard at Brookside and one at Westford station, but his chief business is done at Brookside. His quarries are in the north part, near Flushing Pond. He employs twelve or fourteen men and four horses. Annual sales, $7,000.

The granite dealers send the stone to numerous cities and towns of this Commonwealth, which make the chief demand for it; but it is sometimes sent to New York, New Orleans and Chicago. It is used for paving, for engine-beds, foundations for buildings, street curbing, flagging for city sidewalks, window and door-caps, door-sills and caps, bridge-building and various other purposes. Being free from mineral substances, it holds its color for a long time, and seldom shows any rust or stain; but being hard to bring to an edge, it is not much used for monuments, although it is often prepared for edge-stones around lots in cemeteries. The traffic is an important source of income to the town.

Stores and Store-keepers. The country store is a necessity, albeit the time was when the chief trade was in rum, codfish and molasses. Store-keeping, or shop-keeping, as it was styled, had its favorite haunts to which it clung with much tenacity. The following facts, communicated by Mr. Edward Symmes, relate to one spot on which the business was pursued for a long time:

" *Owners of the Cameron place for the last one hundred and twenty years.* May 5, 1762, Timothy Fletcher sold to Asahel Wyman two acres of land near the meeting-house for £60.

"July 8, 1774, Asahel Wyman, blacksmith, sold to Elizabeth Symmes, shop-keeper, the land and buildings. Her

Granite Quarry of William Reed.

shop was in the north part. The house was evidently built at two different times. The front or east part was originally built for a Sunday *noon-house*. The addition made on the west side was for a kitchen, and her shop, with a glass door, was next to the street. She was then the widow of Captain Caleb Symmes. She was married by her father, Rev. Willard Hall, to Captain Benjamin Fletcher, February 9, 1779—the last marriage recorded by Mr. Hall. The price she paid Wyman for the two acres of land and buildings was £106-13-4. At the time she bought, Capt. James Pollard owned the Sherman D. Fletcher place, and Samuel Gardner the John W. Abbot place. Her conveyance of the place I have not found, but by dates I have, it must have been in the spring of 1793—to Abel Boynton. Boynton, at that time, owned the John W. Abbot place. May 13, 1793, Abel Boynton sold to Samuel Wood for £180. Wood built a store and divided the land, the dividing line running over the centre of the well. October 5, 1799, he sold the western half with the buildings to Isaiah Leighton for $800. I think Samuel Wood was a baker, as well as a trader. February 26, 1806, Isaiah Leighton to Jonas Blodgett for $800. February 1, 1810, Jonas Blodgett to Benjamin Kneeland for $800. August 8, 1811, Benjamin Kneeland to James P. Patten for $1,045.93. January 15, 1825, James P. Patten to Amos Adams for $1,000. October 24, 1828, Amos Adams to Ebenezer Tidd for $1,000. March 31, 1832, Ebenezer Tidd to Edward Symmes for $700. Edward Symmes sold to John W. P. Abbot, and Abbot sold to Allan Cameron." In addition to these ——— Proctor and also Jacob A. Wright kept store there under the lease of the building.

On the opposite side of the street from the site above mentioned, stood the "old red store," which was successively occupied by Benjamin Kneeland, Captain Thomas Read, Samuel M. Newhall, Joseph Keyes, Trueworthy Keyes and Samuel Fletcher. A new store was built on the same site and occupied by Samuel and Sherman D. Fletcher from 1839 to 1860; by Sherman D. Fletcher from 1860 to 1873, and by Wright & Fletcher from 1873 to the present time.

A store once stood on Main Street, near the present residence of Mrs. J. W. P. Abbot, and was occupied by Calvin Fletcher, Willard Reed and William Ditson. A new store took its place and was occupied by Samuel Wright, Isaiah Leighton & Son (George), Peter H. Willard, Fletcher & Tidd, Samuel Fletcher, Trueworthy Keyes & Benjamin F. Keyes, Keyes & Brown (George), Keyes & Parker (Jacob Osgood), Henry Griffin, Butterfield & Hildreth, Alonzo W. Hildreth, David C. Butterfield, Protective Union Company, Cummings & Kimball and Hildreth & Fletcher. The same store was moved to a site near Samuel Wiley's house, and occupied by Fletcher Peckens, Peter Swallow, S. A. Bull, Sidney Parker, Edwin Carter, Samuel Wiley, and Cumings Brothers.

A store in the yard of Mrs. George Prescott was occupied by Benjamin Kneeland, then moved to the site of Mrs. Groce's house and occupied by Joseph Keyes.

Willard Reed had a store in the wing of Ephraim A. Stevens' house, and John Hinckley had one in a part of Mrs. Betsey Day's house.

Albert Leighton built a store in the space near Charles H. Fletcher's house, and occupied it. The building was afterward removed and became a part of John B. Fletcher's house. Mr. Leighton previously occupied a part of the Bancroft house, about 1843.

Caleb M. Blake once had a store in a part of the old Byam house.

Miss Lydia Keyes had a store near the spot on which Greenleaf Drew's house now stands, and this was afterward occupied by Josiah Fairbanks who came from Shrewsbury.

A Mr. Russell came from Boston and occupied a part of Mrs. Abijah Fletcher's house.

Jacob A. Wright began to do business in the "old red store," then moved to the one opposite owned by Edward Symmes, afterward occupied the store in Mrs. Abijah Fletcher's house, and from that he went to the Bancroft house near the First Parish Church.

Residence of Allan Cameron.

In a store east of the common, John B. Fletcher, and after him John M. Fletcher.

In Graniteville, Wright & Co. (N. H. and Arthur Wright), Arthur Wright, Wright & Woods, and Wright & Bemis.

At Cowdry's Corner, in the vicinity of Heart Pond, Nathaniel Sweetser, about 1819-'20.

Luther Reed, in the house now occupied by George Hutchinson.

In the house in the southwest part, sometimes called the Hartwell tavern-stand, Willard Reed, Seth Reed, Jonas Blodgett and Simeon Stevens.

At Chamberlin's Corner, Jacob Osgood, Henry Griffin, ——— Woods, John E. Stevens.

Samuel Adams is early mentioned as a trader. He was concerned in buying and selling land in Cavendish, Vt., to which place he removed and where he lived for a while. His store was probably near the Chelmsford line, hard by Isaac Adams', but he seems also to have been at the Centre.

In Forge Village the merchants have been Jonathan Prescott, Luther Prescott, David P. Lawrence, ——— Butterfield, Gilson, ——— Blodgett & Reiter, Albert King.

CHAPTER X.

ECCLESIASTICAL HISTORY.

THE inhabitants of the west precinct early took measures to secure the settlement of a minister. The following is the earliest hint which the records give of their efforts in this direction: "Chelmsford, December the 15th 1726. At a meeting of the Com^{tee} of the West Precinct of sd Town, it was ordered that Ebenezer Wright, Treasurer of sd Precinct, pay to Joshua Fletcher for money expended about and agoing for ministers the sum of 15s. Pay to Ens. Joseph Keyes, for money expended agoing for Mr. Hall the sum of 8s." Under the same date the treasurer was ordered to "pay to Mr. Willard Hall for Preaching the Gospel amongst us 15^{teen} Sabbaths and the *thanksgiven* the sum of 25£ 05s." Also, " pay to the Reverend Willard Hall for preaching five Sabbaths the sum of 7£ 10s." Here are bills for two periods of service, apparently, making £30 15s. for twenty Sabbaths' preaching. It seems probable, therefore, that he came here in July or August, 1726.

The Invitation to Mr. Hall. "Chelmsford, May the 2nd, 1727. At a meeting of the inhabitants of the westerly Precinct in Chelmsford Regularly Assembled to make choice of a minister to settle with them.

1ly. Chose Dea. John Comings moderator for the work of the day.

2ly. The Reverend Mr. Willard Hall chose for a minister to settle with us.

3ly. Voted to give a hundred pounds money or Bills of Credit to the Reverend Willard Hall, if he seeth cause to take up with us to be our minister, for his settlement, to be paid within six months after he takes up with us to be our minister. Voted to give to the Reverend Willard Hall eighty pounds money or Bills of Credit of this Province for his Sallary." "May 24, 1727. Voted that the Reverend Willard Hall shall have for his Sallary eighty pounds for the first year and then to rise forty shillings per year till it comes to an hundred pounds per year. Voted that he shall have fifty pounds *aded* to the hundred pounds before granted towards his settlement, which shall be in labour or specie. Voted that Dea. John Comings, William Fletcher and Joshua Fletcher shall be a Com^{tee} to carry the votes to the Reverend Willard Hall and to treat with him about settlement with us. Voted that they shall agree with him that his Sallary shall rise and fall according to the vallue of money." *

The Answer to the Call. "Chelmsford Precinct, August 26th, 1727.

To the Com^{tee} to be Communicated:

So certain it is that all ye affairs of the world & of every particular Person and even the most minute circumstances of our lives, are governed by the Providence of him whose Kingdom Ruleth over all, that every wise and every christian man more especially will endeavor in his Designs and Actions to do the Will of God by following the Rule of Scripture wch will certainly entitle him to the favour of God and to the blessing of his providence and will give him Satisfaction and Comfort in the condition which he shall thus put himself into: and thus I have endeavoured to regulate myself in the important affair of settling in the ministry here. I have no farther sought my own Private Interest than the law of nature obliged me to, that I might Secure a tolerably comfortable subsistence which I cannot any longer doubt of since I have so much assurance of the continuance of your good

---

* About three years after his ordination he seems to have complained of this condition as vague and unsatisfactory. The parish explained it by saying that what they meant by money was *silver* at sixteen shillings per ounce.

Disposition toward me w^{h} you expressed by your united Consent.

I do therefore willingly accept of your Call and am well satisfied with the Salary and Settlement you offered, with the addition you afterward made to them, and do now look upon myself to be under peculiar obligation to you more than to others; and when I shall be more formally placed among you and Receive the solemn charge, I will by the grace of God make your spiritual welfare my most important Business, neither shall I count my life dear to myself so that I may finish my course with joy and the ministry which I shall have Received.

WILLARD HALL."

Organization of the Church and Ordination of Mr. Hall. "The Second Church of Christ in Chelmsford was framed of ye members of several of ye neighbouring churches but chiefly of ye first church in this Place. They uniting together (after ye proper Preliminaries to settling a minister) unanimously called Willard Hall* to take ye Pastoral Care of them; and he accepting ye Call, was accordingly ordained their Pastor & Teacher by ye Reverend Elders following, viz: Samson Stoddard who preached & gave ye charge, making ye prayers usually accompanying that solemn Service: Benjamin Shattuck who made ye Ordaining Prayer after ye Sermon: Nathaniel Prentice who made ye first Prayer & gave ye Right Hand of Fellowship: and Thomas Parker who gathered & formed ye Church. This first ordaination was solemnized November 27, 1727."

"As the Custom is, where a number of persons in full communion, desire, for allowable reasons, to seperate from y^{r} respective churches & become a distinct organized church by themselves, for them explicitly to enter into Covenant with God & one another; so here, a Covenant being drawn,

---

* A marginal note reads thus: "Aged 24 years and upward from March 11th to this time."

they who had gotten their Dismissions from ye churches they belonged to, set their hands to it, which is here inserted:

THE COVENANT.

"We whose Names are hereunto subscribed, apprehending ourselves called of God into ye Church-State of ye Gospel, do first of all confess ourselves unworthy to be so highly favoured of ye Lord, & admire that free and rich grace of his which triumphs over so great unworthiness, & then with an humble Reliance on ye Aids of Grace therein promised for them that, in a sense of their Inability to do any good thing, do humbly wait on him for all, we now thankfully lay hold on his Covenant & would chuse ye Things that please him. We declare our serious Belief of the Christian Religion as contained in the Sacred Scriptures, heartily resolving to conform our Lives unto the Rule of that holy Religion as long as we live in ye world. We give up ourselves to the Lord Jehovah who is the Father and the Son and the Holy Spirit, & avouch him this day to be our God, our Father, our Savior & our Leader & receive him as our Portion forever.

"We give up ourselves unto ye Blessed Jesus who is the Lord Jehovah and adhere to him as ye Head of his People in ye Covenant of Grace, & rely on him as our Priest & our Prophet & our King, to bring us unto eternal blessedness.

"We acknowledge our Everlasting and indispensable obligations to glorify God in all the duties of a Godly, a Sober & a Righteous Life, & very particularly in the duties of a Church-State & a Body of People associated for an Obedience to him in all the Ordinances of the Gospel; and we therefore depend upon his gracious Assistance for our faithful discharge of all the Duties thus incumbent on us.

"We desire and intend and (wth Dependence on his promised and powerful Grace) we engage to walk together as a church of ye Lord Jesus Christ, in the faith and order of the Gospel, so far as we shall have the same revealed to us; conscienciously attending to ye publick Worship of God, ye

Sacraments of his new Testament, ye Discipline of his Kingdom, & all his holy Institutions in Communion with one another, and watchfully avoiding sinful Stumbling Blocks and Contentions, as becomes a People whom the Lord has bound together in a Bundle of Life.

"At ye same time we do also present our Offspring with us unto God, purposing with his help, to do our Parts in ye methods of a religious Education, that they may be ye Lord's.

"And all this we do, flying to ye Blood of ye Everlasting Covenant for the Pardon of our many errors & praying that ye glorious Lord who is the great Shepherd, would prepare & strengthen us for every good Work by his Will, working in us that which will be pleasing to him. To whom be glory forever and ever. Amen.

"Willard Hall,   Samuel Chamberlin,
John Comings,   Samuel Fletcher,
William Fletcher,   Aaron Parker,
Joseph Underwood,   John Procter,
Joshua Fletcher,   Jonas Fletcher,
Aquila Underwood,   Nathaniel Boynton,
Jonas Prescott,   his
Jonathan Hildreth,   Benjamin X Robbins,
Andrew Spalding,   mark.
Jacob Wright,   Josiah Whitney."—18.

The date of ordination seems to be the date of the organization of the church. No other can be found on the records. Great deliberation was shown in the action of the parish and of Mr. Hall. He had been with them fourteen or fifteen months, and this gave opportunity for securing a mutual acquaintance. The relation of pastor and people was assumed thoughtfully, and with a sincerity of purpose and aim that is very commendable. It was the custom in those times to observe days of fasting and prayer with reference to the choice of a minister. At such times the neighboring ministers were called in to aid the church in its deliberations, and the records show that such a day was observed here before the call was given.

Of the "reverend Elders" who composed the council, Samson Stoddard was pastor of the old church in Chelmsford; Benjamin Shattuck was the first minister of Littleton; Nathaniel Prentice was minister of Dunstable, and Thomas Parker was the minister of Dracut.

Of the original members of the church, John Comings had been deacon in the First Church in Chelmsford, as it appears from the fact that he is called deacon in the records before the church was formed. Joshua Fletcher, Samuel Chamberlin, John Procter, Benjamin Robbins and perhaps Josiah Whitney had been members of the church in Littleton. It does not appear on the records that any *women* were among the original members; and the fact is noteworthy since they have always constituted so large a part of all the churches. It is fair to presume, however, that persons of that sex were among the number, since the names of women are numerous in the subsequent record of additions. Yet, with the exception of Parker and Procter, the names of the wives of the original members do not appear on the church-books, not even Madam Hall's. It seems to be an omission that was never supplied. It is charitable to suppose this, for surely they could hardly intend to interpret Paul's words so strictly as to merge the wife in her husband in respect to her ecclesiastical relation.

The first pastor, Rev. Willard Hall, was born in Medford, Massachusetts, March 11, 1703. He was the son of Stephen and Grace (Willis) Hall, and belonged to a family of distinction. He graduated at Harvard College in 1722, in the class of Richard Saltonstall and William Ellery. He married Abigail Cotton, of Portsmouth, New Hampshire. Mr. and Mrs. Hall were the parents of eleven children, four sons and seven daughters:

1. Willard, born June 12, 1730, at Portsmouth, N. H.
2. Elizabeth, born October 24, 1732.
3. Abigail, born July 19, 1734.
4. Anne, born April 22, 1736.
5. Mary, born July 30, 1738.

6. Martha, born June 8, 1741; died young.
7. Stephen, born May 28, 1743.
8. Grace, baptized June 30, 1745.
9. Willis, born November 14, 1747.
10. Isaiah, born January 19, 1749.
11. Martha, born July 16, 1752.

As was usual in those days, Mr. Hall became the proprietor of a small farm which he cultivated with great care and success. In 1727 he bought of Josiah Burge eighteen acres of land, and he received by gift one acre from Dea. John Comings. This was situated on the west side of Main Street, and included a tract now severally owned by Charles L. Fletcher, the heirs of Rev. W. F. Wheeler, Charles H. Fletcher, Mrs. Abijah Fletcher, John Lanktree, the heirs of Samuel Wiley and the heirs of the Bancroft estate. This was the homestead, extending probably from the meeting-house to the corner by Greenleaf Drew's house, and perhaps including the land of N. Harwood Wright, Samuel Tilton, Mrs. Asa Hildreth and True A. Bean.

It is difficult to fix the precise spot on which his dwelling stood. An emphatic tradition puts it on the site now occupied by the house of the late Rev. W. F. Wheeler, but there is some evidence in favor of the house now occupied by Austin Wright, or one which stood on that site, for this has been several times in the possession of Mr. Hall's descendants.

It is said that he was a good farmer, cultivating fruit trees bearing plums, apricots, peaches, pears and apples; and that his garden, orchards and fields, years after his death, bore witness to his skill and industry. He also owned land on the north side of Stony Brook, in the vicinity of Thomas Horan's, which, in the old records, is called the *Hall Field*. It is now a forest, but it was once cultivated. He had a few acres in Providence Meadow. In February, 1731, the town voted " that the use and improvement of the Ministry Meadow, lying in our town, shall be given to the Rev. Willard Hall so long as he continues to be our minister."

This was the same lot of ten acres in Snake Meadow which was given up to Westford as their part of the ministerial lands by the old town in 1729. (See page 11.) But this being remote from Mr. Hall's house, the town, in September of the same year, " voted to sell the Ministry Meadow and lay out the money in the most convenient place for the use of the ministry." At the same time it was voted to " pay Mr. Hall's salary *quarterly*," and also " to raise £50 and *give it* to Mr. Hall this present year." These quarterly payments were continued during his ministry, and were generally made with promptness and punctuality. The record of them usually specifies, with noticeable preciseness, that they were made to Mr. Hall " for preaching the gospel and carrying on the work of the ministry." There is recorded, in his own handwriting, a receipt in full which, as a specimen of the times, may be worth transcribing:

" Westford, August 31, 1733. Rec'd at sundry times of Constable & Treasurers of ye town of Westford, ye full sum of all my Demands upon sd Town, upon all accounts *from ye beginning of ye world* to ye first day of September, in ye year one thousand seven hundred & thirty-two. In witness whereof I have hereunto set my hand.

WILLARD HALL."

It would not be easy to go back of this with any demand for service or payment of the same.

On the 6th of March, 1731–'2, Thomas Read, Samuel Chamberlin and Joseph Fletcher were chosen a committee to join with Mr. Hall to sell the Ministry Meadow and lay out the money according to the vote of September, 1731. This committee, May 27, 1735, bought for fifty pounds of Benjamin Blodgett, of Litchfield, and Elizabeth, his wife, a tract of land, being part of the estate of Dea. Joshua Fletcher, deceased, containing by estimation three acres and twenty-five rods, lying in Westford, south of the house of Joshua Fletcher, Jr., deceased.

This lot, situated about one mile south of the First Parish meeting-house and near the house of Stephen E. Hutchins, now belongs to the heirs of Daniel Flagg.

The sliding scale of Mr. Hall's salary occasioned no little difficulty. In 1733 the town voted to add to his salary yearly the sum of fifteen pounds, to be as silver money at twenty shillings per ounce. Mr. Hall asked for this increase "on account of the fall of money in the year 1732." But the year following, at the request of the town, he relinquished this addition; and the town afterward appropriated, from year to year, such a sum as was deemed an adequate fulfilment of their contract, in the fluctuations of the money market in those times. In 1731 they paid him £100 as salary; in 1738 it had increased nominally to £180, and in 1741 to £200 in bills of credit of the old tenor. Yet, such was the depreciation in the value of the Province money, that this sum would probably not be equal to his first year's salary. In 1743 a new issue of money was made and his salary was then reckoned at £50, but it rose in 1749 to £100, and fell the next year to £63.

In 1739 he entered a complaint regarding his salary, and the question came up before the town, "whether they would give any direction to the selectmen about Mr. Hall's complaint; or agree upon some certain method how his salary shall be determined the year past and from year to year; and to raise money, if they see cause, to complete his salary, if it be not completed already—and it passed in the *Negative*." Mr. Hall then appealed to the courts for redress in the matter; and the town appointed a committee, consisting of Jonas Prescott, Esq., Capt. Thomas Read and Jabez Keep "to stand against and answer the complaint of the Rev. Willard Hall against the town, at the Court or Courts, and to vindicate said town as far as possible in the law, or make use of attorneys as they shall think best." (May 16, 1740.)

The town had previously (Sept. 5, 1739) appointed a similar committee, "to take the votes or attested copies from the town book, that are relating to Rev. W. Hall's salary, and his answers to said votes, and go and ask and inquire of Col. Savage, Captain Caleb Lyman and Thomas Hutchinson, Esq., at Boston, and Daniel Russell, Esq., at Charlestown, and Samuel Danforth, Esq., at Cambridge, their judgment, how the Rev. W. Hall's salary is, according to said votes, and his answers to the town about said salary." What the result of this legal controversy was, does not appear from the records. It seems to have been adjusted, however, without much diffiulty; and apparently it did not produce, as it evidently did not spring from, any exasperated or hostile feeling.

At a meeting, however, of the town in the latter part of the year in which this lawsuit arose (November 25, 1740) a proposition to grant "£60 as a gift to Mr. Hall," probably to make up past dues, was voted down, as were also proposals to give £50 or £40. They finally voted "to give nothing."

In 1745 several members of the church were disciplined for "frequently absenting themselves from public worship and from communion at the Lord's table"; also for "attending a private meeting under the ministration of a lay exhorter, in time of public worship on the Lord's day." The names of these members were Joseph Temple and his wife, Aaron Parker, Jr., Jonathan Underwood, Joseph Underwood and his daughter Mary, Aaron Parker, Mrs. Chamberlin and Dorothy Parker, the wife of Aaron Parker, Jr. The meeting was held at the house of Jonathan Underwood, and the name of the lay-exhorter was Paine.*

Some of these made confession and were restored; the others were allowed further time for consideration, but in the meantime were debarred from the Lord's table. It does not appear from the record whether they gave satisfaction and were afterward restored to fellowship or not.

---

* "One Pain, a lawyer, belonging to the Colony of Connecticut, hath lately been introduced into the town by John Burge and Gershom Procter, and divers females of our communion have followed the said Pain, an exhorter, and a very illiterate one, too, to Westford on the Lord's day." (History of Chelmsford, p. 116.)

In 1758, September 19, Mr. Hall, together with William Fletcher, as delegate from this church, attended an Ecclesiastical Council at Haverhill, Mass., which was called to try Rev. Samuel Bacheller for alleged heresy. Mr. Hall dissented from the opinion of the Council in the case, and not long afterward published his views in a small pamphlet entitled "An Answer to Col. Choate: Reasons of Dissent from the Judgment of a Council in a controversy respecting some doctrines advanced by Rev. Mr. Bacheller, of Haverhill—particularly that the work of Redemption as to Price, Purchase and Ransom, was finished when Christ gave up the Ghost. By Willard Hall, A. M., Pastor of the Church in Westforc. Boston: Printed by Edes and Gill, 1761."

This pamphlet was no doubt an important contribution to the polemic theology of the times. It gives evidence that Mr. Hall was a man of strong intellect and of considerable acuteness. The style is vigorous and the reasoning is clear and forcible.

No important incident occurred in Mr. Hall's ministry for a few years after the time of this controversy; but the country was approaching a crisis which severely tried both the pastor and his people.

In 1772, July 6th, the town voted that the selectmen should provide preaching in case Mr. Hall should remain unable to supply the pulpit. This arose probably from his sickness, and the interruption to his labors at this time was comparatively brief. Rev. Deliverance Smith was employed for ten Sabbaths; after this Mr. Hall resumed his ministrations for a time.

But May 17, 1773, the selectmen were again appointed a committee "to provide preaching till the September meeting"; at which time a committee of five was chosen "to treat with Rev. Mr. Hall about his salary, and to provide preaching in his absence." The town at that time granted but £45 for his salary the year ensuing. Mr. John Marsh was paid at this time £4 for preaching three Sabbaths; or at the rate of £70 a year.

March 30, 1774, the town voted "to be in some preparation for settling another minister with Mr. Hall." This is the first intimation that appears of dissatisfaction with his services, either on account of the infirmities of age, or from any other cause. He was then 71 years old.

The remaining years of Mr. Hall's ministry were stormy ones. The essential particulars will be given, but some minor details of the strife will be omitted in the interest of a true charity and a pure taste.

At a meeting of the church, August 10, 1774, Mr. Hall proposed choosing a committee "to assist him in preparing an account of the general disorders which subsisted among them, for the hearing of the church or of an ecclesiastical council, if it should be thought needful." But the church refused to concur in the measure.

November 1, 1774, Mr. Hall read to the church a list of complaints in which he mentioned by name six or seven prominent men, especially the two youngest deacons whom he arraigns for unfaithfulness in their office.

According to some memoranda that have been preserved in connection with the records of the old church, "the selectmen, by desire of several of the town's people, hired Mr. Samuel Ely to preach." He officiated but two Sabbaths; for something derogatory to his character appeared in the newspapers of the day, and "Mr. Hall found so much fault with him that he was sent away." Mr. Hall told them "to take advice of some good minister" concerning a candidate, or "to go to the College [*i. e.*, Harvard] and hire some likely young man to come and preach for them." The selectmen accordingly sent down one of their number "to Cambridge to take Mr. Appleton's advice who to hire." He recommended Mr. John Mellen and Mr. Joseph Thaxter, and they were both engaged to preach, according to a vote of the town. "The next Sabbath," the account goes on to say, Mr. Hall "made a long speech to the congregation, reflecting on the selectmen for hiring a preacher." This opposition, however, was unavailing; for the town proceeded in their course, and afterward employed Mr. Thaxter. His services were acceptable to the people; for he preached in the town for more than a year, and received a call to settle both from the church and the town.

The disaffection toward Mr. Hall still continued, and, September 5, 1774, the town voted "to dismiss the Rev. Willard Hall from any further service in the town as a minister, provided the church should think proper to dismiss him from any further service in his ministerial office in said church."

However, they raised £42 for his support the year ensuing, in case the church should not see fit to dismiss him.

October 27, 1774, the church called in the aid of Rev. Ebenezer Bridge, of Chelmsford, "to assist in moderating a church-meeting." But about a month later the town voted not to take under their consideration the advice of Rev. Mr. Bridge. They also voted "not to hear Mr. Willard Hall any more as a minister of the Gospel," but "to hire preaching further in order to settling a minister with us."

December 27, 1774, the church voted to call an ecclesiastical council, which assembled February 7, 1775, and though no record of their doings is preserved, yet from a document on the town books, it would appear that they advised the settlement of a colleague. "Proposed (1st) that Rev. Willard Hall consent to the settlement of a gospel minister with him. (2nd) That in consideration of his great bodily infirmities, this church expects that he will consent that from and after the time of settlement, the whole exercise of calling and presiding in all church meetings be placed in the latterly settled pastor. (3rd) That with a view to the restoration of the invaluable blessing of peace, this church engage to use their best endeavors that £25 be paid by this town to the Rev.

Willard Hall within ten months, that he enjoy the use of the ministerial pasture, and be paid yearly the sum of £46 13s. 4d. by quarterly payments, during his natural life. (4<u>th</u>) That all past offences subsisting between Pastor and Brethren be mutually forgiven, and that we all will strive together by our prayers and best endeavors that Unity, Love and Peace may prevail here, that the God of Peace may be with us.

"Consented to by the church, *nemine contra dicente*, and by Willard Hall upon condition of the town's compliance."

The town, at a meeting held February 27, 1775, complied with the conditions, except in regard to the use of the ministerial pasture, which was refused; and they also appointed "a day of Fasting in order to give some gentleman a call to settle in the ministry in this town."

These efforts of the church and town did not bring about a final cessation of strife. The political views of Mr. Hall caused great uneasiness among the people, and in September, 1775, the town voted to rescind the pledge to give him £25, and refused to raise any money for his support. After various attempts to effect a reconciliation, the church assembled November 30, 1775, and voted "to dismiss the Rev. Willard Hall from his pastoral relation to this church, for reasons to be given." These reasons are set forth in the records. They relate mainly to Mr. Hall's attitude toward the Colonial Government and the cause of civil liberty. At a meeting of the town, held January 1, 1776, and called for the express and sole purpose of acting in reference to the dismission of Mr. Hall, it was voted "to concur with the vote of the church in this town in the dismission of Rev. Willard Hall from his ministerial office and to dismiss him for the reasons given by the church."

His ministry extended over a period of forty-eight years. There were received into the church during his pastorate 274 persons—256 by profession of faith, 18 by letters of recommendation from other churches, and 34 were dismissed to churches in other towns. The number who " owned the covenant" was 344.

Mr. Hall baptized 1535 children and solemnized 280 marriages.

He united the offices of pastor and physician, thus, in the condition of society at the time, greatly extending his influence and usefulness. He was a strenuous supporter of education for all. The town, on one occasion, considering itself excused by special emergency from levying the required school-tax, he complained to the General Court and arraigned his own charge before that tribunal. In this he offended, as he knew he would, many of his people; but he would make no compromise with delinquency in this matter. Dr. Phillips Payson, pastor of Chelsea, Mass., bore testimony in strong terms to the pleasure of having an acquaintance with him, and mentioned as remarkable the clearness and strength of his mind. He died March 19, 1779, and was buried in the East Burying-Ground. The following is the inscription on his monument:

<blockquote>
ERECTED IN MEMORY OF
THE REVEREND WILLARD HALL,
FIRST PASTOR OF THE CHURCH OF CHRIST
in Westford.
DIED MARCH 19, 1779,
AGED 77 YEARS,*
and in the 52nd year of his
Ministry.

While the pale carcass tho'tless lies
  Among the silent graves,
Some hearty friend shall drop his tear
  On our dry bones and say,
These once were strong as mine appear,
  And mine must be as they.
Thus shall our mouldering members teach
  What now our senses learn;
For dust and ashes loudest preach
  Man's infinite concern.
</blockquote>

---

* According to Mr. Hall's own marginal note in the record of his ordination he was

His widow died October 20, 1789, at the age of eighty-four years. His oldest son, Willard, married Ruth Fletcher, of Westford, and settled in Dunstable.

The second son, Stephen, graduated from Harvard College in 1765 and studied for the ministry, but was not ordained. He was a tutor in Harvard for 6 years, 1772 to 1778, and in the latter year he moved to Portland, Maine, where he married Mary (Cotton) Holt, daughter of Dea. William Cotton and widow of Moses Holt.

His residence at Cambridge shows him to have been a good scholar; but he did not turn his scholarship to much account after settling in Portland. He was a warm politician and a strenuous advocate of the separation of Maine from Massachusetts. He was for two years—1780-'81—a Representative to the General Court from Portland. He died in 1795, aged 51. His widow died in 1803. His son, John H., was the inventor of a valuable improvement in the rifle, and was for many years employed by the government in their armory at Harper's Ferry. His daughter, Martha C., who died unmarried in 1847, left all her property, amounting to $5,500 to the First Parish in her native place. (New England Geneal. Register, 1848, p. 148.)

The third son, Willis, married Mehetabel Poole, of Hollis, N. H., 1779, and lived in Westford on the farm of the late Asia Nutting, near the North Burying-Ground. He was a saddler by trade. His oldest son, Willard, became District Judge of the United States for the District of Delaware.

The fourth son, Isaiah, married Hannah Keep of Westford and settled in Groton. The oldest daughter, Elizabeth, married first, Captain Caleb Symmes of Charlestown, in 1756, and afterward (1779) Captain Benjamin Fletcher, of Westford.

---

then " twenty-four years and upward from March 11 to this time." As the year began March 25th, perhaps the March 11th should be reckoned as March 11, 1726, and in that case his birth took place in 1702, and the headstone is correct in fixing his age at 77 years.

Anne, the third daughter, married Captain Leonard Whiting, of Hollis, N. H., 1761. Mary married Jonas Minot, of Concord, in 1759. Abigail married Oliver Abbot, of Billerica, in 1769. Grace married Benjamin Whiting, Esq., of Hollis, in 1770, and Martha, the youngest child, married Richard Kneeland, about 1775, and lived and died in Westford.

The practice of "owning the covenant," as it was termed, prevailed in this church from the time of its organization to the close of Mr. Hall's ministry. This act entitled a person to certain church privileges, such as baptism for his children, but not to admission to the Lord's table. It will be seen that the number who owned the covenant under Mr. Hall was much larger than the number who were admitted to full communion. But many who took the first step became members in full. Soon after the death of Mr. Hall, the church, at a meeting held June 29, 1779, passed the following vote, apparently without opposition, namely: "that it is the mind of this church that all persons entering into covenant with God, are to be considered as members of the church, and are to be under the discipline of the church; and that the church look upon it that *there is no 'half-way covenant.'*" In this way the church voluntarily freed herself from the custom and ceased to observe it.

As before stated, the church and the town both extended a call to Mr. Joseph Thaxter to settle with them; the church by a vote passed April 7, 1775, and the town by a concurrent vote passed Nov. 30, 1775. The "settlement" offered him, was £133 6s. 8d. and the yearly salary was £75. Here the matter ended; for Mr. Thaxter evidently *declined* the call, although no statement to that effect is recorded on any of the books.*

---

*Joseph Thaxter, the eldest son of Deacon Joseph and Mary (Leavitt) Thaxter, was born in Hingham, April 23, 1742. He graduated at Harvard College in 1768; studied theology with Rev. Dr. Gay in his native place, and was licensed to preach in 1771. He was present at the fight at Concord Bridge and at the battle of Bunker Hill. On the 23rd of January, 1776, he was elected a chaplain in the army, and served in a regiment of

After the dismission of Mr. Hall, various persons were employed to supply the pulpit. Mr. Wheaton of Framingham for one Sabbath ; Manasseh Smith of Hollis for 13 Sabbaths; Josiah Goodhue of Dunstable for 4 Sabbaths ; Samuel Whitman, afterward of Ashby, 8 Sabbaths ; and Mr. Jones 2 Sabbaths. About the middle of November, 1776, Mr. Jesse Read was engaged and served for one year, at the end of which time the church, November 21, 1777, gave him a call to settle by a vote of 21 to 5. The town undoubtedly concurred, for they had previously expressed a wish to have him settled. The acceptance was not received for some months, for the church voted, April 6, 1778, to return thanks to, Mr. Read "for his acceptance of their call." The town agreed to the action of the church May 4, 1778, and the day of the assembling of the council was fixed for June 17, 1778. The churches in Abington, Braintree, Weymouth, Andover, Kingston, Dracut, Townsend, Groton, Concord, Acton, were first invited, but subsequently the church in Concord was dropped and the churches in Medway and Franklin were added, making in all eleven churches. A committee of five was appointed "to prepare matters for the ordination of Mr. Read ; and also to lay all votes of the church and town before the council, that shall be thought proper." The council assembled at the time specified. It was composed of able and discreet men, some of whom were aged fathers in the ministry. This large and honorable body of men

---

which John Robinson, of Westford, was colonel. He was in the ranks at Cambridge, in different parts of New Jersey and at the battle of White Plains, and, as is supposed, went to Lake George and Ticonderoga. He was ordained and settled over the church in Edgartown, Martha's Vineyard, in 1780, where he remained until his death. While he was in Westford, he addressed a detachment of Westford soldiers, twelve in number, as they were about to start for Ticonderoga, and the tradition is, that one of them, Thomas Rogers, refused to stand up when Mr. Thaxter spoke to them, and that of the twelve all returned but Rogers. (See p. 136.) On the 17th of June, 1825, he was called upon to officiate at the laying of the corner stone of the Bunker Hill Monument. This was the last time that he ever left the island. His prayer at Bunker Hill was written out, and may be seen in Sprague's Annals of the Unitarian pulpit. He died July 18, 1827, aged 83 years.

—the "elders" of the churches, together with some of their choicest brethern—had come, some from their distant homes, to take part in the expected solemnities attending the ordination. But for some unexplained reason the anticipated services did not take place.

The council deliberated *four days*, at an expense to the town of £110, but without accomplishing the work for which they were summoned. Apparently violent opposition was made by the small faction in the church who were still adherents of Mr. Hall. So far as the brief and scanty records show, the result of the council was to advise the calling of another council in the selection of which Mr. Hall and his friends might have a share. Accordingly arrangements were made for a mutual council which was to assemble September 1st. Meantime it was inmated that Mr. Hall was desirous of settling the difficulty, and the church voted "to wait on him at a time he shall designate for the purpose." There is, however, nothing in the records to show that any such conference was held by the parties. The mutual council probably met on the day appointed (September 1, 1778) but for some reason voted to adjourn for one month. October 1st, the church voted to abide by the "advice of the council now sitting." What this advice was does not distinctly appear, but, October 12th, the church "voted unanimously to accept the result of the late council." * They had, at least, brought about a truce in the contest, although Mr. Read was not ordained. He seems to have been sacrificed upon the altar of their mutual reconciliation.

Though Mr. Read was given up, the church determined to go on and "have the gospel preached in this town as soon as may be." The neighboring ministers were applied to for assistance; efforts were made to heal internal dissensions, and November 20th, a vote was carried, unanimously, "to pass by all former difficulties and disputes, one amongst

---

* The council was in session five days, at an expense to the town of £170.

another, and to be in full charity one with another, as Christian brethren." These indications were certainly very hopeful. They still prized the institutions of the gospel and deemed them an indispensable part of their social life.*

Mr. Jesse Read was paid, October 23, 1778, the sum of £252 for preaching twenty-eight Sabbaths.†

The Ministry of Rev. Matthew Scribner. December 14, 1778, the town voted " that the selectmen shall hire Mr. Matthew Scribner ‡ two Sabbaths more than he was first agreed with, and then hire some other man to preach with us." This was probably to give opportunity for some other candidate to be presented. Mr. Scribner had commenced preaching about the First of November, 1778, and supplied the pulpit for ten Sabbaths, preaching also the Thanksgiving sermon and one preparatory lecture.

After this, Mr. Jeremiah Barnard preached for seven Sabbaths, receiving £90 for his services. At a meeting of the church, called April 19, 1779, " to see the church's mind, whether they were inclined to give a call to some candidate to settle with us as a minister," it was voted unanimously that it was the mind of the church to settle a minister with them. It was then moved for the brethren of the church to bring in their votes, written for the gentleman they had a mind to have for their minister. There were twenty of the brethren then present who voted, and chose Mr. Matthew Scribner for their minister ; and six voted not to settle him at present. They also chose a committee

---

* In mitigation, somewhat, of the asperities of this conflict, it should be remembered that those were the "times that tried men's souls," and beside these internal divisions, they were subjected to the harrassing anxieties of a protracted struggle for their civil rights. The Tory principles of their minister were specially obnoxious to them.

† "May 10, 1784. Voted to raise 290 pounds money to pay the Debt that the heirs of Mr. Hall have recovered against this town."

‡ February 15, 1780. " Pay to Lieut. Leonard Procter, for a journey to Norwalk and expenses to Imploy the Reverend Mr. Scribner to come and preach in this town, according to town vote, the sum of £60." Also, "pay to Lieut. Procter for a journey to Newburyport and expenses, after the *Result* of Council, the sum of £36."

of five men, to wit: Dea. John Abbot, Maj. Jonathan Minot, Dea. Jonathan Fletcher, Simeon Wright and Ephraim Chamberlin, "to inform Mr. Scribner of the proceedings of the church, and also to inform the selectmen of the town, that the town may act thereon as they think proper. Also to discourse with Mr. Scribner about his principles of religion and church government, and a plan for a minister and people to settle together properly upon."

At a meeting of the town, May 21st, it was voted "that all the inhabitants of this town now present that are twenty-one years of age, shall have the liberty to vote and show their minds respecting the vote of the church in calling Mr. Matthew Scribner to the work of the gospel ministry in this town." It was then voted "to concur with the vote of the church respecting their calling Mr. Matthew Scribner. Also, voted to support Mr. Scribner *decently* as long as he shall carry on the work of a gospel minister for this town; to provide a suitable dwelling house, keeping for a horse and two cows, and twenty cords of wood yearly, and also to give him £90 for his support the first year, *to be settled according to the neccessaries of life*, and to be stated by the Regulating Act, so called, as it was settled in this town; the year to begin on the day of his ordination."

A committee was appointed "to join with the church's committee, to wait on Mr. Scribner with the votes of the town and for further discourse with him." This "discourse" seems to have been satisfactory to all parties, for it procured a favorable response.

The church, at a meeting held July 15th, voted "to return Mr. Scribner thanks for his kindness to this church in his accepting our call to him to settle with us as our minister." They also voted "to send to eleven churches to assist in the ordination of Mr. Scribner, besides the two churches in the place from which Mr. Scribner came," that is, Norwalk, Conn. The churches invited were as follows, viz: Townsend, Rev. Samuel Dix, pastor; Groton, Rev.

Daniel Chaplin, pastor; Dracut, Rev. Nathan Davis, pastor; Acton, Rev. Moses Adams, pastor; Medway, Rev. David Sanford, pastor; Franklin, Rev. Nathaniel Emmons, D. D., pastor; Newbury, Rev. Samuel Spring, pastor; Keene, N. H., Rev. ――― Hall, pastor; Andover, Rev. Jonathan French, pastor; Ashby, Rev. Samuel Whitman, pastor; First Norwalk, Conn., Rev. ―――; Second Norwalk, Conn., Rev. ―――. Afterwards, August 2nd, they voted "to omit to send to the church in Norwalk that is destroyed by the enemy, and to send to the First Church in Kingston instead." Deacons John Abbot and Jonathan Fletcher, and Mr. Nathaniel Boynton were appointed in behalf of the church to issue the letters missive; and these brethern, together with Jonathan Minot and Thomas Kidder, were designated as a committee "to wait on the council for the ordination of Mr. Scribner, and for the defense of the church in all matters that may be laid before said committee." At the same time the town voted "to concur with the church in the appointment of October 5, 1779, for the ordination of Mr. Scribner," and chose a committee to provide for the council.*

There is no further record of the council, so that it is not known by whom the several parts in the ordination services were performed. The church at this time were deprived of their book of records. Mr. Hall had kept possession of it and refused to give it up, after his dismission, although requested several times to give it or a copy of it for their use. After his death they sent once and again to Madam Hall to have it returned to them; but she replied that she "was advised not to deliver up any papers or records till Mr. Hall's estate was settled and that she understood that the church was about to set up a new plan of government and those records would

---

* It cost the town £352, "continental money." The charge or cost at Mr. Hall's ordination was £14. 8s. 2d.

be of no use to them."* What the "new plan of government" was to which she referred, there seems to be no way of knowing with certainty. Perhaps the reference is to the "half-way covenant" practice which had been set aside by the church.

November 1, 1779, "the church came together to consult upon matters respecting the state and condition of the church. It was thought proper and necessary, not only for the satisfaction and benefit of each other, but also that a door might be open to receive members, if any should see fit to offer themselves, to have a confession of faith and a covenant. As the church could not come at their book of records, and consequently were deprived of all papers of this kind," it was deemed needful to prepare a new one. Accordingly a committee of five, consisting of the pastor, Rev. Matthew Scribner, Dea. John Abbot, Nathaniel Boynton, Jonathan Minot, and Thomas Kidder, was appointed "to draw up a confession of faith and a covenant, and lay them before the church for their approbation." This was done, and during Mr. Scribner's ministry, which lasted about ten years, and during Mr. Blake's, also, the following manual was used:

The Confession of Faith. (1.) We believe there is one God, the Lord Jehovah, Father, Son, and Holy Ghost, who are the same in essence, equal in power and glory: and that God is an eternal, unchangeable Being, possessed of a possible perfection, both natural and moral, to an unlimited degree.

---

*The book of records was afterward recovered and is still in existence. It is to be regretted that the volume contains no record of the church during Mr. Scribner's ministry. In the American Quarterly Register, Vol. XI. pp. 385, seq., is an account of the First Church in Westford, in which it is said that the records were kept by Mr. Scribner in a distinct volume, designated volume second. Diligent search and inquiry have been made for this book, but it has not been found. Between the ministry of Mr. Hall and Mr. Blake, who was the third pastor, there is an uncomfortable gap.

(2.) That God is the creator of all worlds and things; and that his providence is over all and extends to all.

(3.) That God has a fixed, eternal, and infinitely wise plan of goverment, which is never frustrated, or in the least degree counteracted by any thing that ever did, or ever will, take place in the system; but all things take place agreeably to the "counsel of his own will," he having foreordained whatsoever comes to pass; yet so as neither violence is offered to the will of the creature, nor can it be said God is the author of sin.

(4.) That the Scriptures of the Old and New Testaments are of divine authority, being written by men inspired by the Holy Ghost; and that they contain all the truths necessary to be known in order to salvation.

(5.) That God created the first man Adam perfectly holy and upright, without the least inclination to transgress the will of his Maker, yet not immutable, but free to stand or fall; and set him as a public head or representative of his posterity; so that in case of his persevering in holiness and obedience, he and all his posterity were to have been forever happy; but by his fall and apostasy from God, they now come into this world in a state of total depravity, condemnation and wrath.

(6.) That the Lord Jesus Christ, who is God and man in one person, as a mediator between God and man, has perfectly obeyed the precepts of the divine law and suffered the penalties of it; whereby he has answered all the ends of the law, has magnified it and made it honorable; and wrought out a perfect and complete rigtheousness, and made an atonement for sin, sufficient for the salvation of the whole world; yet that God hath from eternity determined to apply the redemption of Christ, but to a certain number of mankind, who are in Scripture called the "elect."

(7.) That the whole ground and foundation of our acceptance into the favor of God, is the righteousness and atonement of Christ, in which we become interested by faith alone.

(8.) That in order to faith, or any other gracious exercise, every son and daughter of Adam must be renewed in the temper of their minds, by the immediate power and influence of the Holy Ghost.

(9.) That God hath absolutely promised, and therefore will keep all true saints from total and final apostasy; and cause them by his Spirit to persevere in faith and holiness, till they are made perfect in glory.

(10.) That none but the cordial friends of Christ have a right to partake of the Lord's Supper; and that a confession of faith in Christ and cordial submission to him, is what the church ought to require of those whom they receive to communion.

(11.) That the infant seed of professing believers are proper subjects of Baptism.

(12.) That "God hath appointed a day in which he will judge the world in righteousness by Jesus Christ"; when he will confer on the goodly eternal happiness, but doom the wicked to pains everlasting.

The Covenant. You do now, in the presence of the heart-searching God, and before angels and men, choose the Lord Jehovah, Father, Son and Holy Ghost, for your God and portion; and heartily accept of the Lord Jesus Christ for your Redeemer and only Saviour, as he is offered to sinners in the gospel; solemnly promising, by the grace of God, that you will yield a cordial and universal obedience to his commands; renouncing the vanities of the world and the service of sin and Satan; and approve yourself a disciple of Jesus Christ in all good carriage toward God and man.

You do also submit yourself to the government of Christ in his church, and to the regular administration of it in this church in particular; and promise to walk in communion with it, attending the worship of God and all the ordinances of the gospel in this place, so long as God in his providence shall continue you here.

Rev. Matthew Scribner was the second son of Matthew and Martha (Smith) Scribner, and was born in Norwalk, Conn., February 7, 1746. He graduated at Yale College in 1775, and received the degree of Master of Arts in 1783. He was married in Topsfield, Mass., December 16, 1779, to Sarah Porter, who was born in Topsfield, March 21, 1742. Their children were ten in number — six sons and four daughters:

1. Sarah, born September 15, 1781; died October 4, 1781.
2. Elijah Porter, born October 11, 1782.
3. Nathaniel, born June 30, 1784.
4. Hannah, born February 12, 1786.
5. Sarah, born September 25, 1787.
6. William, born July 27, 1789; died December 11, 1790.
7. Samuel, born December 9, 1790.
8. William, born June 22, 1792.
9. Abigail, born February 16, 1794.
10. Rufus, born August 20, 1795.

In the matter of Mr. Scribner's pecuniary support there would seem to be some deviation from the usual method.

"In consideration of certain Subscription Papers given into my hands for the payment of my salary for the current year, that is to say, from October 5th 1785 to October 5th 1786, I do relinquish all Demands upon the town of Westford for said year.

MATTHEW SCRIBNER.

"Westford, March 27, 1786."

Perhaps these subscription papers were only private pledges in assurance that the salary should be paid. Mr. Scribner was often in trouble about his salary, and these papers were intended to relieve all anxiety. The real intent of them can only be surmised. It is said that Mr. Scribner was never very popular in his parish; that his pastorate was tumultuous and stormy; and that for these reasons it was brief, lasting only ten years, while that of his predecessor continued forty-eight years.

October 6, 1788, the town voted "to choose a committee to try to settle the difficulties respecting some of the inhabitants of this town and the Rev. Mr. Scribner. Chose ten men for said committee, viz: Zaccheus Wright, Jonas Prescott, Timothy Prescott, Francis Leighton, Joshua Read, John Abbot, Jonathan Keep, Isaac Comings, Issachar Keyes and Jonathan Carver." Also, "Voted not to raise any money for Rev. Mr. Scribner's salary, and then the committee of ten made report, and voted to have a council agreeable to sd committee's report." "November 10, 1788, voted to have a mutual council as soon as may be, and to choose a committee to confer with the church's committee respecting the method of calling sd council. Voted that the report of sd committee [of ten] be recorded on the town book."

"*Proposals for a Mutual Council:* 1st. The council is to consist of seven churches; the odd chh to be first agreed upon, and then each party to choose three which shall be mutually consented to.

"2nd. All articles of complaint are to be submitted to the council and left with them to take up or pass by any of sd articles they shall think proper; and having considered and weighed all matters, it is expected that they give their advice whether on the whole it is most expedient for the pastor of this church to ask a dismission and so his pastoral relations to this People be dissolved, or he continue with this people and all contention be laid aside: and as the council shall determine so it shall be: that is, if the council on the whole advise to a dismission, all parties shall acquiesce, and if the council on the whole shall advise all parties to unite and keep their present minister, all parties shall acquiesce, and all contention shall cease.

"3rd. It is further agreed upon that if the pastor is advised to ask a dismission, it shall be submitted to the council what consideration shall be given in addition to the salary already due, or whether any; and if on the other hand it is thought best that the Pastor continue and all submit themselves under his care, to prevent further difficulties it shall be determined what sum is adequate and sufficient for a decent support agreeable to contract, and that shall be the fixed salary for time to come.

"(Signed.) MATTHEW SCRIBNER, Pastor,
In behalf of the Church.
ZACH^s. WRIGHT,
In behalf of the Town.

"The churches agreed upon are the following, viz: Billerica, Concord, Littleton, Groton, Shirley, Lunenburg and Hampshire Dunstable."

The council was "desired to meet on the first Tuesday of December next."

The council met, but there is no record of their proceedings. It may be inferred from the following votes, however, that they advised the pastor to stay.

"January 12, 1879. Voted not to accept the Result of the late Council. Voted to raise two hundred and fifty pounds for the Rev. Mr. Scribner's back salary."

A few days after Mr. Scribner signed the following receipts: "Westford, January 30; 1789. Then rec^d of the town of Westford, Notes of hand signed by the Town's Committee for two hundred and fifty pounds as part of my salary dues from sd town."

"January 30, 1789. Then rec^d of the town of Westford by the hand of sd Town's Committee agreeable to the Town's vote, fifteen pounds eight shillings in full with one other receipt of even date with this receipt for two hundred and fifty pounds, to be in full for salary dues, and for support and house rent and keeping of cows and horse and firewood, which was due to me from sd Westford, agreeable to contract with sd town. I say in full up to the 5th of October, 1788."

The select men ordered these notes to be paid March 18, 1789, and it was done.

The following extracts from the town records point out the conclusion of Mr. Scribner's ministry:

"October 12, 1789. Voted to choose a committee to converse with the Reverend Mr. Scribner respecting his receiving a Compensation for his asking a dismission from this town and church. Chose Lieut. Jonas Prescott, Col. Zaacheus Wright and Joshua Read for sd Committee."

After an adjournment for fifteen minutes, "the committee made report that the Rev. Mr. Scribner would not take anything short of two hundred pounds, and then voted to give the Rev. Mr. Scribner two hundred pounds as a compensation for his being dismissed from his ministerial relation to this town and church, and also to dismiss the Rev. Mr. Scribner as above mentioned; and then voted to give the Rev. Mr. Scribner one hundred and two pounds eighteen shillings and sixpence for his salary for the past year." Having chosen a committee of three men to give to Mr. Scribner security for the payment of his money, the town then voted that "all difficulties respecting Mr. Scribner as minister of this town shall subside. Voted that a council be called by the 10th of November next."

The council was probably called on the day specified, but the town records are silent about it. It is safe to assume that the dismission took place November 10, 1789. In a few months the pecuniary account was settled, and the town took measures to secure preaching. Several years after his dismission Mr. Scribner removed to Tyngsborough, where he took up a lot of wild land just over the line from Westford. This he began to clear up and cultivate, and there he tried an experiment in raising Merino sheep, having bought a few animals at almost fabulous prices. The experiment failed, but he continued to reside on the farm until his death. He and his family were always connected, socially and religiously, with the people of Westford. Here they came to attend public worship, and on one or two occasions Mr. Scribner was chosen moderator of the town meeting. One of the daughters married Leonard Kendall of Tyngsborough, and another, Hannah, married William Usher, of Charlestown, in 1824.

Mr. Scribner died in Tyngsborough, 1813, at the age of sixty-seven years.

November 16, 1789, the town voted " to raise fifty pounds to hire preaching for this town for the present." Also, chose a committee to hire, and instructed the committee " not to engage a candidate for more than four Sabbaths at his first coming into town without knowing the minds of the town." *

After this numerous candidates appeared before the people, and among them were Josiah Burge, son of Ephraim Burge, who went from this town and settled in Hollis. The son, Josiah, graduated at Harvard College in 1787. Read Page; John Simpkins, H. C., 1786; Stephen Baxter, H. C., 1788; Jonathan Osgood, who was born in Westford, and graduated at Yale College, 1787; Thaddeus M. Harris, H. C., 1787; Thomas Worcester, afterwards settled in Salisbury, N. H.; Benjamin Thurston, H. C., 1744 (called Parson Thurstin on the record); Royal Tyler, H. C., 1776; Thomas Moor, H. C., 1787; Hezekiah Packard, H. C., 1787, afterward settled in Chelmsford; Jacob Coggin, afterward pastor at Tewksbury; William Emerson, H. C., 1789, afterward pastor at Harvard, Mass., and transferred to Boston — the father of Ralph Waldo Emerson; and Caleb Blake, H. C., 1784.

The Ministry of Rev. Caleb Blake. Mr. Blake came here, apparently, in the summer of 1791, for he received, August 19th of that year, the sum of £3 5s. for preaching. In September following he received £4 16s. for preaching four days.

The Call. "December 26, 1791. Voted to concur with the church in giving Mr. Caleb Blake a call to settle in

---

* An effort was made to restore Mr. Scribner to the position of minister of the town for, April 4, 1791, the town voted " that it tis not agreebale to this town for Mr. Mathew Scribner to Return Back agin to be a minister of this town."

this town in the gospel ministry by the No. 106 for and 12 against. Voted to Mr. Blake £200 as a settlement: that one hundred pounds be paid in six months after his ordination, and the other hundred pounds in one year; to give £80 a year as salary, to be paid quarterly," &c. The selectmen were appointed a committee " to join with the church's committee to inform Mr. Caleb Blake of the proceedings," and a few weeks later, January 30, 1792, the town voted to " concur with the church in their proceedings for the Council."

The Ordination. Rev. Caleb Blake, the third pastor, was ordained, February 29, 1792. No information can be had respecting the composition of the ordaining council or the names of the ministers who sustained the several parts of the service, for the simple reason that the town records are silent and the church records are missing.

" March 2, 1792. Pay Col. Abel Boynton the sum of £4 20s. for 123 meals of victuals for the Council."* " March 9, 1792. Pay to John Abbot the sum of 18 shillings for pooting up 32 horses for the Council."

Mr. Blake was born in Wrentham, Massachusetts, May 1, 1762, and graduated at Harvard College in 1784. He married, October 13, 1791, Martha Moseley, of Hampton, Connecticut, who was born in 1775, and who was a sister of Hon. Ebenezer Moseley, lately of Newburyport. They had five children, who lived to adult age, two sons and three daughters. One son died in infancy.

1. Martha, or Patty, born April 6, 1793.
2. Caleb Moseley, born April 7, 1795.
3. Sophia Strong, born April 20, 1801.
4. William Herbert, born February 23, 1806.
5. Mary Ann, born December 5, 1809.

Mr. Blake continued in office thirty-four years. His relations to his people were harmonious for about twenty-five years, or until the coming on of that conflict of theological

---

*This is conclusive evidence that the work was done and the dinner was eaten by *somebody*; but *who* did the one and ate the other, the muse of history declines to say.

opinions which marked the early part of the present century. He belonged, it is said, to that class of theologians called Hopkinsians, and when the controversy waxed warm he took a decided stand in defence of his own views. But being ill-fitted and less disposed to engage in disputations, he resigned after a few years and betook himself to a farm. He lived first in the old house (now removed) which stood on the corner of Main and Heywood Streets, and which was successively occupied by Dr. Asaph Fletcher, Jonathan Keep and John Abbot. There all his children were born. He was dismissed, February 28, 1826. In 1817 he bought the Amos Heywood farm, and having repaired the buildings, occupied them until he removed to Bedford, Massachusetts, in 1828. He was in Bedford five years, and returned in 1833. He then purchased what was formerly known as the Bixby farm, now occupied by John Warren Day. After his return he was chosen to represent the town one term in the Legislature. He was not a close student, a fluent speaker, or an easy writer. He published only one sermon, delivered before the Ladies' Charitable Association in 1812 or 1813. He was fond of farming, and attributed his good health in a great measure to that occupation; but his chief pleasure was in reading. He died, May 11, 1847, aged 85 years.

The incidents in his period of service are not very numerous. He seems to have led the quiet life of a country parson, at least until the time of divergence in theological opinions. Soon after his ordination, April, 1793, the church voted " that candidates for admission shall be examined before the church." Also, " that a Chapter or Clause be read in the Bible in the forenoon and afternoon on the Lord's day, as a part of public worship. Col. Wright, at the same time, generously presented the church with a Bible for this purpose."

" March 10, 1794, the church debated on the kind of vessels they would procure for sacramental use, the others having been destroyed when the meeting-house was burnt, and voted to procure ten tankards and three platters."

Beginning of Sabbath School Library. "July 26, 1827. I gave notice that the church voted — it may be a year since or upward — that what money they could spare from sacramental uses should be applied in the purchase of Books for a Sabbath School Library in this place."

During the ministry of Mr. Blake, 124 persons were received into the church, and 17 were dismissed to other churches. He baptized 378 children and officiated at 307 marriages.

December 13, 1827, the church chose Amos Heywood clerk, and adjourned for one week.

December 20th, they chose a committee consisting of Mr. Blake, Dea. John Cutter and Dea. Reuben Leighton to make some alterations in the confession of faith.

"February 28, 1828, the church voted to choose a committee to request Mr. Eber Carpenter to come in and answer questions before the church." Afterward, "Voted that the church are satisfied with the answers made by Mr. Carpenter. Voted to give Mr. Eber Carpenter a call to become the pastor of this church, and to choose a committee to request the selectmen to call a town meeting to see if the town will concur in the call of Mr. Eber Carpenter to the gospel ministry."

The town voted *not* to concur, and this proved to be the last effort to settle a pastor over the church and town together. For one hundred years this had been the order of things, but a change was effected, and the practice was abandoned. It was not, however, until a few years later that the privilege of belonging to any religious society, or the liberty to refuse to be connected with any, was granted by the Legislature without restriction or impeachment. The change in this case was the effect of causes that had long been operating, and the disintegration and separation, though at first unwelcome and disastrous to some cherished customs and familiar associations, came in due time to be acquiesced in as needful and salutary. For many years before the formtion of any new society in this town, persons had connected themselves with Baptist churches in Chelmsford and Littleton, and by furnishing certificates of membership in these, they were released from the obligation to pay a minister tax here. The Baptist Church in South Chelmsford was formed in 1771, and since that time many families in the south and east parts of the town have been connected with it. The following list is without date, but it was probably made out in 1826: "Names of persons that have joined other societies: John Woods, Homer Sawtelle, Peter C. Edwards, Sampson Stevens, Josiah Boynton, Levi Wright, Luther Wright, James Kidder, Gilbert Parker, James Gardner, Dea. Eliakim Hutchins, Thomas Hutchins, John Hutchins, Thomas Hutchins, 3d, Elias Sweetser, Nathaniel Sweetser, Thomas Richardson, Jr., Matthew Griffin, William Cook, Benjamin Haywood, John Osgood, Isaac Patch, Jr., Avery Prescott, Ezra Fletcher, Wid. Anna Pierce, Benjamin Parker, Polly Abbot, Ephraim Chamberlin, Elizabeth Parker, Rufus Flint, Jotham Fletcher, Silas Chandler, Jenner Bird, William Moulton, George Kidder, George S. Messenger, Augustus H. Searles, Thomas Hutchins, 2d, and Salmon Snow."

The following persons are described as "belonging to the first Universalist Society in Westford: Asia Hamlin, Theodore Woodard, William Whiting, William Chandler, Seth Fletcher, Thomas R. Wright, Thomas Spalding, Jr., John Wilson, Luther Trowbridge, Asa Prescott, Jr., Eli Spalding, George Frederick, Thaddeus Blodgett, Parker Woodard, Peter Parker, Jacob Blodgett, Thomas Richardson, Jr., Joseph Fletcher, Solomon Taylor, Cyprian Banister, Timothy Smith, Joel Wright, Oliver Woodard, George W. Spalding, John Wright. April 14, 1826. Recorded the names according to the certificates produced."

About this time a second Congregational Society was formed.

The following belonged to the Baptist Society in Chelmsford: Joshua Hunt, William Laws, Stephen N. Nichols, Samuel H. Nichols, Elisha Bunce, Josiah Webber, Salathiel Adams, Phinehas Chamberlin, Luther Hunt, Erastus Brown,

Isaac Corey, John Fletcher, Edward L. Taylor, Joseph Shed, William Mears, Jr.

The following to the Baptist Society of Littleton: Cyrus Brooks, Eliakim Hutchins, Samuel Farwell, Eliakim Hutchins, Jr.

And these, in addition to the names before given, belonged to the first Universalist Society here: William B. Daniels, Samuel Frederick, Charles Nutting, Samuel Stone, Calvin Green, Jr., John B. Fletcher, Othiel Fletcher, Parker Wright, Nathan Robbins, Eli Green; Avery Prescott, clerk.

Also George Harlow, member of the second Congregational Society in Chelmsford.

This was the attitude of ecclesiastical matters in the winter of 1827-'28. The large number who joined the second Congregational Society indicates some disturbance in the First Parish, the nature of which the records do not reveal. It is evident the elements were in motion, but an effort was soon made to fuse them and secure harmony.

At the annual town meeting, March 5, 1828, a proposition was made to unite all the societies for the purpose of supporting public worship, and the town appointed Jonathan Prescott, Andrew Fletcher and Jesse Minot, Jr., "a committee to confer with the second society committee."

The following paper, apparently embodying the result of a conference of these committees, is on record: (Town Records, vol. vi., p. 19.)

"For the purpose of uniting in supporting preaching for the present, and in the hope that the town may unite in the settlement of a minister, the persons who have subscribed this paper have agreed to recommend to the different Religious Societies in Westford for their adoption the following propositions:

"1st. All the societies shall unite in raising money to support preaching and be assessed together for the same.

"2nd. The manner of raising money shall be such as may be considered legal.

"3rd. The money which shall be voted to be raised thus shall be laid out as follows: A committee of five individuals shall be chosen to procure preaching, two of said committee to be taken from the first Society, two from those who constitute the second, and one from those who constitute the Universalist.

"4th. The two members of the committee taken from those who were the first Society, shall first hire such candidates as they may choose for four Sabbaths; the two members of the committee taken from those who were the second Society shall then hire such candidates as they may choose for four Sabbaths, and the member taken from those who were the Universalist Society shall then hire such candidate as he may choose for two Sabbaths; and so on, till the town shall obtain such candidate as they may agree to settle, it being understood that each denomination in the said committee shall at least have right to hire one candidate before any person shall be settled.

"5th. It is agreed that all money to be raised shall be so raised as to be legally binding on every member of each society that will agree to the union; and that the acceptance of this report is not to bind any society unless accepted by all the societies."

(Signed.) "Jonathan Prescott, Andrew Fletcher, Jesse Minot, Jr., John Abbot, Abram Prescott, Nahum H. Groce, Thomas Richardson, Avery Prescott."

This document is without date, but was evidently prepared after the annual meeting in March, 1828. The town, at a meeting held April 7, 1828, voted "to raise four hundred dollars to support preaching the year ensuing," and chose a committee, consisting of Imla Goodhue, Jacob Osgood, John Abbot, Nahum H. Groce and William B. Daniels, to hire preaching. This seems to indicate a purpose to carry out the recommendation of the joint committee.

January 26, 1829, the church voted to give Mr. Ephraim Randall a call to become their pastor, and on the same day the inhabitants of the *First Congregational Society* * in Westford voted that the society are satisfied with Rev. Ephraim Randall, and that the parish do concur with the church in giving him a call to settle. . . . Voted that the church and society give the Rev. Mr. Randall five hundred dollars as a salary yearly. Voted that the church and society may dismiss Mr. Randall on the vote of two-thirds of the members by giving him six months' notice; and he shall have the same privilege of leaving by giving the church and society the same notice in writing."

Mr. Randall accepted the invitation and was installed, April 30, 1829.

The following churches were represented in the council:
Dorchester, Rev. Edward Richmond, D. D., pastor.

Chelmsford, Rev. Wilkes Allen, pastor; John C. Dalton, M. D., delegate.

Groton, Rev. Charles Robinson, pastor; Joseph Hall, delegate.

Littleton, Rev. William H. White, pastor; Dea. Martin Wood, delegate.

Ashby, Rev. Ezekiel L. Bascom, pastor; Cushing Burr, delegate.

At the services of installation Rev. C. Robinson read the Scriptures and offered the introductory prayer; Rev. Dr. Richmond preached the sermon; Rev. E. L. Bascom offered the installing prayer and gave the right-hand of fellowship; Rev. W. Allen gave the charge, and Rev. W. H. White offered the concluding prayer.

Rev. Ephraim Randall, the fourth pastor, was the son of Hopestill and Submit (Bruce) Randall, and was born in Easton, Massachusetts, November 29, 1785. He graduated at Harvard College in 1812, and was ordained in New Bedford, Massachusetts, August 26, 1814. He was afterward installed at Saugus, Massachusetts, October 3, 1826, and dismissed, August 7, 1827. His connection with the first church of Westford ceased May 1, 1831, by his voluntary resignation

---

* It is "the *town*" no longer, but the *Society*. This is the first time the title appears.

and dismission by act of an ecclesiastical council consisting of Rev. H. Packard, Rev. William Barry, Jr., Rev. Wilkes Allen and Rev. Stephen Hull. He died, December 16, 1871, at Easton.

June 1, 1830, the church by unanimous vote adopted a new profession and covenant, to wit:

"In the presence of Almighty God, the searcher of hearts, and before this assembly, you profess, in the language of the first disciples, to 'believe Jesus Christ is the son of God,' (Acts viii: 37) and do believe the record, 'that God hath given to us eternal life, and this life is in his son,' (1 John v: 11). You receive the 'Scripture given by inspiration of God,' as alone the sufficient and only infallible rule of faith and practice; and do reject all human authority in religion, whether assumed by one man or a body of fallible men, as submission to such authority implies that the Holy Scriptures are not a sufficient rule, and that private Christians are not competent to think and believe for themselves, and is contrary to the declaration of our Lord — 'one is your master, even Christ, and all ye are brethren,' (Matthew xxiii: 8). 'But in vain they do worship me, teaching for doctrines the commandments of men,' (Matthew xv: 9). You do now acknowledge the Lord Jehovah, the one living and true God, to be your God, and, relying upon divine assistance, do promise that you will endeavor 'to walk humbly with God,' (Micah vi: 8).

"Professing repentance towards God, you do sincerely receive the Lord Jesus Christ as he is offered in the gospel, as 'the Teacher come from God,' the High Priest of our profession and 'the King and head over all things to the church,' believing that 'there is none other name under heaven given among men, whereby you must be saved," (Acts iv: 12).

"Depending upon the Holy Spirit for strength and consolation, you will endeavor 'to put off concerning the former conversation, the old man which is corrupt, to be renewed in the spirit of your minds, and to put on the new man, which after God is created in righteousness and true holiness,' (Eph. iv: 22–14).

"In your relation to this church, you will submit to their brotherly care, and to the government and laws of Christ in this church, uniting with them 'with all lowliness and meekness, with long suffering forbearing one another in love, endeavoring to keep the unity of the Spirit in the bond of peace,' (Eph. iv: 2, 3). You do now solemnly give up yourself and all that you have unto God, promising that you will herein exercise yourself to have always ' a conscience void of offence toward God and toward man,' (Acts xxiv: 16).

"On the Part of the Church: I do now declare you to be a member of this church of Christ, who are under solemn obligations to unite with you in seeking the things of peace and love and of a sound mind, and to care for your state, with meekness, fidelity and brotherly kindness."

After Mr. Randall's dismission, Rev. Ephraim Abbot was acting pastor, and continued to act as such until April 3, 1834. "There was preaching but part of the time from October, 1834, to April, 1835. In the summer of 1835, Rev. Jonathan Farr* preached, and after him Rev. Ephraim Abbot supplied the desk until April, 1836."

"Rev. Luther Wilson then preached till April, 1839, assisted the latter part of the time several months, on account of Mr. Wilson's ill health, by Rev. Ephraim Abbot. Rev. Claudius Bradford preached till April, 1840, and then Rev. Ephraim Abbot till April, 1841. Mr. Thurston, Mr. Coolidge and Mr. Buckingham preached as candidates till October, 1841. The Universalists having a right in the meeting-house have had preachers of their denomination a few Sabbaths every year for thirteen years past. Rev. Ephraim Abbot preached from October, 1841, to April, 1845."

---

* Harvard College, 1818. Died in 1845.

"From April to July, 1845, there was preaching in the society only part of the time. Mr. Edward Capen preached from July 20, 1845, to July 7, 1846, and having been invited to settle, declined the invitation. After which, on account of altering and repairing the meeting-house, there was no public worship in the society before the house was dedicated on 7th January, 1847; on which occasion Rev. William H. White, of Littleton, preached the sermon, and Rev. Mr. Thayer, of Chelmsford, made the dedicating prayer. After this, Mr. Putnam preached three Sabbaths, and Mr. Newell one. Rev. Herman Snow began to preach February 7, 1847, and continued for one year." (Church Records.)

June 6, 1847. Rev. E. Abbot and the pastor were appointed a committee to prepare a new covenant for the church.

The Covenant. "In the presence of God and before these witnesses you offer yourself for admission to this Christian church.

"You regard this transaction as a profession of your belief in the one living and true God; a testimony of your faith in Jesus Christ as the son of God and the Savior of the world; and an acknowledgment of the sacred scriptures of the Old and New Testament as containing a revelation from God to man, and a perfect rule of faith and duty.

"And you promise that you will strive to walk with this church in the spirit of charity and brotherly love, and in all things to live as becometh a true disciple of Jesus Christ.

"Thus you profess and promise. We, then, of this church receive you gladly into our number, and will endeavor to aid you in the trials of life and in the work of duty. And may God, our Father, grant that this union formed on earth may continue in heaven and fit us for the fellowship of the saints in the light."

Mr. Snow having declined a re-engagement and accepted a mission to the West, different persons preached until

Mr. John B. Willard began to supply the desk, March 19, 1848. The society, having invited him to become their pastor, and he having given an affirmative answer, a council met at the house of Rev. E. Abbot, May 24, 1848.

The exercises of ordination were as follows: Rev. William Morse presided as moderator; Rev. Joseph C. Smith was the scribe; introductory prayer by Rev. Seth Chandler, of Shirley; reading the Scriptures by Rev. Charles Babbidge, of Pepperell; sermon by Rev. Washington Gilbert, of Harvard; ordaining prayer by Rev. Ephraim Abbot, of Westford; charge by Rev. Mr. Bulfinch, of Nashville, N. H.; right-hand of fellowship by Rev. George M. Bartol; address to the people by Rev. Joseph C. Smith, of Groton; concluding prayer by Rev. William H. White, of Littleton.

Rev. John B. Willard was born in New York city, April 1, 1822. His parents, Luther and Mary (Davis) Willard, were born in Harvard, Massachusetts.* He graduated at Brown University in 1842, and then studied law three years, partly in Syracuse, New York, and partly in Boston, but never entered the legal profession. He studied theology with Rev. Washington Gilbert, then of Harvard. The church records say, "the Rev. John B. Willard dissolved his connection as pastor of the First Parish the first of December, A. D. 1850, without calling a council."

After the retirement of Mr. Willard, the pulpit was supplied by Rev. Mr. Maynard and others until July 1, 1851, when Rev. Jacob Caldwell came and preached about four months. In November, 1851, Mr. Willard† was recalled and officiated until March 25, 1852. Rev. Timothy Elliot preached from April 25, 1852, to April 10, 1853. Rev. Stillman Clark was the acting pastor four years, 1853-'57.

---

* The farm in Harvard (Still River) has been the home of the Willard family since 1675. The mother, Mary Davis, was of a long-established family in Harvard.

† Mr. Willard, after leaving this town, labored, for longer or shorter periods, in Windsor, Vt., in Lowell (Lee Street), in Barnstable, in Lunenburg, Warwick and Norton. He gave up preaching in 1871, and now lives on the old homestead in Still River Village.

April 25, 1858, Rev. George M. Rice began to preach, and, May 23rd, received an invitation to supply the pulpit for one year on a salary of $600. June 20th he delivered a sermon which the record designates as "special and appropriate," and admitted to church communion Harriet Burbank Rogers,* and administered the ordinance of the Lord's supper.

George Matthias Rice was born in Danvers, Massachusetts, June 28, 1814. His parents were residents of Salem, but as war then existed, and Salem was threatened with an attack from the British fleet, they retired to Danvers for the summer. Mr. Rice was fitted for college in the schools of Salem, especially in the grammar schools under the tuition of those renowned masters, Ames and H. K. Oliver. He was intended for Cambridge, but his father having removed to Geneva, New York, he entered Geneva (now Hobart) College in 1829, and graduated in 1832. He then pursued his studies in the Cambridge Divinity School, from which he graduated in 1835. He was ordained as evangelist at Watertown, Massachusetts, being at that time the acting pastor of the First Congregational Church in Lexington. Afterward, and before coming to Westford, he had the pastoral care of the Unitarian Churches in Lunenburg, North Chelsea and Mendon, in this State, and Eastport, Maine, and Lancaster, New Hampshire. His ministry here continued eight years.

On the 17th of March, 1866, the following votes were passed unanimously:

"Whereas, the Rev. George M. Rice has addressed a letter to the Parish Committee, stating that he has accepted a call from the First Congregational Society in Dublin, N. H., and that his Pastorate with this society [will come to an end]

---

* Miss Rogers was then preceptress in the Academy here, and associated with John D. Long. She is now at the head of the Clarke Institution for Deaf-Mutes at Northampton.

after the first Sabbath in April, when his present engagement ceases;

"Voted that we give our thanks to the Great Head of the Church for the pleasure and profit we have received from the able and faithful services of our pastor for the last eight years;

"That we esteem him highly for the ability, zeal, prudence and fidelity with which he has performed all his duties both as a pastor and citizen, and also for the readiness and good sense with which he has uniformly endeavored to promote every benevolent and worthy object;

"That by his amiable temper and discreet conduct he has greatly contributed to the promotion of peace and good will in this parish and in this town, to both of which his leaving is a cause of grief and regret."

On the 7th of August, 1866, the church "voted unanimously that Mr. George H. Young be invited to become the pastor of the First Church of Christ in Westford." He accepted the call and was ordained October 17, 1866. He continued in office nearly six years, and resigned in April, 1872. He was born in Slatersville, Rhode Island, March 14, 1841. He studied in the Theological School at Meadville, Pennsylvania four years, and graduated in June, 1866. After leaving Westford he was pastor of the Unitarian Church in Troy, New York, and of a church in Santa Barbara, California. He is at present a pastor in Woburn, Massachusetts.

Rev. William A. Cram was the next pastor. He came in April, 1872, and remained till April, 1876, a period of four years. He is the son of Joseph and Sarah Cram, and was born at Hampton Falls, New Hampshire, July 10, 1837. He received his education at Hampton and Exeter Academies; studied for the ministry and was ordained in Boston in 1868. He preached in Augusta, Maine, about two years before coming to Westford.

The present pastor, 1882, is Rev. Joseph Sidney Moulton, who was born in Plainfield, New Hampshire, April 12,

1852. He graduated at Kimball Union Academy in his native town, June, 1869, and at Dartmouth College in 1873. He studied theology at Cambridge Divinity School and graduated in 1876. He was ordained here June 12 1878. He preached here nearly two years before his ordination.

Deacons. John Comings, chosen December 7, 1727. Joshua Fletcher, chosen December 7, 1727. Jonas Prescott, chosen January 5, 1733, declined. Paul Fletcher, chosen January 5, 1733. Andrew Spalding, chosen March 5, 1736. Henry Wright, chosen March 5, 1736. John Abbot, chosen March 5, 1762. Nathaniel Boynton, chosen October 9, 1772, declined. Jonathan Fletcher, Jr., chosen October 9, 1772. Nathaniel Boynton, re-elected May 2, 1780, declined. William Hildreth, chosen May 2, 1780. Samuel Fletcher, chosen July 5, 1780. John Prescott, chosen August 20, 1782. Andrew Fletcher, chosen October 10, 1810. Reuben Leighton, chosen October 10, 1810. Caleb Wight, chosen 1824. John Cutter, chosen 1824. Abram Prescott, chosen July 23, 1830. Ebenezer Prescott, chosen July 23, 1830. Dr. Benjamin Osgood, chosen July 23, 1830. Levi Heywood, chosen June 10, 1842. Calvin Howard, chosen June 11, 1848.

Formation of the Union Congregational Society. "August 18, 1828. Pursuant to a warrant issued by Jonathan Prescott, Esq., for the purpose of forming another Religious Society in Westford, among other things the following vote was passed, viz: this society be denominated the Union Society in said Westford.

"I hereby certify that the following persons whose names are hereunto subjoined are members of the Religious Society denominated the Union Society: Andrew Fletcher, Horatio Fletcher, John Goodhue, Reuben Leighton, Jonas Keyes, William W. Goodhue, William Nichols, Timothy

Hartwell, Franklin Hildreth, Jesse Minot, John Cutter, Caleb Wight, Imla Goodhue, Andrew Fletcher, Jr., Simeon Hildreth, John Hildreth, Bill W. Stevens, Timothy P. Wright, Ephraim Harwood, Stephen Wright, Addison Parker, Abijah Hildreth, Oliver Wright, Jr., John Boynton, Ephraim Wright, Oliver Wright, Lemuel Hildreth, Joel Glover, John Davis, George Leighton, Thomas C. Parker, Amos Heywood, Asa Day, Luther Read.

HORATIO FLETCHER,
Clerk of said Society."

October 15, 1828, the following additional names were placed upon the list: Jesse Minot, Jr., Isaiah Prescott, Rachel Prescott, Jonathan Prescott, Isaac Day, Jr., Sophia Prescott, Isaac Day, Ira Pratt, Mary Davis, 2d, John Day, Isaac Durant, Mary Davis, Samuel Fletcher, Luther E. Puffer, Eve Kneeland, Simeon Hildreth, Levi Snow, Rebecca Proctor, Samuel M. Newhall, Aaron Brooks, Sally Peabody, Nahum Wight, Jeremiah J. Carter, Hannah Hamlin, Ezra Carter, Horace Pratt, Abigail Hildreth, Cephas Drew, Lemuel Bicknell, Rebecca Symmes, David Parker, John Bicknell, Maria Wright, Frederic Scott, Jonathan F. Parker, Abigail Fletcher, Amos Day, Thomas Smith, Deliverance Hildreth, Benjamin Robbins, Abijah Reed, Mary Brooks, Lydia Hunt.

The town clerk, after recording these on the town book, adds this note: "Wily Richardson and seventeen others filed in their certificates bearing date, January, 1829. For their names reference is had to the certificates on file. Abram Prescott, Town Clerk." March 4, 1830, these names were added: Trueworthy Keyes, Lydia Keyes, Betsey Keyes, Sally Keyes, Artemas Bailey.

Organization of the Union Church. The Union Congregational Church was formed December 25, 1828. It was composed of members of the First Church,* who withdrew on account of doctrinal differences, and a few others who joined on profession of their faith. The number at the organization was seventy-five.

NAMES OF THE ORIGINAL MEMBERS.

Samuel Fletcher,
Andrew Fletcher,
William Nichols,
Reuben Leighton,
Jonathan Prescott,
Imla Goodhue,
Ira Pratt,
Abijah Hildreth,
Caleb Wight,
John Cutter,
Amos Heywood,
Luther E. Puffer,
Andrew Fletcher, Jr.,
Simeon Hildreth,
Ephraim Harwood,
Oliver Wright,
Stephen Wright,
Bill W. Stevens,
Jonas Keyes,
John Boynton,
Addison Parker,
Nahum Wight,
Abigail Wight,
Mary Davis,
Hannah Hamlin,
Martha Tufts,
Polly Blood,
Eve Kneeland,
Maria Wright,
Mary Brooks,
Betsey Hall,
Sally Hartwell,

Milla Fletcher,
Mary Fletcher,
Ruth Nichols,
Sally Leighton,
Huldah Prescott,
Nancy Goodhue,
Sarah Goodhue,
Susan Hildreth,
Mary Wight,
Sally Peabody,
Amy Richardson,
Fanny Fletcher,
Laura Fletcher,
Ruth Hildreth,
Lydia Harwood,
Elizabeth Cummings,
Molly Hildreth,
Rachel Stevens,
Sally Keyes,
Sarah Boynton,
Hannah Parker,
Lydia Parker,
Elizabeth Hildreth,
Hannah Cummings,
Deliverance Hildreth,
Sarah Stevens,
Huldah Robbins,
Catherine Dupee,
Abigail Bicknell,
Caroline Green,
Mary Perry,
Rebecca Proctor,

---

* "December 25, 1828. Voted that any member of the church who may wish to be dismissed from this church with a view to unite with the Union Church about to be organized in connection with the Union Society, shall be regarded as duly dismissed, and that when they shall be organized into said church, they shall cease to be members of this church." (Records of First Church, p. 220.)

Helena Duraut,
Mary Richardson,
Hannah Keyes,
Almira Keyes,
Mary Cummings,
Esther Goodhue,

Rachel Prescott,
Molly Nutting,
Martha Keyes,
Elizabeth Read,
Martha Leighton.

These were all members of the old church, with the exception of Sally Hartwell and Rebecca Proctor.

The council called to organize the church was composed of the following pastors: Rev. George Fisher of Harvard, Rev. John Todd of Groton, Rev. Phillips Payson of Leominster, Rev. Rufus A. Putnam of Fitchburg, and Rev. Daniel S. Southmayd of Concord. Rev. John Todd preached the sermon.

January 29, 1829, the church " voted unanimously to give Mr. Leonard Luce a call to become the pastor of this church." At the same time they chose Reuben Leighton, Caleb Wight, and John Cutter a standing committee to examine candidates for admission to the church; and Jonathan Prescott, Imla Goodhue and Reuben Leighton a committee to confer with a committee of the old church in this town respecting church property. At that meeting, also, Amos Heywood was chosen clerk.

April 8, 1829, an ecclesiastical council convened at the house of Timothy Hartwell for the purpose of constituting Mr. Leonard Luce pastor of the church.

The following churches were represented:

Mason, N. H., Rev. Ebenezer Hill, pastor; Dea. Isaac Kimball, delegate.

Charlestown, Rev. Warren Fay, D. D., pastor; Dea. Isaac Warren, delegate.

Harvard, Rev. George Fisher, pastor; Bro. Josiah Wetherbee, delegate.

Fitchburg, Rev. Rufus A. Putnam, pastor; Bro. Joseph Downs, delegate.

Groton, Rev. John Todd, pastor; Dea. J. S. Adams, delegate.

Leonard Luce.

Concord, Rev. D. S. Southmayd, pastor; Bro. David Hartwell, delegate.

Bedford, Dea. Michael Crosby, delegate.

Andover, Theological Seminary, John R. Young, delegate.

The services of ordination were as follows: Introductory prayer, Rev. R. A. Putnam; sermon and ordaining prayer, Rev. W. Fay, D. D.; charge to the pastor, Rev. E. Hill; right-hand of fellowship, Rev. D. S. Southmayd; address to the people, Rev. John Todd; concluding prayer, Rev. George Fisher.

The church and society having no house of worship, the exercises of ordination were held at the house of Mr. John Davis, in the south part of the town. It was a clear, warm morning in spring. A platform was erected in the spacious door-yard, and the audience gathered about it, while many occupied the house and listened from the open windows. It was an impressive scene, and many hearts rejoiced that day in the gift of a pastor and spiritual guide.

When they left the old church there was a sum of money to which they were entitled, which was sufficient to pay for preaching for four Sabbaths, and during that time they occupied the First Parish meeting-house. Then they met at the house of Ephraim Wright, and afterward in a building which stood on the site of Wright & Fletcher's store. For a few months, in the summer of 1829, they occupied the hall of the Academy.

The church edifice in which the Union Society now worship was built in that year. The frame was raised July 30th, and religious services were held in it that evening. It was dedicated October 8, 1829.

Rev. Leonard Luce was born May 14, 1799, in that part of Rochester now Marion, Massachusetts. He graduated at Brown University in 1824, and at Andover Theological Seminary in 1828. He came directly from Andover to this place and began his labors here October 1, 1828. From the date of his ordination his pastorate extended over a period of twenty-three years and three months; the whole term of service from the beginning was twenty-three years and nine months. He was dismissed July 8, 1852. His ministry was truly successful. The church and society enjoyed some special tokens of the divine favor. During the whole period not a single year passed by without additions to the chuch; sometimes, indeed, only one person for the year, but often large numbers. The largest number in any one year was sixty-one, in 1840.

At the formation of the Orthodox Congregational Church in Littleton, May 14, 1840, sixteen persons were dismissed from this church and became members in that. The whole number admitted during Mr. Luce's ministry was 257; the number of baptisms was, adults 69, children 144, and the number of marriages was 204.

The second pastor was Rev. Thomas Wilson, born in Paisley, Scotland, June 15, 1822. He graduated at Dartmouth College in 1844, and at Andover Theological Seminary in 1847. He received a call from the church October 9, 1852, which he declined, but accepted an invitation to supply the pulpit for six months. The call was renewed February 8, 1853, and Mr. Wilson accepted it and was installed May 4, 1853. At his installation the sermon was preached by Rev. Amos Blanchard, D. D., of Lowell; installing prayer by Rev. Benjamin Dodge, of Acton; charge by Rev. Willard Child, D. D., of Lowell; right-hand of fellowship by Rev. Lyman Cutler, of Pepperell; address to the people by Rev. B. F. Clark, of North Chelmsford.

The ministry of Mr. Wilson continued not quite three years, and he was dismissed February 13, 1856.*

The pulpit was then supplied by Rev. David O. Allen for about two years, and by Rev. John Whitney for about one year, who closed his labors May 1, 1859.

---

* Mr. Wilson was ordained at Palmer, Mass., March 1, 1848, where he labored till July 1, 1852. After leaving Westford he was pastor in Stoughton, Mass., from March 13, 1856, to March 13, 1876, just twenty years. He is now a pastor in Eaton, Madison County, N. Y.

Rev. Edwin R. Hodgman became acting pastor June 26, 1859, and continued five years, closing his term of service July 3, 1864. He was born in Camden, Maine, October 21, 1819. He graduated at Dartmouth College in 1843, and at Andover Theological Seminary in 1846.

Rev. George F. Stanton then preached for a few months and was followed by Rev. James Fletcher, who supplied the pulpit until April or May, 1865.

Rev. Edwin A. Spence then became acting pastor for nearly two years. He was ordained here as an evangelist in September, 1866.

Rev. Henry D. Woodworth was invited to become pastor August 14, 1867. He accepted the call and was installed October 2, 1867. He graduated at Amherst College in 1855. The ministry of Mr. Woodworth was brief, lasting not quite two years, and closing by his dismission, July 18, 1869.

After the retirement of Mr. Woodworth, Rev. Nathan R. Nichols, a graduate of Middlebury College, supplied the pulpit for one year. After he left, several persons were employed for short periods of service. May 7, 1872, Rev. Henry H. Hamilton received a call from the church to become its pastor, and he was ordained September 11, 1872. Mr. Hamilton was born in Chester, Massachusetts, February 1, 1842. He graduated at Amherst College in 1868, and at Union Theological Seminary, New York city, in 1871. His pastorate continued for almost five years, and terminated by his voluntary resignation and dismission, June 25, 1877.

In November, 1877, Rev. Rufus C. Flagg began his labors in behalf of this church, and continued them until January 1, 1880, when he removed to Fairhaven, Vermont. He was immediately succeeded by Rev. Charles H. Rowley, the present acting pastor. He was ordained here as an evangelist February 23, 1881.

Deacons. Reuben Leighton, Caleb Wight and John Cutter were chosen, January 29, 1829. Ephraim A. Harwood, chosen November 1, 1856. Alden P. Osgood, chosen

January 3, 1868. Daniel T. Atwood, chosen May 3, 1873. Andrew S. Wright, chosen May 1, 1879.

Formation of the Methodist Society. The field occupied by this society is chiefly the village of Graniteville, in which the church edifice is situated. In this village twenty-five years ago there were scarcely half a dozen families. In 1880, according to the returns of the census, there were 105 families containing 540 persons. Formerly it was a part of School District No. 3, but was set off, March 26, 1851, and was called School District No. 10. A small wooden school-house was built soon after, and at the first annual meeting of the district, March 9, 1852, it was voted " to have the school-house opened for public worship." From this date till March, 1856, there was regular preaching, mostly by Methodists, and early in the summer of 1856 a subscription paper was opened, and Rev. John Naylor, of West Chelmsford, was employed, and he held services until the commencement of cold weather. These were the *first regular services* held in the house. In the spring of 1857 Mr. Naylor resumed his work, but was obliged to give it up before autumn on account of ill-health. About this time a Sabbath-school was formed with Mr. David C. Mead as superintendent. Mrs. Knowles, Mrs. Prescott and Miss Nancy M. Hill were teachers. It ceased at the approach of winter, but was re-opened in the following spring. Regular preaching was enjoyed from March, 1858, to March, 1859, but for a year afterward there was no religious service. In 1860, Rev. L. Luce conducted worship in the school-house during the warm months. He reorganized and superintended the Sabbath-school. In 1861 there was no preaching and no Sabbath-school; but in 1862 the school was reopened in charge of Arthur Wright, and was very successful. Regular preaching was likewise enjoyed. Early in the spring of 1863 the services of Rev. Mr. Howarth, a Methodist preacher from Lowell, were secured, and he labored through the summer. The Sabbath-school was held in the afternoon. During the summer of 1864 Rev. George M. Rice held services in the school-house at 4 o'clock, p. m., but there was no Sabbath-school. From March, 1865, to November, 1866, there was neither preaching nor Sabbath-school. In the winter of 1866–'67 Rev. E. A. Spence preached in the school-house several times on Sabbath evenings. Much religious interest was manifested during that winter, and meetings were held in private houses, which were attended by so many that they were appointed at the school-house for greater convenience.

In March, 1867, a Bible-class was formed and taught by Arthur Wright, which was soon changed to a Sabbath-school. In June, 1869, the Sabbath-school was reopened under the care of Josiah K. Proctor. During the same month Mr. Charles G. Sargent expressed his conviction that there ought to be regular preaching in Graniteville, and intimated his readiness to contribute liberally for its support. His opinion was reported to the Methodist churches of Lowell, who, by their pastors, and especially through the active agency of Mr. Charles S. Graves, for many years the conductor on the Stony Brook Railroad, took measures to secure the establishment of a Methodist Episcopal Society in in that village. Application was made to Dr. Patten, of the Boston Theological Seminary, to send a man to preach. Mr. Minor H. A. Evans, a student in that institution, was sent, who preached in the old school-house, July 4, 1869. The congregation filled the room to its utmost capacity, and many stood in the ante-room and around the windows. Mr. Evans, the next morning, drew up a subscription paper for funds to build a church edifice. Mr. Charles G. Sargent promptly headed the list with $2000 and site. Another $1000, in smaller sums, was added during the day. July 12th, Mr. Evans was appointed preacher in charge by the Presiding Elder. July 18th, the congregation being unusually large, a platform was erected and seats arranged in the grove in the rear of Mr. Samuel Fletcher's house, and there the services were held for the remainder of the summer. July

20th, a class was formed, consisting of twenty members, and Arthur Wright was appointed class-leader. August 3rd, a quarterly conference was held, at which Mr. Evans, the preacher in charge, Mr. Wright, the class-leader, and Mr. J. K. Proctor, the Sabbath-school superintendent, were present, and the following persons were chosen trustees: Arthur Wright, Charles G. Sargent, Cyrus Hosmer, William Reed, Samuel Fletcher, Lyman A. Smith and Josiah K. Proctor; stewards, Cyrus Hosmer, Arthur Wright and J. K. Proctor.

August 13th the board of trustees was organized by the choice of Charles G. Sargent president, and Arthur Wright secretary and treasurer. A building committee was elected, consisting of Messrs. Sargent, Wright and Smith, who were duly authorized to build a church. Soon after, the site given by Mr. Sargent was conveyed by deed; a design by S. S. Woodcock, architect, was adopted, and the contract for building was made with Messrs. Mead, Mason & Co., of Concord, New Hampshire, to build the edifice, above the foundation, for $8900.

The society worshipped in the new school-house in the village during the winter.

In March, 1870, Mr. Evans was ordained deacon and appointed to Graniteville.

The work upon the church building steadily progressed, and November, 20, 1870, the society entered the vestry for the first time. The whole building was finished early in the following spring. March 22, 1871, was fixed upon as the day of dedication. Rev. J. M. Buckley, of Stamford, Connecticut, preached the dedication sermon.

The building is of wood, in Gothic style, one hundred feet long and forty-three feet wide. The auditorium is fifty-two feet long and forty-two feet wide, with sittings for three hundred and forty-two persons. The lecture-room is forty-two feet long and twenty-nine feet wide, in the rear of the audience-room. Above the lecture-room is the ladies' chapel, twenty-nine feet long and twenty-three feet wide. The pulpit is of black walnut, and over the arched recess is the

M. E. Church, Graniteville.

inscription "How amiable are thy tabernacles, O Lord of hosts."

Rev. Nathaniel B. Fisk, the second pastor, received his appointment in April, 1871, and remained three years. During his ministry a bell was procured for the church edifice, and $2000 paid on the church debt. In the spring of 1874 Rev. James F. Mears became pastor and remained two years.

In 1871 Mr. C. G. Sargent presented a receipted bill for $1305 for work done and money advanced by him.

The society worshipped in the auditorium for the first time on the Sabbath, March 26, 1871.

Rev. Miner H. A. Evans was appointed to his second pastorate in 1876, and continued three years. The financial crisis proved trying to the church. Mr. Charles G. Sargent, the chief financial patron of the church died July 16, 1878. He had contributed about $5000 and the site to the church, and he left a further pledge of $1000.

The official board passed the following preamble and resolution:

"Whereas, Divine Providence has removed from this life Charles G. Sargent, chairman of our Board of Trustees,

"Resolved, That the official board expresses its profound esteem for the life and character of Mr. Sargent, and its sympathy with the family and the society, which have lost a devoted friend and faithful counsellor."

Since the death of Mr. Sargent the debt incurred by building the church, has been entirely extinguished, partly by the efforts of the society and partly by the generosity of Mr. Sargent's heirs, who paid the last installment of $2400.

A medallion of Mr. Sargent has been placed in the church by Rev. M. H. A. Evans, the first pastor.

Rev. Alfred Woods, a native of St. Johns, Newfoundland, was appointed minister in charge in April, 1879, and remained three years, closing his labors in April, 1882.

CHAPTER XI.

EDUCATIONAL HISTORY.

THE people of Westford have always supported the cause of popular education with commendable liberality. Schools were at first kept in private houses,* and for only one term in the year. At a later date there were two terms each year, but these were short. The town was early divided into school squadrons, of which there were four: the Centre; the South, corresponding to Parkerville; the West, corresponding to Forge Village; and the North, including the region about Long-sought-for Pond. For a long time the selectmen seem to have had the entire control of the schools. They generally made all the contracts with the teachers, and gave the orders to the town treasurer for the payment of their wages. In those early days that long-suffering body of men, now known as the school committee, had no existence.

The first votes of the town respecting schools which appear on the record are these: "March 4, 1733-'34, voted to chose four men for a Commity to provide a schoolmaster for the insuing year. Voted, Ensign Jonathan Hartwell, Joseph Underwood, Ensign Joseph Keyes, and Joseph Hildreth, Jr., Comt. to provide a scool for insuing year."

"March 3, 1734-'35. Voted to raise twenty pounds money to pay ye scool master."

---

*September 23, 1757. "It is agreed that the places for the school to be kept for the year ensuing shall be as follows, to wit: At Mr. Aaron Parker, Jr's., for the southeast part of the town; at Lieut. William Fletcher's, for the southwest part; at Timothy Prescott's, for the northwest part, and at Samuel Burge's, for the northeast part." It is the school, not schools; for they regarded it as one.

May 28, 1735, the selectmen voted to "pay to Mr. Joseph Underwood, Junior, for his keeping scool in this town of Westford, 1734, the sum of £16 to be in full for sd service."

It is apparent, therefore, that the name of Joseph Underwood, Jr., stands at the head of the list of teachers in this town. He graduated at Harvard College in 1735; was the son of Joseph and Susanna (Parker) Underwood, and was born in Reading, Massachusetts, in the year 1708. He studied for the ministry but was never ordained. It is supposed that he died in this town suddenly, about the year 1748.

The name of the second teacher was Ephraim Craft. "April ye 27, 1736. Pay to Mr. Ephraim Craft for his keeping scoll in this town one month, in the year 1736, £2 5s., to be in full for his sarvis."

Josiah Burge was the third teacher. "December 13, 1736, the selectmen agreed with Josiah Burge to keep school in this town one month." This and the preceding extract seem to show that the town had a school for one month only during the year. Josiah Burge was one of the earliest inhabitants and his homestead was near the house of Daniel W. Sherman.

"May 16, 1738, voted that the articol of skool should be dismissed." But, "December 4, 1738, voted to choos a commity to higher a schooll master for keeping schooll this winter," and they chose Captain Thomas Read and Joseph Hildreth, Jr., for that committee.

In the year 1739 William Bowen comes into notice, and he became a teacher of some notoriety. He had more or less to do with the schools from 1740 to 1775, a period of thirty-five years. He travelled over the town, keeping school in three out of the five parts into which the town was divided.*

---

* It is said that he was a retired minister and lived on Frances Hill, near the residence of Warren Hunt. A story is told of him, that, when teaching in Stony Brook squadron, he started for the school-room one morning, after a heavy fall of snow. A huge drift had formed across his path and into this the boys had dug a

In 1741 the town voted to raise £100, old tenor, " £40 for the scholl and the rest for town debts or county rates or taxes and squerls [squirrels] and bords [birds]. The selectmen have liberty to dra [draw] money out of the treasury for these squirls and burds as the law directs."

This was quite a liberal proportion for schools of the whole amount raised, and after paying town and county charges, there was probably little left for the squirrels and birds. In 1742 the number of schools was multiplied by a vote to have six squadrons or districts.

The first woman who taught in the public schools was Mrs. Edward Bates, whose maiden name was Mary Snow. She was employed in the years 1740–'43

Dea. Andrew Spalding was a teacher in 1739, '42 and '54; John Abbot in 1747, and frequently after that year.

GRAMMAR SCHOOL.

In 1647 the General Court " ordered that when any town shall increase to the number of one hundred families or households, they shall set up a grammar school, the master thereof being able to instruct youth so far as they may be fitted for the University."

In order to comply with this law, this town was early compelled to hire graduates from Cambridge to take charge of one school, which was called the grammar school. It does not appear, however, that the graduate or member of college always taught the school at the Centre; but he is sometimes designated, by way of eminence, the grammar school teacher. The names of some of these are given, with their years of service and of graduation:

1750, Jonathan Kidder, a graduate in 1751. He was the son of Thomas Kidder, of Billerica.

---

hole, carefully concealing it by laying blocks of snow over the top, and into it the luckless pedagogue fell, much to his discomfort and greatly to the amusement of the mischievous urchins who set the trap. He died in poverty.

1753, Azariah Faxon, a graduate in 1752.

1753, Joseph Perry, a graduate in 1752. Perhaps he is the man who married Sarah, daughter of Rev. William Lawrence, of Lincoln, and settled in East Windsor, Connecticut, and died in 1783.

1756, Stephen Shattuck, Jr., a graduate in 1756.

1757, John Munroe, a graduate in 1751. He was of Concord; taught in Long-sought-for squadron and Forge Village.

1758, Peter Russell, a graduate in 1758.

1759, Amos Moody, a graduate in 1759. He became a minister; died in 1819.

1759, John Treadwell, a graduate in 1758. He was from Andover; a minister.

1761, Willard Wheeler, a graduate in 1755. He was of Concord; became Episcopal minister of Scituate, and died, 1810, aged 75.

1762, Penuel Bowen, a graduate in 1762. He is supposed to be the man, born in Framingham, who was ordained pastor of the New South Church in Boston, April 30, 1766, and was dismissed May 12, 1772.

1762, William Russell, a graduate in 1758.

1762, Jeremiah Dummer Rogers, a graduate in 1762.

1764, Stephen Hall, a graduate in 1765.

1764, Nathaniel Cooper, a graduate in 1763.

1767, Jonathan Crane, M. D., a graduate in 1762.

1768, William Hobart, a graduate in 1774.

1769, Elijah Fletcher, a graduate in 1769. Born in Westford, 1743; taught for two or three years; minister of Hopkinton, N. H.

1772, Mr. Ebenezer Allen, a graduate in 1771.

1775, Thomas Whiting, a graduate in 1775.

1785, Amos Crosby, a graduate in 1785. He was afterward tutor in the college, 1788–'92.

1787, Jonathan Procter, a graduate in 1789. He was born in Westford and was the son of Nathan Procter; taught several terms.

1787, Ebenezer Hill, a graduate in 1786. He was born in Cambridge in 1766; taught in Stony Brook squadron, at the Centre, and at Forge Village. He married Mary Boynton of this town and settled as a pastor in Mason, N. H., in 1790, where he died in 1854, aged 88 years.

1790, Asa King, a graduate in 1791. He was born in Westford, February 10, 1770; the son of Rogers and Lydia King.

1792, Jacob Abbot, a graduate in 1792. He was a minister in Windham, N. H.

1792, Levi Hedge, a graduate in 1792.

1793, Joseph Prince, a graduate in 1793.

1793, Samuel Thatcher, a graduate in 1793. The records say that Abel Boynton was paid in 1793, "for bringing up two schoolmasters from Cambridge"; probably, Prince and Thatcher.

1793, Abraham Randall, probably a graduate in 1798.

1796, Stephen Cogswell, a graduate in 1797.

1800, Willard Hall, a graduate in 1799. The son of Willis and grandson of Rev. Willard Hall; he taught in Stony Brook District.

In 1748 the number of tax payers had increased to one hundred and forty, and the town was under obligation to have a grammar school. But the people neglected to establish one and were indicted.

December 25, 1750, the town paid Thomas Read, Esq., "for what money he expended in going to court to answer to the presentment against the town for not having a grammar school last summer." It does not appear from the records, however, that any school of that grade was maintained until 1752, when Mr. Azariah Faxon was employed, and perhaps he was, in fact, the first teacher of the kind here.

In 1764, May 23rd, the town voted "to hire a schooldame the following six months from the above date, and to keep the school in six parts of the town." One dame for six parts — and a peripatetic one at that, since it was not easy to divide up this official personage and let her wield the rod in six schools at once! This rotating process was often practised, for in 1765, September 2nd, the selectmen made an agreement with Mr. Stephen Hall, then fresh from college, to keep school in Stony Brook squadron; then called him to the Centre; in December moved him to the school in the southwest part, and in January to the southeast. In the following year they shifted him around in this manner: One month in the Centre, one month in the northwest, so that in one school year he fairly "boxed the compass." Probably this educational *Sartor Resartus* drew a long breath when he reached home from his last pilgrimage.*

December 17, 1787, the town "voted to build school-houses in the several school squadrons, and that each squadron draw their own proportion of the money which shall be raised for that purpose. Voted to raise one hundred and forty-five pounds for the above purpose. Voted to choose a committee to affix the lines of the several squadrons and to proportion the money which is raised for building the school-houses. Chose Joshua Read, Jonathan Keep, David Goodhue, Jonathan Carver, Thomas Richardson, Joseph Keyes and Samuel Wright, committee." The language implies that the town had no school-houses within its limits; but in the following year it was voted "that each school squadron choose a committee for themselves for building *and repairing* the several school-houses in this town." This seems to show that they had some old houses that needed repairing, and the vote hints, also, at the independent district system which prevailed so long in this Commonwealth. That system was adopted by enactment of the Legislature in 1789, and continued in force in this town until the year 1869, when it was abolished — a period of eighty years. The records furnish evidence that the town has ever been careful to nourish and support its common schools. Only on one occasion do they show the least faltering, and that was indicated by

---

*Widow Elizabeth Nutting was the travelling school teacher in 1764. The first teachers were men, but women were soon employed, and they came gradually to be regarded as the best instructors.

postponing action at a certain meeting, but probably the matter was put right at the next meeting. The sum appropriated to the support of schools in those early days will not suffer in point of generosity or liberality when compared with the amount now granted. Wealth had not then accumulated, and to many of the people it was a hard struggle to live in any way, but education was not neglected. From the passage of the Stamp Act in 1768, to the adoption of the Federal Constitution in 1789, the public burdens were very heavy. The depreciation of continental money, the large exactions of England, and the expenses of the Revolutionary War, were a severe test of their attachment to the system of popular education which they early adopted and steadily fostered. It may be that their progress in mental achievement in those troublous times was somewhat retarded, but there is surely reason for gratitude that they did not allow the system to drift upon the lee-shore of barbarism. Here, in the old Bay State, in towns like this, is the seed-bed out of which the germs of educational life have been transplanted to other States to thrive in vigor and beauty there. But not merely in the support of common schools did the people show their appreciation of sound learning. Some of them, near the close of the last century, began to see the need of a school of higher grade, and by their efforts and liberality the Academy was called into existence.

THE ACADEMY.

In 1792, several gentlemen met together and agreed "to form themselves into a society by the name and institution of the Westford Academy." Articles of agreement and subscription were then drawn up and signed by fifty-four persons; and at the head of the list stand the names of Zaccheus Wright, John Abbot and Abel Boynton, each of whom subscribed £30. The town also contributed to the original fund and became entitled to its benefits. "May 7, 1792, voted that the town will have twenty shears in the accademy at six pounds a shair, and the town to have Equal privileges with the other subscribers. Voted to chose a committee to Inspect the Shairs that the town voted to subscribe. Chose Joseph Keyes, Mr. Francis Leighton, Captain Pelatiah Fletcher, Mr. Joshua Read, Lieut. Jonas Prescott for sd committee. Voted that the committee subscrib the twenty shairs the town voted to have in the Cademy in behalf of this town. Voted that the Representive youse his Influence in the general Cort to obtain an act of Incorporation for the acadamy in this town." (Records, vol. iii., p. 78.)

The subscription by the town of twenty shares at six pounds each amounted to one hundred and twenty pounds. In addition to this, Zaccheus Wright gave the sum of three hundred pounds in real estate, the conveyance of which was to be made to the trustees of the Academy as soon as an act of incorporation should be obtained. These several subscriptions amounted to £978.

On the 30th of April, 1792, the subscribers met and organized by the choice of Zaccheus Wright, president; James Prescott, vice-president; Rev. Caleb Blake, Hon. Ebenezer Bridge, Rev. Ezra Ripley, Rev. Moses Adams, Hon. Joseph Bradley Varnum, Sampson Tuttle, Esq., James Prescott, Jr., Mr. John Abbot, Dr. Charles Proctor and Mr. Jonathan Carver, trustees.

The subscribers, or proprietors, as they were afterwards styled in the records of the Academy, held meetings from time to time to urge on the work they had undertaken. Measures were adopted for purchasing a site and erecting thereon a building for the exclusive use of the school or academy. A committee was also appointed to procure an act of incorporation.

November 2, 1792, the town voted :" to give liberty to the subscribers of the accadamy to Build a house on the Common if the Land can't be Bought of Miss Lidy Keyes to set sd house on." *

---

* Miss Lydia Keyes then owned a lot of land near Alvan Fisher's. She was probably the daughter of Joseph Keyes, Jr., born in 1724, and died unmarried.

The land on which the building now stands was purchased in 1793. It was once a part of the farm of Timothy Fletcher, Jr., who lived in the house now occupied by Cyrus Hamlin, or in one that stood on the same spot. Fletcher sold it to Oliver Hildredth in 1781, and Hildreth sold it to Levi Parker in 1785. Parker mortgaged the same to Richard Manning, of Salem, in 1789. When Parker bought, there were buildings on it; Parker's mortgage says, a dwelling-house, barn and blacksmith's shop. In 1793 Parker conveyed it by the following deed which is given in brief:

"I, Levi Parker, in consideration of five pounds paid by Zaccheus Wright, Abel Boynton, Benjamin Osgood, James Prescott, Samuel Fletcher, Abijah Read, Jonathan Keyes, John Prescott, Levi Parker, Isaac Cumings, John Hildreth, Jonathan Carver, Timothy Prescott, Elijah Hildreth, Joel Abbot, Samuel Adams, Joseph Jewett, Matthew Scribner, Nathaniel Boynton, all of Westford, do grant, sell and convey to the forenamed persons a certain piece of land, situated in Westford, beginning at the southeasterly part of Abel Boynton's garden, thence twenty-five feet easterly to the common training field, thence southerly by said common twenty-four feet, thence westerly twenty-five feet by said Parker's land; thence twenty-four feet by said Boynton's land to the first bounds."

This deed does not seem to have been acknowledged until the year 1822, when Parker was living in New Hampshire. He also conveyed to the proprietors or trustees in 1793 another lot, called the shop piece, which he had previously bought of Abel Boynton.

May 6, 1793, the town voted "that Lieut. Levi Parker may move his shop unto the East side of the common." This being removed, the land was unencumbered, and so passed into the hands of the trustees.

August 3, 1792, the proprietors adopted certain rules and by-laws for the regulation and government of the school; and among other things it was provided, "that the English, Latin and Greek languages, together with writing, arithmetic and

Westford Academy.

the art of speaking should be taught, and, if desired, practical geometry, logic, geography and music; that the school should be free to any nation, age or sex, provided that no one should be admitted a member of the school unless able to read in the Bible readily without spelling."

The act of incorporation was passed September 28, 1793. It recites that over £1000 had been given by various parties for the establishment of the Academy; but the records of the early meetings of the subscribers specify only the gifts before mentioned. In the meantime, however, these may have been increased by additional subscriptions.

May 5, 1794, the town voted "to raise the one hundred and twenty pounds the town was to give for the benefit of the Academy, the one half to be paid by the first of October next, and the other half by the first of January next."

The first meeting of the trustees under the act of incorporation was held on the 2nd of April, 1794, at the house of Mr. Joel Abbot, and was continued by several adjournments to the 21st of July following. At this meeting the arrangements seem to have been completed, or nearly so, for the orderly working of the institution. James Prescott, Jr., was chosen secretary of the board, and was re-elected for several successive years. Rev. Moses Adams, of Acton, was chosen president *pro tempore*, and Rev. Edmond Foster, of Littleton, and Rev. Hezekiah Packard, of Chelmsford, were chosen trustees in addition to those before named. John Abbot, Sr., was chosen treasurer and served one year, being succeeded in that office by Jonathan Carver. At this meeting Mr. Levi Hedge was requested to have a public exhibition on the 4th of July. This is the first intimation on record of his being in office as teacher or preceptor.[*]

Public exhibitions seem to have been continued for many years, and tradition says that they were attended with great interest. Academies were rare then, and the attendance

---

[*] In 1806 the town voted "*not* to prevent the Academy scholars from holding exhibitions in the meeting-house." Mr. Hedge had previously taught in the public schools here.

from other towns and from considerable distances was much larger than it now is.

In May, 1797, a committee of the trustees was appointed to attend to and investigate the interest of the corporation in a late grant of land in the district of Maine. It is presumed that this grant was made in pursuance of a policy adopted by the State for aiding and encouraging academic institutions. This grant consisted of half a township in Aroostook County, in the southeast corner and on the border of New Brunswick, "beginning at a spruce tree four miles from the monument at the head of St. Croix River, running north thirteen degrees east, three miles to Groton Academy grant."*

It was sold not long after for $5,810, as appears by the report of the committee. It contained 11,520 acres, and was sold for fifty cents per acre; but as it was sold partly on credit, it was some time before the proceeds of the sale were fully realized.

In tracing the history of this Academy the names of several gentlemen occur who were more or less prominent in public life, and especially in their connection with this school, and a brief notice of their lives and characters very justly forms a part of this history.

First among the early friends and promoters of this institution stands the name of Zaccheus Wright. His interest in it is evinced by the liberality of his gifts; and the estimation in which he was held is apparent from the fact that he was elected the first president of the board of trustees, and was annually re-elected to that office till 1808, when he declined further service. His ancestors came from Woburn, and were among the first settlers of Chelmsford. He was the son of Ebenezer and Deliverance (Stevens) Wright, and was born in Westford October 27, 1738. He died in 1811, aged 72 years and four months. He served in the revolutionary

---

*Groton Academy, now known as the Lawrence Academy, was incorporated the same year, and the land granted to it was situated adjacent to the grant made to this institution.

army and was in the battle of White Plains. He was colonel of a regiment, but did not serve through the war. Returning home he was conspicuous in town affairs, holding nearly every position within the gift of his fellow-citizens; was often selectman; was member of various important committees; representative to the General Court many times; delegate to political conventions, and justice of the peace. In 1773, at the age of 35, he became a member of the church in full communion, and was highly esteemed as such. Long after his decease his name continued to be mentioned with respect as one of the best and most public-spirited men that Westford had produced. He is said to have been a man of uncommon size, weighing, perhaps, two hundred and fifty pounds, yet active and agile, constantly superintending his farm, and capable, when occasion called, of chasing a flock of sheep as nimbly as the most lithe and youthful of his hired men. He married, January 5, 1764, Rachel Parker, of Chelmsford. They had no children.

Next, perhaps, in prominence among the founders of the Academy, stands the name of James Prescott, Jr. He was the youngest son of Col. James Prescott, of Groton, and was born there, April 19, 1766. He was a graduate of Harvard College in the class of 1788; read law and commenced the practice of his profession in Westford, where he was residing at the time the Academy was started and where he spent about ten years. For many years he filled the office of secretary of the board of trustees, in which he was succeeded by Rev. Caleb Blake. He was president of the board from 1815 to 1827, when he declined a re-election. After his return to Groton upon the death of his uncle, Oliver Prescott, who was for many years Judge of Probate for the county, he was appointed to that office, and soon after was made Chief Justice of the Court of Common Pleas for the county. He has been described as one possessed of a strong discriminating mind, a good classical scholar, and a learned lawyer. He died October 14, 1829.

John Abbot, eldest son of John Abbot, was born in Westford, January 27, 1777, and died April 30, 1854, at the age of 77. He graduated at Harvard University in 1798, in a class distinguished for talent, in which he took a high collegiate rank. He immediately became preceptor of this Academy and held that place two years. He then studied law and opened an office in Westford, and about the same time he was chosen a trustee. On the decease of Jonathan Carver in 1805, he was chosen treasurer of the Academy, which office he held by successive annual elections till his death, a period of fifty years, less three or four months. To his careful management and prudent foresight the institution is chiefly indebted for its present funds. During his long administration they increased nearly or quite threefold. The Academy had no wealthy patrons like its neighbor at Groton, but depended for the increase of its means on small but carefully husbanded accumulations. It was the aim of the treasurer to save something from the annual interest of the funds to be added to the principal; and almost every year's report showed some increase in their amount. The trustees had implicit confidence in his integrity, fidelity and skill, and rarely, if ever, interfered with his plans. During this long period his services were rendered gratuitously to the institution whose welfare he had so much at heart, and he will always be remembered as one of its staunchest friends. Mr. Abbot was also held in high respect by his fellow-townsmen, being often chosen to places of trust. He was regarded as a sound lawyer, and a faithful and reliable legal adviser. He served one term as a Senator in the State Legislature, and was a member of the convention for revising the State Constitution in 1820. He was also a distinguished member of the Masonic Order. He was twice Grand Master of the Royal Arch Chapter of the Free Masons of Massachusetts, and in that capacity laid the corner-stone of the monument on Bunker Hill in 1825; General Lafayette being present and assisting in that ceremony.

He was succeeded in the office of treasurer by his son, John William Pitt Abbot, who held it till his death in 1872.

The latter, like his father, gave his services gratuitously, being animated by the same desire to further its prosperity. He was born April 27, 1806, in Hampton, Connecticut, the early home of his mother, Sophia Moseley, a daughter of Ebenezer Moseley, Esq., of Hampton. He was chiefly fitted for college at this Academy and graduated at Cambridge in 1827. After studying law in the Law School at Cambridge he entered his father's office, the business of which was not long after transferred entirely to him. He was a member of the House of Representatives in 1862, and of the State Senate in 1866; and was selectman and town clerk for many years. During the late war his services as a town officer were invaluable. He was particularly interested in the affairs of the First Parish, and for a long time was entrusted with the management of them. In all these relations he was trusted as an able and faithful counsellor and public servant, and he was universally regarded with esteem and affection for his urbanity, benevolence and generosity.

TEACHERS.

	Began.	Ended.
Levi Hedge, LL. D., H. U.	1792	1794
Samuel Thatcher, H. U.	1794	1795
Amos Crosby, H. U.	1795	1798
John Abbot, H. U.	1798	1800
William Warren, D. C.	1800	1802
Benjamin Stone, H. U.	1802	1803
Henry Putnam, H. U.	1803	1804
Benjamin Ames, H. U.	1804	1805
Joseph Hovey, H. U.	1805	1806
Benjamin Burge, H. U.	1806	1807
Joseph Tufts, H. U.	1807	1808
Nahum Houghton Groce, H. U.	1808	1822
Charles Phelps Huntington, H. U.	1822	1823
John Wright, H. U.	1823	1825
Allen Putnam, H. U.	1825	1827
Charles Rollin Kennedy, H. U.	1827	1827
Ephraim Abbot, H. U.	1828	1837
Claudius Bradford	1837	1839
Edmund B. Wilson	1839	1839
John Kebler, H. U.	1839	1841
Henry Colman Kimball, H. U.	1841	1842

320   HISTORY OF WESTFORD.

Francis Lemuel Capen, H. U.	1842	1843
James Dinsmore, D. C.	1843	1845
Henry Colman Kimball, H. U.	1845	1847
William Cushing, H. U.	1847	1850
Charles H. Wheeler, B. C.	1850	1851
Samuel Hilliard Folsom, D. C.	1851	1853
Luther Eastman Shepard, D. C.	1854	1857
John Davis Long, H. U.	1857	1859
Jacob A. Cram	1859	1860
Addison G. Smith	1860	1861
Richard Stone, H. U.	1861	1863
Albert Edwin Davis, B. C.	1863	1868
John Hillis, H. U.	1868	1868
Charles O. Whitman, B. C.	1868	1872
William Edwin Frost, B. C.	1872	

ASSISTANT TEACHERS.

	Began.	Ended.
Susan Prescot	1819	1820
Catherine Abbot	1829	1831
Elizabeth D. Abbot	1832	
Hannah Rogers	1832	1834
Lucy Ann Breck	1833	1834
Eliza Ann Dodge	1834	1835
Clarissa Butler	1835	1836
Martha Kilburn	1836	1837
Charlotte Bradford	1837	
Welthea Bradford	1838	
Lucy Elliot Abbot	1842	1844
Sarah Boynton	1844	
Nancy M. Blackington	1845	1846
Ellen A. Gage	1846	1847
Mary C. A. Cunningham	1848	1849
Ellen A. Gage	1846	1847
Catherine A. Cram	1851	1852
Mary F. Fletcher	1859	
Margaret F. Foley	1853	1854
Harriet B. Rogers	1855	1858
Amanda M. Hale	1857	1859
Olive A. Prescott	1850	
Marietta M. White	1858	1861
Harriet B. Rogers	1861	1863
Alice J. Hardman	1863	1867
Josephine L. Taggart	1867	
Elizabeth McDaniels	1868	
Sarah F. White	1868	1873
Harriet M. Hodgman	1873	1876
Adelaide Baker	1876	

Levi Hedge, the first preceptor, graduated at Harvard University in 1792, a distinguished member in a distinguished class. He came directly to Westford with a high reputation as a scholar, and left two years after with an equally high reputation as a teacher. He returned to Cambridge to take the place of a tutor in the college, and after several years was promoted to a professorship of Logic and Metaphysics. Though not eminent as a writer or thinker, he had a certain reputation as a teacher and disciplinarian. His interest in the Academy never waned. He was chosen a trustee in 1802 and resigned in 1844, in consequence of growing infirmities. He died the same year. It was well known in college that when the annual meeting of the trustees came he would give his class a day — "a miss," as they delighted to call it — while he himself enjoyed no less the pleasure of visiting a spot endeared to him by many agreeable associations. On these occasions he was usually accompanied, after 1811, by Prof. Sidney Willard, the son of President Willard, who was chosen a trustee in 1811, and resigned in 1854. Mr. Hedge, in his later years, was commonly known as Dr. Hedge, having received the honorary degree of LL. D., which was well merited by his long service in the cause of letters.

Amos Crosby, the third preceptor, was tutor in Harvard College for four years, 1788-'92.

Benjamin Burge, the tenth preceptor, was the son of Ephraim Burge, and was born in Hollis in 1782. He graduated at Harvard College in 1805. After leaving Westford, he was a tutor in Bowdoin College, and received the honorary degree of A. M. in 1815 from that college. He studied medicine and settled in Vassalborough, Maine.

Nahum Houghton Groce, the twelfth preceptor, was born in Sterling, Massachusetts, in 1781, but early removed with the family to Salem. He graduated at Harvard in 1808, and coming immediately to Westford, he became principal, and remained such till 1822, when he resigned and became a farmer in Westford, where he died in 1856. His term of service was the longest in the whole line of teachers. It was his misfortune at the age of fourteen to meet with an accident which made him a cripple for life. After years of intense suffering, consequent on this mishap, he fitted for college, and by his own exertions and the aid of friends, worked his way through. His lameness was such as to deprive him of the use of his right foot, and compelled him to use a crutch. It made him morbidly sensitive, perhaps, at times, irritable. But he was generally liked by his pupils, to whose instruction he devoted himself with great industry, fidelity and success, being himself master of the branches he professed to teach, and his judgment being clear and penetrating. His retiring habits, critical judgments and somewhat severe tastes rendered him less popular than some who have preceded and followed him; but he had a high and well-deserved reputation as an instructor, and his school was almost always full. Sometimes he had in one term and at one time sixty or more pupils whom he taught without assistance, or with only such aid as he occasionally sought from some of the older and more advanced members of the school. It was not until 1818 or 1819 that he had any regular assistant. Miss Susan Prescott, daughter of Hon. James Prescott, president of the board of trustees, was the first female assistant employed, and her instructions were confined solely to the classes of young ladies. She was justly regarded as an accomplished teacher, but she held that position only for two successive seasons in summer. She returned to Groton and there opened a school for young ladies, which flourished for several years. She afterward married John Wright, Esq., while he was a lawyer in Groton, and died in Lowell, where the latter years of her life had been passed.

John Wright, Esq., was a native of Westford, the son of Nathan and Betsey (Trowbridge) Wright, and was born November 4, 1797. He fitted for college at Phillips Academy, Andover, and graduated at Harvard in 1823, and came to Westford to take the place of the late Judge Charles P.

Ephraim Abbot,

Huntington. After two years' service Mr. Wright went to Groton, studied law, and having continued at the bar a few years, turned his attention to manufactures and ultimately became the agent of the Suffolk Mills in Lowell, which agency he retained for many years. He died in Lowell in 1869. He was for many years president of the board of trustees, in which position he proved himself an able and judicious counsellor. He was succeeded in that office by the late John C. Bartlett, M. D., of Chelmsford, who, for many years, served as a trustee and also as the general superintendent.

Rev. Ephraim Abbot took charge of the school in 1828, and was the preceptor for nine years. He was born in New Castle, Maine, September 28, 1779, and was the son of Benjamin and Sarah (Brown) Abbot. He graduated at Harvard College in 1806, and at Andover Theological Seminary in 1810, in the first class that left that institution. His name stands at the head of the list of graduates. He was ordained pastor of the Congregational Church in Greenland, New Hampshire, October 27, 1813, and was dismissed on account of ill health, October 27, 1828. While in Greenland he was for a time the principal of the Brackett Academy in that place. During his residence at Westford he represented the town in the State Legislature in 1839. He was a land surveyor and justice of the peace, and was a very useful and philanthropic man and an earnest and devout Christian. He was a true friend of the Academy, and never ceased to take an interest in its prosperity. He died in Westford, July 21, 1870, aged 90 years, 9 months and 23 days.

Hon. John Davis Long, now Governor of the Commonwealth, was born in Buckfield, Maine; graduated at Harvard in 1857, and came at once to Westford, where he remained two years. The school under his management was very prosperous. The number of pupils was unusually large, and the enthusiasm of both teacher and scholars was high-toned and abundant. Mr. Long, during his preceptorship, started a literary society in which debates were held and a paper, called the *Literary Gatherer*, was edited by the members. The versatility of Mr. Long's gifts was shown in his contributions to that paper, and his ready tact in the discussions. The society was kept up for several years after he left. He is remembered with affection and esteem by his pupils and associates, and such of them as yet reside here welcome him to their homes as one whom they honor and love. His honorable career as a lawyer and statesman have won for him golden opinions which many may emulate but which few attain.

The place of preceptor is now filled by Mr. William Edwin Frost, a native of Norway, Maine. He was born December 6, 1842; graduated at Bowdoin College in 1870, and took charge of this Academy, April 26, 1872, being the thirty-sixth in the line of preceptors. He is a very careful and thorough teacher, and a most efficient disciplinarian. His work in the school has been excellent, and for ten years it has secured the just and hearty praise of all who have been familiar with his methods and witnesses of his achievements. During his principalship eleven students have completed the college preparatory course of study; nineteen, the English and classical course, and four, the English course. Five of the graduates have entered Bowdoin College, three of whom graduated with high rank, and two are under-graduates, and one has just entered Amherst College. All of them were admitted without conditions. Seven have entered the Massachusetts Institute of Technology; one, the Worcester Technological Institute, and one, the Cambridge Divinity School. Several other graduates and advanced scholars of the school have become successful teachers in our public schools.

Previous to Mr. Frost's taking charge of the school, the only examinations of the classes were oral ones at the close of each term; and as these were limited to one day's session, some of the classes were not examined at all. The first change made in this matter was to have the oral examinations include all the classes, two and sometimes three days being devoted to this purpose. In order to secure greater care and thoroughness in the preparation of lessons, a system of written examinations was soon introduced in addition to the oral ones, three being held each term at regular intervals. The rank of each student and class is impartially made up from these examinations and kept on record. This judicious system of examining and ranking the students has proved to be a strong incentive to faithful study, and has greatly improved the quality of the work done in the school.

GRADUATES.

1872 — 1882.

COLLEGE PREPARATORY COURSE.

Brinkerhoff, Osgar	Forge Village	1878
Chamberlin, Edward H.	Westford	1877
Cumings, John O.	Westford	1878
Fisher, Frederic A.	Westford	1877
Leighton, Ida E.	Westford	1877
Prescott, Chas. O.	Westford	1878
Robbins, Arthur G.	Carlisle	1882
Stevens, Nettie M.	Westford	1880
Stevens, Emma J.	Westford	1882
Wright, Henry M.	Westford	1880
Wheeler, Leonard W.	Westford	1882

ENGLISH AND CLASSICAL COURSE.

Atwood, Lillie B.	Westford	1877
Abbot, Emma S.	Westford	1882
Drew, George G.	Westford	1879
Drew, Edea J.	Westford	1882
Fisher, Addie M.	Westford	1879
Fisher, Clara A.	Westford	1882
Hildreth, Herbert V.	Westford	1880
Keyes, Rosina	Westford	1877
Kimball, James L.	Westford	1880
Martin, Delia	Westford	1878
Pond, Abby M.	Dedham	1878
Parker, Issie A.	West Chelmsford	1881
Prescott, Albert E.	Westford	1881
Read, Carrie E.	Westford	1879
Reed, Stella E.	Graniteville	1880
Robbins, Carrie M.	Carlisle	1882

Spalding, M. Dora	Westford	1882
Worden, Minnie A.	North Chelmsford	1882
Wiley, M. Ella	Westford	1882

ENGLISH COURSE.

Parkhurst, M. Belle	West Chelmsford	1881
Walker, Edith E.	Burlington	1879
Whidden, Clarence W.	Westford	1881
Worthen, S. Eva	Chelmsford	1882

The number of ladies employed as assistant teachers has been twenty-nine. Some of these served only short terms, but several of them were employed for many years in succession. Among these Miss Margaret F. Foley deserves notice. She was a resident of Lowell while employed here as a teacher; and all the while her thoughts and her spare time were given to the study of sculpture. After leaving Westford she went abroad and spent much time in Rome. She became the intimate friend of Mary Howitt's daughter. She longed for fame as a sculptor and her aspirations were in a measure gratified. Her work received high encomiums at the Centennial Exhibition in Philadelphia in 1876. She died and was buried at Meran, Italy, in 1879. She was one who fell a premature sacrifice in the pursuit of her favorite vocation, and her early death was lamented by numerous friends who had hoped for her a long and prosperous career.

The achievements of Miss Harriet B. Rogers, a native of Billerica, born April 12, 1834, entitle her to notice in these sketches. She was regarded while in the Academy as a teacher of remarkable tact, energy and ability; and she has since won a far wider and well-merited reputation. She has been from its organization in 1867, the accomplished, enthusiastic and successful Principal of the Clarke Institution for Deaf-Mutes at Northampton. She was the first in this country to introduce a system of teaching the use and employment of spoken language or reading from the lips, instead of the sign language. This system, as now developed, is regarded with much favor. In furtherance of her work, Miss Rogers a few years since visited similar schools in Europe; and is steadily employed in her peculiar field of philanthropic endeavor.

The government and general management of the school is left very much to the principal for the time being, aided to some extent by the superintendent; but subject, of course, to the supervision and control of the trustees.

The average attendance for a term, may, perhaps, be stated at forty-five or fifty. It varies with the seasons, and still more with the popularity of teachers, as well as the popularity of neighboring schools or academies. This latter circumstance has now, and long has had, a material influence on its prosperity. While many such have been established or opened within the present century, some have flourished and some have failed; but the bare multiplication of them has doubtless had some effect to retard the growth of this. It has, however, endeavored to hold on the even tenor of its way, aiming to meet the wishes of its friends and achieve the primary objects of its founders, undisturbed by jealousies or petty rivalries.

TRUSTEES.

1882.

President — His Excellency John D. Long, Hingham.
Secretary — Sherman D. Fletcher, Westford.
Treasurer — Edward Prescott, Esq., Westford.

Julian Abbot, Esq., Lowell; Edward Symmes, Westford; George T. Day, Esq., Westford; Rev. Edward A. Horton, Boston; Allan Cameron, Esq., Westford; John William Abbot, Westford; J. Adams Bartlett, Chelmsford; Hon. J. Henry Read, Westford; Hon. Albert L. Coolidge, Boston; Hon. Daniel S. Richardson, Lowell; Hon. Joseph A. Harwood, Littleton; Abiel J. Abbot, Westford.

Superintendent — Rev. Edward A. Horton.
Principal — William Edwin Frost, A. M.
Preceptress — Miss Adelaide Baker.

Ninety years have now elapsed since the foundations of the Academy were laid; and its influence in diffusing knowledge and in promoting true culture has been very great. Its growth and well-being will no doubt be carefully fostered by its guardians and friends. So, when another decade of years shall have rolled by, they will be glad to commemorate the first century of its usefulness with fitting tributes to the philanthropy and zeal of the men and women who established and sustained it.

Meantime, the common schools have surely reaped the benefits of its presence here. As in nature some forces are noiseless, but strong, so in society, some influences are quiet, but potent; and among the good things whose tendency is subtle but powerful, it is safe to place this literary institution which sends its quickening impulse all abroad.

A few particulars need to be added to the history of common schools here. In due time school-houses were built and the lines of the several districts were defined. The term squadron ceased to be used about 1798. That known as Stony Brook was divided in 1795, and that known as the southeast was separated from the south soon after.

In 1808 the town voted to " give to the southeast district (now No. 6) fifty dollars toward erecting a school-house." This was the first school-house in the district. In 1809, voted " to choose a committee to regulate the several schools in their inspection the year ensuing." This looks like a veritable school committee, but the law of the State requiring the election of such a committee was not enacted until 1827. This town plainly anticipated the enactment. The men to whom belongs the credit of being the first school committee of Westford were John Abbot, Esq., Col. Benjamin Osgood, Reuben Leighton, Levi Wright, Nathaniel Hildreth, Jonathan Prescott, Amos Read and Bill W. Stevens. This appointment was not exceptional, but continued to be made year by year.

In 1822 the territory of the town was divided into eight school districts. These were the Centre, Stony Brook,

Forge, the southwest, the south (No. 5), the southeast (No. 6), the northeast (No. 7), and the north (No. 8 and No. 9). In 1826 the north district was divided and one part called the northwest. In 1851 the Forge district was divided. Sometime previous to this division the school-house of that district stood near the poor-house.

April 6, 1835, "Voted that the scholars in the several districts shall be numbered by the committee on the first Monday or Tuesday of November, with the names of the heads of families."

March 7, 1836, the selectmen were made a committee to number the school-houses, and then the present numbers were given. In 1851 Graniteville became No. 10. At the present time (1882) there are eleven public schools in the town, and ten school-houses. The houses, with one exception, have all been built since the repeal in 1869 of the law relating to school districts. The schools are kept for eight months in the year.

The amount of money raised for the support of schools, March, 1882, was $3500.

COLLEGE GRADUATES BORN IN WESTFORD.

HARVARD UNIVERSITY.

	Grad.	Died.
Stephen Hall	1765	1795
John Marston Minot	1767	
Elijah Fletcher	1769	1786
Phinehas Wright	1772	1802
Jonathan Procter	1789	
John Abbot	1796	1854
Willard Hall	1799	1875
Samuel Prescott	1799	1813
Robert Adams	1804	1806
Abel Boynton	1804	1817
Joshua Prescott	1807	1859
Oliver Patten	1814	1822
Aaron Prescott	1814	1851
Jotham B. Wright	1817	1828
Samuel Manning	1822	
Luther B. Lincoln	1822	
John Wright	1823	1869
Julian Abbot	1826	

John W. P. Abbot	1827	1872
Avery Prescott	1827	1830
Oliver Prescott	1828	
James Blodgett	1841	1845
George E. H. Abbot	1860	
Albert E. Davis	1864	1869
George Abbot	1864	
Thomas E. Symmes	1865	

YALE COLLEGE.

Jonathan Osgood	1787

DARTMOUTH COLLEGE.

Otis Caleb Wight	1842

BOWDOIN COLLEGE.

Frederic Alvan Fisher	1881
Edward Henry Chamberlin	1881

RESIDENT COLLEGE GRADUATES NOT BORN IN WESTFORD.

HARVARD UNIVERSITY.

Rev. Willard Hall	1722	1779
Joseph Underwood, Jr.	1735 ab't	1748
Benjamin Stone	1776	
Rev. Caleb Blake	1784	1847
James Prescott, Jr.	1788	1829
Rev. Ephraim Abbot	1806	1870
Nahum H. Groce	1808	

BROWN UNIVERSITY.

Rev. Leonard Luce	1824

AMHERST COLLEGE.

Rev. Winthrop F. Wheeler	1839	1880

DARTMOUTH COLLEGE.

Rev. Edwin R. Hodgman	1843
Edward C. Atwood	1871
Rev. Joseph S. Moulton	1873

BOWDOIN COLLEGE.

William E. Frost	1870
Osgar Brinkerhoff	1877

MIDDLEBURY COLLEGE.

Charles H. Rowley	1868

EDUCATIONAL.

MINISTERS BORN IN WESTFORD.

Phinehas Wright, son of Ebenezer and Deliverance (Stevens) Wright, born May 22, 1747.

Philip Spalding, son of Philip and Elizabeth (Obert) Spalding, born Nov. 18, 1776; died May 25, 1834, aged 58. He settled in Penobscot, Hancock County, Maine, in 1809; afterward at Jamaica, Vermont, in 1815. His son, Samuel T. Spalding, graduated at Amherst, 1839, and is a lawyer in Northampton.

Daniel M. Reed, now living in Rockford, Illinois. He is the son of Jonas Reed, who once owned the Burbeck place.

Phinehas Spalding.

PHYSICIANS.

Thomas Mead, about 1740.
Jeremiah Robinson, 1766; removed to Littleton.
Jonathan Crane, 1768.
Asaph Fletcher, 1770.
Solomon Wheat, 1771; came from Natick.
Nathan Raymond, 1782.
Jonas Marshall, 1783; removed to Fitchburg.
Charles Proctor, 1784; died here in 1817.
William Little, 1785.
Allen Flagg, in Forge Village, 1799; removed to Ashby.
Isaiah Parker, 1800.
Samuel Manning, 1801.
Samuel Stillman Parker, 1801.
Ebenezer Parker, 1802.
Asaph Byam, 1816; died here, May, 1838.
Benjamin Osgood, 1818; died here, February 1, 1863.
Joseph Whitmore, 1840; removed to Lowell.
Sidney Drinkwater, 1845; removed to Sedgwick, Maine.
Darius A. Dow, 1852.
J. T. Buttrick, 1860; removed to Block Island.
Henry Rockwood, 1860.
Morris E. Jones, 1862.

William A. Webster, 1868; removed to Manchester, New Hampshire.
Edward C. Atwood, 1875.
Joseph B. Heald, 1879.

LAWYERS.

John Prescott, Jr., removed to Groton.
John Abbot, died in 1854.
John W. P. Abbot, died in 1872.

CHAPTER XII.

BIOGRAPHICAL SKETCHES.

Rev. Phineas Wright, for seventeen years pastor of the church in Bolton, Massachusetts.* Died, at Bolton, on the 26th of December, 1802, of a paralytic shock, the Rev. Phineas Wright, pastor of the church and congregation there, in the 56th year of his age, and the 18th of his ministry. His remains were respectfully interred on the 30th of the same month. The death of so worthy and useful a minister cannot but be considered as a great infliction, not only to his relatives and the society with which he was immediately connected, but to the public at large.

The Rev. Mr. Wright was born in Westford, of reputable parents, and received the first honors of Harvard University, in Cambridge, at the commencement in the year 1772. During his residence at college, such were his correct morals and amiable deportment that he enjoyed the respect of the students in general, and the approbation of the government to a great degree. His constant attention to his studies was attended with a valuable improvement in all the branches of learning which he pursued. The powers of his mind, taken collectively, possessed greater strength than is common. They were cultivated by reading, much by conversation, and probably most of all, by close observation and deep reflection. A social disposition made an intercourse with the learned, wise and good, always peculiarly pleasing to him. His knowledge of human nature, his penetrating

---

*This sketch is reprinted from a pamphlet giving an account of Mr. Wright's death, and the sermon preached at his funeral. The sketch was by Rev. Daniel Chaplin, of Groton.

sagacity in discovering the characters and designs of men, his fortitude in danger, his address in defeating the purposes of the mischievous, and his perseverance in what he thought to be right, were conspicuous to all who knew him. He seems to have been eminently qualified for the situation which Providence assigned him. Two ministers had been dismissed in Bolton before his settlement there. In consequence of many sharp altercations and long continued divisions, the habits of the people had become extremely unfavorable in a religious and civil view, and their prejudices so great that there appeared scarcely a possibility of their being brought, for many years, into a state of social order. Nevertheless, by the blessing of God on the wise management, the multiplied labors, the manly, unwearied, spirited and persevering exertions of this servant of Christ, the church has become truly respectable for its regularity, peace and unity, for the number of its members, and their religious characters. And the town has established the character of patriotic and federal, harmonious and prudent in the transaction of all public business, and is especially distinguished for the important care of the rising generation that they may be properly educated. He devoted much time to conversation with his people, on moral, religious, political and other subjects; being of opinion himself, as he declared, that he did as much good to them by his private discourses, as by his public preaching. In the pulpit his manner was grave, his style plain and logical. His voice was clear, audible, and of a happy tone for a public speaker. He always studied conciseness and simplicity, rather than prolixity and ornament, in his public exhibitions. He aimed to enlighten the minds of men with knowledge, and make them unwavering, rational and persevering Christians. He paid little regard to confessions of faith, formed by men uninspired; and avowed the adoption of the sacred -oracles as the only standard of his faith and practice. He was independent in his theological principles, claiming and asserting the right to judge for himself; and candidly allowed others to judge for themselves.

He was friendly and accommodating to his brethren in the ministry, disposed to esteem others better than himself; and generously encouraged and assisted youth whose pecuniary circumstances were difficult, but their genius and turn of mind promising, in attaining a public education, to qualify them for usefulness to the community. He was pitiful to the sick and distressed, and ready to do good to all. His sympathy, always awake to the calls of dependence and affliction, made him the prompt benefactor of the wretched and friendless. His house was the seat of order, peace, economy, friendship and generosity. No man ever displayed a more cordial hospitality to friends and others who came under his roof. He was a pleasant and affectionate husband, a sincere and constant friend, a cheerful companion, tender in his feelings toward all his relations, an intrepid advocate for civil and religious liberty, a stable patriot on rational principles, a most valuable citizen, and a devout and exemplary Christian. As the servant of the Lord, he ruled in the church with wisdom, firmness and impartiality; and was a faithful minister of the gospel, as all who judge with candor must necessarily conclude. Pleasure was never his pursuit nor indulgence, except within the limits of due moderation; and the temperance which he habitually observed in the use of ardent spirits of all kinds, was carried to a degree of abstemiousness, through the course of his life, even to the closing scene. He was able to continue his public labors until the Sabbath preceding his death. Notwithstanding the people of his late charge are disposed highly to appreciate the excellency of his character and the usefulness of his ministerial services, yet most certainly they will hereafter in a greater measure perceive the worth of his talents and exertions to them. Indeed it would be difficult, if possible, to name the clergyman, either dead or living, who has done more good than the deceased whose exit we deplore to church and state, since the time of his ordination to the gospel ministry. And though religion and charity oblige us to believe that to him death was the greatest gain, for then he received the reward of a faithful minister of Christ; yet it is natural to the pious, in a prospect of the present state of religion and morals and of politics in this country, to contemplate his death and that of other good ministers of late, as severe frowns of Divine Providence on the public. Under this painful impression, in the language of humble and fervent trust in God, who doth all things with consummate wisdom and unerring rectitude, they will address their prayer to him — " Help, Lord, for the godly man ceaseth; for the faithful fail from among the children of men."

Samuel Chamberlin. He was the son of Samuel and Elizabeth, and grandson of Samuel, of Woburn. He was born in Chelmsford in 1685. His residence was near the house of Wayland F. Balch. Like many of the early settlers he was concerned in the purchase and sale of wild lands. In the year 1736 his name appears on the records of the General Court among others who petitioned for a line of towns on the Connecticut River. The petition was granted and leave was given to the petitioners to meet at Woburn December 7, 1736, to admit proprietors. Ten days after, to wit, December 17th, in the House of Representatives, "Voted that Mr. Samuel Chamberlin, of Westford, be and he is hereby fully authorized and impowered to assemble and convene the grantees or proprietors of township number one." This was Chesterfield, New Hampshire, and the line of towns on the river above it were Westmoreland, Walpole and Charlestown, which was called " Number Four." But difficulties arose between the two colonies, and these towns afterward received charters from New Hampshire. He was known as Lieutenant Chamberlin; was an original member of the First Church, and was one of the first board of selectmen. He died June 6, 1769, in the eighty-fourth year of his age. After his death his son Samuel lived on the homestead.

Col. John Robinson. Reference has already been made to this gallant soldier and to the part he bore at Concord Bridge and at Bunker Hill. A few particulars should be added respecting him. He was the son of Jacob and Mary (Gould) Robinson, and was born in Topsfield, 1735, and died in Westford, June 13, 1805. He married Huldah Perley, of Boxford, November 27, 1764. Their children were:

1. Huldah, born September 23, 1765.
2. Mehitable, born August 9, 1767.
3. Betty, born May 3, 1770.
4. Sally, born May 3, 1772.
5. Rebecca, born July 7, 1774.
6. John, born February 17, 1781.

Col. Robinson was buried in the West Cemetery, and the headstone at his grave bears the following inscription: "Here reposes the body of Col. John Robinson, who expired June 13th, 1805, aged 70 years. In 1775 he distinguished himself by commanding the corps of soldiers who first opposed the menacing attempts of the British troops at Concord Bridge.

> Here rest thine ashes; on thy silent grave
> May dews distil and laurels gently wave;
> Let heralds far proclaim thy soul was fired
> By love of freedom and by Heaven inspired.
> First in the glorious cause our rights to attain,
> Last in our hearts shall thy brave deeds remain."

Rev. Jonathan Osgood. He was born in Westford in 1761; graduated at Yale College in 1787; was ordained as pastor of the church in Gardner, Massachusetts, October 19, 1791, and died May 21, 1821, in the sixty-first year of his age. For nearly thirty years he served that town in the capacity of minister, physician and school-teacher. He rose to considerable eminence in the medical art; and for a number of years he was an officer in the Medical Society. He represented the town in the State Legislature, and was regarded as a man of respectable talents, and one possessed of good knowledge of human nature. It is natural to suppose that the time spent in the school-room or devoted to the practice of medicine must have interfered somewhat with the duties of the clerical profession; and it is said he came to regret in the latter part of his life that he had not given more attention to the duties and studies of the ministerial office.

Charles Proctor, M. D. Was born in Westford, September 13, 1755, and died here in March, 1817. He was the son of Nathan and Phebe Proctor, and the homestead of his father was in the south part of the town, the farm now in possession of Mrs. Desmond. He was among the earliest educated physicians in the town; but in his earlier days had to compete with others who sought to establish themselves here, among whom was Dr. Amos Bancroft, of Groton. He studied his profession in Chelmsford. He did not receive a collegiate education, but was a successful physician and was much esteemed by his fellow-citizens. He was a member of the Massachusetts Medical Society, and was for many years a justice of the peace. He was one of the originators of the Academy, and one of its trustees till his death. He married for his first wife Miss Edea Carver, sister of Jonathan Carver, who died early; and for a second wife the widow Lydia Cummings. By her he had two daughters — Edea, who married Nahum H. Groce and died within a year after marriage; and Sarah, who also married Mr. Groce, December 24, 1815. None of his decendants are now living, but his memory is still cherished by the few who once knew him as a kind and benevolent friend, a dignified and upright man.

Hon. Joseph Read. A brief notice of him appears on page 163, but further particulars are here added. He was the son of Joshua and Mary (Spalding) Read, and was born at the Read homestead on Frances Hill, March 13, 1776. When nearly twelve years of age, being offended and grieved at a slight punishment imposed upon him in school in February, 1788, he asked and obtained leave of his father to go with an uncle, Joseph Read, to Plymouth, New Hampshire, where his uncle then resided. He engaged in the mercantile business in Thetford, Vermont, in 1803; married in 1804, but in a few years obtained a legal separation from his wife (an unfortunate matter); married in 1812 Elizabeth Burnap, daughter of Rev. Dr. Burnap, of Merrimack, New Hampshire, and of this marriage there were two sons, Charles and George W. Read, Esquires, of Montpelier, Vermont. In 1814 he was representative of the town of Thetford, and was chosen to the same office five times afterward. He was elected Judge of the County in 1818 and in the two following years. In 1827 he removed to Montpelier, and in 1830 he was elected Judge of Probate for the District of Washington, and retained the office three years. In 1834 he was chosen one of the council of censors to revise the Constitution of the State, and in 1840 one of the Presidential electors. He held the office of County Treasurer for nearly thirty years. He died February 6, 1859, aged 82 years, leaving a handsome fortune and a character well worthy of esteem and emulation. He was a gentleman of the old school, precise and methodical in his habits; of noble presence and demeanor; honest and sincere in all his dealings; reserved and prudent in his speech; sagacious and comprehensive in his views; of resolute and unflinching perseverance, and wise and ample generosity. Among his marked traits, besides his general honesty and unbending integrity, was his particular and nice conscientiousness.*

Hon. Willard Hall. Born in Westford, December 24, 1780. He was the son of Willis and Mehetabel (Poole) Hall, and grandson of Rev. Willard Hall, the first minister of the town. He entered Westford Academy with its first scholars, was fitted for Harvard College in 1794; was then examined and received, but went back and spent another year in the Academy, and entered Harvard as a freshman in 1795 and graduated in 1799. " Writing in years long after Judge Hall touchingly alludes to his father's sacrifices

---

*For this outline of his life and work and this estimate of his character, the compiler is indebted to the History of Montpelier, Vermont.

to keep his children at school. He also refers, with not a little satisfaction, to the time when a small boy he trudged two miles on foot to school with dinner in his pocket; a discipline to which he ascribed largely his fitness to encounter the stern responsibilities of after life. 'I should like,' he writes, 'to hear something of Levi Hedge, to whose partiality for me I owe my education, through privations and hardships and conflict that placed me in the upper current of the struggle; by which I trust I have done something for the good of others. I remember him with lively gratitude.' He inherited from his ancestry a constitution singularly sound and vigorous in all its parts, physical, intellectual and moral. His entire organization, body, intellect, affections, conscience and will, was healthful, active and symmetrical, a remarkable example of the *mens sana in corpore sano*. The early development of that delicate moral and religious sensibility, which so toned and regulated his character, is directly traceable to the mother's hand. She was a woman of much force of character; trained in early life under the ministry and personal influence of Rev. Daniel Emerson, the pastor of her native town of Hollis." Among his contemporaries at college were Horace Binney, William Ellery Channing, Joseph Story, Washington Allston and Lemuel Shaw.

"His proficiency as a college student must have been excellent in all branches; but there is reason to suppose that his leading interest was in the ancient classics. His appointment to deliver a Latin oration in the junior year would seem to mark some distinction in that department of study. Besides, his style of composition, in its purity, terseness and vigor bore strong traces of early and thorough classical culture."

After graduating he studied law in the office of Judge Dana at Groton, and was admitted to the bar of Hillsborough County, New Hampshire, in 1803. In a remark made to his pupil years afterward, Judge Dana bore this testimony: "When you left my office, I had not a misgiving concerning you. I was as confident of your success as a farmer is of a crop from a well-cultivated field."

In 1802, while a student at Groton, his attention was called to the State of Delaware as one offering some inducements to settlement, and he addressed a note of inquiry to the elder James A. Bayard. The favorable reply of Mr. Bayard induced him to make choice of that State for prosecuting his profession. He left his father's house in Westford, April 7, 1803, and, travelling the whole distance on horseback, reached Wilmington, Delaware, on the 16th of the same month. On motion of Mr. Bayard he was admitted to the bar at Georgetown, and settled at Dover in the following month.

"As a counsellor at the bar he became distinguished for his legal learning, sound judgment and such fidelity to a trust as made a client's interest all his own. He has been represented by the elder lawyers as being on occasions eloquent; yet few, if any, had less of the common arts of oratory. It was once the remark of the late Chancellor Ridgely, made from the bench, that he never called a cause of Willard Hall's in which the answer was 'not ready.' In 1812 he was appointed Secretary of State, which office he held for three years. In 1816 he was elected Representative in Congress and served for two terms. In 1821 he was again Secretary of State; and in 1822 he was elected a member of the State Senate. On the 6th of May, 1823, he was appointed by President Monroe, District Judge of the United States for Delaware District. He retired from the profession, as he himself said, 'wearied with twenty years' labors and anxieties.' He held the office of District Judge through the exceptionally long term of forty-eight years, retiring from it in December, 1871, in his ninety-first year, with his faculties still unimpaired, except that bodily infirmity had disabled him for protracted labor."

In 1822 Mr. Hall, while Secretary of State, took up the interest of popular education in his adopted State, with a grasp which relaxed only after fifty years of labor and under the infirmities of age. It became, thenceforth, truly his lifework. He matured the school system which in 1829 became the law of the State. His biographer says: "It is very far from an adequate estimate of the service of Judge Hall to the cause of popular education to regard him as the founder or organizer of the school system. That was but the commencement of his labors. Not content only to frame and inaugurate the system, he watched its operations with ceaseless vigilance, encouraging effort, conciliating honest dissent, shaming selfish cavils and narrow prejudices, studying to the utmost detail the working of the system, seeking legislation to remedy its defects and improve its efficiency. . . . The principle earnestly maintained by Judge Hall was, that an elementary education at the public expense should be extended to all who might desire it. He enforced it both as a duty to the young and on grounds of high public expediency.

"Through his earnest advocacy the Board of Education for the city of Wilmington was formed in 1852, and he was chosen president of it and continued to hold the office for eighteen years. On the evening of March 28th, 1870, he met with them for the last time. He then announced in few words the necessity, through age, of his retirement, and received from the board, by a unanimous rising vote, its testimony, given in the name of the people and city of Wilmington, to his untiring, faithful and efficient service in the cause of education in the State of Delaware and in the city of Wilmington. Thus he closed the long record of his forty-eight years of service to the educational interests of that State."

Mr. Hall was for forty-eight years president of the Delaware Bible Society, and was also president of the Wilmington Saving Funds Society for many years. He became president of the Delaware Historical Society when he was in his eighty-fourth year, and gave to it the prestige of his revered name.

"He united with the Presbyterian Church of Wilmington in 1827, and in 1829 he was elected a ruling elder, which office he held until his death. He taught a succession of

Bible classes in the Sabbath-school for a period of over forty years. When far advanced in life he accepted an invitation to address the literary societies of Delaware College, having in himself a true sympathy for young men in the pursuit of an education. He gave an ardent support to the temperance cause, and in 1844 he published a 'Plea for the Sabbath,' and in 1846 a pamphlet against lotteries.

"His habits of life were systematic and exact. In one thing he was pre-eminent, that is, his rigorous punctuality to engagements, springing from his acute sense of justice. . . . The crowning excellence of Judge Hall's character was the absolute supremacy of the moral sentiments. Their influence pervaded his entire manhood. . . . The natural force and freshness of his mind, and the warmth of his affections remained to the last. The change came to him on the evening of May 10th, 1875, as gently as sleep comes to an infant." His age was 94 years 4 months and 16 days. [Memorial address by Hon. Daniel M. Bates, President of Delaware Historical Society, 1876.]

Rev. James Blodgett. Died in Lexington, July 16, 1845, aged 33 years. The following obituary of him appeared in the *Christian Register:*

"Few things can be sadder to the friends of liberal Christianity than to see the young servants of the church, before whom the long promise of usefulness is opening, cut off at the very beginning of their labors in the field where the harvesting is plenteous and the laborers are few. This is especially felt in the case of the young clergyman whose death we record. Mr. Blodgett was, both in his natural gifts and by his experience, peculiarly fitted for the office of a Christian teacher. His whole character was ministerial; not of that austere and over-prudent character which is sometimes falsely so named, but the character of a man with whom religion was the crowning grace of a modest, benevolent and honest heart. His judgment was excellent — the result of faculties remarkable for their even balance, and seldom disturbed by any pressure of vanity or passion. He was patient of labor, calm under the common troubles of life, and constant to his main purpose. The turn of his mind was rather to reflection, and his meditations had been from his youth chiefly on religious topics. These kept the first place, not merely as a matter of conscience, but as an intellectual taste; and it might have been said of him, long before he entered the ministry, that he was far in advance of most young clergymen in well-digested theological knowledge. It had been to him, also, more than a mere inquiry; he well knew the experience of a Christian life. Its hopes, its anxieties, its trials had long been written on his heart, and manifested in his daily walk. The result of many anxious and laborious inquiries had been to attach him more and more closely to the Bible, and his hope, the hope of his childhood, had always been to enforce its truths as a Christian preacher. He could hardly fail to be acceptable as such. The topics which it was his office to treat were those which he had long felt as most interesting and vital to himself, and though without any love of display, he had a sound understanding and a vein of strong sense which must have gained him attention as a speaker. His language was plain and he used but little ornament; but he always spoke to the purpose, and had an unusual command of illustrations which were often homely and sometimes humorous, but which always carried him on to his point. But his great fitness for the ministry was, after all, ' the ornament of a meek and quiet spirit,' which naturally sought the tranquillity of a pastor's life, never reaching into the world for a more ambitious occupation, but content to stay where God placed it."

Mr. Blodgett's life had not been without trials. His grand aim had been to fit himself for the ministry, but his studies had been interrupted and he came at last to college late in life and chiefly by the assistance of the late Dr. Follen, whom, in some points, he strongly resembled. He was graduated in 1841 with great credit to himself, and completed his studies at the Theological School in two years. He was ordained at Deerfield in January, 1844; but his eagerness to accomplish the purpose of his life had urged him beyond the strength of a constitution which had already borne unusual fatigue. It was evident to his personal friends, at the time of his ordination, that his days were numbered. But he struggled through a year, and continued to preach until his voice quite failed him. He soon felt that his work was done; he felt, too, the reward of a Christian experience. The doubts, the anxieties concerning his own acceptance with God, which had clouded much of his early life, now gave way to a humble and settled peace. He said to a brother in the ministry, a few days before his death, that he had not felt a moment's despondency; and so he continued to the last, when he fell asleep in Jesus in a "sure and certain hope of a glorious resurrection." Mr. Blodgett fitted for college in the Academy here, under the instruction of Rev. Ephraim Abbot.

James M. Stone. Born in Westford, August 17, 1817; died in Charlestown, Massachusetts, December, 1880, aged 63. He went to Lowell about 1832 and worked for a year in the tailoring store of Francis Hobbs, 17 Central Street. He was afterward in the employ of Samuel Burbank. Then after working for a time with Col. Reed he went to Charlestown. He always had a taste for newspaper work, and during his life wrote more or less for publication. In 1841 he was for six months editor of the *Vox Populi*, just after it started; and in 1843 he began the publication of a small morning paper called *The Herald*, which lived but a few months. He was attached to the Free Soil party, and was also strongly anti-"Know Nothing," when that party came up. He was elected to the Legislature from Charlestown for several years, and in 1866 and 1867 was Speaker of the House. He was one of the most effective men in influencing legislation, and was sometimes called "King of the Lobby," but no one ever accused him of anything dishonorable.

CHAPTER XIII.

RAILROADS — PUBLIC LIBRARY — SKETCH OF FORGE VILLAGE — MILITARY COMPANIES.

THE Stony Brook Railroad was the first one that was built and opened for travel. The preliminary surveys were made in 1846, and the company was organized in the spring of 1847. The final surveys were made and work was begun in the following summer. It was opened July 5, 1848, on which day the proprietors or stockholders passed over the road to Groton Junction, and, by previous arrangement, to Clinton, where they dined. The Worcester and Nashua Railroad was not then completed, but was opened a few months later. Passing from North Chelmsford up the valley of the Stony Brook in a southwest direction, it cuts the township into two nearly equal parts, and forms the main channel of communication with Lowell and Boston on the east, and New York and the wide continent on the west. There are four stations, known as Brookside, Westford, Graniteville and Forge Village. It has been the means of developing much business, especially in Graniteville and Forge Village. In the latter village within a few years, the ice business has been carried on with success. The cost of the building with the engine was $65,000, and the cost of tools $3000. The number of men employed when cutting ice is 175, and the number of horses 50. The amount of ice sent to Boston last year (1881) for John P. Squire was 35,000 tons, and the amount stored for the Southern market was 50,000 tons. The proprietor is Thomas S. Hittinger, of Boston.

The Framingham and Lowell Railroad enters the town on the easterly side, a little south of Heart Pond, and passing what has been known as Dupee's Corner, where for many years a tavern was kept for the benefit of travellers and teamsters, it enters the town of Acton. It furnishes good accommodation to all who live in that section of the town. It was opened for travel October 1, 1871. There is but one station in Westford, that called by the company the Carlisle Station.

The Nashua, Acton and Boston Railroad was opened to the public July 1, 1873. Striking the town near its northwest angle it passes longitudinally and leaves near the southwest corner. It is under the management of the Concord (N. H.) Railroad Company, and is used chiefly for the transportation of freight. It has three stations in town — Graniteville, Westford and East Littleton, so called.

SOCIAL AND PUBLIC LIBRARY.

It is now eighty-five years since the establishment of a library in this town. It was at first the effort of a few benevolent men to secure a wider diffusion of knowledge among the people by means of good books; but that early inception has widened into a large and useful public library. Evidently these men took a just view of the needs of society, and it is gratifying to be able to point to the result of their wise forecast and philanthropy. The following document makes known their purpose in their own words:

"WESTFORD, 14th February, 1797.
" We, the subscribers, Inhabitants of the Town of Westford, feeling ourselves willing to promote Literature and useful knowledge among ourselves and our families, think it for the benefit of us, and for the Town in general to establish a Social Library to be put under such rules and regulations as shall appear to be the most beneficial to the subscribers; and it is proposed that two dollars shall constitute a share to each member that shall subscribe that sum, and so in proportion to those that shall subscribe for a greater sum; and we pledge ourselves each of us severally and Individually to pay all the

monies that we subscribe for, on the first Monday in April next ensuing, when there shall be a general meeting of the subscribers at the house of Mr. Samuel Wood at 6 o'clock afternoon, at which time there will be appointed a Committee to receive the subscription money and to purchase such Books as shall be most likely to subserve the purposes aforesaid, and to act upon all other matters that shall come before us.*

James Prescott, Jr	. D 8 00	Samuel Wood	.	. D 2 00
Samuel Adams	. D 8 00	Issachar Keyes	.	2 00
Joseph Cummings, Jr.	. D 4 00	John Raymond	.	2 00
Eleazer Hamblin	. D 4 00	Ebenezer Prescott	.	2 00
Charles Proctor	. D 4 00	Benjamin Osgood	.	2 00
John Abbot	. D 6 00	Caleb Blake	.	2 00
Jonathan Carver	. D 4 00	Francis Leighton	.	2 00
Abel Boynton	. D 4 00	Reuben Leighton	.	2 00
Zaccheus Wright	. D 8 00	Wyle Richardson	.	2 00
Josiah Boynton, Jr	. D 2 00	Joseph Jewett	.	2 00
Joel Abbot	. D 2 00	Joseph Keyes	.	2 00
Timothy Spalding	2 00	Amos Crosby	.	2 00
Thomas Richardson	4 00			

According to agreement the subscribers held a meeting at Mr. Wood's tavern, April 3, 1797, at which Zaccheus Wright was chosen moderator, and Caleb Blake clerk. Rev. Caleb Blake, Col. Zaccheus Wright, James Prescott, Jr., Francis Leighton and Ebenezer Prescott were appointed "to draw up rules and laws for the intended Library in Westford." At an adjourned meeting held at Mr. Samuel Adams', May 8th, the subscribers "voted to accept the Rules and Regulations that have been drawn up by the committee"; and elected James Prescott, Jr., Rev. Caleb Blake and Dr. Charles Proctor, directors; and Richard Kneeland, librarian and treasurer. The "preamble" to the code of laws recites that "the subscribers being desirous of increasing their own information and promoting useful knowledge in the community, especially among the rising generation, agree to form themselves into a society under the name

---

* The original paper from which this is copied shows the autographs of the subscribers. The letter D, which is prefixed in several cases, indicates dollars, not shares.

of the Westford Library Company"; and the rules state that "the Library shall consist of fifty shares at least, and shall always be kept in the town of Westford; that the Company shall always consist of thirteen members at least, and seven shall constitute a quorum; that there shall be a meeting of the Company on the first Monday in January annually, for the choice of officers and other necessary business; that the Librarian shall provide, at the expense of the Company, a convenient place for the safe keeping of all the books belonging thereto and shall keep a fair catalogue," &c. In a long article the directors are given a supervisory and executive power similar to that now generally recognized and conferred on such officers. Members were entitled to vote according to their shares, allowing one vote to each share, and any member could vote by proxy. No person could become a member until he had actually paid for one share. Any member could "give, sell, transfer or bequeath" his share, and all shares descended to the heirs of a deceased member; but "no person or member shall withdraw any share from the Library or receive the value thereof of the Company under any pretence whatever." "There shall be no books in the library upon civil or religious controversy, or tending to deprave the morals of men." When any members could not agree about the priority of taking books, they must determine it by drawing tickets from a box wherein a number of tickets were kept, numbered in arithmetical order, equal to the whole number of proprietors, and the priority of numbers gave the priority of choice. The annual tax or assessment was twenty cents upon each share, to be used for the purchase of books and payment of expenses.

The first assessment was paid by thirty-six persons on forty-nine shares; and the second by thirty-one persons on forty-one shares. The first book on the list was "Ferguson's Roman Republic," in three volumes. A printed catalogue, issued in 1816, gives the titles of 102 books in 179 volumes. In 1801 a vote was passed "that the members of said Company shall be hereafter called and known by the name and style of 'the proprietors of the social library in the town of Westford.'" With the exception of the year 1800, Zaccheus Wright was president down to the year 1806, when Francis Leighton was chosen, who died the same year and was succeeded by Issachar Keyes.

In 1853 the town chose a committee "to report a plan for establishing a Town Library and ascertaining at what price the Social Library can be purchased." There is no hint on the town records of any report from that committee. The matter was again brought before the town in 1858, November 2nd, when a committee was appointed "to see if any measures can be adopted by which a Town Library can be established and the Proprietors' Library merged in the same." March 7, 1859, this committee made report as follows:

"Your committee met the committee chosen by the Proprietors on the 4th of February, 1859, and after an interchange of views on the subject-matter, received from said committee the following propositions:

"1st. Said Inhabitants shall annually expend in the purchase of books for said Library a sum of money not less than thirty dollars.

"2nd. Said Inhabitants shall provide, furnish and keep in good order a suitable room in the middle of said Westford where said Library shall be kept under the charge of a suitable Librarian.

"3rd. Said Inhabitants shall make suitable and proper regulations respecting the preserving, keeping in repair, and loaning the books in said Library.

"4th. Whenever said Inhabitants shall refuse to make the appropriation before mentioned, said Library shall revert back to said proprietors or their heirs.

"And your committee recommend the acceptance of the above propositions.

"THOMAS RICHARDSON,
"D. C. BUTTERFIELD,
"P. CHAMBERLIN."

On the same day the town voted to accept the report, and chose Leonard Luce, Sherman D. Fletcher and Elbridge G. Parker to carry the vote into effect. Upon these conditions the Social Library came into the possession of the town as a gift, and became in fact and of right a town library.

About twenty-five years ago a collection of books was made, called the Agricultural Library, consisting of one hundred volumes. The funds were obtained by subscription, each person paying three dollars. This also passed into the hands of the town some ten years ago, and was merged in the Public Library. This library is now kept in a commodious apartment in the Town Hall. Three directors, chosen annually, have the entire management of it; and the town makes an annual appropriation of one hundred and fifty dollars. Number of volumes, August, 1882, 4191.

FORGE VILLAGE.

The following interesting incidents and reminiscences have been furnished to the compiler by Capt. David Prescott Lawrence, whose long residence in that village has made him familiar with its history:

"On the west side of Beaver Brook near the bridge was located a house, known as the Cogswell place. It was afterward occupied by Calvin Green, and later by Charles Reed: It was once a hospital for small-pox patients, it being customary at that time for people to go there and be vaccinated for small-pox. Following the road to the village we find the next house, called the Kent place, at the corner of the road leading to Westford Centre, where was also a blacksmith shop. Within my remembrance there lived in the house one Isaac Durant, a revolutionary soldier, who was blind and was guided about the village by a little grandson. Afterward it was owned by Ebenezer Blood, who was noted for telling very improbable stories. Next it was owned by Charles Miner, who was a soldier in the last war and never returned. Some years ago the buildings were burned by an incendiary, and the place is now owned by D. P. Lawrence. Next was the Patch house, occupied by Isaac Patch and Elisha Kent. The latter had two wives and five children; the last wife being a sister of Asa Wright. The house where George Wright now lives was built and occupied by Amos Heywood, who married Lydia Buck. The house nearly opposite was built and occupied by Eben Prescott, who had three wives and a large family. The next house was owned by Col. David Goodhue, the father of Imla Goodhue, who married a sister of Judge Locke, of Lowell. The house nearly opposite was owned by Eben Prescott, but was occupied by Eleazer Wright, a blacksmith, and after by one Pushee, and still later by Horatio Clark, a blacksmith. The next dwelling-house was the " garrison house," so called on account of its being built for defence against the attacks of the Indians, having a brick wall between the woodwork. The house was occupied successively by four generations of the name of Ebenezer Prescott, the last being an uncle of Luther Prescott, and who died where Mr. Sprague now lives. The next house stood where George Henry Prescott's house now stands, and was occupied by Joseph Prescott (a son of Eben Prescott), who was father of several children, one of whom was Avery Prescott, who built the house where Edward Prescott now lives at Westford Centre; and another son built the house where Samuel Blodgett died, now demolished. The next house we find at the extreme west end of the village, occupied by Jonas Prescott, great grandfather of Oliver Prescott, who also lived there and who married Bethiah Underwood. He had four sons and eight daughters; was farmer and innkeeper. At that time Ann Lee had founded a society of Shakers at Harvard, Massachusetts. Through her influence the mother and five daughters were induced to leave home and join them. This circumstance so wrought upon the mind of the deserted husband and father that he became demented, and continued so to the end of his life. Three of the daughters lived and died with the Shakers. The others left at different times and had families. The eldest son removed to

Jaffrey, New Hampshire, where he had a large family. The second son went to Whitestown, now New Hartford, New York, when that country was a wilderness; he also had a large family. The third son, Abram, remained at home, and in the years 1808–'9 built the brick house near the site of the old one. His first wife was Polly Fletcher, of Westford; the second Olive Adams, of Chelmsford. He was captain of a military company; was a representative to the General Court several years in succession; was a deacon of the First Church, town clerk, and held various civil offices.

"Retracing our steps through the village we come to the house where Levi Prescott recently died, now occupied by his son, Nelson L. Prescott. Here was formerly a house inhabited by Jonas Prescott, great grandfather of Levi. He had three wives and nine children. Passing toward Graniteville, at the railroad crossing was the old school-house of the village. Where the poor-house now stands was an old house owned and occupied by Dea. John Prescott, son of Jonas, above named, who exchanged property with John Read, and Read sold it to the town. Next was an old house at David Reed's, owned by Timothy Prescott, also son of the above Jonas, and afterward occupied by his two sons, Isaiah and Amos.

"About fifty-five years ago Forge Village was in a very prosperous condition. It had a store, hotel, three iron forges, two blacksmith's shops, two wool-carding machines, one clothier's mill, a grist mill and a wheelwright's shop, all located near the new worsted mill."

To these interesting statements of Captain Lawrence, it is pertinent to add that this village is situated on one of the great thoroughfares of travel from Vermont to Boston. The great road, as it was called, from Bellows Falls to Boston passed through Groton to Groton Ridges, where there was a choice of routes to Boston, one road leading through Forge Village, Carlisle, Bedford and Lexington, the other through Littleton, Acton and Concord. As all merchandise was then transported in heavy wagons drawn by horses or oxen, the amount of travel on both roads was very great. One man now living says he has counted seventy teams in a line on the road through Forge Village; and another affirms that he has seen a hundred teams on the road in the south part of the town.

There were numerous taverns in town to accommodate the wayfarers, five or six in all. They preferred the route on which they found the best entertainment. In winter when the snow was deep, the people, encouraged and rewarded (with plenty of the " good creature," it is said,) turned out to make a path for the teams; and there was a strong competition between the people living on the two routes for the travel. Sometimes the party from Westford would reach the tavern at Groton Ridges by daybreak, and thus tempt the snowbound teamsters through this town. Taverns were kept at Forge Village, at the house now occupied by Capt. Jacob Smith, at George Yapp's house, Henry P. Ruggles' house and at Dupee's Corner. Among the landlords whose names are remembered, are Willard Reed, who was at Capt. Smith's, and after him Joseph Bailey; Seth Reed at Mr. Yapp's, and Timothy Hartwell, who came from Concord, and was the last one in the business there. He sold to Leonard L. Gibson. John Raymond and Josiah Hayward, who came from Concord, were on the Ruggles place; and Solomon Woods, Samuel Wright, Josiah Boynton, Samuel Lancy and William Dupee (from Dedham) were at Dupee's Corner. These are only a few of the men who were in that business. A living witness testifies that he has known seventy or seventy-five teams to "put up" for the night at the three taverns severally called Reed's, Raymond's and Hartwell's. The times are changed, and the wayside inn is rapidly becoming a thing of the past in this Commonwealth.

Graniteville. Capt. Lawrence has also furnished a few items respecting this village as it was:

" Where Samuel Fletcher's house now stands was an old house occupied by Jacob Abbot. It has been removed to a grove near by. At Charles G. Sargent's was located an old house occupied by Isaac Wright; also a grist-mill and saw-mill. Afterward it was occupied by John Read, and later by Dea. John Prescott. One hundred years ago there was a house and grist-mill at the bridge below Sargent's works, owned by one Thomas Cummings. About sixty years ago the house was burned with three children in it. One hundred years ago, at the Boutwell Brook place, where Eleazer Wright was killed, lived Eleazer Lawrence (grandfather of D. P. Lawrence), who received a lieutenant's commission from Gov. Shirley, dated June 20, 1755, to enlist a company of volunteers for scouting and guarding against the attacks of Indians."

MILITARY COMPANIES.

All that can be gleaned respecting them down to the year 1800 has been given, and but little can be added. The Westford and Littleton Rifle Company flourished for many years, but in the absence of any records it can only be stated that David P. Lawrence once held the rank of captain, and after him John W. P. Abbot. Sherman D. Fletcher was clerk. The company occupied the hall of the old schoolhouse in the Centre as an armory. It was composed of men from both towns.

Company F, Massachusetts Volunteer Cavalry was formed in September, 1864. The men are from Chelmsford, Billerica, Carlisle and Westford. Sherman H. Fletcher of this town is captain, and William L. Kittredge is second lieutenant. This being in part a Westford institution deserves notice as a band of soldierly men, to whom, when liberty is imperilled, war is no pastime, but a stern duty.

CHAPTER XIV.

STATISTICAL AND OFFICIAL.

Citizenship. In 1875 the town had 571 ratable polls, and 479 legal voters, and the aggregate of votes cast for governor was 371, or 77 per cent. In 1880 there were 525 ratable polls, and the estimated number of voters was 433. The number of votes cast for governor in 1881 was 146, or 33 per cent.

Population. No census was recorded, and probably none was taken until the year 1776, and that is known as the colonial census. The second or first national census was taken in 1790. The population of Westford is given in the following table:

1776 1,193	1840 1,436
1790 1,229	1850 1,473
1800 1,267	1860 1,624
1810 1,330	1870 1,803
1820 1,409	1875, State 1,933
1830 1,329	1880 2,148

In 1880 the villages ranked as follows: Graniteville, 540, in one hundred and five families; Centre, 270, in eighty-one families; Forge Village, 260, in sixty families; Brookside, 89, in fifteen families; Westford Corner, 67, in fifteen families. Number of families in the five villages, 276; in the whole town, 477.

Representatives to the General Court. There is no record of any election until the year 1739, when Thomas Read was elected. In 1734 the town " voted that they think they are not obliged by law to send a man to represent them in the great and gineral cort of the province." But the court took action upon their neglect and imposed the usual fine for not sending; and Capt. Thomas Read was sent to vindicate the town, which he did by quoting the above vote and pleading for the remission of the penalty. For the four succeeding years the town voted not to send; and oftentimes subsequently a similar vote was passed. In those days the towns were obliged to pay the expenses of a representative, and when there was no special reason for choosing one, they neglected to do so on the ground of economy.

REPRESENTATIVES.

1739. Thomas Read.	1771. Joseph Read.
1740. Thomas Read.	1772. Joseph Read.
1741. Thomas Read.	1773. None.
1742. None.	1774. Joseph Read.
1743. Thomas Read.	1775. Joseph Read.
1744. Thomas Read.	1776. Joseph Read.
1745. None.	1777. Zaccheus Wright.
1746. Thomas Read.	1778. Joseph Read.
1747. None.	1779. Joseph Read.
1748. None.	1780. Joseph Read.
1749. None.	1781. Joseph Read.
1750. Jonas Prescott, Jr.	1782. Francis Leighton.
1751. None.	1783. Francis Leighton.
1752. Thomas Read.	1784. Francis Leighton.
1753. None.	1785. Francis Leighton.
1754. None.	1786. None.
1755. None.	1787. Samuel Fletcher.
1756. Jabez Keep.	1788. Zaccheus Wright.
1757. None.	1789. Zaccheus Wright.
1758. Jonas Prescott.	1790. Zaccheus Wright.
1759. Jonas Prescott.	1791. Zaccheus Wright.
1760. Jonas Prescott.	1792. Zaccheus Wright.
1761. Jonas Prescott.	1793. Zaccheus Wright.
1762. None.	1794. Zaccheus Wright.
1763. None.	1795. None.
1764. Jonas Prescott.	1796. Abel Boynton.
1765. Jonas Prescott.	1797. Abel Boynton.
1766. Jonas Prescott.	1798. Abel Boynton.
1767. Jonas Prescott.	1799. Abel Boynton.
1768. Jonas Prescott.	1800. Amos Fletcher.
1769. Jonas Prescott.	1801. Abel Boynton.
1770. None.	1802. None.

1803. Jonathan Carver.
1804. Jonathan Carver.
1805. Jonathan Carver.
1806. Thomas Fletcher.
1807. Thomas Fletcher.
1808. Thomas Fletcher.
1809. Thomas Fletcher.
1810. Thomas Fletcher, Jr.
1811. Thomas Fletcher, Jr.
1812. Thomas Fletcher.
1813. Jesse Minot.
1814. Jesse Minot.
1815. Jesse Minot.
1816. Jesse Minot.
1817. None.
1818. None.
1819. None.
1820. None.
1821. Thomas Fletcher.
1822. None.
1823. Jesse Minot.
1824. Jesse Minot.
1825. None.
1826. None.
1827. Jesse Minot.
1828. Abram Prescott.
1829. Abram Prescott.
1830. Jesse Minot.
1831. None.
1832. Abram Prescott.
1833. None.
1834. Abram Prescott.
1835. Abram Prescott.
1836. Caleb Blake.
1837. Jeremiah J. Carter.
1838. Ephraim Abbot.
1839. Samuel Fletcher.
1840. John Cutter.
1841. John Cutter.
1842. William Chandler.
1843. George Harlow.
1844. George Harlow.
1845. Timothy P. Wright.
1846. None.
1847. None.
1848. None.
1849. William Dupee.
1850. None.
1851. Oliver Wright.

1852. Phinehas Chamberlin.
1853. None.
1854. Luther Prescott.
1855. Calvin Howard.
1856. Luther Prescott.

Since 1856 this town has been connected with other towns in a representative district.

1857. John W. P. Abbot, Charles Babbidge, Pepperell.
1858. James P. Longley, Shirley; Charles Babbidge.
1859. George T. Day, Westford; Alpheus Swallow, Dunstable.
1860. George H. Brown, Groton; Samuel L. Shattuck, Pepperell.
1861. David Porter, Shirley.
1863. George S. Gates, Groton; George T. Day, Westford.
1864. George Davis, Shirley; Edward F. Jones, Pepperell.
1865. George W. Fletcher, Dunstable; Benj. F. Taft, Groton.
1866. Ebenezer Swan, Tyngsboro'.
1867. George W. Heywood, Westford.
1868. Asa Clement, Dracut.
1869. J. Wesley Marshall, Tyngsborough.
1870. James T. Burnap, Dunstable.
1871. J. Henry Read, Westford.
1872. J. Henry Read, Westford.
1873. Gayton M. Hall, Dracut.
1874. Gayton M. Hall, Dracut.
1875. James C. Woodward, Dunstable.
1876. Asa S. Lawrence, Groton.
1877. William Read, 1st, Westford.
1878. Sumner P. Lawrence, Pepperell.
1879. Dexter Butterfield, Dunstable.
1880. Asa S. Lawrence, Groton.
1881. Sherman H. Fletcher, Westford.

STATISTICAL AND OFFICIAL. 359

VOTES FOR GOVERNOR AND LIEUTENANT GOVERNOR.

1781. Governor, John Hancock, 57; Lieutenant Governor, Thomas Cushing, 40.
1782. Governor, John Hancock, 21, Thomas Cushing, 5; Lieutenant Governor, Thomas Cushing, 17.
1783. Governor, John Hancock, 35, Oliver Prescott, 4; Lieutenant Governor, Thomas Cushing, 28.
1784. Governor, John Hancock, 29, Oliver Prescott, 2; Lieutenant Governor, Thomas Cushing, 22, Oliver Prescott, 2.
1785. Governor, Thomas Cushing, 26; Lieutenant Governor, Azor Orne, 26.
1786. Governor, John Hancock, 25; Lieutenant Governor, Thomas Cushing, 21.
1787. Governor, John Hancock, 91, Benjamin Lincoln, 5, Thomas Cushing, 1; Lieutenant Governor, Nathaniel Gorham, 91, Benjamin Lincoln, 5, Thomas Cushing, 1.
1788. Governor, John Hancock, 64, Elbridge Gerry, 25, James Warren, 1; Lieutenant Governor, Samuel Adams, 32, James Warren, 28, Benjamin Lincoln, 13, Nathaniel Gorham, 7, Elbridge Gerry, 2.
1789. Governor, John Hancock, 66, James Bowdoin, 1; Lieutenant Governor, Samuel Adams, 46, Benjamin Lincoln, 17, Nathaniel Gorham, 1.
1790. Governor, John Hancock, 61; Lieutenant Governor, Samuel Adams, 60.
1791. Governor, John Hancock, 64; Lieutenant Governor, Samuel Adams, 56, Azor Orne, 2.
1792. Governor, John Hancock, 42, Azor Orne, 8; Lieutenant Governor, Samuel Adams, 42, John Brooks, 9.
1793. Governor, John Hancock, 41, Elbridge Gerry, 1; Lieutenant Governor, Samuel Adams, 17, Elbridge Gerry, 28.
1794. Governor, Samuel Adams, 52, James Sullivan, 3; Lieutenant Governor, Nathaniel Gorham, 24, Moses Gill, 22, William Heath, 2.
1795. Governor, Samuel Adams, 76; Lieutenant Governor, Moses Gill, 62.
1796. Governor, Samuel Adams, 83, Elbridge Gerry, 6, Increase Sumner, 6; Lieutenant Governor, Moses Gill, 80.
1797. Governor, James Sullivan, 51, Increase Sumner, 2, Elbridge Gerry, 9, Moses Gill, 11; Lieutenant Governor, Moses Gill, 56, James Sullivan, 5.
1798. Governor, Increase Sumner, 39, James Sullivan, 12; Lieutenant Governor, Moses Gill, 40, Samuel Dexter, 1, James Sullivan, 1.
1799. Governor, Increase Sumner, 31, William Heath, 93; Lieutenant Governor, Moses Gill, 97, William Heath, 1.
1800. Governor, Elbridge Gerry, 115, Caleb Strong, 29; Lieutenant Governor, Moses Gill, 101, William Heath, 24, Elbridge Gerry, 2.

1801. Governor, Elbridge Gerry, 102, Caleb Strong, 19 ; Lieutenant Governor, William Heath, 96, Edward H. Robbins, 6, Samuel Phillips, 9, Elbridge Gerry, 2, Benjamin Lincoln, 1, William Phillips, 1.

1802. Governor, Elbridge Gerry, 106, Caleb Strong, 28, William Heath, 2 ; Lieutenant Governor, William Heath, 94, Edward H. Robbins, 28, Ebenezer Bridge, 1.

1803. Governor, Caleb Strong, 58, Elbridge Gerry, 9, William Heath, 1 ; Lieutenant Governor, Edward H. Robbins, 54, William Heath, 7, James Bowdoin, 4, Elbridge Gerry, 1.

1804. Governor, James Sullivan, 100, Caleb Strong, 42, Edward H. Robbins, 2 ; Lieutenant Governor, William Heath, 102, Edward H. Robbins, 40, Caleb Strong, 1, James Sullivan, 1.

1805. Governor, James Sullivan, 108, Caleb Strong, 63, William Heath, 2 ; Lieutenant Governor, William Heath, 106, Edward H. Robbins, 57, Ebenezer Bridge, 1, James Sullivan, 1.

1806. Governor, James Sullivan, 128, Caleb Strong, 52, William Heath, 1 ; Lieutenant Governor, William Heath, 133, Edward H. Robbins, 46.

1807. Governor, James Sullivan, 126, Caleb Strong, 49, William Eustis, 1 ; Lieutenant Governor, Levi Lincoln, 130, Edward H. Robbins, 44, John L. Tuttle, 1, Ebenezer Bridge, 1.

1808. Governor, James Sullivan, 110, Christopher Gore, 37 ; Lieutenant Governor, Levi Lincoln, 108, David Cobb, 35, Christopher Gore, 1, Abijah Reed, 1.

1809. Governor, Levi Lincoln, 136, Christopher Gore, 55, David Cobb, 1, Harrison G. Otis, 1 ; Lieutenant Governor, Joseph B. Varnum, 138, David Cobb, 54, Christopher Gore, 1.

1810. Governor, Elbridge Gerry, 121, Christopher Gore, 51, Samuel Wright, Jr., 1 ; Lieutenant Governor, William Gray, 121, David Cobb, 50.

1811. Governor, Elbridge Gerry, 122, Christopher Gore, 42 ; Lieutenant Governor, William Gray, 123, William Phillips, 40.

1812. Governor, Elbridge Gerry, 127, Caleb Strong, 61 ; Lieutenant Governor, William King, 124, William Phillips, 58.

1813. Governor, Joseph B. Varnum, 115, Caleb Strong, 73 ; Lieutenant Governor, William King, 119, William Phillips, 67, Timothy Prescott, 1.

1814. Governor, Samuel Dexter, 118, Caleb Strong, 75 ; Lieutenant Governor, William Gray, 121, William Phillips, 75.

1815. Governor, Samuel Dexter, 123, Caleb Strong, 62 ; Lieutenant Governor, William Gray, 124, William Phillips, 61.

1816. Governor, Samuel Dexter, 125, John Brooks, 64 ; Lieutenant Governor, William Gray, 125, William Phillips, 62.

1817. Governor, Henry Dearborn, 103, John Brooks, 70 ; Lieutenant Governor, William King, 103, William Phillips, 70.

1818. Governor, John Brooks, 60, Benjamin W. Crowninshield, 110; Lieutenant Governor, Thomas Kittredge, 110, William Phillips, 61.

1819. Governor, Benjamin W. Crowninshield, 110, John Brooks, 65 ; Lieutenant Governor, Benjamin Austin, 110, William Phillips, 65.

STATISTICAL AND OFFICIAL. 361

1820. Governor, William Eustis, 107, John Brooks, 46; Lieutenant Governor, Benjamin Austin, 104, William Phillips, 45.
1821. Governor, William Eustis, 101, John Brooks, 47; Lieutenant Governor, Levi Lincoln, 102, William Phillips, 46.
1822. Governor, William Eustis, 96, John Brooks, 49; Lieutenant Governor, Levi Lincoln, 96, William Phillips, 49.
1823. Governor, William Eustis, 140, Harrison Gray Otis, 46; Lieutenant Governor, Levi Lincoln, 138, Daniel Noble, 46.
1824. Governor, William Eustis, 157, Samuel Lathrop, 35; Lieutenant Governor, Marcus Morton, 159, Richard Sullivan, 35.
1825. Governor, Levi Lincoln, 102; Lieutenant Governor, Marcus Morton, 99.
1826. Governor, Levi Lincoln, 117, Charles Jackson, 5; Lieutenant Governor, Thomas L. Winthrop, 115: Richard Sullivan, 2, George Sullivan, 1.
1827. Governor, William C. Jarvis, 121, Levi Lincoln, 21; Lieutenant Governor, Thomas L. Winthrop, 14.
1828. Governor, Levi Lincoln, 95; Lieutenant Governor, Thomas L. Winthrop, 93.
1829. Governor, Levi Lincoln, 85, William C. Smith, 2, John Abbot, 1; Lieutenant Governor, Thomas L. Winthrop, 85, Benjamin Osgood, 1.
1830. Governor, Levi Lincoln, 127, Stag Prescott, 1, Elisha Glitton, 1, Luther E. Puffer, 1; Lieutenant Governor, Thomas L. Winthrop, 128, Marcus Morton, 1, Brother Boaskin, 1, Joel Glover, 1.
1831. Governor, Levi Lincoln, 62, Samuel Lathrop, 49, Marcus Morton, 1; Lieutenant Governor, Thomas L. Winthrop, 99, William Sullivan, 1, John Mills, 1.
1832. Governor, Levi Lincoln, 70, Samuel Lathrop, 61, Marcus Morton, 1; Lieutenant Governor, Samuel T. Armstrong, 69, Timothy Fuller, 58, John Mills, 8.
1833. Governor, John Quincy Adams, 80, John Davis, 38, Marcus Morton 21; Lieutenant Governor, Samuel Lathrop, 78, Samuel T. Armstrong, 41, James Fowler, 21.
1834. Governor, John Davis, 84, John Bailey, 30, Marcus Morton, 9; Lieutenant Governor, Samuel T. Armstrong, 84, George Odiorne, 27, William W. Thompson, 9.
1835. Governor, Edward Everett, 47, Marcus Morton, 46, Samuel T. Armstrong, 1; Lieutenant Governor, William Foster, 90, Geo. Hull, 6.
1836. Governor, Edward Everett, 63, Marcus Morton, 58, Samuel T. Armstrong, 2; Lieutenant Governor, George Hull, 65, William Foster, 58.
1837. Governor, Marcus Morton, 108, Edward Everett, 77, Charles Jackson, 1; Lieutenant Governor, William Foster, 103, Geo. Hull, 79, Samuel T. Armstrong, 1.
1838. Governor, Marcus Morton, 92, Edward Everett, 86, Charles Jackson, 1; Lieutenant Governor, George Hull, 87, Theodore Sedgwick, 93, Samuel T. Armstrong, 1.
1839. Governor, Marcus Morton, 120, Edward Everett, 76, Charles Jackson, 1.

1840. Governor, John Davis, 142, Marcus Morton, 137; Lieutenant Governor, George Hull, 143, Nathan Willis, 135.
1841. Governor, John Davis, 98, Marcus Morton, 121, Lucius Boltwood, 5; Lieutenant Governor, George Hull, 98, Henry H. Childs, 121, Ebenezer Hunt, 5.
1842. Governor, John Davis, 92, Marcus Morton, 144, Samuel E. Sewall, 2; Lieutenant Governor, George Hull, 91, Henry H. Childs, 143, William Jackson, 2.
1843. Governor, George N. Briggs, 108, Marcus Morton, 139, Samuel E. Sewall, 13, Francis Jackson, 1; Lieutenant Governor, John Reed, 104, Henry H. Childs, 141, William Jackson, 14.
1844. Governor, George N. Briggs, 119, George Bancroft, 142, Samuel E. Sewall, 11; Lieutenant Governor, John Reed, 119, Henry H. Childs, 142, William Jackson, 11.
1845. Governor, George N. Briggs, 87, Isaac Davis, 115, Samuel E. Sewall, 4; Lieutenant Governor, John Reed, 87; George Savary, 115, John M. Brewster, 4.
1846. Governor, George N. Briggs, 94, Isaac Davis, 103, Samuel E. Sewall, 13; Lieutenant Governor, John Reed, 95; George Hood, 103, John M. Brewster, 13.
1847. Governor, George N. Briggs, 86, Caleb Cushing, 105, Samuel E. Sewall, 9; Lieutenant Governor, John Reed, 85, Henry W. Cushman, 106, John M. Brewster, 10.
1848. Governor, George N. Briggs, 87, Caleb Cushing, 77, Stephen C. Phillips, 51; Lieutenant Governor, John Reed, 87, Henry W. Cushman, 77, John Mills, 52.
1849. Governor, George N. Briggs, 91, George S. Boutwell, 97, Stephen C. Phillips, 38; Lieutenant Governor, John Reed, 91, Henry W. Cushman, 97, John Mills, 38.
1850. Governor, George S. Boutwell, 94, George N. Briggs, 88, Stephen C. Phillips, 28; Lieutenant Governor, Henry W. Cushman, 93, John Reed, 88, Amasa Walker, 29.
1851. Governor, Robert C. Winthrop, 102, George S. Boutwell, 126, John G. Palfrey, 18; Lieutenant Governor, George Grennell, 101, Henry W. Cushman, 127, Amasa Walker, 18.
1852. Governor, John H. Clifford, 106, Henry W. Bishop, 96, Horace Mann, 45; Lieutenant Governor, James D. Thompson, 116, Elisha Huntington, 89, Amasa Walker, 42.
1853. Governor, Emory Washburn, 101, Henry W. Bishop, 107, Henry Wilson, 34, Bradford L. Wales, 5; Lieutenant Governor, William C. Plunkett, 100, Levi A. Dowley, 107, Amasa Walker, 34, George Osborne, 5.
1854. Governor, Henry J. Gardner, 99, Emory Washburn, 53, Henry W. Bishop, 25, Henry Wilson, 23; Lieutenant Governor, Simon Brown, 101, William C. Plunkett, 53, Caleb Stetson, 24, Increase Sumner, 23.
1855. Governor, Henry J. Gardner, 99, Erasmus D. Beach, 60, Samuel H. Walley, 36, Julius Rockwell, 28; Lieutenant Governor, Henry W. Benchley, 98, Caleb Stetson, 55, Moses Davenport, 42, Simon Brown, 30.

1856. Governor, Henry J. Gardner, 181, Erasmus D. Beach, 62, Luther V. Bell, 12, George W. Gordon, 6; Lieutenant Governor, Henry W. Benchley, 182, Albert Currier, 62, Homer Foote, 18.
1857. Governor, Henry J. Gardner, 82, Erasmus D. Beach, 71, Nathaniel P. Banks, 71; Lieutenant Governor, Alexander De Witt, 82, Albert Currier, 71, Eliphalet Trask, 70.
1858. Governor, Nathaniel P. Banks, 99, Erasmus D. Beach, 62, Amos A. Lawrence, 45; Lieutenant Governor, Eliphalet Trask, 99, Charles Thompson, 62, Increase Sumner, 46.
1859. Governor, Nathaniel P. Banks, 81, Benjamin F. Butler, 60, George N. Briggs, 47; Lieutenant Governor, Eliphalet Trask, 81, Stephen C. Bemis, 58, Increase Sumner, 52.
1860. Governor, John A. Andrew, 159, Amos A. Lawrence, 39, Erasmus D. Beach, 34, Benjamin F. Butler, 30; Lieutenant Governor, John Z. Goodrich, 159, George Marston, 39, Charles Thompson, 34, David N. Carpenter, 30.
1861. Governor, John A. Andrew, 115, Isaac Davis, 93; Lieutenant Governor, John Nesmith, 115, Edwin C. Bailey, 93.
1862. Governor, John A. Andrew, 122, Charles Devens, Jr., 128; Lieutenant Governor, Joel Hayden, 122, Thomas F. Plunkett, 127.
1863. Governor, John A. Andrew, 127, Henry W. Paine, 116; Lieutenant Governor, Joel Hayden, 129, Thomas F. Plunkett, 116.
1864. Governor, John A. Andrew, 186, Henry W. Paine, 115, George Laws, 1; Lieutenant Governor, Joel Hayden, 192, Thomas F. Plunkett, 115.
1865. Governor, Alexander H. Bullock, 118, Darius N. Couch, 87; Lieutenant Governor, William Claflin, 118, Thomas F. Plunkett, 87.
1866. Governor, Alexander H. Bullock, 149, Theodore H. Sweetser, 109; Lieutenant Governor, William Claflin, 149, Horace C. Lee, 109.
1867. Governor, Alexander H. Bullock, 140, John Quincy Adams, 163; Lieutenant Governor, William Claflin, 140, George M. Stearns, 161.
1868. Governor, William Claflin, 190, John Quincy Adams, 131; Lieutenant Governor, Joseph Tucker, 192, Reuben Noble, 130.
1869. Governor, William Claflin, 130, John Quincy Adams, 146; Lieutenant Governor, Joseph Tucker, 129, Samuel O. Lamb, 145.
1870. Governor, William Claflin, 150, John Quincy Adams, 157, Wendell Phillips, 6; Lieutenant Governor, Joseph Tucker, 150, James Chattaway, 157, Eliphalet Trask, 6.
1871. Governor, William B. Washburn, 182, John Quincy Adams, 162, Robert C. Pitman, 1; Lieutenant Governor, Joseph Tucker, 185, Samuel O. Lamb, 160, Eliphalet Trask, 1.
1872. Governor, William B. Washburn, 195, Frank W. Bird, 149; Lieutenant Governor, Thomas Talbot, 199, William L. Smith, 158.
1873. Governor, William Gaston, 163, William B. Washburn, 99; Lieutenant Governor, Thomas Talbot, 127, William L. Smith, 136.
1874. Governor, Thomas Talbot, 144, William Gaston, 210; Lieutenant Governor, Horatio G. Knight, 151, William L. Smith, 204.

HISTORY OF WESTFORD.

1875. Governor, Alexander H. Rice, 129, William Gaston, 215, John I. Baker, 27; Lieutenant Governor, Horatio G. Knight, 163, John Quincy Adams, 209.
1876. Governor, Alexander H. Rice, 217, Charles Francis Adams, 174, John I. Baker, 6; Lieutenant Governor, Horatio G. Knight, 217, William R. Plunkett, 176, Daniel C. Eddy, 6.
1877. Governor, Alexander H. Rice, 156, William Gaston, 159, Robert C. Pitman, 20, Wendell Phillips, 1; Lieutenant Governor, Horatio G. Knight, 159, William R. Plunkett, 160, Elijah A. Morse, 15, Dyer D. Lum, 1.
1878. Governor, Thomas Talbot, 195, Josiah G. Abbott, 25, Benjamin F. Butler, 117, Alonzo A. Miner, 1; Lieutenant Governor, John D. Long, 189, William R. Plunkett, 31, John F. Arnold, 116.
1879. Governor, John D. Long, 176, Benjamin F. Butler, 123, John Quincy Adams, 32; Lieutenant Governor, Byron Weston, 183, Albert C. Woodworth, 114, William R. Plunkett, 34.
1880. Governor, John D. Long, 217, Charles P. Thompson, 103, Horace Binney Sargent, 1; Lieutenant Governor, Byron Weston, 217, Alpha E. Thompson, 163, George Dutton, 1.
1881. Governor, John D. Long, 96, Charles P. Thompson, 50; Lieutenant Governor, Byron Weston, 97, James H. Carleton, 49.

NOTE.— From 1781 to 1831, the election for State officers was held in April; since that date it has been held in November.

TOWN OFFICERS.

1730. Selectmen — Joshua Fletcher, John Comings, Samuel Chamberlin, Joseph Keyes, Thomas Read. Clerk, Joshua Fletcher. Treasurer, Samuel Fassett.
1731. Selectmen — Joshua Fletcher, Jonas Prescott, Jonathan Hartwell, John Comings, Aaron Parker. Clerk, Joshua Fletcher. Treasurer, Paul Fletcher.
1732. Selectmen — Joshua Fletcher, Jonas Prescott, John Comings. Clerk, Joshua Fletcher. Treasurer, Paul Fletcher.
1733. Selectmen — Jonas Prescott, John Comings, Aaron Parker, Paul Fletcher, Andrew Spaulding. Clerk, Jonas Prescott. Treasurer, Samuel Fassett.
1734. Selectmen -- Capt. Jonas Prescott, Samuel Fassett, Jonathan Hartwell, Aaron Parker, Andrew Spaulding. Clerk, Capt. Jonas Prescott. Treasurer, Jonas Prescott, Jr.
1735. Selectmen — Capt. Jonas Prescott, John Comings, Samuel Fassett, Joseph Fletcher, Joseph Hildreth. Clerk, Jonas Prescott. Treasurer, Andrew Spaulding.
1736. Selectmen — John Comings, Thomas Read, Joseph Hildreth, William Chandler, Aaron Parker. Clerk, John Comings. Treasurer, Josiah Burge.
1737. Selectmen — Jonas Prescott, Jr., Thomas Read, Joseph Underwood, Lieut. Samuel Chamberlin, William Fletcher, Jr. Clerk, Jonas Prescott, Jr. Treasurer, Samuel Fletcher, Jr.

STATISTICAL AND OFFICIAL. 365

1738. Selectmen — Jonas Prescott, Jr., Dea. Andrew Spaulding, Capt. Thomas Read, James Hildreth, Jr., Josiah Burge. Clerk, Jonas Prescott, Jr. Treasurer, Samuel Fletcher, Jr.
1739. Selectmen — John Comings, Jonas Prescott, Jr., Thomas Read, Ephraim Hildreth, Josiah Burge. Clerk, Jonas Prescott, Jr. Treasurer, John Abbot.
1740. Selectmen — John Comings, Jonas Prescott, Jr., Thomas Read, John Procter, James Hildreth, Jr. Clerk, Jonas Prescott, Jr. Treasurer, John Abbot.
1741. Selectmen — John Comings, Thomas Read, Jonas Prescott, Jr., Joseph Procter, Ephraim Hildreth. Clerk, Jonas Prescott, Jr. Treasurer, John Abbot.
1742. Selectmen—John Abbot, Jabez Keep, Samuel Fletcher, Jr., Aaron Parker, Jr., Ephraim Chandler. Clerk, John Abbot. Treasurer, Dea. Henry Wright.
1743. Selectmen — Thomas Read, John Comings, John Abbot, William Chandler, Abner Kent. Clerk, John Abbot. Treasurer, Jonas Prescott, Jr.
1744. Selectmen—Samuel Chamberlin, Thomas Read, John Abbot, John Comings, Jabez Keep. Clerk, John Abbot. Treasurer, Jonas Prescott, Jr.
1745. Selectmen — Thomas Read, Esq., John Abbot, William Fletcher, Jr., James Hildreth, Jr., Jabez Keep. Clerk, John Abbot. Treasurer, Jonas Prescott, Jr.
1746. Selectmen — Lt. Jonas Prescott, Jr., Thomas Read, John Abbot, William Fletcher, Jr., Jabez Keep. Clerk, John Abbot. Treasurer, Amos Fletcher.
1747. Selectmen—Thomas Read, Jonathan Hartwell, Jabez Keep, Jonas Prescott, Jr., William Fletcher. Clerk, Jabez Keep. Treasurer, Amos Fletcher.
1748. Selectmen — John Comings, Jonas Prescott, Jr., John Abbot, William Fletcher, Jr., Samuel Chamberlin. Clerk, John Abbot. Treasurer, Amos Fletcher.
1749. Selectmen—Thomas Read, John Abbot, Jonas Prescott, Jr., John Comings, William Fletcher, Jr. Clerk, John Abbot. Treasurer, Ephraim Hildreth, Jr.
1750. Selectmen—John Abbot, Jonas Prescott, Jr., Samuel Chamberlin, Jabez Keep, William Fletcher, Jr. Clerk, John Abbot. Treasurer, Ephraim Hildreth, Jr.
1751. Selectmen— Abner Kent, Jabez Keep, Timothy Fletcher, Amos Fletcher, Ezekiel Proctor. Clerk, Jabez Keep. Treasurer, Joseph Dutton.
1752. Selectmen — Jonas Prescott, Jabez Keep, John Abbot, William Fletcher, Jr., Joseph Read. Clerk, John Abbot. Treasurer, Ephraim Hildreth, Jr.
1753. Selectmen — Henry Wright, Andrew Spaulding, Thomas Adams, Joseph Read, Timothy Fletcher. Clerk, Joseph Read. Treasurer, Gershom Fletcher.

1754. Selectmen — Joseph Read, Jabez Keep, Samuel Fletcher, Samuel Reed, James Pollard. Clerk, Joseph Read. Treasurer, Gershom Fletcher.
1755. Selectmen — Jonas Prescott, John Abbot, Jabez Keep, William Fletcher, Joseph Read. Clerk, John Abbot. Treasurer, Nathaniel Boynton.
1756. Selectmen — Jabez Keep, Jonas Prescott, John Abbot, William Fletcher, Joseph Dutton. Clerk, John Abbot. Treasurer, Nathaniel Boynton.
1757. Selectmen — Jonas Prescott, Jabez Keep, John Abbot, William Fletcher, Amos Fletcher. Clerk, John Abbot. Treasurer, Oliver Prescott.
1758. Selectmen — Joseph Read, Samuel Fletcher, Amos Fletcher, Samuel Read, Nathaniel Boynton. Clerk, Nathaniel Boynton. Treasurer, Oliver Prescott.
1759. Selectmen — Jonas Prescott, John Abbot, Nathaniel Boynton, William Fletcher, Amos Fletcher. Clerk, Nathaniel Boynton. Treasurer, Oliver Prescott.
1760. Selectmen — John Abbot, Jonas Prescott, Nathaniel Boynton, Simeon Wright, Benjamin Carver. Clerk, Nathaniel Boynton. Treasurer, Joshua Fletcher.
1761. Selectmen — Jonas Prescott, John Abbot, Nathaniel Boynton, William Fletcher, Benjamin Carver. Clerk, Nathaniel Boynton. Treasurer, Joshua Fletcher.
1762. Selectmen — Jonas Prescott, William Fletcher, Nathaniel Boynton, Ephraim Hildreth, Jr., Gershom Fletcher. Clerk, Nathaniel Boynton. Treasurer, Timothy Prescott.
1763. Selectmen—Samuel Fletcher, Nathaniel Boynton, Amos Fletcher, Jonathan Minot, Timothy Fletcher, Jr. Clerk, Nathaniel Boynton. Treasurer, Joseph Boynton.
1764. Selectmen — Jonas Prescott, Samuel Fletcher, Thomas Kidder. Benjamin Carver, Oliver Bates. Clerk, Nathaniel Boynton. Treasurer, Pelatiah Fletcher.
1765. Selectmen — Samuel Fletcher, Amos Fletcher, John Abbot, Thos. Kidder, Thomas Comings. Clerk, John Abbot. Treasurer, Henry Wright, Jr.
1766. Selectmen—Nathaniel Boynton, Ephraim Hildreth, Jr., Zaccheus Wright, Ephraim Chamberlin, Benjamin Fletcher. Clerk, Nathaniel Boynton. Treasurer, Henry Wright, Jr.
1767. Selectmen — Nathaniel Boynton, John Abbot, Amos Fletcher, Thos. Kidder, Zaccheus Wright. Clerk, Nathaniel Boynton. Treasurer, Asahel Wyman.
1768. Selectmen — Jonas Prescott, Joseph Read, Benjamin Fletcher, Thomas Comings, Jonathan Fletcher, Jr. Clerk, Joseph Read. Treasurer, Moses Burge.
1769. Selectmen — John Abbot, Nathaniel Boynton, Joseph Read, Timothy Prescott, Zaccheus Wright. Clerk, Nathaniel Boynton. Treasurer, Timothy Spaulding.

1770. Selectmen—Amos Fletcher, Jonathan Minot, Nathaniel Boynton, Zaccheus Wright, Leonard Procter. Clerk, Nathaniel Boynton. Treasurer, Zechariah Hildreth.
1771. Selectmen—Joseph Read, Timothy Fletcher, Zaccheus Wright, Ephraim Hildreth, 3rd, John Robinson. Clerk, Zaccheus Wright. Treasurer, James Fletcher.
1772. Selectmen—Joseph Read, Zaccheus Wright, Timothy Fletcher, Ephraim Hildreth, 3rd, John Robinson. Clerk, Zaccheus Wright. Treasurer, John Abbot, Jr.
1773. Selectmen—Joseph Read, Zaccheus Wright, Timothy Fletcher, Ephraim Hildreth, 3rd, John Robinson. Clerk, Zaccheus Wright. Treasurer, John Abbot, Jr.
1774. Selectmen—John Abbot, Jonathan Minot, Amos Fletcher, Oliver Bates, Jonathan Keep. Clerk, John Abbot. Treasurer, John Abbot, Jr.
1775. Selectmen—Joseph Read, Zaccheus Wright, Nathaniel Boynton, Aaron Parker, Jr., Oliver Bates. Clerk, Nathaniel Boynton. Treasurer, David Goodhue.
1776. Selectmen—Joseph Read, Zaccheus Wright, Zechariah Hildreth, Francis Laughton, Jonathan Keep. Clerk, Zaccheus Wright. Treasurer, Gershom Fletcher.
1777. Selectmen—Asaph Fletcher, Nathaniel Boynton, Jonathan Minot, Timothy Prescott, Francis Leighton. Clerk, Nathaniel Boynton. Treasurer, Aaron Parker.
1778. Selectmen—Joseph Read, Nathaniel Boynton, Asaph Fletcher, Timothy Prescott, Leonard Proctor. Clerk, Nathaniel Boynton. Treasurer, John Abbot.
1779. Selectmen—Joseph Read, Nathaniel Boynton, Asaph Fletcher, Timothy Prescott, Leonard Proctor. Clerk, Nathaniel Boynton. Treasurer, John Abbot.
1780. Selectmen—Joseph Read, Nathaniel Boynton, Timothy Prescott, Leonard Proctor, Francis Leighton. Clerk, Nathaniel Boynton. Treasurer, John Abbot.
1781. Selectmen—Timothy Prescott, Gershom Fletcher, Samuel White, David Goodhue, Samuel Fletcher. Clerk, Gershom Fletcher. Treasurer, John Prescott. "Treasurer for the minister rate," Jonas Proctor.
1782. Selectmen—Nathaniel Boynton, Capt. Joseph Read, Timothy Prescott, Samuel White, Gershom Fletcher. Clerk, Nathaniel Boynton. Treasurer, John Prescott.
1783. Selectmen—Joseph Read, Nathaniel Boynton, Samuel White, Dea. John Prescott, Samuel Wright. Clerk, Nathaniel Boynton. Treasurer, Joseph Jewett.
1784. Selectmen—David Goodhue, Timothy Prescott, Samuel Wright, Joshua Reed, John Prescott. Clerk, David Goodhue. Treasurer, Nathaniel Boynton.
1785. Selectmen—David Goodhue, Timothy Prescott, Samuel Wright, Joshua Read, Gershom Fletcher. Clerk, David Goodhue. Treasurer, Nathaniel Boynton.

1786. Selectmen—Timothy Prescott, David Goodhue, Joseph Keyes, Joshua Reed, John Abbot. Clerk, David Goodhue. Treasurer, John Abbot.
1787. Selectmen—Jonathan Keep, Ebenezer Prescott, Rogers King, Samuel Wright, Isaac Cumings. Clerk, Jonathan Keep. Treasurer, John Abbot, Jr.
1788. Selectmen—Jonathan Keep, Samuel Wright, Samuel Fletcher, Joseph Keyes, Isaac Cumings. Clerk, Jonathan Keep. Treasurer, Benjamin Osgood.
1789. Selectmen—John Abbot, Amos Fletcher, Samuel Wright, Samuel Fletcher, John Prescott. Clerk, Jonathan Keep. Treasurer, John Abbot.
1790. Selectmen—John Abbot, Jr., Amos Fletcher, Abel Boynton, Benjamin Osgood, Jonathan Carver. Clerk, John Abbot, Jr. Treasurer, Richard Kneeland.
1791. Selectmen—John Abbot, Jr., Amos Fletcher, Abel Boynton, Benjamin Osgood, Jonathan Carver. Clerk, John Abbot, Jr. Treasurer, Richard Kneeland.
1792. Selectmen—John Abbot, Amos Fletcher, Abel Boynton, Benjamin Osgood, Jonathan Carver. Clerk, John Abbot. Treasurer, Richard Kneeland.
1793. Selectmen—Abel Boynton, Samuel Fletcher, John Prescott, Thomas Chamberlin, Thomas Fletcher. Clerk, Abel Boynton. Treasurer, Richard Kneeland.
1794. Selectmen—Abel Boynton, John Prescott, Jonathan Carver, Thos. Chamberlin, Thomas Fletcher. Clerk, Abel Boynton. Treasurer, John Abbot.
1795. Selectmen—John Abbot, Abel Boynton, Jonathan Carver. Clerk, John Abbot. Treasurer, Richard Kneeland.
1796. Selectmen—John Abbot, Abel Boynton, Jonathan Carver. Clerk, John Abbot. Treasurer, Richard Kneeland.
1797. Selectmen—Richard Kneeland, Joseph Keyes, Jeremiah Hildreth. Clerk, Richard Kneeland. Treasurer, John Abbot.
1798. Selectmen—Richard Kneeland, Joseph Keyes, Jeremiah Hildreth. Clerk, Richard Kneeland. Treasurer, John Abbot.
1799. Selectmen—Richard Kneeland, Joseph Keyes, Jeremiah Hildreth. Clerk, Richard Kneeland. Treasurer, John Abbot.
1800. Selectmen—Richard Kneeland, Joseph Keyes, Jeremiah Hildreth. Clerk, Richard Kneeland. Treasurer, Jonathan Carver.
1801. Selectmen—Abel Boynton, Jesse Minot, Abraham Prescott. Clerk, Abel Boynton. Treasurer, Abel Hildreth.
1802. Selectmen—John Abbot, Jeremiah Hildreth, Amos Fletcher. Clerk, John Abbot. Treasurer, Jonathan Carver.
1803. Selectmen—John Abbot, Jeremiah Hildreth, Amos Fletcher. Clerk, John Abbot. Treasurer, Jonathan Carver.
1804. Selectmen—Jeremiah Hildreth, Isaiah Prescott, Thomas Fletcher. Clerk, Jeremiah Hildreth. Treasurer, Jonathan Carver.
1805. Selectmen—Jeremiah Hildreth, Isaiah Prescott, Thomas Fletcher. Clerk, Jeremiah Hildreth. Treasurer, Jonas Blodgett.

STATISTICAL AND OFFICIAL. 369

1806. Selectmen—Jeremiah Hildreth, Isaiah Prescott, Thomas Fletcher. Clerk, Jeremiah Hildreth. Treasurer, Jonas Blodgett.
1807. Selectmen—Jeremiah Hildreth, Isaiah Prescott, Thomas Fletcher. Clerk, Jeremiah Hildreth. Treasurer, Jonas Blodgett.
1808. Selectmen—Jeremiah Hildreth, Isaiah Prescott, Thomas Fletcher. Clerk, Jeremiah Hildreth. Treasurer, Jonas Blodgett.
1809. Selectmen—Jeremiah Hildreth, Isaiah Prescott, Thomas Fletcher. Clerk, Jeremiah Hildreth. Treasurer, Jonas Blodgett.
1810. Selectmen—Thomas Fletcher, Jr., Isaiah Prescott, John Cummings. Clerk, Thomas Fletcher. Treasurer, Jonas Blodgett.
1811. Selectmen—Pelatiah Fletcher, John Cummings, Aaron Parker. Clerk, Pelatiah Fletcher. Treasurer, Samuel Read, Jr.
1812. Selectmen—John Cummings, Aaron Parker, Samuel Davis. Clerk, John Cummings. Treasurer, Samuel Read, Jr.
1813. Selectmen—Thomas Fletcher, Isaiah Prescott, Jesse Minot. Clerk, Thomas Fletcher. Treasurer, Samuel Read, Jr.
1814. Selectmen—Thomas Fletcher, Isaiah Prescott, Jesse Minot. Clerk, Thomas Fletcher. Treasurer, John Hildreth.
1815. Selectmen—Thomas Fletcher, Isaiah Prescott, Jesse Minot. Clerk, Thomas Fletcher. Treasurer, Samuel Davis.
1816. Selectmen—Thomas Fletcher, Jesse Minot, Imla Goodhue. Clerk, Thomas Fletcher. Treasurer, Samuel Davis.
1817. Selectmen—Thomas Fletcher, Jesse Minot, Imla Goodhue. Clerk, Thomas Fletcher. Treasurer, John Abbot.
1818. Selectmen—John Abbot, John Cummings, Samuel Wright. Clerk, John Abbot. Treasurer, Thomas Fletcher.
1819. Selectmen—Thomas Fletcher, Samuel Wright, Jr., Imla Goodhue. Clerk, Thomas Fletcher. Treasurer, John Abbot.
1820. Selectmen—Thomas Fletcher, Samuel Wright, Jesse Minot. Clerk, Thomas Fletcher. Treasurer, John Abbot.
1821. Selectmen—John Abbot, Thomas Spalding, Ezra Carter. Clerk, John Abbot. Treasurer, Benjamin Kneeland.
1822. Selectmen—Aaron Parker, Ezra Carter, James P. Patten. Clerk, Aaron Parker. Treasurer, John Abbot.
1823. Selectmen—Aaron Parker, Ezra Carter, James P. Patten. Clerk, Aaron Parker. Treasurer, John Abbot.
1824. Selectmen—Benjamin Osgood, Jr., Ezra Carter, Levi Heywood. Clerk, Benjamin Osgood. Treasurer, John Abbot.
1825. Selectmen—Benjamin Osgood, Levi Heywood, Zaccheus Read. Clerk, Benjamin Osgood. Treasurer, Henry Herrick.
1826. Selectmen—Benjamin Osgood, Levi Heywood, Zaccheus Read. Clerk, Benjamin Osgood. Treasurer, Henry Herrick.
1827. Selectmen—Imla Goodhue, Peter C. Edwards, Jonathan Prescott. Clerk, Imla Goodhue. Treasurer, Henry Herrick.
1828. Selectmen—Abram Prescott, Levi Heywood, Zaccheus Read. Clerk, Abram Prescott. Treasurer, Avery Prescott.
1829. Selectmen—Abram Prescott, Levi Heywood, Zaccheus Read, Jr. Clerk, Abram Prescott. Treasurer, Avery Prescott.
1830. Selectmen—Jonathan Prescott, Thomas Richardson, Eliakim Hutchins. Clerk, Jonathan Prescott. Treasurer, Avery Prescott.

1831. Selectmen—Jonathan Prescott, Thomas Richardson, Eliakim Hutchins. Clerk, Jonathan Prescott. Treasurer, Avery Prescott.
1832. Selectmen—Jonathan Prescott, Thomas Richardson, Samuel H. Nichols. Clerk, Jonathan Prescott. Treasurer, Asaph Byam.
1833. Selectmen—Jonathan Prescott, Thomas Richardson, Samuel H. Nichols. Clerk, Jonathan Prescott. Treasurer, Asaph Byam.
1834. Selectmen—Jonathan Prescott, Jos. Hildreth, Horatio Fletcher. Clerk, Jonathan Prescott. Treasurer, Avery Prescott.
1835. Selectmen—Jonathan Prescott, Horatio Fletcher, Henry A. Prescott. Clerk, Jonathan Prescott. Treasurer, Avery Prescott.
1836. Selectmen—Joseph Hildreth, Henry A. Prescott, William Chandler. Clerk, Asaph Byam. Treasurer, Avery Prescott.
1837. Selectmen—Henry A. Prescott, William Chandler, Thaddeus Blodgett. Clerk, Henry A. Prescott. Treasurer, Avery Prescott.
1838. Selectmen—Thaddeus Blodgett, George Brown, Othiel Fletcher. Clerk, John W. P. Abbot. Treasurer, Avery Prescott.
1839. Selectmen—John W. P. Abbot, Samuel Fletcher, Henry A. Prescott. Clerk, John W. P. Abbot. Treasurer, Amos Heywood.
1840. Selectmen—Zaccheus Read, Jr., John Cutter, Jonas Prescott. Clerk, John W. P. Abbot. Treasurer, Jacob A. Wright.
1841. Selectmen—Zaccheus Read, Jr., John Cutter, Jonas Prescott. Clerk, John W. P. Abbot. Treasurer, Jacob A. Wright.
1842. Selectmen—Zaccheus Read, Jr., John Cutter, Jonas Prescott. Clerk, John W. P. Abbot. Treasurer, Jacob A. Wright. Treasurer, Amos Heywood, November 14.
1843. Selectmen—Thaddeus Blodgett, Eliakim Hutchins, Jr., Henry P. Herrick. Clerk, John W. P. Abbot. Treasurer, Avery Prescott.
1844. Selectmen—William Dupee, Albert Leighton, Eli Tower. Clerk, John W. P. Abbot. Treasurer, Nathan S. Hamblin.
1845. Selectmen—Albert Leighton, Nathan S. Hamblin, Phinehas Chamberlin. Clerk, John W. P. Abbot. Treasurer, Samuel Fletcher.
1846. Selectmen—Albert Leighton, Nathan S. Hamblin, Phinehas Chamberlin. Clerk, John W. P. Abbot. Treasurer, Albert Leighton.
1847. Selectmen—Albert Leighton, Nathan S. Hamblin, Phinehas Chamberlin. Clerk, John W. P. Abbot. Treasurer, Ephraim Wright.
1848. Selectmen—Nathan S. Hamblin, Phinehas Chamberlin, Charles L. Fletcher. Clerk, John W. P. Abbot. Treasurer, Ephraim Wright.
1849. Selectmen—Phinehas Chamberlin, Charles L. Fletcher, Nathan S. Hamblin. Clerk, John W. P. Abbot. Treasurer, Ephraim Wright.
1850. Selectmen—Oren Coolidge, Jonas Prescott, David C. Butterfield. Clerk, Joseph Hildreth. Treasurer, Ephraim Wright.

1851. Selectmen—John Cutter, Amos Heywood, Lewis H. Hildreth. Clerk, Joseph Hildreth. Treasurer, Ephraim Wright.
1852. Selectmen—John Cutter, Amos Heywood, Lewis H. Hildreth. Clerk, Joseph Hildreth. Treasurer, Ephraim Wright.
1853. Selectmen—Joseph Hildreth, Ezekiel Wright, Thaddeus Blodgett. Clerk, Joseph Hildreth. Treasurer, Sherman D. Fletcher.
1854. Selectmen—John Cutter, Alden P. Osgood, Timothy P. Wright. Clerk, Leonard Luce. Treasurer, Sherman D. Fletcher.
1855. Selectmen—John W. P. Abbot, Phinehas Chamberlin, Oliver Wright. Clerk, Leonard Luce. Treasurer, Sherman D. Fletcher.
1856. Selectmen—Joseph Hildreth, Amos Hildreth, 2nd, George Reed. Clerk, Leonard Luce. Treasurer, Sherman D. Fletcher.
1857. Selectmen—George Reed, Lewis H. Hildreth, Ephraim A. Harwood. Clerk, John W. P. Abbot. Treasurer, Sherman D. Fletcher.
1858. Selectmen—Nathan S. Hamblin, John W. P. Abbot, Jonas Prescott. Clerk, John W. P. Abbot. Treasurer, Sherman D. Fletcher.
1859. Seloctmen—John W. P. Abbot, Elbridge G. Parker, Jonas Prescott. Clerk, John W. P. Abbott. Treasurer, Sherman D. Fletcher.
1860. Selectmen—Elbridge G. Parker, Jacob Smith, Phinehas Chamberlin. Clerk, Leonard Luce. Treasurer, Sherman D. Fletcher.
1861. Selectmen—John W. P. Abbot, Jacob Smith, Eli Tower. Clerk, Leonard Luce. Treasurer, Sherman D. Fletcher.
1862. Selectmen—John W. P. Abbot, Jacob Smith, Phinehas Chamberlin. Clerk, Leonard Luce. Treasurer, Sherman D. Fletcher.
1863. Selectmen—John W. P. Abbot, Jacob Smith, Phinehas Chamberlin. Clerk, Leonard Luce. Treasurer, Sherman D. Fletcher.
1864. Selectmen—John W. P. Abbot, Jacob Smith, Phinehas Chamberlin. Clerk, Leonard Luce. Treasurer, Sherman D. Fletcher.
1865. Selectmen—John W. P. Abbot, George T. Day, William Read, 1st. Clerk, Leonard Luce. Treasurer, Sherman D. Fletcher.
1866. Selectmen—Joseph Hildreth, William Read, 1st, J. Henry Read. Clerk, Leonard Luce. Treasurer, Sherman D. Fletcher.
1867. Selectmen—George T. Day, William Read, 1st, J. Henry Read. Clerk, Leonard Luce. Treasurer, Sherman D. Fletcher.
1868. Selectmen—George T. Day, William Read, 1st, J. Henry Read. Clerk, Leonard Luce. Treasurer, Sherman D. Fletcher.
1869. Selectmen—John W. P. Abbot, Luke L. Fletcher, Josiah Reed. Clerk, Leonard Luce. Treasurer, Sherman D. Fletcher.
1870. Selectmen—Isaac P. Woods, J. Henry Read, William Read, 1st. Clerk, Leonard Luce. Treasurer, Sherman D. Fletcher.
1871. Selectmen—Isaac P. Woods, George W. Heywood, William Read, 1st. Clerk, Winthrop F. Wheeler. Treasurer, Sherman D. Fletcher.
1872. Selectmen—William Read, 1st, J. Henry Read, George W. Heywood. Clerk, Winthrop F. Wheeler. Treasurer, Sherman D. Fletcher.

1873. Selectmen — J. Henry Read, George W. Heywood, William Read, 1st. Clerk, Edwin R. Hodgman. Treasurer, Sherman D. Fletcher.
1874. Selectmen — J. Henry Read, George W. Heywood, William Read, 1st. Clerk, Edwin R. Hodgman. Treasurer, Sherman D. Fletcher.
1875. Selectmen — Isaac P. Woods, N. Harwood Wright, Henry Chamberlin. Clerk, Edwin R. Hodgman. Treasurer, Sherman D. Fletcher.
1876. Selectmen — George T. Day, J. Murray Chamberlin, Benjamin G. Brooks. Clerk, Edwin R. Hodgman. Treasurer, Sherman D. Fletcher.
1877. Selectmen — George T. Day, Benjamin G. Brooks, Noah Prescott. Clerk, Edwin R. Hodgman. Treasurer, Sherman D. Fletcher.
1878. Selectmen — George T. Day, Benjamin G. Brooks, Noah Prescott. Clerk, Edwin R. Hodgman. Treasurer, Sherman D. Fletcher.
1879. Selectmen—George T. Day, Arthur Wright, Albert P. Richardson. Clerk, Edwin R. Hodgman. Treasurer, Sherman D. Fletcher.
1880. Selectmen — George T. Day, Arthur Wright, Albert P. Richardson. Clerk, Edwin R. Hodgman. Treasurer, Sherman D. Fletcher.
1881. Selectmen—George T. Day, Arthur Wright, Albert P. Richardson. Clerk, Edwin R. Hodgman. Treasurer, Sherman D. Fletcher.
1882. Selectmen—George T. Day, Arthur Wright, Albert P. Richardson. Clerk, Joseph B. Heald. Treasurer, Sherman D. Fletcher.

RECORD OF MARRIAGES BY REV. WILLARD HALL.

1728. October 28, Samuel Adams, Westford, Elizabeth Butterfield, Chelmsford.
1729. September 17, Samuel Fletcher, Jr., Chelmsford, Mary Lawrence, Littleton.
1730. May 7, Samuel Butterfield, Chelmsford, Tabitha Butterfield, Westford.
May 25, Ebenezer Wright, Westford, Deliverance Stevens, Chelmsford.
November 25, Oliver Spalding, Sarah Reed, Westford.
December 4, Ebenezer Spalding, Hannah Craft, Westford.
1731. January 26, Henry Barton, Littleton, Sarah Bell, Westford.
March 4, Samuel Stevens, Chelmsford, Ruth Wright, Westford.
March 16, William Fletcher, Ruth Remington, Westford.
November 16, Jacob Gragg, Lancaster, Margaret Conn, Littleton.
December 6, Benjamin Perham, Sutton, Esther Butterfield, Westford.
1732. March 7, Samuel Minot, Concord, Sarah Prescott, Westford.
January 20, Benjamin Hildreth, Lydia Fassett, Westford.
January 27, Benjamin Chamberlin, Chelmsford, Esther Fassett, Westford.

STATISTICAL AND OFFICIAL.

1732. March 8, Nathaniel Hammond, Littleton, Abigail Chamberlin, Littleton.
March 16, Ephraim Butterfield, Westford, Elizabeth Davis, Littleton.
April 24, Samuel Fitch, Joanna Kidder, Westford.
November 10, Timothy Read, Mary Comings, Westford.
November 23, Samuel Read, Abigail Comings, Westford.
1733. February 14, Benjamin Blodgett, Chelmsford, Elizabeth Fletcher, Westford.
March 27, Samuel Chamberlin, Westford, Sibel Roper, Marlborough.
May 28, Gershom Fletcher, Lydia Townsend, Westford.
July 2, Josiah Spalden, Chelmsford, Mary Fletcher, Westford.
July 12, Benjamin Robbins, Westford, Ann Johnson, Harvard.
September 11, Zechariah Sartel, Groton, Abigail Bigsby, Westford.
September, 26, Thomas Comings, Sarah Fassett, Westford.
1734. August 28, Samuel Adams, Chelmsford, Esther Fletcher, Westford.
September 3, Stephen Shattuck, Littleton, Elizabeth Robbins, Westford.
December 17, James Pollard, Westford, Abigail Chamberlain, Chelmsford.
1735. May 5, Jonathan Fletcher, Jane Chamberlain, Westford.
May 21, Joseph Fletcher, Elizabeth Underwood, Westford.
November 6, Joseph Dutton, Westford, Rebecca Adams, Chelmsford.
1736. December 2, Philip Wooldry, Dunstable, Lydia Adams, Westford.
1737. January 17, Samuel Searls, Dunstable, Mary Butterfield, Westford.
February 2, Charles Richardson, Oxford, Mary Roper, Westford.
February 3, John Read, Abiel Butterfield, Westford.
April 20, Aaron Parker, Jr., Dorothy Fletcher, Westford.
October 31, Simeon Wright, Westford, Dorcas Hildreth, Chelmsford.
December 7, David Brown, Hannah Bigsby, Westford.
December 21, Obadiah Jenkins, Wilmington, Lydia Bigsby, Westford.
1739. January 22, Samuel Parker, Sarah Fletcher, Westford.
April 26, William Wilson, Weston, Sibel Roper, Westford.
1740. February 27, Nathaniel Jefs, Acton, Esther Foster, Westford.
April 27, John Tuttle, Littleton, Sarah Robbins, Westford.
December 9, James Robbins, Grafton, Deborah Butterfield, Westford.
1741. January 1, Samuel Fassett, Jr., Katharine Read, Westford.
March 3, Samuel Corey, Littleton, Sarah Read, Westford.
July 9, Abiel Richardson, Sarah Boynton, Westford.
September 3, Amos Fletcher, Mary Perham, Westford.
November 30, Ephraim Hildreth, Priscilla Barron, Westford.
December 29, William Read, Thankful Spalding, Westford.

1742. March 11, John Senter, Londonderry, Abigail Parker, Westford.
June 29, Benjamin Fletcher, Bethiah Herrick, Westford.
July 13, Simeon Wheeler, Acton, Sarah Temple, Westford.
August 23, Samuel Craft, Hannah Read, Westford.
1743. January 18, William Tomson, Chelmsford, Mary Fassett, Westford.
February 22, Joseph Hildreth, Westford, Abigail Hill, Billerica.
March 21, Joseph Robbins, Mary Chamberlain, Westford.
May 4, Jonathan Robbins, Mary Proctor, Westford.
October 21, Benjamin Chandler, Hannah Dutton, Westford.
November 18, Joseph Piper, Concord, Esther Wright, Westford.
1744. January 16, Oliver Bates, Ruth Wright, Westford.
February 8, Nathaniel Barrett, Westford, Abigail Searls, Concord.
February 22, Joseph Hildreth, Jr., Westford, Abigail Hill, Billerica.
April 4, Zechariah Robbins, Elizabeth Proctor, Westford.
April 10, Oliver Proctor, Chelmsford, Mary Parker, Westford.
June 6, Moses Parker, Bridget Comings, Westford.
June 6, Stephen Corey, Littleton, Luce Parker, Westford.
June 7, John Bates, Westford, Martha Foster, Littleton.
October 26, Oliver Hildreth, Ann Blasdale, Westford.
November 15, Benoni Jewett, Nottingham, Deborah Fletcher, Westford.
December 17, Benjamin Hosley, Luce Herrick, Westford.
December 20, Enoch Cleaveland, Pomfret, Deborah Fassett, Westford.
1745. January 7, Robert Butterfield, Westford, Mehitable Boynton, Dunstable.
May 23, Benjamin Carver, Eade Fletcher, Westford.
June 25, Benjamin Darby, Concord, Sarah Fletcher, Westford.
August 1, Thomas Richardson, Rebecca Read, Westford.
1746. January 20, Jonathan Keyes, Elizabeth Fletcher, Westford.
March 6, Jonathan Minott, Chelmsford, Esther Proctor, Westford.
May 15, William Warren, Littleton, Hannah Boynton, Westford.
June 4, Ebenezer Patch, Groton, Sarah Wright, Westford.
December 10, Nehemiah Wheeler, Acton, Susannah Proctor, Westford.
December 11, Jacob Fletcher, Ruth Trull, Westford.
1747. January 27, William Barrett, Mary Craft, Westford.
February 10, Philip Proctor, Phebe Hildreth, Westford.
March 19, John Wright, Westford, Mary Kendall, Dunstable.
April 7, Joseph Hildreth, ye 3rd, Lydia Fletcher, Westford.
May 19, James Proctor, Hannah Nutting, Westford.
1748. May 12, Samuel Parker, Mary Robbins, Westford.
June 29, Capt. John Buckley, Groton, Mrs. Mary Underwood, Westford.
September 19, Joseph Blanchard, Dunstable, Betty Spalding, Dunstable.
September 26, Benjamin Butterfield, Westford, Susanna Spalding, Chelmsford.

STATISTICAL AND OFFICIAL. 375

1748. October 12, Jonathan Searls, Nottingham, Thankful Bigsby, Westford.
1749. February 7, John Davis, Chelmsford, Elizabeth Skinner, Westford.
April 4, Aaron Chandler, Ruth Butterfield, Westford.
April 6, Jacob Bigsby, Eunice Heald, Westford.
April 12, Josiah Boyden, Groton, Jane Read, Westford.
June 22, John Underwood, Hannah Wright, Westford.
July 18, John Russell, Jr., Littleton, Abigail Hildreth, Westford.
December 21, Eleazer Butterfield, Mary Wright, Westford.
1750. March 7, Josiah Johnson, Sarah Hunt, Westford.
May 28, Benjamin Hoar, New Ipswich, Anna Brooks, Westford.
June 28, James Dutton, Rebecca Hildreth, Westford.
September 26, Benjamin Knowlton, Westford, Phebe Wright, Westford.
October 2, John Butterfield, Martha Trull, Westford.
October 31, Gershom Heald, Hannah Blood, Westford.
November 28, William Chandler, Jr., Dorcas Blood, Westford.
1751. May 2, Ephraim Wright, Westford, Abigail Whittemore, Dunstable.
July 10, Benjamin Dutton, Mary Rumril, Westford.
1752. January 9, Ephraim Chamberlin, Esther Boynton, Westford.
February 18, John Marshall, Nottingham West, Thankful Baldwin, Westford.
February 24, Robert Butterfield, Westford, Joanna Parker, Chelmsford.
February 27, Samuel Chamberlin, Jr., Westford, Sarah Tinny, Littleton.
February 27, Joseph Kidder, Rebecca Chamberlin, Westford.
April 16, David Taylor, Dunstable, Hannah Fletcher, Westford.
April 16, Eleazer French, Dunstable, Abigail Fletcher, Westford.
August 23, Thomas Penniman, Braintree, Abigail Burge, Westford.

NEW STYLE.

1753. January 12, Josiah Brooks, Westford, Lydia Heywood, Concord.
February 22, Timothy Prescott, Lydia Fletcher, Westford.
April 12, Zechariah Hildreth, Elizabeth Prescott, Westford.
April 12, Ebenezer Corey, Hannah Robbins, Westford.
April 17, Benjamin Fassett, Westford, Rebecca Russell, Litchfield.
November 1, Ebenezer Ball, Townshend, Rebecca Butterfield, Westford.
December 13, Thomas Read, Tertius, Susanna Dutton, Westford.
1754. March 21, Reuben Kidder, Susanna Burge, Westford.
March 22, Eleazer Read, Joanna Fitch, Westford.
March 22, Joseph Bullard, New Ipswich, Sarah Proctor, Westford.
July 3, Lemuel Perham, Littleton, Isabel Marble, Westford.
July 4, Jonathan Johnson, Hollis, Sarah Bates, Westford.

1755. January 2, Benjamin Read, Abigail Fassett, Westford.
January 16, Willard Hall, Jr., Ruth Fletcher, Westford.
January 16, Eleazer Fletcher, Mary Fletcher, Westford.
September 11, Jacob Wright, Jr., Luce Butterfield, Westford.
December 4, Benjamin Warren, Littleton, Eunice Prescott, Westford.
1756. April 7, Joseph Hooker, Jr., Ruth Powers, Westford.
September 21, Caleb Symmes, Charlestown, Elizabeth Hall, Westford.
1757. January 13, Pelatiah Fletcher, Dorothy Hildreth, Westford.
May 23, Joseph Wright, Dorothy Heald, Westford.
June 22, Samuel Read, Wid. Hannah Underwood, Westford.
July 7, Jabez Keep, Jr., Phebe Crosby, Westford.
August 29, Thomas Spalding, Rachel Chandler, Westford,
October 18, Jonathan Perham, Littleton, Hannah Wright, Westford.
1758. February 8, Simeon Hildreth, Hannah Spaulding, Westford.
1759. January 11, Jonathan Spaulding, Lydia Richardson, Westford.
January 16, Jonas Minot, Concord, Mary Hall, Westford.
April 11, Eleazer Taylor, Townshend, Sarah Keyes, Westford.
April 30, Nathaniel Kemp, Wid. Mary Russell, Westford.
July 11, Thomas Adams, Mary Meads, Westford.
October 16, Samuel Parker, Jr., Zeruiah Proctor, Westford.
November 29, William Spalding, Esther Dutton, Westford.
1760. June 11, Francis Fletcher, New Ipswich, Sarah Parker, Westford.
October 20, Francis Leighton, Littleton, Lydia Fitch, Westford.
November 27, Daniel Gilson, Groton, Apphia Kent, Westford.
December 17, Isaac Howe, New Ipswich, Sibel Proctor, Westford.
1761. April 23, Capt. Leonard Whiting, Anne Hall, Westford.
June 11, Pelatiah Wright, Alice Powers, Westford.
October 29, William Bartlett, Marblehead, Mary Raymond, Westford.
November 12, Samuel Butterfield, Dunstable, Hannah Chandler, Westford.
November 19, David Dutton, Esther Heald, Westford.
1762. January 28, Samuel Lawrence, Jr., Rebecca Spalding, Westford.
March 10, Jacob Wendall, resident in Westford, Lora Winslow, Westford.
March 19, Moses Chandler, Westford, Elizabeth Kendall, Litchfield.
May 20, Judah Wheeler, Acton, Lucy Corey, Westford.
June 17, John Procter, Jr., Molly Nutting, Westford.
July 1, Jonathan Keyes, Westford, Wid. Betty Read, Littleton.
July 27, John Hildreth, Abigail Parker, Westford.
October 7, William Read, Jr., Priscilla Emery, Westford.
1763. February 15, Josiah Spalding, Westford, Lydia Cleaveland, Acton.
May 3, William Scott, Dunstable, Elizabeth McLane, Westford.
July 18, Joseph Parker, Susanna Fletcher, Westford.
August 4, Timothy Spaulding, Hannah Richardson, Westford.

1764. January 17, Hezekiah Corey, New Ipswich, Sarah Fletcher, Westford.
March 15, Joshua Parker, Mary Boynton, Westford.
April 10, Samuel Squire, Mary Hildreth, Westford.
November 13, Jonathan Robbins, Mary Fletcher, 3rd, Westford.
November 29, Abner Kent, Jr., Dorcas Hildreth, Westford.
1765. February 28, Solomon Dutton, Sarah Parker, Westford.
May 1, Nathan Hawley, New Milford, Conn., Sarah Kent, Westford.
May 21, Amos Hildreth, Priscilla Hildreth, Westford.
May 23, Jonas Stone, Groton, Rebecca Fletcher, Westford.
June 18, Zaccheus Green, Concord, Elizabeth Kidder, Westford.
September 12, Joseph Cumings, Elizabeth Fletcher, Westford.
October 7, Leonard Keep, Ruth Stone, Westford.
December 6, Andrew Betties, Jr., Chelmsford, Rebecca Farmer, Westford.
1766. June 3, Aaron Parker, Jr., Westford, Lydia Spaulding, Chelmsford.
September 17, Joseph Dutton, Jr., Lucy Biglow, Westford.
November 19, Jonas Barrett, Townshend, Mary Fletcher, Westford.
November 27, Benjamin Wheat, New Ipswich, Sarah Wright, Westford.
1767. January 1, Benjamin Crosby, Chelmsford, Mary Parrot, Westford.
June 22, Rogers King, Lydia Woods, Westford.
June 30, Thomas Wright, New Ipswich, Mary Parker, Jr., Westford.
November 5, David Goodhue, Esther Prescott, Westford.
November 26, Amos Wright, Dorcas Wright, Westford.
December 3, Abraham Taylor, Ashby, Sarah Prescott, Westford.
1768. January 7, Luke Richardson, Sarah Minot, Westford.
January 14, Ezra Jewett, Littleton, Lucy Spaulding, Westford.
May 17, Amaziah Fassett, Eade Richardson, Westford.
June 23, Abel Fletcher, Abigail Hildreth, Westford.
August 25, Henry Morgan, Westford, Hannah Whitney, Chelmsford.
September 1, Aaron Blood, Hannah Marble, Westford.
September 20, Leonard Parker, Mary Foster, Westford.
September 22, Oliver Fletcher, Sarah Fletcher, Westford.
November 15, Thomas Dutton, Sarah Biglow, Westford.
1769. March 23, Abijah Boynton, Pepperell, Sarah Chamberlin, Westford.
April 25, Josiah Boynton, Lucy Raymond, Westford.
May 11, Richard Wait, Charlestown, Hannah Prescott, Westford.
May 17, Isaac Cumings, Elizabeth Trowbridge, Westford.
June 22, Hosea Hildreth, Experience Keep, Westford.
July 11, Gershom Hubbart, Groton, Phebe Patch, Westford.
July 26, Jonathan Keep, Hannah Hildreth, Westford.
July 27, Nathaniel Adams, Charlestown, Susanna Prescott, Westford.

1769. August 1, Oliver Abbot, Billerica, Abigail Hall, Westford.
September 5, Joseph Warren, Littleton, Sarah Hadley, Westford.
September 12, Jonas Kemp, Westford, Joanna Corey, Chelmsford.
September 26, James Spaulding, Jr., Hannah Barron, Jr., Westford.
November 14, Samuel Adams, Wid. Hannah Spaulding, Westford.
November 16, Phineas Chamberlin, Rebecca Dutton, Westford.
November 28, Benjamin Easterbrook, Sarah Heald, Westford.
December 7, Gershom Fletcher, Jr., Sarah Robinson, Westford.
December 28, Silas Richardson, New Ipswich, Lydia Fletcher, Westford.

1770. January 9, Amos Boynton, Mary Parker, Westford.
February 21, James Fletcher, Rebecca Prescott, Westford.
October 22, Issachar Keyes, Elizabeth Richardson, Westford.

1771. January 15, James Spaulding, Wid. Eunice Fassett, Westford.
January 15, Samuel Wright, Esther Minot, Westford.
January 15, Samuel Fletcher, Olive Wright, Westford.
January 24, Isaac Needham, Templeton, Sarah Raymond, Westford.
July 22, Abel Adams, Chelmsford, Olive Richardson, Westford.
October 31, Samson Warren, Littleton, Huldah Wright, Westford.
November 11, Joseph Read, Jr., Martha Fletcher, Westford.
December 24, John Proctor, Jr., Sarah Wright, Westford.
December 30, William Jewett, Littleton, Esther Wright, Westford.

1772. February 27, Paul Thorndyke, Tewksbury, Olive Fletcher, Westford.
March 3, Thomas Smith, Molly Herrick, Westford.
June 2, Silas Read, Hannah Chamberlain, Westford.
June 2, Seth Fletcher, Joanna Fletcher, Westford.
June 4, Thomas Barnes, Chelmsford, Mary Fletcher, Westford.
September 24, Peter Read, Littleton, Dorothy Parker, Westford.
December 1, Josiah Spaulding, Mary Welsh, Westford.
December 3, Isaac Butterfield, Dunstable, Ruth Spaulding, Westford.
December 24, John Hildreth, Betty Gates, Westford.
December 24, Samuel Butterfield, Abigail Petts, Westford.

1773. February 9, Jeremiah Barrett, Ashby, Sarah Fletcher, Westford.
March 18, Samson Read, Lydia Phelps, Westford.
April 22, Oliver Hildreth, Mary Wright, Westford.
May 24, Rev. Elijah Fletcher, Hopkinton, Rebecca Chamberlin, Westford.
October 14, Jacob Bixby, Martha Hardy, Westford.
November 30, John Fletcher, Elizabeth Perry, Westford.
November 30, Henry Fletcher, Deborah Parker, Westford.

1774. March 10, Levi Temple, Rachel Nutting, Westford.
April 7, Daniel Goodhue, Sarah Hildreth, Westford.
May 2, Samuel Farwell, Mary Lawrence, Westford.
November 28, Thomas Richardson, Abigail Spaulding, Westford.

STATISTICAL AND OFFICIAL. 379

1775. January 6, Silas Howard, Sibel Read, Westford.
March 8, Caleb Putnam, Wilton, N. H., Amy Spalding, Westford.
1776. April 24, Ebenezer Wright, Susanna Ayres, Westford.
June 13, Alexander Grey (from Boston), Ann Greenough, Westford (from Boston).
1777. December 11, Levi Parker, Rebecca Fletcher, Westford.
December 17, William Dutton, Westford, Phebe Temple, Acton.
1778. November 24, Abel Read, Rebecca Farrar, Westford.
November 25, Timothy Fletcher, Jr., Hannah Proctor, Westford.
1779. February 9, Capt. Benjamin Fletcher, Wid. Elizabeth Symmes, Westford.

BY REV. MATTHEW SCRIBNER.

1779. October 21, Nehemiah Fletcher, Mary Welch, Westford.
November 18, Phinehas Spaulding, Westford, Rebecca Jaquith, Dunstable.
November 22, David Fletcher, Jr., Sarah Richardson, Westford.
1780. February 15, Stephen Meads, resident, Lucy Wright, Westford.
February 28, Eleazer Lawrence, Sarah Foster, Westford.
May 3, Solomon Spalding, Jemima Read, Westford.
June 21, Thomas Kidder, Mary Fletcher, Westford.
June 22, John Abbot, Jr., Mary Farrar, Concord.
June 27, John Tidd, Elizabeth Wilson, Westford.
October 16, Stephen Temple, Lois Barrett, resident in Westford.
October 26, Asa Bixby, Wid. Elizabeth Wilkinson, Westford.
November 8, Isaac Green, Townshend, Abigail Chamberlin, Westford.
November 27, Thomas Scott, Olive Proctor, Westford.
December 25, Rev. Samuel Whitman, Ashby, Grace Carver, Westford.
1781. March 15, Thomas Adams, Chelmsford, Esther Perry, Westford.
April 12, Joseph Brabrook, Hannah Johnson, Westford.
April 17, Ebenezer Chandler, Ruth Wright, Westford.
April 19, James Wright, Mary Minott, Westford.
May 29, Jesse Perkins, Carlisle, Elizabeth Proctor, Westford.
June 28, Ephraim Dutton, Susanna Bixby, Westford.
July 31, Josiah Burge, Jr., Townshend, Priscilla Barnes, resident in Westford.
September 10, Uriah Drury Pike, Dunstable, Hannah Keyes, Westford.
September 13, Peter Wright, Abigail Read, Westford.
September 18, Timothy Adams, Chelmsford, Joanna Keyes, Westford.
November 1, Abel Russell, Westford, Wid. Sarah Frost, resident in Chelmsford.
December 7, William Dutton, Susanna Read, Westford.
1782. July 28, Abel Boynton, Polly Abbott, Westford.
August 8, Jesse Fletcher, Lucy Keyes, Westford.

1782. September 8, Isaac Patten, Lydia Keyes, Westford.
October 15, Capt. Pelatiah Fletcher, Wid. Betty Keyes, West ord.
1783. January 2, Francis Smith, Hannah Russell, Westford.
January 16, Jacob Robbins, Jr., Dolly Hildreth, Westford.
January 23, Benjamin Robbins, Littleton, Elizabeth Heald, Westford.
January 30, Isaac Proctor, Rebecca Read, Westford.
June 10, Eleazer Parlin, Concord, Olive Hildreth, Westford.
June 22, Jonathan Johnson, Jr., Esther Wright, Westford.
September 17, Jonas Wright, Wid. Rebecca Fletcher, Westford.
November 25, Samuel Adams, Acton, Ruth White, Westford.
1784. January 20, Lieut. Thomas Read, Westford, Wid. Phebe Proctor, Groton.
January 20, James Hall, Cavendish, Vt., Thankful Hildreth, Westford.
January 22, Joel Wheeler, Carlisle, Molly Proctor, Westford.
January 29, Hezekiah Hildreth, Esther Parlin, Westford.
April 30, Dr. Charles Proctor, Wid. Lydia Comings, Westford.
June 3, John Patch, Betty Chandler, Westford.
June 3, Asa Patch, Lydia Lawrence, Westford.
September 7, Jesse Minott, Betty Adams, Westford.
November 4, Ephraim Wright, Mary Blodgett, Westford.
1785. February 1, Sampson Fletcher, Dolly Fletcher, Westford.
February 8, Isaac Parker, Bridget Fletcher, Westford.
March 3, Job Spaulding, Sarah Proctor, Westford.
April 21, Asa Bixby, Elizabeth Wilkinson, Westford.
July 28, Samuel Read, Littleton, Catharine Read, Westford.
December 5, Pelatiah Fletcher, Jr., Patty Keyes, Westford.
1786. February 21, Isaac Patch, Jr., Phebe Fletcher, Westford.
March 23, Abijah Read, Elizabeth Boynton, Westford.
April 9, Josiah Fletcher, Abigail Fletcher, Westford.
May 4, Eleazer Read, Jr., Elizabeth Fletcher, Westford.
May 18, Elijah Nutting, Groton, Susanna Foster, Westford.
July 6, Isaiah Prescott, Westford, Betty Wright, Littleton.
October 5, Asa Wright, Betty Patch, Westford.
December 14, Dea. Samuel Fletcher, Milla Keyes, Westford.
December 26, Oliver Heild, Esther Fletcher, Westford.
1787. April 5, Stephen Wright, Littleton, Sarah Prescott, Westford.
April 30, John Jewett, Elizabeth Comings, Westford.
May 31, Benjamin Clark, Gardner, Martha Minott, Westford.
August 30, Samuel Foster, Mary Fletcher, Westford.
October 29, James Lawrence, 3rd, Pepperell, Anna Wright, Westford.
December 19, Reuben Wright, Sarah Read, Westford.
1788. January 3, Nathaniel Abbot, Phebe Comings, Westford.
March 4, Jacob Wendall, Lydia Read, Westford.
March 6, Jeremiah Hildreth, Abigail Parker, Westford.
March 18, George Frederick, Chelmsford, Rhoda Read, Westford.
March 18, Jonathan Swallow, Groton, Jemima Wilson, Westford.

1788. April 6, Preserved Leonard, West Springfield, Wid. Mary Harwood, Westford.
May 12, Isaiah Hall, Groton, Hannah Keep, Westford.
August 28, Leonard Parker, Jr., Rebecca Fletcher, Westford.
September 22, Pelatiah Fletcher, Ashburnham, Sally Woodward, Westford.
October 21, Nathan Wright, Betty Trowbridge, Westford.
October 23, John Raymond, Phebe Proctor, Westford.
December 2, Silas Johnson, Dunstable, Rebecca Hildreth, Westford.
1789. March 17, Isaiah Hildreth, Lydia Leighton, Westford.
March 17, Ebenezer Barrett, Jane Read, Westford.
June 3, Eleazer Hamlin, Harvard, Mrs. Hannah Fletcher, Westford.
June 9, Peter Read, Sally Parker, Westford.
July 9, Isaac Read, Littleton, Rebecca Fletcher, Westford.
August 2, Thomas Symmes, Rebecca Carver, Westford.
September 3, John Leighton, Hannah Farrar, Westford.
October 8, David Parker, Lydia Hildreth, Westford.

BY ZACCHEUS WRIGHT, JUSTICE OF PEACE.

1784. May 27, Samuel Richardson, Elizabeth Hildreth, Westford.
June 17, David Fletcher, Abigail Wright, Westford.
June 26, Silas Proctor, Olive Read, Westford.
July 12, Henry Richardson, Ruth Bates, Westford.
August 25, Benjamin Robbins, Huldah Robertson, Westford.
September 7, Jesse Minott, Betty Adams, Westford.
September 26, Isaac Fletcher, Westford, Ruth Parse, Groton.
October 4, Jacob Klatter, Joanna Fletcher, Westford.
November 23, Caleb Symmes, Lydia Trowbridge, Westford.
November 25, Andrew Fletcher, Lydia Wright, Westford.
1785. January 26, Thomas Holt, Polly Bevens, Wilmington.
April 14, Zechariah Robbins, Jr., Abigail Hildreth, Westford.
May 31, Jonathan Jones, Abigail Wright, Westford.
June 9, William Bettyes, Olive Corey, Chelmsford.
June 16, Simon Hunt, Acton, Lydia Proctor, Westford.
July 11, Isaac Gliney, Sally Nutting, Westford.
October 24, William Read, Jr., Lydia Stratton, Westford.
November 11, Simeon Kemp, Elizabeth Hildreth, Westford.
December 20, Joseph Jewett, Esther Symons, Westford.
1786. February 7, Thomas Fletcher, Jr., Patty Jewett, Westford.
March 14, Benjamin Dutton, Westford, Elizabeth Freetoe, Dunstable.
March 23, Josiah Howard, Westford, Elizabeth Read, Littleton.
May 23, Abraham Ball, Townshend, Deliverance Perham, Westford.
September 4, Joel Abbot, Lydia Comings, Westford.
December 17, William Whiting, Lucy Hildreth, Westford.

1787. May 29, Ebenezer Parker, Chelmsford, Hannah Fletcher, Westford.
August 14, Oliver Spaulding, Abigail Hall, Westford.
September 10, John Dalrymple, Betty Comings, Westford.
November 11, John Dudley, Sarah Dutton, Westford.
November 25, Jonathan Keyes, Patty Woodard, Westford.

1788. January 24, John Farrar, Lydia Richardson, Chelmsford.
February 25, John Hadlock, Weathersfield, Vt., Sarah Wright, Westford.
July 1, Daniel Raymond, Miriam Proctor, Westford.
July 15, Timothy Howard, Sarah Spaulding, Chelmsford.

1789. August 27, John Sterns, Chelmsford, Lydia Crosby, Carlisle.
September 24, Joseph Foster, Mary Adams, Chelmsford.
October 1, Jeremiah Warren, Chelmsford, Rachel Spalding, Billerica.
November 19, Paul Hunt, Betty Parkhurst, Chelmsford.
November 26, Joseph Rockwood, Jr., Groton, Lucy Fletcher, Westford.

1790. February 22, Amos Read, Westford, Rachel Prescott, Groton.
July 15, Obadiah Foster, Mary Goodhue, Chelmsford.
September 6, Benjamin Hildreth, Polly Kemp, Westford.
September 26, Enoch Cook, Groton, Abigail Butterfield, Westford.
November 3, Joseph Cumings, Jr., Hannah Leighton, Westford.
November 25, Jesse Stevens, Fitchburg, Molly Spalding, Chelmsford.
December 6, Simon Rumril, New Ipswich, Joanna Kemp, Westford.

1791. February 14, Joseph Richardson, Fitchburg, Ruth Stevens, Chelmsford.
March 9, Zebulon Spalding, Jr., Molly Mears, Chelmsford.
March 13, Stephen Wilson, Rachel Mansfield, Chelmsford.
March 13, Solomon Byam, Abi Adams, Chelmsford.
July 5, Simon Parker, Susanna Fletcher, Chelmsford.
November 17, Joseph Fletcher, Lucy Proctor, Chelmsford.
December 22, Henry Spaulding, 3rd, Lydia Proctor, Chelmsford.

1792. April·5, Ephraim Spaulding, Fitchburg, Lydia Spaulding, Chelmsford.
May 3, Josiah Parkhurst, Rachel Stevens, Chelmsford.
May 15, David Keyes, Sarah Bradley, Tyngsborough.
November 29, Bill Wright Stevens, Phebe Gould, Chelmsford.

1793. January 1, Jeduthan Parker, Phebe Gould, Chelmsford.
October 6, Amos Cummings, Betsey Wright, Westford.
December 26, Abijah Read, Susanna Coleman, Westford.

1794. April 7, Joseph Fletcher, Frances Grant Keyes, Westford.
April 22, Levi Wright, Rhoda Hildreth, Westford.
May 10, Jonas Hildreth, Dilly Johnson, Westford.

1795. June 2, Nathaniel Farmer, Littleton, Abigail Bloggett, Westford.
June 18, Jacob Tuttle, Littleton, Betsey Comings, Westford.
September 6, Israel Baley, Abigail Filding, Westford.

STATISTICAL AND OFFICIAL. 383

1795. November 12, Joseph Jewett, Hannah Spalding, Westford.
December 13, Zaccheus Read, Polly Parker, Westford.
1796. January 11, Wilson Comings, Lucy Cowdry, Westford.
February 8, Daniel Blood, Polly Perry, Westford.
March 9, James Chamberlin, Joanna Fletcher, Westford.
March 29, Isaac Day, Lucy Dutton, Westford.
July 3, Thomas Hastings, 3rd, Watertown, Bridget Richardson, Westford.
September 18, Josiah Boynton, Jr., Lydia Perkins, Westford.
December 28, Aaron Blood, Jr., Esther Perry, Westford.
1797. March 30, Oliver Wright, Dolly Prescott, Westford.
April 27, Capt. John Cook, Claremont, N. H., Molly Proctor, Chelmsford.
June 1, Benjamin Stevens, Hannah Parker, Chelmsford.
August 24, Thaddeus Carter, Sandy Stream, County of Lincoln, Betsey Derumple, Groton.
November 16, Daniel Brooks, Westford, Lois Snow, Chelmsford.
1798. May 3, Ezra Corey, Phebe Parker, Chelmsford.
1799. May 12, Parker Stevens, Catharine Parkhurst, Dunstable.
November 28, Samuel Wesson, Hannah Parker, Chelmsford.
November 28, James Keyes, Westford, Abigail Carlton, Chelmsford.
1803. June 7, James Robbins, Phene Osgood, Westford.
September 11, Jacob Shedd, Jr., Tewksbury, Susanna Spalding, Chelmsford.
December 8, Thomas Read, Jr., Rebecca Cummings, Westford.

BY JONAS PRESCOTT, JUSTICE OF THE PEACE.

741. March 19, Benjamin Daves, Sarah Buttrick, Concord.
May 20, Leonard Parker, Abigail Parker, Groton.
July 7, Joseph Baldwin, Townshend, Thankful Spaulding, Westford.
July 8, Gershom Davis, Rebeckah Prescott, Acton.
October 8, Simon Page, Hannah Gilson, Groton.
1742. February 18, Isaac Green, Marthy Boyden, Groton.
March 11, John Roobey, Litchfield, Lyda Richardson, Westford.
October 12, Ephraim Comings, Mary Hildreth, Westford.
October 12. Amiziah Fassett, Eunice Fletcher, Westford.
November 11, Joseph Herrick, Lois Cutler, Townshend.
1743. January 11, Gershom Huboard, Mary Townshend, Groton.
February 14, Oliver Blood, Mary Foster, Concord.
1744. January 3, John McCoin, Mrs. Sarah Heald, Concord.
March 22, David Hubbard, Mrs. Sarah Parker, Groton.
May 30, John Cowdrey, Billerica, Hannah Davis, Groton.
June 27, Joseph Shipley, Eunice Parker, Groton.
July 3, Jacob Warrin, Littleton, Mary Foster, Westford.
1745. June 13, William Preson, Groton, Ann Camble, Winham.
August 13, Robert Parker, Deborah Hubbard, Groton.

1746. February 19, Ebenezer Prescott, Westford, Elizabeth Sprague, Groton.
May 29, Clement Blood, Eunice Gilson, Groton.
July 22, Gershom Proctor, Chelmsford, Elizabeth Parker, Westford.
1747. June 25, Amos Russell, Harvard, Sarah Hildreth, Westford
September 22, Samuel Wood, Jr., Tabitha Wheeler, Groton.
October 20, John Gilson, Jr., Hannah Green, Groton.
December 1, John Nutten, Westford, Mary Adams, Chelmsford.
1748. May 26, Isaac Patch, Groton, Mary Hastin, Dunstable.
November 16, Ephraim Wessen, Wilminkton, Marah Proctor, Chelmsford.
1749. February 16, Jacob Ames, Olive Davise, Groton.
February 21, William Wright, Marah Proctor, Littleton.
June 8, Oliver Prescott, Bethiah Underwood, Westford.
October 31, Ebenezer Kemp, Marah Broadstreet, Groton.
1750. January 11, Nathaniel Edwards, Acton, Hannah Prescott, Westford.

BY CALEB BLAKE, PASTOR.

1792. April 2, John Goodhue, Sarah Tuttle, Westford.
April 17, Benjamin Twist, Chelmsford, Phebe Heald, Westford.
April 30, Josiah Spaulding, Bethiah Read, Westford.
May 5, Henry Wilson, Hannah Spaulding, Westford.
June 17, Thomas Read, Molly Spaulding, Westford.
June 18, Thomas Hutchins, Carlisle, Esther Prescott, Westford.
November 6, Jonathan Johnson, Susanna Heald, Westford.
1793. February 22, Eliakim Hutchins, Carlisle, Mary Prescott, Westford.
April 8, John Pushee, Persia Durant, Westford.
April 16, Moses Woods, Acton, Hazadiah Spaulding, Chelmsford.
July 14, James Cook, Rebecca Read, Westford.
July 23, Paul Wright, Stoddard, N. H., Abigail Kent, Westford.
November 24, Benjamin Green, Olive Hildreth, Westford.
1794. January 29, Caleb Parker, Pepperell, Olive Prescott, Westford.
February 6, Eleazer Wright, Betsey Nutting, Westford.
March 3, Samuel Coburn, Dracut, Meriam Read, Westford.
March 31, Joash Minot, Sally Hildreth, Westford.
April 10, Benjamin Wheeler, Pepperell, Polly Parker, Westford.
June 24, Samuel Sherburn, Chelmsford, Sally Read, Westford.
August 4, Abijah Tarbell, Westford, Eunice Stone, Lexington.
December 24, Abel Brown, Polly Hildreth, Westford.
December 26, Allen Flagg, Sally Goodhue, Westford.
1795. January 20, Amos Prescott, Polly Emerson, Westford.
1796. January 6, Thaddeus Taylor, Grafton, Sally Taylor, Ashby.
February 15, Phineas Whitney, Winchendon, Bethiah Barrett, Westford.
March 2, Amaziah Hildreth, Peggy Marstins, Westford.
April 13, Henry Chandler, Polly Proctor, Westford.

1796. April 28, James Snow, Westford, Sukey Gilson, Groton.
August 2, Abel Prescott, 2d, Concord, Mary Perry, Westford.
October 11, John Tidd Wright, Bedford, Hannah Proctor, Westford.
November 7, Osgood Eaton, Reading, Joanna Leighton, Westford.
November 28, Stephen Fletcher, Betty Hildreth, Westford.
December 13, Thomas Read, Jr., Phebe Wright, Westford.
1797. January 8, Jacob Kidder, Westford, Hannah Davis, Dunstable.
March 4, Hezekiah Sprague, Martha Prescott, Westford.
June 12, Ephraim Dutton, Cavendish, Esther Dutton, Westford.
July 22, Joshua Abbot Jewett, Sally Spalding, Westford.
August 27, Benjamin Fletcher, Mehitable Robinson, Westford.
October 30, Aaron Maynard, Concord, Polly Hildreth, Westford.
October 30, Silas Richardson, Westford, Lydia Marcey, Chelmsford.
1798. May 13, Simeon Hildreth, Ruth Bicknell, Westford.
May 13, Luther Boynton, Nabby Parker, Westford.
May 13, William Chambers, Sally Keyes, Westford.
September 3, Calvin Green, Carlisle, Rebecca Richardson, Westford.
October 21, Abram Prescott, Polly Fletcher, Westford.
November 19, Asa Johnson, Sally Perry, Concord.
November 23, James Baldwin, Dunstable, Priscilla Keyes, Westford.
December 4, Isaiah Leighton, Patty Kneeland, Westford.
1799. February 12, Isaiah Read, Lydia Proctor, Westford.
May 12, Parker Stevens, Catharine Parkhurst, Dunstable.
August 5, William Robinson, Westminster West, Vt., Alice Wright, Westford.
——— Joseph Swasey, Jr., Martha's Vineyard, Mary Stodder, Westford.
——— James Kidder, Patty Cumings, Westford.
——— Thomas Dutton, Hannah Twiss, Westford.
September 22, Buckley Ames, Groton, Lydia Prescott, Westford.
December 28, Calvin Farnsworth, Washington, Lydia Bixby, Westford.
1800. January 1, Willard Read, Miriam White, Westford.
January 6, Moses Wright, Templeton, Hannah Parker, Westford.
February 23, Samuel Stone, Boston, Grace Stoddard, Westford.
March 20, Bradford Norton, Williamsburg, Nabby Blood, Westford.
May 15, Joshua Abbot Jewett, Rebecca Robinson, Westford.
May 18, David Patch, Groton, Sally Heald, Westford.
May 29, Ebenezer Prescott, Hannah Wright (Waite?), Westford.
June 24, Jonathan Lawrence, Ashby, Lydia Boynton, Westford.
July 10, Timothy Prescott, Wid. Rebecca Boynton, Westford.
September 7, Abijah Wright, Polly Fletcher, Westford.
September 14, John Keep, Fitchburg, Lucy Fletcher, Westford.
November 27, Joel Keyes, Polly Boyden, Westford.

1801. January 4, Oliver Hildreth, Betsey Learned, Westford.
January 15, Joseph Harwood, Boston, Patty Gilbert, Westford.
February 3, Jonathan Wooster, Esther Tenny, Westford.
February 24, Caleb Putnam, Wilton, Lydia Spaulding, Westford.
March 24, Jesse Hildreth, Olive Fletcher, Westford.
August 20, John Prescott, Anna Keyes, Westford.
October 28, William Prescott, Westford, Eunice Wheeler, Littleton.
1802. March 30, John Blodgett, Mason, N. H., Mary Prescott, Westford.
June 1, David Dutton, Chelmsford, Hannah Wright, Westford.
October 12, Abel Stevens, Westford, Betsey Putnam, Fitchburg.
October 31, John C. Wilkins, Carlisle, Susanna Leighton, Westford.
November 25, Sampson Keyes, Wilton, Betsey Little, Westford.
1803. February 15, Edmund Boynton, Salem, Betsey Needham, Westford.
February 22, Luther Bancroft, Pepperell, Anna Fletcher, Chelmsford.
March 20, Abel White, Ruth Prescott, Westford.
May 22, David Campernell, Polly Dutton, Westford.
May 29, Jesse Hadley, Brattleboro', Vt., Nabby Fletcher, Westford.
May 31, Ballard Smith, Dunstable, Prudence Griffin, Westford.
June 6, Capt. Eleazer Cummings, New Ipswich, Wid. Mary Hildreth, Westford.
June 23, Pelatiah Fletcher, Jr., Westford, Mrs. Beulah Heywood, Concord.
July 7, James Goodhue, Westford, Asenath Carlton, Chelmsford.
July 12, Zebedee Wright, Dunstable, Hannah Wright, Westford.
September 22, Levi Parker, Betsey Wright, Westford.
November 6, Lieut. Abijah Tarbell, Betsey Hildreth, Westford.
December 25, Joel Fletcher, Abigail Fletcher, Westford.
1804. January 1, Timothy Locke, Ashby, Rebecca Dutton, Westford.
March 20, Seth Read, Rhoda Finny, Westford.
September 9, Samuel White, Cavendish, Vt., Mrs. Rachel Adams, Westford.
November 1, John Read, Sally Wright, Westford.
November 17, Joseph Comy, Boston, Polly Fletcher, Westford.
December 9, Isaac Cumings, Mrs. Polly Richardson, Westford.
1805. March 3, Theophilus Bixby, Westford, Anna Fisk, Groton.
April 18, Asaph Chaflin, Acton, Anna Read, Westford.
October 3, Joseph Wright, Sally Laws, Westford.
November 3, Joseph Adams, Littleton, Mrs. Mehitable Hildreth, Westford.
November 24, Abel Abbot, Catharine Cummings, Westford.
1806. January 15, John Woodward, Tyngsborough, Mrs. Polly Prescott, Westford.
May 5, Avery Prescott, Westford, Lucy Lawrence, Ashby.
May 27, Adams Fletcher, Westford, Betsey Bateman, Chelmsford.
June 5, Joseph Gould, Polly Smith, Westford.

STATISTICAL AND OFFICIAL. 387

1806. June 5, Zebulon Spalding, Carlisle, Dorcas Parker, Westford.
June 15, Eleazer Ingalls, Dunstable, Amy Pearsons, Westford.
September 15, Abraham Morgan, Wilton, Anna Pearsons, Westford.
September, Justus Fletcher, Westford, Sally Glyn, Tyngsborough.
September 28, Thomas Flint, Chelmsford, Betsey Keyes, Westford.
December 9, Richard Adams, Sally Fletcher, Westford.
1807. January 1, Lieut. Nathaniel Hildreth, Mary Pierce, Westford.
March 1, Lieut. Amos Lawrence, Jr., Fitchburg, Sally Fletcher, Westford.
March 18, Jacob Wright, Sally Smith, Westford.
April 2, Jonathan Emerson, Dunstable, Rebecca Nutting, Westford.
April 9, Jacob Osgood, Patty Fletcher, Westford.
June 7, Abraham L. Stevens, Boston, Levina Jenkins, Westford.
June 10, Michael Carter, Dunstable, Hannah Smith, Westford.
June 14, John Osgood, Patty Fletcher, Westford.
August 26, Daniel Patch, Betsey Wright, Westford.
September 14, Moses Wilson, Guildford, Lucy Pierce, Sterling.
October 18, John D. Howard, Boston, Sophia Hinckley, Westford.
November 8, William Sweetser, Charlestown, Sally Raymond, Westford.
November 11, Nathan Green, 2nd, Gardner, Fanny Bicknell, Westford.
1808. January 17, Amos Flint, Jr., Walpole, N. H., Mary Lancey, Westford.
January 25, Samuel Wright, Martha Parker, Westford.
February 14, James Colman, Norridgewock, Me., Betsey Read, Westford.
March 2, Henry Herrick, 2nd, Beverly, Elizabeth Prescott, Westford.
March 8, Abraham Perley, Boxford, Betsey Robinson, Westford.
April 7, Thomas Heald, Rebekah Smith, Westford.
March 29, Samuel Towne, Boxford, Charlotte Fletcher, Westford.
June 12, David Nutting, Charlotte Read, Westford.
June 26, Sherman Dewy, Hartford, Vt., Joanna Fletcher, Westford.
September 4, Capt. Leonard Jarvis, Cambridge, Mary Cogswell, Westford.
November 6, Jonas Keyes, Sally Read, Westford.
1809. January 1, Simeon Stevens, Betsey Fletcher, Westford.
January 1, John Robinson, Hannah Woods, Westford.
January 19, Joel Taylor, Sally Wright, Westford.
January 29, Ensign Jonathan Prescott, Huldah Robbins, Westford.
March 5, William Ditson, Mary Leighton, Westford.
March 30, Isaac Needham, Jr., Rhoda Boynton, Westford.
April 2, Silas Merriam, Polly Abbot, Westford.
April 19, Abijah Hildreth, Susanna Hildreth, Westford.
April 19, Isaiah Prescott, Mrs. Sally Bird, Westford.

1809. October 19, Reuben Wright, Jr., Westford, Esther Woodward, Tyngsborough.
October 25, Levi Prescott, Hannah Prescott, Westford.
November 6, Porter Kimball, Fitchburg, Mary Davis, Westford.
1810. January 7, Joel Read, Joanna Chandler, Westford.
February 15, Solomon Woods, Mary Raymond, Westford.
March 8, Stephen Wright, Jr., Abiah Richardson, Westford.
April 10, Dr. Benjamin Osgood, Nancy Cummings, Westford.
April 19, Thomas C. Parker, Hannah Proctor, Westford.
September 9, Ebenezer Blood, Polly Fletcher, Westford.
November 29, Ensign Thomas Pearson, Esther Wright, Westford.
December 20, Dennis Townsend, Francestown, N. H., Nancy Wilson, Westford.
1811. March 20, Caleb Wight, Mary Osgood, Westford.
April 3, David Walker, Jr., Chelmsford, Lydia Blood, Westford.
April 9, John Smith, Martha Boynton, Westford.
April 25, Daniel Smith, Jr., Exeter, Anna Bead, Westford.
May 1, Rev. Jonathan Cogswell, Saco, Me., Elizabeth Abbot, Westford.
May 9, Thomas Richardson, Jr., Filinda Wright, Westford.
June 18, Jacob O. Parker, Rachel Read, Westford.
September 3, Joseph Wright, Dedham, Sally Snow, Westford.
1812. January, Buckley Prescott, Mrs. Eunice Prescott, Westford.
February 18, David Johnson, Boston, Submit Taylor, Westford.
April 21, Joseph Wright, Jr., Hannah Smith, Westford.
May 20, Levi Warren, Littleton, Betsey Stevens, Westford.
June 3, Laban Hersey, Jr., Hingham, Martha C. Davis, Westford.
June 30, Samuel Brown, Concord, Mrs. Lucy Osgood, Westford.
August 9, Thomas Fletcher, Jr., Orpah Fletcher, Westford.
November 9, Jabez Parker, Roxanna Fletcher, Westford.
November 26, Amos Pierce, Waltham, Mrs. Anna Dutton, Westford.
December 27, Homer Sawtell, Nancy Needham, Westford.
December 31, Samuel Spalding, Polly Read, Westford.
1813. January 5, Isaac Patch, Mrs. Esther Craft, Westford.
January 10, Samuel Farwell, Mary Parker, Westford.
January 24, Francis Leighton, Mary Read, Westford.
January 28, Adams Fletcher, Abigail Davis, Westford.
March 4, Isaac Heald, Ruth Read, Westford.
April 18, Ebenezer Prescott, Charlotte Jones, Westford.
April 18, William Nichols, South Reading, Lavina Kennedy, Fitchburg.
May 19, Elisha Kent, Mrs. Betsey Patch, Westford.
October 12, Nathan Dadmun, Abigail Prescott, Westford.
1814. January 4, Fisher Blackington, Attleboro', Nancy Fletcher, Westford.
January 5, Joseph Wild, Braintree, Lydia Read, Westford.
February 8, Joseph Haynes, Townsend, Lucy Osgood, Westford.
April 27, Frederick Blood, Carlisle, Mary Cummings, Westford.
May 8, Solomon Richardson, Nancy Cogswell, Westford.

STATISTICAL AND OFFICIAL.   389

1814. June 26, Benjamin Kneeland, Eve Cogswell, Westford.
August 14, Nahum H. Groce, Ede Proctor, Westford.
August 18, Nathaniel Adams, Ashby, Paran Goodhue, Westford.
September 22, Abel Stevens, Mrs. Sally Fletcher, Westford.
October 27, Simeon Blanchard, Boxborough, Mary Keyes, Westford.
1815. January 1, Joel Mansfield, Chelmsford, Rebecca Cogswell, Westford.
February 2, John Hunt, Concord, Martha Perry, Westford.
February 7, Nathan Wright, Shelburne, Sally Wright, Westford.
March 23, Andrew Kelly, Concord, Mary Hunt, Westford.
April 4, Samuel Hosley, Pepperell, Mary Reed, Westford.
April 13, Levi Heywood, Martha Keyes, Westford.
April 13, Samuel Fletcher, Beulah Heywood, Westford.
April 23, Samuel Brown, Jr., Malden, Elizabeth Heywood, Westford.
May 2, Thomas R. Wright, Hannah Hall, Westford.
May 4, William Laws, Chelmsford, Lucinda P. Cook, Westford.
May 9, Gardner Fletcher, Chelmsford, Fanny Fletcher, Westford.
May 31, David Eastman, Strafford, Vt., Patty Fletcher, Westford.
September 12, Timothy Smith, Betsey Abbot, Westford.
October 12, Alpheus Spaulding, Chelmsford, Patty Osgood, Westford.
October 14, Benjamin Green, Lucy Bicknell, Westford.
December 24, Nahum H. Groce, Sarah Proctor, Westford.
1816. March 14, Levi Lund, Dunstable, Mary Gilson, Tyngsborough.
April 11, Theodore Woodard, Mehitable Spaulding, Westford.
May 5, Joshua Read, Charlotte Read, Westford.
May 9, Samuel Damon, Ashby, Patty Read, Westford.
July 11, Artemas Rogers, Newton, Lucy Bigsby, Westford.
September 25, Josiah Williams, Mrs. Anna Lawrence, Pepperell.
September 30, Imla Keyes, Hannah Fletcher, Westford.
October 1, Daniel Lincoln, Westminster, Martha Robbins, Westford.
November 10, Jepthah Trowbridge, Milly Chandler, Westford.
November 28, Andrew Fletcher, Jr., Rebecca Hutchins, Westford.
1817. January 12, William Read, Jr., Lucinda Patch, Westford.
February 4, Salathiel Patch, Malden, Ruth Cumings, Westford.
March 9, Abel P. Jones, Mary Corey, Westford.
May 1, Issachar Keyes, Mrs. Abigail Carlton, Westford.
May 4, Capt. Samuel Read, Milton, Phebe Raymond, Westford.
July 3, Asa Bixby, Jr., Mary Gilson, Groton.
October 16, Amos Heywood, Lydia Buck, Westford.
October 21, Capt. John Cutter, Mary Prescott, Westford.
November 16, Ebenezer Brackett, Peterboro', Clarissa Hildreth, Westford.
November 17, Capt. Nathaniel Sweetser, Nancy Hutchins, Westford.

1818. January 15, Prescott Barrett, Concord, Olive Heywood, Westford.
April 26, Asa Read, Betsey Prescott, Westford.
May 3, Thomas Minott, Zoa A. Goodhue, Westford.
June 25, Parker Wright, Mary Gage, Westford.
October 14, William H. Smith, resident, Rachel Blood, Westford.
December 3, Daniel G. Fish, Southborough, Lorenza Pierce, Westford.
December 16, Dr. John Ramsey, Greenfield, N. H., Orphelia Davis, Westford.

1819. March 4, Addison Parker, Fanny Hildreth, Westford.
April 8, John Davis, Lucy Tufts, Westford.
May 27, Samuel Peabody, Lunenburg, Betsey Jones, Westford.
September 5, Charles Hildreth, Westford, Mehitable Trask, Beverly.
September 12, Moses Caryl, Nancy Gage, Westford.
September 14, Horatio Clark, Elizabeth Bixby, Westford.
October 10, Calvin Fletcher, Nancy Read, Westford.
October 21, Nathan Dexter, Mehitable Proctor, Westford.
December 16, Dea. Andrew Fletcher, Westford, Mrs. Mary Hapgood, Acton.

1820. January 23, Willard Jones, Vershire, Vt., Lucy Fletcher, Westford.
March 26, Andrew Gage, Orphelia Read, Westford.
May 28, Charles Marten, resident in Lynn, Fanny Richardson, Westford.
May 31, Gilbert Parker, Acton, Sally White, Westford.
June 1, Ephraim Wright, Asenath Fletcher, Westford.
June 16, Joseph Keyes, Sophia S. Blake, Westford.
July 23, Asa Wright, Bathsheba Dadmun, Westford.
October 18, Jacob P. Kellogg, Shelburne, Lucy Wright, Westford.
November 23, Robert Spaulding, Chelmsford, Joanna Snow, Westford.

1821. January 9, Loammi Parker, Mary Whitcomb, Westford.
January 23, Joel Clark, Stanstead, Lower Canada, Sally Stevens, Chelmsford.
February 1, Ebenezer Prescott, Sally Fletcher, Westford.
March 22, Perley Raymond, New Bedford, Hannah Fletcher, Westford.
April 5, John C. Newell, Concord, Mary Richardson, Westford.
May 3, Benjamin F. Tidd, Lancaster, Nancy Keyes, Westford.
May 3, Joseph Harrington, Concord, Mary Snow, Westford.
August 19, Nathaniel S. Gilson, Groton, Nancy B. Hildreth, Westford.
September 17, John Allen, resident in Danvers, Sally Hunt, Westford.
September 27, Andrew Fletcher, Jr., Laura Chandler, Westford.
December 11, Samuel Dodge, Beverly, Mrs. Esther Conant, Westford.
December 27, Daniel B. Willowby, Hollis, N. H., Mahala Pike, Westford.

STATISTICAL AND OFFICIAL. 391

1822. February 11, Luther Gilson, Groton, Patty Blake, Westford.
March 21, Samuel Frederick, Lucinda Patten, Westford.
April 4, Otis Adams, Chelmsford, Abigail O. Read, Westford.
May 28, Mial Davis, Dunstable, Lucy Hutchins, Westford.
August 29, Andrews Breed, Charlestown, Susan Davis, Westford.
October 24, Daniel Trask, Billerica, Ann Pike, Westford.
November 10, Joseph Hildreth, Parmela Read, Westford.
November 16, Ensign Luther Trowbridge, Abigail Prescott, Westford.
November 28, Zaccheus Read, Jr., Mary Heywood, Westford.
December 26, Kendall Swallow, Dunstable, Patty Keyes, Westford.

1823. January 14, Calvin Spaulding, Sally Wright, Westford.
January 28, Abner Bailey, Tewksbury, Hannah Mears, Westford.
January 31, Simeon Hildreth, Jr., Harriet Prescott, Westford.
March 31, Jonas Heald, Sally Parker, Westford.
April 22, Samuel Wright, Mrs. Rebecca Fletcher, Westford.
April 27, Joel Balcom, Almira Flagg, Westford.
August 3, John Daland, 3rd, Westford, Sarah G. Laine, Salem.
September 14, Jeremy B. Read, Louisa Hildreth, Westford.
October 14, Moses Wheeler, New Ipswich, Lucy Fletcher, Westford.
October 30, Augustus Tuttle, Concord, Almira Robbins, Westford.
December 25, Samuel Dunn, Chelmsford, Charlotte Keyes, Westford.

1824. February 25, William Usher, Charlestown, Mrs. Hannah Scribner, Westford.
April 8, William Coolidge, Natick, Anna Leighton, Westford.
June 8, Dr. Calvin Brown, Ackworth, N. H., Lydia Patten, Westford.
August 17, Peter Hadley, Elizabeth Green, Westford.
September 30, Isaiah Leighton, Jr., Hannah Read, Westford.
October 7, Abram Wright, Maria Hildreth, Westford.
December 2, Thomas Harding, Brighton, Sylvia Leland, Westford.
December 26, Nathan Pennington, Chelmsford, Louise Nutting, Westford.

1825. January 19, Geo. W. Jones, Vershire, Vt., Sophia Fletcher, Westford.
February 16, Bela Wright, Sarah Wright, Westford.
March 31, Walter Wright, Eleanor Wendall, Westford.
April 14, Levi T. Fletcher, Ama Richardson, Westford.
May 29, Leonard Foster, Carlisle, Doranda Tufts, Littleton, N. H.
September 4, Andrew Gage, Stoddard, N. H., Lucy Prescott, Westford.
November 23, Solomon Keyes, Jr., Littleton, Almira Foster, Westford.
November 27, William Babcock, Milton, Rebecca Raymond, Westford.
December 6, Timothy Read, Mary Proctor, Chelmsford.
December 29, Leonard L. Gibson, Boston, Mary Ann Fletcher, Westford.

1826. January 3, Isaac Day, Jr., Betsey Proctor, Westford.
April 6, Ira Leland, Susan Prescott, Westford.
April 20, Calvin Howard, Chelmsford, Betsey Fletcher, Westford.
June 29, Orville Richardson, Leominster, Polly Fletcher, Westford.
July 20, Aaron White, Jr., Sophia E. L. Kendall, Westford.
August 30, Jacob Blodgett, Almira Wright, Westford.
October 10, Dexter Richardson, Lowell, Mary Ann Read, Westford.
December 5, John Edwards, Acton, Mariah Adaline Heald, Westford.
December 7, Joseph Haskell, Lowell, Mary Prescott, Westford.

1827. February 20, Calvin B. Wright, Almira Tenny, Westford.
April 12, Luther Billings, Westford, Maria Proctor, Acton.
April 19, Geo. W. Worcester, Sophia Hildreth, Westford.
June 13, Dr. Geo. Haskell, Cambridge, Eunice P. Edwards, Westford.

BY LEONARD LUCE, PASTOR.

1829. April 9, Samuel C. Tenny, Cynthia Goodhue, Westford.
April, Geo. R. Johnson, Sybil Nichols, Waltham.
May 27, Samuel Perham, Eliza Pratt, Westford.

1830. September 23, Ebenezer Swan, Jr., Tyngsborough, Mary E. Leighton, Westford.
October 28, Nahum H. Groce, Betsey Keyes, Westford.
December 23, Otis Longley, Nancy L. Goodhue, Westford.
December 23, Jesse Minott, Almira Fletcher, Westford.

1831. April 7, William W. Tenny, Charlestown, Esther W. Wright, Westford.
April 14, Dr. Kendall Davis, Reading South Parish, Jane Ann Patten, Westford.
June 7, Sam L. Wilkins, Lowell, Sarah Ann Heald Goodhue, Westford.
December 29, Henry P. Herrick, Betsey Hildreth, Westford.

1832. January 31, Lemuel Whiting, Leominster, Betsey Day, Westford.
February 9, Amos Byam, Chelmsford, Elizabeth Hildreth, Westford.
September 9, Isaac Litchfield, Harriet Hildreth, Lowell.
October 2, Capt. Timothy P. Wright, Elnora Prescott, Westford.
October 30, Gilbert Farmer, Tewksbury, Mary Wright, Westford.
December 20, Henry L. Lawrence, Groton, Martha H. Leighton, Westford.
December 25, Joseph Cummings, Littleton, Rebecca F. Proctor, Westford.
December 30, Silas H. P. Cowdrey, Chelmsford, Catharine P. Johnson, Westford.

1833. April 30, Rogers Ryan, Lowell, Hannah Wight, Westford.
April 30, Burnap Nichols, Gardner, Sarah M. Fletcher, Westford.
June 4, Charles Tuttle, Acton, Maria H. Wright, Westford.

1833. October 8, Jacob Upham, Lowell, Nancy Hildreth, Westford.
November 12, Nahum Childs, Lowell, Elizabeth Wright, Westford.
December 10, Otis Manning, Littleton, Ann C. Carter, Westford.
1834. February 6, Amos Hildreth, 2nd, Martha Parker, Westford.
1835. January 29, Benjamin A. Read, Betsey Hunt, Westford.
April 15, Brackley Rose, Lyndeborough, N. H., Sally Chamberlin, Westford.
June 7, John Denning, Grafton, Betsey Flint, Westford.
December 3, Daniel W. Hemmenway, Concord, Sophia Adams, Westford.
1836. March 10, William S. Walker, Harriet Flint, Westford.
May 29, Christopher Way, Gorham, Me., Susanna Shedd, Westford.
1837. April 9, Trueworthy Keyes, Sophia S. Keyes, Westford.
April 27, Isaac Spaulding, New Ipswich, Mrs. Martha L. Parker, Westford.
July 20, Francis Bartlett, New York City, Caroline C. Kneeland, Westford.
1838. May 1, Henry Wesson, Julia A. Flint, Grafton.
May 15, Francis Richardson, Providence, R. I., Belinda Fletcher, Westford.
June 26, D. Augustus Kimball, Burlington, Vt., Martha Hartwell, Littleton.
September 20, Geo. E. Burt, Harriet S. Hildreth, Westford.
October 4, Thomas D. Pushee, Littleton, Mandana W. Erskine, Westford.
October 11, John Wright, Ursula Brown, Hudson, N. H.
December 5, Samuel A. Wales, Millbury, Sarah E. Read, Chelmsford.
December 13, Dea. Andrew Fletcher, Mrs. Abigail Hildreth, 2nd, Westford.
1839. January 31, Jeremiah J. Carter, Sophia Prescott, Westford.
May 19, Ancil Davis, Caroline Scott, Westford.
May 23, George Brown, Harriet E. Osgood, Westford.
June 18, Dr. Theodore Wells, Sarah E. C. Peabody, Westford.
October 3, Samuel Farwell, Jr., Harriet Horn, Westford.
November 3, Amos Day, Isabella Hildreth, Westford.
1840. April 7, Asaph Mansfield, Chelmsford, Elizabeth S. Griffin, Westford.
April 7, Joseph H. Blanchard, Boxborough, Mary A. Colver, Boston.
May 26, Charles B. Richmond, Lowell, Nancy L. Heywood, Westford.
June 2, Elisha Shaw, Chelmsford, Emily Hildreth, Westford.
June 4, Phineas P. Trowbridge, Eliza S. Jones, Westford.
September 24, Theophilus C. Hersey, Portland, Me., Abigail D. Fletcher, Westford.
November 26, Warren Hunt, Clarissa Wilson, Westford.

1841. January 3, James Hildreth, Sarah R. Tenny, Westford.
January 3, Joel P. Green, Mrs. Almira T. Wright, Westford.
April 7, Massena B. Erskine, Susan Perry, Westford.
April 28, William K. Perry, Charlotte J. Prescott, Westford.
July 15, John H. Spalter, Groton, Martha Ann Hildreth, Westford.
November 14, Daniel Campbell, Lucy Perry, Westford.
1842. April 14, Henry O. Rockwell, Fitchburg, Sarah C. Laws, Westford.
June 9, Nathan Hartwell, Littleton, Mrs. Almira Foster, Westford.
December 22, Benjamin O. Farwell, Westford, Mary Horn, Lowell.
1843. January 3, Joseph Gould, Jr., Quincy, Semantha J. Blodgett, Westford.
March 23, Thomas E. Prescott, Reading, Abigail E. Prescott, Westford.
December 28, Israel Blaisdell, Louisa Vose, Westford.
1844. March 2, Elijah Holmes, Mrs. Mary Green, Windham, N. H.

BY A. G. FAY, MINISTER OF THE GOSPEL, CONCORD.

1845. April 17, Elbridge G. Parker, Westford, Nancy Tuttle, Acton.

BY OLIVER AYER, MINISTER OF BAPTIST SOCIETY, LITTLETON.

1842. May 1, Stephen P. Wiley, Sarah Fletcher, Westford.
May 29, Rufus Bullard, Mary E. Leighton, Westford.
1843. May 21, Josiah K. Webber, Mrs. Betsey M Gates, Westford.

BY BENJAMIN OSGOOD, JUSTICE OF THE PEACE.

1807. January 20, Artemas Parker, Sibel Spaulding, Chelmsford.
March 17, James Spaulding, Westford, Anna Tenna, Tyngsborough.
1812. September 6, Samuel P. Wyman, Tyngsborough, Ruth Wright, Westford.
October 9, Emerson Parker, Dunstable, Eunice Dutton, Westford.
1815. September 14, Thomas Cumings, Jr., Lucinda Wright, Westford.
1817. January 12, William Read, Jr., Lucinda Patch, Westford.
1818. April 7, Greenleaf Gennis Chesby, Canterbury, Vt., resident in Westford, Hannah W. Hildreth, Westford.
May 21, Zaccheus Wright, Olive Fletcher, Westford.
1820. December 21, James Foster, Goffstown, N. H., Hannah Gordon, resident in Westford.
1822. December 9, Henry Mier, Westford, Elizabeth Nutting, Groton.
1824. February 28, Abraham Knowlton, East Sudbury, now resident in Westford, Lucy Hildreth, Westford.

BY JOHN PARKHURST, BAPTIST SOCIETY, CHELMSFORD.

1827. March 5, John R. Green, Martha R. Parker, Westford.
April 29, Elisha Bunce, Priscilla C. Wright, Westford.

STATISTICAL AND OFFICIAL. 395

1827. May 30, Charles P. Kidder, Mary Ann Wright, Westford.
August 30, James Kidder, Jr., Westford, Lucy Pushee, Littleton.
1828. January 10, Jesse Wright, Westford, Sybel Stevens, Chelmsford.
August 31, Walter Fletcher, Mary Chamberlin, Westford.
1829. October 8, William Richardson, Chelmsford, Lucy Ann Webber, Westford.
1830. March 8, Abel Corey, Lucinda C. Jones, Westford.
1831. January 27, Alfred Kemp, Mary Ann Cowdrey, Westford.
March 31, Geo. Kidder, Lydia Sawtelle, Westford.
October 23, Samuel B. Tibbitts, Mrs. Mary Read, Westford.
December 8, Augustus H. Searles, Chelmsford, Rebecca Wright, Westford.
1832. April 12, Thomas Hutchins, 3rd, Hannah Dadmun, Westford.
April 23, Asa Stevens, Chelmsford, Harriet Chamberlin, Westford.
October 28, Joshua Whidden, Lowell, Martha Fletcher, Westford.
1833. June 30, Jedediah Robbins, Eliza Ann Searles, Westford.
August 23, Jonathan S. Hill, Nancy Abbot, Westford.
1834. January 1, Moses P. Worthing, Lowell, Irena Chamberlin, Westford.
November 13, Ira Bicknell, Martha Dadmun, Westford.
November 27, Orville Peckins, Rebecca P. Cowdrey, Westford.
1836. March 3, John B. Gates, Betsey M. Gates, Westford.
1839. February 7, Calvin Green, Susan Dadmun, Westford.
1840. April 1, Sampson Stevens, Jr., Edee P. Wright, Westford.
June 11, Geo. A. Griffin, Eliza T. Wright, Westford.
October 22, Thomas Hutchins, Jr., Sarah Dadmun, Westford.
1843. October 26, Otis H. Penniman, Carlisle, Elizabeth R. Heald, Westford.
November 30, Geo. B. Dupee, Westford, Hannah M. Hutchins, Chelmsford.
December 7, Benjamin Heywood, Jaffrey, N. H., Mrs. Betsey Wright, Westford.

BY AMASA SANDERSON, PASTOR OF BAPTIST CHURCH, LITTLETON.

1827. December 6, John B. Fletcher, Joan Hildreth, Westford.
1828. May 15, Vandolo Emory Whitcomb, Littleton, Sophia Foster, Westford.
October 5, Lyman Gilbert, Boston, Mary Hildreth, Westford.
November 6, Joel Glover, Nancy S. Hildreth, Westford.
1830. February 18, Benjamin Spaulding, Chelmsford, Polly F. Prescott, Westford.

BY EPHRAIM ABBOT, PASTOR.

1832. April 5, Ebenezer Needham, Andover, Sally Wright, Westford.
May 17, Eliel Heywood, Mary Read, Westford.
September 25, Levi Snow, New Ipswich, Louisa Read, Westford.
1833. February 21, Dr. Benjamin Osgood, Eliza Cummings, Westford.
May 23, James M. Wright, Sarah Gould, Westford.

1833. September 12, Geo. Wright, Mary Ann Prescott, Westford.
October 6, Samuel Hoyt, Hannah Cilley, Westford.
December 23, Eli Tower, Concord, Mary Fletcher, Westford.
1834. January 2, Benjamin L. Wright, Elizabeth Wright, Westford.
December 4, John Day, Hannah Wright, Westford.

AS JUSTICE OF THE PEACE.

1836. June 16, Abel Fletcher, Mary Kimball, Westford.
September 20, Joseph V. Wright, Lucy L. Blood, Townsend.
December 2, Rufus Patten, Sarah B. Hall, Westford.
1837. October 10, Jacob A. Wright, Harriet A. Leighton, Westford.
1838. November 23, Joseph Hildreth, 2nd, Sarah Brown, Westford.
1839. May 30, Jonas Prescott, Martha W. Cumings, Westford.
November 28, Sherman D. Fletcher, Emily A. Fletcher, Westford.
1840. January 23, Thomas Richardson, Mary Fletcher, Westford.
May 7, Benjamin F. Adams, Chelmsford, Frances E. Leighton, Westford.
December 29, Geo. Farwell, Lucia Kilburn, Westford.
1841. March 23, Charles Gould, Eliza Ann Trowbridge, Westford.
September 16, Ira G. Richardson, Sarah Dix Hamlin, Westford.
October 31, Amos Bancroft, M. D., Groton, Mary Kneeland, Westford.
1842. March 20, Ebenezer R. Whitney, Newton, Sarah F. Leighton, Westford.
August 24, Hon. John Scott, Detroit, Mich., Jane Abbot, Westford.
December 29, Olvin F. Raymond, Littleton, Julia Ann Prescott, Westford.
1843. April 6, Liberty C. Raymond, Boxborough, Sarah Ann Spaulding, Tyngsborough.
1844. April 4, Trueworthy Heywood, Catharine Richardson, Westford.

BY JEREMIAH HILDRETH, JUSTICE OF THE PEACE.

1809. April 2, Silas Merriam, Polly Abbot, Westford.
May 20, Seth Fletcher, Jr., Sally Proctor, Westford.
August 10, Joel Hunter, Chelmsford, Lucy Read, Westford.
1810. April 1, Samuel Scott, Sally Wetherbee, Westford.

BY JOHN ABBOT, JUSTICE OF THE PEACE.

1813. September 12, Isaiah Spaulding, Patty Byam, Chelmsford.

BY EPHRAIM RANDALL, MINISTER.

1829. June, Ebenezer Tidd, Mrs. Parmelia Trowbridge, Westford.
November, Samuel H. Nichols, Nancy E. Fletcher, Westford.
November, Nathan S. Hamblin, Harriet Fletcher, Westford.
November, William W. Goodhue, Rebecca A. Fletcher, Westford.
1830. Samuel Richardson, Jr., Olive Prescott, Westford.

STATISTICAL AND OFFICIAL. 397

BY JOSEPH WRIGHT, MINISTER.

1834. March 13, Jonathan Wheeler, Acton, Mary Angeline Baker, Westford.

BY W. B. KITTREDGE, PASTOR.

1835. April 2, Chas. P. Kidder, Mrs. Mary Ann Kidder, Westford.

BY NATHANIEL LAWRENCE, MINISTER.

1834. September 7, Samuel Spalding, Tyngsborough, Mary Ann Wright, Westford.
1835. April 15, Asa Robbins, Townsend, Anna Wright, Westford.
November 11, Ephraim Buttrick, Dunstable, Lydia Fletcher, Westford.

BY LUTHER WILSON, PASTOR.

1837. Capt. Henry A. Prescott, Mary M. Fletcher, Westford.
November 28, Luther Prescott, Olive Prescott, Westford.
November 30, Walter Wright, Hannah Webber, Westford.
1838. February 8, Joseph Leland, Louisa Read, Westford.
July 4, Francis J. Barrett, Nancy Bemis, Westford.

BY J. W. PARKIS, PASTOR.

1837. May 25, James R. Davis, Chelmsford, Civonia Adams, Westford.

BY ABEL C. THOMAS, MINISTER.

1841. May 30, Peter B. Prescott, Lowell, Zibiah Richardson, Westford.

BY SAMUEL RIPLEY, MINISTER.

1844. April 21, Samuel W. Hosley, Mary Ann Laws, Westford.

BY TRUEWORTHY KEYES, JUSTICE OF THE PEACE.

1844. April 2, Chas. L. Fletcher, Sophia M. Keyes, Westford.

BY E. PORTER DYER, PASTOR.

1842. November 10, Francis Leighton, Westford, Mrs. Almira Casanas, Stow.

BY JOHN ALBRO, PASTOR.

1829. February 18, Stephen Richardson, Lowell, Betsey Patten, Westford.

BY OLIVER PRESCOTT, JUSTICE OF THE PEACE.

1796. August 29, Dr. Amos Bancroft, resident in Westford, Abigail Whiting, Hollis.

BY WILLIAM LAWRENCE, JUSTICE OF THE PEACE.

1751. May 22, Preserved Leonard, Springfield, Sarah Keep, Westford.

BY DR. HAVEN, AT PORTSMOUTH, N. H.

1770. September 9, Benjamin Whiting, Grace Hall, Westford.

FROM REPORT OF TOWN CLERK OF ACTON.

1741. November 12, Daniel Fletcher, Acton, Sarah Hartwell, Westford.
1742. May 14, Mark White, Acton, Anna Chamberlain, Westford.
1768. May 7, Joseph Keyes, Westford, Ruth Forbush, Acton.
1778. June 16, Smith Foster, Westford, Esther Sartell, Acton.
1794. June 26, Josiah Noyes, Acton, Hetty White, Westford.

FROM REPORT OF TOWN CLERK OF ANDOVER.

1742. June 28, Moses Chandler, Westford, Dorothy Marble, resident in Andover; by Rev. Samuel Phillips.
1745. November 26, Dea. Andrew Spalding, Westford, Mrs. Mehitable Crosby, Andover; by Rev. Samuel Phillips.
1783. May 15, Wiley Richardson, Westford, Frances Poor, Andover; by Rev. William Symmes.

FROM REPORT OF TOWN CLERK OF ASHBURNHAM.

1796. April 20, Lyman Fletcher, Westford, Lois Gates, Ashburnham; by Rev. John Cushing.
1797. March 12, Elijah Prescott, Westford, Eunice Walker, Ashby; by Rev. John Cushing.

FROM RECORDS OF BILLERICA.

1754. August 8, Ebenezer Fletcher, Westford, Joanna Stearns, Billerica; by Rev. John Chandler.
1765. August 20, David Rumrie, Westford, Priscilla Corey, Chelmsford; by William Stickney, Esq.
1789. October 13, Levi Snow, Lucy Fletcher, Westford; by Isaac Stearns, Esq.

FROM RECORDS OF BOLTON.

1788. December 15, Reuben Chaffin, Westford, Eunice Walcott, Bolton; by Rev. Phineas Wright.

FROM RECORDS OF BOXFORD.

1764. November 27, Lieut. John Robinson, Westford, Mrs. Huldah Perley.

FROM RECORDS OF CARLISLE.

1785. November 17, Nathan Wheeler, Carlisle, Ruth Hunt, Westford; by Paul Litchfield.

1791. September 11, Thomas Heald, Carlisle, Abi Hildreth, Westford; by Asa Parlin, Justice of the Peace.
1793. July 4, David Davis, Acton, Polly Hildreth, Westford; by Asa Parlin, Esq.
1794. September 18, Asa Barker, Chelmsford, Sally Foster, Westford; by Asa Parlin, Esq.
1795. January 1, Jacob Robbins, Westford, Annis Taylor, Hollis; by Asa Parlin, Esq.

FROM RECORDS OF CHARLESTOWN.

1756. January 12, Oliver Proctor, Eliza Proctor, Westford; by Thomas Jenner, Justice of the Peace.
1769. April 13, Thomas Richardson, Abigail Reed, Westford; by Isaac Rand, Esq., Justice of the Peace.
1774. November 30, Willard Read, Olive Minot, Westford; by Isaac Rand, Esq., Justice of the Peace.
1798. May 18, Abel Boynton, Polly Pierce, Westford; by Josiah Bartlett, Esq.

FROM RECORDS OF CHELMSFORD.

1681. March 1, Joseph Wheeler, Nashobah (supposed Westford), Mary Powers, Nashobah.
1786. January 26, John Spaulding, 3rd, Lucy Fletcher, Westford; by Abisha Crossman, pastor of Baptist Church.
1799. February, Zaccheus Wright, Westford, Abigail Hildreth; by Rev. Hezekiah Packard.

FROM CHURCH RECORDS, BY REV. EBENEZER BRIDGE.

1753. March 14, Samuel Hildreth, Westford, Sarah Proctor.
June 11, Ebenezer Hadley, Westford, Abigail Spaulding.
1754. September 19, Daniel Keyes, Westford, Abigail Proctor.
1759. November 1, Isaac Chandler, Westford, Betty Proctor.
1760. November 25, Josiah Spaulding, Westford, Esther Adams.
1761. January 22, Jonathan Fletcher, Westford, Sarah Spaulding.
May 28, Joshua Snow, Lois Hildreth, Westford.
1764. January 5, Zaccheus Wright, Westford, Rachel Parker.
July 19, Simeon Stevens, Elizabeth Wright, Westford.
1767. February 12, Zebulon Spalding, Lydia Wright, Westford.
July 2, Jonah Blood, Westford, Tabitha Corsey.
1769. January 16, Ebenezer Emery, Agnes Proctor, Westford.
1771. March 26, Silas Pierce, Lucy Spaulding.
1773. March 11, Nathaniel Cowdry, Westford, Rebecca Parker.
1773. November 25, Ephraim Cumings, Westford, Lydia Adams.
1775. December 26, Willard Fletcher, Abigail Hadley.
1780. February 8, Jacob Chamberlin, Ruth Hall, Westford.

FROM RECORDS OF CHELSEA.

1776. October 8, Asaph Fletcher, Westford, Sarah Green, Chelsea; by Rev. Phillips Payson.

FROM RECORDS OF CONCORD.

1731-'32. March 7, Samuel Minot, Concord, Sarah Prescott, Westford; by Justice James Minot.

1734. October 24, Ezekiel Proctor, Westford, Elizabeth Chamberlin, Chelmsford; by Justice Flint.

1735. September 23, Zachariah Fletcher, Susanna Fasset, Westford; by Justice Flint.

1737. May 30, Joseph Read, Ruth Underwood, Westford; by Justice Flint.

1739. October 29, Isaac Patch, Joanna Butterfield, Westford; by Justice Flint.

December 6, Thomas Prescott, Sarah Robbins, Westford; by Justice Minot.

1740. December 25, Jonas Prescott, Westford, Rebecca Barrett, Concord; by Rev. D. Bliss.

1743. April 3, William Hunt, Concord, Elizabeth Hildreth, Westford; by Justice Flint.

1769. March 21, Samuel Keyes, Molly Davis, Acton; by John Cumings, Esq.

October 31, Solomon Wheat, Hannah Richardson, Westford; by Thomas Whiting, Esq.

1770. January 7, John Hill, Acton, Sarah Harris, Westford; by John Cumings, Esq.

October 9, Samuel Gilbert, Littleton, Elizabeth Robbins, Westford; by John Cumings, Esq.

November 20, John Pushee, Acton, Lucy Blodgett, Westford; by J. Cumings, Esq.

1774. January 9, Nathan Proctor, Westford, Lydia Robbins, Chelmsford; by J. Cumings, Esq.

1775. May 23, Samuel White, Westford, Hepsibah Barrett, Concord; by Rev. William Emerson.

1777. September 3, Jonathan Minot, Westford, Hánnah Eastman, Hollis; by Justice Cumings.

1778. November 3, Thomas Mead, Westford, Sarah Porter, Concord; by Ephraim Wood, Esq.

1783. May 30, Benjamin Reed, Templeton, Olive Robbins, Westford; by Justice Barrett.

1785. November 16, Nathan Wheeler, Carlisle, Ruth Hunt, Westford; by Justice Cumings.

1786. June 28, Ephraim Chamberlin, Westford, Persis Barrett, Concord; by Rev. Ezra Ripley.

1790. December 28, Nathaniel Boynton, Westford, Anna Barrett, Concord; by Rev. Ezra Ripley.

1791. December 29, Thomas Dugan (colored), Concord, Cate Porter, Westford; by Rev. Mr. Ripley.

FROM RECORDS OF DUNSTABLE.

1783. December 11, Jeremiah Fletcher, Westford, Elizabeth Perham, Dunstable; by Joel Parkhurst, Justice of the Peace.

STATISTICAL AND OFFICIAL. 401

FROM CHURCH RECORDS OF DUNSTABLE.

1759. May 29, Samuel Perham, Westford, Mary French, Dunstable.
1760. May 16, Ezekiel Proctor, Jr., Westford, Elizabeth Proctor, Dunstable.
1767. March 5, Benjamin Swallow, Dunstable, Joanna Spalding, Westford.
1767. November 19, Abel Spalding, Dunstable, Lydia Powers, Westford.
1773. February 10, David Bixby, Westford, Alice Haywood, Dunstable.

FROM RECORDS OF DRACUT.

1771. March 7, Reuben Parker, Westford, Sarah Kimball, Dracut.
1792. December 12, Peleg Gardner, Westford, Anna Lue, Dracut; by Solomon Aiken, pastor of Dracut.

FROM RECORDS OF GLOUCESTER.

1786. October 26, Nathan Proctor, Westford, Patience Leighton; by Rev. Eli Forbes.

FROM RECORDS OF GROTON.

1755. December 10, Timothy Steward, Esther Taylor, Westford; by Rev. Caleb Trowbridge.

BY REV. SAMUEL DANA.

1761. June 3, Henry Farwell, Groton, Sarah Taylor, Westford.
1765. November 26, John Pierce, Groton, Sarah ———, Westford.
1767. December 10, Thomas Smith, Westford, Hannah Saunders, Groton.
1768. November 19, John Woods, Jr., Westford, Hannah Goodhue, Groton.
1768. December 27, Samuel Parker, Jr., Groton, Rebecca Hunt, Westford.
1772. May 7, William Beles, Westford, Anna Wood, Groton.
1773. September 14, Peter Stone, Groton, Abigail Fasset, Westford.
1774. January 6, John Hadley, Jr., Westford, Ruth Kemp, Groton.
December 22, Joseph Prescott, Westford, Abigail Derumple, Groton.

BY REV. DANIEL CHAPLIN.

1778. May 7, Samuel French, Dunstable, Mary Johnson, Westford.
September 22, Jonathan Hall, Ashby, Beulah Bigelow, Westford.
1780. January 29, Ezra Prescott, Groton, Dolly Wright, Westford.
December 14, Jonas Hadley, Azubah Prescott, Westford.
1786. April 19, Joseph Keyes, Westford, Sarah Derumple, Groton.
1792. November 22, Philip Robbins, Westford, Ruth Pierce, Groton.
1795. February 16, Robert Wilkinson, Westford, Lydia Sawtell, Groton.
March 10, Abel Wright, Westford, Lefe Trowbridge, Groton.
December 20, Samuel Reed, Jr., Westford, Polly Fitch, resident in Groton.
1793. March 26, Asa Bixby, Jr., Westford, Lucy Gilson, Groton; by William Swan, Esq.

1796. August 29, Dr. Amos Bancroft, Westford, Abigail Whiting, Hollis; by Oliver Prescott, Jr., Esq.

FROM RECORDS OF HARVARD.

1769. December 23, Leonard Proctor, Westford, Mary Keep, Harvard.

FROM RECORDS OF LEXINGTON.

1763. November 3, Joseph Jewett, Littleton, Rebecca Abbot, Westford.

FROM RECORDS OF LINCOLN.

1754. February 17, Jeremy Underwood, Westford, Lucy Wheat, Lincoln.

FROM RECORDS OF LITTLETON.

1761. September 15, Isaac Spaulding, Westford, Susannah Lawrence, Littleton; by Daniel Rogers, minister.

1762. July 28, Jonathan Fletcher, Westford, Mary Lawrence, Littleton; by Rev. Daniel Lawrence.

1768. February 17, Nathaniel Farr, Littleton, Abigail Foster, Westford; by J. Dummer Rogers, Justice of the Peace.

1769. November 8, Simon Lawrence, Littleton, Sibel Robbins, Westford; by J. Dummer Rogers, Justice of the Peace.

1771. October 31, Jeremiah Cogswell, Littleton, Sarah Fletcher, Westford; by Rev. Daniel Rogers.

1773. March 3, John Sterns, Littleton, Martha Cleveland, Westford; by Jeremiah D. Rogers, Justice of the Peace.

1774. January 20, Ebenezer Prescott, Westford, Lydia Wood, Littleton; by Rev. Daniel Rogers.

1779. February 25, Josiah Fletcher, Margaret Fletcher, Westford; by Jonathan Reed, Justice of the Peace.

1780. May 11, Ezra Jewett, Littleton, Rebecca Dutton, Westford; by Jonathan Reed, Justice of the Peace.

1781. September 27, Daniel Raymond, Jr., Naomi Leighton, Westford; by Jonathan Reed, Justice of the Peace.

1782. June 18, David Parker, Martha Carver, Westford; by Jonathan Reed, Justice of the Peace.

1783. July 15, Timothy Adams, Lydia Robbins, Westford.

1786. October 22, Henry Durant, Littleton, Mary Percy, Westford.

1788. November 20, Reuben Leighton, Hannah Hildreth, Westford.

1789. February 24, Sampson Tuttle, Hancock, N. H., Sarah Fletcher, Westford; by Rev. Edmund Foster.

1790. November 25, Samuel Fassett, Westford, Rebecca Powers, Littleton.

1791. May 7, Thomas Brooks, Jr., Billerica, Esther Hildreth, Westford; by Sampson Tuttle, Justice of the Peace.

1797. December 28, Joseph Bayley, Lydia Tilden, Westford; by Rev. Edmund Foster.

STATISTICAL AND OFFICIAL.   403

1799. September 28, Thomas Hartwell, Littleton, Caroline Reed, Westford; by Sampson Tuttle, Justice of the Peace.
Benjamin Prescott, Polly Reed, Westford.

FROM CHURCH RECORDS.
(By what official unknown.)

1734–'35. March 4, Ezra Jewett, Littleton, Mary Herrick, Westford.
1737. May 5, Samuel Lawrence, Littleton, Mary Hildreth, Westford.
1740. August 3, Jabez Keep, Westford, Experience Lawrence, Littleton.
August 12, Robert Proctor, Jr,, Littleton, Elizabeth Reed, Westford.
September 23, Benjamin Blanchard, Littleton, Hannah Keys, Westford.
1745. October 2, William Tenny, Littleton, Sarah Proctor, Westford.
1755. February 20, Thomas Cummings, Westford, Lucy Lawrence, Littleton.
1775. December 17, Lewis Farr, Littleton, Eunice Hadley, Westford.
1779. January 29, Allen Stevens, Molly Berry, Westford.
1779. July 13, Francis Kidder, Westford, Abigail Russell, Littleton.
1798. November 27, John Cumings, Westford, Lois Tuttle, Littleton.

FROM RECORDS OF LUNENBURG.

1798. May 31, Stephen Nichols, Westford, Rebecca Hilton, Lunenburg; by Rev. Zabdiel Adams.

FROM RECORDS OF MEDFORD.

1762. June 22, Capt. William Fletcher, Wid. Susanna Fletcher, Westford; by Stephen Hall, Esq.

FROM RECORDS OE MEDWAY.

1739. June 15, Jonathan Underwood, Westford, Hannah Richardson, Medway; by Mr. Buckman.

FROM RECORDS OF PEPPERELL.
BY REV. JOSEPH EMERSON.

1759. August 15, Thomas Heald, Westford, Elizabeth Boynton, Pepperell.
1773. October 5, Josiah Conant, Pepperell, Lydia Prescott, Westford.

BY REV. JOHN BALLARD.

1783. August 7, Eleazer Heald, Westford, Elizabeth Lawrence, Pepperell.
1794. February 5, John Proctor, Westford, Rachel Shedd, Pepperell.
1795. January 8, Moses Thomas, Westford, Becca Cumings, Dunstable.

FROM RECORDS OF READING.

1762. February 1, Thomas Smith, Jr., Westford, Elizabeth Walton, Reading.

FROM RECORDS OF SCITUATE.

1799. September 1, Rogers King, Westford, Polly Tilden, Scituate; by Rev. Nehemiah Thomas.

FROM RECORDS OF SHIRLEY.

1789. April 21, John Hildreth, Westford, Ruth Bicknell, Shirley; by Rev. P. Whitney.

FROM RECORDS OF SHREWSBURY.

1773. June 24, Abner Miles, Shrewsbury, Deborah Underwood, Westford; by Rev. Joseph Sumner.

FROM RECORDS OF STOWE.

1789. October 7, Jacob Gilson, Stowe, Hannah Hardy, Westford; by Jonathan Wood, Justice of the Peace.

FROM RECORDS OF TOPSFIELD.

1779. December 16, Rev. Matthew Scribner, Westford, Sarah Porter, Topsfield.

FROM RECORDS OF TOWNSEND.

1757. December 22, Jonathan Crosby, New Ipswich, Julia Chandler, Westford; by Rev. Phineas Hemenway.

BY REV. SAMUEL DIX.

1764. April 3, Stephen Hildreth, Westford, Esther Manning, Townsend.
1772. May 20, James Hildreth, Townsend, Esther Fletcher, Westford.
1777. May 7, Joseph Spaulding, Westford, Jemima Shattuck, Pepperell.
September 1, Zachariah Hildreth, Elizabeth Keyes, Westford.
1785. December 25, James Proctor, Esther Wright, Westford.

FROM RECORDS OF TYNGSBOROUGH.

1791. August 18, Thaddeus Davis, Dunstable, Bridget Wright, Westford; by Rev. Nathaniel Lawrence.
1796. June 6, Grant Houston, Tyngsborough, Patty Fletcher, Westford.

FROM RECORDS OF WINCHENDON.

1779. May 27, David Foster, Elizabeth Minot, Westford; by Rev. Joseph Brown.

MARRIAGE INTENTIONS.

In the copying of the following list, the aim has been to give the names of parties whose marriage record cannot be found on the books, and of such parties only. In the record of families it is often extremely difficult to ascertain the full maiden name of the mother, or to determine the date of her marriage. But by turning to the list of intentions the family name is often found and the proximate date of the marriage. In some cases there is no record of intention, or of marriage.

1730. August 16, Ebenezer Spalding and Mary Craft.
November 1, Oliver Spalding and Sarah Read.
November 22, Henry Barton, Littleton, and Sarah Bell.
1730-'31. February 19, Samuel Stevens, Chelmsford, and Ruth Wright.
February 28, William Fletcher and Elizabeth Remington.
March 7, Jonas Prescott and Elizabeth Harwood.
1731. September 14, Ephraim Fletcher and Hannah Roe.
November 6, Benjamin Hildreth and Lydia Fasset.
November 13, Benjamin Perham and Esther Butterfield.
1731-'32. Samuel Minot and Sarah Prescott.
January 8, Benjamin Chamberlin and Esther Fasset.
January 30, Samuel Chamberlin and Mrs. Sybil Roper, Marlborough.
1732. April 3, Samuel Fitch and Joanna Kidder.
October 27, Timothy Read and Marah Comings.
November 18, Samuel Read and Abigail Comings.
1732-'33. January 3, Thomas Wright and Elizabeth Park.
January 20, Benjamin Blodgett and Elizabeth Fletcher.
1733. March 28, Josiah Spalding, Chelmsford, and Marah Fletcher.
April 26, Gershom Fletcher and Lydia Townsend.
June 28, Benjamin Robbins and Anna Johnson, Harvard.
August 7, Zachariah Sartle, Groton, and Abigail Bixby.
August 10, Thomas Cummings and Sarah Fasset.
1734. April 19, Samuel Adams, Chelmsford, and Esther Fletcher.
May 8, Ezekiel Proctor and Elizabeth Chamberlin.
May 11, James Pollard and Abigail Chamberlin.
June 22, Stephen Shattuck, Littleton, and Elizabeth Robbins.
July 12, William Cummings and Lucy Colburn, Dunstable.
1734-'35. January 10, Jonather Fletcher and Jane Chamberlin.
March 5, Joseph Fletcher and Elizabeth Underwood.
1735. August 29, Samuel Craft and Margaret Richardson.
September 6, Zachariah Fletcher and Susanna Fasset.
September 13, Nathaniel Boynton and Elizabeth Shedd, Billerica.
September 20, Joseph Dutton and Rebecca Adams, Chelmsford.
December 6, Aaron Parker, Jr., and Marah Barrett, Chelmsford.
1736. May 15, Richard Hildreth, and Hannah Wright.
September 18, James Spalding and Amy Underwood.
November 11, Philip Woodard, Dunstable, and Lydia Adams.
November 26, Samuel Searls, Dunstable, and Mary Butterfield.
December 1, John Read and Abigail Butterfield.
December 28, Charles Richardson, Oxford, and Mary Roper.

1737. April 9, Josiah Butterfield and Hannah Farnsworth, Harvard.
May 3, Joseph Read and Ruth Underwood.
1737-'38. March 17, Aaron Parker, Jr., and Dorothy Fletcher.
1738. November 11, David Brown and Hannah Bixby.
November 24, Obadiah Jenkins, Wilmington, and Lydia Bixby.
January 6, Samuel Parker and Sarah Fletcher.
1739. November 24, Joshua Preston, Littleton, and Agnes Peacock.
1740. November 22, Samuel Hosley, Billerica, and Elizabeth Keep.
1741. June 12, Henry Willard, Lancaster, and Sarah Procter.
July 18, Thomas Kidder and Elizabeth Wheeler, Littleton.
October 2, Samuel Comings and Sarah Spalding, Chelmsford.
1742. November 11, David Fletcher and Mary Butterfield, Chelmsford.
1744. October 13, Samuel Blodgett and Sarah Spencer, Groton.
1745. May 4, Reuben Fletcher and Susanna Chandler.
January 11, Eleazer Heald, Concord, and Elizabeth Barrett.
February 15, Timothy Fletcher, Jr., and Bridget Richardson, Chelmsford.
1746. April 12, Elias Foster, Jr., and Abigail Wheeler, Acton.
May 3, Ebenezer Park, Groton, and Sarah Wright.
May 10, Samuel Barrett and Rebekah Dutton.
November 29, Benjamin Hadley and Sarah Adams, Lexington.
February 21, Thomas Read, Jr., and Olive Howard, Chelmsford.
1747. September 18, Nathaniel Lawrence, late of Woburn, and Bathsheba Butterfield.
November 12, Ephraim Chandler and Wid. Abigail Blood, Groton.
1747-'48. March 5, Benjamin Nutting, Medford, and Anna Brooks.
1749. September 9, Deliverance Davis, Acton, and Hannah Hildreth.
October 28, Joseph Jenkins, Wilmington, and Sarah Barron.
November 25, Jacob Robbins and Lydia Heald, Acton.
1750. June 20, Philip Robbins and Anna Minot, Chelmsford.
October 5, Clode Dupay and Sarah Wrise. (Wright?)
February 16, Jonas Prescott, Jr., and Rebecca Parker, Groton.
1751. March 29, John Glene, Dunstable, and Thankful Adams.
May 5, John Robbins and Sarah Davis, Acton.
October 27, Joseph Swallow, Dunstable, and Esther Robbins.
November 23, Nathaniel Boynton and Rebecca Barrett.
1752. December 9, David Prescott and Abigail Wright.
1753. January 13, Henry Wright, Jr., and Sarah Spalding.
January 20, Enoch Cleaveland, Jr., Chelmsford, and Martha Butterfield.
August 25, Ephraim Hildreth, 3rd, and Elizabeth French, Hollis.
November 24, Benjamin Hildreth and Eunice Willis.
December 22, Charles Eames, Leominster, and Hannah Robbins.
1754. March 23, John Nutting and Hannah Read.
August 17, John Rider and Susanna Winslow.
1755. February 1, James Blodgett and Abigail Keyes.
June 28, Joshua Fletcher and Elizabeth Raymond.
June 28, Josiah Nutting and Kezia Butterfield.
October 25, James Tarbell, Pepperell, and Esther Fletcher.

STATISTICAL AND OFFICIAL.   407

1756. April 17, Asa Bixby and Susanna Howard.
April 24, Nathan Procter and Mehitable Varnum, Dracut.
December 3, Samuel Adams and Elizabeth Blood.
1757. January 15, Clark Brown, Harvard, and Lucy Davis.
March 19, Joseph Chamberlin and Anna Davis, Acton.
April 15, David Procter, Acton, and Lydia Hildreth.
October 15, Jonah Crosby, New Ipswich, and Lydia Chandler.
October 29, William Sweetser, Reading, and Lydia Smith.
1758. February 16, Joshua Atwood and Esther Chamberlin, Chelmsford.
May 27, Joshua Read and Mary Spalding.
July 28, Samuel Parker and Hannah Fletcher.
October 28, Simeon Fletcher and Rachel Fletcher.
1759. February 3, Benjamin Spalding, Dorchester, Canada, and Sarah Chandler.
July 7, Oliver Fletcher and Olive Procter.
July 14, Elijah Robbins, Dunstable, and Lucy Adams.
1760. March 29, Zaccheus Barrett, Narragansett, No. 6, and Elizabeth Sprague.
March 29, Caleb Wright and Elizabeth Cleaveland, Acton.
April 25, Phinehas Byham, Narragansett, No. 6, and Tabitha Chamberlin.
June 14, Isaac Patch and Elizabeth Avery.
September 6, Leonard Procter and Lydia Nutting.
1761. January 3, Zachariah Willis and Abigail Russell, Acton.
May 30, Amaziah Hildreth and Ruth Read.
August 22, Zechariah Fletcher and Eunice Keep.
November 21, William Hartwell and Abigail Stratton, Concord.
1762. April 10, Philip Spaulding and Elizabeth Obert, Acton.
April 10, Lieut. Joseph Boynton and Sarah Tarbel, Groton.
December 11, Abel Wright, New Ipswich, and Eunice Wright.
December 24, Josiah Spaulding and Lydia Cleaveland, Acton.
1763. January 16, Thomas Fletcher and Wid. Sarah Hildreth.
February 5, Charles Lawrence and Naomi Stone.
March 4, Eleazer Dows, Billerica, and Lucy Proctor.
March 26, Thomas Mead and Lucy Read.
April 16, William Hildreth and Dorothy Parker.
July 8, Aaron Parker, Jr., and Lucy Hildreth.
November 15, Zaccheus Wright and Rachel Parker, Chelmsford.
December 15, John Phillips, Cambridge, and Lydia Kemp.
1764. January 6, Joseph Spalding, Westminster, and Bridget Crosby.
January 14, Silas Wright and Mary Craft.
May 5, Capt. Joseph Fletcher and Wid. Kezia Nutting.
May 25, William Barrett and Abigail Cowdry.
October 20, John Jewell, Chelmsford, and Margaret Parret.
November 28, Nathan Hawley, New Milford, Conn., and Sara Kent.
1766. June 21, Benjamin Green, Groton, and Ruth Keep.
July 25, Ezekiel Fletcher, Groton, and Bridget Parker.
September 4, Zebulon Spalding, Jr., and Lydia Wright.

1766. September 27, Benjamin Swallow, Dunstable, and Joanna Spaulding.
1767. February 14, Samuel Craft and Margaret Parrot.
June 20, David Fish and Sarah Barron, Acton.
September 3, Henry Adams, Dunstable, Edie Adams.
December 5, Joseph Keyes, and Ruth Furbush, Acton.
1768. August, Amos Hardy and Lydia Stratton.
November 5, William Proctor, Chelmsford, and Mary Proctor.
November 12, Joshua Fassett and Sarah Priest, New Ipswich.
1769. July 8, John Abbot, Jr., and Lucy Proctor, Chelmsford.
October 28, Peter Larkin, Boston, and Wid. Hannah Cowdry.
November 18, James Fletcher and Rebecca Prescott.
November 25, Leonard Reed and Bethiah Herrick.
1770. June 23, Joseph Tuker, New Ipswich, and Rebecca Wyman.
July 14, Thomas Beal and Molly Kimble, New Ipswich.
September 4, Parker Emerson, Chelmsford, and Rebecca Pollard.
September 15, Samuel Gilburd, Littleton, and Elizabeth Robbins.
1771. February 26, Silas Pearce, Chelmsford, and Lucy Spaulding.
November 6, James Hildreth, Townshend, and Esther Fletcher.
1772. March 28, Joseph Farrar and Rebecca Wyman.
June 8, Jeremiah Barrit, Ashby, and Sarah Fletcher.
August 25, Simeon Sartill, Townshend, and Abigail Corey.
November 14, Josiah Kemp and Wid. Lydia Robinson.
November 27, David Bireby and Ellis Howard.
December 5, David Danforth, Camblin, N. H., and Hannah Proctor.
1773. August 20, Josiah Conant, Pepperell, and Lydia Prescott.
August 28, Thomas Wood, Littleton, and Sibyl Hildreth.
September 16, Josiah Heald, Concord, and Tryphena Corey.
November 8, Joseph Wright and Hannah Kemp.
November 12, John Fletcher and Elizabeth Perry.
1774. March 8, Joshua Parker and Hannah Kidder, Cambridge.
March 19, Thaddeus Read and Anna Sartle.
March 21, Benjamin Fletcher, Jr., and Rebekah Boynton.
April 11, Ezekiel Hildreth and Luce Robbins, Chelmsford.
May 14, Timothy Fletcher, Jr., and Huldah Pearly, Boxford.
July 5, Jonathan Carver and Mary Proctor.
July 30, Silas Biglow and Rachel Petts.
October 27, David Fletcher, Jr., and Joanna Stevens.
October 28, Henry Spaulding, Jr., Chelmsford, and Mary Fletcher.
1775. April 15, Thaddeus Gaffel, Weston, and Mary Barrett.
August 25, Ephraim Bixby and Martha Barker.
October 21, Stephen Patch, Ashby, and Thankful Bennett.
November 18, Jonas Holden and Sarah Read.
1776. January 13, Elijah Hildreth and Molly Read.
February 15, Simeon Barrett, Chelmsford, and Ruth Wright.
March 5, Timothy Comings and Katherine Fasset.
March 8, Jonathan Harwood, Chelmsford, and Mary Comings.
March 30, Isaac Parker and Sarah Hardy.

1776. April 6, Ephraim Heald and Sarah Hardy.
June 15, Amos Fletcher and Rebecca Prescott.
June 29, Asaph Fletcher and Sarah Green, Chelsea.
July 4, Phineas Chamberlin and Sibil Hildreth.
August 24, John Tidd and Rebecca Richardson.
September 5, William Bixby and Lydia Farrington.
November 16, John Prescott and Martha Hildreth.
December 17, Philip Smith and Frances Bacon. (?)
December 20, Benjamin Huckins, Putney, N. Y., and Sarah Richardson.

1777. March 15, Timothy Hildreth and Hannah Hildreth.
April 18, Matthew Griffin, Pepperell, and Wid. Mary Adams.
June 26, Samuel Fletcher, Jr., and Lucy Jones, Concord.
July 5, Calvin Blanchard and Abigail Read.
October 10, Henry Richardson and Wid. Lucy Wright.
November 1, Ebenezer Parker, and Wid. Experience Hildreth.

1778. February 4, Joel Esterbrooks and Abigail Underwood, Chelmsford.
February 5, John Crice (?), Littleton, and Abigail Blodgett.
February 28, Ensign Josiah Fletcher and Margaret Fletcher.
February 28, Dr. Charles Proctor and Edie Carver.
April 18, Jonathan Hall, Ashby, and Beulah Biglow.
April 18, Samuel French, Dunstable, and Mary Johnson.
May 6, Samuel Dutton and Wid. Rhoda Bacon.
May 30, Smith Foster and Esther Sartel, Acton.
August 1, Samuel Read, Jr., and Elizabeth Raymond.
August 15, Dr. William Little and Betty Fletcher.
September 5, Thomas Meads and Sarah Foster.
October 31, Benjamin Osgood and Tryphena Comings.
November 17, Jonas Proctor and Lydia Brooks.
December 30, Jonathan Jones, Jr., Dracut, and Bethiah Fletcher.

1779. January 16, Thomas Comings, 3rd, and Elizabeth Hildreth.
January 21, Simeon Read and Sarah Comings.
February 6, Asa Shedd, Ashby, and Elizabeth Comings.
February 16, John Whitney and Mary Skiffington.
March 15, Eleazer Blood and Lydia Fletcher.
April 3, John Underwood and Mary Fasset.
April 6, Jeremiah Willard, Harvard, and Bethiah Prescott.
April 8, Stephen Read and Mary Derumple, Groton.
April 13, Oliver Read and Abigail Read.
June 3, Abijah Hildreth, Townsend, and Joanna Keyes.
June 26, Francis Kidder, Jr., and Abigail Russell, Littleton.
August 11, Moses Blanchard, Athol, and Azubah Blodgett.
August 14, Jonathan Hildreth and Eunice Warren.
August 20, Lieut. Moses Parker and Wid. Anna Barrett.
September 4, Willis Hall and Mehitable Pool, Hollis.
December 8, Stephen Wright and Sarah Carter, Hollis.

1780. January 18, Daniel Osgood, Littleton, and Lucy Comings.
February 11, Thomas Robbins and Bridget Wright.

1780. February 12, Samuel Richardson, Methuen, and Lucy Parker.
February 22, Samuel Hale, Stowe, and Molly Parlin.
April 24, Ezra Jewett, Groton, and Wid. Rebecca Dutton.
April 24, Amos Russell, Jr., and Wid. Hannah Foster.
December 2, Jeremiah Robbins and Elizabeth Keele.
1781. February 24, Jonathan Straton and Hepzibah Prentiss, Concord.
May 25, Josiah Esterbrooks and Molly Perry.
July, Jonas Blodgett and Sarah Fletcher.
August 4, Elnathan Read and Anna Prescott.
August 31, Thomas Nutting and Sibil Prescott.
August 31, Joshua Read, Jr., and Rebecca Wright.
1782. January 19, William Blaisdell and Lydia Robbins.
February 20, Solomon Fletcher and Abigail Melven.
March 23, William Munroe, Jr., Lexington, and Wid. Molly Rogers.
April 6, Abel Boynton and Molly Abbot.
April 8, Benjamin Pearce and Rebecca Wright.
July 6, Ezra Blodgett and Sarah Wright.
October 30, John Taylor, Stoddard, N. H., and Mary Blodgett.
1783. January 4, Levi Fletcher and Jerusha Morton, Athol.
January 24, Nathaniel Bowen and Wid. Lydia Bixby.
October 13, Asa Brown, New Ipswich, and Mary Hunt.
1784. April 4, Robert Spaulding and Hepsibah Ramond.
July 16, Henry Richardson and Wid. Ruth Bates.
September 11, Abraham Breising and Bridget Brown, Dunstable.
1785. January 1, Henry Blaisdell and Mary Robbins.
April 15, Eleazer Ames and Suza Wendall.
May 9, Lieut. Levi Parker and Mrs. Nabby Pool, Hollis.
October, Nathan Wheeler, Carlisle, and Ruth Hunt.
November 9, Pelatiah Fletcher, Jr., and Patty Keyes.
December 28, John Spaulding, 3rd, Chelmsford, and Lucy Fletcher.
1786. January 28, Ephraim Chamberlin, Jr., and Persis Barrett, Concord.
March 6, Joseph Keyes and Wid. Sarah Derumple.
August 19, Nathan Proctor and Patience Leighton, Gloucester.
September 8, Henry Durrent, Littleton, and Wid. Mary Perry.
1787. July 8, Jacob Abbot, Cavendish, Vt., and Molly Cumings.
September 26, William Chandler, Jr., and Joanna Read.
1788. February 9, Peter Robbins and Rachel Robbins, Dunstable.
November 8, Reuben Leighton and Hannah Hildreth.
December 6, Thomas Chamberlin and Polly Barritt, Ashby.
1789. January 8, Sampson Tuttle, Hancock, and Sarah Fletcher.
March 22, Jacob Gibson, Stowe, and Hannah Hardy.
March 29, John Hildreth and Wid. Ruth Bicknell.
May 3, Capt. Eleazer Hamlin, Harvard, and Wid. Hannah Fletcher.
July 8, Nehemiah Gilson, Dunstable, and Esther Keyes.
August 4, John Stearns, Chelmsford, and Lydia Crosby, Carlisle.
September 20, Levi Snow and Lucy Fletcher.
October 25, Joseph Rockwood, Jr., and Lucy Fletcher.

1790. March 1, Ebenezer Parker, New Ipswich, and Lydia Richardson.
June 11, Thomas Pike and Ruth Keyes.
July 10, Samuel Fasset and Rebecca Powers, Littleton.
October 24, Nathaniel Boynton, Jr., and Anna Barrit, Concord.
October 24, Rev. Ebenezer Hill and Molly Boynton.
1791. March 12, Capt. Aaron Parker and Joanna Fletcher.
March 26, Ebenezer Persons and Polly Swan.
November 16, James Prescott and Hannah Champney, New Ipswich.
1792. April 4, Phillip Robins and Wid. Ruth Peirce, Groton.
June 2, Lieut. Thomas Read and Molly Spaulding.
1793. May 15, Lieut. John Hildreth and Elizabeth Leighton.
June 20, David Davis, Acton, and Polly Hildreth.
September, John Proctor and Rachel Shedd, Pepperell.
1794. February 24, David Jones Nichols and Leah Levet, Hingham.
February 24, Jacob Robins and Annis Taylor, Hollis.
June 24, Jesse Barker, Chelmsford, and Sally Foster.
1795. April 8, James Chamberlin and Joanna Stevens Fletcher.
June 21, Ira Spaulding, Chelmsford, and Joanna Fletcher.
December 6, Nathaniel Hildreth, Cavendish, and Bridget Hildreth.
1796. January 14, Daniel Blood and Polly Perry.
May 5, Isaac Prescott and Lucy Hinckley.
October 20, Ensign Elias Parker and Dolly Fletcher.
October 20, Stephen Fletcher and Betty Hildreth.
December 7, Thomas Richardson and Polly Noice, East Sudbury.
1797. April, Seth Hildreth and Mehitable Hildreth.
July 24, Peter Hildreth and Bridget Comings.
August 14, Joseph Fletcher, Dunstable, and Wid. Abigail Read.
October 2, Joel Spaulding and Sylvia Lawrence, Ashby.
December 5, Daniel Read and Betsy Clenny.
December 17, Joseph Bailey and Lydia Tilden.
1798. March 18, Rogers King and Polly Tilden.
September 28, Jonas Barrett, Jr., Ashby, and Sarah Chamberlin.
October 6, Samuel Hastings and Arville Patch.
1799. June 10, Timothy Cummings, Jr., and Alice Ditson.
August 7, Bradford Norton, Williamsburg, and Mary Blood.
December 7, Joseph Perham, Tyngsborough, and Mary Nutting.
1800. May 25, Aaron White and Sally Griffin.
June 19, Levi Hildreth and Rebecca Hildreth.
June 19, Elisha Kent and Fanny Crouch, Littleton.
July 8, Joel Keyes and Polly Boyden.
August 22, John Hinckley and Ennis Warren, Littleton.
1801. February 23, Samuel Hilton, Sr., Lunenburg, and Nancy Braybrook.
September 15, Dr. Samuel Manning and Lucy Cogswell, Littleton
October 10, Ephraim Chamberlin and Sarah Howard, Chelmsford.
October 15, Joseph Tuttle, Littleton, and Mary Peirce.
November 12, Lieut. Abraham Prescott and Olive Adams, Chelmsford.

1802. January 18, Willard Richardson and Mary Griffin, Sudbury.
June 5, Imla Goodhue and Nancy Locke, Ashby.
June 20, Lemuel Hildreth and Molly Dutton.
August 14, Isaac Hamblin and Mary Walnut, Bolton.
October 3, Francis Leighton and Hannah Jones, Acton.
October 8, John Nutting and Eunice Peirse.
October 18, Silas Chandler and Mary Brown, Billerica.
November 24, Abel Hildreth and Ruth Hildreth.

1803. February 1, Joel Fletcher and Mary Stone.
February 6, James Wright and Wid. Sarah Tower, Carlisle.
September 2, Samuel Richardson and Amy Fletcher, Dunstable.
October 4, Joshua Adams and Anna Woods, Pepperell.

1804. January 30, Jonas Kemp, Jr., and Nancy Lawrence.
March 16, Joseph Heald, Carlisle, and Mary Procter.
July 15, Salathiel Patch and Polly Cummings.
October 7, James Cummings, Wilton, Me., and Edee Spalding.
October 20, David Patch, Littleton, and Susanna Parker.
December 22, Timothy Cummings, Jr., and Betsey Whitman, Groton.

1805. January 8, Jonas Kemp and Margaret Craft.
March 2, Peter Wyman, Pelham, and Hannah Nutting.
March 4, Reuben Leighton and Sally Wilson.
March 4, Samuel Fletcher, Jr., and Lydia Webber, Bedford.
March 4, Charles Stoddard and Fayette Turner, Pembroke.
April 8, Henry Butterfield and Betsey How, Hollis.
June 1, Jonas Nutting and Mary Spalding, Ashburnham.
June 4, Frederic Fausell, Salem, and Sally Read.
December 11, Samuel Read and Lois Brooks.

1806. January 2, John Blodgett and Mary Prescott, Groton.
February 17, Samuel Stearns and Amma Billash, Brookline.
February 27, William Griffin and Olive Read.
September 27, Sampson Klatter and Sally Gilman, Mason.
November 29, Elisha Fletcher and Abigail Wright, Littleton.

1807. January 9, Jonathan Emerson, Dunstable, and Rebecca Nutting.
July 2, Jacob Prescott and Bathsheba Dadmun, Framingham.
September 7, Joel Wright, and Sally Wright, Dunstable,
September 20, John Day Haywood, Boston, and Sophia Hinkley.
October 26, Jesse Reed and Nancy Pratt.

1808. February 15, Willard Fletcher, Jr., and Sally Spalding, Chelmsford.
March 26, James Searles and Betsey Peirce, Waltham.
April 22, Ephraim Heald, Jr., and Lydia Patch, Groton.
June 18, Eleazer Blood, Jr., and Betsey Parker.

1809. October 9, Ralph Nutting and Hannah Wright, Hollis.

1810. January 3, Charles Read and Beulah Gilson.
March 10, Capt. Joseph Read and Abigail Winn, Tewksbury.
October 19, Matthew Griffin and Sally Adams, Chelmsford.
November 3, Leonard Read, Jr., and Lucy Powers, Peterborough.

1811. January 13, Elias Sweetser and Mary Adams, Chelmsford.
May 30, Daniel Procter and Esther Spalding.

STATISTICAL AND OFFICIAL. 413

1811. June 23, Jonathan Snow and Sarah Parker.
September 20, Lemuel Lawrence, Chelmsford, and Polly Burge.
October 21, Isaac Patch and Hannah Dudley.
November 16, Obadiah Perry and Lavina Piper, Rindge.
November 16, John Pushee and Abigail Williams.
1812. December 11, Francis Kidder, Littleton, and Lydia Abbot.
1813. March 7, Joash Keyes and Mary Ann Le Grosse.
May 9, Nathan Davis, Boston, and Wid. Mary Carver.
June 13, Timothy Cummings and Elizabeth Farrar, Pepperell.
June 24, Roswell Read and Sybil Gilson, Groton.
September 5, Jonathan Snow and Sally Bohonon, New Chester, N. H.
1814. March 11, Jonas Wright and Anna Jones, Littleton.
May 29, Phinehas Wright and Betsey Whitcomb, Templeton.
1815. March 4, Joshua Fletcher and Lucy Jones, Ashburnham.
April 6, Joshua Fletcher Read and Betsey Fletcher, Ashburnham.
November 13, Avery Prescott and Betsey Capen, Leominster.
December 30, John Osgood and Sarah Perham, Chelmsford.

RECORD OF DEATHS.

1704. May 17, Sarah, daughter of Joshua and Dorothy Fletcher.
1706. November 17, Esther, daughter of Joshua and Dorothy Fletcher.
1723-'24. January 3, Aquila, son of Aquila Underwood, and Margaret, his wife.
1727. September 15, Joshua, son of Joshua and Dorothy Fletcher.
1729. December 24, Jonathan, son of Timothy and Hannah Barron.
1730. August 1, Peter Procter.
August 29, Samuel, son of Samuel and Hannah Fletcher.
September 3, Joanna, daughter of Samuel and Hannah Fletcher.
October 1, Esther, wife of Jonas Prescott.
October 12, Susanna, daughter of Samuel and Hannah Fletcher.
October 13, John Wright, late of Chelmsford.
1731. December 9, Hannah, wife of Benjamin Robins.
1731-'32. March 24, Sarah, wife of Josiah Heald.
1732. March 11, Elijah, son of Jonas and Elizabeth Prescott.
August 14, Josiah, son of Timothy and Rebecca Spalding.
October 19, Joshua Fletcher, deacon.
October 20, Thomas, son of Joseph and Susanna Underwood.
1733. May 6, Josiah Heald.
July 19, Sarah, wife of John White.
September 16, Mrs. Hannah Boynton, daughter of Joseph and Dorothy Perham.
1734. April 3, John, son of John and Abigail Cowdry.
April 11, Timothy, son of Timothy and Rebecca Spalding.
December or September 14, Ephraim, son of Jacob and Abigail Wright.
1735. August 16, Ebenezer, son of John Wright and his wife.
October 12, Dorothy, daughter of Samuel and Dorothy Hildrick.

1736. January 8, Dea. Paul Fletcher.
March 28, Sarah, wife of Samuel Craft.
October 14, Agnes, daughter of Joseph and Agnes Proctor.
October 17, Lydia Hildreth.
October 20, Olive Hildreth, daughter of James and Lydia Hildreth.
October 28, Ruth Hildreth, daughter of James and Lydia Hildreth.
December 3, Abigail, daughter of Jonathan and Jane Fletcher.

1736-'37. March 13, Susanna, daughter of Jonathan and Jane Fletcher.
March 15, Sarah, daughter of Thomas and Sarah Heald.
March 25, Hannah, daughter of Thomas and Sarah Heald.

1737. February 20, Mary, wife of Aaron Parker.
April 14, Sybil, daughter of Joseph and Agnes Proctor.
October 17, Elizabeth Hildreth, daughter of Ephraim and Mary Hildreth.
October 27, Thankful Hildreth, daughter of Ephraim and Mary Hildreth.

1738. January 4, Zechariah, son of Zechariah and Susanna Fletcher.
January 13, Susanna, daughter of Zechariah and Susanna Fletcher.
February 19, Jonathan, son of Ensign Jonathan and Sarah Hartwell.
September 17, Isaac, son of Jonas and Elizabeth Prescott.
October 5, Hannah, daughter of John and Hannah Abbott.

1738-'39. March 9, Sarah, wife of Jabez Keep.

1739. December 27, Elizabeth, wife of Jonas Prescott.

1740. May 7, Samuel, son of Samuel and Margaret Craft.

1741. February 14, Silas and Abel, sons of James Hildreth, Jr.
February 19, Thankful, daughter of James Hildreth, Jr.
March 30, Thomas Blodgett.
April 3, Benjamin, son of Jonas Prescott, Jr.
Joseph Butterfield, Jr.
November 2, Benjamin, son of Jacob and Abigail Wright.

1742. December 3, Sarah, daughter of William Fletcher, Jr., and Elizabeth, his wife.

1743. January 11, Sarah, wife of William Barrit.

1744. February 11, Hannah, wife of Andrew Spalding.
February 21, Lois, daughter of Jacob Taylor.
June 1, Dorothy, daughter of Moses and Dorothy Chandler.
June 11, Susanna, daughter of Moses and Dorothy Chandler
July 11, Joseph Keyes, Jr.

1745. September 9, Abel, son of Benjamin Butterfield.
October 11, James Hildreth, Jr., at Cape Breton.
October 16, Esther, daughter of Timothy Fletcher.

1746. June 24, Joseph, son of Ezekiel and Elizabeth Proctor.
October 12, Sarah, wife of Samuel Parker.

1747. August 2, Esther, daughter of Ezekiel and Elizabeth Proctor.

1748. July 17, Samuel, son of James Hildreth.
October 12, Susanna, daughter of James and Amy Spalding.

1749. February 17, Mary, wife of Jonas Prescott.
February 25, Lois, daughter of William Barrit.
October 2, John, son of Josiah and Susanna Burge.

1749. October 30, Samuel, son of Samuel Fletcher.
December 11, Sarah, daughter of Ezekiel Proctor.
1749–'50. January 24, Olive, daughter of William and Bathsheba Butterfield.
1750. April 17, Susanna, wife of Josiah Burge.
July 4, Josiah, son of Josiah Burge.
1751. December 10, Rebecca, daughter of Ensign Samuel and Mary Fletcher.
1752. March 6, Margaret, daughter of Ensign Samuel and Mary Fletcher.
March 20, Samson, son of Ensign Samuel and Mary Fletcher.
May 15, Sarah, daughter of Thomas Wright and Elizabeth, his wife.
May 22, Peter, son of Thomas and Elizabeth Wright.
October 9, Abraham, son of Ephraim Wright.
October 17, Silas, son of James and Ama Spalding.
1753. June 17, Joanna, daughter of Jonathan and Elizabeth Keyes.
June 17, Isaac, son of Moses and Bridget Parker.
July 3, Susanna, daughter of Jonathan and Jane Fletcher.
July 9, Wiley, son of Jonathan and Jane Fletcher.
July 11, Sarah, daughter of Josiah Burge.
July 17, Susanna, daughter of Moses and Dorothy Chandler.
July 25, Hannah, daughter of Simeon and Dorcas Wright.
July 28, Jane, daughter of Jonathan and Jane Fletcher.
August 1, Aaron, son of Jonathan and Elizabeth Keyes.
August 3, Thankful, daughter of Oliver and Sarah Spalding.
October 8, Joshua, son of John and Hannah Abbott.
1754. January 16, Joseph Proctor.
February 14, John, son of Joseph Dutton.
1755. January 20, Samuel son of Samuel and Abigail Read.
August 13, Lydia, daughter of Josiah and Lydia Brooks.
October 12, Timothy, son of Timothy and Mary Fletcher.
1756. April 24, Jesse, son of Timothy and Mary Fletcher.
June 30, Isaac, son of Aaron Parker, Jr.
October 16, Josiah Burge.
October 23, Robert Butterfield, late of Westford, died near Lake George.
1757. January 9, Joseph, grandfather of Jonathan Keyes.
July 27, Oliver Spalding.
September 29, Oliver Spalding, Jr., son of the above.
November 22, Mary, wife of Samuel Parker.
1758. March 31, Joanna, grandmother of Jonathan Keyes.
August 3, Stephen, son of Jonathan Keyes.
September 27, John, son of Thomas and Sarah Cummings.
October 11, Azubah, daughter of Simeon and Dorcas Wright.
December 12, Joel, son of Ebenezer and Deliverance Wright.
1759. April 27, Dea. John Comings.
April 30, Elizabeth, widow of Dea. John Comings.
September 14, Isaiah, son of Thomas and Elizabeth Kidder.
September 23, Esther, daughter of Timothy and Lydia Prescott.

1759. September 25, Timothy, son of Timothy and Lydia Prescott.
September 26, James, son of Samuel and Sarah Hildreth.
October 3, Samuel Hildreth.
October 21, Lucy, daughter of Timothy and Lydia Prescott.
December 4, Bethia, wife of Lieut. Timothy Spalding.
December 22, Reuben, son of Thomas and Elizabeth Wright.
1760. March 6, Anna, wife of Daniel Brooks.
April 11, Dorothy, wife of Moses Chandler.
September 6, Daniel, son of Timothy and Mary Fletcher, at Crown Point.
September 24, Abraham, son of William and Bathsheba Butterfield.
December 15, Elias Foster, Sr.
1761. January 24, Deliverance, widow of Dea. Paul Fletcher.
January 29, Joseph Underwood, aged 79 years.
February 25, James Hildreth.
April 12, Daniel, son of Daniel and Anna Brooks.
November 21, Jacob Wright, aged 65 years.
November 30, Abigail, wife of Jacob Wright, aged 65 years.
1762. February 4, Sarah, daughter of Ephraim and Abigail Wright.
March 30, Hannah, daughter of Josiah and Lydia Brooks.
September 30, Aaron Parker, Jr., aged 49 years.
December 1, William, son of Thomas Wright.
1763. March 30, Jonathan Keyes.
April 14, Timothy Spalding.
1764. November 17, Joseph Hildreth.
1767. John Read, aged 82 years.
1768. July 1, Mehitable, wife of Dea. Andrew Spalding.
1769. March 17, Daniel, father of Josiah Brooks.
December 10, Thomas Wright, aged 63 years.
1770. Annie, wife of James Spalding, aged 53 years.
October 22, Thomas Wright.
1771. Mary, wife of Joshua Parker.
April 13, Dea. Henry Wright, in his 72nd year.
Ebenezer Prescott, aged 71 years.
James Burn, in his 81st year. When he was 80 years of age he was baptized at his own house by Rev. Willard Hall.
1773. Dorothy, wife of Joseph Wright.
Luke Richardson, aged 28 years.
December 24, Thomas Read, Esq., in his 80th year.
1774. August 19, Capt. Jabez Keep, in Harvard.
David Prescott, aged 45 years.
William Blodgett, aged 50 years.
1775. September 5, Jonathan Spalding.
Ephraim Wright.
1776. Priscilla, wife of Henry Richardson, aged 63 years.
Mary, wife of Edward Bates, aged 78 years.
October 17, Lieut. Thomas Rogers, killed by the bursting of a cannon on Lake Champlain.
Ezra, son of Ezekiel Proctor, Jr., aged 15 years.

STATISTICAL AND OFFICIAL. 417

1777. February 8, Mrs. Ruth, wife of Capt. Joseph Read.
February 11, Joseph Wright, son of Joseph and Dorothy, at White Plains, in the army.
February 21, Ezekiel Proctor, Sr.
December 25, John Nutting, son of John and Hannah, at Albany, in the service of his country.
Samson, son of Capt. Joseph Read, aged 23 years.
1778. September 18, Joanna, wife of David Fletcher.
October 7, Lucy, daughter of Gershom Fletcher, Jr.
October 8, Jacob, son of Gershom Fletcher, Jr.
October 11, Gershom, son of Gershom Fletcher, Jr.
1779. Gershom Fletcher, Jr.
April 3, Joseph Minot Wright, son of Samuel and Esther Wright.
1780. Capt. Samuel Fletcher, aged 73 years.
Timothy Fletcher, aged 72 years.
Joseph Hildreth, aged 80 years.
1781. Susanna, wife of Lieut. Thomas Read.
1783. December 25, Hannah, daughter of Dea. John Abbot.
1784. Rebecca, wife of Levi Parker.
Capt. William Fletcher, aged 82 years.
Zachariah Hildreth, aged 58 years.
1785. February 22, Oliver Harris, son of Oliver and Mary.
William Butterfield, aged 80 years.
1787. May 10, Abigail Read, wife of Benjamin.
1788. August 7, Martha, wife of David Parker.
1789. Capt. Benjamin Fletcher, aged 72 years.
June 3, Esther, wife of Hezekiah Hildreth.
July 13, Simeon Wright, at New Ipswich.
October 20, Madam Abigail Hall.
1790. Richard Read.
1791. February 27, Ephraim Hildreth, Jr.
June 20, Oliver Read.
October 22, Dea. John Abbot, son of Joshua, of Billerica.
Nathan Ames.
1792. Amaziah Hildreth.
1793. Bathsheba, wife of William Butterfield.
William Butterfield, aged 58 years.
1794. Asa Nutting.
1795. Hannah, widow of Dea. John Abbot.
1796. David Keyes.
1797. July 12, Lieut. Moses Parker, aged 79 years.
1798. Ensign Nathaniel Boynton, aged 73 years.
Col. David Goodhue, aged 56 years.
Lydia Prescott, wife of Timothy.
1800. March 8, Richard Kneeland, drowned in Concord River.
September 15, Daniel Brooks.
1801. February 13, Lydia (Fitch), wife of Francis Leighton.
December 19, Polly, wife of Abram Prescott.
1802. January 26, Anne, wife of John Prescott, aged 21 years.

1803. January 1, Dea. Oliver Prescott, aged 77 years.
November 1, Hannah, wife of Dea. Reuben Leighton.
Patience Fish, pauper.
Nehemiah Fletcher, Jr.
1804. February 13, Elizabeth, wife of Isaac Cummings.
March 4, Mehitable, wife of Willis Hall.
July 17, Samuel, son of Francis Leighton.
Elizabeth Wilson, pauper.
Philip Robbins, pauper.
1805. April 19, Widow Catherine Fassett.
March 30, Rebecca, wife of Timothy Prescott.
January, Thankful, widow of William Read, aged 84 years.
Sarah Hildreth, pauper, aged 84 years.
1806. Francis Leighton, aged 72 years.
May 3, Betsey, wife of Isaiah Prescott.
May 9, Jonathan Keyes, aged 49 years.
April 12, Joel Abbot, aged 48 years.
Jonathan Minot, aged 83 years.
1807. February 23, Capt. Pelatiah Fletcher.
January, Jeremiah Temple, pauper.
1808. October 7, Stephen, son of John Prescott, aged 24 years.
1809. June 23, Jacob Wendell.
November 7, Hezekiah Hildreth, at St. Vincent, W. I.
James Proctor.
Samuel Craft.
1810. Abel Abbot.
Oliver Fletcher.
Nathaniel Adams.
Daniel Patch.

RECORDED BY DEA. REUBEN LEIGHTON.

1811. January 23, William, son of Rebecca Cummings, aged 3 years.
January 23, Ebenezer Prescott, aged 63 years.
January 24, Dolly, daughter of Nathaniel Hildreth, aged 10 years.
March 3, Josiah, son of Josiah Vose, aged 4 years.
March 7, Hannah, widow of Samuel Read, aged 81 years.
March 10, Mrs. Isaac Patch.
March 14, child of Solomon Woods, 5 weeks.
March 18, Amos Leighton, aged 21 years.
March 20, Zaccheus Wright, Esq., aged 72 years.
April 9, John Tidd, aged 59 years.
May 7, Pelatiah Fletcher, aged 44 years.
May 8, Lucy Parker, aged 20 years.
May 23, Mrs. John Pushee, aged 50 years.
May 27, Mitta Blodgett, aged 19 years.
June 8, Leonard Read, aged 61 years.
June 23, Thomas Patten, aged 21 years.
July 8, daughter of Thomas Read, aged 5 years.

1811. July 24, Jesse Patten, Jr., aged 26 years.
August 9, Philip Jackson.
August 11, Anna Clatter.
September 4, Benjamin Dutton, aged 92 years.
October 17, Jeremiah Robbins, aged 58 years.—Total, 23.
1812. January 13, Miss Whiting, aged 94 years.
January 15, Mrs. Brooks.
January 27, Mrs. Anna Wright.
February 2, Hartwell Hildreth, aged 23 years.
February 2, child of Levi Prescott.
March 24, Polly Wilkinson, aged 43 years.
April 12, Mrs. Sawtell, aged 22 years.
April 18, John Dutton, aged 51 years.
May 1, Mrs. Zachariah Hildreth, aged 77 years.
June 21, Aaron Blood, aged 73 years.
July 2, Seth Fletcher, aged 68 years.
July 22, child of Ebenezer Prescott.
August 5, Huldy Robinson, aged 70 years.
August 15, ———— Hinkley.
September 4, child of Mr. Sawtell.
September 8, Mrs. Ebenezer Prescott, aged 29 years.
October 15, Mrs. Timothy Cummings.
October 15, child of William W. Stephens.
November 14, child of David Johnson.
November 20, Mrs. Isaac Patch.
December 10, child of James Spalding.
December 12, child of Willard Fletcher.
December 18, Mrs. Elisha Kent.—Total, 23.
1813. January 6, Rev. Matthew Scribner.
January 7, Willard Fletcher.
January 9, Simeon Kemp.
February 2, Myma (Jemima) Fletcher.
February 8, child of Mr. Blake.
February 13, child of Elisha Kent.
February 27, Mrs. Sarah Johnson, aged 78 years.
March 10, child of Mrs. Norris, aged 4 years.
March 12, Peter Prescott.
March 23, Jonas Prescott, aged 80 years.
March 28, child of William W. Stevens.
April 1, Joseph Prescott.
April 3, Mrs. Thomas Fletcher, aged 76 years.
April 16, child of Joseph Wright.
April 22, Suky Symmes.
May 6, Widow Mary Reed.
May 23, Willis Hall.
June 9, Mrs. Dea. Amos Fletcher.
July 13, child of Capt. Timothy Cummings.
July 20, Thomas Fletcher, aged 92 years.
August 1, Clarissa Fletcher, aged 17 years.

1813. August 3, child of Asia Hamlin.
August 10, child of Capt. Timothy Cummings.
August 13, Mrs. Edea Carver, aged 38 years.
August 29, child of Joel Taylor.
August 30, sister of Lydia Hildreth, aged 45 years.
September 30, Mrs. Dorothy Hildreth.
December 14, Ebenezer Wythe.
December 14, Mrs. Kittredge.—Total, 31.

1814. January 7, Mrs. Shepard.
January 14, Mrs. Sarah Cogswell, aged 67 years.
January 14, child of David Prescott.
February 9, Willard Reed.
February 23, child of Mr. Hamlin.
March 15, Joseph Cummings, aged 77 years.
March 16, child of Asa Wright.
March 20, child of Capt. Joseph Reed.
March 20, child of Silas Merriam.
March 24, Abigail Wright, mother of Nathan, aged 84 years.
April 2, Abner Kent, aged 77 years.
April 7, Widow Phebe Proctor, aged 84 years.
April 27, child of Mr. Dadman.
May 4, Dick Reed.
May 18, Mrs. Beulah Fletcher.
May 25, Mrs. Stephens.
May 30, Lucy, daughter of Samuel Reed.
June 28, wife of Avery Prescott.
July 13, Mrs. Rogers King.
July 28, child of Mr. Scott.
August 12, child of Jacob Prescott.
September 25, child of Capt. Stoddard.
December 6, daughter of Lemuel Bicknell.
December 13, grandchild of Capt. Brown.
December 15, son of Nathaniel Dutton, aged 16 years.
December 16, John Parker.
December 18, Mrs. Nahum H. Groce.—Total, 27.

1815. February 16, child of Henry Fletcher.
February 20, child of Benjamin Hildreth.
February 20, daughter of Ebenezer Prescott.
February 21, child of Ebenezer Prescott.
February 23, child of Ebenezer Prescott.
February 26, Mrs. ——— Abbot.
February 26, ——— Prentice.
March 19, Mrs. Sarah Scribner, in Tyngsborough.
March 20, Lucy Green.
April 11, Jacob Abbot.
July 24, Sister Green.
August 25, Mrs. ——— Richardson.
August 29, Mrs. Phebe Stevens.
October 8, child of Asa Prescott.

1815. October 18, Mrs. Patty Osgood.
October 28, Mrs. Thomas Cummings.
October 31, child of Mr. Buttrick.
November 4, Mrs. Fletcher, aged 76 years.—Total, 18.
1816. January 7, Mrs. ——— Keyes.
January 28, Jeptha Prescott, aged 37 years.
February 7, Bill Gould Stevens, aged 20 years.
February 13, Mr. Marvel's blind child.
March 27, Widow Abner Kent.
March 25, Mrs. Thaddeus Read.
April 1, Thaddeus Read.
June 8, Patty Hildreth.
June 28, Josiah Boynton, aged 72 years.
August 17, Silas Read, aged 79 years.
August 29, Mrs. Henry Wilson.—Total, 12.
1817. January 14, Capt. Nathan Davis, aged 73 years.
January 19, Mrs. Issachar Keyes.
February 16, Mrs. Joshua Fletcher, aged 80 years.
March 3, child of ——— Cowdrey.
March 6, Dr. Charles Procter.
March 7, Joseph Dutton.
March 7, child of James Kent.
March 13, child of James Kent.
April 17, Jeremiah Hildreth, Esq.
April 29, William Proctor.
June 22, child of Levi Hildreth.
June 20, child of Samuel Richardson.
July 30, Mrs. Hutchins.
July 30, child of Salome Sherron.
August 8, daughter of Stephen Wright, aged 17 years.
August 23, Mrs. Amos Prescott.
August 22, old Mrs. Chandler, aged 90 years.
August 31, daughter of Wid. Richards.
September 1, Thomas Symmes.
September 14, Isaac Jipson. (Gibson?)
September 21, Mrs. Stephen Wright.
October 16, Isaac Needham.
October 16, child of Asa Prescott.
October 23, daughter of Stephen Wright, aged 13 years.
November 7, child of Benjamin Green.
November 14, child of Benjamin Hildreth.
December 12, child of Jeremiah Vose.
December 26, Ephraim Pratt.—Total, 28.
1818. January 19, Child of Levi Prescott.
February 4, son of Mr. Taft, or Tuft, aged 22 years.
March 30, child of Thomas Richardson.
March 10, David Dutton, aged 87 years.
March 30, Martha Tufts, aged 27 years.
April 7, Mrs. Amos Wright.

1818. May 24, Mrs. Mirot. (Miers?)
June 26, Mrs. Bixby.
July 12, Mrs. William Reed, Jr.
July 13, daughter of Amaziah Hildreth.
August 12, Mrs. Andrew Fletcher, aged 53 years.
August 22, wife of Mr. Dexter.
September 13, child of Solomon Richardson.
September 15, child of Ezra Fletcher.
September 15, Betsey Minot.
October, child of Silas Farmer.
November, child of Elisha Kent.
November 8, daughter of Mrs. Campernell.
November 14, Betsey Read.
November 16, child of Mrs. Campernell.
November 16, Thomas Cummings, aged 86 years.
December 27, Eleazer Read, Jr. — Total, 22.

1819. January 4, Samuel Tufts.
March 8, child of Amos Heywood.
March 10, Mr. Thompson.
March 26, Mrs. White.
April 10, child of Imly Keyes.
April 24, child of Eliakim Hutchins.
April 28, Mrs. Foster, aged 70 years.
May 27, child of David Nutting.
May 28, three children of Thomas Cummings. [They perished by the burning of their father's house, in his absence.]
May 29, Peter Hildreth, aged 66 years.
June 16, Amos Wright.
July 19, child of Mr. Keyes.
September 10, child of Dr. Osgood.
September 10, child of Joel Taylor.
September 10, child of Thomas Prescott.
Edy Hildreth.
September 21, Asa Bixby.
September 22, Joanna Spalding.
September 25, Samuel Conant.
September 25, " Widder " Patience Proctor.
October 1, Mrs. Adams.
October 1, Mr. Pierce.
October 2, child of Isaac Chamberlin.
October 3, Moses Carroll.
October 8, child of Mr. Harward.
October 9, Mrs. Needham.
November, child of Dr. Osgood.
November, child of Mrs. Windal. — Total, 27.

1820. February 1, David Stephens.
March 1, Mrs. Eben Prescott.
April 17, Mr. Cogswell.
April 20, Issachar Keyes.

STATISTICAL AND OFFICIAL. 423

1820. Mrs. Willard Fletcher.
Mrs. Joel Taylor.
Mrs. Herrick.
September 1, child of Eben Prescott.
September 2' Jonas Prescott.
October 2, Benjamin Hildreth.
October 4, child of Andrew Fletcher.
October 8, Benjamin Hildreth, Jr.
October 11, daughter of Amaziah Hildreth.
October 26, Mrs. Griffin.
Mrs. Wood. — Total, 15.

1821. January 2, Theodore Peabody.
January 24, Wid. Oliver (?) Fletcher.
February, child of Col. Timothy Cummings.
March 26, Mrs. Abbot.
March 29, Caleb Symmes.
April 14, Mr. Simon Hunt.
May 5, sister of Captain Prescott.
May 6, daughter of Mr. Dexter.
May 8, son of Mr. Gardner.
Mr. Walker.
Son of Andrew Fletcher.
Eleazer Wright.
June 9, child of Charles Hildreth.
June 18, son of Dr. Osgood.
August 8, Mr. Stoddard.
Son of Mr. Gardner.
Oliver Hildreth.
Harry Wilson.
December 20, Mr. Snow.
December 27, daughter of Mr. Mears.
December 29, Mrs. S. Wright. — Total, 22.

1822. March, [Jacob] Osgood Parker.
April 3, Liberty Cutter.
April 5, Wid. Ephraim Hildreth.
May, Fletcher Read.
May, child of Avery Prescott.
July 12, child of Abner Fisher.
August 29, Daniel Hayward, aged 29 years.

1823. December 29, Capt. Aaron Parker, aged 61.

1824. January 12, Miss Dutton.
February 15, Mrs. Buckley Prescott.
March 13, J. Patch.
March 16, Mr. Kidder.
May 30, Mr. Farwell.
May 30, Reuben Leighton, Jr.
June 30, Elisha Kent.
August 15, Mrs. Thomas Fletcher.
September 15, Mrs. Snow.

1824. September 16, child of Seth Fletcher.
September 17, child of Asa Prescott.
Child of Mr. Mead.
December 9, Col. Benjamin Osgood, aged 70.
1825. January 16, Levi Hildreth, aged 49.
Child of Mr. Snow.
Asa Blood.
March 11, Ann Peabody, aged 18 years.
Child of Jacob Osgood.
March 19, Amos Wright, aged 81 years.

RECORDED BY REV. LEONARD LUCE.

1828. October 17, Jesse Minot, Esq.
November 23, Abijah Richardson.
December 3, Mrs. John Dudley.
1829. January 5, Ruth Hildreth.
January 17, child of Luther Read.
January 18, child of Jeremy B. Read.
January 29, child of Daniel Patch, Jr.
February 15, Mary Ann Blodgett.
February 18, Benjamin Cummings.
February 20, Mrs. Abel Hildreth.
February 20, Betsey Parker.
March 1, Mrs. Benjamin Hall.
March 2, Ebenezer Shedd.
April 23, Jacob Osgood, Jr.
April 24, Jonas Wright.
May 29, Joseph Cummings.
June 6, Abel Corey.
June 13, Dr. Horace Parker.
July 8, Abram Boynton.
July 13, child of Jacob Blodgett.
July 16, Mrs. Ephraim Abbot.
July 16, George Read.
July 28, John Hunt.
September 1, Susanna Bradstreet.
September 12, child of George Leighton.
September 14, Isaiah Leighton, Esq.
September 17, Polly Mears.
September 24, child of Abram Wright.
October 21, Levi Felton.
November 4, Eliza Green.
November 19, Thomas Smith, aged 91 years.
December 9, Mrs. Joseph Souther. — Total, 29.
1830. February 27, John Wright.
March 22, Thomas Brown.
March 25, Mrs. John Leighton.
June 9, child of Jacob Wright.

1830. June 15, Mrs. Jeremy B. Read.
July 5, Charles L. Hildreth.
July 11, Timothy Read.
August 15, Lucy Wilson.
August 21, George Leighton.
September 22, child of Abel Jones.
September 23, widow of Dr. Charles Proctor.
September 23, Avery Prescott, Jr.
September 29, Mrs. Joel Glover.
September 29, child of Jesse Wright.
December 3, Mrs. Walter Wright. — Total, 15.

1831. January 4, Augustus Parker, aged 18 years.
January 5, Ephraim Spalding (pauper).
January 14, Mrs. Adams (pauper).
February 10, child of Abijah Hildreth.
May 29, Mrs. Farwell (pauper).
May 30, Lucy Hildreth, aged 18 years.
June 6, Mrs. Flint, aged 69 years.
June 20, Mrs. Abigail Wright, aged 55 years.
June 27, Elizabeth Trowbridge, aged 86 years.
August 18, Jane Day, aged 3 years.
August 26, child of John Hutchins.
August 30, Homer Sawtell.
September 10, Abigail Read (by suicide), aged 19 years.
October 7, Mrs. Benjamin Osgood.
October 20, child of Robert Wiley.
October 29, Abby Maria Abbot.
November 5, Priscilla Wright.
December 29, Ebenezer Parker, aged 83 years. — Total, 18.

1832. January 1, Amaziah Hildreth (pauper).
January 4, Peter C. Edwards.
February 5, Martha Tufts.
May 5, Mrs. Tibbetts.
June 14, Albert Patch.
June 21, Mrs. Wright, aged 84 years.
June 27, Mrs. Spalding (pauper).
July 18, Mrs. Dexter.
July 20, Eleazer Blood (pauper), aged 87 years.
July 30, Nathan Dexter, aged 90 years.
August 16, child of Asa Prescott.
August 29, child of Timothy Smith, aged 4½ years.
September 17, William Mears, aged 71 years.
October 12, Timothy Cummings, aged 81 years.
November 12, John Raymond. — Total, 16.

1833. January 2, Leonard Gibson, aged 30 years.
April 4, Mrs. Reuben Wright.
May 7, child of Charles Wright.
May 18, Horatio Clark.
June 11, Esther Goodhue, aged 91 years.

1833. July 12, Charles Blodgett, aged 9 years.
July 22, ——— Banister.
August 17, child of Asa Hildreth.
August 18, child of Asia Nutting.
August 28, Lydia Blood (pauper).
August 29, Sally Wood.
August 31, child of Imlah Keyes.
September 5, Cephas Drew.
September 5, child of Mr. Woods.
September 13, child of Charles Wright.
September 20, child of Thomas Fletcher.
September 25, child of Jedediah Robbins.
September 18, Amos Prescott (pauper).
October 6, Charlotte Lucretia Flint, aged 4 years.
October 1, Cynthia Puffer.
November 20, Ruth Hildreth.
Mrs. Wright (pauper).
Child of P. Kidder.
December 12, Lucy Prescott, aged 24 years.
December 22, William Pool (pauper).
Child of Parker Woodward.—Total, 26.

1834. January, child of Knowlton.
Child of Samuel Temple.
Child of Mr. Phillips.
Child of Mr. Cushing.
Augustus Dane, aged 11 years.
Child of Abel Corey, aged 3 years.
Widow Sampson Prescott.
Phinehas Trowbridge.
Child of Artemas Parker, Jr.
Eli Green.
Oliver Wright.
Child of John Fletcher.
Lydia Parker.
David Parker.
Helena Durant.
Eliza Osgood.
Joel Wright.
Martha Gibson, aged 2 years.
Son of James Spalding, aged 14 years.
August 27, Deidamia Rogers, aged 50 years.
Child of Capt. Trowbridge.
Nahum Wight, aged 89 years.
Abijah Wright.
Samuel Read.
A child from Lowell, name not known.
Child of John Cummings.
Child of Mr. Fisher.
Child of George Fletcher.

1834. Child of Othiel Fletcher.
November 12, Lucretia Atherton, aged 63 years.
December 29, Lowell Atherton, aged 21 years.
Mary Alzina Wright, aged 1 year.
Lucy Miranda Nichols.
[The dates, with few exceptions, are not given for this year.]
1835. January 14, Luther Warren Read, aged 3 years.
January 24, Sarah Jewett, aged 22 years.
January 25, Amos B. Abbot, aged 1 year.
Feburary 2, Charles Read.
February 2, Otis Wright, aged 11 years.
February 7, child of Mr. Bruce.
February 9, Elvira Melvina Read.
April 17, Caroline Green.
May 17, Sarah F. Kneeland, aged 15 years.
July 7, son of Theodore Woodward, aged 11 years.
July 13, Relief Wright.
July 16, Mrs. Nathan Wright.
Levi Snow, aged 79 years.
August 24, William Nichols, aged 88 years.
September 6, Franklin Wright (drowned), aged 21 years.
September 20, Mrs. Chandler (pauper).
Isaac Cummings, aged 34 years.
Reuben Wright.
Molly Smith.
1836. January, Joseph Keyes.
Alzina Read (pauper).
Francis Heywood, aged 3 years.
Hannah Richardson (pauper).
Mrs. Abel Fletcher.
Julian T. Abbot, aged 4 months.
April 11, Daniel Nutting, aged 80 years.
May 16, Addison Parker, aged 43 years.
Child of Peter Read (pauper).
Anna Boynton.
Mrs. Nancy Carroll.
Mrs. Johnson.
Child of Benjamin Prescott.
Child of John Bicknell.
Child of Peter Read.
Child of Proctor Kidder.
Child of Mr. Marble.
Mrs. William Adams.
Child of William Adams.
September 2, Sally Peabody, aged 52 years.
Child of Samuel Nichols.
Mrs. Mary Green.
Isaac Patten, aged 75 years.
Child of Mr. Gilson.

1837. January 5, child of Luther Read.
January, Mrs. Dea. Andrew Fletcher.
January, Benjamin Robbins, aged 78 years.
January, Miss Hannah Richardson.
January, Mrs Matilda Horne.
February 12, child of Levi T. Fletcher.
April, Miss Lucy Day.
July, Mrs. Hannah Hamlin, aged 90 years.
July, Miss Abigail Hildreth, aged 45 years.
Child of Peter Read, aged 1 year, 8 months.
Child of Peter Read, aged 10 months.
Mr. Farmer, died at Mr. Edwards'.
September 22, Susan Read, aged 5 years.
Child of Benjamin Wright.
Child of Benjamin Prescott.
Miss Sarah Haywood.
Two children of Asa Prescott, aged 5 and 3 years.
Grandchild of Mr. Vose.
Child of Dr. Osgood.
December 13, Samuel Richardson, aged 81 years.
George Osgood, aged 19 years.
Ann Parker, aged 45 years.
Lydia Hunt aged 78 years.
Rufus Hildreth, aged 19 years. — Total, 25.

1838. January 8, Lydia Chandler (pauper), aged 70 years.
Elizabeth Daisey, died in Grafton, aged 25 years.
Child of Rev. L. Wilson, aged 3 years.
Lydia Patten, aged 73 years.
Child of J. Robbins, aged 2 years, 6 months.
Widow of Benjamin Hildreth (pauper).
Child of Peter Reed.
Mary Webber, aged 23 years.
Mrs. Thomas Hutchins.
Child of Samuel Nichols.
May, Doct. Asaph Byam.
George S. Flagg, aged 5 years. Killed by accidental discharge of a gun.
July, Nabby Richardson (pauper).
Horace Adams.
Sarah Pierce.
William Whiting.
William Sanborn, of Vermont.
August 1, Augusta M. E. Kneeland; died in New York; buried in Westford.
August 18, Mary H. P. Hall; died in Boston; buried in Westford.
August 26, Dea. Samuel Fletcher, aged 86 years.
August 27, Isaiah Prescott; died in Concord; buried in Westford.
Benjamin Green.
August 30, wife of Thomas Richardson, aged 48 years.

1838. Edwin Read; died at sea; aged 24 years.
September 5, child of Abel Corey, aged 2 years.
Mrs. Betsey D. Whiting; died at Groton; buried in Westford; aged 26 years.
Asa Day, aged 30 years.
Mrs. Goodhue (pauper), aged 53 years.
Mrs. Mary Nutting, aged 79 years.
Mr. Wheeler, aged 30 years.
Joseph Proctor, aged 59 years.
Child of John Davis.
Ephraim Read. — Total, 53.

1839. January 6, Mary M. Wright, aged 2 years.
January 13, T. Gilbert Wright, aged 5 years.
Mrs. Levi Heywood, aged 50 years.
Maria Heywood, aged 15 years.
Mrs. Cook, aged 87 years.
Mrs. Henry A. Prescott, aged 26 years.
Child of Mr. Barker.
Mrs. Timothy Cummings, aged 58 years.
Wid. Dilla Hildreth, aged 65 years.
May 7, Levi Prescott, aged 67 years.
May, Mrs. Hunter; died in Tyngsborough.
May 23, Mary A. Nelson, aged 15 years.
Child of Mr. Blodgett.
Child of James M. Wright.
Mrs. R. Raymond.
Mrs. Dadmun.
Wid. Reuben Wright.
Mrs. Hutchins.
Calvin Wright.
Thomas Cummings.
Nehemiah Cummings.
Laurinda Keyes, aged 28 years.
Catherine Johnson, aged 61 years.
Child of John Davis.
Child of Charles Osgood.
Mr. Appleby.
Miss Appleby.
Mr. Johnson.
Mrs. Mary Davis.
Silas Chandler.
Capt. Reuben Foster.

1840. Mrs. Mary Ditson (Boston), aged 49 years.
Mr. Tileston.
Mrs. Wiley Richardson.
Mrs. Banister (pauper).
John Green (pauper).
Mrs. Othiel Fletcher.
Mrs. Brown.

1840. Mrs. Davis.
Phinehas Chamberlin.
Bill W. Stevens.
April 22, Jesse Hildreth, aged 67 years.
April 25, Andrew Leland, aged 37 years.
Mrs. Ruth Nichols, aged 88 years.
Samuel E. Fletcher, aged 12 years.
Child of George Frederick, aged 2 years.
Zilpha Wright, aged 13 years.
Elihu Read (pauper).
Three children of Samson Stevens.
Benjamin Prescott.
Nancy Pierce (pauper).
Child of Peter Read (pauper).
Mr. Gilson.
Lucy Jones; died in Lowell.
Mrs. Low. (?)
George Prescott.
Mrs. Frost.
Child of Joseph Leland.
William Hildreth.
Child of W. Hildreth.
Varnum Fletcher; died in Illinois.
Calvin Green; died in Chelmsford.
Lois Reed.
Jack Wilson.

1841. Ebenezer Prescott.
Mrs. Boynton.
Mrs. Proctor Kidder.
Jackson Prescott, aged 22 years.
Lydia Read (pauper), aged 92 years.
April 4, Mrs. Betsey H. Herrick, aged 29 years.
Ephraim E. P. Abbot, aged 6 years.
George Frederick, aged 49 years.
Child of Erastus Wright.
Charles Groce, aged 21 years.
Lorenzo Tidd, aged 6 years.
Mrs. Tidd, aged 50 years.
Patty Keyes, aged 75 years.
Abel Wright, aged 70 years.
Rachel Prescott, aged 83 years.
James Bunce, aged 11 years; killed by discharge of a gun.
Child of Amos Day.
Child of Mr. Whitney.
Child of J. A. Wright.
Mrs. Lawrence; died in Groton; buried in Westford.
Mrs. Corey, aged 86 years.
Mrs. Mary Davis, aged 86 years.
George Richardson, aged 32 years.

1841. Child of George Kidder.
John Robinson, aged 72 years.
Child of Mr. Tower.
Elizabeth Cummings.
Child of George Farwell. — Total, 26.
1842. Mrs. Chandler, aged 86 years.
John Goodhue, aged 74 years.
Mrs. Mary Leighton.
Mr. Hildreth (pauper).
Othiel Fletcher.
June 12, Alfred Ellery Luce, aged 9 years.
June 14, Nancy Reed, aged 11 years.
Mrs. Betsey Howard.
Child of Samuel Temple.
Two children of Mr. Gates.
Samuel H. Nichols, aged 41 years.
Andrews Breed Davis, aged 1 year.
Mrs. Bicknell.
Stephen Hutchins, aged 35 years.
Mrs. Fletcher, aged 96 years.
Seth Fletcher.
Abel Hildreth.
Luther Hildreth, aged 24 years.
Walter Wright, aged 31 years.
Mrs. Charlotte Dunn, aged 45 years.
Thomas Day, aged 33 years.
Stephen Keyes, aged 35 years.
Child of Mr. Wiley.
Betsey Boynton (pauper).
Mrs. Charles (pauper).
Child of Mr. Lawrence.
Sarah A. Leighton.
Peter Hadley (pauper).
Mrs. Lemuel Hildreth.
Child of Luther Prescott.
Child of Isaac Day, Jr.
Mrs. Otis Farwell.
1843. Joseph Fletcher, aged 73 years.
Caroline A. Heywood, aged 20 years.
Mrs. Mary Cummings, aged 86 years.
Child of Mr. Lawrence.
Lucy Ann Day.
Pelatiah Osgood, aged 31 years.
George Fletcher, aged 12 years.
Warren Leighton, aged 7 years.
Maria Wright, aged 7 years.
Sarah Jane Farmer, aged 5 years.
Mr. Dudley (pauper).
Child of David Whitney.

1843. Sally Keyes, aged 40 years.
Mrs. Thaddeus Blodgett, aged 42 years.
Child of Thomas Hutchins.
Child of Mr. Marble.
Albert M. Longley, aged 3 years.
Sophia Abbot, aged 2 years.
Dea. Andrew Fletcher, aged 85 years.
Jonas Leland.
Emily H. Shaw.
Othiel Fletcher, aged 11 years.
Avery Prescott, aged 62 years.
Hannah Cummings; died in Boston.
Mary Adams; died in Carlisle.
Mrs. Lawrence.

1844. John A. Davis, aged 18 years.
Child of Mr. Bunce.
Child of Samuel Temple.
Mrs. Sarah D. H. Richardson, aged 23 years.
Andrew Edes, aged 15 years.
Abijah Reed, aged 90 years.
Child of Isaac Minot.
Mrs. Sophia M. Keyes, aged 40 years.
Child of R. Patten.
Mrs. Susan Hamlin, aged 62 years; died in Groton.
Child of Mr. Pressey.
Jonathan Fletcher; died in Pepperell.
Mrs. Mary Byam Saville, aged 26 years; died in Boston.
Child of George Wright.
Mrs. Mary Perry, aged 92 years.
September 9, Dea. Reuben Leighton, aged 82 years.
Catherine B. Keyes, aged 16 years.
Mrs. Benjamin Parker, aged 81 years.
Trueworthy Heywood, aged 24 years.
Isabella Phelps, aged 16 years.
George Fletcher; died in Georgetown.
Mary Jane Reed, aged 17 years.
Mrs. Nancy Nichols, aged 36 years.
Susan F. Hildreth.
Alden Woodward, aged 9 years.
William Chandler, Jr., aged 25 years.
Deaths in town, 22; burials, 26.

1845. Samuel Fletcher, aged 20 years; died in Groton.
Ann Woods, aged 38 years.
Mrs. Oliver Woodward.
Thomas Richardson (pauper).
Aronette Reed (pauper), aged 29 years.
—— Blodgett, aged 15 years.
Jonathan Keyes.
Mrs. Whiting, aged 80 years.

1845. Mrs. Luther Prescott, aged 30 years.
Child of T. Hutchins.
Child of Massena Erskine; died in Chelmsford.
Mrs. J. J. Carter.
Mrs. Ebenezer Prescott, aged 95 years; died in Dracut.
Mr. Drake.
Eliza Reed; died in Boston.
Mrs. Chamberlin; died in Cambridge.
Child of Mr. Chamberlin.
Mrs. Jeremiah Hildreth, aged 72 years.
Mr. Proctor.
Mrs. Francis Leighton.
Abram Prescott; died in Utica, N. Y.
Martha S. Keyes.

1846. Wiley Richardson, aged 92 years.
Josiah Vose, aged 62 years.
Miss Knight.
Mrs. Asa Wright (pauper), aged 84 years.
Sidney E. Wright.
Nathan Wright; died in Lowell.
Mr. Sherwin; died in Lincoln.
Samuel B. Law; died in Lowell.
Child of G. Griffin; died in Lowell.
Nathan Wright, Jr.
Alvah Prescott.
Mrs. Snow.
Child of Joseph Ingalls.
Levi B. Heywood.
Child of James Flint.
John Keyes (pauper).
Mr. Edes; died in Lowell.
Mrs. Andrew Fletcher.
Mrs. Joseph Gould.
Samuel Reed; died in Boston.
Child of Tilly Flint.
Thomas Symmes; lost in the "Atlantic," on Long Island Sound, Thanksgiving Day, November 26, 1846; interred in this town, January 10, 1847.

1847. Charles Wiley.
Sarah Reed.
Elizabeth Fletcher.
Mrs. Isaiah Prescott (pauper).
Mrs. Jacob Clatter (pauper), aged 94 years.
Mrs. Spalding; died in Tyngsborough.
Chester H. Osgood.
Mr. Kemp; died in Littleton.
Betsey Reed.
Mrs. Martha Lincoln.
Nancy M. Day.
Lucy E. Day.

1847. Augusta V. Patten.
Child of Amos Hildreth.
Deborah Wright (pauper).
Bill Richardson (pauper).
An Irishman (pauper). Name not known.
Child of Mrs. Comey.
Thomas Hutchins.
May 11, Rev. Caleb Blake, aged 86 years.
Martha Heywood.
Mrs. Zaccheus Read.
Child of C. Nutting.
Mr. Fletcher, aged 26 years.
Calvin Cummings.
Child of William Taylor.
Whole number of those who died in town, 22.

1848. Mrs. Huldah Robbins.
Child of Mr. Bruce, from Boston.
Joseph Richardson, aged 49 years.
Sally Stevens; died in Littleton.
John Bruce, aged 20 years; brought from Boston.
Mrs. Sylvester Hildreth, aged 47 years.
Mrs. Isaiah Leighton; died in Tyngsborough.
Mrs. Clark, aged 96 years.
Mr. Parmenter, aged 84 years.
Mrs. George Griffin; died in Lowell.
Mr. Spalding, aged 22 years.
Benjamin Parker, aged 81 years.
Child of Sampson Stevens, Jr.
Child of Mr. Sprague.
Child of George Farwell; died in Concord.
Child of Eli Tower, aged 2 years.
Child of Augustus Hildreth.
Child of Mr. Walker, from Peterborough.
Mrs. Cyrus Fletcher, aged 42 years.
Isaac Durant, from Boston, aged 80 years.
Mrs. Richie, aged 33 years.
An Irishman.
Child of Newton Chandler, Charlestown.
Mrs. Lowell.
Daughter of Edward Symmes.
Son of Mr. Symmes; both buried in the same grave.
Miss Green; brought from Lowell.
Levi Heywood, aged 49 years.
Patty Cummings, aged 40 years.
Child of Mr. Rouillard.
Mrs. Andrew Fletcher.
Mr. Gage.
Mrs. Tenney.
Mrs. Ephraim A. Harwood, aged 26 years.
Patty Dutton (pauper).

Residence of Abiel J. Abbot.

HISTORY OF WESTFORD.

PART II.

GENEALOGY OF THE EARLY FAMILIES.

" Who counts himself as nobly born
  Is noble in despite of place,
And honors are but brands to one
  Who wears them not with Nature's grace.

Then, be thou peasant, be thou peer,
  Count it still more thou art thine own;
Stand on a larger heraldry
  Than that of nation or of zone."

THE materials for the genealogy of the principal families that were here before the year 1800 have been gathered from several sources. The records of births and marriages have been copied with care, and much information has been secured by personal inquiry. The compiler has had access to the records of Chelmsford and of the neighboring towns, and the facts have been carefully collected and arranged. Researches have been made in various ways so as to verify everything that seemed susceptible of proof, and nothing has been admitted on mere conjecture. Doubtless errors will be found, but the utmost care has been taken to secure accuracy.

ABBOT. 1. John, son of Dea. Joshua Abbot, of Billerica, where he was b. 1713, May 5. He joined the church 1735, Dec. 5, and was chosen deacon 1762, Mar. 5. He was a school teacher, town clerk, and selectman, for many years. He lived in the centre of the town. He m. Hannah Richardson, who d. 1795, Nov. 29. He d. 1791, Oct. 22, aged 78. Children: (1) *Hannah,* b. 1736-37; d. 1738. (2) *Rebecca,* b. 1738-39;

m. Joseph Jewett, of Littleton, 1763. (3) *Hannah*, b. 1740-41; d. 1783. (4) *John*, 2, b. 1743. (5) *Joshua*, b. 1750; d. 1753. (6) *Martha*, b. 1755.

2. John was enterprising and useful as a citizen and town officer; captain. He m., 1st, Lucy Proctor, and had (1) *John*, 3, b. 1777. He m., 2nd, Mary Farrar, of Concord, 1780, and had (1) *Abel*, 7, b. 1781. His wife, Lucy, d. 1779. He d. 1804. His widow, Mary, d. 1815.

3. John, grad. H. U., 1798; counsellor-at-law and state senator. He m. Sophia Mosely, daughter of Ebenezer Mosely, of Hampton, Conn. Children: (1) *John William Pitt*, 4, b. 1806. (2) A son b. and d. 1807. She d. 1821; He d. 1854.

4. John W. P., grad. H. U., 1827; attorney-at-law, Westford; state senator; judge of court for Northern Middlesex; selectman and town clerk for many years, and treasurer of the academy. He m. Catherine Abbot, daughter of Rev. Jacob Abbot, of Windham, N. H. Children: (1) *John William*, 3, b. 1834. (2) *Julian Thayer*, b. 1836; d. 1836. (3) *Julian*, b. 1837; d. 1857; he came to his death by reason of an accident on the Boston and Lowell railroad. (4) *Sophia Elizabeth*, b. 1841; d. 1843. (5) *George*, b. 1845; grad. H. U., 1864; m. (6) *Abiel Jacob*, 6, b. 1850.

5. John W., m. Elizabeth R. Southwick, daughter of Philip R. Southwick, of Boston, 1857. Children: (1) *Catherine Mabel*, b. 1861; m. Abbot L. Kebler, of Cincinnati, O., 1881. (2) *Emma Southwick*, b. 1863. (3) *Lucy Kebler*, b. 1870. (4) *John Cameron*, b. 1872.

6. Abiel J., m. Mary Alice Mosely, daughter of Edward S. Mosely, of Newburyport. Child: *Edward Mosely*, b. 1882.

7. Abel, m. Catherine Cummings, daughter of Timothy Cummings, 1805. Child: *Julian*, b. 1806; grad. H. U., 1826; attorney-at-law, Lowell, Mass.

8. Joel, b. Hollis, N. H., 1757, Dec. 4; son of Capt. Benjamin Abbot; m. Lydia Cumings, of Westford, 1786, daughter of Isaac Cumings, and lived on the place now occupied by Mrs. Catherine Abbot. Children: (1) *Betsy, or Elizabeth*, b. 1787; m. Rev. Jonathan Cogswell, D. D., professor in the theological seminary, East Windsor, Conn., and d. 1837. (2) *Joel*, b. 1793; captain, U. S. Navy; m. Mary Wood, of Newburyport. (3) *Walter*, b. 1795; lieutenant, U. S. N.; d. 1825, of a wound received on the Chesapeake. (4) *Lydia*, b. 1798; m. Daniel W. Lord, Kennebunkport, Me. (5) *Mary Phillips*, b. 1801. (6) *Isaac Houghton*, b. 1804. He d. 1806. His widow m. Capt. Francis Kidder, of Littleton, and d. 1813.

9. Jacob, brother of Joel, b. Hollis, N. H., 1760; m. Polly Cummings, 1787, Sept., daughter of Thomas Cummings, Jr. Children: (1) *Mary*, b. 1788; m. Silas Merriam, 1809. (2) *Cummings*, b. 1790; d. 1797. (3) *Betsey*, b. 1792; m. Timothy Smith, of Westford, 1815. (4) *Jacob Cummings*, b. 1798; wharfinger, Boston; m. Mary Todd. (5) *Nancy*, b. 1804; m. Jonathan S. Hill, Westford. (6) *Samuel B.*, b. 1812; a dentist, Lowell; m. H. Eastman, and d. 1865.

ADAMS. The Adams family of Chelmsford and Westford is descended from Henry, who was in Braintree in 1630, and who was the ancestor of two presidents of that name. Three of his sons went to Concord about 1640. Two of them, Samuel and Thomas, removed to Chelmsford in 1654, and were leading men in that town. They were both men of property and contributed much to the prosperity of the new plantation. Samuel built the first mill in the town, on River Meadow Brook, and Thomas settled in the westerly part, near the present residence of Charles Adams. From these two brothers there are two lines of descent, so involved and intricate that no investigator without access to private records can trace them satisfactorily. They cross each other by intermarriages, and the given names in each line are so often alike that the difficulty is greatly increased. In giving the genealogy of the Westford branches it is scarcely practicable to show their connection with the one or the other of the two brothers.

1. Samuel, who was probably a descendant of Thomas and son of Timothy, of the third generation, m. Elizabeth Butterfield, of Chelmsford, 1728. This was the first marriage recorded by Rev. Willard Hall.

GENEALOGY.

Children: (1) *Thankful*, b. 1728; m. John Glene, Dunstable, 1751 (pub. March 29). (2) *Samuel*, 2, b. 1731. (3) *Elizabeth*, b. 1733. (4) *Lucy*, b. 1734. (5) *Henry*, b. 1741. (6) *Ede*, bap. 1746. He m. a second wife, Wid. Hannah (Craft) Spalding, 1769.

2. Samuel, m. Elizabeth Blood, 1756 (pub. Dec. 8). Child: (1) *Jonathan*, b. 1757.

3. Thomas, m. Mary Mead, or Meads, daughter of Doct. Thomas Mead, 1759. Children: (1) *Betty*, b. 1760; m. Jesse Minot, 1784. (2) *Timothy*, b. 1762; m. Lydia Robbins, daughter of Jacob Robbins, 1783. They were married at Littleton, by Jonathan Reed, Esq., and rem. to Cavendish, Vt. (3) *Mary*, b. 1764. (4) *Ruth*, b. 1766. (5) *Isaac*, b. 1769.

4. Samuel is generally designated on the books as Samuel *tertius*, or third, "trader." (See p. 251.) He was probably the son of Samuel, who m. Esther Emerson, in 1746; and there is ground for the supposition that he m. Thankful Chamberlin, about 1770. Children: (1) *Samuel*, b. 1773. (2) *Tutty* (*Thankful*), b. 1775; d. 1791. (3) *Polly*, b. 1778. (4) *Lucretia*, b. 1782; d. 1783. (5) *Sophia Charlotte*, b. 1784. (6) *Nancy*, b. 1786. (7) *Sukey*, b. 1789; d. 1790. (8) *Sophia*, b. 1793. (9) *Patty*, b. 1771, in Chelmsford; d. 1773.

5. Thomas, of Chelmsford, m. Esther Perry, of Westford, 1781. Perhaps he was the son of John. The record of his family stands thus: Children: (1) *Thomas*, b. 1781. (2) *Joshua*, b. 1783; d. in Westford. (3) *Asa*, b. 1784; d. in Carlisle. (4) *Amos*, b. 1788. (5) *Isaac*, b. 1793. (6) *Polly*, b. 1795. (7) *John*, b. 1798; d. 1801. Thomas, the father, d. 1824. Esther, the mother, d. 1843, aged 83.

6. Richard, son of Robert, m. Sally Fletcher, daughter of Pelatiah, 1806. Children: (1) *Robert*, b. 1807. (2) *Sally*, b. 1809.

BALDWIN. James, Lieut., of Dunstable, m. Priscilla Keyes, daughter of Issachar, 1798. Children: (1) *Stephen*, b. 1799. (2) *Josiah*, b. 1801. (3) *Josephus*, b. 1803. These were born in Dunstable. Josephus was the first mayor of Nashua, and deacon of the Baptist Church. (4) *Eliza*, b. 1805. (5 and 6) *Edwin* and *Caroline*, b. 1807. (7) *Nancy*, b. 1809. (8) *James*, b. 1812. (9) *Priscilla*, b. 1814. (10) *John*, b. 1817. James, the father, d. at Dunstable, N. H., 1827.

BARRETT. 1. William, son of Samuel and Sarah, b. in Chelmsford, 1689; m. Sarah ———. Children: (1) *Nathaniel*, b. 1717. (2) *Samuel*, b. 1718. (3) *Elizabeth*, b. 1721. (4) *William*, b. 1724. (5) *Sarah*, b. 1728-29. (6) *Benjamin*, b. 1731. (7) *Lois*, daughter of second wife, Mary Craft, b. 1749; m. Stephen Temple, 1780.

2. Nathaniel, probably son of William, above; m. Abigail Searles, of Concord, 1744. Children: (1) *Nathaniel*, b. 1745. (2) *Zaccheus*, b. 1748. Probably he is the one who was in Templeton, 1762 (see p. 170), or he may be the Zaccheus who was in Mason, N. H., in 1773, and m. Sarah Hodgman; and the Zaccheus of Templeton may be the son of Thomas, of Chelmsford, who was born in 1728.

3. Nathaniel, probably the son of Joseph and Mary, of Chelmsford; b. 1724. He married Martha [Wheeler] (?) and lived in the vicinity of Flushing Pond. Children: (1) *Mary*, b. 1753. (2) *Nathaniel*, b. 1763. (3) *Levi*, b. 1769. (4) *Joseph*, b. 1769. (5) *Sarah*, b. 1773. There is evidence almost conclusive, that there was an *Ebenezer*, b. 1762, and *Jonathan*, *Oliver*, and perhaps others.

BARRON. Timothy, m. Hannah [Fletcher] (?). Children: (1) *Sarah*, b. 1726. (2) *Jonathan*, b. 1727; d. 1729. (3) *Joshua*, b. 1729; d. young. (4) *Jonathan*, b. 1730. (5) *Moses*, b. 1732. (6) *William*, b. 1738. (7) *Timothy*, b. 1740. (8) *Dorothy*, b. 1742. (9) *John*, b. 1744. (10) *Hannah*, b. 1747; m. James Spalding, of Westford, 1769, and rem. to Ashburnham, where she d. 1814. (See p. 160.) (11) *Joshua*, b. 1749. (12) *Nathan*, b. 1750.

BATES. Edward, son of John, who lived in the vicinity of Parkerville. In the year 1722 the small-pox appeared in his family, and most of them died. (See Allen's History of Chelmsford, p. 37.) This is the earliest mention of that disease in the history of that town. Edward was b. 1796; m. Mary Snow. Children: (1) *Oliver*, b. 1720-21; m. Ruth

Wright, daughter of Ebenezer and Hannah Wright, 1744. He was captain of one of the Westford companies that pursued the British red coats in their retreat from Concord Bridge, and received a wound which caused his death, July 4, 1775. (2) *Sarah*, b. 1733; m. Jonathan Johnson, of Hollis, N. H., 1754.

BAYLEY. Joseph and Deborah, from Bradford. Child: *Thomas*, b. 1767.

BEALE. 1. Thomas, and Molly, his wife, came here from Ipswich. Children: (1) *Jesse*, b. 1772. (2) *Josiah*, b. 1773.

2. **William**, probably a brother of Thomas; m. Anna Wood, of Groton, 1772. Child: *Abel*, b. 1773. Both removed.

BICKNELL. Lemuel, m. Abigail ———. Children: (1) *Lucy*, b. 1794, at Waterford, Vt. (2) *John*, b. 1797. (3) *Deborah*, b. 1798. (4) *Cynthia*, b. 1801. (5) *William Cutler*, b. 1803. (6) *James*, b. 1804. (7) *Mary*, b. 1806.

BIGELOW. John, was born in Framingham; probably settled first in Weston, and afterward in Acton, from which place he came here about 1762. He lived in the south part. His wife's name was Grace. Children: (1) *Lucy*; m. Joseph Dutton, Jr., 1766. (2) *Bulah*; m. Jonathan Hall, of Ashby. (3) *Sarah*; m. Thomas Dutton, 1768. (4) *Silas*; rem. to New Ipswich and had children, viz: Silas, Daniel, Samuel, Joel and John; these were born before he resided in Acton. Also, Simeon, b. 1752; Molly, b. 1754; Grace, b. 1757; and Eunice, b. 1760, all in Acton. John, and his son, Silas, and his daughters, Bulah and Eunice, were in New Ipswich in 1787.

BIXBY. This family probably came from Boxford or Topsfield. It still exists in both towns, but it has been found difficult to establish the connection.

1. **David** was here before the precinct was formed. He took up a large tract of land, which included the farms now occupied by George O. Wright (late Waldo Cumings), and John W. Day. He m. Abigail ———. Children: (1) *Abigail*, b. 1715; m. Zechariah Sartle, Groton, 1733. (2) *Lydia*, b. 1717; m. Obadiah Jenkins, Wilmington, 1738. (3) *Hannah*, b. 1719; m. David Brown, 1738. (4) *Joseph*, b. 1721; rem. to Marblehead. (5) *Thankful*, b. 1724-25; m. Jonathan Searls, Nottingham, 1748. (6) *Jacob*, **2**, b. 1728. (7) *David*, b. 1729; m. Alice Haywood, of Dunstable, 1773, and rem. to Ludlow, Vt. (8) *Asa*, **3**, b. 1734-35. (9) *William*, **4**, b. 1737.

2. **Jacob**, m. Eunice Heald, daughter of Thomas and Sarah Heald, 1749. Children: (1) *David*, b. 1749; a soldier of the Revolution. (2) *Levi*, b. 1750; rem. to Wilton, N. H. (3) *Ephraim*, **5**, b. 1753. (4) *Jacob*, b. 1754.

3. **Asa**, m. Susanna Howard, 1756. (Pub. April 17.) Children: (1) *Susanna*, b. 1757; m. Ephraim Dutton, 1781; rem. to Ludlow, Vt. (2) *Asa*, **6**, b. 1761. (3) *Thomas*, b. 1762; rem. to Ludlow, Vt. (4) *Abigail*, b. 1764. (5) *Joseph*, b. 1766; m. in Ludlow, Vt., 1791, but was afterward of Mt. Holly, where he was surveyor in 1798.

4. **William**, m. Mary ———. Children: (1) William, b. 1762. (2) *John*, b. 1767. Probably rem. to Springfield, Vt.

5. **Ephraim**, m. Martha Barker, of Acton, 1775. (Pub. Aug. 25.) Children: (1) *Patty*, b. 1776; d. young. (2) *Patty*, b. 1779. (3) *Abishar*, b. 1781. (4) *Tryphene*, b. 1783.

BLAKE. Rev. Caleb, m. Martha Moseley, of Hampton, Conn. Children: (1) *Martha*, b. 1793; m. Luther Gilson, of Groton, 1822. (2) *Caleb Mosely*, b. 1795; m. ———. (3) *Sophia Strong*, b. 1801; m., 1st, Joseph Keyes, 1820; m., 2nd, Trueworthy Keyes, 1837. (4) *William Herbert*, b. 1806; m.———. (5) *Mary Ann*, b. 1813; m. True A. Bean, 1848. Mrs. Blake was a niece of Governor Caleb Strong, who came once or twice on a visit to the family here.

BLODGETT. 1. **Thomas**, and his wife Tabitha. He lived on the Amos Heywood place, and d. 1741. Children: (1) *Tabitha*, b. 1719-20. (2) *Thomas*, b. 1729. (3) *John*, **2**, b.——.

2. John, m. Abigail ———. Children: (1) *Esther*, b. 1730. A pauper for many years. (2) *James*, **3**, b. 1733.

3. James, m. Abigail ——— Children: (1) *Jonas*, b. 1757. (2) *Azubah*, b. 1761; m. Moses Blanchard, Athol. (3) *Isaiah*, b. 1764. (4) *Mary*, b. 1766; m. Ephraim Wright, 1784. (5) *Elizabeth*, b. 1768. (6) *Sarah*, b. 1770. (7) *Olive*, b. 1774. (8) *Hannah*, b. 1778.

4. Jonas, m. Sarah Fletcher, 1781. (Pub. July 23.) Children: (1) *John*, **5**, b. 1782. (2) *Ama*, b. 1784. (3) *Joshua*, b. 1785. Settled in Littleton. (4) *James*, b. 1787. (5) *Jesse*, b. 1789. (6) *Mitta*, b. 1791; d. 1811. (7) *Sally*, b. 1793. (8) *Hannah*, b. 1795. Jonas, the father, d. in Swanzey, N. H., 1826.

5. John, m. Mary Prescott, daughter of David, 1802, March 30. The record says he was "of Mason," at the time of his marriage; but he afterward lived in Groton, on the "Crue place." Child: (1) *John Prescott*, b. 1806.

BLOOD. Eleazer, m. Lydia Fletcher. Children: (1) *Lydia*, b. 1779. (2) *Ebenezer*, b. 1782. (3) *Eleazer*, b. 1787. (4) *Rachel*, b. 1792. (5) *Abigail C.*, b. 1797.

BOYNTON. 1. Nathaniel. The proof is not absolute but strongly presumptive, that he came from Rowley, and was the son of Joseph and Bridget (Harris) Boynton, b. 1694. He m. 1720, Hannah, daughter of Joseph and Dorothy Perham. Children: (1) *Sarah*, b. 1721; m. Abiel Richardson, 1741. (2) *Elizabeth*, b. 1722. (3) *Nathaniel*, **2**, b. 1724. (4) *Hannah*, b. 1726; m. William Warren, Littleton, 1746. (5) *Bridget*, b. 1727. (6) *Esther*, b. 1729. (7) *Joseph*, **3**, b. 1731. (8) *Dorothy*, b. 1733. Hannah, the mother, d. 1733, and he m. Elizabeth Shedd, of Billerica. Children, by 2nd wife: (9) *Nathan*, b. 1736; d. young. (10) *Mary*, b. 1737; m. Joshua Parker, 1764, March 15. (11) *Abijah*, b. 1740; m. Sarah Chamberlin, 1769; rem. to Pepperell. (12) *Nathan*, b. 1742; rem. to New Ipswich. (13) *Amos*, b. 1744; m. Mary Parker, 1770; rem. to Plymouth, Vt. (14) *Isaiah*, b. 1746.

2. Nathaniel, m., Rebecca Barrett, of Concord, 1750. Children: (1) *Rebecca*, b. 1753; m., 1st, Benjamin Fletcher, Jr., 1774; 2nd, Jonas Wright, 1783. (2) *Abel*, **4**, b. 1755. (3) *Lydia*, b. 1757; m. Jonathan Lawrence, Ashby, 1800. (4) *Elizabeth*, b. 1760; m. Abijah Reed, 1786. (5) *Nathaniel*, b. 1763; m. Anna Barrett, Concord, 1790; rem. to Mason, (6) *Mary*, b. 1765; m. Rev. Ebenezer Hill, Mason, 1791. (7) *Jeremy*, b. 1767. (8) *John*, b. 1770; m. Nabby Parker, 1798; rem. to Washington, N. H. (9) *Salla*, b. 1772; d. 1772. (10) *John*, b. 1776.

3. Joseph, m. Sarah Tarbell, of Groton, 1762. Children: (1) *Joseph*, b. 1764. (2) *Samuel Tarbell*, b. 1766.

4. Abel, m., 1st, Polly Abbot, 1772. Children: (1) *Abel*, b. 1783; graduated at H. U., 1804; lawyer, Bath, Me.; m. Sarah Leland; no children; d. 1817. (2) *Polly*, b. 1785. (3) *Betsey*, b. 1787. (4) *Benjamin Abbot*, b. 1790; d. 1790. (5) *Benjamin Abbot*, b. 1791. (6) *Isaac Newton*, b. 1793. (7) *Sally*, b. 1794.

5. Josiah, b. in Groton; m. Lucy Raymond, 1769. Children: (1) *Josiah*, **6**, b. 1770. (2) *Samuel*, b. 1772. (3) *Joel*, b. 1774.

6. Josiah, Jr., m. Lydia Perkins, 1796. Children: (1) *John*, b. 1797. (2) *Federal*, b. 1799. (3) *Myra*, b. 1801. (4) *Edmund*, b. 1805. Josiah, Jr., lived at the Centre, in the house now owned by Mrs. George Prescott, where he kept tavern. The family rem. to East Cambridge.

BROOKS. Josiah came from Acton, son of Daniel; m. Lydia Heywood, Concord, 1756. Children: (1) *Lydia*, b. 1754; d. 1755. (2) *Josiah*, b. 1756. (3) *Lydia*, b. 1758. (4) *Hannah*, b. 1760. (5) *John*, b. 1762; frozen to death 1785. (6) *Daniel*, b. 1764; d. 1800. (7) *Mary*, b. 1769; d. 1853. Josiah, the father, d. 1771; Daniel, father of Josiah, d. 1769; Anna, mother of Josiah, d. 1760.

BURN or BOURNE. The only person, bearing this name, was James, who lived on the place lately occupied by Samuel N. Burbeck. A pasture near Rattlesnake Hill is still called the "Burn's Pasture." He was a potter by trade. (See p. 242.)

BURGE. This family came from Weymouth to Chelmsford. John, of Chelmsford, m. Trial Thayer, of Braintree, about 1682, and had ten children, whose births are recorded on Chelmsford books. Of these, Josiah, b. 1696, lived on the farm now occupied by Daniel W. Sherman. He owned a large tract of two or three hundred acres, which abutted on Main Street, and ran north-west over Stony Brook. It has been variously subdivided, but included "the Crancum Pasture," and the "Dughill Lot." The farm of Rev. W. Hall was taken from the upper end. Samuel, cousin of Josiah, owned the land in the vicinity of Burge's Pond. Very little is known of him. Probably he had no family, and was not a permanent citizen.

1. Josiah, m. Susanna Jaquith, of Bradford, 1724, and he and his wife became members of the church, 1728. Children: (1) *Samuel*, b. 1726. (2) *Moses*, b. 1728. (3) *Abigail*, b. 1730-31; m. Thomas Penniman, of Braintree, 1752; settled in Washington, N. H. (4) *Josiah*, b. 1733; d. 1750. (5) *Susanna*, b. 1736; m. Reuben Kidder, 1754; settled in New Ipswich. (6) *Ephraim*, b. 1738; he settled in Hollis, where he m. Anna Abbot, 1762, Jan. 7, and had ten children. His two sons, Josiah and Benjamin, were graduates of Harvard University; Josiah became a minister, but died in 1790, in his 24th year. Benjamin became a physician. (7) *Ruth*, b. 1739; m. Joseph Pollard, 1767; lived in New Ipswich. (8) *Sarah*, b. 1741; d. 1753. (9) *Elizabeth*, b. 1743. (10) *John*, b. 1747; d. 1750. There seems to have been a second Josiah, whose birth was not recorded; for Josiah Burge, Jr., of Townsend, m. Priscilla Barnes, of Westford, in 1781. Josiah, the father, d. 1756, and Susanna, the mother, d. 1750.

BUTTERFIELD. Two persons of this name, Nathaniel and Benjamin, came from Woburn and settled in Chelmsford. There were many families, and it is hard to trace those that became residents here back to the original stock.

1. Josiah is the first that appears on the record, whose wife was Hannah ———. Children: (1) *Josiah*, b. 1738. (2) *Simeon*, b. 1740.

2. John and Mary. Children: (1) *Mary*, b. 1728. (2) *Thomas*, b. 1730-31. (3) *John*, b. 1733. (4) *Charles*, b. 1735. (5) *Sarah*, b. 1737.

3. Benjamin, m. Kezia ———. Children: (1) *Ruth*, b. 1724; m. Aaron Chandler, 1749. (2) *Benjamin*, 4, b. 1726. (3) *John*, b. 1728. (4) *Timothy*, b. 1730. (5) *Kezia*, b. 1733. (6) *Mary*, b. 1735. (7) *Abel*, b. 1737; d. 1745. (8) *Jonas*, b. 1740. (9) *Isaac*, b. 1742. (10) *James*, b. 1744. Benjamin, the father, d. 1747. This family lived on the margin of Boutwell's meadow, near the house of the Coolidge brothers. (See p. 162.)

4. Benjamin, m. Susanna Spalding, 1748, Sept. 26. Child: (1) *Benjamin*, b. 1749. (See p. 169.)

5. Robert was probably the son of Jonathan and Elizabeth; b. 1716; m., 1st, Mehitable Boynton, of Dunstable, 1745. Children: (1) *Mehitable*, b. 1745. (2) *Robert*, b. 1747. He was a pauper, sick and disabled for many years. (3) *Joel*, b. 1749. (4) *Betty*, b. 1752. He m., 2nd, Joanna Parker, Chelmsford, 1752. (5) *James*, b. 1755. Robert, the father, d. near Lake George, 1756, Oct. 23.

6. William, on tax list, 1730; m. Bathsheba Shepard, Concord; lived on Frances Hill. Children: (1) *Rebecca*, b. 1729. (2) *Lucy*, b. 1731; m. Jacob Wright, Jr. (3) *William*, b. 1734. (4) *Hannah*, b. 1737. (5) *Peter*, b. 1739; m. Hannah Buttrick, Townsend, and settled there, 1768. (6) *Abraham*, b. 1741; d. 1760, at Crown Point. (7) *Olive*, b. 1743; d. 1749-50. (8) *Samuel*, b. 1745.

7. Joseph, Jr., on tax list, 1730; lived near Calvin Howard's; m. Dorothy Heald. Children: (1) *Eleazer*, b. 1727-28; m. Mary Wright, 1749; settled in Townsend. (2) *Hannah*, b. 1729. (3) *Martha*, b. 1731-32. (4) *Joseph*, b. 1733. (5) *Ebenezer*, b. 1736; perhaps settled in Hardwick. (6) *Dorothy*, b. 1739.

8. John, son of Benjamin and Kezia; m. Martha Trull, 1750. Children: (1) *Benjamin*, b. 1751. (2) *John*, b. 1753. (3) *Abel*, b. 1756, at Narragansett, No. 6 (Templeton). (4) *Henry*, b. 1759, in Groton. (5) *Abraham*, b. 1766. (6) *Ruth*, b. 1769.

GENEALOGY.   441

CARVER. 1. Robert, said to be brother of Gov. John Carver, was born in England, 1594; came to Marshfield, 1638; d. there 1680, aged 86. His son, John, b. 1637, m. Melicent Ford, of Marshfield. He died 1679, aged 42, leaving children: William, John, Robert, Eleazer, David, Elizabeth, Mercy and Anna. David d. in 1727, in Canterbury, Conn. By his second wife, Sarah Butterfield, of Chelmsford, he had a son, Benjamin, born in Canterbury, 1722, Dec. 10. His mother, after his father's death, returned to her native Chelmsford. He passed his life in Westford, where he owned a valuable farm, near the Centre, being the land about the house of Nathan P. Prescott, 1882. (See Symmes' Memorial p. 104.) He m., 1745, Edith Fletcher, daughter of Capt. Joseph, b. 1725. Children: (1) *Sarah*, b. 1746; d. in Ashby, 1831. (2) *Benjamin*, b. 1748; d. young. (3) *Jonathan*, **2**, b. 1751. (4) *Thomas*, b. 1755; m. Esther Tarbell; physician in Ashby; no children; d. 1815. (5) *Edith*, b. 1757; m. Charles Proctor, physician; d. without issue, 1781. (6) *Martha*, b. 1759; m. David Parker; d. 1788. (7) *Benjamin*, b. 1761. (8) *Mary*, b. 1764; d. 1767. (9) *Rebecca*, b. 1766; m. Thomas Symmes; d. 1836. (10) *Joseph*, bap. 1754. Benjamin, the father, d. 1804, in his 86th year. Edith, the mother, d. 1813, aged 89.

2. Jonathan, m., 1774, Aug. 16, Mary Procter; they removed to Ashby but returned. Children: (1) *Mary*, b. 1779; d. 1793. (2) *Sally*, b. 1783; d. 1837. He d. 1805, and his widow m. Capt. Nathan Davis. She d. 1841, aged 88. Capt. Davis d. 1817, aged 72.

CHAMBERLIN. 1. Henry. The ancestor of this family in New England was probably Henry of Hingham. Thomas, Edmund and Samuel came from Woburn to Chelmsford, and were among the first settlers. The first to be noticed here was Lieut. Samuel, of whom a sketch has already been given. His wife was Rebecca Whitcomb, of Lancaster, but it seems probable that he was first married to Anna —— by whom he had several children. Children: (of Samuel and Rebecca) (1) *Samuel*, **2**, b. 1723. (2) *Ephraim*, **3**, b. 1725. (3) *Wilder*, b. 1730; rem. to Hollis.

2. Samuel, m. Sarah Tenney, Littleton, 1752, Feb. 27. Children: (1) *Martha*, b. 1753. (2) *Wilder*, b. 1754. (3) *Sarah*, b. 1755. (4) *Elizabeth*, b. 1758. (5) *Sibel*, b. 1759; d. 1760. (6) *Molly*, b. 1762. (7) *Asaph*, b. 1764. (8) *Submit*, b. 1766. (9) *Samuel*, b. 1767. (10) *Jesse*, b. 1770.

3. Ephraim, m. Esther Boynton, 1752. Children: (1) *Hannah*, b. 1752; m. Silas Read, 1772. (2) *Rebecca*, b. 1754; m. Rev. Elijah Fletcher, 1773. (3) *Ephraim*, b. 1756; (?) m. Persis Barrett, Concord, 1786. (4) *Nathaniel*, b. 1758; was a school teacher here in 1783. (5) *Abigail*, b. 1760; m. Isaac Green, of Townsend, 1780, and rem. to Cavendish, Vt. (6) *John*, b. 1762. (7) *Thomas*, **4**, b. 1764. (8) *James*, **5**, b. 1767. (9) *Elijah*, b. 1770; dismissed to the church in Dunstable, 1814. (10) *Sarah*, b. 1776.

4. Thomas, m. Mary ———. Children: (1) *Thomas*, b. 1789. (2) *Jonas*, or *James*, b. 1791. (3) *Elijah*, b. 1793. (4) *Luther*, b. 1795. (5) *Lucinda*, b. 1797. Thomas, the father, was dismissed to the church in Ashby, 1800. Perhaps he went from Ashby to Cavendish.

5. James, m. Joanna, daughter of David Fletcher, 1796. Children: (1) *Joanna Stevens*, b. 1797. (2) *Becky Stevens*, b. 1799. (3) *Jarvis*, b. 1801. (4) *Sally Porter*, b. 1805. (5) *Porter*, b. 1809. He was dismissed to the church in Wallingford, 1803.

6. Ephraim, son of Phinehas, of Chelmsford; lived near Thomas Drew's; m. Sally Howard, of Chelmsford. Children: (1) *Joel*, b. 1802. d. 1803. (2) *Phinehas*, **7**, b. 1803. (3) *Sally*, b. 1806. (4) *Mary*, b. 1808; m. Walter Fletcher, 1828.

7. Phineas, m., 1st, Mary Parker, 1827; m., 2nd, Louisa Webber, 1865. Children: (1) *Maria*, b. 1828. (2) *Julia Ann*, b. 1830; m. Edward Z. Read, 1852. (3) *Joel*, b. 1832. (4) *Sophronia*, b. 1834; m. Franklin A. Fletcher, 1857. (5 and 6) *Charles* and *Henry* (twins), b. 1836; Charles m. ———. *Henry* m. Mary E. Read, 1857. (7) *Marietta*, b. 1838; m. Henry M. Hutchins, 1856. (8) *John Murray*, b. 1840; m. Eunice F. Hutchins, 1862.

CHANDLER. Two persons of this name settled in Westford, William and Ephraim, who were cousins, and lineal descendants of William of Roxbury. They were both born in Andover, and came to this town before the date of its incorporation.

1. **William** was the son of William and Eleanor (Phelps), grandson of Thomas, and great-grandson of the first William, being of the fourth generation. He m. Susanna Burge, of Chelmsford, daughter of John and sister of Josiah Burge. He lived at Brookside. (See page 12.) Children: (1) *Benjamin*, b. 1718; m. Hannah Dutton, of Westford, 1743. (2) *William*, **2**, b. 1719. (3) *Moses*, **3**, b. 1720; rem. to Wilton, Me. (4) *Aaron*, **4**, b. 1722; m. Ruth Butterfield, 1749. (5) *John*, b. 1725; m. Lydia Taylor, of Townsend, and settled in New Ipswich. (6) *Henry*, b. 1727; killed by the Indians near Fort Dummer, 1748. (7) *Joseph*, b. 1728–29; d. in 1807, at Winthrop, Me., and left his property to his niece, Deborah Jennings. (8) *Isaac*, **5**, b. 1730. (9) *Rachel*, b. 1732; m. Thomas Spalding, 1757. (10) *Sarah*, b. 1734; d. young. (11) *Lydia*, b. 1735; m. Jonah Crosby, of New Ipswich, son of Robert Crosby and Mehitable (Chandler), of Andover, and daughter of Joseph and Mehitable (Russell) Chandler. (12) *Samuel*, b. 1736. (13) *Sarah*, b. 1738–39; m. Benjamin Spalding, and rem. to Jaffrey, and d. 1796. (14) (?) *Jacob*.

2. **William**, m. Dorcas Blood, 1750. Children: (1) *William*, **6**, b. 1751. (2) *Ebenezer*, **7**, b. 1753. (3) *Silas*, **8**, b. 1755.

3. **Moses**, m., 1st, Dorothy Marble, Andover, 1742; and 2nd, Elizabeth Kendall, Litchfield, 1762. Children: (1) *Hannah*, b. 1742; m. Samuel Butterfield, Dunstable, 1761. (2 and 3) *Dorothy* and *Susanna*, "being twins," b. 1744. Dorothy and Susanna d. 1744. (4) *Samuel*, b. 1745; m. Rebecca Walton, and settled in Farmington, Me. (5) *Susanna*, b. 1747; d. 1753. (6) *Henry*, b. 1749; d., Amherst, N. H., 1764. (7) *Dorothy*, b. 1752; m. Bunker Clark, who was taxed in New Ipswich, 1774, but rem. and settled in Farmington, Me. (8) *Susanna*, b. 1754; m. Jacob Reed, Jr., Farmington. He was born "near Dunstable." (9) *Moses*, b. 1757; rem. to Farmington, Me.; was known as Colonel; m. Sarah Berry. (10) *Jacob*, b. 1763; rem. to Farmington; m., 1st, Rhoda Pollard, of Jay, Me.; 2nd, Judith Pettis, of Winthrop, Me. (11) *Henry*, b. 1765; rem. to Wilton, Me.; m. Mehitable Bean, of Winthrop.

4. **Aaron**, who m. Ruth Butterfield, rem. to Petersham. His wife was dismissed from the first church here in 1752, and recommended to the church in Nitchawage, Petersham. Children: (1) *Abel*, b. 1752. (2) *Susanna*, b. 1754. (3) *Mary Ann*, b. 17—; m. Timothy Butterfield, Westmoreland, N. H. (4) *Ruth*, b. ——; m. Jonas Butterfield, Westmoreland, 1787. (5) *Susanna*, b. 1761; m. Samuel Works. The children of Aaron and Ruth were all born in Petersham. [See Chandler Memorial.]

5. **Isaac**, m. Betty Proctor, Chelmsford, 1759. Children: (1) *Isaac*, b. 1760. (2) *Betty*, b. 1763; m. John Patch, Jr. (3) Lydia, b. 1765. (4) *Henry*, b. 1768. (5) *John*, b. 1771.

6. **William**, m. Joanna, daughter of Eleazer Reed, 1787 (pub. Sept. 26). Children: (1) *Joanna*, b. 1789; m. Joel Read, 1810. (2) *William*, b. 1791. (3) *Milley*, b. 1793; m. Jeptha Trowbridge, 1816. (4) *Nancy*, b. 1795; m. J. Boynton Read, 1831. William, the father, was a clothier, at Brookside, as his father and grandfather had been before him. In 1805 he removed to the farm of Ephraim Chandler, near Flushing Pond. He d. 1826, aged 75. His widow, Joanna, was on the list of pensioners in 1840, aged 85.

7. **Ebenezer**, m. Ruth Wright, 1781; he was at White Plains, in Col. Zaccheus Wright's regiment; settled in Reading, Vt., about a mile from the South Village. Children: (1) *Ebenezer*, b. at Westford, 1782. (2) *Jesse*, b. 1784; d. at Reading. (3) *Sally*, b. 1787; lived with her sister, Laura, at Westford. (4) *Silas*, b. 1788. (5) *Elijah*, b. 1790. (6) *Lydia*, b. 1791. (7) *Polly*, b. 1793; m. Mr. Dickinson, of Weathersfield, Vt. (8) *Joel*, b. 1796; m. Sally Hooper. (9) *Laura*, b. 1800; m. Andrew Fletcher, Westford, 1821.

8. **Silas** was out two days in the Lexington alarm, and was at White Plains, under Col. Wright; m. Mary Brown, of Billerica, 1803. Child: (1) *Mary*, b. 1804; m. Benjamin F. Morse.

9. Ephraim. He was born in Andover, 1696, and was the son of Thomas and Mary (Peters) Chandler. Like his cousin, William, he was a great-grandson of William and Annis, of Roxbury. In 1720, Samuel Corey, of Littleton, sells land to Ephraim Chandler, of Andover, *tanner*, 40 acres lying in Chelmsford. In 1721, Ephraim Chandler, of Chelmsford, tanner, sells to Benjamin Chamberlin, 40 acres. There is some ground for the supposition that this land was on Frances Hill, and perhaps on, or near the spot on which a tannery was afterward built, near Chamberlin's Corner.

10. Ephraim, m., 1st, Sarah Adams, Chelmsford. Children: (1) *Sarah*, b. 1724; owned the covenant, 1745. (2) *Phebe*, b. 1733. He m., 2nd, widow Abigail Blood, of Groton.

CLEAVELAND. Enoch, Jr., m. Martha Butterfield, perhaps the daughter of Joseph, Jr. Children: (1) *Martha*, b. 1753; m. John Sterns, Littleton, 1773. (2) *Enoch*, b. 1754.

COOK. 1. Capt. Enoch, of Groton, m. widow Abigail (Petts) Butterfield, 1790. Lived on the place now owned by Mrs. Eunice Hildreth. Children: (1) *Betsy T.*, b. 1791. (2) *William*, 2, b. 1793. (3) *Lucinda*, b. 1795; m. William Laws, of Chelmsford, 1815.

2. William, m. Anna ———. Children: (1) *Stephen*, b. 1827. (2) *Levi*, b. 1828. (3) *Nathan*, b. 1830.

COREY. 1. Abel, son of Stephen and Lucy (Parker) Corey, of Littleton; m. Hannah ———. Children: (1) *Lucy*, b. 1778; (2) *Abel*, 2, b. 1781; d. 1856. (3) *Isaac*, b.——. He once held some office in the State prison; perhaps overseer, or deputy warden; d. 1839. (4) *Mary*, b. 1795. (5) *John*, b. 1798; d. 1827. Abel, the father, d. 1829. Hannah, the mother, d. 1841.

2. Abel, m., 1830, March 8, Mrs. Lucinda C. Jones. Children: (1) *Abel*, b. 1832. (2) *Lucy H.*, b. 1833. (3) *Isaac*, b. 1837. (4) *Mary Jane*, b. 1841.

COWDREY. 1. John, from Billerica; m., 1st, Abigail ———. Children: (1) *John*, b. 1731-32; d. 1734. (2) *Samuel*, b. 1734. (3) *Abigail*, b. 1737. (4) *Susanna*, b. 1739. He m., 2nd, Hannah Davis, of Groton, 1744. (5) *Nathaniel*, 2, b. 1745. (6) *Mary*, b. 1747. (7) *John*, b. 1750. (8) *Jonathan*, b. 1752. (9) *David*, b. 1756.

2. Nathaniel, m. Rebecca Parker, Billerica, 1773. Children: (1) *Lucy*, b. 1774; m. Wilson Cummings, 1796. (2) *Nathaniel*, b. 1776. (3) *Rebekah*, b. 1778. (4) *Joseph*, b. 1781. (5) *Mighill*, b. 1784. (6) *Naomi*, b. 1787. (7) *Betty*, b. 1790. (8) *Charlotte*, b. 1794.

CRAFT. 1. Ephraim came from Roxbury, and took land near the present residence of Alvan Fisher.

2. Samuel, supposed to be the son of Ephraim, m. Margaret ———. Children: (1) *Margaret*, b. 1737. (2) *Ephraim*, b. 1739. (3) *Mary*, b. 1741. (4) *Hannah*, b. 1744. A son, *Samuel*, d. in 1740, and a second *Samuel*, 3, was baptized 1747.

3. Samuel was a soldier of the Revolution; he m., 1767, Margaret Parrot. The town supported his family while he was in the army; after his return went to Weare, N. H., where he owned land. He returned, and becoming a pauper, the land in Weare was sold for the benefit of the town. His wife seems to have had a title to land in Gilmanton, N. H., which was also sold. The names of his children were *Mary* and *Margaret* (or *Peggy*.)

COMINGS, Cumings, Cummings. These are variations in the mode of spelling the same name. There is presumptive evidence that the family came from Topsfield or Boxford, and were related to the Cummings family, of Dunstable.

1. John Comings was a member of the church in Chelmsford, and a deacon of the same. Also, an original member of the church here and the first deacon. He was moderator of the first town meeting, and was chosen one of the selectmen; also, town clerk in 1736. His farm included the land around Westford Station on both sides of the brook, and is now occupied in part by Sarah Cummings and George F. Dupes.

It extended up the hill to William Kittredge's, and perhaps farther. His dwelling was probably near Mr. Dupee's and the great elm. He m., about 1705, Elizabeth Adams, supposed to be the daughter of Capt. Samuel Adams, of Chelmsford, who was born 1680. Children: (1) *Elizabeth*, b. 1706. (2) *John*, **2**, b. 1710. (3) *William*, b. 1712; (?) rem. to Groton. (4) *Thomas*, **3**, b. 1714. (5) *Abigail*, b. 1716. (6) *Samuel*, **4**, b. 1718. (7) *Ephraim*, **5**, b. 1720; (8) *Bridget*, b. 1722; m. Moses Parker, 1744. (9) *Mary*, b. 1724 (?). (10) *Ebenezer*, b. 1726. Dea. John Comings and his wife, Elizabeth, d. 1759.

2. **John** was admitted to the church, 1729, Dec. 7; dismissed to Groton, 1740; he m. Sarah Lawrence, daughter of Eleazer, of Littleton, 1736. Children: (1) *John*, b. 1737. (2) *Eleazer*, b. 1739. (3) *Sarah*, b. 1741. (4) *Peter*, b. 1744. (5) *Mitty*, b. 1751. (6) *Reuben*, b. 1757. (7) *Sybil*, b. 1760.

3. **Thomas**, m. Sarah Fassett, 1733 (pub. Aug. 10). She was (probably) the daughter of Josiah, and niece of Samuel, of Westford, and was born in Billerica, 1716. Children: (1) *Thomas*, **6**, b. 1734. (2) *Joseph*, **7**, b. 1736. (3) *Sarah*, b. 1738. (4) *Isaac*, **8**, b. 1742. (5) *Elizabeth*, b. 1743. (6) *John*, b. 1745; d. 1758. (7) *Bridget*, b. 1749. (8) *Timothy*, **9**, b. 1752. (9) *Molly*, b. 1755.

4. **Samuel**, m., 1741, Dec. 1, Sarah, daughter of Dea. Andrew Spalding. Children: (1) *Samuel*, b. 1742. (2) *Abigail*, b. 1744. He was dismissed and recommended, 1757, but no church or town is mentioned.

5. **Ephraim**, m. Mary Hildrith, 1742 (pub. Aug. 6). Children: (1) *Abigail*, b. 1744. (2) *Ephraim*, **10**, b. 1747. (3) *Wilson*, b. 1753; d. young. (4) *Abigail*, b. 1755.

6. **Thomas**, m., 1755, Lucy Lawrence, daughter of Eleazer, Jr., Littleton. Children: (1) *Tryphena*, b. 1756. (2) *Thomas*, b. 1757; settled in Tyngsboro'. (3) *Lucy*, b. 1760. (4) *Sarah*, b. 1762. (5) *Betty*, b. 1764; m. John Dalrumple, 1787. (6) *Phebe*, b. 1766; d. 1766. (7) *Molly*, b. 1767. (8) *Phebe*, b. 1770; m. Nathaniel Abbot, 1788.

7. **Joseph**, m., 1765, Elizabeth, daughter of Capt. William Fletcher. Children: (1) *Joseph*, **11**, b. 1768. (2) *Elizabeth*, b. 1769; m. Jacob Tuttle, Littleton, 1795. (3) *Bridget*, b. 1772. (4) *Polly*, b. 1776. (5) *William*, **12**, b. 1778. Joseph, the father, d. 1814, aged 78.

8. **Isaac**, m., 1769, May 17, Elizabeth Trowbridge. Children: (1) *Lydia*, b. 1769. (2) *John*, **13**, b. 1772. (3) *Isaac*, b. 1774; d. young. (4) *Betsey*, b. 1778. (5) *Isaac*, b. 1780. (6) *Nancy*, b. 1783. Isaac, the father, d. 1817, aged 75. Elizabeth, the mother, d. 1804, aged 60.

9. **Timothy**, m., 1776, Catherine, daughter of Benjamin Fassett. Children: (1) *Timothy*, **14**, b. 1776. (2) *Catherine*, b. 1780; m. Abel Abbot, 1805. (3) *Rebecca*, b. 1783. (4) *Polly*, b. 1784. (5) *Benjamin*, b. 1786. (6) *Ruth*, b. 1790. (7) *Sarah*, b. 1791. (8) *Thomas*, b. 1794. (9) *John*, **15**, b. 1797. (10) *Betsey*, b. 1799.

10. **Ephraim**, m. Lydia Adams, of Chelmsford, 1773. Children: (1) *Wilson*, b. 1775; m. 1796, Lucy Cowdrey; no children. (2) *Patty*, b. 1777; m. James Kidder.

11. **Joseph**, m., 1790, Hannah, daughter of Francis Leighton. Children: (1) *Charles*, b. 1792. (2) *Daniel Leighton*, b. 1794; d. 1794. (3) *George*, b. 1795; d. 1798. (4) *Lydia*, b. 1798. (5) *Daniel*, b. 1800. (6) *Angelina*, b. 1802. (7) *George*, b. 1805.

12. **William**, m., 1798, Rebecca, daughter of Wiley Richardson. Children: (1) *Rowland*, b. 1799. (2) *Louisa*, b. 1801. (3) *Wiley Richardson*, b. 1803.

13. **John**, m. Lois Tuttle. Children: (1) *Isaac*, b. 1800. (2) *Eliza*, b. 1803; (3) *John Waldo*, b. 1809. (4) *Martha Whitcomb*, b. 1811; m. Jonas Prescott. John, the father, d. 185 . Lois, the mother, d. 1867, aged 94.

14. **Timothy, Col.**, m. Elizabeth, or Betsey Whitman, of Groton. Children: (1) *Nehemiah Whitman*, b. 1806. (2) *Timothy*, b. ——. (3) *Artemas*, b. 1810; d. 1813. (4) *Catherine*, b. 1812; d. 1813. (5) *Sarah*, b. 1812. (6) *Artemas Ward*, b. 1815; m., 1st, Sarah E. Groce, who d. 1864; m., 2nd, Sarah Peabody Wright, 1874. (7) *Charity Ames*, b. 1818. (8) *Isaac*, b.

1821. (?) *Frances*, b. 1822; m. Rev. Seth W. Banister, and d. at Weare, 1856. Col. Timothy Cummings d. 1856, aged 80. His wife, Elizabeth. d. 1839, aged 58.
15. **John**, m. Sally Boynton. Child: *John Boynton*, b. 1838.
(Unconnected.) **Nathaniel**, m. Rebecca ———. Children: (1) *Nathaniel*, b. 1778. (2) *John*, b. 1781.

DAY. 1. Isaac came from Ipswich; m. Lucy Dutton, 1796. He d. 1856, aged 84. Children: (1) *Isaac*, **2**, b. 1797; d. 1856. (2) *Amos*, **3**, b. 1799. (3) *Lucy*, b. 1803; d. 1837. (4) *John*, **4**, b. 1805. (5) *Asa*, b. 1807; d. 1838. (6) *Thomas*, b. 1809; d. 1842. (7) *Betsey*, b. 1812; m. Lemuel Whiting, Groton, 1832; d. 1838.

2. Isaac, m. Betsey Proctor, daughter of Nathan Proctor, Jr. She was born in Dunstable, 1801. Children: (1) *Isaac Edmund*, b. 1826; m. 'Lucy Maria Whiting. (2) *Betsey Jane*, b. 1828; d. 1831. (3) *George Thomas*, b. 1833; m. Cornelia A. Fletcher, 1867. Isaac, the father, d. 1856, aged 59. Betsey, the mother, d. 1878.

3. Amos, m. Isabella Hildreth, daughter of Elijah, 1839. Child: *Mary Elizabeth*, b. ——; m. Jonathan T. Colburn, 18—.

4. John, m. Hannah Wright, daughter of Jacob, 1834. Children: (1) *John Warren*, b. 1837; m. Emma M. Sprague. (2) *Lucy Elizabeth*, b. 1839. (3) *Sarah Ann*, b. ——, m. Warren S. Jones.

DENNIS. Arthur, m. Mary ———. Child: *John*, b. 1771; was in New Ipswich, 1790.

DUDLEY. Daniel, m. Hannah ———. Children: (1) *Ebenezer*, b. 1759. (2) *Jesse*, b. 1761; d. in the army, 1778. (3) *Sarah*, b. 1763. (4) *John*, b. 1765; m. Sarah Dutton, 1787. (5) *Isaac*, b. 1770.

DUTTON. 1. Thomas, son of Thomas, b. in Billerica, 1681; came here after 1738. He and his sons lived in the vicinity of Jonathan T. Colburn's, one on the Flagg place, and one near Colburn's. He d. 1759.

2. Joseph, son of Thomas, b. in Billerica, 1711; m. Rebecca Adams, Chelmsford, 1735. Children: (1) *Esther*, b. 1738; m. William Spalding, 1759. (2) *Joseph*, **7**, b. 1741. (3) *Salmon*, b. 1743-44; settled in Cavendish, Vt., where he d., aged 80. (4) *Rebecca*, b. 1746; m. Phinehas Chamberlin, 1769; rem. to Bedford. (5) *Thomas*, b. 1747-48; m. Sarah Bigelow, 1768; rem. to Jaffrey. (6) *William*, b. 1750; m. Phebe Temple, of Acton, 1777; rem. to Cavendish. (7) *John*, b. 1753; d. 1754.

3. Thomas, son of Thomas, b. in Billerica, 1713; m. Mary Hill, Billerica, 1737. Children: (1) *Mary*, b. in Billerica, 1737. (2) *Silas*, b. 1739, in Westford. (3) *Sarah*, b. 1741, in Westford.

4. James, son of Thomas, b. in Billerica, 1721; m. Rebecca Hildreth, 1750. Children: (1) *Samuel*, b. 1751. (2) *Lucy*, b. 1753. (3) *Rebecca*, b. 1755; m., 1780, Ezra Jewett, Littleton. (4) *James*, b. 1757. (5) *Esther*, b. 1758. (6) *Jesse*, b. 1762. (7) *Hildreth*, b. 1764.

5. Benjamin, son of Thomas, b. in Billerica; m. Mary Rumrill, 1751. Children: (1) *Mary*, b. 1753. (2) *Benjamin*, b. 1755; m. Elizabeth Freetoe, Dunstable, 1786. (3) *Sibel*, b. 1758. (4) *Martha*, b. 1761; a pauper.

6. David, son of Thomas, b. in Billerica; m. Esther Heald, 1761. Children: (1) *Esther*, b. 1762; m. Ephraim Dutton, 1797. (2) *Sarah*, b. 1764; m. John Dudley, 1787. (3) *David*, b. 1766; m. Hannah Wright, 1802; settled in Chelmsford. (4) *Thomas*, b. 1769; settled in Deering, N. H. (5) *Eunice*, b. 1773; d. 1775. (6) *Eunice*, b. 1777.

7. Joseph, m. Lucy Bigelow, 1766. Children: (1) *Lucy*, b. 1768; m. Isaac Day. (2) *Molly*, b. 1770; d. young. (3) *Patty*, b. 1773; d. young. (4) *Rebecca*, b. 1775; m. Timothy Locke, of Ashby, 1804. (5) *Molly*, b. 1779. (6) *Patty*, b. 1782; m. David Campernell.

8. Thomas, m. Hannah Twiss, 1799. Children: (1) *Luther*, b. 1800; d. 1802. (2) *Hannah*, b. 1801. (3) *Lydia*, b. 1803.

ESTHERBROOKS. 1. Benjamin, son of Thomas and Prudence, b. in Dunstable, 1744-45; m. Sarah Heald, 1769. Children: (1) *Thomas*, b. 1770. (2) *Joel*, b. 1772. (3) *Benjamin*, b. 1773. (4) *Hosea*, b. 1779. (5) *Sarah*, b. 1781. (6) *Rhoda*, b. 1783.

2. Joel, brother of Benjamin, b. 1748–49; m. Abigail Underwood, Chelmsford, 1778 (pub. Feb. 4.) Children: (1) *Abigail Underwood*, b. 1779. (2) *Sophia*, b. 1781. (3) *Polly*, b. 1782. (4) *Susanna*, b. 1784. (5) *Joel*, b. 1788. (6) *Sarah*, b. 1790.

ELIOT. John, and Rachel, his wife. Children: (1) *Thomas*, b. 1783. (2) *David*, b. 1787. (3) (?) *Andrew*.

FARMER. Benjamin, m. Rebecca ———. Children: (1) *Rebecca*, b. 1743; m. Andrew Bettys, Jr., Chelmsford, 1765. (2) *Benjamin*, b. 1746. (3) *Minot*, b. 1751; rem. to Hollis; m. 1775, Abigail Barron.

FASSET. 1. Samuel, the first town treasurer. He was a son of Patrick, of Billerica, where he was born, 1679; m. Lydia Parker, 1705–06. He doubtless had children born before his settlement here; for Samuel, Jr., had a family, whose record appears on the books; and also, Amaziah and Benjamin who were born here, 1729.

2. Samuel, m. Catherine Read, daughter of Thomas and Sarah, 1740. Children: (1) *Catherine*, b. 1741. (2) *Samuel*, b. 1743. (3) *Thomas*, b. 1745. (4) *Joshua, 5*, b. 1747.

3. Amaziah, m. Eunice Fletcher, 1742. Children: (1) *Amaziah*, b. 1742; settled in Groton; in the battle of Bunker Hill (see p. 111); m. Ede Richardson, 1768. (2) *Eunice*, b. 1744. (3) *Abigail*, b. 1745. Wid. Eunice m. James Spalding, 1771,

4. Benjamin, m. Rebecca Russell, of Litchfield, 1753. Children: (1) *Rebecca*, b. 1754. (2) *Catherine*, b. 1757. (3) *Mara*, b. 1759.

5 Joshua, a soldier of the Revolution; m. Sarah Priest, of New Ipswich, 1768. Children: (1) *Samuel*, b. 1769; m. Rebecca Powers, Littleton, 1790. (2) *Catherine*, b. 1771.

FITCH. Samuel, came from Bedford; m. Joanna Kidder, 1732; and settled at Nashoba Hill, close to Littleton line. Children: (1) *Samuel*, b. 1733; rem. to Acton. (2) *Joanna*, b. 1735; m. Eleazer Read, 1754. (3) *Lydia*, b. 1737; m. Francis Leighton, 1760.

FLETCHER. The ancestor of this family was Robert, who came from England and settled in Concord, 1630. William, his son, was born in England, 1622, and was among the first settlers of Chelmsford, 1653. Paul, the son of William, lived in Westford, near Boutwell's meadow. He m. Deliverance Stevens, 1705; was deacon of the church; d. 1736. Joshua, grandson of William, settled in Westford on the farm now occupied by Robert J. Taylor. He had sons, Joshua, Gershom, Ephraim and Zechariah. Joshua d. 1727; Gershom m. Lydia Townsend and lived for a time in Groton. Ephraim and Zechariah enlisted in the war against the Indians and never returned. (For further information of the line of Joshua, see the Fletcher Genealogy). Paul, the grandson of William, settled in the Stony Brook Valley on the farm now occupied by Clarence Decatur, and his son Ebenezer lived on the farm of the late Levi Snow. Jonathan, grandson of William, m. Jane Chamberlin, and settled near Thomas Horan's. Jonas, another grandson of William, settled near the present village of Graniteville. Samuel, the son of Robert, m. Margaret Hailston, and settled in that part of Chelmsford, which is now Westford. His grandson William (son of William), settled in Westford on the farm now owned by Henry A. Hildreth. Samuel, the grandson of Samuel and also the son of William, settled in Westford on the farm of Calvin Howard. This family is very numerous and it has always been so. It is not convenient for the purposes of this registry to arrange the families in the order of their pedigree, nor is there space to give them all in detail. It is thought expedient to follow the order of the record, and indicate the lineal descent as far as practicable. The records begin with:

1. Samuel, son of William, and grandson of Samuel. He m. Mary Lawrence, of Littleton, 1729. Children: (1) *Samuel*, b. 1730; d. 1749. (2) *Eleazer*, b. 1731–2. (3) *Peter*, b. 1733. (4) *Oliver*, b. 1735. (5) *Abel*, b. 1737. (6) *Mary*, b. 1739. (7) *Ezekiel*, b. 1741. (8) *Phebe*, b. 1742; d. 1759. (9) *Margaret*, b. 1744; d. 1752. (10) *Sarah*, b. 1746. (11) *Samson*, b. 1748; d. 1752. (12) *Rebecca*, b. 1750. (13) *Samuel*, b. 1754. (14) *Margaret*, b. 1755. (15) *Samson*, b. 1758.

GENEALOGY. 447

2. Joshua and Dorothy. Children: (1) *Joshua*, b. 1701. (2) *Sarah* b. 1703–4; d. 1704. (3) *Elizabeth*, b. 1704–5; m. Benjamin Blodgett, Litchfield. (4) *Hannah*, b. 1706; m. Timothy Barron. (5) *Esther*, b. 1708; d. 1708. (6) *Ephraim*, b. 1709–10. (7) *Gershom*, b. 1712. (8) *Zechariah*. b. 1714. (9) *Dorothy*, b. 1715–16. (10) *Sarah*, b. 1719. (11) *Eunice*, b. 1720. Deacon Joshua, the father, d. 1736.

3. Joshua, son of Dea. Joshua; m. Elizabeth ———. Children: (1) *Joshua*, b. 1724; d. young. (2) *Esther*, b. 1726; d. young.

4. Jonathan, the grandson of William. Children: (1) *Wyle*, b. 1728; d. 1753. (2) *Susanna*, b. 1733; d. 1753. (3) *Abigail*, b. 1735; d. 1753. (4) *Jonathan*, b. 1736. (5) *Rachel*, b. 1740. (6) *Jane*, b. 1742. (7) *Susanna*, b. 1744. (8) *Elizabeth*, b. 1746.

5. Zechariah, son of Joshua, m. Susanna Fasset, 1735. Children: (1) *Zechariah*, b. 1735; d. 1738. (2) *Susanna*, b. 1737; d. 1738. (3) *Zechariah*, b. 1740. (4) *Susanna*, b. 1743. (5) *Joshua*, b. 1745; d. 1747. (6) *Abigail*, b. 1747. (7) *Elizabeth*, b. 1755.

6. William, son of William, m., 1st, Elizabeth Remington. Children: (1) *William*, b. 1731. (2) *Jonathan*, b. 1733–4. (3) *Caleb*, b. 1735. (4) *Elizabeth*, b. 1737. (5) *Sarah*, b. 1739; d. 1742. (6) *Lydia*, b. 1741; m. Silas Richardson, New Ipswich. (7) *Joel*, b. 1742. (8) *Seth*, b. 1744. (9) *Asaph*, b. 1746. (10) *Oliver*, b. 1749. (11) *Sarah*, b. ———.

7. Joseph, son of Joshua, and grandson of William; m. Sarah Adams, Concord, 1712. Children: (1) *Joseph*, b. 1713. (2) *Benjamin*, b. 1716. (3) *Timothy*, b. 1719. (4) *Thomas*, b. 1721. (5) *Edith*, b. 1725; m. Benjamin Carver. (6) *Pelatiah*, b. 1727. (7) *Joshua*, b. 1731. (8) *Ruth*, b. 1733. (9) *Mary*, b. 1735; m. Eleazer Fletcher.

8. Timothy, son of Paul, m. Mary ———. Children: (1) *Jesse*, b. 1730; d. 1756. (2) *Timothy*, b. 1732; d. 1780. (3) *Daniel*, b. 1735; d. at Crown Point, 1760. (4) *Simeon*, b. 1737; rem. to New Ipswich. (5) *Mary*, b. 1739; m. Jonas Barrett. (6) *Rebecca*, b. 1741. (7) *James*, b. 1743. (8) *Esther*, b. 1745; d. 1745. (9) *Sarah*, b. 1749. (10) *John*, b. 1751.

9. Gershom, son of Dea. Joshua, m. Lydia Townsend. Children: (1) *Lydia*, b. 1733; m. Timothy Prescott. (2) *Esther*, b. 1735; m. James Tarbell. (3) *Gershom*, b. 1737, in Groton. (4) *Olive*, b. 1741, in Groton. (5) *Sarah*, b. 1744; m. Hezakiah Corey; settled in New Ipswich. (6) *Mary*, b. 1746; m. Jonathan Robbins; settled in Plymouth, N. H. (7) *Lucy*, b. 1751. (8) *Martha*, b. 1754; m. Joseph Reed, 1771. Gershom, the father, d. 1779.

10. Ephraim, m. Hannah Roe. Children: (1) *Joshua*, b. 1734. (2) *Peter*, b. 1736. (3) *Lois*, b. 1741. (4) *Sarah*, b. 1742. (5) *Ephraim*, b. 1743.

11. Amos, son of William, and grandson of Samuel; m. Mary Perham, 1741. Children: (1) *Amos*, b. 1755. (2) *Mary*, b. 1757; m. Henry Spalding, Chelmsford, 1774. (3) *Nehemiah*, b. 1758. (4) *Lucy*, b. 1761.

12. Ebenezer, son of Paul; m., 1754, Joanna Stearns, in Billerica. Children: (1) *Joanna*, b. 1755. (2) *Josiah*, b. 1757. (3) *Solomon*, b. 1760. (4) *Esther*, b. 1762. (5) *Lucy*, b. 1765. (6 and 7) *Rebecca* and *Rachel*, b. 1769.

13. David, son of Samuel, m. Mary Butterfield, 1742. Children: (1) *Oliver*, b. 1743; settled in Shirley, but returned. (2) *Samuel*, b. 1745; m. Olive Wright; rem. to Hollis. (3) *Joanna*, b. 1747; m. Seth Fletcher. (4) *Willard*, b. 1749; m. Abigail Hadley. (5) *David*, b. 1752; m. Joanna Stevens, Chelmsford. (6) *Jeremiah*, b. 1756; rem. to Wilton, Me. (7). *Andrew*, b. 1761.

14. Reuben, son of William, m. Susanna Chandler. Children: (1) *Mary*, b. 1746; m. Thomas Barnes, Universalist Minister. (2) *Sarah*, b. 1747. (3) *William*, b. 1749; d. 1754. (4) *Henry*, b. 1751. (5) *Susanna*, b. 1753; m. Henry Thompson, settled in Jaffrey, N. H. (6) *William*, b. 1755; d. unmarried, about 1776. (7) *Lydia*, b. 1757; m. Eleazer Blood. (8) *Rachel*, b. 1761; m. Asa Thompson, settled in Jeffrey. (9) *Phebe*, b. 1763; m. Isaac Patch.

15. Zechariah, son of Zechariah, m. Eunice Keep. Children: (1) *Eunice*, b. 1763. (2) *Susanna*, b. 1765. (3) *Abigail*, b. 1768.

16. Thomas, son of Capt. Joseph, m. Sarah Goodhue. Children:
(1) *Thomas,* b. 1764. (2) *Patty,* b. 1771; d. 1779. Thomas, the father, d. 1813, aged 92. Sarah, the mother, d. 1813, aged 76.

17. Pelatiah, son of Capt. Joseph, m., 1st, Dorothy, daughter of James Hildreth. Children: (1) *Betty,* b. 1757. (2) *Dorothy,* b. 1759; m. Sampson Fletcher. (3) *Joseph,* b. 1761; d. 1765. (4) *Sarah,* b. 1763; d. 1783. (5) *Lucy,* b. 1765; d. 1765. (6) *Pelatiah,* b. 1767. (7) *Joseph,* b. 1769. (8) *Lucy,* b. 1771; m. Joseph Rockwood, Groton. (9) *Adams,* b. 1773; d. 1775. (10) *Ezra,* b. 1774. (11) *Polly,* b. 1776; m. Abram Prescott. (12) *Adams,* b. 1779. Capt. Pelatiah, the father, d. 1807.

18. Benjamin, son of Capt. Joseph, m. Bethiah Herrick, 1744. Children: (1) *Benjamin,* b. 1747. (2) *Joseph,* b. 1749. (3) *Bethiah,* b. 1751. (4) *Rebecca,* b. 1755; m. Levi Parker (?).

19. Timothy, son of Capt Joseph, lived where Cyrus Hamlin now lives; m. Bridget Richardson, daughter of Capt. Zachariah, of Chelmsford. She was a woman of distinguished piety, and the author of a small volume of hymns published by her son about 1774. Children: (1) *Elijah,* b. 1747, grad. H. U., 1769; was the second Congregational minister, Hopkinton, N. H. (2) *Josiah,* b. 1749; a soldier of the Revolution, in the battles of Bunker Hill, White Plains, Bennington and Ticonderoga; settled in Ludlow, Vt. (3) *Bridget,* b. 1751; d. young. (4) *Lucy,* b. 1754. (5) *Bridget,* b. 1760; m. Isaac Parker; settled in Cavendish, Vt. (6) *Jesse,* b. 1762; m, Lucy Keyes, and settled in Ludlow.

20. Joshua, son of Capt. Joseph, m. Elizabeth Raymond (pub. 1755). Children: (1) *Levi,* b. 1756. (2) *Lyman,* b. 1758. (3) *Joshua,* b. 1760. (4) *Paul Raymond,* b. 1761; in the War of the Revolution; d., Valley Forge. (5) *Isaac,* b. 1763. (6) *Elizabeth,* b. 1766. (7) *Abigail,* b. 1768. (8) *Polly* b. 1771. (9) *Sally,* b. 1773.

21. Levi, son of Joshua and Elizabeth, m. Jerusha ———. Child: (1) *Raymond,* b. 1783.

22. Jonathan, son of William, who lived on the farm of Henry A. Hildreth, was deacon of the First Church; m. Sarah Spalding, Chelmsford. Children: (1) *Sarah,* b. 1762. (2 and 3) *Jonathan* and *Joanna,* b. 1764; Jonathan d., unmarried, 1844; Joanna m. Capt. Aaron Parker.

23. Jonas, son of Joshua and grandson of William, m. Elizabeth ———. Children: (1) *Jonas,* b. 1729. (2) *Jonas,* b. 1735.

24. Samuel, son of Samuel, m. Hannah ———. Children: (1) *Samuel,* b. 1713; d. young. (2) *Jacob,* b. 1715; d. young. (3 and 4) *David* and *Hannah,* b. 1718. (5) *Elizabeth,* b. 1720; m. Jonathan Keyes, 1746. (6) *Samuel,* b. 1722. (7) *Susannah,* b. 1723. (8) *Jacob,* b. 1725; m. Ruth Trull 1746. (9) *John,* b. 1727; lived in Dunstable. (10) *Joanna,* b. 1729; d. 1730. (11) *Abigail,* b. 1731. (12) *Sarah,* b. 1833. [See Gen. p. 128.]

25. James, son of Timothy; lived on the Patten place; m. Rebecca Prescott. Children: (1) *Jonas,* b. 1770. (2) *Rebecca,* b. 1772.

26. Gershom, son of Gershom, m. Sarah Robinson. Children. (1) *Sarah,* b. 1770. (2) *Gershom,* b. 1771; d. 1778. (3) *Jacob,* b. 1773; d. 1778. (4) *Lucy,* b. 1775; d. 1778. (5) *Stephen,* b. 1776. (6) *Dorothy,* b. 1778. (7) *Gershom,* b. 1780.

27. Benjamin, son of Benjamin, m. Rebecca Boynton. Children: (1) *Benjamin,* b. 1775. (2) *Rebecca,* b. 1778. (3) *Sewall,* b. 1780; m. Mary Stone, and settled in Cortland Co., N. Y.

28. David, son of David, m. Joanna Stevens. Child: (1) *Joanna,* b. 1774.

29. Seth, son of Capt. William, m. Joanna Fletcher. Children: (1) *Seth,* b. 1775. (2) *Joel,* b. 1777. (3) *Joanna,* b. 1779. (4) *Mary,* b. 1781. (5) *Elizabeth,* b. 1784. (6) *Noah,* 1786.

30. Amos, son of Amos, m. Rebecca Prescott. Children: (1) *Amos,* b. 1777; d. 1778. (2) *Amos,* b. 1778. (3) *Abel,* b. 1782. (4) *Elisha,* b. 1784. (5) *Jesse,* b. 1786. (6) *Rebecca,* b. 1790. (7) *Mary,* b. 1792.

31. Asaph, son of Capt. William, m. Sarah Green, Chelsea. Children: (1) *Sarah,* b. 1778. (2) *Asaph,* b. 1780. (3) *Salome,* b. 1783. (4) *Rebecca,* b. 1785. He rem. to Cavendish, Vt., where other children were born. [See Fletcher Genealogy.]

GENEALOGY. 449

32. Samuel, son of Capt. Samuel, m., 1st, Lucy Jones. Children: (1) *Samuel*, b. 1778. (2) *Lucy*, b. 1781; m. John Keep, 1800. (3) *Polly*, b. 1783; m. Joseph Corey, 1804. He m., 2nd, Miriam Keyes. (4) *Anna*, b. 1788; m. Seth Whitmore, Lockport, N. Y. (5) *Betsey*, b. 1791; m. Calvin Howard. (6 and 7) *Horatio* and *Clarissa*, b. 1796. (8) *Mary Ann*, b. 1798. (9) *Almira*, b. 1805; m. Jesse Minot, Lockport, N. Y. (10) *Elbridge*, b. 1807; rem. to Clarksville, Mo.

33. Nehemiah, son of Capt. Amos, m. Mary Wheeler. Children: (1) *Patty*, b. 1780. (2) *Polly*, b. 1781. (3) *Nehemiah*, b. 1783. (4) *Abijah*, b. 1784.

34. Willard, son of David, m. Abigail Hadley. Children: (1) *Mary*, b. 1776; m. Abijah Wright. (2) *Willard*, b. 1778. (3) *Abigail*, b. 1781; m. Jesse Hadley. (4) *Abby*, b. 1782. (5) *Loammi*, b. 1788. (6) *David*, b. 1791. (7) *Orpah*, b. 1794; m. Thomas Fletcher. (8) *Nancy*, b. 1797. (9) *Cyrus*, b. 1802; rem. to Townsend.

35. Jeremiah, son of David; m. Elizabeth Perham, of Dunstable. Children: (1) *Betsey*, b. 1785. (2) *Polly*, b. 1786. (3) *Asa*, b. 1787. (4) *Rebecca*, b. 1789. (5) *Jeremiah*, b. 1791. The family rem. to Wilton, Me.

36. Andrew, son of David, m., 1st, Lydia Wright. Children: (1) *Andrew*, b. 1785. (2) *Jotham*, b. 1787. (3) *Patty*, b. 1790; m. David Eastman, Strafford, Vt. (4) *Lucy*, b. 1793; m. Willard Jones, Vershire, Vt. (5) *Hannah*, b. 1796; m. Imla Keyes. (6) *Sophia*, b. 1798; m. George W. Jones, Vershire, Vt. (7) *Asenath*, b. 1800; m. Ephraim Wright. (8) *Jesse*, b. 1804; was drowned in Nubanussuck Pond. (9) *Lydia*, b. 1808; m. Ephraim Buttrick. Dea. Andrew Fletcher, d. 1843, aged 82.

37. Samson, son of Samuel, m. Olive Spalding. Child: *Justus*, b. 1785.

38. Lyman, son of Joshua; m. Lois or Louisa Gates. Children: (1) *Lyman*, b. 1796. (2) *Levi T.*, b. 1798. (3) *Hosea*, b. 1799; d. 1800. (4) *Louisa*, b. 1802. (5) *George W.*, b. 1803. (6) *Walter*, b. 1805. (7) *Patty*, b. 1807. (8) *Paul Raymond*, b. 1809. (9) *Sally*, b. 1813.

39. Thomas, son of Thomas, m. Patty Jewett. Children: (1) *Patty*, b. 1787; m. John Osgood. (2) *Thomas*, b. 1791. (3) *Rebecca Abbot*, b. 1796; m. William W. Goodhue. (4) *Sally*, b. 1799; m. Sewall Parkhurst, Chelmsford. (5) *Jefferson*, b. 1802.

40. Joseph, son of Capt. Pelatiah, m. Frances Grant Keyes. Children: (1) *Joseph*, b. 1794. (2) *Frances Grant*, b. 1796; m. Gardner Fletcher, Chelmsford. (3) *Walter*, b. 1797. (4) *Louisa*, b. 1799. (5) *Charles Hartwell*, b. 1801. (6) *Polly*, b. 1802; m. Orville Richardson, Leominster. (7) *Nancy*, b. 1805; d. young. (8) *Abijah*, b. 1807. (9) *Nancy*, b. 1808; m. Samuel J. Nichols. (10) *Jonathan Varnum*, b. 1812.

41. Pelatiah, son of Capt. Pelatiah, m., 1st, Patty Keyes. Children: (1) *Joel*, b. 1786. He m., 2nd, Sally Woodward. (2 and 3) *Sally* and *Patty*, b. 1789. (4) *Wiley*, b. 1791; rem. to Albany, N. Y. (5) *Samuel*, b. 1792. (6) *Timothy*, b. 1795; rem. to Charlestown, Mass. (7) *Calvin*, b. 1797; rem. to Groton. (8) *Harriet*, b. 1800; m. Nathan S. Hamblin. (9) *Mary*, b. 1803; m. Thomas Richardson. He m., 3rd, Mrs Beulah Heywood. (10) *Pelatiah*, b. 1804. (11) *Lucy Wheeler*, b. 1806; m. Abel Stevens.

42. Sampson, son of Capt. Samuel, m. Dorothy Fletcher. Children: (1) *Sally*, b. 1786. (2) *Abel*, b. 1789. (3) *Dolly*, b. 1792; m. Calvin Holmes; rem. to Western New York. (4) *Sampson*, b. 1795. (5) *George*, b. 1797. (6) *Asa*, b. 1799. (7) *Lucy*, b. 1803.

43. Seth, son of Seth, m. Sally Proctor, 1809. Children: (1) *Sherman Dewey*, b. 1810. (2) *Mary E.*, b. 1815. (3) *Asaph*, b. 1818; d. 1820.

44. Thomas, son of Capt Thomas, m. Orpah Fletcher, 1812. Children: (1) *Mary*, b. 1813; m. Eli Tower, 1833. (2) *William E.*, b. 1815; d. 1828. (3) *Francis*, b. 1818; m. Esther B. Wright; rem. to Utah. (4) *Charles Leonard*, b. 1820; m. Sophia M. Keyes, 1844. Child: Ella Sophia.

45. Ezra, son of Capt. Pelatiah, m. Hannah Bateman, of Chelmsford, 1800. Children: (1) *John Bateman*, b. in Chelmsford, 1802. (2) *Othiel*, b. 1806. (3) *Mary*, b. 1809; m. Gilbert Harwood. (4) *Maria*, b. 1815; d. 1818. (5) *Timothy*, b. 1820; m. Sarah Gould, 1851.

46. Levi Thomas, son of Lyman, b. 1798; m. Ama Richardson, 1825. Children: (1) *Ama Elizabeth,* b. 1826; d. 1847. (2) *Susan Augusta,* b. 1828; m. Reuben J. Butterfield. (3) *Edward T.,* b. 1831; d. 1833. (4) *Sarah Jane,* b. 1836; d. 1837. (5) *Lydia Henrietta,* b. 1888; d. 1860.

47. Horatio, son of Dea. Samuel, m. Nancy Edwards, of Acton. Children: (1) *Caroline,* b. 1827; d. 1853. (2) *Samuel E.,* b. 1829; d. 1840. (3) *Julia M.,* b. 1830; m. Luther B. Morse, M. D., of Watertown. (4) *Mary Edwards,* b. 1832; m. W. P. Brazer, of Lowell. (5) *Horatio Richmond,* b. 1835. (6) *Clara Augusta,* b. 1841; m. John E. Humphrey, Rockford, Ill.

48. Sherman D., son of Seth, m. Emily Augusta Fletcher, 1839. Children: (1) *Cornelia A.,* b. 1841; m. George T. Day, 1867. (2) *Emily Frances,* b. 1843. (3) *Sherman Heywood,* b. 1846; m. Mary E. Richardson 1874.

49. Abel, son of Sampson, m., 1st, Susan Richardson. Children: (1) *Oliver R.,* b. 1821; res. in Waltham. (2) *Abel Bancroft,* b. 1823. (3) *Sampson,* b. 1829. He m., 2nd, Mary Kimball. (4) *Mary K.,* b. 1838; m. Edwin E. Heywood. (5) *Albert Wright,* b. 1840; killed at Port Hudson. (6) *Lucy Adelaide,* b. 1842; d. 1881. (7) *Edward E.,* b. 1857.

50. Abijah, son of Joseph, m. Louisa Lawrence, of Hollis. Children: (1) *Luke L.,* b. 1832; m. Lucy J. Walker, of Burlington, 1864. (2) *Elizabeth C.,* b. 1834; m. George W. Heywood, 1860. (3) *Charles H.,* b. 1843; m. Mary E. Leighton, 1865.

FOSTER. 1. Elias, jr., m. Abigail Wheeler, Acton. Children: (1) *Abigail,* b. 1746-7. (2) *Mary,* b. 1749. (3) *Elias,* b. 1751. (4) *Samuel,* b. 1756.

2. Samuel, m. Mary ———. Child: (1) *Polly,* b. 1788.

3. Benjamin, m. Abigail ———. Children: (1) *Benjamin,* b. 1765. (2) *Susanna,* b. 1768.

4. Smith, son of Henry, of Billerica, m. Esther Sartell, of Acton. Children: (1) *Luther,* b. 1778. (2) *Ephraim,* b. 1781.

GLENE. John, m. Thankful Adams. Children: (1) *John,* b. 1751. (2) *Sarah* b. 1757. (3) *William,* b. 1758. (4) *Isaac,* b. 1761; m. Sally Nutting. (5) *Molly,* b. 1763.

GOODHUE. 1. David, probably came from Ipswich; m. Esther Prescott. Children: (1) *John,* 3, b. 1768. (2) *Amos,* b. 1771. (3) *Sally,* b. 1774; m. Dr. Allen Flagg; rem. to Ashby. (4) *Imla,* b. 1776; d. 1859; m. Nancy Locke, (no children). (5) *Paron;* m. Nathaniel Adams, of Ashby. (6) *David,* b. 1782. (7) *Senir* (?) *Asenath,* b. 1786. Col. Goodhue d. 1798, aged 56. Esther, his widow, d. 1833, aged 91.

2. Daniel, perhaps a brother of David; m. Sarah Hildreth. Children: (1) *Daniel,* b. 1774. (2) *Samuel,* b. 1776. (3) *James,* b. 1779. (4) *Thomas Fletcher,* b. 1784.

3. John, m. Sally Tuttle. Children: (1) *Alinda,* b. 1792; d. young. (2) *Zoa A.,* b. 1774; m. Thomas Minot. (3) *Cynthia,* b. 1795; m. Samuel C. Tenny. (4) *Alinda,* b. 1798. (5) *David,* b. 1800. (6) *William W.,* b. 1803; m. Rebecca A. Fletcher. (7) *Nancy L.,* b. 1809; m. Otis Longley. (8) *Harriet M.,* b. ———.

GREEN. Benjamin, m., 1st, Olive Hildreth. Children: (1) *Benjamin,* b. 1794. (2) *Amos,* b. 1796. (3) *Lucy,* b. 1798; d. 1815. (4) *Huldah,* b. 1801. (5) *Caroline,* b. 1803. (6) *Eliza,* b. 1805. (7) *Abel,* b. 1807. (8) *Jabez,* b. 1809. (9) *William,* b. 1812. He m., 2nd, Lucy Bicknell. (10) *Charles,* b. 1816. (11) *Lucy,* b. 1817; d. 1817. (12) *Lewis,* b. 1818. (13) *George,* b. 1820.

GRIFFIN. 1. Matthew, from Pepperell, m. Wid. Mary Adams, 1777. Children: *Matthew,* 2, b. 1779. (2) *Sally,* b. ———; m. Aaron White. (3) *Prudence;* m. Ballard Smith, Dunstable, 1803.

2. Matthew, m. Sally, daughter, of Samuel and Sally (Kidder) Adams, 1810. Children: (1) *Matthew T. A. K.,* b. 1812. (2) *Susanna,* b. 1814. (3) *Joseph,* b. 1816. (4) *Mary A.,* b. 1819; m. Jacob Burnham Smith, 1840. (5) *Benjamin K.,* b. 1821. (6) *Sylvia E.,* b. 1824; m. Asaph Mansfield, 1840. (7) *Timothy Lilley,* 3, b. 1827. (8) *George A.* b. ———; m. Eliza T. Wright, 1840.

Residence of Sherman D. Fletcher.

3. Timothy L., m. Lydia S. Gates, 1852. Children: (1) *Sarah J.*, b. 1853; m. Frank C. Hildreth. (2) *Augusta Ann*, b. 1856; d. 1857. (3) *Clara S.*, b. 1861. (4) *Frank Artemas*, b. 1864. (5) *Viola Mabel*, b. 1868. (6) *Isaac Adams*, b. 1871.

HADLEY. 1. John, probably b. in Groton, 1719; m. Eunice ——. Children: (1) *Sarah*, b. 1745; m. Joseph Warren, Littleton. (2) *John*, 3, b. 1746. (3) *Eunice*, d. young. (4) *Eunice*, b. 1750; m. Levi Farr. (5) *Peter*, b. 1752; rem. to Marlborough, N. H. (6) *Jonathan*, b. 1754; killed at Bunker Hill. (7) *Jonas*, b. 1756; settled in Mt. Holly, Vt. (8) *Lucy*, b. 1758. (9) *Ruth*, b. 1760. (10) *Tryphena*, b. 1762. (11) *Joseph*, b. 1764. (12) *Benjamin*, b. 1766. (13) *Amos*, b. 1768; rem. to Mt. Holly.

2. Ebenezer, m. Abigail Spalding, Chelmsford. Children: (1) *Jesse*, b. 1753; m. Nabby Spalding; rem. to Brattleborough, Vt. (2) *Ebenezer*, b. 1755. (3) *Abigail*, b. 1757; m. Willard Fletcher. (4) *Martha*, b. 1760. (5) *Jacob*, b. 1762. (6) *Susanna*, b. 1764. (7) *Benjamin*, b. 1766; d. 1767. (8) *Benjamin*, b. 1769. (9) *Sarah*, b. 1771.

3. John, m. Ruth Kemp, Groton. Children: (1) *Sarah*, b. 1774. (2) *John*, b. 1777.

HALL. Rev. Willard. 1. His birth and parentage have already been given. His marriage to Miss Abigail Cotton, took place some time in 1720, the precise date not certain. She was probably descended from William Cotton, of Portsmouth, N. H., who came from England at some time prior to 1657, and who died in 1678. There is some evidence to show that she was his granddaughter, but the relationship cannot be positively affirmed. If such was the fact, she must have been the daughter of John and Sarah Cotton, of Portsmouth. She is said to have been "a woman aristocratic in her feelings, and somewhat severe with her domestics." Children: (1) *Willard*, b. 1730, in Portsmouth, N. H.; m. Ruth Fletcher, of Westford, and settled in Dunstable. (2) *Elizabeth*, b. 1732; d. 1813; m., 1st, Capt. Caleb Symmes; m., 2nd, Capt Benjamin Fletcher. (3) *Abigail*, b. 1734; d. 1804; m. Oliver Abbot, of Billerica. (4) *Anne*, b. 1736; d. 1801; m. Capt. Leonard Whiting. (5) *Mary*, b. 1738; d. 1792; m. Capt. Jonas Minot. (6) *Stephen*, b. 1740; d. young. (7) *Martha*, b. 1741; d. young. (8) *Stephen*, b. 1743; m. Mary (Cotton) Holt. (9) *Grace*, b. 1745; d. about 1783; m., 1st, Benjamin Whiting; m., 2nd, Burpee Ames, of Hollis. (10) *Willis*, b. 1747; m. Mehitabel Poole. (11) *Iraiah*, b. 1749; lived in Groton. (12) *Martha*, b. 1752; d. 1840; m. Richard Kneeland.

2. Willis, son of Rev. Willard, b. 1747; m. Mehitabel Poole, of Hollis. Children: Willard, b. 1780. (See sketch p. 339.) (2) *William*, b. 1782. (3) *Elizabeth*, b. 1787. (4) *Mehitabel*, b. 1789. (5) *Hannah*, b. 1791. (6) *Francis*, b. 1793. (7) *Benjamin*, b. 1796.

HAMLIN. The first of this name in Westford was Eleazer, who came here from Harvard; but the family is said to have been early established in Plymouth County. Eleazer m. Lydia Bonney, probably in Bridgewater, Mass. They had fifteen children, whose names were Asia, d. young; Betty, Alice, Africa, Europe, America, Lydia, Molly, Cyrus, (twin,) Hannibal, (twin,) Sally, Isaac, Asia, Green and George. Five of these graduated at Harvard, and of his descendants fourteen or fifteen have graduated from some college. Isaac removed to Waterford, Me. Besides him, several of the sons removed to Maine. Cyrus was the father of ex-Vice President Hamlin, and Hannibal was the father of Rev. Cyrus Hamlin, D. D., now President of Middlebury College. Eleazer m., 2nd, 1789, Mrs. Hannah Fletcher, wid. of Timothy Fletcher, Jr.

1. Asia, son of Eleazer and Lydia, b. 1780; m., 1st, Susanna Read. Children: (1) *Nathan Sumner*, b. 1806. (2) *Susan*, b. 1808; m. ——. (3) *Hannibal*, b. 1812. (4) *Cyrus*, b. 1815. (5) *Sarah Dix*, b. 1820; m. Ira G. Richardson. (6) *Mary Antoinette*, b. 1821.

2. Nathan S., son of Asia, b. 1806; m. Harriet Fletcher, daughter of Pelatiah, 1829. Children; (1) *Edward S.*, b. 1830; res. in Boston. (2) *Samuel A.*, b. 1832.

HEALD. 1. Josiah, lived on the farm now owned by Artemas W. Cummings; m. Sarah ——. Child: (1) *Sarah*, b. 1730; (?) m. Benjamin Estherbrooks, 1769. Josiah the father, d. 1733.
2. Thomas, m. Sarah Butterfield, and lived first near Forge Village, afterward in the valley near Jeptha Wright's. Children. (1) *Ephraim*, bap. 1729. (2) *Eunice*, b. 1730–31; m. Jacob Bixby, 1749. (3) *Dorothy*, b. 1731–32; m. Joseph Wright. (4) *Esther*, b. 1736–37; m. David Dutton. (5) *Oliver*, b. 1740,—also *Sarah* and *Hannah*, who died young.
3. Gershom, m. Hannah Blood. Children: (1) *Sarah*, b. 1751. (2) *Ephraim*, **4**, b. 1753. (3) *Hannah*, b. 1756. (4) *Oliver*, b. 1758. (5) *Elizabeth*, b. 1761; m. Benjamin Robbins. (6) *Eleazer*, b. 1763; m. Elizabeth Lawrence, Pepperell. (7) *Susanna*, b. 1767; m. Jonathan Johnson. (8) *Phebe*; m. Benjamin Twist, Chelmsford.
4. Ephraim, m. Sarah ——. Children: (1) *Sarah*, b. 1777; (?) m. David Patch, Groton. (2) *Thomas*, **5**, b, 1779; (?) m. Rebecca Smith. (3) *Ephraim*, b. 1782; d. 1784. (4) *Ephraim*, b. 1785. (5) *Susanna*, b. 1788; d. 1789. (6) *Isaac*, b. 1791; m. Ruth Read, daughter of Elnathan, settled in Cavendish, Vt.
5. Thomas, m. Rebecca Smith. (?) Child: *Thomas Smith*, b. 1808.

HILDRETH. The ancestor of this family was Richard, from whom all bearing the name in this country have descended. The first notice of him is his admission as a freeman of the colony of Massachusetts Bay, May 10, 1643, when he was thirty-five years old. There was a Richard of Cambridge, whose wife, Sarah, died in 1644; and this was probably the Richard who settled in Woburn, and married Elizabeth. His name appears among several inhabitants of Woburn, as one of the petitioners to the General Court for a new township, which was granted and called Chelmsford. On the supposition that Richard of Cambridge and Richard of Woburn and Chelmsford, are identical, there can be little doubt that *James* who was an early settler of Chelmsford, was the son of Richard and Sarah, and was born in Cambridge. The homesteads of Richard and James in Chelmsford, were south of the centre village and near South Chelmsford.* From Chelmsford they or their children came to Westford and early secured a large tract of land on the eastern border. (See p.)

1. Ephraim. He is supposed to be the son of Richard, and half-brother of James. The deeds show that he once owned land near Providence Meadow. He married Anna Moore, of Lancaster. Children: (1) *Joseph*, b. 1688. (2) *Abigail*, b. 1691. (3) *James*, b. 1692; d. young. (4) *Ebenezer*, **2**, b. 1696. (5) *James*, **3**, b. 1698. (6) *Anna*, b. 1703. (7) *Thomas*, b. 1707. (8) *Jacob*, b. 1709. (9) *David*, b. 1711. (10) *Josiah*. (?) This is perhaps the Ephraim who moved to Dracut about 1710, but who seems to have returned, at least, to reside awhile. Ephraim Hildreth, of Chelmsford, was one of the grantees of Concord, N. H.

2. Ebenezer, lived in the south part in or near "Texas." He m. Sarah ——. Children: (1) *Sarah*, b. 1720. (2) *Ebenezer*, b. 1721. (3) *Hannah*, b. 1729. (4) *Mary*, b. 1733.

The foregoing families are not found in the Westford books, but were obtained from Chelmsford. The following is the first family recorded here.

3. James. He lived on the place lately occupied by J. Boynton Reed. He m. Dorothy ——. Children: (1) *Rebecca*. (2) *Zechariah*, b. 1728. (3) *Dorothy*, b. 1732; d. 1735. (4) *Dorothy*, b. 1736; m. Pelatiah Fletcher. (5) *Amos*, b. 1730. (6) *Lucy*, b. 1742. (7) *Samuel*, b. 1744; d. 1748.

4. Ephraim, son of Joseph and Abigail, and grandson of the first Richard; m. Mary ——. Children: (1) *Ephraim*, b. 1725. (2) *Sarah*, b.

---

*See a brief account of "the American Hildreths" in the New England Genealogical and Antiquarian Register for 1857. (p. 7.) It was written by Richard Hildreth, the historian, who is a descendant of the Westford Hildreths.

1726. (3) *Simeon*, b. 1728; d. young. (?) (4) *Abigail*, b. 1730; m. John Russell, Jr., Littleton. (5) *Elizabeth*, b. 1732; d. 1737. (6) *Thankful*, b. 1734; d. 1737. (7) *Simeon*, b. 1736. (8) *John*, b. 1738. (9) *William*, b. 1741. (10) *Peter*, b. 1743. (11) *Hannah*, b. 1744. (12) *Sybil*, b. 1746.

5. Joseph, son of Joseph and Abigail and grandson of the first Richard; m., 1st, Deliverance ——. Children: (1) *Ephraim*, b. 1718. (2) *Jonathan*, b. 1722 (?). (3) *Phinehas*, b. 1725. (4) *Hannah*, b. 1726. (5) *William*, b. 1728. (6) *Wilson*, b. 1731. (7) *Hannah*, b. 1738. Joseph is supposed to have married a second wife, Abigail Hill, of Billerica. (8) *Ezekiel*, b. 1744; d. young. (9) *Hosea*, b. 1744–45. (10) *Timothy*, b. 1746; d. young. (11) *Abigail*, b. 1747. (12) *Hannah*, b. 1750. (13) *Ezekiel*, b. 1753. (14) *Timothy*, b. 1756. The historian says of this Joseph, that he was grandson of the first Richard, and that he was the father of Timothy, who was the youngest of the family of children by two successive wives, being born in his father's old age, at Westford, 1756. Timothy was the grandfather of the historian. Joseph lived at Minot's corner.

6. Jacob, son of Ephraim and Anna, m. Abigail ——. Children: (1) *Ephraim*, b. 1732; d. young. (2) *Ephraim*, b. 1735. (3) *Jacob*, b. 1737. (4) *William*, b. 1740. (5) *David*, b. 1746. (6) *John*, b. 1748. (7) *Lucy*, b. 1752. He rem. to Litchfield.

7. Ephraim, son of Joseph and Deliverance, m. Priscilla Barron. Children: (1) *Priscilla*, b. 1742. (2) *Hannah*, b. 1744; d. 1746. (3) *Peter*, b. 1746; d. 1752. (4) *Hannah*, b. 1749; d. 1752. (5) *Elijah*, b. 1750. (6) *Peter*, b. 1753. (7) *Rebecca*, b. 1755. (8) *Jonathan*, b. 1757. (9) *Lydia*, b. 1760. (10) *Lucy*, b. 1762; d. 1766. (11) *Isaiah*, b. 1767.

8. Samuel, son of Richard and Dorcas, m. Sarah Proctor. Children: (1) *Sarah*, b. 1758. (2) *James*, b. 1758. Only these two appear; probably there were others who were born earlier.

9. James, son of Richard and Dorcas, m. Lydia Wright, probably the daughter of Ebenezer and Hannah. Children: (1) *Elizabeth*, b. 1728. (2) *Olive*, b. 1729. (3) *Lydia*, b. 1732. (4) *Ruth*, b. 1734. (5) *Samuel*, b. 1736. (6) *Thankful*, b. 1738. (7) *Lois*, b. 1739. (8) *Silas* (twin), b. 1741; d. 1742. (9) *Abel* (twin), b. 1741; d. 1742. (10) *Stephen*, b. 1743. (11) *James*, b. 1745. He is called Junior in the records to distinguish him from James, son of Ephraim and Anna. He d. at Cape Breton, 1745, aged 44.

10. Amaziah, son of Benjamin, m. Ruth Read. Children: (1) *Esther*, b. 1761. (2) *Ruth*, b. 1763. (3) *Susanna*, b. 1766. (4) *Benjamin*, b. 1768. (5) *Thomas*, b. 1770. (6) *Amaziah*, b. 1772. (7) *Mary*, b. 1775. (8) *John Parker*, b. 1778. (9) *Joseph*, b. 1780. (10) *William*, b. 1783. This family lived on the east side in the vicinity of Heart Pond.

11. Joseph, called 3rd on the books. He was probably the son of Joseph, and grandson of Ephraim and Anna (Moore). If so, he was born in 1724. It is difficult to trace his parentage, but this supposition makes no break in the chronological order. He m. Lydia Fletcher, 1747. Children: (1) *Joseph*, b. 1747. (2) *Phebe*, b. 1751. (3) *Lydia*, b. 1753. (4) *Deborah*, b. 1755. (5) *Jesse*, b. 1757. (6) *Mary*, b. 1761. (7) *Anna*, b. 1761.

12. Zechariah, son of James and Dorothy, m. 1753, Elizabeth Prescott, daughter of Jonas and Elizabeth. Children: (1) *Zechariah*, b. 1754. (2) *Elizabeth*, b. 1755. (3) *Hannah*, b. 1758. (4) *Timothy*, b. 1760. (5) *James*, b. 1762. (6) *Lucy*, b. 1764. (7) *Jonas*, b. 1766. (8) *Ruth*, b. 1768. (9) *Edy*, b. 1771, (10) *Jesse*, b. 1773. (11) *Hita*, b. 1775.

13. Simeon, son of Ephraim and Mary, m. Hannah Spalding; rem. to New Ipswich. Child: (1) *Simeon* b. in New Ipswich, 1758.

14. Stephen, son of James and Lydia (Wright), m. Esther Manning, of Townsend, and settled in New Ipswich.

15. Amos, son of James and Dorothy, m. Priscilla Hildreth, daughter of Ephraim and Priscilla (Barron). Children: (1) *Abel*, b. 1766. (2) *Patty*, b. 1768. (3) *Hannah*, b. 1770. (4) *Olive*, b. 1772; d. 1772. (5) *Olive*, b. 1773; m. Benjamin Green. (6) *Levi*, b. 1775. (7) ——, b. 1779; d. 1801. Amos, the father, d. 1807.

16. John, son of Ephraim and Mary, m., 1st, Abigail Parker. Children: (1) *John*, b. 1763. (2) *Abigail*, b. 1765; m. Zechariah Robbins,

Jr. (3) *Sarah*, b. 1768; d. 1770. He m., 2nd, Betty Gates, daughter of Stephen, 1772. (4) *Sarah*, b. 1773; m. Joash Minot, 1794. (5) *Simeon*, b. 1776. (6) *Stephen*, b. 1777. (7) *Betty*, b. 1779. (8) *Lemuel*, b. 1781.

17. Hosea, son of Joseph and his 2nd wife, Abigail Hill, and twin brother of Ezekiel, m. Experience Keep, 1769. Children: (1) *Nathaniel*, b. 1770. (2) *Peda* (Experience,) b. 1771. (3) *Rhoda*; m. Levi Wright. (4) *Hosea*, b. 1774; rem. to Pepperell. (5) *Ruth*, b. 1776. Hosea, the father, d. 1776, and his wid. m. Ebenezer Parker.

18. William, son of Ephraim and Mary, m. Dorothy ——. Children: (1) *Dolle*, b. 1762. (2) *Bridget*, b. 1768. (3) *Peter*, b. 1771

19. Timothy, son of Joseph and his 2nd wife, Abigail (Hill), m. Hannah Hildreth, daughter of Zechariah Hildreth. Richard, the historian, says of him. "My grandfather emigrated to Cavendish, Vt., and there cut for himself a farm in the woods; but he soon returned to Massachusetts, and passed the larger part of his life on a farm in Sterling." He had ten children; Hosea, the third son, was father of the historian.

20. Ephraim, "3rd," son of Ephraim and Mary, m. Elizabeth French, Hollis, N. H. Children: (1) *Elizabeth*, b. 1754; m. Samuel Richardson. (2) *Thankful*, b. 1756; m. James Hall, Cavendish, Vt. (See p. 166.) (3) *Hezekiah*, b. 1758. (4) *Jeremiah*, b. 1761. (5) *Olive*, b. 1763; m. Eleazer Parlin, of Concord. (6) *Mary*, b. 1765. (7) *Aby*, b. 1768; m. Thomas Heald, of Carlisle, 1791. (8) *Sibbel*, b. 1772. (9) *Thomas Greenough*, b. 1775; rem. to Cavendish, Vt.

21. Elijah, son of Ephraim and Priscilla, m. Mary Reed, daughter of Peter Reed, Littleton, 1776. Children: (1) *Elijah*, b. 1770. (2) *Mary*, b. 1777; m. —— Champney, Billerica. (3) *Salla*, b. 1779. (4) *Rebekah*, b. 1781. (5) *Abijah*, b. 1783. (6) *Betsey*, b. 1786. (7) *Jonathan Hartwell*, b. 1788; d. 1810. (8) *Hannah*, b. 1792; d. 1823. (9) *Charles*, b. 1794. (10) *Ephraim*, b. 1796; rem. to Mason, N. H. (11) *Joseph*, b. 1798. Elijah, the father, d. 1798, aged 47.

22. Oliver. His parentage has not been ascertained. There was an Oliver who m. Ann Blasdale [Blaisdell] (?) 1744, and Oliver and Anne Hildreth, of Townsend had Sarah, b. 1745. There is scarcely any reason to doubt the identity of the parties. This Oliver was probably son of James and Dorothy. An Oliver m. Mary Wright, 1773. His parentage is also unknown. (Oliver of Townsend had no Oliver.) He owned the land on which Nathan S. Hamblin's house stands, and sold a small strip to the Proprietors of the Academy. Children: (1) *Sarah*, b. 1773. (2) *Seth*, b. 1775. (3) *Polly*, b. 1777. (4) *Oliver*, b. 1780; d. 1780. (5) *Oliver*, b. 1781. (6) *Luke*, b. 1783. (7) *Betsey*, b. 1786. (8) *Lucy*, b. 1788. (9) *Dolly*, b. 1791. (10) *Amos*, b. 1793. (11) *Nancy*, b. 1795. The names given to the children are in part similar to those found in the families of James and Dorothy, and of Zechariah, and this strengthens the supposition that he was connected with them. But it is possible that he was son of Ephraim and Mary.

23. Isaiah, son of Ephraim and Priscilla, m. Lydia Leighton, 1769. Children; (1) *Susanna*, b. 1789; m. Abijah Hildreth, 1809.

24. John, Lieut., son of John and Abigail, m. Elizabeth Leighton, 1793. Children: (1) *Augustus*, b. 1794; m. Lydia B. Sargent; d. in Boston. (2) *Francis Leighton*, b. 1797; m. Elizabeth Armstrong; d. in Boston. (3) *Elizabeth*, b. 1798; m. Amos Byam, 1832, and lived in Chelmsford. (4) *John*, b. 1801; m. Elizabeth Gray, Boston. (5) *Mary*, b. 1803; m. Lyman Gilbert, Boston, 1828. (6) *Joanna*, b. 1805; m. John B. Fletcher, 1827. (7) *William*, b. 1807; m. Emeline Hunnewell. (8) *Nancy*, b. 1809; m. Joel Glover, res. in Boston and Dedham. (9) *George B.*, b. 1811; m. Nancy Childs, Cambridgeport. (10) *Emily*, b. 1817; m. Elisha Shaw, Middleboro', Mass. Augustus d. in Boston, 1836. Francis L. d. in Boston, 1832. John d. in Arlington, 1872. Mary d. 1860. Joanna, d. 1868. William d. 1840. Emily d. 1843.

25. Jeremiah, son of Ephraim 3rd, and Elizabeth (French), m. Abigail Parker, 1788. Children: (1) *Jeremiah*, b. 1789, in Cavendish, Vt.; d.

1789. (2) *Abigail*, b. 1790. (3) *Betsey Parker*, b. 1792. (4) *Fanny*, b. 1794. (5) *Franklin*, b. 1797. (6) *Jeremiah*, b. 1802. (7) *Patty*, b. 1805 (8) *Caroline*, b. 1808. (9) *Mary Ann*, b. 1810; m. Isaac Minot.

26. **Simeon**, son of John and Abigail; lived on the farm of James O. Kidder; m. Ruth Bicknell, 1798. Children: (1) *Simeon*, b. 1799. (2) *Maria*, b. 1801; m. Abram Wright, 1824. (3) *Asa*, b. 1803. (4) *Nancy*, b. 1805; d. 1808. (5) *Betsey*, b. 1807; d. 1808. (6) *Amos*, b. 1809. (7) *Nancy*, b. 1811; m. Jacob Upham, Lowell. (8) *Betsey Ann*, b. 1814.

27. **Lemuel**, son of John and Abigail, m. Mary Dutton, 1802. Children: (1) *Mary*, b. 1803. (2) *Horace*, b. 1804. (3) *Otis*, b. 1806. (4) *Ai*, b. 1808; d. 1810. (5) *Ai*, b. 1810; d. 1810. (6) *Betsey*, b. 1811. (7) *Elvira*, b. 1813. (8) *Lucy*, b. 1815. (9) *Zoa*, b. 1818. (10) *Rufus*, b. 1820; d. 1821. (11) *Nancy*, b. 1822.

28. **Hezekiah**, son of Ephraim 3rd, m. Esther Parlin, 1784. Children: (1) *Susanna*, b. 1784. (2) *Hezekiah*, b. 1785. (3) *Susanna*, b. 1787. Hezekiah, the father, rem. to Tynsborough. Died at St. Vincent, W. I., 1809, aged 52. Esther, the mother, d. 1789.

29. **Levi**, son of Amos and Priscilla, m. Rebecca Hildreth, 1800. Children: (1) *Louisa*, b. 1802. (2) *Amos*, b. 1807. (3) *Jonathan*, b. 1816; d. 1819. (4 and 5) *Rufus and Luther*, b. 1818.

30. **Joseph**, son of Elijah, m. Permelia Reed, 1822. Children: (1) *Joseph Barnard*, b. 1823; d. 1864. (2) *Mary Ann*, b. 1825. (3) *Caroline Augusta*, b. 1827; m. Abel Prescott. (4) *William Edward*, b. 1829. (5) *Maria Theresa*, b. 1831. (6) *Rosalia Elizabeth*, b. 1838; d.

31. **Horace**, son of Lemuel, m. Eveline ——. Children: (1) *Horace Newell*, b. 1831. (2) *Mary Eveline*, b. 1838. (3) *Susan Frances*, b. 1843. (4) *George Everett*, b. 1845. (5) *Susan Elizabeth*, b. 1847.

32. **Jonas**, son of Zechariah, m. Deliverance Johnson, 1791. Children: (1) *Nancy*, b. 1794. (2) *Betsey*, b. 1796. (3) *Samuel*, b. 1797. (4) *Jonas*, b. 1798. (5) *James*, b. 1800. (6) *Orin*, b. 1802. (7) *George*, b. 1803; d. 1805. (8) *Susan Anthony*, b. 1805. (9) *Harriet*, b. 1807. (10) *George*, b. 1808. Jonas, the father, d. 1808.

33. **Amaziah**, son of Amaziah, m. Margaret Marstins, 1796. Children: (1) *Hannah Wright*, b. 1797. (2) *Margaret Webb*, b. 1799. (3) *Sally Hart*, b. 1801. (4) *Martha Mary Webb*, b. 1803. (5) *John Parker*, b. 1805. (6) *Elizabeth King*, b. 1807. (7) *Samuel Webb*, b. 1811. (8) *Thomas William*, b. 1817.

34. **Nathaniel**, son of Hosea, m., 1st, Bridget Hildreth, daughter of William, 1795. He went to Cavendish, Vt., and was of that place in 1796. He returned and lived on the place now occupied by Julian Hildreth. He afterward built the house now owned by Elisha Bunce and son; went South, and d. in Virginia. He m. for a 2nd wife, Miss Mary Pierce, of Westford, 1807. Children: (1) *Clarissa*, b. 1797. (2) *Zimri*, b. 1799; d. (3) *Dolly*, b. 1801. (4) *Elmira*, b. 1805. Mrs. Bridget Hildreth, d. 1806. By 2nd wife, Mary: (5) *Zimri*, b. 1807; d. 1807. (6) *Rebecca*, b. 1809.

35. **Abijah**, son of Elijah, m. Susanna Hildreth, 1809. Children: (1) *Abijah Edwin*, b. 1809. (2) *Louis Hartwell*, b. 1813. (3) *Harriet Susannah*, b. 1818; m. George E. Burt; d. 1849, at Harvard. (4) *Martha Ann*, b. 1820. (5) *Henry Albert*, b. 1823. (6) *Frances A.*, b. 1831, and d. same day. Abijah, the father, d. 1869. Susanna, the mother, d. 1861.

36. **Sylvester**, adopted son of Abel, born in Townsend. He m. Mary Hildreth, of Townsend. Children: (1) *Augustus Sylvester*, b. 1821. (2) *Olive Augusta*, b. 1823. (3) *Alonzo Whiting*, b. 1825. (4) *Mary Ann*, b. 1827. (5) *Emeline Elizabeth*, b. 1828. (6) *Lucy Jane*, b. 1830. (7) *Harriet Sophia*, b. 1832. (8) *Martha Maria*, b. 1834. (9) *Edward Stow*, b. 1835. (10) *Caroline Dix*, b. 1837. (11) *Henry Abel*, b. 1841.

37. **Jesse**, son of Jesse, grandson of Zechariah, m. Lucretia Ingalls. Children: (1) *Eliza Ann*, b. 1832. (2) *Jesse Alonzo*, b. 1837. (3) *George H.*, b. 1846. (4) *Abby F.*, b. 1849. (5) *Ellen A.*, b. 1851.

38. **James**, son of Jesse, and grandson of Zechariah, m. Sarah Tenney. Children: (1) *Sarah R.*, b. 1842. (2) *James Henry*, b. 1845. (3) *Samuel T.*, b. 1849. (4) *Martha M.*, b. 1854.

HORSLEY. Samuel, son of James, and b. in Billerica 1719, m. Elizabeth Keep, probably the sister of Capt. Jabez Keep, 1740. Children: (1) *Aaron*, b. 1742. (2) *Betty*, b. 1743. (3) *Lydia*, b. 1745. (4) *Bridget*, b. 1747. (5) *Timothy* (twin), b. 1749. (6) *Samuel* (twin), b. 1749. (7) *Joshua*, b. 1753. (8) *John*, b. 1755. (9) *Lydia*, b. 1756, in Pepperell. (10) *Stephen*, b. 1758, in Pepperell. (11) *Martha*, b. 1761. (12) *Thomas*, b. 1764. The family rem. to Pepperell.

HUNT. Simon, was born in Acton, ——, and d. 1821. He m., 1st, Lydia Brooks, daughter of Daniel, who lived near the East Burying Ground. By this marriage there were two children, Nancy who m. a Wood, and Lucy. He m., 2nd, Wid. Lydia Procter, 1785. Children: (1) *Mary*, b. 1788; m. —— Kelly. (2) *Simon*, b. 1790. (3) *Timothy*, b. 1792. (4) *John*, b. 1793. (5) *Luther*, b. 1795; d. young. (6) *Sally*, m. John Allen, of Danvers, 1821. (7) *Warren*, b. 1801; m. Clarissa Wilson, 1840; one child, George W. (8) *Betsey*, b. 1803; m. Benjamin Abbot Read, 1835.

JEWETT. 1. Joseph, from Littleton, m. Rebekah Abbot, 1763. Children: (1) *Jonathan*. (2) *John*, 2, b. 1766. (3) *Patty*, b. 1768; (?) m. Thomas Fletcher, Jr. 1786. (4) *Leonard*, physician in Athens, O. (5) *Joshua Abbot*, 3, b. 1772. (6) *Ahimaaz*, ——.

2. John, m. Elizabeth Cummings, 1787; and rem. to Peterboro', N. H. Children, b. in Westford: (1) *John*, b. 1787. (2) *Jonathan*, b. 1791; d. young. (3) *Ahimaaz*, b. 1794; m. Eliza Scott. (4) *Rebecca*, b. 1795. Others were born in Peterboro'.

3. Joshua Abbot, m. Rebecca Robinson, daughter of Col. John, 1800. Children: (1) *Joshua Abbot*, b. 1800; rem. to Sterling, Mass. (2) *George*, b. 1802. (3) *Eliza*, b. 1804. (4) *Clarasy*, b. 1807. (5) *Harriet*, b. 1809. (6) *Sally*, b. 1812. (7) *William*, b. 1814. "Joshua Abbot Jewett, found dead in an old building in Concord, Mass., March 23, 1838."

JONES. Jonathan, m., 1st, Bethiah Fletcher, probably daughter of Capt. Benjamin. Children: (1) *Adams Fletcher*, b. 1779. (2) *Susanna*, b. in Dracut, 1782. He m., 2nd, Abigail Wright, 1785. (3) *Abigail*, b. 1786. (4) *Jonathan*, b. 1787. Jonathan, the father, was at the seige of Yorktown, and witnessed the surrender of Cornwallis. He rem. in 1794 to Reading, Vt., where his grandson, Daniel Parker Jones, is now living. (1882.)

KEEP. 1. Capt. Jabez. He was born in Springfield, Mass., 1706, and was the son of Samuel and Sarah; m., 1st, Sarah ——, who d. 1739. Children: (1) *Sarah*, b. 1731; m. Preserved Leonard, Springfield. (2) *Samuel*, b. 1732. (3) *Lucy*, b. 1734. (4) *Jabez*, b. 1736; m. Phebe Crosby, 1757. He m., 2nd, Experience Lawrence, of Littleton, 1740. (5) *Eunice*, b. 1741. (6) *Leonard*, b. 1742; m. Ruth Stone, daughter of Ebenezer, and rem. to Westmoreland, N. H. (7) *Mary*, b. 1743-44; m. Leonard Proctor, rem. to Cavendish, Vt. (8) *Jonathan*, 2, b. 1745. (9) *Ruth*, b. 1746-47. (10) *Experience*, b. 1748; d. young. (11) *Elizabeth*, b. 1750. (12) *Experience*, b. 1752; m. Hosea Hildreth, 1769. (13) *John*, b. 1753. (14) *Jemima*, b. 1755. (15) *Rebecca*, b. 1758.

2. Jonathan, m. Hannah Hildreth, 1769. Children: (1) *Hannah*, b. 1770; m. Isaiah Hall, of Groton, 1788. (2) *Abigail*, b. 1771. (3) *Jonathan*, b. 1773. (4) *Charlotte*, b. 1775. (5) *Sylvia*, b. 1777, at Harvard. (6) *John*, b. 1779; m. Lucy Fletcher. (7) *Samuel*, b. 1781. (8) *Susanna*, b. 1783. (9) *Imla*, 1785. (10 and 11) *Luther and Lucinda* (twins), b. 1787. (12) *Matilda*, b. 1789.

KEMP. This family came here·from Chelmsford and Billerica. It has been somewhat noted for the pauperism of its members, many of them being supported for long periods by the town. The first in order on the records, but not in the order of time, is

1. Jonas, who m. Joanna Corey, 1769. Children : (1) *Jonas*, b. 1770; d. young. (2) *Polly*, b. 1771; m. Benjamin Hildreth, 1790. (3) *Jonas*, 2, b. 1782, at Chelmsford.

2. Jonas, m. Anna ——. Children: (1) *Alfred*, b. 1804; m. Mary Ann Cowdry, 1831. (2) *Ezekiel*, b. 1806. (3) *Hartwell*, b. 1808. (4) *Jonas Avery*, b. 1810. (5) *Francis*. (?)

GENEALOGY. 457

3. Josiah, Jr. His connection with the foregoing is not known; m. Sarah ——. Children: (1) *Sarah*, b. 1759. (2) *Rachel*, b. 1761. He d. before March, 1763, and his widow m. William Fletcher, of Concord, and settled in Norridgewock, Me.

4. James, his relationship unknown, m. Margaret Craft. Children: (1) *Joanna*, b. 1805. (2) *James*, b. 1807; d. young. (3) *Ansil*, b. 1808. (4) *James*, b——.

Kent. 1. Abner, m. Elizabeth ——. Children: (1) *Apphia*, b. 1731; m. Daniel Gilson, Groton, 1760. (2) *Abigail*, b. 1733–34. (3) *Abner*, **2**, b. 1737. (4) *Sarah*, b. 1739. (5) *Deborah*, b. 1742.

2. Abner, m. Dorcas Hildreth, 1764. Children: (1) *Dorcas*, b. 1765. (2) *Mary*, b. 1767. (3) *Abigail*, b. 1769; m. Paul Wright, of Stoddard, N. H. (4) *Susanna*, b. 1772. (5) *Lydia*, b. 1775. (6) *Abner*, b. 1777. (7) *Elisha*, **3**, b. 1779.

3. Elisha, m., 1st, Fanny Crouch, Littleton. Children: (1) *Elisha Sewell*, b. 1800. (2) *Dorcas*, b. 1802. (3) *Justin*, b. 1808. (4) *Fanny*, b. 1811; d. young. He m., 2nd, Mrs. Betsey Patch, wid. of Daniel Patch, and daughter of Asa Wright. (5) *Fanny*, b. 1813. (6) *Almira*, b. 1815. (7) *George*, b. 1820.

KEYES. This, according to the best information now in hand, is the oldest family in the order of actual settlement. As early as 1664, Solomon Keyes was in possession of land on Frances Hill. He came from Newbury where he married Frances Grant in 1653. There was a Joseph, probably his brother. The Westford families are descended from Solomon, whose son Solomon was born, as it seems reasonable to suppose within the limits of this town in 1665. This second Solomon had a son Solomon, born in 1701, who was wounded in the battle of Lovewell's Pond. He, the third Solomon, married and had eight children, two of whom, Solomon and David, were born here. (See pp. 52, 53.)

1. Joseph, second son of the first Solomon, b. 1667, m. Joanna Cleveland. Children: (1) *Lydia*, b. 1693. (2) *Joanna*, b. 1695. (3) *Joseph*, **2**, b. 1698.

2. Joseph settled on the west side of Keyes Pond, as early as 1722. He m. Elizabeth ——. Children: (1) *Elizabeth*, b. 1730. (2) *Jonathan*, **3**, b. 1721. (3) *Sarah*, b. 1723. (4) *Lydia*, b. 1724. (5) *David* ——.

3. Jonathan. He settled on the old place on Frances Hill, and m., 1st, Elizabeth Fletcher in 1746. Children: (1) *Joseph*, **4**, b. 1746. (2) *Joanna*, b. 1748; d. 1753. (3) *Aaron*, b. 1751; d. 1753. (4) *Stephen*, b. 1754; d. 1758. (5) *Joanna*, b. 1757; m. Timothy Adams, Chelmsford, and became the mother of the late Joel Adams, of Chelmsford. (6) *Elizabeth*, b. 1759; m. Capt. Zaccheus or Zechariah Hildreth, of Townsend. (7) *Hannah*, b. 1761; m. Uriah Drury Pike, of Dunstable, 1781, and was the grandmother of Hon. Austin F. Pike, of Franklin, N. H. He m., 2nd, Mrs. Betty (Hartwell) Reed, of Littleton, 1762. (8) *Jonathan*, **5**, b. 1763. (9) *Lydia* (twin), b. 1765; m. Isaac Patten. (10) *Lucy* (twin), b. 1765; m. Jesse Fletcher. (11) *Miriam*, b. 1767; m. Dea. Samuel Fletcher, and d. 1871, aged 102 years, 11 months, 18 days. (12) *Patty*, b. 1769; m. Pelatiah Fletcher, Jr., 1785. (13) *Frances Grant*, b. 1771; m. Joseph Fletcher, 1794. (14) *Aaron*, d. young.

4. Joseph, m., 1st, Ruth Forbush, of Acton, 1768, and settled on the homestead of his grandfather, near Keyes Pond. Children: (1) *Ruth*, b. 1769; m. —— Pike, 1799. (2) *Joseph*, b. 1771; d. 1775. (3) *Stephen*, b. 1772; d. 1775. (4) *Rebecca*, b. 1774; d. 1775. (5) *Joel*, b. 1776; m. Polly Boyden, 1800, and rem. to Tyngsboro'. (6) *Salla*, b. 1778; m. William Chambers, 1798. (7) *Anna*, b. 1780; m. John Prescott, 1801. (8) *Jonas*, b. 1782; m. Saily Reed of Chelmsford, 1808. He m., 2nd, Sarah Boyden, of Groton. (9) *John*, b. 1787; rem. to Concord, Mass., where he became a man of much distinction. (10) *Joseph*, b. 1789; d. 1796. (11) *Polly*, b. 1791. (12) *Imla*, **9**, b. 1793. (13) *Patty*, b. 1797.

5. Jonathan, m. Patty Woodward, of Dunstable. Children: (1) *Martha*, b. 1787; m. Levi Heywood, and d. 1839. (2) *Jonathan*, **6**, b. 1789. (3) *Aaron*, b. 1791; rem. to Townsend, and m. Martha Warren, 1824. (4)

Lydia, b. 1792; d. unmarried, 1874. (5) *Betsey*, b. 1794; m. Nahum H. Groce, 1830; d. 1881. (6) *Joseph,* **7,** b. 1796. (7) *Charlotte,* b. 1797; m. Samuel Dunn, of Chelmsford, 1823. (8) *Nancy,* b. 1799; m. Benjamin F. Tidd, 1821, and lived in Lancaster. (9) *Benjamin F.*, b. 1801; m. Catherine Wight, of Dedham, where he lived. (10) *Sally,* b. 1803; d. unmarried, 1843. (11) *Trueworthy,* **8,** b. 1805. (12) *Stephen Adams,* b. 1807; d. unmarried, 1843, in Townsend. (13) *Wright Sumner,* b. 1809; m. Maria Cummings, 1832, and rem. to Boston. (14) *Laurinda,* b. 1811; d. 1839.

6. Jonathan, m. Irene Harriman, of Maine. Children: (1) *Jonathan Hartwell,* b. 1842; killed at Fredericksburgh. (2) *John Harriman,* b. ———; was a Lieutenant in the war; d. of yellow fever, at Galveston, Texas. (3) *Ellen,* b. ———; m. G. H. Burt, and rem. to Hillsdale, Ill. (4) *Nancy E.,* b. ———; m. Thomas Clissold; rem. to Pennsylvania.

7. Joseph, m. Sophia Strong, daughter of Rev. Caleb Blake, 1820. Children: (1) *Sophia Moseley,* b. 1821; m. Charles L. Fletcher, 1844. (2) *Martha Strong,* b. 1824; d. 1845. (3) *Joseph Hammond,* b. 1826; m. Sarah A., daughter of Rev. Liba Conant, and res. in Bristol, N. H. (4) *Catherine Blake,* b. 1828; d. 1844. (5) *Julian Victor,* b. 1830; m.

8. Trueworthy, m. Sophia S. Keyes, the widow of his brother Joseph, 1837. Children: (1) *Josephine* (twin), b. 1838. (2) *Clementine* (twin), b. 1838; m. Charles E. Swett, 1866. Trueworthy, the father, d. 1871.

9. Imla, m. Hannah Fletcher, 1816. Children: (1) *George,* b. 1817. (2) *Lydia,* b. 1819; d. young. (3) *Joseph Warren,* b. 1820; m. Rebecca H. Fletcher, 1868; d. 1879. (4) *Liberty* (twin), b. 1822; m. Rebecca P. Davis, and d. 1856. (5) *Lydia* (twin), b. 1822; m. Thaddeus Uriah Davis, 1846, and rem. to Tyngsborough. (6) *Otis,* **10,** b. 1824. (7) *Rufus,* b. 1826. (8) *Edward,* b. 1827; m. Lucy Richardson. (See p. 217.) (9) *Martha Maria,* b. 1829; d. 1856. (10) *Emeline,* b. 1831; m. Francis A. Proctor, 1858, and rem. to Lunenburg, Mass. (11) *James,* b. 1833; d. young. (12) *Cornelius Freeman,* b. 1834. (13) *Sarah Elizabeth,* b. 1839. (See p. 216.)

10. Otis, m. Lucy Ann Turrell, of Nashua, 1854. Children: (1) *Rosina,* b. 1856. (2) *Henry Otis,* b. 1859. (3) *Alice May,* b. 1861. (4) *Edward H.,* b. 1863.

11. Moses, son of Moses, and grandson of the first Solomon, lived here awhile. He m. Susanna ———. Child: *Ruth,* b. 1729.

12. Samuel, probably son of David, m. Molly Davis, of Acton, 1768; killed in the war of the Revolution. (See p. 130.) Children: (1) *Samuel,* b. 1769. (2) *John,* b. 1774. There was a Charles, and perhaps a Judith, whose births are not recorded.

13. Daniel, youngest son of Moses, Jr., m. Abigail Procter, 1754, granddaughter of Robert and Jane Procter. Children: (1) *Israel,* b. 1756; rem. to Washington, N. H. (2) *Jacob,* b. 1758.

14. Issachar, son of Zechariah and grandson of Moses, Jr., b. 1747; m. Elizabeth Richardson, 1770. Children: (1) *Solomon,* b. 1771; rem. to Littleton. (2) *Priscilla,* b. 1772; m. James Baldwin, of Dunstable, 1798. (3) *James,* **15,** b. 1775. (4) *Samson,* b. 1777; m. Betsey Little, 1802; rem. to Wilton, Me. (5) *Elizabeth,* b. 1780; m. Thomas Flint, of Chelmsford, 1800; rem. to Wilton, Me. (6) *Stephen,* b. 1784. (7) *Jonas,* b. 1788; m. Sarah P. Read, of Stoddard, 1808; rem. to Pelham, N. H. (8) *Joash,* **16,** b. 1792.

15. James, m. Abigail Carlton, of Chelmsford, 1799. Children: (1) *Abigail,* b. 1800; m. Samuel Wheeler, and rem. to Bolton, Mass. (2) *Ivory,* b. 1805; m. Lucy Robbins; rem.

16. Joash, m. Mary Ann LeGross, 1812. Children: (1) *Zoa Ann,* b. 1813; m. George Bulmer, Lowell. (2) *Mary Ann,* b. 1815; m. Asa G. Farwell; rem. to Fitchburg. (3) *Francis J.,* b. 1817; d. 1820. . (4) *Aaron,* b. 1819. (5) *Moses,* b. 1821; m. Martha Aldrich, printer, in Lowell. (6) *Joshua,* b. 1823; rem. to California. (7) *Maria,* b. 1825; m. Amos Green, of Lowell. (8) *Shepherd* b. 1827; rem. to St. Lawrence Co., N. Y. (9) *Daniel,* b. 1829; d. 1843.

KIDDER. 1. The first of this name who lived in this town was Thomas,* son of John and Lydia (Parker), b. 1690, in Chelmsford. John was son of James, and came from Billerica about 1685. Thomas m. Joanna Keyes, 1816. Children: *Thomas*, 2, *Aaron*, *Reuben*, *Joseph* and *Josiah*. (See History of New Ipswich, p. 405.)

2. Thomas, m. Elizabeth Wheeler, Acton. Children: (1) *Elizabeth*, b. 1743; m. Zaccheus Green, Concord, 1765. (2) *Isaiah*, b. 1749; d. 1759. (3) *Sarah*, b. 1761. This record is evidently imperfect. There were other children whose births were not recorded, bearing the names of Francis, James, Jacob, Mary and perhaps Isaac. Thomas, known as "Cornet Kidder," d. in 1793, aged 75.

3. James, supposed to be the son of Thomas and Elizabeth, m. Patty Cummings, 1799. Children: (1) *James*, **4**, b. 1800. (2) *Charles Proctor*, **5**, b. 1801. (3) *George*, **6**, b. 1803. (4) *John Lewis*, b. 1805. (5) *Martha Caroline*, b. 1808. (6) *William*, b. 1811. (7) *Nancy*, b. 1814. (8) *Mary Ann*, b. 1817.

4. James, m. Lucy Pushee, Littleton, 1827. Children: (1) *James Otis*, **7**, b. 1831. (2) *Sarah Jane*, b 1834. (3) *Elizabeth Ann*, b. 1836.

5. Charles Proctor, m. Mary Ann Wright, 1827. Children: (1) *Harriet*, b. 1836. (2) *Nancy*, b. 1837. (3) *Charles*, b. 1839. (4) *Mary Ann*, b. 1841.

6. George, m. Lydia Sawtell, 1831. Children: (1) *Lydia Maria*, b. 1836. (2) *Laura Ann*, b. 1840. (3) *Almira*, b. 1849. (4) *Andrew J.*, b. 1852.

7. James Otis, m. Charlotte F. Bruce. Child: *Josephine A.*, b. 1849.

KING. 1. Rogers, came from Littleton, and lived on the Asaph B. Cutter place; m. Lydia Woods, Westford, 1767. Children: (1) *Rogers*, **2**, b. 1768. (2) *Asa*, b. 1770; grad. Harvard College. (3) *Lydia* b. 1774. Rogers, the father, d. 1797.

2. Rogers, m. Polly Tilden, Scituate, 1799. Children: (1) *Lydia*, b. 1800. (2 and 3) *Mary and Maria* (twins), b. 1802. (4) *George Rogers*, b. 1804. (5) *Rufus Tilden*, b. 1807.

KNEELAND. 1. Joseph, m. Miriam ——. Child: *Lydia*, b. 1747.

2. Richard, m. Martha Hall. Children: (1) *Martha*, b. 1776. (2) *Richard*, b. 1778. (3) *Benjamin*, b. 1780. (4) *William*, b. 1782. (5) *John*, b. 1784. (6) *James*, b. 1786. (7) *Mary*, b. 1789. (8) *Edward*, b. 1791. (9) *Samuel*, b. 1794. (10) *Bartholomew*, b. 1797; d. 1826. Richard (the father) was drowned in Concord River, March 8, 1800. He held the office of Town Treasurer at the time of his death; a thoroughly honest man.

3. Benjamin, m. Eve Cogswell, 1814. Children: (1) *Caroline*, b. 1815. (2) *Augusta Maria Eve*, b. 1818. (3) *Sarah Fletcher*, b. 1820. He d. 1828, aged 48. Caroline m., 1st, Francis Bartlett; m., 2nd, —— Wyeth, of Baltimore.

LANCEY. Samuel, m. Elizabeth ——. Children: (1) *John*, b. 1798. (2) *Betsey*, b. 1801. (3) *Isaac Hurd*, b. 1803. (4) *Dorothy*, b. 1806. These four children by the death of their parents, were left in the care of the town. The father kept the "Wheat Sheaf Inn" at the Centre and also the tavern at Carlisle station.

LAWRENCE. 1. Samuel, son of Eleazer, and b. 1714 in Littleton; m. Mary Hildreth, and after the birth of three children, came to this town where the following children were born: (1) *John*, b. 1744. (2) *Thomas*, b. 1746–47. (3) *Mary*, b. 1749; m. Samuel Farwell, 1774. (4) *William*, b. 1751; d. young. (5) *Sarah*, b. 1754. (6) *William*, b. 1757; rem. to Ashby. (7) *Jabez*, b. 1759.

---

* He lived in the south part, beyond Parkerville, and near Nonesuch Hill. He is said to have been a man of considerable wealth, and his house was an unusually fine one for the times, having much architectural symmetry with some adornments. His sons were enterprising men, especially Col. Reuben who bore so conspicuous a part in the settlement of New Ipswich. (See p. 158 ante.) Owing to the defective record, it is difficult to trace the remaining families.

2. James, son of James, and b. in Pepperell, 1767; m. Anna Wright, of this town, and had (1) *Anna,* b. 1788; rem. to Pepperell where had four children, *Luther, Matilda, James* and *Aaron.* He returned to Westford, and had (2) *Noah,* b. 1799. (3) *Charles,* b. 1801. (4) *John Wright,* b. 1804.

3. Eleazer, son of Eleazer, was born in Littleton. He lived in Littleton for many years, but rem. to Westford, where he m., for a 2nd wife, Sarah Foster, in 1780. Children: (1) *Joel,* b. 1781. (2) *Silas,* b. 1784. (3) *Sally,* b. 1786. He lived near Boutwell's Brook, on the plain which is covered with forest. Died 1789.

4. Simon, son of Eleazer, by his first wife, Lucy Tuttle, was born in Littleton, 1739. He m. Sybil Robbins, 1769. Children: (1) *Sybil,* b. 1770. (2) *Simon,* b. 1772. (3) *Rebecca,* b. 1774. (4) *Zechariah,* b. 1776. (5) *Lucy,* b. 1783; m. Avery Prescott, 1806. (6) *Lydia,* b. 1785. (7) *Sarah,* b. 1788. (8) *Lucinda,* b. 1790. (9) *Olive,* b. 1792.

5. Silas, son of Eleazer and Sarah (Foster), m. Hepsibah Prescott, 1808. Children: (1) *Silas,* b. 1809; lived in Westford; d. in Lowell, 1871. (2) *David P.,* b. 1810; m. Sarah Prescott, daughter of Dea. Abram, 1853. (3) *Alpheus,* b. 1813; lost at sea, 1837. (4) *Imla,* b. 1815. (5) *Harriet,* b. 1818; m. Seth Drake, 1840. (6) *Sarah,* b. 1821. (7) *Hannah,* b. 1824. (8) *Benjamin,* b. 1827; res. in Lowell.

LEIGHTON. This family came to New England in 1650. They were descended from Rev. Alexander Leighton, D. D., the father of Archbishop Leighton. William, one of the ancestors, received the honor of Knighthood; and the sword with which he was knighted was in the possession of Gen. Samuel Leighton, of Alfred, Me., in 1850. John, William and Samuel, who were brothers, came from England to Ipswich, Mass., in the autumn of 1650. John, the oldest, settled in Ipswich; William in Kittery, Me., and Samuel went to Virginia. John had two children, John and Martha, but Martha d. young. John, the son of John, had a son who was born in 1689. He was sea captain. He m., 1st, Sarah Perkins, and 2nd, Hannah Treadwell. The wife Hannah had six sons, viz: John, Thomas, William, Samuel, Daniel and Francis. He had also three daughters. Of the sons, John, Thomas and William were lost at sea. Capt. John, the father, becoming weary of sea-faring life, removed to Littleton, taking with him his youngest son, Francis, b. 1734, and his daughters Hannah, Martha and Sarah. The date of his removal was 1748. He was a member of Rev. Mr. Rogers' church. He died at the age of 84. His daughter Hannah m. —— Stone, of Groton; Martha m. —— Lawrence, of Littleton, and Sarah m. —— Hunt, of Littleton. Elizabeth, a granddaughter of Capt. John, came to Littleton and m. John Tuttle.

1. FRANCIS, b. in Ipswich, 1734, m. Lydia Fitch, of Westford, 1760. Children: (1) *Naomi,* b. 1761; m. Daniel Raymond, Jr., 1781. (2) *Reuben, 2,* b. 1762. (3) *John, 3,* b. 1764. (4) *Isaiah, 4,* b. 1766. (5) *Lydia,* b. 1768; m. Isaiah Hildreth, 1789. (6) *Hannah,* b. 1770; m. Joseph Cummings, Jr., 1790. (7) *Elizabeth,* b. 1774; m. Lt. John Hildreth. (8) *Joanna,* b. 1776; m. Osgood Eaton, of Reading, Mass., 1796. (9) *Daniel,* b. 1778. (10) *Susanna,* b. 1781; m. John C. Wilkins, of Carlisle. (11) *Samuel,* b. 1784; d. 1804.

2. Reuben, m., 1st, Hannah Hildreth, 1788. Children: (1) *Amos,* b. 1789; d. young. (2) *Francis, 5,* b. 1791. (3) *Patty,* b. 1794; m., 1st, Addison Parker; m., 2nd, Isaac Spalding, of New Ipswich. (4) *Abel,* b. 1795; settled in Roxbury. (5) *Ephraim,* b. 1797; rem. to New Jersey. (6) *Anna,* b. 1799; m. William Coolidge. (7) *Lydia,* b. 1801; m. Alexander Coolidge, 1823. He m., 2nd, Sally Wilson. (8) *Samuel,* b. 1809; a Baptist clergyman; d. in West Townsend, 1860. (9) *Amos, 6,* b. 1814. (10) *Sarah Augusta,* b. 1818.

3. John, m. Hannah Farrar, 1789. Children: (1) *Mary,* b. 1789; m. William Ditson, 1809, and had one son, George L. Ditson, who resides in Malden. (2) *Almaria,* b. ——; lived in Boston; d. in Malden, 1881. (3) *Caroline,* b. ——; m. —— Regally; d. in Malden, 1881. (4) *Frances,*

GENEALOGY.   461

kept a boarding house in Boston, where she d. in 1857. (5) *John*, b. ——;
went to California, and d. there. (6) *Rufus*, b.——; was a policeman in
Boston, where he d. about 1862.

4. **Isaiah**, m. Martha Kneeland, 1798. The births of the children
are not recorded. Their names were: (1) *Martha*, who d. young. (2)
Isaiah. (3) *George*. (4) *Mary*. (5) *Martha*. (6) *Daniel*. (7) *Harriet A.*,
who m. J. Austin Wright. (8) *Francis*. (9) *Maria A*.

5. **Francis**, m. Mary Reed, daughter of Willard. Children: (1)
Albert, **7**, b. 1813. After the birth of his first child he rem. to Salem. (2)
Mary Minot, b. 1815. (3) *Reuben Minot*, **8**, b. 1816. (4) *Sarah Flint*, b.
1819; m. Ebenezer Whitney. (5) *Benjamin Flint*, b. 1820; res. in Haverhill. (6) *Susan Poor*, b. 1823. (7) *Mary E.*, b. 1825, in Danvers; m., 1st,
Rufus Bullard, and 2nd, Samuel Tilton. (8) *George F.*, b. 1827, in Danvers; res. in Haverhill. (9) *Lowell E.*, b. 1829, in Natick. Francis, the
father, d. in 1862.

6. **Amos**, m. Elvira Bacon of West Cambridge, 1839. At the time
of his marriage he was living in Carlisle. Children: (1) *Elvira*, b. 1840;
m. Gilmer Stone. (2) *Mary E.*, b. 1843; m. Charles H. Fletcher. (3)
Sarah, b. 1845; m. Chancey Favor. (4) *Ida E.*, b. 1857. (5) *Amos Richmond*,
b. 1859.

7. **Albert**, m. Hannah Perry, 1832. Children: (1) *Henry*, b. 1833,
in Natick. (2) *Warren*, b. 1834, in Westford; d. 1843. (3) *Elbert*, b. 1837.
(4) *Warren*, b. 1843. (5) *Frank*, b. 1848. (6) *Charles*, b. 1850, in Pepperell,
whither the family removed.

8. **Reuben Minot**, m. Abigail Wright, of Chelmsford, and rem.
to Germania, Wis.

LELAND. 1. Jonas, b. in Sherborn, 1767; m. Olive ——. Children: (1) *Ira*, b. 1798. (2) *Sylvia*, b. 1800; m. Thomas Harding, Brighton,
1824. (3) *Andrew*, b. 1803; d. 1840. (4) *Joseph*, b. 1808; m. Louisa Read, 1838.
(5) *Henry Bullard*, b. 1811. Jonas d. 1843, aged 76. Olive, his wife, d. 1861,
aged 90.

2. **Ira**, m. Susan Prescott, 1826. Children: (1) *Andrew*, b. 1827; d.
1827. (2) *Susan Amelia*, b. 1834; d. unmarried, 1862. (3) *Martha Elizabeth*,
b. 1845; m. Hiram Whitney, 1868.

LUFKIN. Samuel, m. Sarah ——. Children: (1) *Samuel*, b.
1788. (2) *Cyrus*, b. 1789. (3) *Ezra*, b. 1791. (4) *Sarah*, b. 1793.

MEAD. 1. Thomas, m. Ruth ——. Children: (1) *Thomas*, **2**, b.
1742. (2) *Susanna*, b. 1744. (3) *John*, b. 1746. (4) *Ruth*, b. 1749. (5) *Stephen*, b.
1752. Probably there was a Mary, who was born before the father
moved here. He was the first physician in town. He was in the French
and Indian war, and d. before 1760. (See p. 65.) Lived on the place now
occupied by Mrs. Eunice Hildreth.

2. **Thomas**, m. Sarah Porter, Concord, 1778. No record of any
children. He lived in the south part.

MINOT. The ancestor of this family in this country, was George
of Dorchester, who was son of Thomas Minot, of Saffron-Walden, Essex,
England. Jonathan, of the fourth generation from George, was of Concord, where he m. Elizabeth Stratton, and is said to have lived and died
in Westford.

1. **Samuel**, the oldest son of Jonathan, was a resident here. He m.
Elizabeth ——. Children: (1) *Benjamin*, b. 1744. (2) *Sarah*, b. 1745. (3)
Samuel, b. 1748. After the birth of his third child, he went to Westmoreland, N. H. He was one of the grantees of that town in 1752. He did
not, however, make a permanent settlement there, but removed to Putney, Vt., where he was a deacon in the church, and where he died.

2. **Jonathan**, son of Jonathan, and brother of Samuel, m. Esther
Procter, daughter of Joseph and Agnes, b. 1725. The date of their publishment on Chelmsford records is 1745. They lived in Parkerville, near
Nonesuch Meadow. Children: (1) *John Marston*, b. 1746; grad. at Harvard, 1767. He settled in Castine, Me., where he was deputy sheriff. (2)
Esther, b. 1747; d. unmarried, 1821. (3) *Jonathan*, b. 1749, a soldier; m.
Hannah Eastman, Hollis, and rem. to Westminster, Mass., where he

died. (4) *Joseph*, b. 1751; killed at Bunker Hill. (5) *Olive*, b. 1753; m. Willard Read, 1774. (6) *Elizabeth*, b. 1755; m. David Foster, Winchendon, 1779. (7) *Mary*, b. 1757; m. James Wright; rem. to Maine. (8) *Jesse*, 2, b. 1759. (9) *Joanna*, b. 1762. (10) *Martha*, b. 1764; m. Benjamin Clark, Gardner, 1787. (11) *Joash*, b. 1769; m. Sally Hildreth, 1794; rem. to Hillsboro', N. H.

2. Jesse, m. Betsey, daughter of Thomas and Mary (Mead) Adams, 1784. Children: (1) *Betsey*, b. 1784; d. unmarried. (2) *Jesse*, b. 1787; m. Almira Fletcher, and rem. to Lockport, N. Y., where he died. (3) *Joseph*, b. 1789; m. Fanny Hildreth, res. in Manchester at the time of his death. (4) *Thomas*, b. 1791; m. Zoa A. Goodhue, 1818. He was a baker, and carried on business in the Centre, but rem. to Boston. (5) *Isaac*, 3, b. 1795. (6) *Jonathan*, b. 1797; m. —— Giles, Boston. (7) *Rufus*, b. 1800; m. Rebecca Townsend, Boston. (8) *Otis*, b. 1803; m. Elizabeth Bartlett, Boston; res. in Malden. (9) *Mary Ann*, b. 1807; d. 1809. Jesse and Almira had one child, Edward Jesse, b. 1833, before their removal.

3. Isaac, m. Mary Ann Hildreth, daughter of Jeremiah, 1844. Children: (1) *Isaac Warren*, b. 1845. (2) *Mary Ann*, b. 1847. (3) *Alma*, b. 1849; m. Albert P. Richardson, 1874.

4. John, brother of Jonathan 1, m. Rachel ——. Child: *Rachel*, b. 1754. This is the only birth recorded here.

NICHOLS. 1. William, came from Concord, m. Ruth ——, 1773. Children: (1) *Stephen* 2, b. 1774; d. 1826. (2) *Ruth*, b. 1777; d. 1801. (3) *William*, b. 1787. (4) *Mary*, b. 1790; d. 1823.

2. Stephen, m. Rebecca Hilton, of Lunenburg, 1798. Children: (1) *Stephen Norman*, b. 1800. (2) *Samuel Hilton*, 3, b. 1802. Stephen, the father, d. 1826. Stephen Norman, d. in California. He m. Nancy Hilton (?) who d. 1826. They had one son, Charles, d. 1826, aged 32 days.

3. Samuel H., m. Nancy E. Fletcher, daughter of Joseph, 1829. Children: (1) *Maria Rutha*, b. 1831. (2) *Sarah Miranda*, b. 1834; d. 1834. (3) *Norman Samuel*, b. 1836; d. 1836. (4) *Sarah Augusta* (twin), b. 1838. (5) *Samuel Augustus* (twin), b. 1838; d. 1838.

NUTTING. 1. Josiah, m. Mary ——. Children: (1) *Mary*, b. 1736. (2) *Benjamin* (?).

2. John, of Westford; m. Mary Adams, of Chelmsford, 1747, but no record of any children.

3. John, m. Hannah ——. Children: (1) *Hannah*, b. 1755. (2) *John*, b. 1756; d. at Albany, 1777, in the service of his country. (3) *Thomas*, 4, b. 1758. (4) *Mary*, b. 1761. (5) *Benjamin*, b. 1764; d. 1777, aged 13. (6) *Sarah*, b. 1767.

4. Thomas, m. Sibbel ——. Children: (1) *John*, b. 1782. (2) *Jonas*, b. 1783. (3) *Hannah*, b. 1785. (4) *Thomas*, b. 1787. (5) *Rebecca*, b. 1789; m. Jonathan Emerson, Dunstable, 1807. (6) *Benjamin*, b. 1791. (7) *Sibbel*, b. 1794. (8) *Buckley*, b. 1796. (9) *Abel*, b. 1799; m.

5. Daniel 3rd, son of Daniel, Jr., of Groton, b. 1756, m. Mary Lawrence, who was born in Townsend, 1763, and d. 1807. Children: (1) *Ede*, b. in Groton, 1780. (2) *Rebekah*, b. in Groton, 1782; m., 1st, —— Emerson; m., 2nd, Phinehas Trowbridge. (3) *Samuel*, b. 1784. (4) *Mary*, b. 1785. (5) *Ralph*, b. 1787. (6) *Stephen*, b. 1789. (7) *Daniel*, b. 1791. (8) *Sibel*, b. 1793; m., 1st, —— Carpenter, m., 2nd, —— Flint, rem. to Oneida, N. Y. (9) *Luther*, b. 1795. (10) *Asia*, 6, b. 1796. (11) *Nancy*, b. 1798; m. John H. Young. (12) *William*, b. 1801. (13) *Louisa*, b. 1804. (14) *Roxey*, b. 1805. Daniel, the father, d. 1836, aged 80. Mary, the mother, d. 1838, aged 79.

6. Asia, m. Clarissa ——. Children: (1) *Clarissa*, b. 1823. (2) *Alden Bradford*, b. 1825. (3) *Stephen Henry*, b. 1826. (4) *Sybil*, b. 1828. (5) *Luther Lawrence*, b. 1830. (6) *Mary*, b. 1832. (7) *Sally Ann*, b. 1833. (8) *Samuel Lawrence*, b. 1835. (9) *Daniel Washington*, b. 1837. (10) *Martha Cole*, b. 1839. (11) *Benjamin Franklin*, b. 1841.

OSGOOD. 1. Benjamin, Col., b. in Andover, 1754; m. Tryphena Cummings, daughter of Thomas, Jr., 1778. Children: (1) *Phena*, b. 1779; m. James Robbins, 1803. (2) *Benjamin*, 2, b. 1781. (3) *Josiah*, b. 1782; d.

GENEALOGY. 463

1784. (4) *John*, **3**, b. 1784. (5) *Jacob*, **4**, b. 1787. (6) *Patty*, b. 1790; m. Alpheus Spalding, of Chelmsford, 1815.
2. Benjamin, M. D., m., 1st, Nancy Cummings, daughter of Isaac, 1810. She d. 1831. Children: (1) *Benjamin Franklin*, b. 1812; d. unmarried. (2) *Zaccheus Wright*, b. 1814; d. 1821. (3) *Nancy*, b. 1816; d. 1819. (4) *George Stuart*, b. 1819; d. 1837. (5) *Nancy Houghton*, b. 1821. (6) *Elizabeth Mayhew*, b. 1823. (7) *Isaac Cummings*, b. 1826; d. at Racine, Wis., 1854. (8) *John Mason*, b. 1828. He m., 2nd, Eliza Cummings, daughter of John, 1833. (9) *Augustus Holyoke*, b. 1833. (10) *Judith Pickman*, b. 1836; d. 1837. (11) *Ellen Appleton*, b. 1840. Benjamin Osgood, M. D., d. 1863.
3. John, m., 1st, Patty Fletcher, daughter of Capt. Thomas, 1807. Children: (1) *John Hamilton*, b. 1807; res. in Chelsea. (2) *Josiah*, b. 1809; res. in Chelsea. (3) *Martha*, b. 1811; m. Rev. Thomas Laurie, D. D., and went as a Missionary to Turkey; d. 1843. He m., 2nd, Mrs. Sarah (Spalding) Perham, of Chelmsford, 1816. (4) *Harriet Emma*, b. 1817; m. George Brown, 1839, and rem. to Winchendon. (5) *Edward Henry*, b. 1829. John the father, d. 1858. Mrs. Sarah, d. 1878, aged 91 years, 11 months.
4. Jacob, m. Patty, daughter of Pelatiah Fletcher, 1807. Children: (1) *Joel Fletcher*, b. 1807. (2 and 3) *Jacob* and *Patty*, b. 1809. Jacob d. 1820. (4) *Pelatiah Fletcher*, b. 1811. (5) *Charles*, b. 1815; rem. to Townsend. (6) *Maria*, b. 1817. (7) *Alden Pitt*, **5**, b. 1819. (8) *Eliza Jane*, b. 1821; d. 1834. (9) *Isaac Newton*, b. 1823; d. 1825. (10) *Augusta Ann*, b. 1827. (11) *Jacob Newton*, b. 1829. (12) *Chester Houghton*, b. 1832; d. 1847. (13) *Benjamin Everett*, b. 1835.
5. Alden P., m., 1st, Sarah S. Baker, 1840. She d. 1857; m., 2nd, Nancy, daughter of Dea. Caleb Wight, 1858. Children: (1) *Houghton Gilbert*, b. 1859. (2) *Ida Maria*, b. 1861. (3) *Sarah Josephine*, b. 1863; d. 1878. He d. 1880.

PARKER. The ancestor of this family was Abraham, who is supposed to have come from Wiltshire, Eng. He first settled in Woburn, where he married Rose Whitlock, 1644; was admitted freeman in 1645; and rem. to Chelmsford, probably upon its incorporation in 1653, with his brothers, Jacob, James and Joseph. His homestead of 24 acres was set off to him in 1662 and was near the middle of Chelmsford. His son, Moses, b. in Chelmsford about the year, 1657; m. Abigail Hildreth, daughter of Richard.
1. Aaron, was the first of the name in Westford, and was the son of Moses, b. 1689. His name is among the orginal members of the first church. He m. Abigail Adams, about, 1712. Children: (1) *Aaron*, **2**, b. 1713. (2) *Samuel*, **3**, b. 1717. (3) *Moses*, **4**, b. 1718. (4) *Abigail*, b. 1720; m. John Senter, of Londonderry, N. H. (5) *Mary*, b. 1723; m. Oliver Procter, of Chelmsford. (6) *Lucy*, b. 1725-26; m. Stephen Corey, of Littleton. (7) *Elizabeth*, b. 1728; m. Gershom Proctor, of Chelmsford. (8) *Isaac*, b. 1731. (9) *Joseph*, b. 1735; m. Susanna Fletcher, 1763. (10) *Esther*, b. 1738. He lived on the farm now owned by George Hutchins, which was the original homestead of the family in thistown. He d. in 1772, aged 83.
2. Aaron, m., 1st, Mary Barret, who d. in 1737. He m., 2nd, Dorothy Fletcher, 1738. Children: (1) *Aaron*, **5**, b. 1739. (2) *Joshua*, **6**, b. 1740. (3) *Dorothy*, b. 1742; m. ———. (4) *Mary*, b. 1744; m. Amos Boynton, 1767. (5) *Abigail*, b. 1745; m. John Hildreth, 1762. (6) *Sarah*, b. 1747. (7) *Ebenezer*, **7**, b. 1749. (8) *Deborah*, b. 1751; m. Henry Fletcher, 1773. (9) *Isaiah*, b. 1752. (10) *Isaac*, b. 1755; d. 1756. (11) *David*, **8**, b. 1757. He d. 1762, and his widow m. Peter Reed, of Littleton.
3. Samuel, m., 1st, Sarah Fletcher, daughter of Dea. Joshua, 1739. He lived on the Horace Pratt farm. Children: (1) *Samuel*, b. 1739; d. in Maine. (2) *Sarah*, b. 1740; m. Solomon Dutton, of Antrim, N. H., 1765. (3) *Joseph*, b. 1742; rem. to New Ipswich. (See p. 160.) (4) *Silas*, b. 1743; d. at Mt. Desert. (5) *Leonard*, **9**, b. 1745. He m., 2nd, Mrs. Mary (Proctor) Robbins, 1748. (6) *Mary*, b. 1749; m. Thomas Wright, of New Ipswich,

1766. (7) *Jonathan*, b. 1751; rem. to Rindge, N. H., where he d. unmarried, 1820. (8) *Abel*, b. 1753. He, with his father's family rem. to Pepperell about 1767, where he m. Edith, daughter of Jedediah Jewett. In 1780, he rem. to Jaffrey, where he d. in 1831. He was called to fill many offices of public trust, and "it was his highest pride that every office came to him unsought." He was the father of Hon. Edmund Parker, of Nashua, Judge of Probate; of Hon. Isaac Parker, a distinguished merchant of Boston; and of Hon. Joel Parker, once Chief Justice of N. H. and afterward professor of law in Harvard College. (9) *Elizabeth*, b. 1755; m.———Tenny. (10) *Lydia* b. 1757; d. unmarried, 1774.

4. Moses, Lieut., m. 1744, Bridget Cummings, daughter of Dea. John, b. 1722. Children: (1) *Bridget*, bap. 1745. (2) *Bridget*, b. 1746. (3) *Elizabeth*, b. 1749; d. unmarried, 1829. (4) *Isaac*, b. 1751; d. 1753. (5) *Lucy*, b. 1753. (6) *Moses*, b. 1755. (7) *John*, **10**, b. 1757; d. 1778. (8) *Isaac*, **11**, b. 1760. (9) *Aaron*, **12**, b. 1762. (10) *Abigail*, b. 1765. He m., 2nd, wid. Anna Barrett, 1779.

5. Aaron, m., 1st, Lucy Hildreth, 1763, who d. the same year. Children: (1) *Hildreth*, b. 1763; d. 1764. He m., 2nd, Lydia Spalding, of Chelmsford, 1766. (2) *Aaron*, b. 1767. (3) *Lydia*, b. 1771.

6. Joshua, Capt., (see pp. 111 and 165.) m., 1st, Mary Boynton, 1764. Children: (1) *Joshua*, b. 1764; rem. to Cavendish, Vt. He m. Hannah Jackman, of Lunenburg, 1790, and had Polly, Betsey, Levi, Abner, Joshua and John W.———. The third Joshua had a son Charles G., now a merchant at Proctorsville, Vt. (2) *Patty*, b. 1766; m. Daniel Coffin, of Cavendish. (3) *Mary*, b. 1769; m. Abel Kimball, of Cavendish. He m., 2nd, Hannah Kidder, of Cambridge, 1774. She was left an orphan and lived for a time with her sister in Brighton, Mass. (4) *Amariah Fassett*, b. 1775. (5) *Hannah*, b. 1778. She became the second wife of Isaiah Boynton, of Plymouth, Vt., and had two children. Capt. Joshua Parker d. in the state of New York.

7. Ebenezer, m. Mrs. Experience Hildreth, who was the daughter of Capt. Jabez Keep, and the widow of Hosea Hildreth, 1777. Children: (1) *John*, b. 1778; rem. to Cavendish, Vt., where he m. Nancy Atherton. (2) *Ebenezer*, b. 1780; rem. to Cavendish, Vt., where he m. Sally Bowers. (3) *Sarah*, b. 1782; m. Thomas Brown, of Plymouth, Vt. (4) *Rebecca*, b. 1784; d. 1808, aged 24. (5) *Jabez*, b. 1788; m. 1812, Roxana Fletcher, daughter of Benjamin and Mehitabel (Robinson) and settled in Richmond, Va.; physician. (6) *Mary*, b. 1790; m. Samuel Farwell, 1813. (7) *Dorothy*, b. 1792; m. Asa Stratton, of Cavendish, Vt. (8) *Salome*, b. 1793; m. Asa Stratton, after the death of her sister. (9) *Loammi*, b. 1795. (10) *Eri*, b. 1797; settled in Littleton.

8. David, m. Martha Carver, 1782. Children: (1) *Thomas Carver*, **13**, b. 1783. (2) *Benjamin*, b. 1784; d. 1785. (3) *Benjamin*, b. 1785; rem. to Acworth, N. H.; physician. (4) *Martha*, b. 1787; d. 1788. (5) *Lucy*, b. 1791. (6) *Addison*, b. 1793; m. Martha Leighton, 1819; d. 1836. (7) *Horace*, b. 1796; rem. to Acworth; physician; d. 1829. (8) *Ephraim Hildreth*, b. 1798; d. 1801. (9) *David*, b. 1802; rem. to Gardner, Mass.; physician.

9. Leonard, m. Mary Foster, 1768. Children: (1) *Leonard*, b. 1769; m. Rebecca Fletcher, 1788. (2) *Elias*, b. 1771. (3) *Abel*, b. 1773. (4) *Polly*, b. 1775; m. 1794, Benjamin Wheeler, of Pepperell. (5) *Sally*, b. 1777; d. young. (6) *Sally*, b. 1778. (7) *Rebecca*, b. 1780; d. young. (8) *Rebecca*, b. 1782. (9) *Silas*, b. 1785. (10) *Mille*, b. 1787. (11) *Lydia*, b. 1793. Leonard, the father, d. in the "Holmes Purchase," Me., and it may be that the sons Elias, Abel, and Silas, rem. thither, and the younger daughters, likewise.

10. John, m. Abigail———. Child: *John*, b. 1788. This is all that appears; probably rem.

11. Isaac, m., 1st, Bridget Fletcher, daughter of Timothy and Bridget (Richardson), 1785. Children: (1) *Hannah*, b. 1785, in Concord. (2) *Grace*, b. 1786; d. young. (3) *Isaac*, b. 1789 in Cavendish, whither the family rem. (4) *Betsey*, b. 1789; m. Jabez Proctor. (5) Nancy, b. 1791; m. ——— Bates. (6) *John*, b. 1795; d. in Chicago. (7) *Sally*, b. 1797; res. in

Proctorsville, Vt., unmarried. (8) *Timothy*, b. 1798 (physician), Warren, Penn. (9) *Abigail*, b. 1800. (10) *Elijah Fletcher*, b. 1804; lived in Cavendish; Vt. He m., 2nd, Catherine Wilson, and had Hiram, Warren, and Lydia. Isaac, the son, kept school in Westford one winter. He settled in Coventry, Vt. The father, d. in Byron, N. Y. His wife, Bridget, d. in Weathersfield, Vt.

12. **Aaron**, Capt., m. Joanna ———, 1792. Children: (1) *Anna*, b. 1793; d. 1837. (2) *Jonathan Fletcher*, b. 1795; d. unmarried, 1854. He lived a hermit's life. His house or camp stood on the road leading from Forge Village to Carlisle, on the north side between the old Luther Read place, and the old Farwell place. It is said that he had a small orifice in his door which could be covered with a slide, and which was closed when he saw any one coming. (3) *Aaron*, b. 1799; d. 1802. Capt. Aaron d. 1823. His wife d. 1838.

13. **Thomas Carver**, m. Hannah Proctor, 1810. Children. (1) *Augustus*, b. 1812; d. 1830. (2) *Lucy*, b. 1814; d. 1821. (3) *Martha*, b. 1816; m., Amos Hildreth, 2nd, and had Julian, b. 1852. (4) *Hosea*, b. 1820; d. 1820.

14. **Isaac**, parentage not ascertained, probably son of William, of Groton, m. Bridget Cummings, 1776. Children: (1) ——, b. 1779, at Litchfield, N. H. (2) *Thomas Cummings*, b. 1781, at Chelmsford. (3) *Sarah*, b. 1787.

15. **Levi**, Lieut., parentage not ascertained, but perhaps the son of William, of Groton; m., 1st, Rebecca Fletcher, 1777. She d. 1784. Children: (1) *Levi*, 16, b. 1778. (2) *Bille*, b. 1780. (3) *George*, b. 1783. He m., 2nd, 1785, Abigail Pool, daughter of William and Hannah (Nichols) Pool, of Hollis. (4) *James*, b. 1787. (5) *Luther*, b. 1789. (6) *Calvin*, b. 1790; d. 1790. (7) *Betsey*, b. 1792. He, the father, res. awhile in N. H., perhaps at Hollis, but rem. to Cambridge.

16. **Levi**, m. Betsey Wright, 1808. Children: (1) *Martha*, b. ———; m. Edmund Boynton. (2) *William*, b. ———; d. at Cambridge. (3) *Anna Wright*, b. 1813. (4) *Luther L.*, b. 1815.

17. **Benjamin**, came from Chelmsford, m. Betsey ———. Children: (1) *Asa*, b. 1797. (2) *Joel*, b. 1799. He lived on the place now occupied by John Wayne.

PARRIT or PARROT. Thomas, m. Sarah Robbins, 1739. Children: (1) *Sarah*, b. 1739. (2) *Thomas*, b. 1742; settled in New Ipswich. (3) *Mary*, b. 1743; m. Benjamin Crosby, of Chelmsford, 1767. (4) *Margaret*, b. 1744.

PATCH. 1. Isaac, of Westford, m. Joanna Butterfield in 1739. They were married in Concord by Justice Flint. The family of Isaac and Joanna appears on the records of Groton; the children were: Isaac b. 1739, and Hannah, Phebe, Edith, and Stephen. Isaac, the son, probably came from Pepperell here, where he had m. Elizabeth ———. Children (on Westford book): (1) *John Avery*, b. at Pepperell, 1761. (2) *Isaac*, 2, b. 1762. (3) *Asa*, b. 1764, at Groton; m. Lydia Lawrence, 1784. (4) *Elizabeth*, b. 1766. (5) *Abel*, b. 1769, at Groton.

2. **Isaac**, m. Phebe Fletcher, 1786 and rem. to Cavendish, Vt. Children: (1) *Ralph*, b. in Cavendish, 1788. (2) *Abijah*, b. in Cavendish, 1790. After the birth of the second child, he seems to have returned. (3) *Lucinda*, b. 1792; m. William Read, Jr., 1817. (4) *Salome*, b. 1794. (5) *Phebe*, b. 1797. (6) *Alvah*, b. 1799. (7) *Albert*, b. 1801. (8) *Sophronia*; m. Moses Titus, of Lyman, N. H., 1831. They settled in Pepperell and celebrated their golden wedding, 1881.

3. **John**, of Westford, m. Betty Chandler in 1784, but there is no record of any children.

4. **Daniel**, of Westford, m. Betsey Wright, 1807. He d., and she m. Elisha Kent, 1813.

PATTEN. 1. Isaac, was born in Chelmsford; m. Lydia Keyes, 1782. Children: (1) *James Pollard*, b. 1783. (2) *Isaac*, b. 1784. (3) *John*, b. 1786. (4) *Oliver*, b. 1788, in Ashby. (5) *Thomas*, b. 1792, in Ashby. (6) *Lydia*, b. 1794; m. Dr. Calvin Brown, of Acworth, N. H. (7) *William*,

b. 1796. (8) *Mary*, b. 1798. (9) *Rufus*, **2**, b. 1802. (10) *Joseph*, b. 1804; was found dead in Spencer, Mass, 1837. (11) *Jane Ann*, b. 1807; m. Dr. Kendall Davis, of South Reading, Mass, 1831. Isaac, the father, d. 1836. Lydia, the mother, d. 1838.

2. Rufus, m. Sarah B. Hall, 1836. Children: (1) *Augusta Virginia*, b. 1838; d. young. (2) *Mary Olivia*, b. 1839. (3) *Georgiana*, b. 1840; m. Isaac Henry Stone; rem. to Illinois. (4) *William Oliver*, b. 1842; res. in Worcester. (5) *Rufus Orlando*, b. 1844; d. 1846. (6) *Sarah Jane*, b. 1846; m. Albert F. Conant, of Littleton.

PEARSON. 1. Thomas, m. Ame (Putnam). (?) Children: (1) *Anna*, b. 1783; m. Abraham Morgan, of Wilton, N. H., 1806. (2) *Thomas*, **2**, b. 1785. (3) *Caleb*, b. 1786. (4) *Amy*, ——; (?) m. Eleazer Ingalls, of Dunstable, 1806.

2. Thomas, Lieut., m. Esther Wright, 1810.

PERRY. James, m. Hepsibah ——. Children: (1) *Sarah*, b. 1765. He seems to have m., 2nd, Mary ——. (2) *Mary* b. 1770; m. Daniel Blood, 1796. (3) *Esther*, b. 1773; m. Aaron Blood, Jr., 1796. (4) *Rachel*, b. 1778.

PRESCOTT. The ancestor of this family was John, who came from Standish, England, landed at Boston, 1640; was for a time at Watertown, but settled at Lancaster, Mass., 1643. He married in England Mary Platts, in 1629, and she came to this country with him. Their son Jonas, b. in Lancaster, 1648; m. Mary Loker, of Sudbury, in 1672, and settled in Groton. He was a blacksmith by trade. He became a large landholder in Groton. "Upon the resettlement of the town after its destruction by the Indians, in 1676, he built mills and a forge for the manufacture of iron from the ore, at Forge Village."

1. Jonas, son of Jonas and Mary (Loker), lived at Forge Village. He m., 1st, Thankful Wheeler, of Concord, 1699. The record of his family is not on the Westford book, and it is copied from the Prescott memorial. Children: (1) *Ebenezer*, **2**, b. 1700. (2) *Jonas*, **3**, b. 1703. (3) *Thankful*, b. 1705; m. Timothy Spalding. (4) *Mary*, b. 1711; m. Joseph Stone, of Groton. (5) *Sarah*, b. 1712; m. Samuel Minot, Concord. (6) *Dorcas*, b. 1714; m. Samuel Minot, being his second wife.

2. Ebenezer, m. Hannah Farnsworth, 1721. Children: (1) *Ebenezer*, **4**, b. 1723. (2) *Oliver*, **5**, b. 1725. (3) *Sarah* (twin), b. 1726; m. John Edwards, of Lancaster. (4) *Joseph* (twin), b. 1726. (5) *David*, b. 1728; m. Abigail Wright and lived in Groton, near to Westford line. (6) *Hannah*, b. 1730. (7) *Rebecca*, b. 1732. (8) *Eunice*, b. 1734.

3. Jonas, m., 1st, Esther Spalding, 1726. Children: (1) *Jonas*, **6**, b. 1727. (2) *Timothy*, **7**, b. 1728. He m., 2nd, Elizabeth Howard, of Chelmsford, 1731. (3) *Elijah*, b. 1732; d. young. (4) *Elizabeth*, b. 1734; m. Zechariah Hildreth, 1753. (5) *Isaac*, b. 17 ; d. young. (6) *Benjamin*, b. ——; d. young. He m., 3rd, Mrs. Rebecca (Jones) Barrett, of Concord, 1740. (7) *Esther*, b. 1742; m. Col. David Goodhue, 1767. (8) *Sarah*, b. 1744; m. Abraham Taylor, of Ashby, 1776, and d. at the age of 93. (9) *John*, **8**, b. 1752.

4. Ebenezer, m. Elizabeth Sprague, 1746. Children: (1) *Ebenezer*, **9**, b. 1747. (2) *Joseph*, **10**, b. 1749. (3) *Rebecca*, b. 1751; m. James Fletcher, 1770.

5. Oliver, m. Bethiah Underwood, 1749. Children: (1) *Susanna*, b. 1750; m. Nathaniel Adams, of Charlestown, 1769. (2) *Hannah*, b. 1752; m. Richard Wait, 1769, and joined the Shakers. (3) *Benjamin*, Col. b. 1754; m. Rachel Adams, of Chelmsford, 1775; and rem. to Jaffrey, N. H. (See Prescott Memorial, p. 101.) (4) *Betsey*, b. 1756; joined the Shakers, but afterward left them. (5) *Bethia*, b. 1758; joined the Shakers and d. among them. (6) *Oliver*, b. 1760; rem first to Jaffrey, and afterward to Oneida Co., N. Y. (7) *Polly*, b. 1762; d. 1766. (8) *Phebe*, b. 1763; joined the Shakers, but left them, and d. unmarried. (9) *Lucy*, b. 1765; joined the Shakers and d. among them. (10) *Mary*, b. 1767; m., 1st, Eliakim Hutchins, 1793; m., 2nd, Hezekiah Sprague, of Littleton. (11) *Abram*, **11**, b. 1769. (12) *Isaac*, **12**, b. 1771.

6. Jonas, m. Rebecca Bulkley, of Groton, 1751. He was a forgeman at Forge Village, where he d. 1813, aged 86. Children: (1) *Jonas*, b. 1851; d. in Groton unmarried. (2) *Rebecca*, b. 1753; m. Amos Fletcher. (3) *Sybil*, b. 1756; m. Thomas Nutting, 1781. (4) *Abigail*, b. 1757; m. Thomas Hutchins as his 2nd wife. (5) *Abel*, b. 1759; m. Hannah Spalding, of Ashburnham, and lived in Groton. (6) *Peter*, b. 1761; d. unmarried, 1813. (7) *Esther*, b. 1763; m. Thomas Hutchins, who was after her death, the husband of her sister, Abigail, above. (8) *Bulkley*, **13**, b. 1766. (9) *Mary*, b. 1768; d. young. (10) *Levi*, **14**, b. 1771, (11) *Benjamin*, **15**, b. 1774.

7. Timothy, m., 1st, Lydia Fletcher, 1753. Children: (1) *Lydia*, b. 1754; settled in Pepperell where she m., 1st, Josiah Conant. (2) *Timothy*, b. 1755; d. 1759. (3) *Esther*, b. 1757; d. 1759. (4) *Lucy*, b. 1759; d. 1759. (5) *Anna*, b. 1761; m. Elnathan Read, of Westford, and rem. to Cavendish, Vt. (6) *Isaiah*, **16**, b. 1763. (7) *Sarah*, b. 1765; m. Stephen Wright, 1787. He d. at Shelburne, Mass., 1857, aged 92. (8) *Elijah*, b. 1767; m. Eunice Walker, of Ashby, where he lived and died. (9) *Ruth*, b. 1769; m. Abel White and rem. to Washington, N. H. (10) *Amos*, **17**, b. 1771. (11) *Olive*, b. 1774; m. Caleb Parker, of Pepperell. Timothy m., 2nd, Mrs. Rebecca Boynton, 1800.

8. John, m. Martha Abbot, 1776. Children: (1) *John*, b. 1779; m. Anna Keyes, and rem. to Dunstable. (2) *Joshua*, b. 1780; grad. at Harvard, 1807, and was a lawyer in Reading. He was a member of the General Court in 1826 and '27. (3) *Samuel*, b. 1782; grad. at Harvard, 1799, and was a lawyer in Keene, N. H. (4) *Stephen*, b. 1784, was a mechanic in Boston, where he d. unmarried, 1808. (5) *Hannah*, b. 1786; d. unmarried, 1841. (6) *Aaron*, b. 1787; grad. at Harvard, 1814, and was a lawyer in Randolph, Mass. Representative in the General Court several years. (7) *Thomas*, **18**, b. 1791.

9. Ebenezer, m. Lydia Wood, of Littleton, 1775. Children: (1) *Ebenezer*, **19**, b. 1776. (2) *Asa*, **20**, b. 1778. (3) *Lydia*, b. 1780; m. Bulkley Ames, of Groton. (4) *Jonathan*, **21**, b. 1783. (5) *Elizabeth*, b. 1788; m. Henry Herrick, 1808. She d. 1862. (6) *Nancy*, b. 1791; m. —— Varnum, of Dracut. (7) *Lucy*, b. 1793; m. Andrew Gage, 1825.

10. Joseph, m., 1st. Abigail Dalrymple, 1774. Children: (1) *Ede*, b. 1775; d. unmarried. (2) *William*, **22**, b. 1777. (3) *Jeptha*, b. 1779; d. unmarried. (4) *Avery*, **23**, b. 1781. (5) *Jacob*, b. 1783; rem. to Bennington, Vt. He m., 2nd, Rachel Cobleigh (or Cutter ?). (6) *Sophia*, b. 1804; m. Jeremiah J. Carter, and d. 1845.

11. Abram, m., 1st, Polly Fletcher, 1798. Children: (1) *Polly Fletcher*, b. 1799; m. Benjamin Spalding, Chelmsford, 1830. (2) *Martha*, b. 1800; d. 1801. He. m., 2nd, Olive, daughter of Abel Adams, of Chelmsford, 1801. (3) *Olive*, b. 1802; m., 1st, Samuel Richardson, 1830; m., 2nd, Calvin Howard, 1851. (4) *Bethia*, b. 1804; m. Eliel Heywood, 1834. (5) *Oliver*, b. 1806. He studied law and settled in New Bedford; has been judge of Probate for Bristol Co., etc. (6) *Abram*, b. 1809; d. 1854, unmarried. (7) *Henry Adams*, **24**, b. 1811. (8) *Sarah*, b. 1813; m. Capt. David Prescott Lawrence, 1853; had one child, Grace, b. 1859. (9) *Abel*, b. 1816; m. Caroline Hildreth, 1855, and rem. to Ayer. Is a justice of the peace. (10) *Jackson*, b. 1819; d. 1841, aged 22. (11) *Edward*, **25**, b. 1821.

12. Isaac, m. Lucy Hinkley, 1797. Children: (1) *Lucinda*, b. 1797; m. Mason Pierce. (2) *Harriet*, b. 1799; d. 1800. (3) *Harriet*, b. 1801; d. 1802. (4) *Harriet*, b. 1804 ; m. David Plaisted. (5) *Charles*, b. 1805. (6) *Ann*, b. 1807. (7) *Lucy b.* 1810; m. Rev. Stephen Manning; d. 1867. (8) *Isaac*, b. 1812. (9) *Joseph*, b. 1816; d. 1828.

13. Bulkley, m. Mrs. Eunice, wid. of William Prescott, 1812. Children: (1) *Rebecca*, b. 1812; m. Charles Prescott, 1831. (2) *Peter Bulkley*, **26**, b. 1813; m. Zebiah Richardson, daughter of Thomas, 1841. (3) *Joseph Henry*, b. 1819.

14. Levi, m. Hannah Prescott, daughter of David, 1809. Children: (1) *Jonas*, **27**, b. 1810. (2) *Caroline*, b. 1812; d. 1812. (3) *Mary Ann*, b. 1813; m. George Wright, 1833. (4) *Olive*, b. 1815; m. Luther Prescott, 1837. (5) *Hannah*, b. 1817; d. 1818. (6) *Levi*, b. 1823.

15. Benjamin, m. Polly Read, 1799. Children: (1) *Benjamin,* b. 1800; m. Mary S. Flagg, of New Ipswich, 1834. He lived in Westford. (2) *Charles,* b. 1803; m. Lucy Ann Flagg, of New Ipswich, 1830; rem. to Mason, N. H., and d. in 1861.

16. Isaiah, m., 1st, Betsey Wright, of Littleton, 1786. He resided ten years in Ashby, then returned to Westford where his wife d. 1806. He m., 2nd, Wid. Bird who d. and he m., 3rd, Wid. Matilda French. He was influential in town affairs and was one of the selectmen for nearly twenty years. Children: (1) *Timothy,* b. 1787; m. Abigail D. Wood, of Stow; she d. and he m., 2nd, Maria King, of Westford. He lived first in Littleton, afterward in Concord. (2) *A child; still-born.* (3) *Betsey,* b. 1790; d. young. (4) *Lydia* (twin), b. 1792; m. Nathan Wright, 1834. (5) *Mary* (twin), b. 1792; m. Dea. John Cutter, 1817. (6) *Isaiah,* b. 1793; m. Roxana Craig, of Windsor, Vt.; res. first in Littleton, then in Charlestown, N. H. (7) *Nathan,* b. 1795; d. 1796. (8) *Betsey,* m., 1st, Asa Read, 1817; m., 2nd, Elijah Mason Read, of Lowell. (9) *Candace,* b. 1799; d. 1852. (10) *A son,* b. 1802; d. same day. (11) *Harriet,* b. 1803; m. Simeon Hildreth, Jr., 1823, rem. to Deerfield, N. H.

17. Amos, m. Polly Emerson, 1793. Children: (1) *Polly,* b. 1796; m. Joseph Haskell, 1826. (2) *Sally,* b. 1797; d. 1862, unmarried. (3) *Lydia,* b. 1799. (4) *Louisa,* b. 1801; m. Warren Ware, of Lowell, 1829. (5) *George,* b. 1803; d. young. (6) *Lucinda,* b. 1805; in Ashby; m. Gardner Brown, of Acworth, N. H. (7) *Oliver,* b. 1807. (8) *Martha Triphosa,* b. 1810; m. Jacob Puffer, 1836. (9) *Amos Emerson,* b. 1812; m. Mary Shepard. (10) *Timothy,* b. 1815; m. Harriet Stone, 1853.

18. Thomas, m. Sarah Hale, 1814. Children: (1) *Aaron Abbot,* b. 1815; m. Betsey Hunt, of Randolph, Mass., 1839. (2) *Sarah Ann Hale,* b. 1817; m. Edwin Bassett, of Gloucester. (3) *Abigail Eaton,* b. 1820; m. her cousin, Thomas Eaton Prescott, of Reading.

19. Ebenezer, m., 1st, Hannah Wait, 1800. Children: (1) *Asa,* b. 1800. (2) *George,* b. 1801; d. 1801. (3) *Susan,* b. 1802; m. Ira Leland, 1826. (4) *Almira* (twin), b. 1806; d. 1815. (5) *Elnora* (twin), b. 1806; m. Timothy Prescott Wright, 1832. (6) *Franklin,* b. 1808; drowned 1812. (7) *Ebenezer,* b. 1810; d. 1810. (8) *Ebenezer,* b. 1811; d. 1815. He m., 2nd, Charlotte Jones, 1813. (9) *Franklin,* b. 1813. (10) *Timothy,* b. 1815. (11) *Nathan Pollard,* 28, b. 1817. (12) *Charlotte,* b. 1819. d. 1858. He m., 3rd, Sally Fletcher, 1821. (13) *Samuel,* 29, b. 1822. (14) *Joseph Fletcher,* b. 1823; m. Sarah P. Lawrence, of Pepperell, 1848. One son, Joseph Elwin, b. 1851. (15) *Simeon,* b. 1826; rem. to Maine.

20. Asa, m. Sophia Derbe, 1821. Children: (1) *Julia Ann,* b. 1822; m. Calvin F. Raymond, of Littleton. (2) *Augustus Asa,* b. 1823. (3) *Charles Franklin,* b. 1825; d. 1827. (4) *Charles Abbot,* b. 1828. (5) *Mary Jane,* b. 1830; d. 1832. (6) *George Albert,* b. 1831. (7) *Augusta Maria,* b. 1834; d. 1837. (8) *Ebenezer,* b. 1836; d. 1837. (9) *Melvina,* b. 1838. (10) *Elias,* b. 1840. (11) *Martha Jane,* b. 1842.

21. Jonathan, m. Huldah Robbins, daughter of Benjamin, 1809. Child: *Luther,* 30, b. 1809.

22. William, m. Eunice Wheeler, of Littleton, 1801. Children: (1) *Alvah,* b. 1803; d.——. (2) *George Gilbert,* b. 1805; d. young. (3) *William,* b. 1807; d. young.

23. Avery, m., 1st, Lucy Lawrence, of Ashby, 1806. She d. 1814, and he m., 2nd, ——. Child: *Charles Henry,* b. ——; others were born and d.

24. Henry Adams, m. Mary M., daughter of Henry Fletcher, 1837. Children: (1) *George Henry,* b. 1838; m. Sophia P. Carter, 1861. He m., 2nd, Olive E. Read, 1843. (2) *Edward Mason,* b. 1848; d.. 1860. (3) *Clara Frances,* b. 1855. (4) *Emma Louisa,* b. 1861. (5) *Sarah Elizabeth,* b. 1863; res. in Lawrence, Mass.

25. Edward, m. Augusta Babbitt. Children: (1) *Charles Oliver,* b. 1855. (2) *Albert Edward,* b. 1864.

26. Peter Bulkley, m. Zebiah Richardson, daughter of Thomas, 1841. Children: (1) *Helen Zebiah,* b. 1842, d. young. (2) *Helen Zebiah,* b. 1843; d. 1845. (3) *Clara,* b. 1846. (4) *Horace A.,* b. 1849; an apothecary in Boston.

27. Jonas, m. Martha W. Cummings, daughter of John, 1839. Children: (1) *Hannah,* b. 1840; m. Warren A. Wyeth. (2) *Jonas Melbourne,* b. 1843; d. 1882.

28. Nathan Pollard, m. Bethia Sargent, 1842. Children: (1) *Lucinda,* b. 1843; d. 1846. (2) *Noah,* b. 1845; m. —— Tower. (3) *Lucinda,* b. 1847. (4) *Ebenezer* (twin), b. 1849; m. —— Webster. (5) *Eugene DeCosta* (twin), b. 1849. (6) *Charlotte,* b. 1852, (7) *Ellen F.,* b. 1855; m. Henry Going, of Townsend. (8) *Nathan,* b. 1858. (9) *Elnora,* b. 1862.

29. Samuel, m. Parazina Hayden, 1843. Children: (1) *Samuel Austin,* b. 1845. (2) *Mary Eliza,* b. 1847. (3) *Louis Warren,* b. 1852. (4) *Ida Luella,* b. 1858.

30. Luther, m., 1st, Olive Prescott, 1837. Children: (1) *Sherman Luther,* b. 1839. (2) *Olive Ann,* b. 1841.

31. James, son of James, of Groton, came to Westford and established himself as a lawyer. He m. Hannah Champney, daughter of Ebenezer, of New Ipswich, 1792. Children b. in Westford: (1) *Susanna,* b. 1793; d. 1795. (2) *Hannah,* b. 1795; d. 1801. (3) *Susanna,* b. 1796; m. John Wright, of Lowell, a native of Westford, who grad. at Harvard, 1824. (4) *Lucretia,* b. 1798; m. James McWilliams, and rem. to Alton, Ill. (5) *Lucy,* b. 1800; m. Joseph Reynolds, M. D., and rem. to Gloucester, Mass.; afterward res. in Concord.

PROCTER. The ancestor of this family was Robert, of Concord, who m. Jane Hildreth, 1645. He rem. to Chelmsford in 1654 and was one of the first settlers. He had four children b. in Concord, viz: Sarah, Gershom, Mary and Peter, and seven were born in Chelmsford, to wit: Elizabeth, James, Lydia, Thomas, John, Samuel and Israel.

1. Samuel. He was probably the son of Samuel, and grandson of Robert. He was b. 1696-97, and he lived near Sparks' Hill. (See p. 27). His name stands at the head of the tax list of 1730, but there is no record of his family on the books.

2. Joseph, a grandson of Robert, but the name of his father has not been found. He m. Agnes ——. Children: (1) *Susanna,* b. 1723-24; m. Nehemiah Wheeler, of Acton, 1746. (2) *Esther,* b. 1725; m. Jonathan Minot, 1746. (3) *Sibel,* b. 1732; d. 1737. (4) *Agnes,* b. 1734-35; d. 1736. (5) *Rebecca,* b. 1737. (6) *Zerviah* or *Zeruiah,* b. 1739; m. Samuel Parker, Jr., 1759. (7) *Agnes,* b. 1742; m. Ebenezer Emery, of Chelmsford, 1769. (8) *Sibil,* b. 1744; m. Isaac How, of New Ipswich, 1760. He d. 1754.

3. John, son of John and Miriam, and b. 1694; m. Mary ——. Children: (1) *Mary,* b. 1719; m. Jonathan Robbins, 1743. (2) *James,* 4, b. 1720. (3) *Phinehas,* b. 1722. (4) *Elizabeth,* b. 1724; m. Zecharich Robbins, 1744. (5) *Sarah,* b. 1726; m. Samuel Hildreth, 1753. (6) *Oliver,* **5,** b. 1729. (7) *John,* **6,** b. 1733.

4. James, m. Hannah Nutting, 1747. Children: (1) *Hannah,* b. 1748. (2) *Josiah,* b. 1749; d. 1753. (3) *Silas,* b. 1750; rem. to Mt. Holly, Vt. He m. Olive Read, of Westford, 1784. (See p. 167). (4) *Stephen,* b. 1752; d. 1753. (5) *Martha,* b. 1754. (6) *Lydia,* b. 1756; m. Simon Hunt. (7) *Mary,* b. 1758. (8) *Olive,* b. 1760. (9) *Sarah,* b. 1762. (10) *James,* b. 1764. A James Procter, of Townsend, m. Esther Wright, of Westford, 1783. (11) *Elizabeth,* b. 1766.

5. Oliver, m. Mary Parker, 1744. There is doubt, however, whether this Oliver is the one who m. Mary Parker, although a marginal note in the records hints that he was the son of John.

6. John, m., 1st, Mary Nutting, 1762. Children: (1) *Josiah,* b 1762. (2) *Isaiah,* b. 1764; d. young. (3) *John,* b. 1765; m. Rachel Shedd, of Pepperell, 1794. He m., 2nd, Sarah Wright, 1771. (4) *Jesse,* b. 1773; d. 1777. (5) *Polly,* b. 1775; m. Henry Chandler, 1796. (6) *Hosea,* b. 1777; d. 1796. (7) *Joseph,* b. 1779. (8) *Sally,* b. 1782; m. Seth Fletcher, Jr., 1809. (9) *Hannah,* b. 1784; m. Thomas C. Parker, 1806.

7. Thomas, son of Samuel, and grandson of Robert, m. Hannah ——. Children: (1) *Philip,* **8,** b. 1725-26. (2) *Leonard,* **9,** b. 1734. (3) *Olive,* b. 1737-38; m. Thomas Scott, 1780. (4) *Lucy,* b. 1732-33.

8. Philip, m. Phebe Hildreth, perhaps the daughter of Joseph and Phebe. Children: (1) *Hannah,* m., 1st, Timothy Fletcher, Jr., and m., 2nd, Eleazer Hamlin, 1789. (2) *Jonas,* b. 1749; d. at Louisburg or Cape Breton, 1788. He m. Lydia ——, and they had one child, Anna, b. and d. 1783, aged 9 weeks. (3) *Reuben,* b. 1751. (4) *Charles,* 10, b. 1755. (5) *Isaac,* b. 1758.

9. Leonard, m., 1st, Lydia Nutting, 1760. Children: (1) *Philip,* b. 1761. (2) *Abel,* b. 1762. (3) *Leonard,* b. 1764. (4) *Asa,* b. 1766. Mrs. Lydia Proctor, d. 1767, and he m., 2nd, Mary Keep, daughter of Capt. Jabez, 1769. (5) *Mary,* b. 1770. (6) *Lydia,* b. 1772. (7) *Solomon,* b. 1774. (8) *Thomas,* b. 1776. Capt. Leonard, the father, rem. with all his family to Cavendish, Vt., where other children were born. (See p. 164).

10. Charles, m. Wid. Lydia Comings, 1784. Children: (1) *Ede,* b. 1785; m. Nahum H. Groce. (2) *Sarah,* b. 1788, became the second wife of Nahum H. Groce.

11. Jonathan, son of Gershom; m. Elizabeth ——. Children: (1) *Elizabeth,* b. 1721. (2) *Jonathan,* b. 1722. (3) *Jacob,* b. 1724. (4) *Ephraim,* b. 1726. (5) *Job,* b. 1730. Jonathan, the father rem. to Harvard, 1741.

12. Ezekiel, son of ——, and grandson of Robert, m. Elizabeth Chamberlin about 1734. Children: (1) *Ezekiel,* 13, b. 1735. (2) *Abijah,* b. 1736–37. (3) *Mary,* b. 1738. (4) *Elizabeth,* b. 1741. (5) *Joseph,* b. 1743; d. 1746. (6) *Sarah,* b. 1745; d. 1749. (7) *Abigail,* b. 1747. (8) *Ezra,* b. 1752. Ezekiel, the father, d. in Hollis, N. H., 1777.

13. Ezekiel, m. Elizabeth Procter, of Dunstable, 1760. Children: (1) *Ezra,* b. 1761; d. 1776. (2) *Elizabeth,* b. 1762. (3) *Ezekiel,* b. 1764; d. 1766. (4) *Mary,* b. 1766. (5) *Joseph,* b. 1770. Ezekiel, the father, rem. to Hollis where other children were born.

14. Nathan. His birth and parentage have not been ascertained, but perhaps he was the son of Samuel who settled near Sparks' Hill. He m. Phebe Green, of Stoneham, 1761. Children: (1) *Nathan,* 15, b. 1762. (2) *Phebe,* b. 1764; m. John Raymond, 1788. (3) *Jonathan,* b. 1766. (4) *Mehitable,* b. 1768; m. Nathan Dexter, 1819.

15. Nathan, m. Patience Leighton, of Gloucester, 1786. Children: (1) *Sally,* b. 1787; d. unmarried, 1875. (2) *Lydia,* b. 1788. He rem. to Dunstable and had other children, among whom was *Betsey,* b. 1801, who m. Isaac Day, Jr., and d. 1878.

16. Daniel, Lieut., probably from Chelmsford, m. Esther ——. Children: (1) *Esther,* b. 1812. (2) *Daniel,* b. 1814.

PUSHEE. 1. John, of Acton, m. Lucy Blodgett, 1770. Children (1) *John,* 2, b. 1771. (2) *Lucy,* b. 1773; m. James Kidder, Jr., 1827. (3) *Daniel,* b. 1775.

2. John, m. Abigail ——. Children: (1) *James Madison,* b. 1812. (2) *Henry Clay,* b. 1815. (3) *Luther,* b. 1818. (4) *Betsey,* b. 1820. (5) *Almira,* b. 1822. (6) *Gilman,* b. 1826.

RAYMOND. 1. Daniel, was admitted, 1760, to the first church by letter from Concord. He lived on the Abbot Read place.

2. Daniel, Jr., m. Noami Leighton, 1781. Children: (1) *Daniel,* b. 1784; d. 1784. (2) *Sally,* b. 1785; m. William Sweetser, of Charlestown, 1807. (3) *Daniel,* b. 1787. (4) *Lydia,* b. 1789. Noami, the mother, d. 1806, aged 48.

READ. The ancestor was Esdras. For an account of him, see pp. 7, 8.

1. Thomas, son of Obadiah, and grandson of Esdras, had children: (1) *John,* b. 1685. (2) *Thomas,* b. 1687. (3) *Jonathan,* b. ——. (4) *William,* b. ——. (5) *Esdras.* (By his second wife, Hannah.) (6) *Benjamin.* (7) *Timothy.*

2. John, son of Thomas, and born 1685, m. Jane Chamberlin, 1707. Children: (1) *Samuel,* b. 1711. (2) *Thomas,* b. 1713. (3) *William,* b. 1715. (4) *Jane,* b. 1717. (5) *Sarah,* b. 1719. (6) *Betsey,* b. 1721. (7) *Hannah,* b. 1723. (8) *Lucy,* b. 1727. (9) *Jacob,* b.

3. Thomas, son of Thomas, and born 1687; m. Sarah Fletcher, 1709. Children: (1) *Sarah,* b. 1711; d. young. (2) *Sarah,* b. 1712; m. Samuel Corey (?), of Littleton, 1741. (3) *Timothy,* b. 1714. (4) *Joseph,* b. 1716.

GENEALOGY.   471

(5) *Catherine*, b. 1718; m. Samuel Fassett (?), 1740. (6) *Eleazer*, b. 1731. (7) *Benjamin*, b. 1732. (8) *Jacob*, son of Thomas, Jr., was baptized by Mr. Hall in 1749.

4. **Jonathan**, son of Thomas 1st, m. Margaret ——. Children: (1) *Hannah*, b. 1715. (2) *Betsey*, b. 1717.

5. **William**, son of Thomas 1st, m. Hannah Bates and settled on the farm now owned by the Coolidge Brothers. Children: (1) *Robert*, b. 1720; m. Hannah Abbot, of Andover, and rem. to Litchfield and afterward to Amherst, N. H. (2) *William*, b. 1725; m. Lucy Spalding, and rem. to Merrimack, N. H. (See p. 158).

6. **Timothy**, son of Thomas and Sarah, m. Mary Cummings. Children: (1) *Elizabeth*, b. 1733. (2) *Mary*, b. 1734. (3) *Timothy*, b. 1736; settled in Putney, Vt. (4) *Catherine*, bap. 1738. (5) *Eleazer*, b. ——. Timothy, the father, rem. to Chelmsford.

7. **Joseph**, son of Thomas and Sarah, b. 1716, m. Ruth Underwood, 1737. Children: (1) *Joshua*, b. 1737. (2) *Ruth*, b. 1740. (3) *Benjamin*, b. 1742. d. at Crown Point, 1760. (4) *Joseph*, b. 1746. (5) *Leonard*, b. 1750. (6) *Samson* b. 1754; d. 1777. (7) *Mary*, b. 1761; d. 1777.

8. **Eleazer**, son of Thomas and Sarah, m. Joanna Fitch, 1754. Children: (1) *Joanna*, b. 1754. (2) *Samuel*, b. 1756. (3) *Eleazer*, b. 1760. (4) *Eliakim*, b. 1762; m. Sarah Mansfield, of Chelmsford, and rem. to Stoddard, N. H. (5) *Catherine*, b. 1764; m. Samuel Read, of Littleton, 1785. (6) *Elihu*, b. 1766; a soldier of the Revolution; m. Lucy Reinsford, of Boston, where he lived for a few years; then returned and afterward rem. to Tyngsborough. He became poor and was brought back and supported in the almshouse, where he died. Children: William, b. in Boston, 1792; Josiah, b. ——; George W., b. ——; Mary, who m. James Bates. (7) *Lydia*, b. 1768; m. Jacob Kendall, 1788. (8) *Rhoda*, b. 1770; m. George Frederick, 1788. (9) *Miriam*, b. 1772; m. Samuel Coburn, of Dracut. (10) *Sarah*, b. 1776. (11) *Aaron*, b. 1778.

9. **Benjamin**, son of Thomas and Sarah, m. Abigail Fassett, 1755. Children: (1) *Sybel*, b. 1755. (2) *Abel*, b. 1757. (3) *Abigail*, b. 1759. (4) *Rebecca*, b. 1761; m. Isaac Procter, 1783. (5) *Thomas*, b. 1766; served in the war of the Revolution; m. Mary Spalding, and rem. to Londonderry, Vt. (6) *Benjamin*, b. 1768; rem. to Weathersfield, Vt.

10. **Samuel**, son of John and Jane, b. 1711, m., 1st, Abigail Cummings, 1732. Children: (1) *Thomas*, b. 1733. (2) *Samuel*, b. 1735; d. 1755. (3) *Silas*, b. 1737. (4) *William*, b. 1739. He m., 2nd, Wid. Hannah Underwood, 1757. (5) *Abigail*, b. 1758. (6) *Olive*, b. 1760; m. Silas Procter and rem. to Mt. Holly, Vt. (7) *Bridget*, b. 1762. (8) *Samuel*, b. 1764, probably rem. to Littleton.

11. **Jacob**, son of John and Jane, m. Lucy ——. Children: (1) *Benjamin*, b. 1752. (2) *Priscilla*, b. 1756. (3) *John*, b. 1758. Probably the family rem. from town.

12. **William**, son of John and Jane, b. 1715, m. Thankful Spalding, 1741. Children: (1) *Thaddeus*, b. 1742; a soldier of the Revolution; little is known of him. (2) *William*, b. 1743. (3) *Oliver*, b. 17—; d. 1791.

13. **Thomas**, son of John and Jane, b. 1713, m. Olive Howard, of Chelmsford. Children: (1) *Sarah*, b. 1747. (2) *Jacob*, b. 1748. (3) *Catherine*, b. 1750. (4) *Thomas*, b. 1752. (5) *Hannah*, b. 1754. (6) *Rachel*, b. 1756. (7) *Martha*, b. 1758. (8) *Levi*, b. 1760. (9) *Howard*, b. 1762.

14. **Thomas**, Lieut., son of Samuel, b. 1733, m., 1st, Susanna Dutton. Children: (1) *Stephen*, b. 1754; settled in Ludlow, Vt. (2) *Abigail*, b. 1757. (3) *Susanna*, b. 1759; d. 1762. (4) *Jemima*, b. 1761. (5) *Susanna*, b. 1764; m. William Dutton, 1781. (6) *Sarah*, b. 1766; m. Reuben Wright, 1787. (7) *Thomas*, b. 1768; m. Phebe Wright, and rem. to Nelson, N. H. (8) *Lucy*, b. 1771. (9) *Anna*, b. 1773. He m., 2nd, Wid. Phebe Procter, of Groton, 1784. (10) *Phebe*, b. 1784. (11) *Charles*, b. 1785. (12) *Charlotte*, b. 1787; m. David Nutting, 1808. He m., 3rd, Polly Spalding, 1792. (13) *Roswell*, b. 1793. (14) *Polly*, b. 1795; m. Samuel Spalding, 1812. (15) *Alenath*, b. 1797; d. 1802. (16) *Lydia*, b. 1798; m. Joseph Wild, of Braintree, 1814. (17) *Phicinda*, b. 1803.

15. Silas, son of Samuel, b. 1737, m. Hannah Chamberlin, 1772. Children: (1) *Betsey*, b. 1773; d. 1777. (2) *Silas*, b. 1775; d. young. (3) *Hannah*, b. 1777; d. ———. (4) *Silas*, b. 1778. (5) *Ephraim*, b. 1780; d. 1781. (6) *Ephraim*, b. 1782. (7) *Betsey*, b. 1784. (8) *Hannah*, b. 1786. (9) *Abigail*, b. 1788. (10) *Samuel*, b. 1789. (11) *John Cummings*, b. 1792. (12) *Rebecca*, b. 1794. (13) *Bridget*, b. 1796; d. 1798. (14) *Luther*, 1799. (15) *Bridget*, b. 1801. (16) *Harriet*, b. ———.

16. Joshua, son of Joseph, b. 1737, m. Mary Spalding. Children: (1) *Elnathan*, b. 1758; "was in the Revolutionary War during the whole term, and was discharged in North Carolina." He m. Anna Prescott, and rem. to Cavendish, Vt., where he d. aged 82. (2) *Benjamin*, b. 1760; rem. to Templeton. (3) *Joshua*, b. 1763; settled in Stoddard. (4) *Phinehas*, b. 1765; served in the Revolution and settled at Fitzwilliam, N. H. (5) *Amos*, b. 1768. (6) *Isaiah*, b. 1770; d. 1777. (7) *Zaccheus*, b. 1773. (8) *Joseph*, b. 1776; rem. first to Plymouth, N. H., then to Thetford and Montpelier, Vt. (9) *Isaiah*, b. 1778; rem. to Stoddard.

17. Joseph, son of Joseph, and b. 1746; m. Martha Fletcher. Children: (1) *Ruth*, b. 1771. (2) *Patty*, b. 1773.

18. Leonard, son of Joseph, b. 1750; m. Bethiah Herrick. Children: (1) *Bethiah*, b. 1770; m. Josiah Spalding, 1792. (2) *Lois*, b. 1771. (3) *Ruth*, b. 1774. (4) *Joel*, b. 1776.

19. Eleazer, son of Eleazer, b. 1760; m. Elizabeth Fletcher, 1786. Children: (1) *Eleazer* (twin), b. 1786. (2) *Joshua* (twin), b. 1786. (3) *Jepthah*, b. 1790. Of these Eleazer (twin), m. Mary Putnam, of Fitchburg, 1814, and Joshua, m. Charlotte Thomas, 1816.

20. Abel, son of Benjamin, b. 1757; m. Rebecca Farrar, 1778. Children. (1) *Benjamin*, b. 1779. (2) *Olive*, b. 1781. (3) *Abel*, b. 1782. (4) *Timothy*, b. 1785. (5) *Rebecca*, b. 1786. (6) *Peter*, b. 1788.

21. Oliver, son of William and Thankful, m. Abigail ———. Children: (1) *Oliver*, b. 1779. (2) *Abigail*, b. 1780. (3) *Patty*, b. 1782. (4) *Lucy*, b. 1785; m. Joel Hunter. (5) *Richard*, b. 1789; d. 1790. Oliver, the father d. 1791.

22. Amos, son of Joshua, b. 1768, m. Rachel Prescott, of Groton, 1790. Children: (1) *Rachel*, b. 1790; m. Jacob O. Parker. (2) *Bethuel*, b. 1792; served in the War of 1812. (3) *Amos*, b. 1792. (4) *Joshua*, b. 1796. (5) *Stephen*, b. 1799; d. 1804. (6) *Otis*, b. 1807. (7) *Francis*, b. 1809. (8) *Augusta Maria*, b. 1812. Amos, the father, rem. to Sodus, N. Y.

23. Zaccheus, son of Joshua, b. 1773, m. Mary Parker, 1795. Children: (1) *Zaccheus*, b. 1796. (2) *Mary*, b. 1798; m. Eliel Heywood. (3) *Abigail*, b. 1801. (4) *Josiah*, b. ———. (5) *Elmira*, b. 1811. (6) *Edwin*, b. 1814. Zaccheus, the father, d. 1854, aged 81.

24. Joel, son of Leonard, m. Joanna Chandler, 1810. Children: (1) *William Chandler*, b. 1810. (2) *Joel*, b. 1811. (3) *Charles Grandison*, b. 1813. (4) *Edwin Ransom*, b. 1815. (5) *Joanna*, b. 1817. (6) *Bethiah*, b. 1818. (7) *Leonard*, b. 1821; rem. to Charlestown. (8) *Nancy Chandler*, b. 1822. (9) *Sarah Rosina*, b. 1824.

25. Benjamin, son of Abel, b. 1779, m. Bridget Abbot, daughter of William, of Chelmsford. Child: *Benjamin Abbot*, b. 1819.

26. Timothy, son of Abel, b. 1785; m. Mary Proctor, 1825. Children: (1) *Timothy F.*, b. 1826. (2) *Mary Ann Manning*, b. 1827; m. ——— Longley.

27. Zaccheus, son of Zaccheus, b. 1796, m. Mary Heywood, 1822. Children: (1) *Mary Elizabeth*, b. 1823; m. Silas N. Heywood, 1845. (2) *Edward Zaccheus*, b. 1825; m. Julia A. Chamberlin, 1852, and d. 1852. (3) *Martha Ann*, b. 1828; m. Edmund F. Dupee. 1845. (4) *Joseph Henry*, b. 1835; m. Mary E. Falls. (5) *Emily F.*, b. 1837.

28. Benjamin, son of Jacob and Lucy, b. 1752, m. ——— Powers. Children: (1) *Benjamin*, b. 1776; rem. to Cherry Valley, N. Y. (2) *Polly*, b. 1777. (3) *Jacob*, b. 1778; rem. to Maine. Benjamin, the father, rem. to Princeton, Mass., 1780, where other children were born.

29. Samuel, son of Eleazer, and b. 1756, m. Elizabeth Raymond, 1777. Children: (1) *Thomas*, b. 1778; m. Rebecca Cummings, 1803. (2) *Jesse*, b. 1779. (3) *Lucy*, b. 1781.

Residence of William Reed.

GENEALOGY. 473

30. Benjamin Abbot, son of Benjamin, b. 1810; m. Betsey Hunt, daughter of Simon. Children: (1) *Mary Elizabeth,* b. 1835; m. Henry Chamberlin, 1857. (2) *Warren Abbot,* b. 1837; d. 1875. (3) *Sarah Ann,* b. 1839. (4) *Albert S.,* b. 1845.

31. Roswell, son of Thomas, and b. 1773, m. Sybel ——. Children: (1) *Joanna,* b. 1815. (2) *Hannah,* b. 1817; m. Joseph Wright. (3) *Cynthia,* b. 1820. (4) *Merrick,* b. 1821. (5) *Abram,* b. 1824. (6) *Elbridge,* b. 1826; m. Hannah F. Davis. 1858. (7) *Clarissa,* b. 1828. (8) *Elmira,* b. b. 1830. (9) *Laura,* b. 1833.

32. Luther, son of Silas and Hannah, b. 1799; m. Ann Thaxter, of Boston, 1828. Children: (1) *Luther Warren,* b. 1828; d. 1829. (2) *Nancy Thaxter,* b. 1829. (3) *Anna Rebecca,* b. 1831. (4) *Luther Warren,* b. 1832; d. 1835. (5) *Silas Cummings,* b. 1834. (6) *Joseph Warren,* b. 1836; d. 1837. (7) *Luther Felton,* b. 1838; m. Lizzie F. Swift, 1861; d. 1862, soldier. (8) *Catherine Manley,* b. 1840; d. 1862.

REED. The ancestor was Elias, supposed to be son of William and Lucy, of Maidstone, county of Kent, Eng., who first appears in Woburn. His son Philip settled first in Lynn, but rem. to Concord, where he d., 1696. Peter, the great-grandson of Philip, settled in Littleton, where he m. Betty or Elizabeth Hartwell.

1. Abijah, son of Peter, m., 1st, Elizabeth Boynton, 1786. Children: (1) *Elizabeth,* b. 1787. (2) *Abijah,* b. 1789; d. 1789. He m., 2nd Susan Colman, of Ashby, 1793. (3) *Susan,* b. 1794; m. ——. (4) *Abijah C.,* 2, b. 1796. (5) *Orpah,* b. 1798. (6) *Permelia,* b. 1799; m. Joseph Hildreth, 1822. (7) *Jeremy Boynton,* 3, b. 1801. (8) *Charles Hartwell,* b. 1804. (9) *Harriet,* b. 1806. (10) *Mary Ann,* b. 1808; d. 1832. (11) *Nancy Irene,* b. 1810. (12) *James Madison,* b. 1813. (13) *Elvira M.,* b. 1816; d. 1835. Abijah, the father, d. 1844, aged 89.

2. Abijah C., son of Abijah, b. 1796, m. Sarah Locke, of Boston. Children: (1) *Sarah Matilda,* b. 1831; d. 1847. (2) *Susan Colman,* b. 1833; d. 1837. (3) *James Henry,* b. 1835. (4) *Frances Adelaide,* b. 1836. (5) *Georgiana R.,* b. 1839.

3. Jeremy B., son of Abijah, and b. 1801; m. Louisa Hildreth, 1823. Children: (1) *Elizabeth Hartwell,* b. 1824; d. 1829. (2) *Harriet Augusta,* b. 1825; m. Joseph E. Wright, 1844. (3) *Martha Louisa,* b. 1827; d. 1827. He m., 2nd, Nancy Chandler. (4) *Nancy Maria,* b. 1831; d. 1842. (5) *Charles Boynton,* b. 1833; d. 1862, a soldier. (6) *Alvisa Melvina,* b. 1835. (7) *Ellen Amanda,* b. 1839; m. John H. Lackey.

4. John, son of Philip, and b. 1714; m. Abiel Butterfield, 1737, and settled in the south part on the farm now occupied by Mrs. Desmond. Children: (1) *Sarah,* b. 1738. (2) *John,* b. 1740. (3) *Willard,* 5, b. 1746. (4) *Abigail,* b. 1748. (5) *Simeon,* b. 1756; m. Sarah, daughter of Thomas Cummings, 1778, and rem. to Ludlow, Vt.

5. Willard, son of John, and b. 1746; m. Olive Minot, 1774, at Charlestown. Children: (1) *John,* 7, b. 1775. (2) *Willard,* 6, b. 1777. (3) *Joseph,* 8, b. 1779. (4) *Seth,* 9, b. 1781. (5) *Sally,* b. 1786; m. Frederic Fausel (6) *Anna,* b. 1788; m. —— Smith. (7) *Polly,* b. 1790; m. Francis Leighton, 1813. (8) *Asa,* 10, b. 1792.

6. Willard, son of Willard, and b. 1777; m. Miriam White, 1800, daughter of Dea. Mark White and sister of Aaron. Children: (1) *Jonathan Minot,* b. 1804; m. Sarah Fausel, 1840; rem. to Lowell. (2) *Joseph,* b. 1806; rem. to Chelmsford ; was justice of the peace and member of the Legislature.

7. John, son of Willard and Olive, and b. 1775; m. Sally Wright. Children: (1) *John,* b. 1805; res. in Nashua. (2) *Walter,* b. 1807; rem. to Merrimack, N. H. (3) *Lowell,* b. 1810; rem. to Salem, N. H. (4) *Sally,* b. 1712. (5) *Dana,* b. 1814. (6) *Willard,* b. 1816; rem. to Merrimack. (7) *Olive,* b. 1824.

8. Joseph, Capt., son of Willard and Olive, b. 1779; m. Abigail Winn, of Wilmington. Children: (1) *Abigail Winn,* b. 1811; d. 1831. (2) *Alpheus,* b. 1813; d. 1814. (3) *Alpheus Joseph,* b. 1815; m. Sarah S. Parker, 1849. He d. 1872. (4) *Anan,* b. 1818; m. Almira H. Fletcher, 1850.

He d. 1860. (5) *Betsey Wheat*, b. 1819. (6) *Alonzo*, b. 1823; d. 1824. (7) *Amanda Jane*, b. 1827. Capt. Joseph Reed d. 1854.
   9. **Seth**, son of Willard, and b. 1781; m. Rhoda Finney. Children: (1) *Juliana*, b. 1806. (2) *George*, b. 1807. (3) *Orison*, b. 1809. (4) *Mary Augusta*, b. 1811. (5) *Harrison*, b. 1813; was governor of Florida, 1876. (6) *Cortes*, b. 1815; rem. to Milwaukee.
   10. **Asa**, son of Willard and Olive, b. 1792; m. Betsey Prescott, daughter of Isaiah. Children: (1) *Rufus*, b. 1818; m. Martha E. Dodge, of Nashua. (2) *Olive*, b. 1821. He d. 1826, and his widow m. Elijah M. Read of Lowell.
   11. **Barnard**, son of Thomas and Lucy (Farrar), b. in Littleton, 1780; m. Mary —— who was born in Concord, 1794. Children: (1) *George*, b. 1819, in Acton. (2) *William*, b. 1820, in Acton; m. Mrs. Rachel L. Beaman, 1871. (3) *Josiah*, b. 1822, in Acton. (4) *David*, b. 1824; m. Harriet R. Hayden, 1851. (5) *Mary Jane*, b. 1827; d. 1844. (6) *Barnard*, b. 1829; d. 1855. (7) *Deidamia*, b. 1834; m. Ashley A. Farr, of Townsend, Vt., 1859.
   RICHARDSON. The ancestor was Ezekiel, of Woburn.
   1. **Thomas**, son of James, of the fifth generation from Ezekiel settled in Westford, where he m. Rebecca Read, 1745. Children: (1) *Thomas*, **2**, b. 1746. (2) *Abijah*, **3**, b. 1748. (3) *Hannah*, bap. 1750. (4) *Rebecca* b. 1752. (5) *Wiley*, **4**, b. 1754.
   2. **Thomas**, son of Thomas, and b. 1746; m., 1st, Abigail Read, 1769. Children: (1) *Thomas*, b. 1770. (2) *Abigail*, b. 1772. (3) *Jesse*, b. 1773. (4) *Willard*, b. 1774. (5) *Hannah*, b. 1776.
   3. **Abijah**, son of Thomas, m. Elizabeth. Children: (1) *William*, b. 1782; d. unm., 1847. He was a pauper and d. at the poor farm. (2) *Thomas*, b. 1789; m. Philinda Wright, 1811.
   4. **Wiley**, son of Thomas, m., 1st, Bridget Farrar, daughter of Joseph Farrar, of Chelmsford, 1776. Children: (1) *Bridget*, b. 1777; m. Thomas Hastings, of Watertown, 1796. (2) *Rebecca*, b. 1779; m., 1st, Zaccheus Green, of Carlisle, and 2nd, William Cummings, son of Joseph. Wiley, m., 2nd, Frances Poor, of Andover, 1783. (3) *Peter*, b. 1784. (4) *Sally*, b. 1786. (5) *Solomon*, **12**, b. 1790. (6) *Betsey*, b. 1792. (7) *Fanny*, b. 1794; m. Charles Marten, of Lynn, 1820. (8) *Hannah*, b. 1796; d. in Lowell, 1860. (9) *Mary*, b. 1799; m. Rev. John C. Newell, of Concord, who d. 1836. (10) *Nancy*, b. 1803. Wiley, the father, d. 1847.
   5. **Silas**, son of Josiah, and b. in Chelmsford, 1772; m. Lydia Marcy, of Dracut, 1797. Children: (1) *Silas Marcy*, b. 1798; d. 1800. (2) *Lydia Warren*, b. 1800; d. 1802. He rem. to Greene, Me.
   6. **Henry**, parentage not ascertained, m. Priscilla ——. Children: (1) *Lydia*, b. 1738; m. Jonathan Spalding, 1759. (2) *Olive*, b. 1742; m. Abel Adams, 1771. (3) *Luke*, **8**, b. 1744. (4) *Elizabeth*, b. 1747; m. Issachar Keyes, 1770. (5) *Sarah*, b. 1750; m. David Fletcher, 1779.
   7. **Abiel**, parentage not known, m. Sarah Boynton, 1741. Children: (1) *Sarah*, b. 1742. (2) *Hannah*, b. 1743; m. Timothy Spaulding (?), 1763. (3) *Ede*, b. 1745; m. Amaziah Fassett, 1768. (4) *Thomas*, b. 1851, at Pepperell. (5) *Abigail*, b. 1754.
   8. **Luke**, son of Henry; m. Sarah Minot, 1767. Children: (1) *John*, b. 1768; d. 1769. (2) *Betty*, b. 1770. (3) *John*, b. 1772.
   9. **Samuel**, son of Eleazer and Lydia (Perham), m., 1st, Elizabeth Hildreth, daughter of Ephraim 3rd, 1784. She d. 1803, leaving no children. He m., 2nd, Amy Fletcher, of Dunstable. Children : (1) *Amy*, b. 1805; m. Levi T. Fletcher, 1825. (2) *Samuel*, b. 1806 ; m. Olive Prescott, 1830, and d. 1872. (3) *Mary*, b. 1808; m. Jonathan Stow Hildreth, of Townsend, and lived in Groton. (4) *Betsey*, b. 1810 ; m. John S. Buck. (5) *Lydia*, b. 1812; m. Walter Wright, 1841. (6) *Lucy*, b. 1814; d. unm., 1873. (7) *Susan*, b. 1816 ; d. 1817. (8) *Sarah*, b. 1818.
   10. **Thomas**, son of Abijah, m. Philinda Wright, 1811. Children: (1) *George W.*, b. 1811. (2) *Warren*, b. 1814. (3) *Philinda*, b. 1818; m. George R. Moore. (4) *Zibiah*, b. 1820; m. Peter B. Prescott. (5) *John Gilbert*, b. 1822. (6) *Mary Jane*, b. 1824. (7) *Maria*, b. 1826. (8) *Sarah*

Residence of John W. Abbot.

GENEALOGY. 475

Elizabeth, b. 1828. He m., 2nd, Mary Fletcher, 1840. (9) *Milton Thomas*, b. 1843.
11. Willard, son of Thomas, m. Mary ——. Child: *Thomas*, b. 1803.
12. Solomon, son of Wiley, m., 1st. Nancy Cogswell, 1814. No children. He m., 2nd, Sarah E. Tufts. Children: (1) *Charles N.*, b. 1839, in Jaffrey, N. H. (2) *Sarah F.*, b. 1841; m. Wayland F. Balch. (3) *Albert Pierce*, b. 1843, m. Alma Minot, 1874. (4) *Mary E.*, b. 1847; m. Sherman H. Fletcher.

ROBBINS. The ancestor of this family was Robert, of Concord, whose son George settled in Chelmsford.
1. Benjamin, son of George settled in Westford, near Nashoba Hill. He. m. Hannah ——. Children: (1) *Benjamin*, b. 1708. (2) *Joseph*, b. 1711. (3) *Joseph* (twin), b. 1717. (4) *Jonathan* (twin), b. 1717. (5) *Zechariah*, **2**, b. 1720. (6) *Sarah*, b. 1723-24. (7) *John*, **4**, b. 1727.
2. Zechariah, son of Benjamin, m. Elizabeth Procter. Children: (1) *Elizabeth*, b. 1747; m. Samuel Gilbert, of Littleton, 1770. (2) *Sibel*, b. 1749, m. Simon Lawrence, of Littleton, 1769. (3) *Sarah*, b. 1751. (4) *Rebecca*, b. 1753; m. Samuel Tuttle, of Littleton. (5) *Zechariah*, b. 1756. (6) *Benjamin*, **3**, b. 1758. (7) *Lydia*, b. 1760 ; m. Timothy Adams, 1783. Zechariah, Jr., m. Abigail Hildreth, 1785, but there is no record of any family.
3. Benjamin, Lieut., son of Zechariah, m. Huldah Robinson, daughter, of Col. John Robinson, 1784. Children: (1) *Huldah*, b. 1785 ; m. Jonathan Prescott, 1809. (2) *Perley*, b. 1786; d. 1820. (3) *Martha*, b. 1788; m. Daniel Lincoln, of Westminster, 1816. (4) *Nathan* (twin), b. 1790. (5) *Levi* (twin), b. 1790. (6) *Jedediah*, b. 1793; m. Eliza Ann Searles, 1833; rem. to Phillipston or Templeton. (7) *Almira*, b. 1800; m. Augustus Tuttle, of Concord. (8) *Eliza*, b. 1805.
4. John, son of Benjamin, and b. 1727; m. Sarah ——. Children: (1) *John*, b. 1752; perhaps rem. to Dunstable. (2) *Peter* b. 1755. (3) *Hannah*, b. 1757. (4) *Samuel*, b. 1759. (5) *Ezekiel*, b. 1761. (6) *Timothy*, b. 1763. (7) *Benjamin*, b. 1766. (8) *Abel*, b. 1769. (9) *Willard*, b. 1771. (10) *Sarah*, b. 1774; m. James Pierce and lived in Portland.
5. Jacob, son of Thomas, who lived in the south east part, near John Hutchins; m. Lydia Heald, of Acton. Children: (1) *Jacob*, bap. 1753; d. —— (2) *Jacob*, **8**, b. 1755. (3) *Lydia*, b. 1757. (4) *Thomas*, b. 1759. (5) *Jacob*, b. 1762. (6) *Mary*, b. 1767.
6. Philip, son of Thomas and b. 1725; m. Anna Minot. Children: (1) *Jeremiah*, b. 1758. (2) *Anna*, b. 1760.
7. Jeremiah, son of Philip; m. Elizabeth Keele. Children: (1) *Jeremiah*, b. 1781. (2) *Philip*, b. 1783.
8. Jacob, son of Jacob, m. Dorothy Hildreth, 1783. Children: (1) *William*, b. 1783. (2) *Dorothy*, b. 1785.

ROBINSON. 1. John, Col., m. Huldah Perley, of Topsfield. Children: (1) *Huldah*, b. 1765; m. Lieut. Benjamin Robbins, 1784. (2) *Mehitable*, b. 1767; m. Benjamin Fletcher, 1797. (3) *Betty*, b. 1770. (4) *Sally*, b. 1772. (5) *Rebecca*, b. 1774; m. Joshua A. Jewett, 1800. (6) *John*, **2**, b. 1781.
2. John, son of Col. John, m. Hannah Woods, 1809. Children: (1) *John*, b. 1810. (2) *Francis Perley*, b. 1812. (3) *Walter*, b. 1814. (4) *Harriet* (twin), b. 1818. (5) *Huldah* (twin), b. 1818.

ROGERS. Thomas, m. Mary ——. Children: (1) *Mary*, b. 1774; d. 1775. (2) *Mary*, b. 1777. Thomas was killed by the bursting of a cannon, on Lake Champlain, Oct. 17, 1776. His widow seems to have married William Monroe, Jr., of Lexington, 1780.

SKINNER. William, m. Elizabeth ——. Children: (1) *Samuel*, b. 1731. (2) *Sarah*, b. 1733. (3) *Elizabeth*, b. 1735-36.

SMITH. Thomas. There are some facts which seem to indicate that he came from Reading. He m., 1st, Lydia ——. Children: (1) *Sarah*, b. 1749. (2) *Hannah*, b. 1751. (3) *Francis*, b. 1753. (4) *Ephraim*, b. 1756. (5) *Timothy*, b. 1759. He m., 2nd, Mrs. Hannah Sanders, of

Groton, 1767. (6) *Asa*, b. 1770. (7) *William*, b. 1774. (8) *Phillip* (?), Francis m. Hannah Russell, 1783. No births recorded.

  2. **Thomas**, probably son of Thomas, for he is called Jr. in the record of his marriage. He m., 1st, Elizabeth Walton, of Reading, 1762. Children: (1) *Elizabeth*, b. 1763. (2) *Hannah*, b. 1765. (3) *Lydia*, b. 1768. He m., 2nd, Mary Herrick, 1772. (4) *Thomas*, b. 1772; d. 1775. (5) *William*, b. 1774; d. 1775. (6) *Polly* (twin), b. 1778; m. Joseph Gould. (7) *Ruth* (twin), b. 1778; d. 1778. (8) *Samuel*, b. 1780. (9) *John*, b. 1783. (10) *Rebecca*, b. 1784; m. Thomas Heald, 1808. (11) *Sally*, b. 1787. (12) *Timothy, 3*, b. 1789. (13) *Joseph*, b. 1793. Thomas, the father, d. 1829, aged 91. Mary, the mother, d. 1835, aged 92.

  3. **Timothy**, son of Thomas, m. Betsey Abbot, 1815. Children: (1) *Timothy A.*, b. 1816. (2) *Elizabeth M.*, b. 1818; m. —— Chamberlin, and d. of a fever, 1845, aged 27. (3) *Mary Ann*, b. 1820. (4) *Harriet J.*, b. 1822. (5) *Nancy A.*, b. 1824. (6) *Samuel C.*, b. 1826. (7) *George H.*, b. 1828; d. 1832. (8) *Martha A.*, b. 1830. (9) *Laura A.*, b. 1832. (10) *George*, b. 1834.

  SNOW. 1. Jonathan, m. Sarah ——. Children: (1) *Jonathan*, b. 1786. (2) *Sarah*, b. 1788; m. Joseph Wright, of Dedham, 1811. (3) *Polly*, b. 1791; m. Joseph Harrington, of Concord, 1821. (4) *Parker*, b. 1792; d. 1796. (5) *Lucy*, b. 1795. (6) *Nancy*, b. 1797. (7) *Jonas Parker*, b. 1880; d. in Littleton, 1881. He, the father, lived on the Abbot Read place.

  2. **Levi**, probably brother of Jonathan, m. Lucy Fletcher, daughter of Ebenezer. Children: (1) *Levi*, b. 1790; d. 1791. (2) *Levi*, b. 1792; d. 1793. (3) *James*, b. 1794; d. 1794. (4) *Levi*, b. 1795; d. 1802. (5) *Lucy*, b. 1797; d. 1802. (6) *Salmon, 3*, b. 1799. (7) *Joanna*, b. 1801; m. Robert Spalding, of Chelmsford. (8) *Daniel Brooks*, b. 1803; d. 1803. (9) *Joshua*, b. 1805. (10) *Joseph B. Varnum*, b. 1807; d. 1807. (11) *Levi*, b. 1808.

  3. **Salmon**, son of Levi and Lucy, m. Nancy ——. Children: (1) *Lucy*, b. 1822. (2) *Maria*, b. 1822. He rem. to Saugus. (?)

  4. **Levi**, son of Levi and Lucy, m. 1832, Louisa Read, daughter of Eliakim and Sarah (Mansfield) Read, of Stoddard. Children: (1) *Louisa Ann*, b. 1836; m. Samuel Madison Hutchins, of Carlisle, 1871. (2) *George Franklin*, b. 1841; m. Abbie C. Long.

  SPALDING. The ancestor was Edward who came from Braintree and was one of the original founders of Chelmsford.

  1. **Andrew**, son of Andrew and great-grandson of Edward, settled on the John Morrison place, near Keyes Pond. He m., 1st, Hannah ——. Children: (1) *Andrew*, b. 1729; rem. to New Ipswich. (2) *Hannah*, b. 1731. (3) *Abigail*, b. 1734; d. young. (4) *Mary*, b. 1736; m. Joshua Read, 1758. (5) *Joanna*, b. 1738; m. Benjamin Swallow, Dunstable, 1767. (6) *Henry*, b. 1740; d. young. (7) *Ephraim*, b. 1742. (8) *Benjamin*, b. 1744. He m., 2nd, Mrs. Mehitable Crosby, 1745. Her maiden name was Chandler, of Andover, Mass., and she was the widow of Robert Crosby (9) *Ruth*, b. 1746; m. Isaac Butterfield, of Dunstable. (10) *Solomon*, b. 1748. (11) *Henry*, b. 1750. (12) *Abigail*, b. 1754; m. Oliver Taylor.

  2. **Timothy**, son of John and grandson of Edward, settled on the Abijah Fletcher place. He m., 1st, Rebecca Winn, of Woburn, 1700. Children: (1) *Timothy*, b. 1700. (2) *Rebecca*, b. 1708. (3) *Esther* b. 1705. (4) *Deborah*, b. 1707. (5) *Oliver*, b. 1710. (6) *Josiah*, b. 1712; d. 1732. (7) *Lucy*, b. 1716; d. 1717. (8) *Bridget*, b. 1718; d. 1720. (9) *Thankful*, b. 1730; m. William Read, 1741. (10) *Jonathan*, b. 1731. The last child was the son of a second wife, Bethiah.

  3. **Ebenezer**, son of Joseph and grandson of Edward, m. Hannah Craft, and lived near Jefferson Wheeler's. Children: (1) *Esther* b. 1731. (2) *Thomas*, b. 1733; rem. to New Ipswich. (3) *Philip*, b. 1736. (4) *Ebenezer*.

  4. **Oliver**, son of Timothy, b. 1710, m. Sarah Read. Children: (1) *Sarah*, b. 1732. (2) *Rebecca*, b. 1737. (3) *Oliver*, b. 1739; d. 1757. (4) *Timothy*, b. 1741. (5) *Lucy*, b. 1744. (6) *Bridget*, b. 1746; d. young. (7) *Thankful*, b. 1752.

GENEALOGY. 477

5. Timothy, son of Timothy, b. 1700; d. 1734; m. Thankful Prescott. Children: (1) *Reuben*, b. 1726; d. young. (2) *Leonard*, b. 1728. (3) *Samuel*, b. 1730. (4) *Josiah*, b. 1732. (5) *Timothy*, b. 1734; d. 1734.

6. Josiah, son of Dea. Andrew, m. Mary Fletcher, and settled at the foot of Nubannusuck Pond. Children: (1) *Josiah*, b. 1734. (2) *Isaac*, b. 1735; settled in Littleton. (3) *William*, b. 1737. (4) *Elizabeth*, b. 1739. (5) *Lucy*, b. 1741. (6) *Mary*, b. 1746.

7. James, son of Dea. Andrew, of Chelmsford, and b. 1714; m., 1st, Ama Underwood. Children: (1) *Benjamin*, b. 1738. (2) *James*, b. 1739; d. 1747. (3) *Susanna*, b. 1741; d. 1743. (4) *Silas*, b. 1744; d. 1752. (5) *Caleb*, b. 1747; d. 1747. (6) *James* (twin), b. 1748. (7) *Susanna* (twin), b. 1748; d. 1748. (8) *Anna*, b. 1754; d. 1777. (9) *Silas*, b. 1757; rem. to Granville, N. Y. (10) *Phinehas*, b. 1759; m. Rebecca Jaquith, of Dunstable, 1779, and rem. to Western Reserve, Ohio. He was a Baptist minister.

8. William, son of Josiah, b. 1737, m. Esther Dutton, 1759. Children: (1) *John*, b. 1760; d. in Cavendish, Vt., aged 99. (2) *William*, b. 1762. (3) *Mary*, b. 1764. (4) *Esther*, b. 1767. (5) *Asa*, b. 1769. (6) *Joseph*, b. 1770. (7) *Zedekiah*, b. 1775. (8) *Betty*, b. 1777. (9) *Zaccheus*, b. 1779. The entire family rem. to Cavendish, Vt.

9. Josiah, son of Josiah, b. 1734, m., 1st, Lydia Cleaveland, of Acton, 1763. Children: (1) *Lydia*, b. 1764. (2) *Josiah*, b. 1765; rem. to Townsend. (3) *Rebecca*, b. 1767. (4) *Sarah*, b. 1770; m. Jonathan Stevens, of Hollis, and rem. to Hardwick, Vt. (5) *Moses*, b. 1778; rem. to Pepperell, to which place the father rem. after his second marriage to Jemima Shattuck, of that place.

10. Leonard, son of Timothy, and b. 1728, m. Margaret Love. Children: (1) *Reuben*, b. 1756. (2) *Betty*, b. 1758. (3) *Leonard*, b. 1760. Others were born after he rem. to Putney, Vt. (See p. 168.)

11. Jonathan, son of Timothy, and b. 1731, m. Lydia Richardson, 1759. Children: (1) *Esther*, b. 1760. (2) *Olive*, b. 1763. (3) *Jonathan*, b. 1769; rem. to Temple, N. H. (4) *Jesse*, b. 1771. (5) *Lydia*, b. 1774. Jonathan, the father, d. 1775.

12. Timothy, Lieut., son of Oliver, b. 1741, m. Hannah Richardson, 1763. Children: (1) *Oliver*, b. 1764; rem. to Groton. (2) *Levi*, b. 1766; rem. to Farmington, Me. (3) *Timothy*, b. 1769; rem. to Groton. (4) *Hannah*, b. 1771; m. Henry Wilson, 1792. (5) *Sarah*, b. 1773; m. Abbot Jewett, 1797. (6) *Amaziah*, b. ——; d. unm. (7) *Joel*, b. 17—; d. before 1806. (8) *Ede*, b. ——; m. James Cummings, rem. to Farmington, Me.

13. Thomas, son of Ebenezer, m. Rachel Chandler, 1757. Child: *Levi*, b. 1758. The family rem. to New Ipswich.

14. Philip, son of Ebenezer, and b. 1736; m. Elizabeth Obert, of Acton, 1762. Children: (1) *Elizabeth*, b. 1765; m. Joshua Baldwin. (2) *Hannah*, b. 1767; m. Obadiah Shumway, 1793. (3) *Philip*, b.1770; d. young. (4) *Asaph*, b. 1774; rem. to Leominster. (5) *Philip*, b. 1776; became a minister. (6) *Samuel*, b. 1779; lost at sea.

15. Solomon, Lieut., son of Dea. Andrew, lived on the early homestead, near Keyes Pond. He m. Jemima Read, 1780. Children: (1) *Solomon*, b. 1780; rem. to Saratoga Springs. (2) *Jemima*, b. 1782; m. William Worcester, of Tyngsboro'. (3) *James*, b. 1785. (4) *Andrew*, b. 1788; rem. to Shelburne, Vt., and Bangor, N. Y. (5) *Anna*, b. 1790; d. 1790. (6) *Thomas*, b. 1791. (7) *Mehitable*, b. 1793; m. Theodore Woodward, 1816, and rem. to Westville, N. Y. (8) *George W.*, b. 1796. (9) *Susanna*, b. 1797; m. Joseph Smith, and rem. to Minnesota. (10) *Eli*, b. 1799; rem. to Tyngsborough. (11) *Eliza*, b. 1805; m. Parker Woodward and rem. to Iowa.

16. James, son of Lieut. Solomon, m. Anna Tenny, of Tyngsborough. Children: (1) *Evilina A.*, b. 1807; m., 1st, Pierce Dunn, of Chelmsford; and m., 2nd, Samuel Boynton, of Charlestown. (2) *Jemima Read*, b. 1810; m. John H. Smith, of New Hampton, N. H. (3) *James S.*, b. 1812; d. 1813. (4) *Solomon H.*, b. 1813; res. in Boston. (5) *Eliza Tenny*, b. 1816; m. John Ingalls, of Tyngsborough. (6) *Andrew J.*, b. 1819; d. 1834. (7) *Sarah Ann*, b. 1821; m. Liberty C. Raymond, of Boxborough.

(8) *Susan S.*, b. 1824; m. Eri C. Raymond, of Boxborough. (9) *Samuel T.*, b. 1826; rem. to Dunstable. (10) *Esther P.*, b. 1830; d. 1851.

17. **Thomas**, son of Lieut. Solomon, m., 1st, Mary Hilton, of Lunenburg. Children: (1) *Lovina N.*, b. 1819; m. Joseph Smith, Jr., of Lunenburg. (2) *Thomas W.*, b. 1821; rem. to Madrid, Me. (3) *Nancy B.*, b. 1823. He rem. to Lunenburg, where other children were born. "Capt. Spalding enlisted in the U. S. service at the meeting house in Westford, and served five years in the last war with England."

18. **George W.**, son of Lieut. Solomon, m. Rhoda Frederick, of Tyngsborough. Children: (1) *George F.*, b. 1822. (2) *Solomon*, b. 1823; (3) *John L.*, b. 1828; rem. to Mt. Holly, Vt.

SQUIER. Samuel, m. Mary Hildreth, 1764. Children: (1) *John*, b. 1765. (2) *Samuel*, b. 1768. (3) *Solomon*, b. 1770. The family rem. to Mason, N. H.

STEVENS. Bill Wright, m. Phebe Gould, of Chelmsford, 1792. Children: (1) *Betsey*, b. 1793; m. Levi Warren, (?) of Littleton, 1812. (2) *Bill Gould*, b. 1796; d. 1816. (3) *Phebe Gould*, b. 1798. (4) *Zilpah*, b. 1800. (5) *Sally*, b. 1805; m. Joel Clark, (?) of Stanstead, Can. (6) *Amelia*, b. 1807; d. 1813. (7) *Richard*, b. 1812; d. 1812.

STONE. 1. Ebenezer, who came from Wenham, m. Sarah Crowell, in Wenham. Children: (1) *Naomi*, b. 1743, in Wenham; m. Charles Lawrence, 1765. (2) *Ruth*, b. in Westford, 1745; m. Leonard Keep, 1765. (3) *Waldron*, b. 1749; was first in Ashby, but settled in Union, Me. (4) *Ebenezer*, b. 1754. (5) *John*, b. 1756; rem. to Ashby. (6) *Isaiah*, b. 1760. (7) *Allen*, b. 1762. (8) *Sarah*, b. 1766.

2. **Samuel**, who came from Cohasset, was the son of Samuel and Sally (Ridgway) Stone, and was born in 1771. He m., 1st, —— Webb, and had *Samuel W.*, b. 1796, and *Elias R.*, b. 1799. He m., 2nd, Grace Stoddard, of Cohasset. Children: (1) *Grace*, b. 1800; d. 1800. (2) *Ebenezer W.*, b. 1801. Lived in Charlestown, was Adjutant General of the Commonwealth; d. 1880. (3) *Mary B.*, b. 1803; d. 1870. (4) *Stephen S.*, b. 1805. (5) *Nancy L.*, b. 1807; d. 1879. (6) *William M.*, b. 1809. (7) *Elizabeth T.*, b. 1811. (8) *Benjamin F.*, b. 1813. (9) *James M.*, b. 1817; d. 1880. (See sketch p. 345.)

SYMMES. 1. Caleb, b. in Charlestown, m. Elizabeth Hall, daughter of Rev. Willard, 1756. Child: *Caleb*.

2. **Caleb**, son of Caleb, b. ——, m. Lydia Trowbridge, 1784. Children: (1) *Caleb*, b. 1786. (2) *Betsey*, b. 1788. (3) *Lydia*, b. 1791.

3. **Thomas**, son of Caleb, and b. ——, m. Rebecca Carver, 1789. Children; (1) *Thomas*, b. 1789; perished in the stranding of the steamer "Atlantic" on Gardner's Island, Long Island Sound, Nov. 27, 1846. (2) *Susanna Bancroft*, b. 1793; d. 1813. (3) *Edee*, b. 1795; m. Cephas Drew, who was born in Halifax, Mass.. (4) *Patty*, b. 1797; d. 1820. (5) *Caleb*, b. 1800; d. 1821. (6) *Elizabeth Hall*, b. 1803. (7) *Edward* (twin), b. 1806. (8) *Edmund* (twin), b. 1806; d. 1878 unm.

4. **Edward**, son of Thomas, b. 1806, m. Rebecca Pierce Fletcher. Children: (1) *William Edward*, b. 1841. (2) *John Kebler*, b. 1845; d. 1848. (3) *Sarah Rebecca*, b. 1847; d. 1848. (4) *Thomas Edmund*, b. 1842; grad. Harvard College, 1865; m. Nancy Almira Hale, 1881. (5) *Carver*, b. 1851. (6) *Fletcher*, b. 1852. (7) *Harriet E.*, b. 1855; m. James M. Sargent, Jr., of Lynn, 1877.

THOMPSON. William, m. Mary ——. Children: (1) *William*, b. 1743. (2) *Mary*, b. 1745.

TIDD. 1. John, m. Elizabeth Wilson, 1780. Children: (1) *John*, b. 1781. (2) *Betsey*, b. 1783. (3) *Joel*, b. 1785. (4) *Ebenezer*, b. 1788. (5) *George Clifford*, b. 1791. (6) *Charles Louis*, b. 1793. (7) *Benjamin Franklin*, b. 1796; m. Nancy Keyes, 1821, and rem. to Lancaster. (8) *Warren*, b. 1799; d. young.

2. **Ebenezer**, son of John, b. 1788, m. Permelia Trowbridge, 1829. Children: (1) *Nancy Elizabeth*, b. 1830. (2) *Jacob Alonzo*, b. 1835; d. 1841. The father d. in 1873 at the almshouse.

UNDERWOOD. 1. Joseph, son of Joseph and Elizabeth, was born in Reading, 1681, and died in Westford, 1761, aged 80. He was one of the original members of the first church; was active in all public affairs, and was evidently a man of character and influence. He was a farmer and innholder, and owned a large tract of land on the eastern slope of the hill on which the Central Village now stands, reaching up to the Common, and including the Osgood farm, together with the farms of the Spalding Brothers, of the Ira Leland heirs, and of Albert P. Richardson. It was the best land near the centre, and is now occupied by several houses, and by large orchards. His dwelling stood nearly opposite Mrs. Leland's, where a cellar-hole yet remains. He was also largely concerned in the settlement of Litchfield, N. H., although he did not remove his family thither. He married in Reading, 1707, Susanna Parker, of that place, and probably four of their children were born there. Children: (1) *Joseph*, b. 1708; grad. at Harvard College, 1735, and studied for the ministry but probably was never ordained. According to the supposition of Eaton in his Genealogy of the Reading families, he m. Ruth Bancroft, 1739, and had one son, Joseph. He d. in Westford, 1745, aged 37. (2) *Thomas*, b. 1709; d. 1732. (3) *Mary*, b. 1711; m. Col. Buckley. (4) *Elizabeth*, b. 1714; m. Joseph Fletcher, 1735, and rem. to Dunstable. (5) *Jonathan*, 2. b. 1716. (6) *Amy*, b. 1717; m. James Spalding, 1736; d. 1770. (7) *Ruth*, b. 1719; m. Joseph Read; d. 1775. (8) *Phinehas*, b. 1722; d. at Merrimack, N. H., 1757. (9) *Timothy*, 3, b. 1724. (10) *Susanna*, b. 1725; d. 1729. (11) *John*, 4, b. 1727; d. 1750. (12) *Bethiah*, b. 1729; m. Oliver Prescott. (13) *James*, 5, b. 1731.

2. Jonathan, m. Hannah Richardson, of Medway, 1739. Children: (1) *Hannah*, b. 1740. (2) *Jonathan*, b. 1744. (3) *Susannah*, b. 1747. Jonathan the father, d. in Marlborough, N. H.

3. Timothy, m. Rachel Russell. Children: (1) *Rachel*, b. 1747; m. —— Bigelow. (2) *Timothy*, b. 1749; d. young. (3) *Joseph*, b. 1751; d. young. (4) *Deborah*, b. 1754: m. Abner Miles of Shrewsbury, 1773. (5) *Joseph*, b. 1757. When he was not quite eighteen years of age, he was a soldier under Gen. Putnam, on Long Island. He m. —— Reynolds, and their children were: Timothy, b. 1782, who m. Lucy Hubbard; Sally, b. 1784, who m. Moses Johnson; Joseph, b. 1786, who m. Sally Hubbard; Phinehas, b. 1787, who m. Fanny Reed; Polly, b. 1788; Elizabeth, b. 1790; and James, b. 1792, who lived in New York City and d. 1828. (6) *Timothy*, b. 1759. He was a soldier — this is well attested — and, probably, he is the Timothy Underwood, whose name appears in the list of Capt. Joshua Parker's company who served from July 5, 1777, to January 1, 1778. There are some things that indicate his removal to Ashby. He married and had, it is said, a family of seven daughters. (7) *Susanna*, b. 1762; m. John Moore. (8) *Phinehas*, b. 1764; settled in New York City. (9) *Russell*, b. 1766; lived in Putney, Vt., but afterward rem. to New York. (10) *Mary*, b. 1768; m. —— Brigham. (11) *James*, 6, b. 1771. Timothy, the father, was captain of a company of men in the Concord fight. (See pp. 106, 107.) He rem. with all his children, except one, to Putney, Vt. (See also p. 168.) There is an error on this page in stating that his son Timothy settled in Westborough. It should be Westford.

4. John, b. 1727; m. Hannah Wright, daughter of Dea. Henry and Esther (Adams) Wright, and lived in Westford. Children: (1) *Jeremy*, 7, b. 1750. (2) *Hannah*, b. 1752. (3) *A son that d. young*. (4) *John*, b. 1755. John, the father, was drowned while in the army, 1756. His widow married Samuel Read, 1757.

5. James, b. 1731; m. Mary ——, and rem. to Litchfield, N. H., where the births of three children are recorded, viz: (1) *Mary*, b. 1755. (2) *Thomas*, b. ——. (3) *Susanna*, b. 1761.

6. James, the youngest son of Capt. Timothy, settled in Swanzey, N. H. His children were: (1) *Anna*. (2) *Israel*, who rem. to Salina, N. Y. (3) *Harriet*, who m. —— Bryant. (4) *Rachel*, who m. —— Wright. (5) *Timothy*. (6) *Hiram*. (7) *James*; d. young.

7. Jeremy, son of John, m. at Lincoln, 1774, Lucy Wheat, who was born in Concord. They removed to Jaffrey, N. H., 1777. Children: (1) *John*, b. in Westford, 1775; d. 1776. (2) *John*, b. 1777. (3) *A son b.*

and d. 1779. (4) *A daughter* b. and d. 1780. (5) *Jeremy*, b. 1781. The descendants of Jeremy, the father, are still living in Jaffrey. "Mr. Underwood was a distinguished man in town and church affairs. When the church was incorporated in 1780, he and his wife were members. He held, from time to time, most of the public offices in the gift of the town; was a member of the Board of Selectmen six years, five in succession. He was also a lieutenant in the military service, and a soldier in the Revolution; was at West Point in 1780, when Arnold sold that important post to the British officers, and being an artificer by trade, was ordered by Washington to open the traitor's trunk after Arnold's escape to the British lines. At the expiration of his term of enlistment he returned to Jaffrey, where he spent the remainder of his days at work on his farm and at his trade. He d. 1827, aged 77." (See History of Jaffrey, by Daniel B. Cutter, M. D., pp. 501, 502.)

8. Aquila, son of Samuel and probably grandson of William, who removed from Concord to Chelmsford in 1654; was a tax-payer in 1730. This family is probably distinct from that of Joseph whose ancestor settled in Watertown. He, Aquila, m. Margaret ———. Children: (1) *Samuel*, b. 1722. (2) *Aquila*, b. 1723; d. 1724. (3) *Mary*, b. 1724. (4) *Sarah*, b. 1725. (5) *Hannah*, b. 1727. (6) *William*, b. 1728. (7) *Parker*, b. 1730; settled in Littleton. (8) *Lucy*, b. 1731. Aquila, the father, rem. to Litchfield, N. H., 1731. (See p. 157.)

WENDELL. It seems probable that this family is related to Col. Jacob Wendell, of Boston. The Jacob who first appears on the records, brought a letter of dismission from the church in Ashburnham, and joined the first church here in 1773. But one bearing the name of Jacob, "a resident of Westford," married Lora Winslow "of said town" in 1762. It may be that after marrying, they rem. to Ashburnham, where a son Jacob was born whose family is recorded here as follows:

1. Jacob, m. Lydia Read. Children: (1) *Lydia*, b. 1788. (2) *Jacob*, b. 1790. (3) *Anull*, b. 1798. (4) *Pottifer*, b. 1801. (5) *Eleanor*, b. 1803. Jacob, the father was drowned in the Merrimack River, 1809. A pencilled note below the record says, "came from Boston."

WHITE. 1. Samuel, son of Mark and Anna, was born in Acton, 1744. He m., 1st, Dorothy Billings, of Acton, in 1772. Children: (1) *Dorothy*, b. 1773; d. young. Mrs. Dorothy White d. 1773, and he m., 2nd, Hepsibah Barrett, of Concord, in 1775. (2) *Dorothy*, b. 1776; m, Edmund Ingalls, of Concord, and d. 1853. (3) *Hepsibah*, b. 1779; m. Ira Duren, of Weathersfield, Vt., and d. in 1841, at Ann Arbor, Michigan. (4) *Samuel*, b. 1781; was a saddler by trade and lived at Whitesville, Vt. He d. at Cambridge, Vt., 1836. (5) *John*, b. 1781; d. in Cavendish, Vt. 1859. Samuel, the father, rem. to Cavendish, in 1786. (6) *Joseph*, b. 1786, in Cavendish, m. Susan Adams, 1810, and had Susan who m. Otis Robbins, of Cavendish, in 1834; and Joseph Adams who m. Ellen L. Proctor, had three children, and d. 1879. (7) *George W.*, b. 1788; d. 1875. (8) *Benjamin F.*, b. 1791; d. in Boston, 1874. (9) *Anna*, b. 1794; m. Sewall Kenney, of Weathersfield, and d. 1831. Samuel, the first, m., 3rd, Mrs. Rachel Adams, of Westford.

2. Aaron, son of Mark and Mary (Read), of Acton, and b. 1772; m. Sally ———. Children: (1) *Sally*, b. 1801; m. Gilbert Parker, 1820. (2) *Aaron*, b. 1802; m. Sophia E. L. Kendall, 1826. (3) *Otis*, b. 1805.

WHITING. 1. Leonard, Capt., m. Anna Hall, daughter of Rev. Willard, 1761. Child: *Leonard*, b. 1762.

2. Benjamin, m. Grace Hall, daughter of Rev. Willard, 1770. Child: *Frances Wentworth*, b. 1771.

3. William, m. Lucy Hildreth, 1786. Children: (1) *William*, b. 1787; d. 1838. (2) *Augustus*, b. 1795; d. 1795. (3) *Augustus*, b. 1796; rem. to New York City. (4) *Isaac Newton*, b. 1799. (5) *Alonzo*, b. 1803; d. 1804. (6) *Alonzo*, b. 1805; d. 1828.

WILSON. Henry, m. Hannah Spalding, 1792. Children: (1) *John*, b. 1795. (2) *Sophia*, b. 1797. (3) *Sally*, b. 1799. (4) *Timothy*, b. 1801, lives in Fitchburg. (5) *Henry*, b. 1803. (6) *Hannah*, b. 1807. (7) *Levi*, b. 1811.

GENEALOGY. 481

WINN. Hezekiah, m. Bathsheba ———. Children: (1) *Polly*, b. 1792. (2) *Joseph*, b. 1793. (3) *Rebekah*, b. 1795.

WRIGHT. The ancestor was John, of Woburn, who married in 1661, Abigail Warren, of Woburn. He was among the first settlers of Chelmsford, where all his children were born. Children: (1) *John*, b. 1662. (2) *Joseph*, b. 1663. (3) *Ebenezer*, b. 1665. (4) *Jacob*, b. 1667. (5) *Abigail*, b. 1668. (6) *Priscilla*, b. 1671. (7) *Josiah*, b. 1674. (8) *Samuel*, b. 1683, probably rem. to Groton. (9) *Lydia*, b. 1686.

2. **John**, son of John, m., 1st, Mary Stevens. Children: (1) *Jacob*, b. 1692; d. young. (2) *Ebenezer*, b. 1693. (3) *Edward*, b. 1695. (4) *Jacob*, b. 1698. (5) *Henry*, b. 1700. (6) *John* (twin), b. 1701; d. young. (7) *Mary* (twin), b. 1701; d. young. He m., 2nd, Hannah Fletcher. (8) *Hannah*, b. 1704. (9) *Thomas*, b. 1707. (10) *Simeon*, b. about 1710.

3. **Ebenezer**, son of John, and born in 1693, was the first of the family to establish a home within the bounds of Westford. His farm was on the eastern border, being the same that was occupied by the family for successive generations, and on which Edwin E. Heywood now lives. When the old town was divided, a part of it fell within the limits of Chelmsford. He m. in 1730, Deliverance Stevens, of Chelmsford. Children: (1) *Abigail*, b. 1731. (2) *Hannah*, b. 1732; m. Jonathan Perham, of Littleton, 1757. (3) *Ebenezer*, b. 1734; rem. to Templeton. (4) *Caleb*, b. 1735. (5) *Joshua*, b. 1737; rem. to Templeton. (6) *Zaccheus*, b. 1738. (7) *Joel*, b. 1740; d. 1758. (8) *Silas*, b. 1742. (9) *Amos*, b. 1744. (10) *Lydia*, b. 1745; m. Zebulon Spalding (?), 1767. (11) *Phinehas*, b. 1747; pastor in Bolton. (12) *Olive*, b. 1748; m. Samuel Fletcher, 1771.

4. **Jacob**, son of John, and b. 1698; settled in the north part, on the farm recently owned by Bradley V. Lyon. He m. Abigail ———. Children: (1) *Sarah*, b. 1721. (2) *John*, b. 1723. (3) *Ephraim*, b. 1725. (4) *Mary*, b. 1727. (5) *Sarah*, b. 1730. (6) *Jacob*, b. 1732. (7) *Pelatiah*, b. 1734. (8) *Joseph*, b. 1736. (9) *Benjamin*, b. 1738; d. 1741.

5. **Henry**, son of John, and b. 1700; m. Esther Adams. Children: (1) *Hannah*, b. 1730; m. John Underwood, 1749. (2) *Henry*, b. 1732. (3) *Sibel*, b. 1734. (4) *Olive*, b. 1736. (5) *Rachel*, b. 1738. (6) *Eunice*, b. 1740. (7) *Philip*, b. 1742. (8) *Mary*, b. 1745. (9) *Sarah*, b. 1747. (10) *Huldah*, b. 1749; m. Samson Warren (?), of Littleton, 1771. Thus far the record; but there was a *Phebe*, b. 1728, who m. Benjamin Knowlton, 1750.

6. **Thomas**, son of John and Hannah, b. 1707; m. Elizabeth Parker, and settled on the Asia Nutting place. Children: (1) *Thomas*, b. 1734; m. Mary Parker, Jr., 1767, and rem. to New Ipswich. (2) *Abel*, b. 1735; rem. to New Ipswich. (3) *William*, b. 1736; d. 1762. (4) *Oliver*, b. 1738; rem. to New Ipswich. (5) *Reuben*, b. 1740; d. in the army, 1759. (6) *Elizabeth*, b. 1742. (7) *Sarah*, b. 1744. (8) *Ebenezer*, b. 1746. (9) *Peter*, b. 1748; d. 1752. (10) *Hannah*, b. 1750. (11) *Peter*, b. 1752. (12) *Jonas*, b. 1759.

7. **Simeon**, son of John and Hannah, and b. about 1710; m. Dorcas Hildreth, 1738. Children: (1) *Lydia*, b. 1739. (2) *Simeon*, b. 1741; rem. to New Ipswich. (3) *Dorcas*, b. 1743; m. Amos Wright, 1767. (4) *Samuel*, b. 1745. (5) *Sarah*, b. 1747. (6) *Hannah*, b. 1749; d. 1753. (7) *Ruth*, b. 1751. (8) *James*, b. 1754; m. Mary Minot, 1781, and rem. to Maine. (9) *Levi*, b. 1756; d. 1766. (10) *Azubah*, b. 1758; d. 1758. (11) *Betty*, b. 1759; d. 1760.

8. **Caleb**, son of Ebenezer, m. Elizabeth Cleaveland, 1760. Children: (1) *Jonathan*, b. 1761; d. 1761. (2) *Paul*, b. 1762; m. Abigail Kent, and rem. to Stoddard. (3) *Hannah*, b. 1768; d. 1769. (4) *Elizabeth*, b. 1771.

9. **Henry**, son of Henry, and b. 1732; m. Sarah Spalding, 1753. Children: (1) *Mary*, b. 1753. (2) *Thankful*, b. 1754. (3) *Stephen*, b. 1758; rem. to Littleton. (4) *Bridget*, b. 1760. (5) *Esther*, b. 1762; m. Jonathan Johnson, Jr. (?), 1783. (6) *Rebecca*, b. 1763. (7) *Sarah*, b. 1765. (8) *Henry*, b. 1767. (9) *Hannah*, b. 1768. (10) *Abel*, b. 1770. (11) *Elijah*, b. 1771, "and was the first child baptized in the new meeting house"; rem to Ashby.

10. **Jacob**, son of Jacob, and b. 1732; m. Lucy, daughter of William and Bathsheba Butterfield, 1755. Children: (1) *Lucy*, b. 1756; m. Stephen

Mead, 1780. (2) *Jacob*, b. 1758; settled in Washington, N. H., where he d. at the age of 85; was known as Col. Wright. (3) *Abraham Butterfield*, b. 1760; settled in Ashby, but rem. to Mason, N. H., where he d., aged 72. (4) *Olive*, b. 1762; m. Mr. Lowell, of Washington, N. H. (5) *Lavisa*, b. 1764; d. 1777. (6) *Naomi*, b. 1766; m. —— Read, and rem. to Gardner, Mass. (7) *Ziba*, b. 1770; settled in Littleton, N. H., and d. there. (8) *William*, b. 1771, after his father's decease. Jacob, the father, "was accidentally cut with a scythe, while mowing, and died from hemorrhage of the wound at the age of 45; a very pious, good man."

11. Joseph, son of Jacob, and b. 1736; m., 1st, Dorothy Heald, b. in Groton, daughter of Thomas and Sarah. Children: (1) *Joseph*, b. 1758; d. at White Plains, 1777, aged 19. (2) *Dorothy*, b. 1761. (3) *Reuben*, b. 1763. (4) *Asa*, b. 1767. (5) *Abel*, b. 1770. (6) *Phebe*, b. 1778. He m., 2nd, Hannah Kemp, 1774. (7) *Hannah*, b. 1776. (8) *Joseph*, b. 1778; d. 1781. (9) *Ruth*, b. 1781. (10) *Joel*, b. 1783. (11) *Jacob*, b. 1786.

12. Pelatiah, son of Jacob, and b. 1734; m. Alice Powers, 1761. Children: (1) *Rebecca*, b. 1764. (2) *Bridget*, b. 1765. (3) *Esther*, b. 1768. (4) *Benjamin*, b. 1770. (5) *Lydia Powers*, b. 1772. (6) *Susanna*, b. 1774. (7) *Alice*, b. 1778. (8) *Abijah*, b. 1780.

13. John, son of Jacob, and b. 1723; m., in Dunstable, Sarah ——. Children: (1) *Sarah*, b. in Dunstable, 1755. (2) *Mary*, b. in Dunstable, 1757. (3) *Oliver*, b. 1759. (4) *Deborah*, b. 1762. (5) *John*, b. 1764. (6) *Eleazer*, b. 1765. (7) *Rachel*, b. 1767. (8) *Isaac*, b. 1770. (9) *Anna*, b. 1772. (10) *Elizabeth*, b. 1773. (11) *Ebenezer*, b. 1777.

14. John, m. Mary Kendall, of Dunstable. Children: (1) *John*, b 1748. (2) *Zebedee*, b. 1749. (3) *Benjamin*, b. 1751. (4) *Isaac*, b. 1754. These are recorded. Mr. Hall baptized the following: (5) *Nehemiah*, bap. 1756. (6) *Oliver*, bap. 1758. (7) *Sarah*, bap. 1762.

15. Ephraim, son of Jacob, and b. 1725-26; m. Abigail Whittemore, of Dunstable, 1751. Children: (1) *Abraham*, b. 1752; d. 1752. (2) *Abigail*, b. 1753. (3) *Ruth*, b. 1755. (4) *Sarah*, b. 1757; d. 1762. (5) *Ephraim*, b. 1761; rem. to Littleton. (6) *Nathan*, b. 1763. (7) *Lydia*, b. 1765; m. Andrew Fletcher, 1784. (8) *Jotham*, b. 1767. (9) *Hannah*, b. 1770; d. 1775. (10) *Jacob*, b. 1772.

16. Silas, son of Ebenezer, and b. 1742; m. Mary Craft, 1764. Children: (1) *Joel*, b. 1765. (2) *Silas*, b. 1767. (3) *Benjamin*, b. 1769. (4) *Samuel*, b. 1770.

17. Amos, son of Ebenezer, and b. 1743-44; m. Dorcas Wright, daughter of Simeon, 1767. Children: (1) *Levi*, b. 1768. (2) *Amos*, b. 1771; d. 1775. (3) *Zaccheus*, b. 1774. (4) *Hannah*, b. 1776. (5) *Ruth*, b. 1783; m. (6) *John*, b. 1785. (7) *Phinehas*, b. 1788. (8) *Ebenezer*, b. 1791; d. 1795.

18. Samuel, son of Simeon, and b. 1745; m. Esther Minot, 1771. Children: (1) *Abel*, b. 1771, "and the 2nd child christened in the new meeting house." (2) *Luther*, b. 1773; m. Priscilla Emery, of Hollis, N. H. (3) *Joseph Minot*, b. 1778; d. 1779. (4) *Betty*, b. 1779; m. Levi Parker, 1803. (5) *Joanna*, b. 1781; d. 1812. (6) *Samuel*, b. 1784; m. Martha Parker, 1808; he kept a store and tavern at the Centre; rem. to Orono, Me. (7) *Esther*, b. 1786; m. Ens. Thomas Pearson, 1810. (8) *Hannah*, b. 1789. (9) *Sally*, b. 1792; m. Joel Taylor.

19. Oliver, son of John, and b. 1759; m. Dorothy Prescott, widow of Ezra, 1797. Children: (1) *Oliver*, b. 1798; d. (2) *Sarah*, b. 1799; m. Bela Wright, 1825. (3) *Jesse*, b. 1800, at Groton.

20. Nathan, son of Ephraim, and b. 1763; m. Betsey Trowbridge, 1788. Children: (1) *Nathan*, b. 1789. (2) *Parker*, b. 1791. (3) *Jotham Bruce*, b. 1792; grad. at Harvard. (4) *Edmond*, b. 1794; d. young. (5) *Edmond*, b. 1796; d. young. (6) *John*, b. 1797. (7) *Walter*, b. 1800. (8) *Martin*, b. 1806. (9) *George Sumner*, b. 1810.

21. Abel, son of Joseph, and b. 1770; m. Lefe Trowbridge, of Groton, 1795. Children: (1) *Bela*, b. 1796. (2) *Phinehas*, b. 1798. (3) *Lefe*, b. 1800. (4) *George*, b. 1802. (5) *Jeptha*, b. 1804. (6) *Abel*, b. 1808.

22. Joel, son of Joseph, and b. 1783; m. Sally ——, 1808. Children: (1) *Roxana*, b. 1809. (2) *Sophia*, b. 1811. (3) *Relief T.*, b. 1813.

(4) *Joel A.*, b. 1815. (5) *William O.*, b. 1816. (6) *Sarah M.*, b. 1818.
(7) *Zebedee E.*, b. 1820. (8) *Ezra W.*, b. 1822. (9) *Clarissa J.*, b. 1823.
(10) *Julian E.*, b. 1825. (11) *Zilpah A.*, b. 1827; d. 1840. (12) *Pelatiah J.*,
b. 1829. (13) *Martha E.*, b. 1832.

23. Reuben, son of Joseph, b. 1763; m. Sarah Read, daughter of Thomas and Susanna, 1787. Children: (1) *Reuben*, b. 1788. (2) *Thomas Read*, b. 1790. (3) *Philinda*, b. 1792; m. Thomas Richardson. (4) *Newell*, b. 1795. (5) *Lucinda*, b. 1797; m. Thomas Cummings, 1815. (6) *Calvin Blanchard*, b. 1800; m. Almira Tenney, 1827. (7) *Sally*, b. 1803; m. Calvin Spalding. (8) *Almira*, b. 1805; m. Jacob Blodgett, 1826. (9) *James M.*, b. 1809; m. Sarah Gould, 1833.

24. Abijah, son of Pelatiah, and b. 1780; m. Polly Fletcher, 1800. Children: (1) ———, b. 1801. (2) *Archibald*, b. 1803; m. Elvira Chapman. (3) *Erastus*, b. 1806. (4) *Benjamin Loring*, b. 1808. (5) *Warren*, b. 1812; m. Sarah Farwell; rem. to Sycamore, Ill. (6) *Laura Ann*, b. 1815; m. Joel Ingalls, of Tyngsborough.

25. Horatio, son of Abijah, and b. 1801; m. Anna Gass. Children: (1) *Stuart Park*, b. 1827; m. Eliza S. Cutter, 1850. (2) *Horatio Gass*, b. 1829. (3) *Alpheus Fletcher*, b. 1833. (4) *Francis Ballard*, b. 1837; m. Maria Wright, 1861.

26. Parker, son of Nathan, and b. 1791; m. Mary Gage, 1818. Children: (1) *Lydia*, b. 1819; m. Samuel Folsom, of Lowell. (2) *Nathan*, b. 1822. (3) *Mary Elizabeth*, b. 1823. (4) *William Artemas*, b. 1825; res. in Lowell.

27. Phinehas, son of Amos, and b. 1788; m. Betsey Whitcomb, 1814. Children: (1) *Maverick Wyman*, b. 1815; m. Jane Heywood, and lives in Tremont, Ill. (2) *Laura Maria*, b. 1817; m. Elbridge Dutton, of Chelmsford. (3) *Eliza Thompson*, b. 1819; m. George A. Griffin. (4) *Edwin*, b. 1822. Phinehas, the father, d. at Albany, N. Y.

28. Levi, son of Amos, and b. 1768; m. Rhoda Hildreth, 1794. Children: (1) *Amos*, b. 1795; d. unmarried. (2) *Sophronia*, b. 1796; d. unmarried, 1864. (3) *Hosea*, b. 1797; m. Lucinda Minot, 1824, and had one child named Leonora. (4) *Washington*, b. 1799; m. Mary Wright, 1825; had five children; d. near Tremont, Ill. (5) *Lydia*, b. 1803; m. George W. Aldrich. (6) *Rhoda*, b. 1805; d. unmarried. (7) *Levi*, b. 1807; d. 1808. (8) *Rebecca*, b. 1811; m., 1st, Augustus H. Searles, 1831, and had one son; she m., 2nd, Jed Mayo, 1842. (9) *Levi*, b. 1813; m. Hannah Blanchard, of Brookfield, Ohio, and had four children.

29. Zaccheus, son of Amos, and b. 1774; m. Abigail Hildreth, 1802. Children: (1) *Mary*, b. 1803; m. Washington Wright. (2) *Rachel*, b. 1805; m. —— Hawley, of Chicago. (3) *Lucy Susan*, b. 1807. (4) *Ezekiel*, b. 1808; d. (5) *Zaccheus*, b. 1809; d. 1809.

30. Jonas, son of Thomas, and b. 1759; m. Rebecca Fletcher, widow of Benjamin Fletcher, and daughter of Nathaniel Boynton, 1783. Children: (1) *Ralph*, b. 1784. (2) *Rebecca*, b. 1786; m. Aaron Wood, of Mason, N. H. (3) *Sally*, b. 1788; m. Jonas Adams, of Mason. (4) *William*, b. 1790; rem. to Mason. (5) *Luther*, b. 1798; went to the Sandwich Islands; m. and d. there. (6) *John Boynton*, b. 1797.

31. Asa, son of Joseph, and b. 1767; m. Betsey Patch, 1787. Children: (1) *Betsey*, b. 1787. (2) *Joseph*, b. 1789; did he rem. to Dedham? (3) *Huldah*, b. 1791. (4) *Salathiel*, b. 1794. (5) *Rhoda*, b. 1796. (6) *Asa*, b. 1798. (7) *Sophronia*, b. 1802.

32. Asa, son of Asa, and b. 1798; m. Bathsheba Dadmun, 1820. Children: (1) *Ede P.*, b. 1821; m. Simeon Stevens, Jr. (2) *Jefferson*, b. 1825; rem. to Utah. (3) *Esther B.*, b. 1827; m. Francis Fletcher, 1839. (4) *Kendall Asa*, b. 1831. (5) *Arthur*, b. 1837. (6) *Emily Augusta*, b. 1841.

33. Reuben, son of Reuben, and b. 1788; m. Esther Woodward, of Tyngsborough, 1809. Children: (1) *Esther*, b. 1810; m. William Tenney. (2) *Reuben*, b. 1811; m. —— Flint; lives at Tyngsborough. (3) *Mary Ann*, b. 1814; m. Samuel Spalding, of Tyngsborough. (4) *John Woodward*, b. 1817; m. —— Bond, of Nashua, N. H. (5) *Sally Read*, b. 1819; m. Charles Fellows, Lowell. (6) *Almira*, b. 1822. (7) *Horace*

H. W., b. 1826. (8) *George Newton*, b. 1828. (9 *Margia Ann*, b. 1830. (10) *Isaac Sumner*, b. 1833. These all lived until the youngest was 35 years old.

34. Jacob, son of Joseph, by his second wife, Hannah, m. Sally ———. Children: (1) *Miriam*, b. 1806. (2) *Sally*, b. 1808. (3) *Jacob Austin*, b. 1811. (4) *Hannah*, b. 1813; m. John Day, 1834. (5) *Anna*, b. 1816. (6) *Phebe*, b. 1818; m. J. J. Carter, 1856. (7) *George Porter*, b. 1821; m. Adeline Moore. (8) *Joseph Eldredge*, b. 1823; m. Harriet A. Reed, 1844.

35. Ephraim, son of Ephraim, and b. 1761; m. Mary Blodgett. Children: (1) *Abigail*, b. 1786; m. Elisha Fletcher, of Littleton. (2) *Mary*, b. 1788; d. unmarried, 1814. (3) *Sarah B.*, b. 1791; m. Jacob Harrington, of Shirley. (4) *Ephraim*, b. 1793. (5) *Abram*, b. 1797; m. Maria Hildreth, and d. 1827. (6) *Imlah*, b. 1799, rem. to Antrim, N. H. (7) *Jesse*, b. 1802; m., for a second wife, Mrs. Mehitable Davis. (8) *James Mansur*, b. 1807; d. 1824.

36. Ephraim, son of Ephraim, and b. 1793; m. Asenath Fletcher, 1820. Children: (1) *Mary Fletcher*, b. 1821; d. 1826. (2) *Henry Otis*, b. 1824; d. 1825. (3) *Abram*, b. 1828; res. in Clinton. (4) *George Fletcher*, b. 1831; res. in Clinton. (5) *Mary Alsina*, b. 1833; d. 1834. (6) *Martha Asenath*, b. 1835. (7) *Sarah Peabody*, b. 1838; m. Artemas W. Cummings.

37. Stephen, son of Henry, Jr., and b. 1758; m. Sarah Prescott, 1787. Children: (1) *Stephen*, b. 1787; m. Zebiah Richardson, of Westford, and settled in Ludlow, Vt. (2) *Sally*, b. 1791; m. Nathan Wright, of Shelburne. (3) *Lucy*, b. 1795; m. Jacob P. Kellogg, of Shelburne. These three b. in Ashby. (4) *Ezekiel Conant*, b. 1797. (5) *Lydia*, b. 1799; d. unmarried, 1817. (6) *Mary*, b. 1801; m. Gilbert Farmer. (7) *Rebecca*, b. 1803; d. unmarried, 1817. (8) *Timothy Prescott*, b. 1806. (9) *Elizabeth*, b. 1809; m. Nathan Childs, Wilton, N. H.

38. Ezekiel Conant, son of Stephen, and b. 1797; m. Susan Stevens, of Chelmsford, 1821. Children: (1) *Susan Emily Hester*, b. 1822; m. George W. Wood, of Littleton, 1852. (2) *Ezekiel Atwood*, b. 1824. (3) *Sarah Maria*, b. 1826. (4) *Atwell Freeman*, b. 1829. (5) *Nahum Harwood*, b. 1831. (6) *Stephen Eugene*, b. 1834. (7) *Merrill Stevens*, b. 1837. (8) *Harriet Elizabeth*, b. 1841; m. George F. Wright, 1860.

39. Timothy Prescott, son of Stephen, and b. 1806; m. Elnora Prescott, 1832. Children: (1) *Gilbert T.*, b. 1833; d. 1838. (2) *Elnora G.*, b. 1834; m. Elihu Smead, of Shelburne, 1861. (3) *Mary*, b. 1836; d. 1839. (4) *Gilbert T.*, b. 1838. (4) *Edward P.*, b. 1840. (5) *Alfred O.*, b. 1847.

40. Jesse, son of Oliver, and b. 1800; m. Sybil Stevens, of Chelmsford, 1828. Children: (1) *Gilman Jesse*, b. 1829; m. Harriet H. Hales, 1871. (2) *Andrew Stevens*, b. 1833; m. Abby Garvin. (3) *Harriet Maria*, b. 1836; d.

41. Archibald, son of Abijah, b. 1803; m. Elvira Chapman. Children: (1) *Henry O.*, b. 1832, at Lexington. (2) *Elvira Angela*, b. 1836, at Boston. (3) *Laura A.*, b. 1840, at Westford.

42. Benjamin L., son of Abijah, and b. 1806; m. Elizabeth Wright. Children: (1) *Loring*, b. 1835; d. 1835. (2) *Oscar*, b. 1837; d. 1837. (3) *Oscar*, b. 1838; d. 1853. (4) *Hannibal H.*, b. 1839. (5) *Malvina E.*, b. 1841. (6) *Morton G.*, b. 1843. (7) *Rosilla*, b. ———. (8) *Augustus A.*, b. 1854.

43. Erastus, son of Abijah, and b. 1806; m. Elizabeth M. Carr, of Charlestown, 1831. Children: (1) *Everett E.*, b. 1832. (2) *Josiah Osgood*, b. 1834. (3) *Wilbur Fisk*, b. 1837. (4) *Elisabeth*, b. 1839. (5) *Gilman Fessenden*, b. 1841. (6) *Albion LeForest*, b. 1842. (7) *Almaette L.*, b. 1845; d. 1865. (8) *Eugene H.*, b. 1850.

44. Martin, son of Nathan, and b. 1806; m., 1st, Abigail Jones, 1830. Children: (1) *Abigail R.*, b. 1831; m. Charles W. Brooks, of Lowell. (2) *Ellen W.*, b. 1832; m. Joseph C. Healey, of Lowell. (3) *Lovey M.*, b. 1834; m. Charles S. Coburn, of Tyngsborough. He m., 2nd, Eliza Ingalls, of Tyngsborough. (4) *Eliza Ann*, b. 1838; m. Joseph C. Healey, of Lowell.

GENEALOGY.

45. Bela, son of Abel; m. Sarah Wright, and rem. to Nelson, N. H., where he res. until after the birth of his third child, when he returned. Children: (1) *Sarah Ann*, b. 1826. (2) *Jeptha*, b. 1828. (3) *George*, b. 1830. (4) *Varnum*, b. 1833. (5) *Maria* b. 1841; m. Francis B. Wright, 1861.

46. James Madison, son of Reuben, and b. 1809; m. Sarah Gould, 1833. Children: (1) *Sarah June*, b. 1833; m. Hezekiah Cummings. (2) *Mary M.*, b. 1835; d. 1838. (3) *Susan Elmira*, b. 1837; m. Kendall A. Wright. (4) *Mary M.*, b. 1840; d. 1853. (5) *Philinda Ellen*, b. 1842; m Israel S. Worcester.

47. Jacob Austin, son of Jacob, and b. 1811; m. Harriet Leighton, 1837. Children: (1) *Albert Austin*, b. 1838; (2) *George Henry*, b. 1840. (3) *Edwin Elliot*, b. 1841; (4) *Emory Augustus*, b. 1844; m. Emily Curtis.

48. George Porter, son of Jacob, and b. 1821; m. Adeline Moore. Children: (1) *Charles Aloah*, b. 1854; m. Celia J. Smith, 1872. (2) *Willey Merton*, b. 1857; m. Addie S. Hosmer, 1878.

49. Joseph Eldridge, son of Jacob, b. 1823; m. Harriet A. Reed, 1844. Children: (1) *Sidney E.*, b. 1845; d. young. (2) *Sidney B.*, b. 1856. (3) *Charles Henry*, b. 1858. (4) *Frank C.*, b. 1860.

50. Levi, son of Levi, and b. 1813; m. Hannah Blanchard. Children: (1) *Horace Washington*, b. 1837, in Brookfield, Ohio. (2) *Sophronia*, b. 1838, in Brookfield. (3) *Louisa*, b. 1840.

51. John, son of Amos, and b. 1785; m. Betsey Haywood, of Chelmsford. Child: *John Franklin*, b. 1821.

52. John F., son of John, b. 1821; m. Lavinia Frye, of Dracut. Children: (1) *Marion L.*, b. 1845. (2) *Lucius F.*, b. 1848; d. 1880. (3) *Albert J.*, b. 1852; d. 1882. (4) *Gilbert F.*, b. 1857.

53. Eleazer, son of John, b. 1765; m. Elizabeth Nutting, daughter of Ebenezer, of Pepperell, 1793. Children: (1) *Joel*, b. 1794, rem. to Charlestown; m. Elmira Hosmer, of Concord. (2) *Ebenezer*, b. 1796; m. Sarah Holman, rem. to Lowell. (3) *Betsey*, b. 1797; m. Charles Shepard, Bedford, N. H. (4) *Benjamin*, b. 1799; m. Althea Gilson, 1831. (5) *Sophia*, b. 1801; m. True Richards, of Goffstown, N. H. (6) *George*, b. 1803; m. Mary Ann Prescott; d. 1882. (7) *Mary*, b. 1805; d. young. (8) *Martha*, b. 1805. (9) *Walter*, b. 1811; m. Hannah Webber, and had one son, George W., b. 1841; he, Walter, d. 1842. (10) *Franklin*, b. 1813; drowned in Forge Pond 1835, aged 22.

54. Col. Samuel, son of Samuel, and b.——; m. Martha Parker, 1808. Children: (1) *Rufus Samuel*, b. 1810. (2) *Martha Ann*, b. 1811. (3) *Lucy Parker*, b. 1819.

ADDITIONS.

CHANDLER. 11. William, son of William, **6**, and b. 1791; m. Rhoda, daughter of Gershom Procter, of Dunstable, 1816. Children: (1) *Amos Newton*, b. 1818; m. Jane Cabot, Hartland, Vt. (2) *William Procter*, b. 1820; d. 1844. (3) *Mary Ann*, b. 1821; m. Asaph B. Cutter, 1849. (4) *John Murray*, b. 1823; m. Mary Pike, of Maine, 1856. (5) *Jerome*, b. 1825; m. Charlotte Cooper, 1855; res. in Iowa. (6) *George Washington*, b. 1826; m. Abbey Ness, 1857. (7) *Augustus Hiram*, b. 1828; m. Mary Carkin. He d. 1880. (8) *Eliza June*, b. 1830; m. Alfred Perham, Tyngsboro', 1864. (9) *Caroline Maria*, b. 1832; m. James Miller, Peterboro', N. H., 1866. (10) *Charles Edwin*, b. 1833; rem. to Nevada. (11) *Emily Melissa*, b. 1835; m. John B. Fletcher, 1860. (12) *Warren*, b. 1836; m. Frances Ingalls, 1870. (13) *Marcus Morton*, b. 1839; m. Jenny Pattison. (14) *Henry Harrison*, b. 1840.

PARKER. 2. Aaron. (p. 463.) .... (3) *Dorothy*, b. 1742; (add) m. Salmon Dutton, who was b. in Westford, 1744. (See p. 164.)

18. Isaiah, son of Aaron 2; m. Sybil Willard, 1773. Children: (1) *Rachel Willard*, b. 1773; d. young. (2) *Isaiah*, b. 1774; d. 1802. (3) *Samuel Stillman*, b. 1776. He was a physician; (See p. 331.) m. Rebecca Thomas, and d. at River Raisin, Michigan, 1811. (4) *Sally*, b. 1778; m. Joseph Bullard; d. in New York City, 1840. (5) *Luther*, b. 1781; m., 1st, Sophia Hartwell; m., 2d, Sarah Hull, and d. in Michigan. (6) *Sewall*, b. 1783; m. Sally Willard; d. in New York City, 1845. (7) *Miranda*, b. 1785; m. Maj. Joseph Edgarton, and d. 1808. (8) *Rowland*, b. 1787; drowned in Concord River, 1806. (9) *Orsamus*, b. 1789; m. ——, and d. in Otsego, N. Y., 1820. (10) *Isaac Senter*, b. 1791; m. Louisa McClure; d. in Cooperstown, N. Y., 1875. (11) *Rosalinda*, b. 1793; m., 1st, Calvin Whitney; m., 2d, ——, Townsend, of Lancaster, Mass.; d. 1876. (12) *Augustus Granville*, b. 1796; m. Marian Hazen. He was a physician in Shirley, Mass., where he d. 1848. He m., 2nd, Betsey Whitcomb. (13) *Betsey Miranda*, b. 1823; m. Samuel L. Adams, of Cavendish, and rem. to St. Charles, Ill. (14) *Isaiah Whitcomb*, b. 1832; m., 1st, Mary Thompson, of Whitehall, N. Y.; m., 2nd, Lucia E. Barton, of Ludlow, Vt.; d. 1864.

Isaiah, the father, was a physician. He commenced practice in Harvard, Mass., 1772; he also preached, first as a Baptist, and afterwards as a Universalist; was a volunteer surgeon in the Revolution; published a political newspaper in Boston; rem. 1806, to Cavendish, Vt., where he spent the rest of his life, which reached almost to a century. He d. 1848 aged 96. His children by the first marriage were born in Harvard. (Fletcher Genealogy, p. 501.)

INDEX OF TOPICS.

Andrew, the Indian	3
Allotments, earliest	7
Additional Territory from Groton	24
Agreeing to the Articles of Association Drawn Up by the Continental Congress	103
Advice to Representative	114
Articles of Confederation	119
Allowance to Soldiers	119
Applicants for Pensions	136
Alphabetical List of Soldiers in the War of the Revolution	137–9
Acceptance of the First Article of the Declaration of Rights	141–2
Amendment of the Third Article	143
Action in Regard to Shay's Rebellion	149
Annual Reckoning	162
Action of the Town in Regard to the Civil War	189
Alphabetical List of Soldiers in the Civil War	198
Assassination of President Lincoln	220
Annulling the School District System	231
Advent Corner	236
Agricultural Products	239
Abbot Worsted Mills, Enlargement of, by Purchase of Water Power and Buildings at Forge Village	245
Answer of William Hall to the Call of the Church	253
Acceptance to Call by Matthew Scribner	272
Action of Board of Trustees of Methodist Society	305
Academy	312–13
Academy, Town Subscribes 20 Shares to Fund of, and Gives Liberty to Build a House on the Common for	313
Assistant Teachers of Academy	320
Agricultural Library	351
Brief History of the Precinct	17
Brookside	12
Boundary Line Disputed	25
Bounty on Squirrels	70
Bounty on Wolves	72
Bates', Captain, Company	107
Bunker Hill	110
Bills of Credit	118
Bank Proposed	119
Bounty	120
Beef, Committee to Provide	121
Brown's, Captain, Company	126
Butterfield's, Captain, Company	127
Brooks', Colonel, Regiment; and Ballard's, Captain, Company	128–31
Belfry	151
Burning of the Second Meeting House	151
Bounty to Soldiers	153
Burning of Joshua Read, Jr.'s, House	154
Barn at the Poor Farm	184
Boundaries	231
Brookside	235
Buffalo	236
Brick-Making	242
Beginning of Sabbath School Library	264
Building of Methodist Church	304
Biographical Sketches.—Rev. Phineas Wright, Samuel Chamberlin, Col. John Robinson, Rev. Jonathan Osgood, Charles Proctor, M. D., Hon. Joseph Read, Hon. Willard Hall, Rev. James Blodgett, and James M. Stone	323–45
Charter of the Town	21
Copying Records	79
Civil Action	80
Cowdry Estate	95
Committee of Inspection	103
Committee of Correspondence	104
Concord Bridge	108
Congress, Provincial, Delegate to	110
Cæsar Bason	113
Census, 1776	115
Campaigns	116
Committee of Correspondence, 1780	120
Classes, Town Divided into Five; Heads of	121
Committee of Correspondence, 1781	122
Companies of Capt. Fletcher and Capt. Wright	125
Companies of Captains Fletcher, Ford, Brown and Minot	126
Companies of Capt. Butterfield and Capt. Parker	127
Companies of Captains Cole, Jewett and Ballard	128
Companies of Captains Woods, Hunt, Lawrence and Nutting	132
Companies of Captains Porter, Barnes and Sargent	133
Committee to Consider the New Form of Government	139
County House	147
Convention at Boston	150
County Road	154
Copying Records	179
Common Land	181
Copying Record of Marriages	183
Celebration at Acton	183
Career of the Sixteenth Regiment	201
Casualties to Soldiers	210
Citizens' Meeting	224
Celebration at Concord, 1875	225
Centennial Exposition, 1876	226
Completion of 150 Years	227
Central Village	234
Chamberlin's Corner	236
Coopering	242

Carpet-Weaving	242
Chauncey Mills for Making Shaker Socks	246
Conclusion of Mr. Hall's Ministry	265
Call to Mr. Thaxter	268
Call to Mr. Jesse Read	269
Council Fail to Ordain Mr. Read	270
Conference	272
Church Book of Records Held by Mr. Hall	273
Confession of Faith and Covenant	274-6
Complaint of Mr. Hall	263
Conclusion of Mr. Scribner's Ministry. His Removal	280
Candidates	281
Call to Mr. Eber Carpenter	284
Call to Mr. Ephraim Randall	287
Covenant, 1847	291
Call and Ordination of Mr. John B. Willard	292
Council to Organize Union Church	296
Church Edifice Built by Union Society.	299
College Graduates Born in Westford	329
Citizenship	356
Deer-Killing	69
Deeds of Charity	79
Delegate to Provincial Congress	110
Declaration of Independence to be Recorded	115
Declaration of Rights Considered Substitute for the Third Article Proposed	141
Death of an Indian	156
Death of George Washington	155
Disposition of Surplus Revenue	181
Draft	208
Destination of Articles for the Soldiers	215
Disorders	263
Difficulties with Mr. Scribner	278
Dismission of Mr. Randall	288
Deacons of First Church	295
Deacons of Union Church	301
Division into School Districts	328
Deed of Land to the Academy	314
Date of Incorporation of Academy	314
Early Settlers	4
Extension	5
Early Homesteads	8-10
Expedition Against Cuba	54
Extracts from Town Records	67
Early Burying Grounds	80
Even Pay	120
Effect of the War of the Revolution upon the People of the Town	146
Extract from Minott's History of the Insurrections	146
Enrollment and Apportionment	206
Elsewhere	236
Ecclesiastical History	252
Ecclesiastical Council at Haverhill, Mass.	262
Effort to Unite the People in Support of a Minister	286
Educational History	306
Early Friends of the Academy	316
From the Settlement to the Incorporation	1
Frances Hill, Origin of the Name	8
First Mill	11
Fulling Mill	12
Families Annexed to the Parish of Littleton	15
First Meeting House	17
First Town Meeting	22
First Tax List	25
French Neutrals	57
French Family, Removal of	69
Fishways	69
First Bell-Ringer	79
First Committee of Correspondence	91
Field Officers of Middlesex Regiments	124
Formation of State Government	139
First Vote for State Officers	144
Fire Arms	149
Fencing the Common, Subscription for the Purpose of	182
First Martyr for Westford in the Civil War	202
Funding the Town Debt	227
Flowers	240
First Fulling Mill	241
First Church Covenant	255
First Deacons of Mr. Hall's Church	257
First Congregational Society	288
Formation of Union Congregational Society and List of Members	295
Formation of Methodist Society	302-4
First Pastor of	304
Second Pastor	305
First Meeting of Trustees and First Preceptor of Academy	315
And First Preceptress	322
First School Committee	328
Forge Village, Recollections of	351
Framingham & Lowell Railroad	346
Grist Mill at Brookside	12
Garrison House, First	12
Gloves at Funerals	79
Graniteville	235
Geology	236
Grammar School	308
Teachers of	309
Grant of Land to Academy	316
Graduates of Academy, 1872-1882	325
Good Influence of Academy	328
Graniteville, Recollections of	354
Genealogy of Early Families, (part second)	435
Hunting Ground of Indians	2
Homesteads	8-10
Hildreth Row	9
Highway from Chelmsford to Groton	12
Highway to Salem	13
Homesteads in 1730, with Map	27-33
Horse Stables, Proprietors of	154
Hills	231
Hyde's Hole	236
Half-Way Covenant Set Aside	268
History of Westford, (part second)	435
Indian Haunts	3
Industry, Vote to Encourage	90
Independence, Nothing Short of	114
Independence Secured	122
Instructions to Francis Leighton, Representative	122
Instructions to Representative	150
Items from Town Records	178
Idleness and Intemperance, Efforts to Suppress	180
Inauguration of the Conflict	189
Invitation to Concord, 1875	204
Industries and Manufactures	241
Invitation to Mr. Hall	262
Inscription upon Monument of Rev. W. Hall	266
Ice Business at Forge Village	346
Land Bank	69
List of Prices for Labor and Articles of Common Necessity	117
List of Rates	131
List of Seamen	136

INDEX OF TOPICS. 489

Land in Plymouth, N. H.	147
Loss of Military Stores	155
Land of Samuel Craft	155
List of Paupers	155
Losses by Fire	155
List of Soldiers in the War of 1812	177
List of Persons Drafted	208
Ladies of Westford; Their Work for the Soldiers	212-215
Localities	235
Lime-Burning	242
Lineage and Family of Mr. Scribner	277
List of Teachers in Academy	319
List of Trustees of Academy	327
Lawyers	332
Library, Social	347
List of Town Officers, 1730-1882	364
Ministry Lot	11
Millstone Hill	11
Manufacture of Tar and Turpentine	14
Meeting-House Bell	74
Mending the Bell	80
Minot's Company	108
Marshall's Regiment	131
Massachusetts, The Part of, in the Revolution	145
Minot's History of Insurrections	147
Military Review	155
Muster	156
Migration from Westford to Other Towns	156
Migration to Towns in New Hampshire, Litchfield	157
Hollis, Wilton, Mason and New Ipswich	158
Temple, Ackworth, Deering, Amherst, Nashua, Pelham, Warner, Rochester, Swanzey, Keene, Hillsboro', Westmoreland	162
Marlboro', Jaffrey, Fitzwilliam, Stoddard, Rindge, Peterboro', Nelson, Hopkinton, Washington, Littleton, Plymouth	163
Migration to Vermont	163
Cavendish	164
Ludlow	166
Mount Holly	167
Plymouth, Londonderry, Weathersfield, Reading, Putney	168
Brattleboro', Bennington	169
Migration to Maine	169
Portland, Sanford, Farmington, Anson, Wilton, Winthrop	169
Pittston and other Places	170
Migration to Towns in Massachusetts, Templeton, Littleton	170
Groton, Dunstable, Tyngsboro', Pepperell, Townsend, Ashby, Ashburnham, Shirley, Harvard,	171
Lunenburg and other Towns	172
To other States	173
Map of the Town	184
Monument Proposed	226
Massachusetts; Her Part in the Civil War	218
Memorial Day	230
Mackrill Cove	235
Moraines	238
Ministry Lot	247
Ministry Meadow	258
Ministry of Rev. Mr. Scribner	271
Ministry of Rev. Caleb Blake	281
Members of Baptist Society, South Chelmsford	285
Members of Universalist Society	285
Members of Baptist Society in Littleton	286
Ministry of Rev. Luther Wilson	290

Ministry of Rev. Stillman Clark	292
Ministry of Rev. George M. Rice	293
Medallion of Charles G. Sargent	305
Ministry of Rev. James F. Mears and Rev. Alfred Woods	305
Ministers Born in Westford	331
Military Companies	356
Marriage Intentions	404-413
Marriage of Parties from Westford Reported by Clerks of other Towns	398-404
Nonesuch	7
Names of Snow-Shoe Men	53
New County Road	68
No Supper	71
North Burying Ground	84
Nothing Short of Independence	114
New Form of Government Sanctioned, Provided	139
New Meeting-House	151
Number of Men Sent into the War	201
New Burying Ground	230
Nashoba	235
New " Profession and Covenant," 1830	289
Names of Original Members of the Union Church	297
Names of Early Teachers	307
Numbering of School-Houses	329
Nashua & Acton Railroad	347
Once Part of Chelmsford	2
Old Roads	33-52
Objections to the Third Article of the Bill of Rights	141
Occupation of Water-Power at Forge Village	243
Owners of the Cameron Place for 120 Years	248
Organization of First Church and Ordination of Mr. Hall	254
Original Members of First Church	256
Ordination of Mr. Blake	282
Ordination of Rev. George H. Young	294
Organization of Union Church	296
Organization of Proprietors of Academy, Zaccheus Wright, President	313
Providence	7
Providence Meadow	9
Precinct Established	16
Plan for a New County	67
Powder and Bullets	87
Personal Testimony to Col. Robinson	109
Prescott's Testimony	113
Pay of Soldiers	120
" Picking up the Tools "	123
Petition Respecting Public Grievances	147-8
Painting the Meeting-House	151
Plan of the Town	153
Poor-Farm	178
Project for a New County	180
Poor House	181
Printing Town Report	182
Prosperity	221-2
Ponds and Brooks	232
Paradise	234
Parkerville	235
Post Offices	235
Pottery	242
Potash	243
Preparing to Settle Another Minister	263
Proposals to Mr. Hall	264
Pastorate of Rev. Herman Snow	291
Rev. W. A. Cram and Rev. Joseph S. Moulton	294
Rev. Thomas Wilson, Rev. D. O. Allen and Rev. John Whitney	300

Pastorates of Rev. E. R. Hodgman, Rev. James Fletcher, Rev. Edwin A. Spence, Rev. Henry D. Woodworth, Rev. Nathan R. Nichols, Rev. Henry H. Hamilton and Rev. Rufus C. Flagg 301
Preceptors, Notice of Levi Hedge, Amos Crosby, Benjamin Burge and Nahum H. Groce; . . . 321
John Wright, Esq., Rev. Ephraim Abbot, Hon. John D. Long and William E. Frost . . . 322–5
Physicians 331
Population, 1776–1880 356
Part Second of History . . . 435

Remonstrance Against the Stamp Act. 87
Robinson, Col., in Concord Fight . . 104
   Personal Recollections of . . 109
   Testimony to His Bravery at Bunker Hill 113
Regulation Act 117
Restitution 117
Response to Circular from the Town of Concord 146
Revising the Constitution . . . 154
Raising the Flag-Staff on the Common, Speeches, etc 186
Regiment, The Sixteenth; Its Work . 201
Roll of Honor 210
Remodelling Town House . . . 228
Rededication of Town House . . 229
Reading the Bible in the Pulpit . 283
Repairing of Meeting-House and Rededication 291
Rules for the Academy . . . 314
Resident Graduates 330
Representatives to General Court, 1729–1881 356–7
Record of Marriages, 1728, seq. . 372–404
Record of Deaths . . . 413–18
Record of Deaths, by Deacon Leighton 418–24
Record of Deaths, by Rev. L. Luce 424–34

Struggle for a Precinct . . . 14
Soldiers in Lovewell's Expedition . 52
Soldiers at Louisburg in 1745 . . 55
Soldiers in the French and Indian Wars 61
Singing Ruleable 79
Second Meeting-House . . . 96
Salt 114
Soldiers' Families 118
   Allowance to 119
Soldiers on the Rolls of Different Companies 123
Six Months' Levies 134
Soldiers at Valley Forge and Yorktown 136
"Sincere Protestation" in Regard to Religious Liberty 142

Shay's Rebellion 148
Shire-Town 150
Selectmen, to be Three in Number . 154
Singers 154
Stove 154
Spruce and Pine Trees on the Common, Set Out by Eliakim Hutchins, Jr. 183
Sale of Land in Plymouth, N. H. . 183
Subscribers to the Fund for a Flag-Staff 187
Sixth and Sixteenth Regiments . 186
Soldiers, Alphabetical List of . 193–200
Sixth Regiment Reorganized; Its Achievements and Men in it from Westford 202–3

Statement of John W. P. Abbot . . 260
Sketch of Sarah E. Keyes . . . 215
Sketch of Edward Keyes . . . 217
Summary of the Town's Contribution to the War 218
Sequel to the Rebellion . . . 220
Sackatere 235
Soil 239
Stone-Quarrying 246
Stores and Store-Keepers . . 245–51
Salary of Mr. Hall, Difficulties About. 260
Selectmen to Provide Preaching . 262
Sons and Daughters of Mr. Hall . 267
Sketch of Rev. Joseph Thaxter (note). 268
Sketch of Mr. Randall . . . 268
Salary of Mr. Scribner . . . 272
Sketch of Rev. John B. Willard . 292
Sketch of Rev. George M. Rice . 293
Second Congregational Society . 285
Sketch of Rev. George H. Young . 294
Sketch of Rev. Leonard Luce . 299
School-Houses Built, 1787 . . 311
Sketches of Zaccheus Wright and James Prescott, Jr. . . . 316
Sketches of John Abbot and John W. P. Abbot 318
Sketches of Margaret Foley and Harriet B. Rogers 325
Stony Brook Railroad . . . 346
Social and Public Library, Subscribers to 348
Social Library Merged in Town Library 350
Statistical and Official . . . 356

Tadmuck 2
Tar and Turpentine 14
Tar-Kiln Hill 14
Territory Annexed from Groton . 24
Training Field 71
Tony's Island 72
Three Companies in Concord Fight, Bates', Underwood's, and Minot's . 106
Thanks for a Donation . . . 116
Three Months' Levies . . . 135
Twenty-Sixth Regiment; The First Loyal Volunteer Regiment to Reach the Department of the Gulf . 204
Thirtieth Regiment 205
Thirty-Third Regiment; Its Valor and Heroism, Made the Greatest Charge of the War 205
Thirty-Fifth Regiment . . . 206
Teacher of Freedmen . . . 217
Tyngsboro' Bridge 223
Town History 227
Topography 231
"Texas" 235

Vote to Abide by the Advice of the Boston Committee of Correspondence 104
Villages 233
Vote of Esteem to Rev. George M. Rice 293
Votes for Governor, 1781–1861 . . 359

Warning Out Strangers . . . 73
West Burying-Ground . . . 85
Warned Out 85
Wyman's Company 112
Watch Appointed 115
War of 1812 175
War of the Rebellion . . . 185
Westford Well Represented in All Branches of Military Service . 207
Westford Corner 236

INDEX OF NAMES.

The following index of surnames in Part First is designed to furnish the means of easy reference to any name that may be desired. Where lists occur, these are not cited, but the reader is referred to the lists themselves, which may be found on pages 26, 27, 28, 33, 53, 54, 63, 65, 75, 76, 107-9, 111, 112, 124-37, 139, 138, 182, 187, 194-200, 201, 203-8, 210-212, 256, 285, 297, 298, 309, 310, 319, 320, 325, 326, 327, 329-32, 348, 357-434.

No name is given from any page more than once, although it may appear several times on the page.

In Part Second the names of families are arranged in alphabetical order.

Abbot, 35, 53, 58, 60, 74, 75, 76, 79, 83, 89, 90, 91, 92, 94, 96, 97, 103, 115, 116, 139, 148, 152, 154, 155, 166, 177, 178, 182, 183, 188, 208, 209, 223, 242, 244, 245, 247, 249, 250, 272, 273, 274, 278, 282, 283, 287, 290, 291, 292, 295, 312, 313, 314, 315.
Abercrombie, 63.
Adams, 4, 7, 16, 25, 37, 45, 46, 113, 164, 166, 229, 235, 249, 251, 273, 298, 313, 314, 315, 348, 353.
Allen, 5, 6, 16, 288, 289, 300.
Allston, 340.
Ames, 73, 293.
Amherst, 63.
Appleton, 263.
Armstrong, 218.
Atwood, 10, 170, 239.
Avery, 74, 85.
Babbidge, 292.
Bacheller, 262.
Bailey, 85, 354.
Balch, 38, 40.
Baldwin, 144, 162.
Bancroft, 63, 105, 250.
Barrister, 42, 236.
Barnard, 271.
Barrett, 5, 15, 16, 34, 44, 46, 50, 86, 87, 105, 155, 158, 170.
Barron, 40, 160.
Barry, 289.
Bartlett, 323.
Bartol, 292.
Bascom, 288.
Bason, 112, 113.
Bates, 5, 11, 42, 43, 77, 85, 96, 163, 107, 108, 110, 160, 171, 308, 343.
Baxter, 281.
Bayard, 341.
Beal, 86, 87.
Bean, 258.
Belcher, 34.
Bemis, 251.
Bennett, 87, 161.
Bicknell, 34, 38, 187.
Bigelow, 62, 73, 120, 161.
Bixby, 10, 16, 35, 37, 44, 158, 167, 168, 172, 177.
Blake, 34, 38, 156, 172, 250, 274, 281, 282, 284, 313, 317, 348.

Blanchard, 73, 105, 300.
Blodget, 7, 9, 34, 37, 38, 39, 44, 46, 48, 62, 64, 79, 85, 112, 162, 171, 249, 251, 259, 343, 344, 345, 352.
Blood, 64, 228, 243, 351.
Bond, 247.
Boutwell, 10, 13, 35, 37, 38, 44, 46, 233, 238.
Bowdoin, 144.
Bowen, 47, 307.
Boynton, 34, 38, 43, 44, 47, 58, 59, 60, 61, 75, 76, 78, 79, 80, 91, 96, 97, 99, 101, 104, 139, 143, 151, 153, 158, 161, 163, 164, 166, 168, 170, 171, 172, 178, 242, 249, 273, 274, 282, 296, 312, 314, 354.
Bradford, 290.
Bradstreet, 64.
Bridge, 264, 313.
Brooks, 62, 82, 83, 84, 86, 144.
Brown, 24, 73, 148, 163, 177, 250, 323.
Buck, 352.
Buckingham, 290.
Buckley, 304.
Bunce, 9, 210, 239.
Burbeck, 239, 242.
Burge, 10, 39, 54, 81, 96, 158, 159, 162, 171, 232, 258, 261, 281, 307, 321.
Burgoyne, 160.
Burke, 42, 43.
Burnap, 339.
Burns, or Burne, 16, 34, 40, 53, 113, 242.
Burr, 288.
Burt, 184.
Butler, 243.
Butterfield, 5, 8, 10, 11, 16, 18, 35, 38, 41, 57, 62, 63, 86, 100, 158, 162, 169, 171, 172, 184, 250, 350.
Buttrick, 105, 106.
Byam, 165.
Caldwell, 167, 292.
Calvert, 244.
Cameron, 229, 244, 245, 249.
Campbell, 171.
Capen, 291.
Carkin, 246.
Carpenter, 284.
Carter, 250.
Carver, 77, 78, 154, 162, 171, 278, 311, 313, 315, 338.
Caryl, 244.

Chamberlin, 5, 8, 12, 15, 16, 17, 18, 33, 35, 37, 38, 40, 49, 67, 85, 103, 118, 154, 158, 159, 162, 166, 167, 225, 226, 236, 251, 261, 272, 336, 350.
Chandler, 12, 35, 46, 61, 158, 159, 160, 161, 162, 168, 169, 171, 292.
Channing, 340.
Chaplin, 273, 333.
Chase, 78, 87.
Child, 300.
Choate, 282.
Clark, 16, 292, 300, 352.
Cleaveland, 56, 57, 72.
Coggin, 281.
Cogswell, 351.
Colburn, 43, 155, 246.
Comings or Cummings, 10, 16, 22, 35, 39, 44, 45, 46, 48, 62, 68, 78, 83, 84, 90, 97, 98, 99, 100, 101, 113, 118, 120, 154, 159, 162, 166, 171, 250, 252, 253, 278, 295, 314, 338, 355.
Conant, 9, 37, 39.
Cookson, Cuckson, 45, 239.
Coolidge, 3, 38, 61, 163, 290.
Corey, 62, 86, 161.
Cotton, 257, 267.
Cowdry, 48, 85, 153, 232, 247, 251.
Craft, 155, 172.
Cram, 226, 294.
Crosby, 155, 159, 321.
Crouch, 9, 11, 37, 41, 42.
Curtis, 87, 106.
Cushing, 95.
Cutler, 300.
Cutter, 10, 183, 243, 284, 295, 296, 301.
Dakin, 62.
Dalton, 288.
Daly, 244.
Dana, 340.
Dane, 43.
Danforth, 60, 261.
Daniels, 287.
Davis, 57, 62, 105, 106, 172, 184, 273.
Day, 10, 13, 44, 155, 188, 190, 225, 226, 227, 235, 250, 283.
Decatur, 36.
Dennis, 87, 161.
Derby, 116.
Desmond, 338.
Ditson, 178, 250.
Dix, 73, 272.
Dodge, 74, 85, 225, 300.
Downs, 298.
Drake, 113.
Drew, 3, 9, 38, 44, 45, 222, 250, 258.
Dudley, 15, 73, 177.
Dummer, 22, 61.
Dupee, 10, 39, 346, 354.
Durant, 351.
Dutton, 48, 59, 78, 153, 155, 162, 163, 164, 165, 171.
Edes, 262.
Edwards, 47.
Eliot, 5, 242, 292.
Ellery, 257.
Ely, 283.
Emerson, 37, 38, 95, 106, 281, 340.
Emmons, 273.
Endicott, 215.
Esterbrooks, 86.
Evans, 228, 246, 303, 304, 305.
Falls, 210.
Farmer, 49, 86, 158.
Farnsworth, 74.
Farr, 86, 161, 290.
Farwell, 41, 86, 153, 239.
Fassett, 22, 23, 48, 51, 63, 111.
Faxon, 310.
Fay, 298, 299.
Ferguson, 349.

Fish, 73, 74.
Fisher, 225, 227, 298, 299.
Fiske, 4, 50, 305.
Fitch, 34.
Flagg, 34, 156, 171, 260, 301.
Fletcher, 4, 10, 11, 12, 13, 15, 16, 17, 18, 20, 22, 23, 33, 34, 35, 36, 37, 38, 39, 40, 41, 43, 44, 45, 47, 49, 50, 52, 53, 54, 57, 59, 62, 68, 74, 75, 76, 77, 78, 81, 82, 83, 84, 85, 86, 87, 88, 89, 90, 91, 92, 96, 97, 98, 100, 163, 113, 114, 116, 120, 122, 139, 140, 144, 147, 148, 149, 153, 154, 158, 161, 163, 164, 165, 166, 167, 168, 170, 171, 172, 173, 177, 181, 183, 184, 188, 190, 214, 222, 225, 226, 227, 247, 248, 249, 250, 251, 252, 253, 258, 259, 267, 272, 273, 283, 286, 287, 295, 299, 301, 303, 313, 314, 351, 353, 354, 355.
Flint, 169, 187.
Foley, 326.
Foster, 5, 15, 16, 22, 33, 39, 41, 86, 87, 153, 155, 315.
Foye, 71.
French, 74.
Frost, 225, 227, 228, 324.
Fuller, 144.
Gardner, 91, 94, 96, 249.
Gay, 268.
Gibson, 354.
Gilbert, 292.
Gill, 107, 108, 262.
Gilson, 85, 251.
Glenny, 25.
Good, 8.
Goodhue, 87, 100, 103, 106, 121, 140, 151, 269, 287, 295, 296.
Gorham, 144.
Gould, 51, 337.
Grant, 8.
Graves, 303.
Gray, 96.
Green, 153, 163, 166, 351.
Griffin, 251.
Groce, 69, 250, 267, 321, 338.
Gunning, 237.
Hadley, 51, 112, 163, 167, 168, 169.
Hall, 45, 47, 72, 95, 100, 101, 102, 110, 117, 154, 166, 169, 171, 249, 252, 253, 254, 256, 257, 258, 250, 260, 261, 262, 263, 264, 265, 266, 273, 311, 339, 341, 342, 343.
Hamblin, 184, 222, 225, 239, 242, 314.
Hamilton, 226, 301.
Hancock, 92, 144.
Hapgood, 236.
Hardy, 85.
Harris, 168, 187.
Hartford, 10, 43.
Hartwell, 4, 10, 40, 62, 181, 296, 298, 299, 306, 354.
Harwood, 74, 301.
Haskins, 244.
Hayward, 354.
Haywood, 179.
Hazen, 52.
Heald, 37, 48, 166.
Hedge, 153, 315, 321, 340.
Henchman, 4, 5, 11.
Heywood, 8, 9, 35, 37, 42, 49, 181, 225, 239, 283, 284, 295, 296, 352.
Hill, 13, 298, 299, 302.
Hildreth, 5, 9, 10, 12, 15, 16, 22, 23, 34, 38, 40, 42, 45, 49, 56, 62, 64, 74, 78, 98, 99, 106, 114, 115, 151, 153, 154, 155, 156, 158, 161, 162, 164, 166, 171, 190, 237, 250, 258, 295, 306, 307, 314, 328.
Hinckley, 250.
Hitchcock, 237, 238.
Hittinger, 346.
Hobbs, 345.
Hodgman, 188, 217, 223, 224, 225, 226, 227, 228, 239.

INDEX OF NAMES. 493

Holden, 161, 168.
Hollis, 246.
Holmes, 13, 54, 56, 58, 112.
Holt, 73, 267.
Hooker, 50, 62, 172, 230.
Horan, 36, 39.
Horsley, 171, 210.
Hosmer, 179.
How, 87.
Howard, 10, 12, 37, 153, 295.
Howarth, 302.
Howitt, 326.
Hudson, 106.
Hull, 289.
Hunt, 13, 41, 47, 57, 62, 87, 172, 307.
Huntington, 323.
Huston, 64.
Hutchins, 10, 49, 178, 225, 242, 247, 260.
Hutchinson, 251.
Ingalls, 210.
Jacobs, 120.
Jewett, 163, 172, 173, 314.
Johnson, 120, 163.
Jones, 86, 136, 269.
Keep, 59, 68, 69, 75, 78, 95, 115, 148, 150, 163, 171, 260, 267.
Keller, 228.
Kemp, 73, 86, 177.
Kent, 23, 51, 73, 78, 351, 352.
Keyes, 4, 5, 8, 10, 11, 12, 22, 35, 36, 39, 41, 46, 49, 50, 51, 52, 53, 86, 154, 155, 156, 157, 158, 162, 163, 171, 172, 173, 177, 215, 216, 217, 232, 236, 249, 250, 252, 278, 295, 306, 311, 313, 314, 350.
Kneeland, 152, 156, 249, 250, 268, 348.
Kidder, 10, 42, 57, 62, 77, 80, 98, 90, 101, 118, 122, 158, 159, 170, 171, 273, 274, 306.
Kimball, 250, 296.
King, 62, 118, 140, 156, 161, 186, 188, 251.
Kittredge, 237, 355.
Lafayette, 318.
Lancy, 354.
Langley, 10, 36.
Lanktree, 239, 258.
Lane, 87.
Larkin, 86.
Lawrence, 64, 73, 74, 86, 246, 251, 351, 352, 353, 354, 355.
Lee, 220, 352.
Leighton, 33, 34, 40, 42, 52, 62, 115, 122, 139, 177, 249, 250, 278, 284, 295, 298, 301, 313, 328, 348, 350.
Leland, 9, 41.
Lincoln, 172, 216, 220.
Long, 229, 323, 324.
Longley, 12.
Love, 73.
Lovewell, 52, 53.
Luce, 188, 226, 298, 300, 302, 351.
Lyon, 11, 43.
Mace, 230.
Manning, 161, 314.
Mansfield, 74.
Marble, 73.
Marden, 229.
Marsh, 262.
Mason, 304.
Maynard, 292.
McGuire, 177.
Mead, 64, 163, 171, 302, 304.
Mears, 305.
Mellen, 263.
Merriam, 172.
Merrill, 246.
Millard, 10.
Miner, 34, 44, 51.
Minot, 9, 34, 38, 42, 91, 96, 97, 108, 110, 112, 116, 140, 147, 163, 168, 242, 263, 272, 273, 274, 286, 287.
Monckton, 57.

Monroe, 341.
Montcalm, 62, 63.
Moor, 281.
Morgan, 87.
Morrison, 42, 50, 190.
Morse, 292.
Mosely, 282, 319.
Moulton, 228, 294.
Murphy, 34, 52.
Naylor, 302.
Needham, 170.
Newell, 291.
Newhall, 249.
Nichols, 87, 153, 181, 295, 301.
Nutting. 5, 11, 86, 153, 163, 181, 311.
Oliver, 94, 170, 293.
Osgood, 5, 61, 153, 154, 179, 222, 241, 242, 250, 251, 281, 287, 295, 301, 314, 328, 337.
Packard, 281, 289, 315.
Paine, 261.
Page, 177.
Palmer, 230, 246, 247, 248.
Park, 73.
Parker, 5, 9, 13, 14, 22, 38, 39, 40, 53, 74, 85, 87, 100, 101, 106, 111, 112, 116, 120, 121, 150, 153, 158, 160, 162, 164, 165, 166, 170, 171, 172, 173, 177, 181, 242, 243, 250, 254, 257, 261, 306, 314, 317, 351.
Parkhurst, 41.
Patch, 62, 73, 120, 166.
Patten, 10, 34, 44, 165, 172, 173, 238, 249.
Payson, 266, 206.
Pearson, 177.
Perham, 38, 46, 86, 172.
Perkins, 85, 144.
Perley, 337.
Pepperell, 55, 56, 62.
Perry, 57, 74, 85, 86, 162.
Phelps, 86.
Pike, 153.
Pollard, 64, 71, 81, 82, 97, 90, 160, 249.
Polley, 47.
Poole, 339.
Porter, 277.
Powers, 15.
Pownal, 59.
Pratt, 10.
Prescott. 12, 16, 23, 34, 35, 44, 45, 46, 48, 54, 56, 57, 59, 60, 63, 67, 68, 69, 71, 74, 75, 76, 77, 78, 81, 82, 83, 88, 90, 98, 99, 100, 101, 103, 105, 106, 107, 108, 109, 111, 112, 113, 117, 120, 139, 140, 148, 151, 153, 154, 158, 163, 169, 171, 172, 178, 181, 184, 188, 225, 228, 237, 243, 247, 250, 251, 260, 278, 280, 287, 295, 298, 302, 306, 313, 314, 315, 317, 322, 328, 348, 352, 353, 355.
Procter, 4, 9, 16, 33, 40, 44, 45, 46, 53, 56, 62, 85, 120, 121, 140, 148, 153, 158, 162, 164, 167, 171, 257, 271, 303, 304, 313, 338, 348.
Pushee, 362.
Putnam, 291, 298, 299.
Raiter, 51.
Rand, 210.
Randall, 287, 288, 290.
Raymond, 49, 98, 110, 122, 153, 354.
Read, 7, 8, 11, 15, 16, 25, 33, 35, 36, 40, 49, 50, 51, 54, 59, 67, 68, 69, 71, 81, 82, 95, 98, 100, 103, 104, 110, 113, 121, 122, 139, 140, 154, 155, 158, 162, 163, 165, 167, 168, 170, 171, 172, 173, 178, 179, 190, 223, 225, 228, 249, 259, 260, 269, 270, 271, 278, 280, 307, 310, 311, 313, 314, 328, 338, 339, 353, 355, 356, 357.
Reed, 22, 23, 34, 33, 110, 173, 225, 236, 247, 248, 250, 251, 345, 351, 353, 354.
Reynolds, 178.
Rice, 188, 293, 303.
Richards, 187.
Richardson, 9, 11, 40, 41, 47, 46, 53, 69, 149, 153, 162, 170, 171, 179, 183, 239, 242, 287, 311, 350.

Richmond, 286.
Ridgely, 341.
Ripley, 105, 313.
Robbins, 10, 15, 16, 20, 23, 34, 45, 49, 50, 53, 56, 57, 69, 101, 162, 177, 257.
Robinson, 80, 85, 98, 105, 106, 110, 113, 119, 120, 148, 171, 225, 226, 269, 288, 336, 337.
Robisheau, 58, 59, 61.
Roby, 164, 165.
Rogers, 111, 293, 326.
Rollins, 86.
Rowley, 301.
Ruhard, 59.
Ruggles, 10, 354.
Rumrill, 11, 54, 161, 171.
Runels, 248.
Russell, 60, 62, 73, 86, 163, 250, 261.
Salstonstall, 257.
Sanford, 273.
Sargent, 223, 244, 245, 303, 304, 305, 354, 355.
Sartell, 87.
Sawtelle, 188.
Savage, 261.
Scribner, 151, 171, 271, 272, 274, 277, 278, 279, 280, 281, 314.
Searls, 74.
Shattuck, 15, 54, 85, 148, 177, 251.
Shaw, 340.
Shays, 148, 149.
Sheahan, 8, 187.
Sherburne, 46, 51.
Sherman, 307.
Shirley, 55, 355.
Simpkins, 281.
Skinner, 54, 57, 262, 280, 292, 304, 354.
Smith, 13, 51, 57.
Smylie, 74.
Snow, 40, 41, 158, 201.
Southmayd, 298, 299.
Southwick, 215, 217.
Spalding, 9, 10, 11, 13, 18, 23, 35, 39, 42, 43, 44, 45, 46, 48, 49, 51, 53, 54, 120, 158, 160, 161, 162, 164, 165, 167, 168, 169, 170, 171, 172, 173, 232, 295, 308, 338.
Sparks, 40.
Spence, 217, 301.
Sprague, 64, 352.
Spring, 273.
Squier, 158, 346.
Stanley, 85.
Stanton, 301.
Stevens, 222, 250, 251, 316, 328.
Stoddard, 17, 254, 257.
Stone, 75, 77, 78, 79, 87, 90, 144, 166, 170, 171, 172, 345.
Story, 340.
Stratton, 73.
Strong, 176.
Swallow, 177.
Sweetser, 13, 251.
Swett, 113.
Symonds, 150.
Symmes, 9, 184, 223, 248, 249, 250, 267.
Taggart, 86.
Tarbell, 153, 177.
Taylor, 34, 36, 41, 47, 50, 51, 61, 73, 162, 163.

Temple, 46, 86, 155, 169, 261.
Thaxter, 106, 263, 268, 269.
Thomas, 152.
Thurston, 281.
Tidd, 249, 250.
Tilton, 258.
Tinker, 113.
Todd, 296, 299.
Tony, 72.
Tower, 3, 12, 41, 190.
Townsend, 23, 158.
Trowbridge, 172, 322.
Tucker, 163.
Turner, 74.
Tuttle, 313.
Tyler, 86, 281.
Tyng, 21, 23, 24, 53.
Underwood, 9, 16, 20, 22, 34, 44, 54, 67, 71, 72, 78, 106, 107, 111, 157, 158, 168, 170, 261, 306, 307, 352.
Varnum, 313.
Vose, 49, 51.
Waldo, 5.
Warren, 60, 298.
Washington, 155, 216.
Wayne, 50.
Webb, 8.
Webster, 163, 225.
Weeks, 215.
Wentworth, 208.
Wetherbee, 298.
Wheat, 86, 87, 161.
Wheaton, 269.
Wheeler, 49, 64, 73, 74, 172, 258.
White, 62, 115, 123, 140, 162, 163, 164, 166, 288, 201.
Whiting, 268.
Whitman, 269.
Whitney, 13, 15, 16, 37, 50, 51, 242, 257, 300.
Wight, 178, 181, 295, 298, 301.
Willard, 21, 53, 250, 292, 321.
Williams, 57.
Wiley, 222, 242, 250, 258.
Willis, 62.
Wilson, 38, 153, 155, 168, 242, 290, 300.
Winslow, 57, 61.
Wood, 156, 173, 249, 288, 348.
Woodbury, 184.
Woodcock, 304.
Woods, 86, 113, 162, 225, 226, 247, 305, 354.
Woodward, 173, 178.
Woodworth, 301.
Worcester, 281.
Wright, 5, 7, 9, 11, 14, 18, 23, 24, 34, 42, 43, 48, 49, 50, 51, 57, 64, 71, 73, 79, 81, 82, 84, 85, 92, 94, 95, 96, 100, 101, 103, 114, 115, 116, 118, 120, 122, 140, 151, 152, 153, 158, 161, 162, 163, 166, 167, 170, 172, 173, 177, 180, 181, 184, 210, 236, 236, 241, 246, 249, 250, 251, 252, 258, 272, 278, 279, 280, 283, 295, 299, 302, 303, 304, 311, 312, 313, 314, 316, 322, 323, 328, 333, 348, 350, 352, 354, 355.
Wyer, 64.
Wyman, 78, 86, 112, 248.
Yapp, 243, 354.
Young, 223, 228, 294, 290.

CORRECTIONS.

Page 6. In the note, read 1715 instead of "1714."

Page 10. Last line at the bottom. — The residence of Josiah Burge was near the house of Daniel W. Sherman (1882).

Page 14. Sixth line from the bottom, read 1715 instead of "1714."

Page 157. Line 10, for "rightousness" read righteousness.

Page 201. In the fifth line, after the word "by," insert the words *ties of*, so it shall read, "by ties of greater or less strength."

Page 224. In sixth line, read 1875 instead of "1872."

Page 337. *Rev. Jonathan Osgood*. Later information shows that he was born in Andover. He probably came to Westford when quite young, and lived in the family of Col. Osgood. Sprague's Annals of the American Pulpit give authority for saying he was born in Westford.

Page 445. Line 14. — Mary Elizabeth was born in 1841, and married Jonathan T. Colburn, 1874. John Day married Hannah Wright, 1834. Line 17. — Sarah Ann, born in 1849, and married Warren S. Jones, 1874.

Page 452. Near the middle. — "See p. —." Supply 9.

Page 459. Line 4, read 1716 instead of "1816."

www.ingramcontent.com/pod-product-compliance
Lightning Source LLC
Chambersburg PA
CBHW021812300426
44114CB00009BA/138